SPECIALIZED TECHNIQUES IN INDIVIDUAL PSYCHOTHERAPY

Specialized Techniques in Individual Psychotherapy

Edited by

TOKSOZ B. KARASU, M.D.

*Director, Department of Psychiatry,
Bronx Municipal Hospital Center; Associate
Professor of Psychiatry and Vice Chairman
of the Department of Psychiatry,
Albert Einstein College of Medicine*

and

LEOPOLD BELLAK, M.D.

*Clinical Professor of Psychiatry,
Albert Einstein College of Medicine;
Clinical Professor of Psychology,
New York University*

BRUNNER/MAZEL, *Publishers* • New York

Library of Congress Cataloging in Publication Data

Main entry under title:

Specialized techniques in individual psychotherapy.

Includes bibliographical references and index.
1. Psychotherapy. I. Karasu, Toksoz B. II. Bellak, Leopold, 1916-
RC480.S65   616.8'914   79-19970
ISBN 0-87630-201-0

Published by
BRUNNER/MAZEL, INC.
19 Union Square
New York, New York 10003

Contents

Contributors

LEOPOLD BELLAK, M.D.
Clinical Professor of Psychiatry, Albert Einstein College of Medicine; Clinical Professor of Psychology, New York University.

VICTOR BERNAL Y DEL RIO, M.D.
Executive Director, The Puerto Rico Institute of Psychiatry, San Juan.

HUGH F. BUTTS, M.D.
Director, Bronx Psychiatric Center; Professor of Psychiatry, Albert Einstein College of Medicine; Supervisor and Training Analyst, Post Graduate Center for Mental Health; Collaborating Psychoanalyst, The Columbia Psychoanalytic Center; Lecturer, Department of Psychiatry, Columbia University, College of Physicians and Surgeons.

ALLAN COOPER, Ph.D.
Assistant Clinical Professor of Psychiatry, Albert Einstein College of Medicine; Training and Supervising Analyst, William Alanson White Psychoanalytic Institute.

THOMAS DETRE, M.D.
Professor of Psychiatry, University of Pittsburgh School of Medicine.

STEPHEN FLECK, M.D.
Professor of Psychiatry and Public Health, Yale University School of Medicine.

MICHEL HERSEN, Ph.D.
Professor of Psychiatry, University of Pittsburgh School of Medicine.

JAMES R. HODGE, M.D.
Adjunct Professor of Psychology, University of Akron, Ohio; Council of Scientific Advisors, International Graduate School of Behavioral Sciences of Florida Institute of Technology.

MARDI J. HOROWITZ, M.D.
Professor of Psychiatry, University of California Medical School, San Francisco.

DANIEL JOSEPHTHAL, M.D.
Clinical Associate Professor of Psychiatry, University of Virginia Medical Center, Charlottesville.

RALPH J. KAHANA, M.D.
President, Boston Society for Gerontologic Psychiatry; Assistant Clinical Professor of Psychiatry, Harvard Medical School; Associate Psychiatrist, Beth Israel Hospital, Boston.

NANCY B. KALTREIDER, M.D.
Associate Director, Psychotherapy Evaluation and Study Center, University of California Medical School, San Francisco.

TOKSOZ B. KARASU, M.D.
Director, Department of Psychiatry, Bronx Municipal Hospital Center; Associate Professor of Psychiatry and Vice Chairman, Department of Psychiatry, Albert Einstein College of Medicine.

OTTO F. KERNBERG, M.D.
Medical Director, The New York Hospital—Cornell Medical Center, Westchester Division; Professor of Psychiatry, Cornell University Medical College; Training and Supervising Analyst, Columbia University Center for Psychoanalytic Training and Research.

STANLEY LESSE, M.D., Med. Sc.D.
Editor-in-Chief, *American Journal of Psychotherapy*

MYER MENDELSON, M.D.
Professor of Clinical Psychiatry, University of Pennsylvania School of Medicine; Senior Attending Psychiatrist, The Institute of the Pennsylvania Hospital, Philadelphia.

JON K. MEYER, M.D.
Associate Professor of Psychiatry, Director, Sexual Behaviors Consultation Unit, The Johns Hopkins Medical Institutions, Baltimore.

KENNETH PORTER, M.D.
Director, Group and Family Therapy, St. Luke's Hospital Center; Instructor in Clinical Psychiatry, Columbia University Faculty of Medicine, New York.

LEON SALZMAN, M.D.
Clinical Professor of Psychiatry, Georgetown University School of Medicine.

GERALD J. SARWER-FONER, M.D.
Professor and Chairman, Department of Psychiatry, University of Ottawa School of Medicine Faculty of Health Sciences, Ottawa.

SAUL SCHEIDLINGER, Ph.D.
Professor of Psychiatry, Albert Einstein College of Medicine; Editor, *International Journal of Group Psychotherapy.*

ARTHUR M. SCHWARTZ, M.D.
Associate Attending Psychiatrist, Montefiore Hospital and Medical Center.

EDWIN S. SHNEIDMAN, Ph.D.
Professor of Thanatology, University of California at Los Angeles.

VAMIK D. VOLKAN, M.D.
Medical Director, Blue Ridge Hospital, University of Virginia; Professor of Psychiatry, University of Virginia School of Medicine, Charlottesville.

ROBERT WEINSTOCK, M.D.
Assistant Attending Psychiatrist, McLean Hospital; Clinical Instructor in Psychiatry, Harvard Medical School; Deputy Medical Director and Director of Treatment, McLean Hospital Program at Bridgewater State Hospital.

SHELDON ZIMBERG, M.D.
Associate Professor of Psychiatry, Mount Sinai School of Medicine, New York.

Introduction

Psychotherapy is a process of interaction between a therapist and a patient. The interaction must be guided by the therapist, as part of the fulfillment of the therapeutic contract and his role as a responsible professional. Karasu has recently devised a system of categorizing the complexities of psychotherapeutic endeavors (see Chapter 1).

To qualify as a scientific endeavor, psychotherapy must be predicated upon clearly formulated hypotheses, which must, at least in principle, be verifiable or disprovable, as any scientific hypothesis should be. The principle of verifiability is even more important than demonstrated verification. Psychotherapy does not stand alone among therapeutic modalities in its need for more research. That, however, should not keep us from continuously striving for operational definitions and verifications of psychotherapeutic propositions.

Psychotherapy is an applied science. To be sound, its propositions must be clearly derived from more general ones of a theory of psychopathology which, in turn, must be derived from a general theory of the psychology of personality (1). There are many theories of psychotherapy, though the clarity of the relationship between a theory of psychopathology and a theory of personality often leaves much to be desired. Moreover, few of the underlying theories of personality attempt to explain the broad spectrum of human behavior. Except for psychoanalysis, it is hard to think of any theory that ever tried to explain, however dubiously, wit, humor and comedy in relation to the rest of human behavior. Aesthetics, on the other hand, was especially addressed by Gestalt psychology, as well as by psychoanalysis, albeit rather reductionistically. And yet, to treat an artist, it may be quite important to have a general theory of personality and psychopathology to understand the patient and formulate psychotherapeutic interventions.

With respect to this interrelationship of theory of personality, psychopathology and psychotherapy, the field of psychological therapeutics is not different from the rest of medical therapeutics. We expect medical students to learn about physics, chemistry, general biology, anatomy and physiology before we expose them to pathology, and eventually let them practice therapeutics based on the understanding of these underpinnings.

Lest anyone be concerned about this seemingly radically medical model, let us hasten to say that a good medical school program must teach its students to see patients in terms of their social environment in the broadest sense and in terms of epidemiology and public health in a narrower sense. Even more specifically, Selye's field theory provides an interactional model of organisms that could keep any social psychologist, sociologist or ecologist quite happy.

To the extent to which psychotherapy involves symbolic *operations,* the surgical model is especially serviceable. Before engaging in surgical intervention, a careful diagnosis must be made in terms of anatomical structure and physiological processes. A thorough workup of the biochemical status is essential and the provision of optimal preoperative enabling conditions, in terms of hematology, cardiac status, etc., is essential.

Part of the need for specificity in the psychotherapeutic operation must be a similarly careful diagnostic workup in terms of psychodynamics, structure, and the external milieu as well as the internal somatic ones. There should also be a careful assessment of psychological liabilities and assets, possibly in term of ego function (3), and a clear formulation of the therapeutic goal and the steps necessary to reach it. For this purpose, a specific formulation for each patient of the *areas* of intervention, *methods* of intervention, and the sequence of areas and methods of intervention is necessary (1, 2, 4).

A word about therapeutic success may not be amiss here. Strupp and Hadley (5) have made clear that there are at least three facets of success: the subjective feelings of the patient, the assessment by society and, finally, success in terms of the technical expectations of the therapist. Many a patient might feel greatly improved, at least temporarily, if he has, for instance, succeeded in changing some of his ego-alien symptoms,

such as shyness or excessive conscientiousness, into ego-syntonic brash-
ness and self-centeredness, with the help of some of the current fads in
quick cures, such as "taking care of number one" and cathartic self-
expression. Society might take a different view of such a "cure."

Therapeutic success in terms of theoretical expectations is, in turn,
hardest to fulfill by psychoanalytic criteria. While the patient might be
feeling happy about being symptom-free, with both his family and society
sharing in this appraisal, a psychoanalyst might consider his improvement merely the result of flight into health or of a positive transference,
the stability of which he doubts. Or he might consider symptomatic improvement only a small part of the desirable change which he sees as a
structural and dynamic one that would enable the patient—in the time
honored phrase—to function better in work, love and play.

So far, all that has been said holds true for general psychotherapeutic
propositions. Like the rest of the field of medicine, psychotherapy has
had to develop many subspecialties. In the field of psychotherapy, a
broad basic understanding of human behavior is essential, and the more
clinical psychology, sociology and anthropology, ethology, philosophy
and linguistics it includes, aside from medicine, so much the better.

Such is the complexity of human behavior, however, that there are
many precise things to be aware of and many highly individualized
techniques to be mastered in order to work successfully with infants,
children and adults. Even restricting oneself to the psychotherapy of
adults, efficiency and success are based on very precise knowledge of
unique problems. Moreover, it does seem as if our world has become increasingly complex. The number of special problems seems to have mul-
tiplied, bringing along with it the need for more specialized knowledge
and management.

The quest for health and happiness has burgeoned dramatically since
World War II, particularly in the American culture. Affluence has
stirred the desire for orthodontia as much as for orthopsychiatry—the
desire to grow up "straight" emotionally. The post world war period
changed value systems radically, with a resultant change in character
structure and symptomatology, and a pressing need for different and
specialized psychotherapeutic techniques. Along with sexual freedom
came awareness of sexual problems, the quest for greater sexual fulfillment, and a market for various and sundry sex therapies. Along with
equal rights for women came a changing job market, a shift in traditional
marital roles, a quest for greater marital bliss, an increase in the divorce
rate, and the extensive development of marital therapy.

The "culture of plenty" provided fertile ground for the narcissistic revolution. This led to an explosion of character disorders and borderline conditions, and the need for special forms of therapy. Traditional psychoanalysis has to broaden its scope. Superego structure as well as ego structure became looser, and feelings of emptiness became the most frequently voiced psychiatric complaint. The myriad attempts at self-cure consisted too often of trips into the drug culture, with its many psychiatric complications and the need for special treatment designs. A parallel development was a tremendous increase in the population over age 65, having passed the 20 million mark at present. Psychiatric care of the elderly became another special field. The Community Mental Health Act (which created Community Mental Health Clinics) and the greater concern with emotional health had much to do with the development of brief and emergency psychotherapy and of group modalities.

Consumerism and the entry of third party payment were some of the forces responsible for the heightened concern with accountability. Concepts such as "goal directed psychotherapy" and "target symptoms" have become popular, as have peer review and PSRO. Some of these developments, to be sure, have bordered on the ridiculous. One major effort to study the effectiveness of psychotherapy was undertaken by a nationally prominent research organization, which attempted to introduce methods of cost accounting to the evaluation of psychotherapy. Failing entirely to arrive at some measures of quality control, it was simply reduced to measuring the "delivery" of psychotherapeutic services by the number of patients seen per therapist, with no measure of quality at all.

Thus, one has to guard against excesses in the development of psychotherapy, as in all forms of endeavor. The need for instant gratification in our culture has found its counterpart in instant therapies, such as primal scream, EST, scientology and others, and they are probably as valuable as all other attempts at miracle cures.

On the other hand, if social and economic developments and the complexities of our culture force us to develop better, more specific, and more successful psychotherapies, this is only to be welcomed. The more specific and better conceptualized the hypotheses concerning a given form of psychopathology and its treatment, the more effective a therapy it is likely to be. The present volume is dedicated to that proposition. We have asked a large number of psychotherapists with particular knowledge and experience to write about the specific problems and special techniques necessary for the treatment of patients with unique kinds of problems.

We hope that the accumulated expertise of so many distinguished contributors will make this an outstandingly valuable volume.

REFERENCES

1. Bellak, L. Once over: What is psychotherapy? *J. of Nerv. Ment. Dis.*, 1977, 165:295-299.
2. BELLAK, L. Kombinierte Psycho- und Pharmakotherapie unter besonderer Berücksichtigung von Kurz—und Notfalltherapie. *Psychiatria Clinica*, 1977, 10:102-113.
3. Bellak, L., Hurvich, M., and Gediman, H. K. *Ego Functions in Schizophrenics, Neurotics, and Normals.* New York: John Wiley & Sons, 1973.
4. Bellak, L. and Small, L. *Emergency Psychotherapy and Brief Psychotherapy.* Revised edition. New York: Grune & Stratton, 1978.
5. Strupp, H. H. and Hadley, S. W. A tripartite model of mental health and therapeutic outcomes. *American Psychologist*, March 1977, 187-196.

SPECIALIZED TECHNIQUES IN INDIVIDUAL PSYCHOTHERAPY

1

Psychotherapies: An Overview

Toksoz B. Karasu, M.D.

The emergence of numerous competing systems of psychotherapy during the last few decades has been cited as one of the principal problem areas in the field (1). In 1975 Parloff polled more than 140 presumable forms of currently practiced psychotherapy (2). Although London described this confusing proliferation as a reflection of changing times in answer to pervasive repression, anxiety, and/or boredom of man (3), the specific ways in which each new modality may or may not differ from its precedessors are far from clear. For the most part, dogmatic partisan claims of the superiority of each successive system continue to persist in spite of increasing evidence that such separatist claims may be largely unfounded (4, 5).

In attempts to comprehend the therapeutic influence in the total range of psychological treatments that have made their appearance at various points in the course of time, many authors have focused on the nonspecific or uncommon elements that all psychotherapies are presumed to share (4, 6-19). The following features have been repeatedly cited as basic to all psychotherapies: an emotionally charged, confiding relationship; a therapeutic rationale (myth) that is accepted by patient

Reprinted by permission from *The American Journal of Psychiatry*, Vol. 134, pp. 851-863, 1977. Copyright 1977 American Psychiatric Association.

and therapist; the provision of new information, which may be transmitted by precept, example, and/or self-discovery; the strengthening of the patient's expectation of help; the provision of success experiences; and the facilitation of the arousal of one's emotions (9).

Alternatively, Wittkower and Warnes pointed out that "while such universal features undoubtedly exist, it seems absurd to minimize differences in psychotherapy" (19). The originators and strong proponents of individual systems of psychotherapy who felt the need to differentiate and/or dissociate themselves from their predecessors and peers to justify their efforts might share this view (20-23). In addition, comparative conceptual studies of various forms of psychotherapy typically cite striking contrasts among various therapies (24-33). More recently, experimental studies of different schools have lent some scientific support to the separatist stance. Exemplary of such findings are the systematic studies of analytically oriented psychotherapy versus behavior therapy supporting the view that these are, in total, highly contrasting styles of treatment (34, 35). Moreover, the treatment procedures created, developed, and chosen in one society or within the context of a particular belief system may not be transposable to another. This is especially evident in attempts at cross-cultural psychotherapy (19, 36).

The current state of the art attests to the lack of clarity and lack of resolution of the specificity versus common elements controversy in explaining what is the quintessence of the therapeutic cure. This conflicting state of affairs is further compounded by those comparative studies of various psychotherapies which suggest that one's espoused theoretical orientation regarding the nature of the healing process may not always be synchronous with one's actual practices (37-39). For example, a comparison study of Freudian, Kleinian, Jungian, and Gestaltist therapists found that descriptive ratings of the different approaches in action did not differentiate the respective schools of thought as well as the investigators (and, no doubt, the proponents themselves) would have expected (39).

As treatments useful in one area of human disturbance are found to be less valuable in another (5, 40), efforts are made to arrive at better criteria for selecting patients for particular forms of therapy and for modifying existing forms. Here the stated task for the future is to achieve greater specificity concerning the effects of particular kinds of interventions (13). Thus the tantalizing need for increased examination and clarification of the therapeutic process continues.

Doubtless there are many ways to slice the therapeutic pie. In early attempts to schematize the many psychotherapeutic methods and techniques throughout history, Menninger (41) and Bromberg (42) ultimately subsumed the various forms under two dichotomous heads: those which they thought used a principle of suppression in their treatment approach versus those which represented the use of a principle of expression.

Beginning where Menninger and Bromberg left off, Harper's descriptive overview of 36 established Freudian and post-Freudian psychotherapeutic schools, or systems of psychotherapy, attempted to divide the various approaches into two overriding categories: those which reflected emotionally oriented or affective forms of treatment versus those which Harper considered essentially intellectually oriented or cognitive (28). On a more philosophical plane, Rychlak addressed the possible implications of ideology for methodology and assessed psychotherapies on the basis of whether they represented therapeutic models that were essentially Lockean (mechanistic) or Kantian (humanistic) (43). Rychlak also conceptualized psychotherapies according to a comparison of their respective motives: those with a scholarly motive, which are primarily concerned with unraveling the depths of man's nature; those with an ethical motive, which concern themselves primarily with man's self and his values; and those with a curative motive, which directly aim at scientifically derived cure (44). Offenkrantz and Tobin's configuration is more implicit. They suggested that all learning (including psychotherapeutic learning) occurs in three modes: by identification, by conditioning, and by insight (45). Thus one might assume to unite the various psychotherapies on the basis of their primary modes of therapeutic learning or the major ways in which they presume to effect change in or cure of the patient.

With the preceding topographies in mind, I shall organize the morass of systems practiced today according to a troika of basic themes around which each school may be said to broadly, but distinctively, pivot. These, representing a composite of dimensions, are referred to as dynamic, behavioral, and experiential (see Table 1). Although these rubrics per se are not completely new (2, 46), to my knowledge no study has attempted to portray schematically their respective features in relation to the increasing array of modalities being practiced today. A number of contrasting dimensions constitute or reside behind these three themes (see Table 2). Each theme represents something of a unity, that is, one's conceptual framework or belief system regarding the nature of man and his ills will have a bearing on one's concept of therapeutic modes or curative pro-

TABLE 1

Examples of Three Therapeutic Themes in the Psychotherapies and Their Variations*

Dynamic		Behavioral		Experiential	
Theme or Variation	Representative	Theme or Variation	Representative	Theme or Variation	Representative
Classical psychoanalysis	Freud	Reciprocal inhibition therapy	Wolpe	Existential analysis	Binswanger
Analytical psychology	Jung	Implosive therapy	Stampfl	Daseinanalysis	Boss
Will therapy	Rank	Conditioned reflex therapy	Salter	Logotherapy	Frankl
Active analytical therapy	Stekel	Learning theory therapy	Dollard	Client-centered therapy	Rogers
Individual psychology	Adler	Social learning psychotherapy	Rotter	Gestalt therapy	Perls
Interpersonal psychiatry	Sullivan	Modeling therapy	Bandura	Psycho-imagination therapy	Shorr
Intensive psychotherapy	Fromm-Reichmann	Directive psycho-therapy	Thorne	Experiential therapy	Whitaker
Character analysis	Horney	Direct decision therapy	Greenwald	Experiential therapy	Gendlin
Cultural school	Fromm	Confrontation problem-solving	Garner	Primal scream therapy	Janov
Ego analysis	Klein	Assertion-structured therapy	Phillips	Bioenergetic analysis	Lowen

TABLE I (continued)

Therapy	Source	Therapy	Source	Therapy	Source
Chicago school	Alexander, French	Personal construct therapy	Kelly	Structural analysis	Rolf
Sector therapy	Deutsch	Rational therapy	Ellis	Autogenic training	Luthe
Objective psychotherapy	Karpman	Integrity therapy	Drakeford	Transcendental Meditation	
Short-term psychotherapy	Sifneos, Malan, Bellak	Reality therapy	Glasser	Nirvana therapy	
Direct analysis	Rosen	Philosophical psychotherapy	Sahakian	Zen psychotherapy	Watts
Psychobiological therapy	Meyer	Biofeedback training	Green	Psychedelic therapy	Osmond
Biodynamic therapy	Masserman				
Adaptational psychodynamics	Rado				
Hypnoanalysis	Wolberg				
Character analysis, vegetotherapy	Reich				

* Although some of the more recent psychotherapies may combine individual and group techniques, this organization of psychotherapeutic systems focuses on modalities that are essentially dyadic in nature. It therefore does not include family, group, or milieu therapies per se, nor such adjunct therapies as art, music, and dance.

cesses and the nature of the therapeutic relationship between patient and therapist and, ultimately, on one's methods or techniques of treatment.

THE DYNAMIC THEME

The Nature of Man and His Ills

The dynamic point of view, as originally conceived in the context of physics, subscribes to the idea that all mental phenomena are the result of an interaction of forces (47). It pertains to an appreciation of the complexity of man as reactor to or victim of turbulent intrapsychic forces from which he continually struggles to be set free. Freud described the major force of this struggle in the origin of the neuroses of man according to the theory of instinctual conflict: "From the very first we have said that human beings fall ill of a conflict between the claims of instinctual life and the resistance which arises within them against it" (48, p. 57). More specifically, Freud considered the etiology of the neuroses of man to be decidedly sexual in nature: "No neurosis is possible with a normal *vita sexualis*" (49, p. 276). In the orthodox dynamic tradition man is portrayed as fraught with inner and unknown urgings and contradictions, subject to and resisting against a reservoir of impulses largely inaccessible to his conscious self.

The psychoanalytic perspective typically incorporates five fundamental principles, i.e., dynamic, economic, structural, developmental, and adaptive (50). Taken together, these principles offer an analytic legacy that includes the following allegiances: 1) a primary concern with the vicissitudes of man's instinctual impulses, their expression and transformation, and, more crucially, their repression, by which is meant the pervasive avoidance of painful feelings or experiences by keeping unpleasant thoughts, wishes, and affect from awareness; 2) the belief that such repression is of an essentially sexual nature and that the roots of disturbance reside in faulty libidinal or psychosexual development; 3) the idea that faulty psychosexual development has its origins in early past and childhood conflicts or traumata, especially those concerning a parental oedipal configuration as manifested in the classic desire for one's opposite-sexed parent; 4) the belief in the resilience, persistence, and inaccessibility of oedipal yearnings (i.e., these underlying conflicts remain alive and ever active but out of awareness or unconscious; man's consciousness describes the exceptional rather than the standard state of affairs); 5) the idea that we are dealing essentially with the psychic

TABLE 2

Summary of Thematic Dimensions of Three Kinds of Psychotherapy

Theme	Dynamic	Behavioral	Experiential
Prime concern	Sexual repression	Anxiety	Alienation
Concept of pathology	Instinctual conflicts: early libidinal drives and wishes that remain out of awareness, i.e., unconscious	Learned habits: excess or deficit behaviors that have been environmentally reinforced	Existential despair: human loss of possibilities, fragmentation of self, lack of congruence with one's experiences
Concept of health	Resolution of underlying conflicts: victory of ego over id, i.e., ego strength	Symptom removal: absence of specific symptom and/or reduction of anxiety	Actualization of potential: self-growth, authenticity, and spontaneity
Mode of change	Depth insight: understanding of the early past, i.e., intellectual-emotional knowledge	Direct learning: behaving in the current present, i.e., action or performance	Immediate experiencing: sensing or feeling in the immediate moment, i.e., spontaneous expression of experience
Time approach and focus	Historical: subjective past	Nonhistorical: objective present	Ahistorical: phenomenological moment
Type of treatment	Long-term and intense	Short-term and not intense	Short-term and intense
Therapist's task	To comprehend unconscious mental content and its historical and hidden meanings	To program, reward, inhibit, or shape specific behavioral responses to anxiety-producing stimuli	To interact in a mutually accepting atmosphere for arousal of self-expression (from somatic to spiritual)
Primary tools techniques	Interpretation: free association, analysis of transference, resistance, slips, and dreams	Conditioning: systematic densitization, positive and negative reinforcements, shaping	Encounter: shared dialogue, experiments or games, dramatization or playing out of feelings
Treatment model	Medical: doctor-patient or parent-infant (authoritarian), i.e., therapeutic alliance	Educational: teacher-student or parent-child (authoritarian), i.e., learning alliance	Existential: human peer-human peer or adult-adult (egalitarian), i.e., human alliance
Nature of relationship to cure	Transferential and primary for cure: unreal relationship	Real but secondary for cure: no relationship	Real and primary for cure: real relationship
Therapist's role and stance	Interpreter-reflector: indirect, dispassionate, or frustrating	Shaper-adviser: direct, problem-solving, or practical	Interactor-acceptor: mutually permissive or gratifying

struggle and torments of biological man's innate impulses or instincts (id), their derivatives, and the primarily defensive mediation with external reality (ego) in light of one's moral precepts or standards (superego); and, finally, 6) an adherence to a concept of psychic determinism or causality according to which mental phenomena as well as behaviors are decidedly not chance occurrences but meaningfully related to events that preceded them and, unless made conscious, unwittingly subject to repetition.

Therapeutic Change or Curative Processes

In accordance with these tenets, for the dynamic therapist the ultimate task in its most parsimonious and famous form is to make conscious the unconscious. This means that it is the ongoing therapeutic charge of the therapist who subscribes to the dynamic view to facilitate the emergence and comprehension of unconscious and largely libidinal content. That is, the dynamic therapist seeks to undo the essentially sexual repression of the patient and to overcome the patient's natural resistances to this endeavor. The dynamic therapist attempts to accomplish this by means of a slow and scrupulous unraveling of the largely historical meanings of mental events and the devious ways in which they may serve to ward off the underlying conflicts through defensive camouflage. Understandably, the dynamic goal is thereby a long-range one, perhaps even interminable. At best this concept of cure means opting for total personality reorganization in the final resolution of neurotic conflicts. The most crucial manifestation of this is the resolution of the oedipal conflict, which is traditionally regarded as requisite for a healthy personality. This ultimate integration of personality would translate itself into final mastery of ego over id impulses or, as classically stated, where id was, there ego shall be.

Greenson defined the therapeutic process as "an interrelated series of psychic events within the patient, a continuity of psychic forces which have a remedial aim or effect" (51, p. 7). The dynamic psychotherapeutic systems have consecutively considered as their hallmarks of change the processes of catharsis (following abreaction) and insight. Harper broadly defined insight as "the process by which the meaning, significance, pattern, or use of an experience becomes clear—or the understanding which results from this process" (28, p. 163). He defined catharsis as "the release of tension and *anxiety* by recounting and/or *acting out* past experiences" (28, p. 158; author's italics).

Although both processes have been considered in the psychodynamic tradition, it may be noted that Freud never used the term "insight" per se. The therapeutic process transferred its emphasis from the primary importance of abreaction (catharsis) to the removal of amnesia and the recovery of repressed memories. Following this shift, Greenson pointed out, "catharsis [is] no longer the ultimate aim of therapy" (51, p. 13). In its stead, the process of insight has been extensively singled out not only to refer to a phenomenon specially applicable to the psychodynamic therapies in contrast to other therapies (51-53) but also as the patient's ultimate aspiration.

According to Hutchinson, there are four successive stages in attaining therapeutic insight: 1) a stage of preparation, which is characterized by frustration, anxiety, a feeling of ineptness, and despair and may be followed by much trial-and-error activity relevant to the solution of a certain problem and the falling into habitual patterns or ways of thinking, foreseeing no apparent solution to the problem; 2) a stage of incubation or renunciation in which one desires to hide or escape from the problem and one is resistant or unmotivated in therapeutic or insightful efforts; 3) a stage of aspiration or illumination in which the whole problem becomes illuminated and a solution or solutions suggest themselves (often there is a flood of vivid ideas and a sense of finality accompanied by a conviction in the truth of the insight) ; and 4) a stage of elaboration and evaluation in which the validity of the insight is checked against external reality (54).

Although the third stage tends to be most frequently identified with the idea of insight (suggesting an essentially eureka phenomenon), Ludwig pointed out that

> during the typical course of psychotherapy, it is much more common for the patient to experience insight in a . . . drawn out emotionally attenuated form. The sudden tidal wave of illumination or enlightenment is rare compared to the numerous small ripples of insights which are experienced and intellectually assimilated over a long period of time. Moreover, the therapeutic insights tend to be circumscribed and specific to certain problem areas that the profound and general eureka experiences, such as those described to occur during religious conversion or revelation in which the "whole truth" suddenly is revealed (55, p. 315).

In terms of the therapeutic value of the process of insight, Ludwig noted that "there is no necessary relationship between the truth or falseness of insight and therapeutic results" (55, p. 313). In addition, since intellectual insight alone is felt to be of minimal value, attempts have been made to distinguish between intellectual and emotional insight. However, it is difficult to validate such a distinction (56).

In brief, Ludwig hypothesized that insight is therapeutic when it meets all of the following specifications: 1) consistency, that is, the deductions based on the original insight are stable and logically sound regardless of the truth or falsity of the particular content of the insight; 2) continuity, that is, insights must take place within some existing theoretical framework or stream of tradition in which the insight can be tested; 3) personal consequences, that is, the insight must be judged by the fruit it bears in terms of the ultimate use to which the insight is put; and 4) social consequences, that is, the acquisition of insight should allow the person to interact with others in a more honest and meaningful manner (55).

Although analysts have confidence in the role of insight as a therapeutic agent, doubt has been cast on the "insight leads to change" dictum. Schonbar, for example, has observed that "not all change is attributable to insight" and "not all insight leads to change" (57). However, the fact that insight, even as an ultimate change agent, does not occur in isolation is more important for consideration of the analytic therapies. Intricately embedded in the psychodynamic curative process is the critical role of the therapeutic relationship, expressly manifested in the phenomenon of the transference relationship.

The Nature of the Therapeutic Relationship

In 1970 Strupp noted, "There can be no doubt that the patient's relationship to the therapist . . . embodies one of the most powerful forces in the therapeutic enterprise. . . . Psychotherapuetic changes always occur in the context of an interpersonal relationship, and are to some extent inextricable from it" (13, pp. 396, 400). The specific therapeutic agent, according to Rosen, seems to be the "complex, emotionally-charged parent-child kind of relationship between the psychiatrist and the individual whom he is treating" (58, p. 126). In terms of the special nature of that therapeutic relationship, it should be pointed out that deliberate systematic attention to the vicissitudes of the special relationship between therapist and patient is crucial to the conduct of the psychoanalytic psychotherapies. It constitutes both the subject and the object of analysis.

Historically, two roles or stances for the therapist have been described in portraying the psychodynamic psychotherapies: the primary stance with regard to the making of the transference relationship and, more recently, the secondary stance with regard to the making of a working or therapeutic alliance. Despite increasing acceptance of the latter into the therapeutic situation, these represent dual postures, which Greenson explicitly depicted as antithetical to each other, both in their essential purposes and in the actual requirements they make of the therapist (51).

The primary stance reflects Freud's original recommendations 1) that the analyst be like a mirror to the patient, reflecting only what is reflected to him/her by the patient and not bringing his/her own feelings (attitudes, values, personal life) into play (59) and 2) that the analyst follow a posture of privation or rule of abstinence, that is, technical motives must unite with ethical ones in preventing the therapist from offering the patient the "love" that the patient will necessarily come to crave (59, pp. 157-171).

These dictums have been taken to mean that two basic requirements are traditionally made of the analyst if he/she is to best accomplish the therapeutic task: 1) he/she must continue to judiciously frustrate and avoid gratifying the wishes of the patient; and 2) he/she must remain relatively removed and anonymous, a deliberately dispassionate observer and reflector of the patient's feelings. The therapeutic relationship is asymmetrical. Henry and associates described the relationship as follows:

> Only the patient is supposed to reveal the intimate details of his life. The psychotherapist is not only free to determine what he will reveal and conceal about himself, but also to choose how to react to what the patient is saying, if indeed he decides to respond at all. The relationship is also asymmetrical in that only the therapist is supposed to interpret and impute meaning to what the patient is saying and only the therapist can evaluate the degree to which therapeutic objectives are being achieved in the relationship (60, p. 218).

Conversely, within the same framework, the more recent concept of a working or therapeutic alliance reflects an alternatively nonregressive, rational relationship between patient and therapist. Although still in the service of analyzing transference and resistances, according to Chessick it means "that the therapist aims at forming a real and mature alliance with the conscious adult ego of the patient and encourages him to be a scientific partner in the exploration of his difficulties" (53). The real object need of the patient, deliberately frustrated by the transference relationship, is satisfied by the therapeutic alliance.

Techniques and Methods

Bellis' statement that "no technique is therapeutic in itself. . . . Every clinician must understand and calibrate his own instruments" (61) bears repeating in a discussion of the techniques of dynamic psychotherapy.

The major instruments of the prototypic dynamic approach are primarily verbal in nature. They rest in part on the proverbial talking cure and may be regarded as free asociation on the part of the patient and analysis of transference reactions and resistances on the part of the therapist. Analysis, the task of the therapist, is facilitated by four specific procedures: confrontation, clarification, interpretation, and working-through. It is the third of these, interpretation, that, according to Greenson, is regarded as the "ultimate and decisive instrument" (51).

With regard to the input of the patient, the technique of free association early reflected the major vehicle for the communication of uncensored content from patient to therapist. It has constituted the primary procedure for eliciting the raw material on which the analysis ultimately rests. This includes the eliciting of dreams, which Freud regarded as "the royal road to a knowledge of the unconscious activities of the mind" (62, p. 608). Methodically, the attempt to solicit free associations and dreams from the patient accounts for the most notorious material ingredient of the analytic method in classical analysis—the couch. Having the patient in a supine position out of direct view of the therapist and without extrinsic environmental intrusions is meant to create conditions of relative sensory deprivation that in turn serve to maximize the evocation of repressed memories.

With regard to the therapist's task and response to the verbal material elicited from the patient, the crux of the psychoanalytic method remains the analysis of transference, which comprises the major instrument of analysis as well as its major obstacle. The deliberate elucidation of transference reactions results in inevitable resistances to this endeavor, which must also be overcome as part of the treatment. Methodologically, the reflective, ambiguous stance of the therapist in concert with the high frequency and regularity of contacts between patient and therapist are meant to encourage the regressive transference process and the intensity of feelings in the treatment situation.

Despite the endowment of the value of interpretation, the therapeutic path must be carefully paved in order for it to have its most beneficial effects. In this regard, the role of the techniques of confrontation, clarification, and working-through have been noted. Confrontation refers to having the patient discern or face the particular mental event to be investigated: clarification refers to placing the same event in sharp focus, separating important aspects from insignificant ones (both of these processes prepare for the actual interpretation) ; interpretation then goes beyond the manifest material by assigning an underlying meaning or cause to the event or phenomenon in question; finally, working-through refers to the repetitive, progressive, and elaborate explorations of the interpretations and resistances to them until the presented material has become fully integrated into the patient's understanding. This is perhaps the most time-consuming aspect of dynamic psychotherapy. Although the major thrust of treatment occurs within the therapist's office, working-through necessarily includes the tacit work done by the patient outside of the therapeutic hour.

In terms of comparisons with other forms of treatment and their reputed curing powers, certain techniques or procedures are considered to be expressly anti-analytic, i.e., to block or lessen one's understanding or insight rather than facilitating it. Foremost in this regard are (perhaps ironically) abreaction, which may still be used but is not felt to directly bring insight; direct suggestion or advice, which is only useful to the extent that it is openly acknowledged and analyzed within the therapy setting; manipulation, allowable only to the extent that it can be brought into the analytic arena and does not occur without the ultimate knowledge of the patient; and the deliberate or conscious assumption of roles or attitudes that create an unanalyzable situation by their very nature.

Variations on the Dynamic Theme

The prototypic embodiment of the psychodynamic theme is, of course, classical psychoanalysis. The variations on the dynamic theme reflect overt and covert modifications of theoretical conceptualizations as well as methodological and technical applications in practice. These include attempts to partially or completely transcend the biological focus of Freud with more interpersonal, social, ethical, and cultural considerations (e.g., Adler, Horney, Sullivan, Fromm, Fromm-Reichmann, Meyer, and Masserman) ; to extend or enhance the ego with earlier or more adaptive endowments (e.g., Federn and Klein) ; to enlarge man's temporality with a time focus on his primordial past (e.g., Jung), his present, and/or his future (e.g., Adler, Stekel, Rank, and Rado) ; to expand treatment procedures by altering the range and goals of treatment (e.g., Rank, Alexander, Deutsch, and Karpman) ; to develop guidelines for his short-term psychotherapy with anxiety-provoking techniques (e.g., Sifneos) and even brief treatment of serious illness within the context of a single interview (e.g., Malan) (63-67); to revise the role of the therapist's personality and relationship to the patient by making the therapist a more direct, flexible, and/or active participant (e.g., Adler, Sullivan, Rank, Alexander, Stekel, Ferenczi, and Rosen); and, at perhaps the opposing end of the analytic spectrum, to restore the psychophysical balance of man by focusing equally on the physical half of the psychophysical split (e.g., Rado and Masserman) and/or substituting an approach to therapeutic cure from the somatic side by trading the traditional change mode of insight for a reversal back to the earlier catharsis by means of the bodily release of conflictual tensions (e.g., Reich).

THE BEHAVIORAL THEME

The Nature of Man and His Ills

The behavioral theme presumes that all behavior, both normal and abnormal, is a product of what man has learned or not learned. Neuroses or neurotic symptoms are construed as simple learned habits, involuntarily acquired, repeated, reinforced responses to specific stimuli in the environment. Indeed, Eysenck said, "there is no neurosis underlying the symptom, but merely the symptom itself" (68). Conversely, since external behaviors constitute the essence of the therapeutic problem, the therapeutic cure is simple: "Get rid of the symptom and you have eliminated the neurosis" (68).

Behavioral psychotherapy is an outgrowth of animal laboratory experiments on classically conditioned responses in which animals were observed to have habits that were like human phobias. Traditionally, behavioral psychotherapy also presumes that human neuroses have the same basic vicissitudes as those of the animal, in which anxiety (equated with fear) is regarded as its central manifestation (69).

Thus behavioral man is reducible to stimulus-response connections that can be isolated and altered in a piecemeal manner by reinserting new associations. Viewed in this way, behavioral man is infinitely manipulable and therefore controllable by external events in the environment.

The prototype of orthodox behavior therapy is exemplified in Wolpe's reciprocal inhibition therapy, which is based on a classical conditioning paradigm.* Wolpe's main thesis is that neurotic symptoms are all essentially phobias based on the adverse learning of unrealistic fears. In behavioral theory this means that anxiety has been conditioned during highly disturbing or traumatic experiences. Wolpe would regard a complex symptom like neurotic passivity as a learned fear of rejection or disapproval reflecting one form of a phobic or anxious reaction to others.

Therapeutic or Change Processes

For the behaviorist all problems are construed as pedagogical in nature and therefore alterable only through direct teaching and learning of new behavioral associations, i.e., stimulus-response connections. The patient must be taught new alternatives that must be repeated and practiced within as well as outside of the therapy situation. These alternative modes of functioning do not occur simply as a concomitant of cognitive or emotional understanding of one's problems; the patient must rehearse the new alternatives directly. Thus, in direct contrast to the psychodynamic schools, the behavioral approaches, according to Cautela, tend to sustain the view that insight is not only unnecessary but usually hinders the treatment for deviant behavior (70). Wolpe's principle of reciprocal inhibition implies the rejection of catharsis as well. Wolpe sees abreaction (the symbolic re-evocation of a fearful past experience) as a special case in point, asserting that no permanent effects are achieved if unrelieved terror is the only emotional factor involved and is not counterposed by relaxation responses.

One implication of this view of the mode of therapeutic change is that change can presumably occur within a short period of time. In contrast to the dynamic theme, Eysenck stated that "all treatment of neurotic disorders is concerned with habits existing in the present; their historical development is largely irrelevant" (68). Moreover, Cautela stated, "In fact, it is possible to have a situation in which symptoms have been removed with no knowledge at all of the etiology" (70).

Although all behaviorists may be viewed as seeking change through direct conditioning, shaping, or training, Wolpe, in accordance with his classical conditioning paradigm, sees all therapeutic learning or change (not just behavior therapy) as occurring within the reciprocal inhibition framework per se. All therapies necessarily incorporate the substitution

---

* The terms "classical" versus "operant" conditioning procedures refer essentially to the respective sequence in the application of the stimulus. In classical conditioning the stimulus precedes and in operant conditioning the stimulus follows the behavioral response to be changed.

of relaxation for anxiety in the reduction or elimination of symptoms. However, more critically, the difference between behavior therapy and other therapeutic situations is that in the latter, counterconditioning of relaxation over anxiety occurs fortuitously or unsystematically, whereas in behavior therapy this process is overt, systematic, and under the direct control of the therapist.

The Nature of the Therapeutic Relationship

The nature of the therapeutic relationship between therapist and patient in the behavioral therapies is, according to Hollander, an essentially "educative, teacher-pupil relationship" (71). In contrast to the psychodynamic transferential relationship but comparable to the working or therapeutic alliance in certain respects, the behavioral relationship may be portrayed as a deliberately structured learning alliance, in which, at its best, attention is drawn to the more current and presumably constructive aspects of the patient's personality in collaborating on the course of therapy.

Krasner depicted the behavior therapist as a learning technician or "social reinforcement machine" (72). Although this rubric may apply to all therapies to greater or lesser degrees, usually the behavioral therapist openly regards himself/herself as an instrument of direct behavioral influence or control, one who directly and systematically manipulates, shapes, and/or inserts his/her own values in the therapeutic encounter. In a comparable context, the therapist shapes his/her own behavior so as to be a social reinforcer for the patient. If the therapy does not proceed smoothly and effectively, the behavior therapist revises the behavioral plan or schedule to better fit the patient to treatment (71).

Behavior therapy deliberately does not dwell on the therapist-patient relationship; at most, it does so secondarily, that is, according to APA's Task Force on Behavior Therapy, "only to the extent that this is seen to be important in securing the patient's cooperation with the therapist's treatment plan" (73, p. 27).

The behavior therapist's use of warmth, acceptance, and any other relationship skills is common but relegated to the realm of secondary "relationship skills" that are not crucial therapeutic requirements for desired change to occur in the patient (71).

Techniques and Methods

In Ehrenwald's words, the behavioral schools of psychotherapy actively relinquish "the methods of the couch" and replace them with "the methods of the classroom and the pulpit" (7). The behavior therapist has at his/her disposal a large variety of conditioning, training, and other directive techniques. This repertoire may include any or all of the following: the more classical conditioning techniques of systematic desensitization combined with deep muscle relaxation, implosion, or assertiveness training; the operant techniques of positive or negative reinforcement; aversiveness training; shaping or modeling; and/or the more flexible directive techniques pertaining to the direct transmission of advice, guidance, persuasion, and exhortation. The latter methods more typically reflect the means by which behavior modification has been extended recently to the teaching or conditioning of cognitive behaviors or attitudes underlying specific behaviors, methods of philosophical indoctrination, or cognitive programming.

More generally, the behaviorist initially sets out to identify the patient's specific target behaviors or responses that need to be modified. These, in conjunction with the stimuli or environmental situations that give rise to the specific behaviors, constitute a behavioral formulation that may be regarded as the behaviorist's counterpart of psychodynamic formulation. The behavioral formulation is used for the purpose of setting specific treatment goals, which are usually made explicit to the patient at the outset. The initial interview typically aims to specify what situations or factors contribute to the maintenance of the particular responses in question and on what occasions those responses are most likely elicited. On this basis the behavioral conditioning program can then begin.

Wolpe's classical reciprocal inhibition therapy, which has as its direct aim the reduction or inhibition of anxiety responses through the substitution of relaxation responses for anxiety, typically uses two basic techniques for the purpose of juxtaposing relaxation with anxiety. The first technique is progressive deep muscle relaxation training and the second is systematic desensitization of anxiety through imagination. The patient is instructed to relax and then tense up for intervals of 10-15 seconds each; the patient repeats this maneuver using various different muscle groups or parts of the body followed by breathing exercises. Then, after discussing with the patient which real-life situations arouse the phobic symptoms, the therapist incorporates each scene into an anxiety list or anxiety hierarchy; this list constitutes the basic therapeutic tool. (Each scene or situation is arranged hierarchically on the basis of level of anxiety generated in the patient, with a ranking system of 1-10). Starting with the weakest elicitor of anxiety in the hierarchy, the therapist asks the patient to imagine the anxious circumstance for a few minutes and then instructs the patient to concentrate on relaxing; this process is repeated until the patient can imagine the scene without feeling any anxiety. The therapist ascends the anxiety list item by item in the same manner. When this process is finished, the real-life situation that has created the phobia has lost its capacity to elicit anxiety.

A more recent variation of this approach is, ironically, a direct reversal of this procedure. The therapist starts not with the bottom but with the top of the anxiety continuum; the patient is flooded with the strongest anxiety-eliciting stimulus situation of his/her imagination and keeps this in mind until the anxiety dissipates. Then, with successive repetitions of the same scene, the patient's anxiety progressively lessens until he/she is immune to anxiety in that situation. This basic technique is referred to as implosion (Stampfl's implosive therapy).

A cognitive variation of this approach is the technique of thought-stopping. In this variation the patient puts into words the anxiety-producing situations instead of merely imagining them. As the patient speaks about himself/herself in these situations the therapist suddenly interrupts the train of anxious verbalizations by shouting "Stop!" This procedure is repeated on successive occasions until the patient validates the fact that this overt suppression has indeed served to reduce the frequency of the anxiety-loaded thoughts. Ellis' rational therapy represents an elaboration of this cognitive approach on a larger and more varied scale.

The behavioral counterpart of the psychodynamic procedure of working-through is behavioral rehearsal within the confines of therapy as well as assignments to be worked on outside of therapy; these are important parts of the total behavioral treatment. For example, the patient might be directly trained in certain social skills that may first be role-played or rehearsed within the course of therapy as well as explicitly instructed, tested out in outside real-life situations, and reviewed in subsequent sessions.

A special instance of this method is assertiveness training, a technique of instruction and practice of interpersonal behaviors involving the relatively direct expression of one's positive and negative responses to others. Wolpe claimed that assertive responses constitute a major class of behaviors that could be used as an alternative to relaxation responses in the function of reciprocally inhibiting anxiety. Assertive training by means of behavior rehearsal, whether or not it is used as a technique for expressly countering anxiety, has been incorporated into a variety of schools that use the methods of the behavioral laboratory.

Variations on the Behavioral Theme

Three broad types of behavior therapies or behavior modification are considered under the umbrella of the behavioral theme (74) : one, based on the early classical Pavlovian paradigm, primarily uses systematic desensitization or extinction of anxiety techniques (e.g., Wolpe's reciprocal inhibition therapy) ; a second type, based on an operant Skinnerian paradigm, uses direct reinforcement by means of reward/punishment procedures (e.g., Allyon and Azrin's token economy) ; and a third type, based on a human social learning paradigm, is contingent on direct modeling or shaping procedures (e.g., Bandura's modeling therapy). The latter type of therapy extends to a variety of new systems of directive psychotherapy that expressly aim at attitudinal or philosophical restructuring, using methods of the behaviorist's laboratory. Such so-called integrity therapies, although they share the fundamental learning or problem-solving stance, are usually more actively advisory and/or exhortative in their therapeutic techniques (e.g., Ellis' rational therapy, Glasser's reality therapy, and Sahakian's philosophic psychotherapy).

Another way of viewing the scope of these behavioral variations is through the evolution of their targets of change from external to internal alterations in man's learnings. The earlier behavior therapeutic systems addressed overt behaviors and fears (e.g., Wolpe); the more recent systems are directed to more covert values and beliefs (e.g., Ellis). The most recent approaches venture into the reaches of the most inaccessible and involuntary mental and physiological states and responses, such as heart rate, blood pressure, and brain waves (e.g., biofeedback).

THE EXPERIENTIAL THEME

The Nature of Man and His Ills

In terms of therapeutic ideology, a major source of divergence and disagreement for the founders of schools of psychotherapy since Freud has been their inability to reconcile what they regard as a largely deterministic or defeatist image of man. This includes the renunciation of a dynamic conceptualization of man as a predominantly passive or instinctually regressive recipient of his conflictual drives, subservient to the less conscious aspects of himself. The experientialists criticize classical psychotherapy's overcommitment to the canons of science and its concurrent underplaying of man's ethical dimension, that is, his will, choices, and moral relation to others. Through psychotherapeutic practices and overemphasis on technique, man becomes impersonalized, compartmentalized, calculated, managed, and/or analyzed and thereby diminished instead of truly experienced by others or himself (20, 26, 53, 75).

Haigh, an experientialist, has criticized the behavioral conceptualization as follows:

> The therapeutic process [is] essentially concerned with the experiential anguish of isolation and alienation. These experiences of isolation, encapsulation, alienation derive from social programming. . . . The central problem cannot be understood exclusively at the level of overt behavior, [but] must be understood as involving incongruence between overt behavior and inner experience. Reinforcement learning theory is inadequate for translating this central problem because it doesn't include concepts representing human experience. The behavioral therapy techniques associated with reinforcement learning theory are potentially harmful because they involve the very same programming approach which induced these neurotic problems in the first place (76).

The experiential conceptualization represents an increasingly emerging exaltation of man in order to counter alienation, that is, the fostering of the fullest exploration of the unique and universal nature of man's self. It is expressly devoted to the self-transcendent quality of human experience. In Frankl's words, "Man is basically striving to find and fulfill meaning and purpose in life" (77, p. 252).

This reaching out involves a transpersonal as well as intrapersonal dimension. According to Arendsen-Hein, the intrapersonal refers to an "ego-centered level . . . where the main concern is the discovery of one's individuality, of one's emotional states and their representation in the physical body"; the transpersonal, on the other hand, is "spiritually oriented towards ultimate reality, . . . unity on the human, universal, or cosmic plane . . . in which [the person] experiences a transcendence of his ego boundaries into a universal consciousness" (78).

The experientialist tends to view man as an inherently active, striving, self-affirming, and self-potentiating entity with almost limitless capacity for positive growth, and the experiential therapies typically opt for growth and not mere healing of illness. Their therapeutic goal is attaining maximal awareness or a higher state of consciousness, in which, according to May and associates, "to be aware of one's world means at the same time to be designing it" (20, p. 60). Experientialists therefore direct themselves to such expansive dimensions as self-determination, creativity, and authenticity and make use of a potpourri of methodologies that aspire to an ultimate integration of the mind, body, and more recently, soul of fragmented man.

The experiential stance historically reflects the incorporation of the basic philosophy of the European existentialist, with his/her concern for the essential issues of man's being or becoming; the methodology of the phenomenologist, who attempts to address data as given in order to tap their meaning and to examine patients on their own terms without recourse to preconceived theoretical formulations of a causal or diagnostic nature; and, now more than ever, the religious teachings and techniques of the Eastern mystic, who presumes to bridge the mind-body split in seeking man's spiritual center. All, according to May and associates, focus on "man's most immediate experience . . . [i.e.,] that to fully know *what* we are doing, to feel it, to experience it all through our being, is much more important than to know *why*. For they hold, if we fully know the *what*, the *why* will come along by itself" (20, p. 83).

Pathology is regarded as the reduced expression of one's potential, the result of blocking and the loss of congruence with or repressing of one's internal self-experience. Both the psychodynamic and the experiential (essentially existential) themes depict the neurotic personality as suffering from repression and fragmentation. The dynamic view postulates repression of instinctual drives, especially sexual ones, while the experiential view construes repression as an ontological phenomenon, "the loss of a sense of being, together with the truncation of awareness and the locking up of potentialities which are the manifestation of this being" (20, p. 86).

Neurosis is a fundamental universal despair resulting from the individual's estrangement from himself and his society (or world). Comparably, anxiety, in marked contrast with the behavioral equation of anxiety with specific circumscribed fears, refers to "the anxiety of man facing the limits of his existence with the fullest implications . . . death, nothingness" (20, p. 118). Such anxiety manifests itself at every moment as man stands against the reaches of his own possibilities. Moreover, the origin of guilt accrues from the forfeiting of one's potential, for which the person alone is responsible.

In Maslow's words, pathology is "human diminution" (instead of neurosis), "the loss or not-yet-actualization of human capacities and possibilities" (79, p. 124). Thus health and illness, including all of the standard psychiatric categories, reside on a continuum—the differential between what one construes himself to be versus what one can become. The overall ideal or ultimate state of health refers to man as maximally conscious and real at every moment, to wit, according to Denes-Rado-misli, man as "vital, immediate, spontaneous, authentic, and active" (80, p. 104).

Therapeutic or Change Processes

The experiential schools of psychotherapy trade intellectual cognition and insight for emotion and experience, forsaking the there-and-then of the distant past for the here-and-now of the immediate present.

Experiencing is a process of feeling rather than knowing or verbalizing; occurs in the immediate present; is private and unobservable but can be directly referred to by an individual as a felt datum in his own phenomenal field; acts as a guide to conceptualization; is implicitly meaningful, although it may not become explicitly so until later; and is a preconceptual organismic process. The many implicit meanings of a moment's experiencing are regarded not as already conceptual and then repressed; rather, they are considered in the awareness but as yet undifferentiated. In total, according to Gendlin, "therapeutic change occurs as a result of a process [of experiencing] in which implicit meanings are in awareness, and are intensely felt, directly referred to, and changed, without ever being put into words" (81, p. 239).

Therapeutic change through experiencing usually occurs by means of a real or congruent interpersonal relationship between the patient and therapist. In the latter regard, May and associates said,

> Beyond all considerations of unconscious determinism—which are true in their partial context—the only thing that will grasp the patient, and in the long run make it possible [for him/her] to change, is to experience fully and deeply that [he/she] is doing precisely this to a real person ... in this real moment (20, p. 83).

One variation of this thesis, especially applicable to Rogers' client-centered therapy, reflects the underlying positive belief that every organism has an inborn tendency to develop its optimal capacities as long as it is placed in an optimal environment. Thus, according to Hoehn-Saric, the patient is offered "an optimistic self-image; he understands that he is basically good and full of potentials. . . . Therefore, the therapist does not need to challenge or shape the patient, he has only to provide the warm and understanding milieu which will enable the patient to unfold his latent potentials" (82, p. 261).

Unlike transference, which is dependent on the revival of a former interpersonal relationship, experiential encounter works "through the very fact of its novelty." Through encounter the therapist serves as a catalyst in whose presence the patient comes to realize his own latent and best abilities for shaping his own self (20).

The Nature of the Therapeutic Relationship

Although methods may vary, the real here-and-now therapeutic dialogue or mutual encounter between therapist and patient is the sine qua non of many of the experiential schools. It is, according to Ford and Urban, "an emotionally-arousing human relationship in which each person tries to communicate honestly with the other both verbally and nonverbally" (26, p. 470).

Rogers described the flavor of the therapeutic encounter as follows:

> I let myself go into the immediacy of the relationship where it is my total organism which takes over and is sensitive to the relationship, not simply my consciousness. I am not consciously responding in a planful or analytic way, but simply in an unreflective way to the other individual, my reaction being based (but not consciously) on my total organismic sensitivity to this other person. I live the relationship on this basis (83, pp. 267-268).

These approaches to psychotherapy ideologically aspire to an egalitarian treatment model. The human alliance is not of physician to patient or teacher to student but of human being to human being. May and associates presented the following rationale: "The therapist is assumedly an expert; but, if he is not first of all a human being, his expertness will be irrelevant and quite possibly harmful" (20, p. 82). Rogers stated that if the patient is viewed as an object the patient will tend to become an object (83). Therefore, the therapist says, "I enter the relationship not as a scientist, not as a physician who can accurately diagnose and cure, but as a person, entering into a personal relationship" (83, p. 267). Naturally, what one construes to fall within the domain of personal or real in a therapeutic relationship is open to interpretation.

In sum, although Seguin pointed out that the quality of the healer-patient relationship (and the form of therapeutic love or eros that is transmitted) is "different from the one between father and son, teacher and pupil, friends, and, of course, lovers" (84), the experiential theme rejects the paradigm of the parent-child relationship of the dynamic theme and the teacher-student paradigm of the behavioral theme and opts for something closer to the latter conceptualization (i.e., friends and lovers) in its paradigm of the therapeutic relationship.

Techniques and Methods

There is an assortment of schools of psychotherapy within the experiential theme that recoils at the idea of therapeutic technology. These schools, which are predominantly existential, renounce technique as part of their philosophy of understanding human existence. They feel that the chief block in the understanding of man in Western cultures has been an overemphasis on technique and a concomitant tendency to believe that understanding is a function of or related to technique. Rather, according to May and associates, they feel that "what distinguishes [forms of] existential therapy is not what the therapist would specifically do, . . . but rather the *context* of his therapy" (20, p. 77). That is, according to Chessick, it is "not so much what the therapist says [or does] as what he *is*" (58, p. 243). Indeed, in this regard the existential schools of psychotherapy have been criticized for their vagueness regarding technical matters in the conduct of psychotherapy. Ford and Urban's analysis of their approach concluded that "they have developed a new way of thinking about patients, but it does not lead them to *do* anything different in treatment" (26, p. 469).

Less harshly, the experiential schools aspire to flexibility or innovation in their actual methods as long as these methods are useful in the therapist's attempt to experience and share as far as possible the being of the patient. Here the aim or rationale of all techniques would be to enter the phenomenological world of the patient. In direct contrast to the view of the dynamic therapist, the experiential therapist does not concern himself/herself with the patient's past, the matter of diagnosis, the aspiration of insight, the issue of interpretation, or the subtle vicissitudes of transference and countertransference. Unlike the behavioral therapist, the experiential therapist expressly does not set goals for the patient and does not direct, confront, or otherwise impose his/her personality on the patient with directives in the form of behavioral instructions or problem-solving preferences. Techniques that involve placing the therapist's judgments or values above those of the patient are considered anathema to the requirements of unconditional acceptance of the patient and placing the locus of control within the patient. It may also be noted here that Rogerian methods as well as others within the more classically existential framework retain a methodological framework of essentially verbal interchange between therapist and patient.

Although they share the same basic faith in the therapeutic encounter and the emphasis on feelings, other schools under the experiential umbrella are often antiverbal in approach. Such schools (e.g., Gestalt therapy), view overintellectualization as part of the patient's problem, i.e., a manifestation of defense against experiencing or feeling, and discourage it as part of the therapeutic endeavor. These therapies attempt to accentuate activity over reflection, emphasize doing rather than saying, or, at the minimum, aim to combine action with introspection. The goal of experiencing oneself includes developing the patient's awareness of bodily sensations, postures, tensions, and movements, with an emphasis on somatic processes. Awareness of oneself as manifested in one's body can be a highly mobilizing influence. The main thrust of therapy is therefore to actively arouse, agitate, or excite the patient's experience of himself/herself, not simply let it happen.

Among the techniques for expressing one's self-experience in such schools is the combination of direct confrontation with dramatization, i.e., role-playing and the living out of fantasy in the therapeutic situation. This means that under the direction (and often the creation) of the therapist the patient is encouraged to play out parts of himself/ herself, including physical parts, by inventing dialogues between them. Performing fantasies and dreams is typical and considered preferable to their mere verbal expression, interpretation, and cognitive comprehension. In variations of the somatic stance, body and sensory awareness may be fostered through methods of direct release of physical tension and even manipulations of the body to expel and/or intensify feeling.

In yet other attempts to unify mind, body, and more especially, spirit, the immediate experience of oneself by focusing on one's spiritual dimension is sought. This is most often accomplished through the primary technique of meditation. The ultimate state of profound rest serves to transcend the world of the individual ego in that it is a higher reality or state of consciousness that the individual ego subserves. Major methods of will training and attention focused on a special word-sound or mantra, for example, serve to create an egoless or nonegocentered transcendent state.

Variations of the Experiential Theme

The therapeutic systems that have evolved under the experiential theme represent various approaches, each propelled by the immediate moment and geared toward the ultimate unity of man. These include the following: 1) a philosophic type, which reflects existential tenets as a basis for the conduct of psychotherapy and pivots on the here-and-now mutual dialogue or encounter while retaining essentially verbal techniques (e.g., Rogers' client-centered therapy and Frankl's logotherapy); 2) a somatic type, which reflects a subscription of nonverbal methods and aspiration to an integration of self by means of focusing attention on subjective body stimuli and sensory responses (e.g., Perls' Gestalt therapy) and/or physical-motor modes of intense abreaction and emotional flooding in which the emphasis is on the bodily arousal and release of feeling (e.g., Lowen's bioenergetic analyses and Janov's primal scream therapy); and, finally, 3) a spiritual type, which emphasizes the final affirmation of self as a transcendental or transpersonal experience, extending man's experience of himself to higher cosmic levels of consciousness that ultimately aim to unify him with the universe. This is primarily accomplished by means of the renunciation of the individual ego in the establishment of an egoless state by meditation (i.e., relaxation plus focused attention), in which one reaches a state of profound rest (e.g., Transcendental Meditation), a spiritual synthesis that may be amplified by various techniques of self-discipline and will-training and practice of disidentification (e.g., Assagioli's psychosynthesis).

CONCLUSIONS

Individual names given to different schools of psychotherapy often attempt to capture, if not exalt, their uniqueness; at the same time, the very names may serve to mask their derivations and the similarities they share with other systems. The schema presented here subsumes a large array of therapeutic schools that have proliferated under three broad themes since Freud. Each major theme as depicted here in its prototypic or pure form has a unity of its own; each dimension is broadly congruent with the others in its domain and is overtly antithetical to those dimensions described in the other two themes. However, in reality these are rarely categorical distinctions. Therapeutic boundaries in actual practice can and do overlap.

The systematic approach presented in this paper allows us to consider the dimensions of greatest departure as well as convergence in the ever-expanding field of the psychotherapies. In so doing, it is hoped that psychotherapeutic schools and their therapeutic processes will be more closely and critically explored.

REFERENCES

1. Strupp, H. Psychoanalytic psychotherapy and research. In: L. Eron, R. Callahan (Eds.), *The Relation of Theory to Practice in Psychotherapy*. Chicago: Aldine Publishing Co., 1969, pp. 21-62.
2. Parloff, M. Twenty-five years of research in psychotherapy. New York: Albert Einstein College of Medicine Department of Psychiatry, Oct. 17, 1975.
3. London, P. The psychotherapy boom. *Psychology Today*, June 1974, pp. 63-68.
4. Marmor cites common factors in therapies. *Psychiatric News*, Nov. 5, 1975, pp. 1, 15.
5. Luborsky, L., Singer, B., and Lukorsky, L. Comparative studies of psychotherapies. *Arch. Gen. Psychiat.*, 1975, 32:995-1008.
6. Calestro, K. Psychotherapy, faith healing and suggestion. *Int. J. Psychiat.*, 1972, 10:83-114.
7. Ehrenwald, J. *Psychotherapy: Myth and Method, An Integrative Approach*. New York: Grune & Stratton, 1966.
8. Frank, J. *Persuasion and Healing: A Comparative Study of Psychotherapy*. Baltimore: Johns Hopkins Press, 1961.
9. Frank, J. Therapeutic factors in psychotherapy. *Amer. J. Psychother.*, 1971, 25:350-361.
10. Frank J. Common features of psychotherapies and their patients. *Psychother. Psychosom.*, 1974, 24:368-371.
11. Frank, J. An overview of psychotherapy. In: G. Usdin (Ed.), *Overview of the Psychotherapies*. New York: Brunner/Mazel, 1975, pp. 3-21.
12. Leighton, A., Prince, R., and May, R. The therapeutic process in cross-cultural perspective—a symposium. *Amer. J. Psychiat.*, 1968, 124:1171-1183.
13. Strupp, H. Specific vs. nonspecific factors in psychotherapy and the problem of control. *Arch. Gen. Psychiat.*, 1970, 23:393-401.
14. Strupp, H. Toward a reformulation of the psychotherapeutic influence. *Int. J. Psychiat.*, 1973, 11:263-327.
15. Strupp, H. On the basic ingredients of psychotherapy. *Psychother. Psychosom.*, 1974, 24:249-260.
16. Strupp, H. Psychoanalysis, "focal psychotherapy" and the nature of the therapeutic influence. *Arch. Gen. Psychiat.*, 1975, 32:127-135.
17. Tseng, W.-S. and McDermott, J. F., Jr. Psychotherapy: Historical roots, universal elements, and cultural variations. *Amer. J. Psychiat.*, 1975, 132:378-384.
18. White, R. W. Five basic processes in psychotherapy. In: W. S. Sahakian (Ed.), *Psychopathology Today: Experimentation, Theory and Research*. Itasca, Ill.: F. E. Peacock, 1970, pp. 596-599.
19. Wittkower, E. D. and Warnes, H. Cultural aspects of psychotherapy. *Amer. J. Psychother.*, 1974, 28:566-573.
20. May, R., Angel, E., and Ellenberger, H. *Existence: A New Dimension in Psychiatry and Psychology*. New York: Basic Books, 1958.
21. Janov, A. *The Primal Scream*. New York: G. P. Putnam's Sons, 1970.
22. Eysenck, H. J. Learning theory model. In: W. S. Sahakian (Ed.), *Psychopathology Today: Experimentation, Theory and Research*. Itasca, Ill.: F. E. Peacock, 1970, pp. 73-85.
23. Ellis, A. Rational-emotive therapy: A comprehensive approach to therapy. In: D. Bannister (Ed.), *Issues and Approaches in the Psychological Therapies*. New York: John Wiley & Sons, 1975, pp. 163-186.
24. Bannister, D. (Ed.). *Issues and Approaches in the Psychological Therapies*. New York: John Wiley & Sons, 1975.
25. Bry, A. (Ed.). *Inside Psychotherapy: Nine Clinicians Tell How They Work and What They Are Trying to Accomplish*. New York: Basic Books, 1972.

26. Ford, D. and Urban, H. *Systems of Psychotherapy: A Comparative Study.* New York: John Wiley & Sons, 1965.
27. Goldman, G. and Milman, D. *Innovations in Psychotherapy.* Springfield, Ill.: Charles C Thomas, 1972.
28. Harper, R. A. *Psychoanalysis and Psychotherapy: 36 Systems.* Englewood Cliffs, N.J.: Prentice-Hall, 1959.
29. Harper, R. A. *The New Psychotherapies.* Englewood Cliffs, N.J.: Prentice-Hall, 1975.
30. Herscher, L. *Four Psychotherapies.* New York: Appleton-Century-Crofts, 1970.
31. Loew, C., Grayson, H., and Loew, G. *Three Psychotherapies: A Clinical Comparison.* New York: Brunner/Mazel, 1975.
32. Patterson, C. H. *Theories of Counseling and Psychotherapy.* New York: Harper & Row, 1973.
33. Sahakian, W. (Ed.). *Psychopathology Today: Experimentation, Theory and Research.* Itasca, Ill.: F. E. Peacock, 1970.
34. Staples, F., Sloane, R. B., Whipple, K., et al. Differences between behavior therapists and psychotherapists. *Arch. Gen. Psychiat.,* 1975, 32:1517-1522.
35. Sloane, R. B., Staples, F., Cristol, A., et al. Short-term analytically oriented psychotherapy versus behavior therapy. *Amer. J. Psychiat.,* 1975, 132:373-377.
36. Neki, J. S. Gurū-chelā relationship: The possibility of a therapeutic paradigm. *Amer. J. Orthopsychiatry,* 1973, 43:755-766.
37. Fiedler, F. E. The concept of an ideal therapeutic relationship. *J. Consult. Psychol.,* 1950, 14:239-245.
38. Murray, E. J. A content-analysis method for studying psychotherapy. *Psychological Monographs,* 1956, 70(13):1-32.
39. Naftulin, D., Donnelly, F., and Wolkon, G. Four therapeutic approaches to the same patient. *Amer. J. Psychother.,* 1975, 29:66-71.
40. Crown, S. Psychoanalytic psychotherapy. In: D. Bannister (Ed.), *Issues and Approaches in the Psychological Therapies.* New York: John Wiley & Sons, 1975, pp. 187-199.
41. Menninger, K. *The Human Mind.* New York: Alfred Knopf, 1955.
42. Bromberg, W. *The Mind of Man.* New York: Harper & Row, 1959.
43. Rychlak, J. Lockean vs. Kantian theoretical models and the "cause" of therapeutic change. *Psychotherapy: Theory, Research and Practice,* 1969, 6:214-222.
44. Rychlak, J. The motives to psychotherapy. *Psychotherapy: Theory, Research and Practice,* 1965, 2:151-157.
45. Offenkrantz, W. and Tobin, A. Psychoanalytic psychotherapy. *Arch. Gen. Psychiat.,* 1974, 30:593-606.
46. Parloff, M. Shopping for the right therapy. *Saturday Review,* Feb. 21, 1976, pp. 14-20.
47. Freud, S. *Introductory Lectures on Psycho-Analysis, Parts I and II* (1915-1917). *The Complete Psychological Works, Standard Ed.,* vol. 15. Translated and edited by J. Strachey. London: Hogarth Press, 1963.
48. Freud, S. New introductory lectures on psycho-analysis (1933 [1932]). *Ibid.,* vol. 22, 1964, pp. 1-182.
49. Freud, S. My views on the part played by sexuality in the aetiology of the neuroses (1905). In: Joan Riviere, (trans.), *Collected Papers,* vol. 1. London: Hogarth Press, 1950, pp. 272-283.
50. Rapaport, D. and Gill, M. M. The points of view and assumptions of metapsychology. *Int. J. Psychoanal.,* 1959, 40:153-162.
51. Greenson, R. *The Technique and Practice of Psychoanalysis,* vol. 1. New York: International Universities Press, 1967.

52. Birk, L. and Brinkley-Birk, A. Psychoanalysis and behavior therapy. *Amer. J. Psychiat.*, 1974, 131:499-510.
53. Chessick, R. *The Technique and Practice of Intensive Psychotherapy.* New York: Jason Aronson, 1974.
54. Hutchinson, E. D. Varieties of insight. In: P. Mullahy (Ed.), *A Study of Interpersonal Relations.* New York: Hermitage Press, 1950, pp. 56-77.
55. Ludwig, A. M. The formal characteristics of therapeutic insight. *Amer. J. Psychother.*, 1966, 20:305-318.
56. Richfield, J. An analysis of the concept of insight. In: *Psychoanalytic Clinical Interpretation.* New York: Free Press, 1963, pp. 1-41.
57. Schonbar, R. A. Interpretation and insight in psychotherapy. *Psychotherapy: Theory, Research and Practice,* 1964, 4:78-83.
58. Rosen, J. N. Direct psychoanalysis. In: J. H. Masserman (Ed.), *Handbook of Psychiatric Therapies.* New York: Science House, 1972, pp. 125-131.
59. Freud, S. Papers on technique (1911-1915). In: J. Strachey (Trans. and Ed.), *The Complete Psychological Works, Standard Ed.,* vol. 12. London: Hogarth Press, 1958, pp. 85-171.
60. Henry, W. E., Sims, J. H., and Spray, S. L. *Public and Private Lives of Psychotherapists.* San Francisco: Jossey-Bass, 1973.
61. Bellis, J. Emotional flooding and bioenergetic analysis. In: P. Olsen (Ed.), *New Directions in Psychotherapy: Emotional Flooding.* New York: Human Sciences Press, 1976, pp. 136-150.
62. Freud, S. The psychology of the dream-processes. In: J. Strachey (Trans. and Ed.), *The Complete Psychological Works, Standard Ed.,* vol. 5. London: Hogarth Press, 1958, pp. 509-621.
63. Sifneos, P. E. *Short-Term Psychotherapy and Emotional Crisis.* Cambridge: Harvard University Press, 1972.
64. Sifneos, P. E. Short-term, anxiety-provoking psychotherapy: An emotional problem-solving technique. *Semin. Psychiat.,* 1969, 1:389-398.
65. Sifneos, P. E. An overview of a psychiatric clinic population. *Am J. Psychiat.,* 1973, 130:1033-1035.
66. Malan, D. H. *A Study of Brief Psychotherapy.* New York: Plenum Press, 1975.
67. Malan, D. H. Psychodynamic changes in untreated neurotic patients: II. Apparently genuine improvements. *Arch. Gen. Psychiat.,* 1975, 32:110-126.
68. Eysenck, H. J. Learning theory and behavior therapy. *J. Ment. Sci.,* 1959, 105:61-75.
69. Wolpe, J. *The Practice of Behavior Therapy.* New York: Pergamon Press, 1969.
70. Cautela, J. Behavior therapy. In: L. Herscher (Ed.), *Four Psychotherapies.* New York: Appleton-Century-Crofts, 1970, pp. 85-124.
71. Hollander, M. Behavior therapy approach. In: C. Loew, N. Grayson, and G. Loew (Eds.), *Three Psychotherapies: A Clinical Comparison.* New York: Brunner/Mazel, 1975, pp. 220-236.
72. Krasner, L. The therapist as a social reinforcement machine. In: H. Strupp and L. Luborsky (Eds.), *Research in Psychotherapy,* vol. 2. Washington, D.C.: American Psychological Association, 1962, pp. 61-94.
73. American Psychiatric Association Task Force Report 5: Behavior Therapy in Psychiatry. Washington, D.C.: APA, 1973.
74. Mowrer, O. H. The behavior therapies, with special reference to modeling and imitation. *Amer. J. Psychother.,* 1966, 20:439-461.
75. Arieti, S. Psychiatric controversy: Man's ethical dimension. *Amer. J. Psychiat.,* 1975, 132:39-42.
76. Haigh, G. Learning theory and alienation. *Psychotherapy: Theory, Research and Practice,* 1965, 2:147-150.

77. Frankl, V. E. Logotherapy and existential analysis—a review. *Amer. J. Psychother.*, 1966, 20:252-261.
78. Arendsen-Hein, G. W. Psychotherapy and the spiritual dimension of man. *Psychother. Psychosom.*, 1974, 24:290-297.
79. Maslow, A. H. Neurosis as a failure of personal growth. In: W. S. Sahakian (Ed.), *Psychopathology Today: Experimentation, Theory and Research.* Itasca, Ill.: F. E. Peacock, 1970, pp. 122-130.
80. Denes-Radomisli, M. The context of psychotherapeutic innovations: A Gestalt therapist's view. In: G. Goldman and D. Milman (Eds.), *Innovations in Psychotherapy.* Springfield, Ill.: Charles C Thomas, 1972, pp. 104-117.
81. Gendlin, E. Experiencing: A variable in the process of therapeutic change. *Amer. J. Psychother.*, 1961, 15:232-245.
82. Hoehn-Saric, R. Transcendence and psychotherapy. *Amer. J. Psychother.*, 1974, 28:252-263.
83. Rogers, C. R. Persons or science? A philosophical question. *Amer. Psychol.*, 1955, 10:267-278.
84. Seguin, C. A. What folklore psychotherapy can tell us. *Psychother. Psychosom.*, 1974, 24:293-302.

2

General Principles of Psychotherapy

Toksoz B. Karasu, M.D.

The therapist's ultimate commitment to the welfare of his patient governs and directs his therapeutic interventions toward what he understands to be ultimately in the patient's best interests. This principle implies that the therapist always uses his best therapeutic skills to promote and accomplish for his patient the most effective course of treatment (2, p. 364).

DEFINITION AND SCOPE

Broadly, psychotherapy can be described as a mutual therapist-patient endeavor to investigate and understand the nature of the latter's mental distress for the purpose of providing relief from his suffering. The suffering may take the form of attitudes, feelings, behaviors or symptoms that are causing difficulties; the major purpose of psychotherapy is to produce changes in the person which will enable him to maintain a more stable and less painful adaptation to himself and the world around him. Although psychotherapy mainly focuses on the source and manifestations of the patient's difficulties, maladaptations or psychopathology, it need not restrict itself to the healing of the psychological illness per se; rather, it may simultaneously aim for the individual's growth, that is, the attainment of his maximum mental health or best human potential.

It should be pointed out that numerous forms of psychotherapy are being practiced today, with different and often conflicting conceptualizations about the fundamental nature of man and his mental ills, therapeutic processes or change agents, the requirements of the doctor/patient relationship, and the primary techniques and methods that are utilized. Often, each tends to exclusively emphasize either dynamic or behavioral or experiential aspects of treatment (1, Chapter 1). Other more common dichotomies include insight versus supportive therapies; the treatment of psychotic versus neurotic patients, inpatients versus outpatients, etc. However, in reality, these approaches are rarely categorical distinctions. Therapeutic boundaries in actual practice can and do overlap. Thus, if these aspects of the psychotherapies were integrated, the common ground of psychotherapy would currently refer to the treatment of mental and emotional disorders based primarily on verbal (and nonverbal) communication (2) within the context of a special therapeutic relationship between two persons, wherein the one seeking help is the recipient of affective experiences (catharsis, abreaction, etc.), behavioral regulations (advice, control, etc.), and cognitive mastery (insight, explanations, etc.) in relation to his presenting and/or underlying problems (3).

More specifically, psychotherapy as defined above represents a theoretical midpoint of psychological treatment within a large and varied *continuum* of clinical approaches and techniques. While the focus is on general principles, the actual practice of psychotherapy is further delineated by descriptions of two hypothetical endpoints of psychotherapeutic treatment—intrapsychic conflict resolution within the context of a fantasized and frustrating transference relationship; and adaptation to current reality within the context of a real and gratifying therapeutic alliance. (Approaches emphasizing each goal will be elaborated upon in the last section of the paper.)

THEORY OF MENTAL FUNCTIONING

Basic psychotherapeutic theories have as their working concepts the dynamic, genetic, structural, economic, developmental and adaptive nature of mental functioning. In brief, man's affects, thoughts and behavior reflect the expression and transformation of his innate instincts, and more crucially, their repression, as well as the ways in which man defends himself (and adapts) in the face of his moral standards and the demands of external reality. Not only is man a product of inner conflicts —that is, both subject to and resisting against a reservoir of impulses largely inaccessible to his conscious self—but he is also a product of his environment, his learned or unlearned behaviors, values and beliefs which he has acquired through identifications, conditioning and training. Beyond these unconscious determinants and internal and external alterations through learning, man strives not only for stability, but for self-determination, growth, and authenticity; at the same time, he seeks to find some meaning and purpose in life.

There are no procrustean therapeutic beds in which the patient should be fitted. The therapist must formulate an independent therapeutic rationale and working hypothesis for each patient undertaking psychotherapy.

DIAGNOSIS AND ASSESSMENT

Psychotherapy is applicable to a large and complex range of emotional disorders, including a variety of situational crises, personality disorders, neuroses, reconstituted psychoses, psychoses, and chronic mild organic condition. The categories in most current use are described in DSM III.

However, in establishing the therapeutic assessment and plan, a good clinician should avoid the simple attachment of one of the above diagnoses to the patient, since this often prematurely relegates him to a fixed position within that diagnostic label and may produce closure on how the patient is subsequently viewed and treated. Not only do few patients really fit DSM categories, but often this expedient but clinically limited method of assessing illness offers little of practical psychotherapeutic value. Psychotherapy-oriented diagnosis and assessment in a more constructive sense attempt to emphatically portray the patient and his inner world, his strengths as well as weaknesses, his capacities for health as well as illness. Throughout the therapeutic process, therefore, the therapist reexplores and refines his diagnosis by carefully observing the patient's interactions, his relationship to himself and others, his adaptability and accessibility for particular therapeutic interventions.

PSYCHOTHERAPEUTIC OBJECTIVES

Psychotherapy can have any or all of the following goals: 1) relief of immediate crisis, 2) reduction or removal of symptomatology, 3) strengthening of defenses and integrative capacities, 4) resolution or rearrangement of underlying conflicts, and 5) modification of personality organization towards an adaptive and mature functioning.

Based upon the therapist's ongoing assessment of the particular patient, objectives may be modest, restricted, narrowly focused short-term goals, such as reduction of specific symptomatology, brief problem-solving, crisis intervention, or achievement of limited insight into a well-circumscribed area of conflict, or longer-term objectives such as a reduction in the intensity of conflict, rearrangement of defensive structures, resolution of therapeutic dependence, and modification, or, at times, even resolution, of basic and unconscious conflicts. In some cases, where the immediate need is to sustain the patient during a particular crisis or period of stress, the major aim may be to provide a supportive relationship. Supportive efforts can be of brief duration or may extend over a long period, particularly with patients whose capacity for therapeutic work and for adequate functioning without a sustained therapeutic relationship is limited.

Of course, goals set at the beginning of therapy may be—and, indeed, must be—modified or replaced by new ones as therapy progresses. In most instances, the patient should participate in the setting of goals. Both therapist and patient should be aware that the aims of treatment are subject to change throughout its course, and that either overestimating or underestimating the goals of treatment at any one time is not irrevocable. Overrating the patient's capacities may place undue pressure on him during treatment; on the other hand, settling for modified objectives may result in difficulties for the patient later on and necessitate additional therapeutic work at that time.

THE PSYCHOTHERAPEUTIC RELATIONSHIP

Psychotherapeutic change invariably occurs within the context of an interpersonal relationship between the patient and therapist. In fact, some approaches focus almost exclusively on the therapeutic relationship (i.e., it is the subject and object of analysis); others focus primarily on the patient's life situation and only secondarily on the therapeutic relationship per se. Three significant aspects of the therapeutic relationship in psychotherapy are: 1) real-object relationship, 2) therapeutic alliance, and 3) transference relationship.

Real-Object Relationship

The calm, interested, helpful and empathic attitudes of the therapist are essential for providing a warm and understanding milieu which will enable the patient to undertake the tasks of treatment. This milieu also serves to maintain the patient's contact with objects and with reality, constituting the real-object relationship.

The primary task of the therapist here is the establishment of trust.

In his initial contact, the therapist offers to fill the needs of the patient through the possibility of being understood and begins to develop a mutual interaction and rapport that will allow the patient to view him as a constant, reliable, and predictable person. The therapist also supplies to the patient certain moral standards and values. These are not usually expressed directly; rather, they are implicit in the character and behavior of the therapist—that is, it is "not so much what the therapist says or does as what he is" (4, p. 243). The therapist is a model for identification by the patient, while providing the necessary gratification from a real object during the therapeutic encounter.

Therapeutic Alliance

Any successful therapeutic venture requires the close working together of two minds—the therapeutic alliance. This essentially involves the conscious, rational, and non-regressive aspects of the relationship between patient and therapist. It means "that the therapist aims at forming a real and mature alliance with the conscious adult ego of the patient and encourages him to be a scientific partner in the exploration of his difficulties" (4, p. 72). The therapeutic alliance is based on the mutual explicit or implicit agreement to work together according to the requirements of the therapeutic situation.

This therapeutic alliance is an essential part of the therapeutic process. One of the major tasks of the therapist is to foster its development and to indicate to the patient that it is necessary for the psychotherapeutic work of observation, evaluation, judgment, reasoning, and reality-testing in relation to the material revealed in the sessions.

For the maximal development of this working relationship, both therapist and patient must be capable of controlled ego-splitting in the service of the treatment (5). That is, there are times when the real-object relationship between the patient and therapist would interfere with the therapeutic alliance; there is need to oscillate between the two. To accomplish both tasks, the therapist must judiciously set up a barrier against the patient's need to revert to the real-object relationship because he wishes to remain gratified by the therapist. The matter is further complicated because certain aspects of the working relationship are real. The patient learns real things about the therapist both in and out of the office, and the therapist behaves in a real and human way toward the patient (6). Therefore, the reality of certain aspects of the treatment relationship, as well as its place in the formation and maintenance of the therapeutic alliance, must be understood by both partners. If both the real-object relationship and the therapeutic alliance are properly handled by the therapist, they can constitute useful and complementary parts of the treatment situation.

The Transference Relationship

How well the therapeutic alliance has been established determines in large measure the therapist's use of transference as a therapeutic tool. The real object need of the patient, satisfied by the former relationships, is deliberately frustrated by the transference relationship. The deprivations produced by interpretations of transference result in loss of gratification and comfort from an infantile object relationship. The patient is confronted with the pain of his warded-off affects and conflicts and is required to think and begin to deal with these.

Only under certain circumstances should the therapist focus upon and encourage transference feelings: when he feels that such regression will not impair the patient's reality-testing, i.e., his capacity to distinguish reality from fantasy; when the therapeutic alliance is sufficiently established to withstand the frustration entailed in confronting the transference resistance; and, finally, when the therapist's time commitment allows him to assist the patient in working through and resolving the transference dependency.

In summary, the real-object relationship, the therapeutic alliance and the transference relationship between patient and therapist must be carefully balanced at all times as an essential part of treatment.

PSYCHOTHERAPEUTIC TECHNIQUES

No technique is therapeutic in itself. The choice of a particular therapeutic approach for a specific human disturbance at a particular time is crucial. Each technical step must have a conceptual rationale adapted to the specific patient, and the therapist must leave room for flexibility from his own hypothetical standard. In short, a good clinician must be able to calibrate the use and timing of his therapeutic instruments.

The therapist's capacity to listen attentively and empathically is indispensable. He listens not only to the patient's manifest content, but also to the latent, unconscious meanings. Observation of the patient, with sensitivity to what he means as well as to what he says, provides the foundation for therapeutic endeavor. Upon initial evaluation, the therapist must indicate clearly to the patient what his needs for treatment are and clarify proposed purposes and limitations of that particular form of treatment. This should include a statement about what is expected of both parties—their respective roles and relationship—in order to define as explicitly as possible the nature of treatment. The establishment of regularly scheduled appointments is a necessary, albeit obvious, requirement. The frequency with which a patient is seen will depend upon his specific needs (e.g., the nature of his psychopathology, capacity to maintain the therapeutic relationship, etc.), the nature of his particular treatment, and goals considered.

Once treatment is initiated, it is necessary for the therapist to encourage the patient to verbalize his thoughts and feelings despite inherent difficulties in doing so. For this purpose, the therapist at times may need to be fairly active—by asking questions, guiding the patient to focus on certain material, and responding calmly as the patient finds ways of expressing his thoughts and feelings. Here, the issue of whether and when a patient should sit facing the therapist or lie down on a couch may arise. This decision must be based upon consideration of what will be most facilitating to the particular patient. While some patients find it easier to verbalize emotional material when they are not facing the therapist, the couch may be threatening to other patients. In either event, the potential for regression of the patient must be carefully assessed.

Therapeutic techniques are naturally dependent upon, and inextricable from, the therapeutic relationship. (See section on The Psychotherapeutic Relationship.) The therapist should continually reinforce the therapeutic alliance between himself and the patient, while gauging how much regression the patient can tolerate at any one time. Essentially, the development of excessive transference reactions should be prevented. In this regard, some important and necessary defenses should be left undisturbed, and others supported and strengthened. When to stabilize the patient's defenses and when to confront them; when to frustrate the patient and when to gratify him; and when to focus on real events and relationships and when to encourage transferential manifestations—these are inevitable questions to be asked by every therapist throughout the course of treatment.

The therapist has a variety of potential techniques at his disposal, whose purposes may be explanatory, cathartic, or directly educative. Interpretation (of transference, resistance, repressed conflicts) is often considered to be the major psychodynamic tool. The therapeutic path must be carefully paved by a series of steps in order for interpretations to have their most elucidating effects. In this regard, the roles of confrontation and clarification are critical. Confrontation refers to requiring the patient to discern or face the particular mental event to be investigated; clarification refers to placing the same event in sharp focus, separating important aspects from insignificant ones. Interpretation then goes beyond manifest material by assigning an underlying meaning or cause to the event or phenomenon in question. In offering interpretations, the therapist must pay careful attention to the way they are presented, including the actual wording, the timing, the sequence and the dosage.

Interpretations should deal with the psychological realities of the patient, that is, his specific individual experiences in relation to a conflict. They should go from manifest or current connections to progressively more latent material—from what is accessible or partially accessible to what is unknown. The patient should be relatively removed from an anxiety-provoking emotional experience before an attempt at interpretation. A premature interpretation may backfire, in that it may increase the patient's resistance to insight rather than further it. Finally, the interpretation should be reintroduced at various junctures throughout the therapy; it may be that only after several doses can an interpretation become integrated completely into the patient's understanding.

The therapist may also wish at times to use techniques which can be considered essentially non-interpretive, that is, which may serve to block or lessen insight rather than facilitate it. Foremost in this regard are: *abreaction,* which may still be used but is not felt to bring insight directly; *direct suggestion or advice,* which is only useful to the extent that it is openly acknowledged and analyzed within the therapy setting; *manipulation,* allowable only to the extent that it can be brought into the explorative arena and does not occur without the ultimate knowledge of the patient; and the *deliberate* or *conscious assumption of roles or attitudes* that create an unanalyzable situation by their very nature.

In addition, some patients (or all patients at some time) may need to be directly instructed in matters pertaining to their life outside of therapy, e.g., the nature of certain reality events and relationships—at work, at school, at home. Such educative interventions may interfere with access to depth material, but they contribute to the patient's defenses and enlarge the scope of his ego.

DESCRIPTIONS OF TWO PSYCHOTHERAPEUTIC PARAMETERS

Emphasis on Transference and Intrapsychic Conflict

This hypothetical end of the psychotherapy pendulum aims at major changes in the patient's adaptive functioning and personality organization and relatively firm resolution of intrapsychic conflicts. Applicability of such an approach is felt to require some degree of the following characteristics: the capacity for therapeutic alliance—that is, a reasonably well-integrated ego and some ability to relate effectively; sufficient resourcefulness for effective therapeutic work; the capacity to sustain therapeutic regression and to master the resulting anxiety; the capacity to maintain the distinction between fantasy and reality; and the capacity to form a transference (2).

This form of exploratory or depth psychotherapy can play an effective role in treating a large range of psychopathology, although the patients best suited to this approach are those suffering from neurotic conflicts and symptom complexes, reactive conditions, and the whole realm of non-psychotic character disorders. It is also the treatment of choice for patients with borderline personalities, but the management of these patients' regressive episodes may require occasional modifications of this approach.

The patient is seen at least twice a week, preferably more, for 50 minutes each time, in the therapist's office. Typically, it is an environment with minimal extrinsic intrusions in order to create conditions of relative sensory deprivation. This serves to maximize the evocation of repressed memories, free association, uncensored content of the patient's life material, dreams, etc. The crux of this method is the analysis of transference, which comprises the major instrument of the psychotherapeutic treatment as well as its major obstacle.

The therapist maintains the development of transference by judiciously frustrating the patient and avoiding gratifying his wishes, and by remaining relatively removed and anonymous. His basic therapeutic stance is as a deliberately dispassionate observer and reflector of the patient's feelings. The encouragement of transference reactions results in inevitable resistances to this endeavor, which must also be overcome (e.g., interpreted) as part of the treatment. This frustrating stance, in conjunction with the high frequency and regularity of contacts between patient and therapist, encourages an essentially regressive process and tends to increase the intensity of feelings within the treatment situation. In contrast to psychoanalysis, however, a full-blown transference neurosis should be prevented from developing; interpreting the transference as resistance is attempted only partially and in strictest accordance with the needs and capacities of the patient; further, the therapist does not attempt to completely resolve the original conflict.

The ultimate goal of therapy is, of course, working-through, which refers to the repetitive, progressive, and elaborate explorations and testing out of the interpretations and resistances to them until the presented material has become fully integrated into the patient's understanding. This is perhaps the most time-consuming aspect of dynamic psychotherapy. Although the major portion of such therapeutic work occurs within the therapist's office, working-through necessarily includes the tacit work done by the patient outside of the therapeutic hour.

Emphasis on Therapeutic Alliance and Adaptation to Current Reality

Patients who require such an approach are those whose ego impairment is considerable, whose basic conflicts are of the more primitive and narcissistic types, and who are highly unlikely to tolerate further regression. The patients who fall into this group may be psychotic, especially those in remission, borderline cases, or patients with severe characterological problems, whose potential for decompensation is high. Treatment aims at the reconstitution and stabilization of the patient's functioning. This process may require short-term involvement or a relationship extending over a considerable period of time.

The therapeutic posture of the therapist essentially is dispassionate, but must be relatively active. He offers himself in a firmly but gently authoritative way to be a protective, supportive, and real object to the patient. He is generally accepting of the patient's dependency rather than trying to explore or change it. Thus, the nature of the therapeutic relationship differs in emphasis from the model which focused upon the transference relationship, in which the therapist serves primarily as a surrogate ego, a constant object that the patient can rely on. Throughout the therapy, the focus is upon the establishment and maintenance of rapport and a good therapeutic alliance.

Since conflicts over the patient's attachment to the therapist may develop, the intensity of therapeutic involvement can be minimized by limiting the frequency and duration of psychotherapy visits. In addition, minimal interpretation of intrapsychic conflict is attempted, and nonanalytic efforts are made to influence the patient directly through advice, encouragement, reassurance, direct suggestion, inspiration and active persuasion.

This stabilizing type of treatment aims to support the patient's defenses and provide controls for his overwhelming anxiety or destructive impulses. The least amount of frustration and deprivation is imposed upon the patient, especially in terms of not having to relinquish the therapist as a source of real object gratification. In attempting to supply stability, the therapist seeks to mobilize the patient's presently available adaptive resources and strengths. One approach is an examination of stressful aspects of the patient's environment, whereby he may then be advised as to how to lessen these stresses or increase his capacity to cope. The therapist may also supply stability by providing ego support. This can be accomplished by guiding the patient in differentiating reality from his inner distortions, validating, where possible, the correctness of the patient's perceptions and thinking. In addition, the therapist may allow the patient to use temporary displacements (transferential, projective or introjective) (7). Education and information also strengthen the patient's ego by enlarging its scope.

In such therapy, the therapist may wish to use extrapsychotherapeutic means. He should consider medication and/or hospitalization to temporarily help the patient to control his behavior, or to remove him from excessive stimulation which may be contributing to a crisis reaction or stress and causing the patient to decompensate. The therapist may also utilize family and group approaches as adjunctive therapeutic measures. The inclusion of the family can serve to reduce the stresses on significant persons in the patient's living situation, allowing them to collectively participate in the establishment of a less conflict-ridden environment.

With a supportive group approach, concrete efforts can be made to reduce disturbances in interpersonal relationships by providing information and direction with regard to everyday problems of living. The multiplicity of transference opportunities may be beneficial for the patient to test out more effective ways of relating to others; he may also be directly trained in certain social skills which can be rehearsed within the course of therapy, as well as tested in outside real-life situations, and then reviewed in subsequent sessions.

Finally, it is certainly possible in working with these patients to tap intrapsychic conflicts and transference, as long as the individual's abilities and limitations are kept clearly in mind.

In conclusion, the prior section has elaborated upon two hypothetical ends of a psychotherapeutic spectrum. These alternate modes of intervention are by no means antithetical. In actual practice these emphases should overlap and, in the best of all possible therapeutic worlds, complement one another.

44   *Specialized Techniques in Individual Psychotherapy*

REFERENCES

1. Karasu, T. B. Psychotherapies: An overview. *Amer. J. Psychiat.*, 1977, Vol. 134, No. 8.
2. Meissner, W. and Nicholi, Jr., A. The psychotherapies: Individual, family, and group. In: *Harvard Guide to Modern Psychiatry*. Cambridge: Harvard University Press, 1978.
3. Karasu, T. B. Applied science of psychotherapy, visiting lecturer, grand rounds. Ottawa University School of Medicine, Department of Psychiatry, November 23, 1977.
4. Chessick, R. *The Technique and Practice of Intensive Psychotherapy*. New York: Jason Aronson, 1974.
5. Gill, M. M. Psychoanalysis and exploratory psychotherapy. *J. Amer. Psychoanal. Assoc.*, 1954, 2:771-797.
6. Glover, E. *The Technique of Psychoanalysis*. New York: International Universities Press, 1955.
7. Tarachow, S. and Stein, A. Psychoanalytic psychotherapy. In: B. Wolman (ed.), *Psychoanalytic Techniques*. New York: Basic Books, 1967.

3

Brief and Emergency Psychotherapy

LEOPOLD BELLAK, M.D.

SOME BASIC PROPOSITIONS

Psychotherapy is basically a simple process of learning, unlearning, and relearning, based upon 1) a sound theory of the psychology of personality, 2) a set of hypotheses concerned with the development of psychopathology, and 3) an interrelated series of propositions concerned with optimal restructuring. Using a general theory of psychology and a general theory of psychopathology, the therapist attempts to help the patient to restructure his past apperceptions from maladaptive ones to more adaptive ones (1).

For psychoanalysts, the guiding propositions in trying to understand a contemporary personality and its adaptive problems center on the attempt to establish *continuity* between childhood and adulthood, between waking and sleeping thought, and between normal life and pathology. The entire attempt to understand a personality and the problems in its functioning is predicated upon establishing these continuities, finding common denominators in the acquisition of apperceptive distortions, and helping the patient attain better configurations.

Now, all this sounds basically simple and, indeed, it is a simple process. Complications arise from the fact that the adult patient, especially,

The author is greatly indebted to Helen Siegel, M.A., for her editorial assistance.

45

has had years of accumulation of apperceptive distortions. These apperceptive distortions interact with each other so that they form configurations which are a Gestalt, a new configuration which needs to be analyzed, i.e., broken down into its previous components. Furthermore, aside from the basic complexity of the personality, the burdens of psychotherapy lie in the fact that much of pathological learning has started early, has been often repeated, and has some primary as well as secondary gains for the patient, which he may be reluctant to give up.

Therefore, psychoanalysis and psychotherapy are usually of necessity drawn-out, long-lasting procedures of many years' duration. The many cults and faddish quick-help methods, such as scientology, dienetics, EST, primal scream, or a variety of encounter groups, are unlikely to bring about fundamental changes. The learning and relearning they provide usually rely on the immediate effects of catharsis and on a kind of "permission" to ease the superego and permit narcissistic behavior and, to some extent, acting-out. These "therapies" provide, at best, some short-lived relief.

It is understandable, therefore, that for a long time brief psychotherapy, in general, was held in low esteem, especially by psychoanalysts and other dynamically trained therapists. The theoreticians cried of reductionism, and the practitioners thought of it as merely supportive, or as comparable to providing emotional band-aids.

Brief psychoanalytically conceived psychotherapy, however, has genuine merit. It can, indeed, bring about some dynamic and structural changes, often in as few as five or six sessions. To do this, it has to be extremely carefully conceptualized and all interventions have to be carefully planned for optimal effect. Brief therapy can be effective because it is predicated upon very close conceptualization of what ails the patient. The idea is to understand everything, if possible, and then to do only the very little bit that will make a difference. A very old story which demonstrates this point: A general's car broke down and army mechanics were called to fix it. When they were unable to repair the car, they turned for help to an old village smith. The smith took a look at the car, rattled it a little and then banged it sharply. Immediately, the car started up. The general asked, "What do I owe you?" The village smith replied, "A hundred bucks." "A hundred bucks for one bang?" said the general. "No," replied the smith, "One buck for the bang, ninety-nine for knowing *where* to bang." That's the way I see brief and emergency psychotherapy. As a modality, I see *brief therapy relating to traditional long-term therapy the way a short story relates to a novel!*

The process of brief therapy is aided by the fact that most major psychopathological conditions can be understood in terms of a basic set of hypotheses, as I point out below. What varies in the individual patient's psychopathology is the relative importance and role that one or another factor plays, for instance, in a depression. This determines the rank order of therapeutic attention paid to each variable. This conception is not asking more of the psychotherapeutic operation than one would of any medical or surgical intervention. One can expect that a surgeon approaching potential gall bladder surgery has a good grasp of the general propositions involved in the anatomy, physiology and pathology of the gall bladder and its surrounding structures, and has a notion about the sequence of his interventions; he will modify the operation only as the individual circumstances demand.

Similarly, I expect that a psychotherapist dealing with depression is aware of the fact that six, seven or eight factors may play a dominant role: 1) problems of *self-esteem;* 2) *aggression* in the presence of 3) a *severe superego* manifesting itself mostly as intra-aggression; 4) a feeling of *loss* —of love, of a love object, or part of oneself; 5) a feeling of *disappointment,* which Edith Jacobson (3) has also related to a feeling of having been deceived; 6) instead of the narrower concept of *orality,* I like to speak of *stimulus hunger* and the fact that the depressed personality tends to be more dependent on positive input than other people*; 7) the depressed personality, in a broader sense, is more dependent specifically on *narcissistic* nutrients; 8) the outstanding defense mechanism in depression is usually *denial.*

Though these are the main factors in all depressions, they play a varying role in each depression. For instance, sometimes problems of self-esteem may play the primary role, and insult to the self-esteem is the primary factor in precipitating the current depression. In other cases, a feeling of disappointment or deception may have triggered aggression which, in the presence of the severe superego, leads to intra-aggression and not only depression but potential suicide.

In the brief psychotherapy of depression, it is important to listen for the presence and role of these factors in the individual patient, and to see the historical common denominators between the precipitating situa-

---

* In speaking of the depressed personality, I have compared it often to the poikylotherm in distinction to the homoiotherm. In the latter, there is something like an emotional thermostat built into the psychic structure in the form of positive introjects which provide a certain measure of love and self-approval, almost independent of external circumstances. This is similar to the warm-blooded animal which maintains its body temperature to a considerable extent even if the temperature outside is higher or lower, in distinction to the cold-blooded or poikylotherm.

tion and historical circumstances. By vigorously working through the relevant factors with the appropriate methods of intervention and sequence of methods of intervention, depression, in my experience, lends itself very well to brief psychotherapy most of the time.

As they do for depression, certain general propositions hold true for the victim of any violence, be it mugging, rape or a violent accident. A history of past experiences with violence will be crucial or, more broadly, the specific personality structure will be crucial. The new event will, to a large extent, be interpreted in terms of the preexisting experience and personality structure. Someone who already has a great fear of passivity will respond differently from someone who has little. The particular experience that brings the patient to us has to be brought into relation to earlier insults to his or her integrity, such as violence inflicted by older siblings, a parent, or others. The specific features of the assault have to be brought into relation to specific preexisting personality problems, be they fears of castration, a problem of poorly defined self-boundaries, or other factors. Presumably, the impact of the contemporary crisis has its particular effect in terms of those preexisting problems and produces in the patient a feeling of depersonalization, guilt or panic, depending on the circumstances.

Therefore, in all instances, treatment consists of helping the patient understand his symptomatology as an attempt to adapt to his contemporary problem in terms of the past. This is often a maladaptive anachronism, and we offer the patient better problem-solving. It is, indeed, possible that the patient will acquire new strength, and reconstitute with a better capacity for tolerating certain stresses than he or she had prior to his particular emergency. In a broader sense, one could say that the brief psychotherapy permits a working-through of an old problem and leads potentially to a better form of dealing with it than existed premorbidly. In that sense, brief psychotherapy can not only be effective for an existing problem, but may also lead to truly better general integration. Elsewhere, we have described a great number of problems and conditions which can be clearly conceptualized and the treatment of which can then follow a broad outline (2). This should not lead one to adhere to a rigid program as if it were a train schedule. It should be considered as a perspective with which to approach a patient and his problems heuristically. One must remain flexible for finding the best possible fit or be ready for a complete change of hypothesis should circumstances call for it. In that way, the psychotherapist is not in a different situation than the microbiologist who looks through the microscope with a certain knowledge of cell structure and certain expectations which help him see what is there. Without having such a preconceived notion of what to look for under the microscope, however, one would hardly be able to see anything.

Based on such conceptions, I believe it is possible to listen carefully to a detailed history in the first session, to formulate a general treatment plan in terms of the general dynamics and structure of the condition, and to make an individual plan for the *areas of intervention* and *methods of intervention* suitable for the particular patient. By areas of intervention I mean: in a depression, I may choose to address myself in one patient to the loss of self-esteem and only after that to his aggression, intra-aggression and severe superego. In another patient, I may primarily address myself to his severe superego and the intra-aggression, and turn only later to orality and the feeling of deception and other factors. The method of intervention may be interpreting or any others on the list further below.

METHODS OF INTERVENTION

1) *Interpretation*—While this is the classical method of intervention in dynamic psychotherapy, it is by no means the only one.

2) *Catharsis* certainly has its role to play even if it plays an exaggerated one in such faddist therapies as primal scream and others. The mistake is simply to believe that catharsis alone will have a therapeutic effect, when the fact is that it is one form of intervention which, by itself, is probably never enough.

3) *Mediate Catharsis* is a term which I like to use when I express emotionally charged propositions for the patient. For instance, with a depressed patient with a severe superego and a good deal of aggression, I may say, "Certainly if the foreman had done that to me, I would have kicked him." In this instance, I am expressing sentiments for the patient which might be too strong for his sensitive superego but, by virtue of my saying them, I take the superego responsibility for them. I hope that I also convey to the patient that if an authority such as I, the therapist, can permit himself such an aggressive thought, that it may not be so unacceptable. Identification and introjection of the therapist as a more benign part of the superego then play an important role in this part of the therapeutic process. Other forms of indirect or mediate catharsis: "Of course, a conscientious person like yourself would not permit himself to think so, let alone to do it, but somebody else might

certainly feel like killing the son-of-a-bitch." By this statement, I give the patient a double message: 1) I reassure him that he would never lose such control and that, as a matter of fact, he is a person of strict conscience and 2) I convey the idea that in this instance, such aggressive sentiments are not inappropriate.

4) *Reality Testing* is the more necessary the more disturbed a patient is, and the greater the need for the therapist to play the role of an auxiliary reality tester, interpreting the patient's distortions of reality, and functioning as an auxiliary ego for him.

5) *Drive Repression* may play a role if we have a patient who feels that he ought to be able to do as the Jones' do, i.e., with regard to promiscuity, but has reacted with a panic in such a situation. I will flatly say— for instance, to an adolescent girl who feels she has to engage in a certain amount of promiscuity in order to have social standing in her high school—that she simply should not. I will then help her to accept that she does not have to be promiscuous in order to be accepted by her peers. By this means, I hope to actually take a burden off her mind—or, at least, to arrange for a pause in which she can reconstitute.

By selective inattention, one may sometimes discourage some forms of behavior and encourage others, in effect bringing about selective repression in the patient. It must be kept in mind, however, that repression has a normal role to play in daily functioning and that insufficient repression is, of course, as least as much a problem as is excessive repression.

6) *Sensitization to Signals* is concerned with making the patient aware that certain behavior on his part, be it acting out or panic, occurs when there is a specific dynamic constellation. It may not involve anything more sophisticated than pointing out to a patient that she always has a flare-up with her husband in the two or three days preceding her period.

7) *Education* might involve acquainting the patient with the facts about sodium retention and irritability and advising her to reduce her salt intake, etc. I might possibly prescribe a mild sedative for the two or three premenstrual days to help avoid a serious marital conflict.

8) *Intellectualization* plays a greater role in brief therapy than in traditional longer term therapies. At times, I use it to increase the therapeutic alliance. At other times, it is useful—for instance, with a very panicky patient—to give him at least the feeling of intellectually understanding his symptom—and with this, at least some control over what otherwise seems to him totally disruptive and ego-alien behavior.

9) *Support* in terms of the therapist's accepting certain feelings expressed by the patient, be they aggression, sexuality or greed, makes it easier for him to bear anxiety. Making reassuring statements has its role to play at certain times in therapy, but it can never be all that is called for, if one expects to provide something more than just ad hoc help.

10) *Conjoint Sessions and Family Network Therapy* are special techniques which I cannot go into here, except to say that I use them in connection with brief therapy in a very specific way. I try to conceptualize very clearly what I want to accomplish in a joint session, and then arrange for it to accomplish circumscribed goals. In other words, it becomes one of the overall planned forms of intervention, if the joint session seems to be the most economical and most appropriate method, and I feel that it is likely to lead to the best learning or unlearning experience for the patient.

11) *Psychoactive Drugs. See Enabling Conditions.*

THE THERAPEUTIC PROCESS AND THE THERAPEUTIC RELATIONSHIP

Since I see all psychotherapy as a form of unlearning, learning, and relearning, by insight, conditioning, and identification-internalization, it is part of my conception of the therapeutic relationship that it should provide and create optimal circumstances for unlearning, learning, and relearning. This methodology, of course, affects the therapeutic relationship as defined within the terms of the 1) *transference/countertransference relationship,* 2) *the therapeutic alliance,* and 3) *the therapeutic contract.* I would like to discuss these propositions within the framework of brief psychotherapy as a chronological process.

The First Session

In the first session, I expect a great deal of work to be accomplished. Of this, the establishment of the three aspects of the therapeutic relationship is but one of the tasks.

1) *Transference/countertransference relationship*

To be sure, in the broad meaning of the term transference relationship, the patient already comes programmed with certain apperceptive distortions derived from the past, which he ascribes to the as yet unknown therapist, e.g., by dreaming the preceding night of going to the dentist. Certainly, more personal transference/countertransference relations form as soon as the patient and therapist meet in the waiting room.

As an integral part of establishing a relationship in the first session, I expect to hear from the patient as *complete a history as possible,* an exhaustive account of the patient's current problems, their onset and the life situation in which they arose. I consider the history-taking reasonably complete only if I can see the person now sitting opposite me at various stages of his development in the concrete settings of the places he lived in and their general cultural, ethnic and geographic aspects, and can reasonably well relate his current chief complaint and the dynamic situation surrounding its onset in terms of this past history. In inquiring about precipitating events, I also ask specifically why the patient happens to be here *today.* I include in my questions almost routinely one concerning any dream the patient might have had the night before the appointment, thus hoping to get an idea of the preformed transference expectations.

In the course of the history-taking, a significant interpersonal relationship is established, including positive or negative countertransference features—more or less of a rescue fantasy on my part, including cognitive closure and possible critical feelings. For the patient, the intensive interest in his history is often a form of narcissistic gratification. It conveys the genuine interest of the interviewer and thus contributes to the establishment of a positive transference.

At the end of the first session, I review the salient features of the history and the complaint or problem which brought the patient into therapy. I try to point out some common denominators that one can easily perceive between the history and the current problem, and the relationship of these factors to me as therapist as expressed by the patient.

I consider it important to give the patient at least an intellectual understanding of what his problem might be, thus decreasing his feeling of helplessness and giving him the feeling that whatever ails him can at least be understood and that *I can understand it.* This further contributes to the development of an interpersonal relationship between the patient and myself.

In order to get a meaningful history, I am not inactive in eliciting it; I let the patient talk only as long as I feel the information is immediately relevant and then redirect the interview. It is part of my hypothesis concerning very close conceptualization that I formulate some general notion of what the dynamics and structure might be like and attempt to follow up these heuristic hunches. I remain, I hope, flexible for altering my notions as other data come in.

With the careful history-taking and my review of the salient features, I create an atmosphere of *compassionate empathy*. This has luckily remained entirely genuine because of my seeing life somewhat in terms of a Greek drama, all of us being, to some extent, helpless victims of circumstances to which we adapt in various ways. I perceive my job as helping the patient to achieve a little better adaptation than he had achieved before.

I also *create some feeling of hope predicated upon my understanding of the patient's problems,* mixing it with realistic limitations as formulated in the statements concerning the therapeutic alliance and the therapeutic contract.

To be sure, part of the therapeutic relationship involves appropriate *identification of positive and negative transference,* as in psychoanalysis or analytic psychotherapy, but this must be adapted to the needs of brief therapy: This is, in essence, a matter of style, where clear and often concrete formulation plays an especially important role.

2) *The therapeutic alliance*

I introduce the therapeutic alliance with a specific formula: *"The rational and intelligent part of you needs to sit together with the irrational unconscious part of you that causes you problems."* I may briefly explain the nature of the *therapeutic process* as I see it, in the first or second session, to increase this alliance. I briefly convey some basic ideas: The *first* idea is that we can understand behavior if we understand that there is *continuity between childhood and adulthood,* between *waking and sleeping thought,* and between *normal and pathological behavior.* I illustrate this fact with an example or two from the patient's account. Dreams, of course, are especially valuable for this purpose because they show the relationship between the day residue, the dream, and past history, and possibly something about the transference relationship.

My *second* main explanation of the therapeutic process involves an account of the acquisition of dynamics and structure via apperception and apperceptive distortions and role identification. I will compare the experiential process to the laying down of thousands and thousands of transparencies, e.g., of mother feeding, of mother cleaning, of mother punishing, fused with pictures of other significant people in the patient's life, and suggest that his contemporary apperception of various figures is structured to a greater or lesser degree by the Gestalten acquired in the past.

I may at times use a Thematic Apperception Test (TAT) picture and strive to demonstrate this phenomenon, especially since I tend to use the TATs sometimes as a device for aiding communication, interpretation and insight in the process of brief psychotherapy; this is likely to happen in the second session or the third session. The procedure is, of course, that I ask the patient to tell me a story about what is going on in the TAT picture, what led up to it and what the outcome will be; then I point out common denominators in his responses, highly specific features of his story as compared to some others that I can relate, or some specific features, such as his not seeing the gun or the pregnancy, etc.

I explain to the patient that the success of the therapy depends to a large extent on the *ability of part of him to work in alliance with me.* So as not to make patients feel overburdened, I may add that their main job is just to talk and that it is mostly my job to lead the way or to facilitate the rest of the process of understanding. Many people are, of course, not accustomed to the dissociative process that is involved in good analytic reporting and giving what I call an *"internal travelogue."* I frequently convey the idea by relating the story of a delinquent who was being prepared by a social worker for a consultation with me. When she asked him if he knew what a psychiatrist was, he said, "Yeah, that's the guy who makes you squeal on yourself." I explain to patients that what is expected is that they squeal on themselves—in a sense, tell things that they observe about themselves. If this is difficult, I have them give a concrete account of their day and then ask them what they thought at different points. I speak of starting with an *"external* travelogue" and turn next to an *"internal* travelogue." I also have a standard set of questions that help patients report and contribute their part to the therapeutic alliance. I may inquire as to what they were thinking while engaged in any number of semi-automatic tasks such as driving, shaving, or putting on make-up. I may ask patients what the last thought was that they had before falling asleep, and what they first thought of upon waking up.

In this respect, I hold myself responsible for *facilitating the therapeutic process,* which does not necessarily mean only making it go. To the contrary, I consider regulating the flow of the interview one of my crucial tasks, analogous to giving gas and putting on the brakes when driving a car. Selective inattention to some material, dilution by a little more general talking, or, on the other hand, silence and interpretation of defenses, are some of the main instruments I can employ to control the therapeutic process as my part of the therapeutic alliance.

3) *The therapeutic contract*

During the first session, in addition to taking an extensive history and establishing the basics of the transference relationship and the therapeutic alliance, the therapist begins the formulation of the therapeutic contract. As in so many other respects, the therapeutic contract in brief psychothrapy is much more clear-cut and specifically stated than it is in longer forms of psychotherapy. I explain to the patients that I hope that we will be able to deal with their problems in five sessions, each of them lasting approximately 50 minutes, and that I shall want to hear from them about a month after the fifth session, by telephone, letter or in person, telling me how they are faring. I add that I have reason to believe that five sessions may well be sufficient and successful, but if it should turn out that they are not enough, it will be part of my responsibility to see that the patient gets whatever further therapy is necessary either by myself, or, if that is impossible, by somebody else. I add to this that if I need to transfer the patient to someone else, that second person will be seeing the patient through therapy and that I will personally introduce the patient to the therapist and, with his permission, sit in on the first session, and, incidentally, give a brief account to the other therapist in the patient's presence. Of course, I also mention that if there should be a real reason for contacting me before the month is up following the fifth session, then the patient should by all means do so. However, in order to interfere with the *secondary gain of continued transference feelings and dependence,* I add here that it is best to give the treatment process a chance; I quite genuinely believe that often the treatment process opens up some painful areas which are only partially healed by the time the actual therapy stops. I convey to the patient that it is best to permit the therapeutic process to come to its own conclusion spontaneously and that it is best for the patient to try to give the treatment results a chance to solidify rather than for him to call me the first time anything disturbing is experienced, possibly just because he feels abandoned. I thus try to convey—*as part of the contract*—that I will continue to be interested and do whatever is necessary, while I try at the same time to create a situation in which the patient feels motivated to attempt to achieve optimal results in the five sessions—in essence, by my conveying the idea that the *good patient* gives up secondary gains and passivity. Clearly, this is a situation which behavior therapists would consider, appropriately, a matter of reward for giving up some secondary gains.

In essence, this covers the establishment of the three aspects of the therapeutic process in the first session of therapy.

Second Session

In the *second session* we explore further, get better closure and re-examine the basis for choosing areas and methods of intervention (2).

I attempt to strengthen the positive therapeutic relationship—both transference and alliance—and interpret negative transferences, watching for disappointment and negative transference in myself as well as for excessive zeal. If possible, I ask the patient at the beginning of the second session what he thought about after he left the first session. I often refer to the "esprit d' escalier": As one walks down the stairs, one thinks of things that one might have said and of things one might have replied.

Furthermore, as a matter of routine, I ask the patient what he dreamt the night after the first appointment and what he dreamt the previous night, and I especially look for clues concerning the therapeutic relationship. I get a high yield of dreams because even after the patient tells me he didn't have one, I ask whether he at least recalls some feeling, or some word or picture, and thereupon the patient will very often report an entire dream.

Aside from other therapeutic operations, I attempt to modify the superego, the ego ideal and introject by lending myself as modifier. I may tell anecdotes about myself or offer opinions, contrary to the most customary procedure in psychoanalysis or prolonged psychotherapy. I use vivid concrete stories to convey certain ideas with colorful imagery, best delivered in an understated way. For example, to attempt to make some narcissistic behavior ego-alien, I might tell the story of Rothschild and a poor bum who told him the heartbreaking story of his life. As tears roll down Rothschild's cheeks and he finally reaches for the bell to summon the butler, the poor bum's hopes soar. When the butler appears, Rothschild turns to him and says, "Throw the bum out; he's breaking my heart." Or I may illustrate self-harming behavior by telling the story of the guy who stands in front of his burning house laughing uproariously. His neighbor comes over and says, "Hey, Joe, are you crazy? Your house is burning. How come you're laughing?" He says, "Oh, that's okay, the bed bugs are finally getting it!"

I consider it part of the technique of brief psyhcotherapy to have a suitable style likely to facilitate optimal learning.

Third and Fourth Sessions

In the third and fourth sessions, more of the same methodology continues. From the third session on I start referring to the *impending sep-*

aration by mentioning to the patient that there will be only two more sessions. I often predict—in order to be wrong—that in response to this expected separation the patient might even feel worse next time and that this might be due to a fear of separation and a fear of abandonment. Again, I will try to make this acceptable by talking about the fact that so many people call a doctor late at night, though they had some complaint most of the day, because suddenly they become afraid that next morning might be too late or that they may not be able to get hold of the doctor.

Fifth Session

In the fifth session, I review with the patient what we have learned, and address myself to loose ends. Very often we learn of some new aspects, despite all attempts to conceptualize in advance. All work, however, is especially directed towards aspects of the therapeutic alliance and the transference and towards the reaffirmation of the contract as stated before.

I aim to terminate with a positive relationship. As mentioned earlier, I also ask the patient to get in touch with me a month later and let me know how he is faring. This is accompanied by the statement that, of course, if the patient should have difficulties before that time, he should by all means contact me. At the same time, however, I caution the patient that the wish not to be abandoned may make one call more readily than may be necessary. There is some benefit in trying to go it alone rather than be dependent. The patient is again reassured that if it turns out that further therapy is necessary, it will be carried on either by myself or by someone else, whom I will introduce to the patient.

ENABLING CONDITIONS

At times, one may have to provide enabling conditions within which the psychotherapeutic relationship can take place. *Psychotropic drugs* may play a chief role in this. I have previously written (2) of the various roles drugs may play for clinical reasons, for metapsychological considerations, and, at times, for physiological reasons. By *clinical reasons,* I mean that if a patient is so crippled by agoraphobia that he cannot come to my office when no one is available to come with him, I am likely to prescribe enough medication to decrease the anxiety so that the patient can at least come to the session without a companion. Among the *metapsychological reasons,* I consider the prescription of chlorpromazine if I feel that impulse control needs to be improved in order to enable one to perform the psychotherapeutic intervention. This holds true for some psychotics. With them, at times, *environmental intervention* in the life situation is necessary: If the patient's sole contact with reality is via a TV set and that TV set breaks down, I consider it essential to see to it that his TV set is fixed promptly.

Returning to drugs specifically: I like to think of them as enabling conditions for psychotherapy, very similar to the role anesthesia plays for the surgeon. Sometimes they make interventions bearable and create the field within which one can intervene psychotherapeutically. One may stop the drugs as soon as they are not necessary to carry on the psychodynamic intervention.

Naturally, the role of drug giving has to be considered dynamically and especially in terms of the transference role, but generally they play a role in regulating the therapeutic process in psychotherapy and psychoanalysis. For psychotics, this has been described best by Ostow (5).

SOME ADMINISTRATIVE ASPECTS OF BRIEF THERAPY

I believe brief therapy to be useful in all settings—in private practice as well as in clinics and social agencies. A measure of improvement can be produced in acute conditions of all kinds, even chronic psychosis. Naturally, longer therapies are indicated for complex restructuring of personalities.

In public clinics, Leighton's admonition, "Action on behalf of one must be within the framework of calculations for the many" (4, p. 110), is very appropriate. I cannot accept the fact that many clinics and agencies have a year-long waiting list because only a few patients are seen in long-term therapy. Upon inspection, this therapy often turns out to be of poor quality because of insufficient conceptualization of the process or simply lack of therapeutic skill.

I urge the adoption of brief psychotherapy as the *intake procedure of choice*. If used properly, this method avoids waiting lists with their ensuing chronicity of pathology, and leaves enough time for well-thought-out longer therapies when they are indicated.

With regard to the *indications* for brief therapy: Instead of selecting patients or diagnostic categories, *I rather select the treatment goals.* In that framework, brief therapy can be useful for virtually any patient for primary, secondary and tertiary prevention. In the latter instance, for example, I have found it very useful in the treatment of acute exacerbations of chronic psychotics. In such cases, it may make the difference between someone needing to be hospitalized, or being able to remain in the community.

Brief Therapy as the Intake Method of Choice

There are at least two basic forms of intake for brief therapy as the method of choice:

> 1) A Clinic Director sees all patients at intake, and then turns them over to a staff member who is both available and particularly likely to do well with a given patient.
> 2) Whichever staff member is free takes the next patient and continues therapy.

Both methods have advantages and disadvantages. In the first method, one advantage is that the presumably most experienced person does the initial assessing. Also, if the therapist chosen for the patient should become ill, go on vacation or leave the position, the chief (director) can serve automatically as auxiliary therapist to see the patient through, having already met the patient and formed some relationship.

The disadvantage of this method is, of course, the discontinuity: The first relationship is formed with the clinic head and then another one with the actual therapist. To minimize the problem of the transfer, I suggest that, at the end of the intake, the director actually call in the person he has in mind to see the patient through and, in the presence of the patient, run through the salient features of the chief complaint, history, and whatever understanding of the problem has been arrived at. At the end of his presentation, the therapist would then ask some questions of the patient and the clinic director. Thus, a dialogue is started between patient and therapist, which ends with the setting of a date for the next session.

The second method, where whoever does the intake sees the patient through, has the advantage of direct continuity. Whatever supervision is indicated can be obtained in the usual way, by reviewing the case with a senior at any given time.

The disadvantage to this method is that there is no selection process concerning the most suitable therapist for a given patient. No one else is directly familiar with the patient in case the actual therapist is not available. Above all, there may be an administrative as well as a technical disadvantage: Many clinics are organized with one M.D. as the head, most of the other therapists being psychologists or social workers. If the patient is not first screened by the M.D. in charge, there may be a greater chance of overlooking a medical condition which might play a primary or secondary role in the patient's complaints. In many instances, medical screening may also be a legal requirement. Furthermore, if the medical director has at least brief intake acquaintance with the patient, he has a sounder basis for prescribing psychotropic medication if it is called for later on, rather than if he does so only on the basis of secondhand information.

One rationale for brief therapy, which I see as five-session therapy (with a sixth session as a follow-up a month later) is the fact that statistics from outpatient clinics suggest that most patients break off treatment after five sessions. Generally, people are not attuned to the idea of long-range psychotherapy. Among other things, they are accustomed to the medical model of usually rather prompt and brief treatment. In view of this fact, it is better to tailor-make therapy for the number of sessions the majority of patients are actually likely to appear, rather than to plan long-range therapy, which is too frequently prematurely interrupted.

Another basis for such time-limited therapy is the fact that this temporal goal setting, as part of the contract, seems to work well. It increases motivation, forces the therapist to conceptualize clearly, and avoids the secondary gain of passivity and dependence. Also, brief therapy can be offered to many more patients than can long-term therapy, and it can be made available very promptly, without the long waiting lists which cause pernicious chronicity. Moreover, it may indeed free therapy time for that percentage of patients who turn out to need longer therapy and are both willing and able to engage in it.

CONCLUSIONS

Brief psychotherapy (when used in emergencies it becomes emergency therapy) is a form of therapy with a status of its own. When it is predicated upon a comprehensive theory of personality, psychopathology and therapy such as psychoanalysis, it can be effective for unlearning and relearning because of the careful conceptualization of the dynamics and the process of therapy itself. The aim is to understand "everything" and to select carefully the few interventions which are likely to be crucially effective. The therapeutic relationship, carefully defined, and planfully utilized, plays an important role. Brief therapy is probably the intake method of choice, at least for clinics. It offers reasonable help to the largest number of those in need.

REFERENCES

1. Bellak, L. Once over: What is psychotherapy? *Journal of Nervous and Mental Disease*, 1977, 165:295-299.
2. Bellak, L. and Small, L. *Emergency Psychotherapy and Brief Psychotherapy*. New York: Grune & Stratton, 1965.
3. Jacobsen, E. *Depression: Comparative Studies of Normal, Neurotic and Psychotic Conditions*. New York: International Universities Press, 1971.
4. Leighton, A. H. *An Introduction to Social Psychiatry*. Springfield, Ill.: Charles C Thomas, 1960, p. 110.
5. Ostow, M. *Drugs in Psychoanalysis and Psychotherapy*. New York: Basic Books, 1962.

APPENDIX:
SAMPLE INTERVIEW

Following is a transcript of an initial interview, which may serve to illustrate some of my basic principles and methods. The interviewee is a 30-year-old Vietnam veteran amputee who was interviewed before an audience of 400 people, as part of a seminar on brief therapy. These circumstances limited some avenues of inquiry. All possible identifying characteristics have been deleted and the interview was videotaped with the patient's permission.

Dr. Bellak: Would you be kind enough and tell me what brought you here in the first place?

Patient: My marriage . . . Me and my wife separated due to problems of mine where I became passive to the point where if she wanted to do something, I just agreed with her to avoid arguments. When I was in Vietnam I had got blown up by a mine. And I did a lot of things in Vietnam that I don't really like myself for. And I've just become a mental pacifist because I'm afraid that if I do get mad, of what I would do, because in Vietnam I had killed at times due to various strenuous circumstances behind it, like having several of my comrades blown away. Being put in a position where I had killed . . . had done things that fell between being justifiable just to stay alive and what is not. And I got to a point where I developed a resistance in myself to the point where I would not love, would not hate. And it just got to . . . got to the point where I just could not live in that atmosphere. I had to let out some of the hate or some of the fear. Because I held myself to a point where I did not love. You can't love without hating.

Dr. Bellak: OK. That gives me a bit of an idea. It's my job to ask you questions and try to understand as much as possible. Under the circumstances, if there is something that you don't want to go into, that's your privilege.

All right, you gave me a bit of a general background. Exactly when did you come here. Do you remember the date?

Patient: December 10.

Dr. Bellak: December 10. What was the final push that got you here?

Patient: The final push was that I had been separated from my wife since July before I came here, and from July to December my nerves had gotten to the point where I drank quite a bit. And I'd be sitting at the bar and my hands would be shaking to the point where I couldn't control them. I'd crush a glass just trying to hold them steady. My nerves . . . I was afraid of violence. I was having blackouts. My nerves were catching up with me.

Dr. Bellak: And what would you say made you that nervous? Between July and December especially?

Patient: Not knowing whether I could live with me.

Dr. Bellak: That's too fancy.

Patient: I was trying to make myself not love or hate. Totally blocked it all out. I got to a point where I had no emotions. Didn't feel.

Dr. Bellak: Where did you live at the time?

Patient: I had an apartment in Wallingford.

Dr. Bellak: Did you live by yourself?

Patient: I lived by myself.

Dr. Bellak: Still, there must have been something extra. Something that make you come in here one day in December, after being upset all that while.

Patient: My wife had come in here before and basically she talked me into coming, with the idea that they could give me some better answers.

Dr. Bellak: But was there something extra special that made you come in December and not in July?

Patient: I had got to the point where I had left . . . when I felt that I could finance it myself . . . Then by December, I had found out that I could not rationalize some of the things I did by myself. When I was married, I had made myself think that they were rational.

Dr. Bellak: Like?

Patient: Dealing with Nam. I was in several positions where we'd been hit. I worked on what we called hunter-killer teams in Vietnam. You went out with one other man. I went on five missions. Two missions I came back by myself. Lost two men . . . friends of mine.

Dr. Bellak: So that was still really on your mind.

Patient: This was why I felt . . . I had gotten to the point where I was afraid to love anybody, for the fear of losing them. In Nam, we got attached to each other very quick. All the guys I worked with. All the guys that worked with me. I knew things about them that I didn't know about my own brother, and they knew things about me. And after losing so many people, I just refused to get close to anybody . . . afraid to be close for fear of losing them.

Dr. Bellak: OK. Did you live all by yourself or did you see friends? From the time you and your wife separated. . . .

Patient: Matter of fact, from the time I was strictly by myself. For the first three or four months.

Dr. Bellak: When did you actually come back from Vietnam?

Patient: I've been back a few years . . . from 1971.

Dr. Bellak: 1971. And the difficulties with your wife developed then?

Patient: I wasn't married at the time.

Dr. Bellak: Oh, I see.

Patient: I was from New Year's Eve till June 28th in the hospital. Just getting back together . . . about six months . . . had one leg cut off . . . that a mine blew off. . . . I basically got back or got home and my wife and parents had already sort of set up the wedding arrangements. I didn't know about it.

Dr. Bellak: But you knew the girl, I hope.

Patient: Yeah, I knew the girl. (*Laughs*)

Dr. Bellak: OK. (*Laughs*) I was thinking of some Japanese friends of mine where the mother selects the girl.

Patient: I went from 210 pounds down to 105 pounds, during a period of being in the hospital.

Dr. Bellak: In the hospital?

Patient: And there wasn't too much arguing. I didn't really want to fight or argue with anybody anymore. And I still basically stayed that way.

Dr. Bellak: They arranged it and you accepted it? Is that what you're telling me?

Patient: Yeah, we were good friends and we knew each other and had dated. Well, really only about a month before I went into the Army, but I would have postponed it awhile. Two or three months.

Dr. Bellak: Do I hear between the lines that if you had not been in your particular shape that you might not have agreed to the marriage?

Patient: More than likely, because when I was in the hospital I didn't even ask about it and they were talking about it then. They waited a year . . . she waited . . . we waited . . . to give me time to adjust to life and its problems.

Dr. Bellak: OK, so you agreed to go along with it, though. But what were your misgivings? What were your doubts?

Patient: Well, much of my life I had been very athletic. I ran track the first year I was in the Army. I had run cross-country. I didn't know if I could accept not running, not being able to go out and play. Basically, the thought of work . . . I could probably work as well as anybody, but I didn't know if I could do the other things in my life that always seemed to be so important to me.

Dr. Bellak: How did that affect the matter of whether you would or would not get married?

Patient: I basically didn't know if I wanted anybody else to support me that way and I wasn't sure that I even wanted to be that way.

Dr. Bellak: And then how did the marriage go?

Patient: Well, basically until the day I left, my wife felt that we had a great marriage. I usually agreed to whatever she wanted to do. I really didn't want to argue for fear of being mad because I was afraid of what I might do if I got mad. I just gave in and let her have her way. But it eventually just got to the point where I started hating myself even more because I gave in to things that I really didn't want to do, really didn't like.

Dr. Bellak: Could you give me some examples?

Patient: Well, like she was Catholic and I was Baptist. She never insisted that I go to Church, but she always wanted me to and I, basically, the times I did go . . . not really, I guess you'd say, under duress . . . but I really didn't want to go. . . . But I got tired of saying no.

Dr. Bellak: Other things? How about the conflict between you two?

Patient: Well, basically, I liked to horseback ride and I liked athletic things. I still do. I like to water-ski and boat ride and every time I tried to get something that we could do together, she was always afraid of it. Like just horses. I bought two horses and she rode it about a hundred yards and stopped and she got thrown off it and she never would get back on it. It aggravated me that she would not try to do the things that we could do together. I just got to the point where I thought about what I wanted to do and just did it by myself.

Dr. Bellak: And towards the end, in July, what was the main point of the differences?

Patient: I had . . . we had drawn up blueprints for a house we were building and every time I would get through with them, she decided that she wanted to change things a little and we sent them back to the drawing board five times. And I started to agree with her, just not to argue and basically it wasn't the way I would have liked. I know about houses because I used to build them.

Dr. Bellak: Is that your field? What do you do?

Patient: A carpenter. I build furniture.

Dr. Bellak: That's what you still do?

Patient: As a hobby. I'm basically military retired.

Dr. Bellak: OK, what would you say ails you most right now?

Patient: (*Long pause*) Now I can never get to the point where I like me.

Dr. Bellak: OK, let's look into that. What is it, if you had to make a list, that makes you dislike yourself the most especially?

Patient: I'm very closed . . . I've just gotten passive. (*Starts to cry*) You know, that's not my way normally. Normally I speak out, right? I'm very straightforward.

Dr. Bellak: So you dislike yourself for that. Having given in.

Patient: It got to the point where I didn't like me for giving in all the time.

Dr. Bellak: OK, what else? Is that what *still* bothers you? Do you think about it?

Patient: Yeah.

Dr. Bellak: Today?

Patient: Yeah.

Dr. Bellak: Yesterday?

Patient: Yeah . . . Well, we didn't talk yesterday.

Dr. Bellak: Are you and your wife still on talking terms?

Patient: We're still on talking terms. I keep my kids on the weekend.

Dr. Bellak: But what of the things that you dislike about yourself kept running through your mind?

Patient: I guess part of it is the fear of me. Not being able to control me.

Dr. Bellak: And then what would you do?

Patient: Rather than be around people where I would be put into a position where I would be afraid that I would . . . I'd rather be by myself.

Dr. Bellak: I can understand that. But—and I know this is painful for you—but could you try and spell out specifically what you are afraid of? Of doing?

Patient: Disintegrating. Just accidentally becoming mad.

Dr. Bellak: And *then* what would you do?

Patient: Killing somebody out of instinct rather than . . .

Dr. Bellak: How? How?

Patient: With my hands.

Dr. Bellak: How?

Patient: There are several methods that the Army taught us.

Dr. Bellak: Which ones did you think of using?

Patient: There are certain areas. Like the person's Adam's apple. Taking your two hands and breaking off the windpipe. And several methods of crushing a man's ribcage and breaking his back. Hands over his neck, pull back. I had caught myself twice going for a man's throat when I had got angry.

Dr. Bellak: We want to understand. Could you be a little more graphic?

Patient: OK, the first time I was in a bar. Somebody else had come in (*sighs*) . . . he was a homosexual and made a proposition to me. And I got mad. If there weren't two guys in there that were friends of mine, and stopped me, I would have killed him.

Dr. Bellak: How, in this case?

Patient: Well, I had grabbed him by his throat and had him up against the wall. I had my hands around his throat (*voice cracks*), and I was trying to. . . . And the other one. I had come into the bar and a man and another woman there were arguing and I just went for him. I tried to kill him. I had him by the inside of his throat rather than the outside . . . and this scared me to the point where I refused to get mad. That happened in the first year after coming back from the hospital. I got to the point where I just did not go out and socialize with people at all. I just basically stayed home.

Dr. Bellak: And has it become better now?

Patient: I have more control now. Of my feelings. I can take and block everything out. But also by blocking out, it leaves me in a situation where I have to fight myself.

Dr. Bellak: Well, you described that very clearly—that empty feeling that is left after you have tried to push away both love and hate. You made that very clear. Do you have friends at this point?

Patient: I have about four people that I trust enough to call a friend.

Dr. Bellak: Guys?

Patient: Three are male, one's a female.

Dr. Bellak: What did you dream last night?

Patient: I don't remember if I had a dream. I only dreamed twice since I came back from Vietnam.

Dr. Bellak: Do you want to tell me those? Anytime that you feel too uncomfortable . . .

Patient: One was four years ago when me and my wife separated for awhile. I guess it was the day after I had taken her back to Pittsburgh and left her with her parents. I took the train back. That night . . . when I was in Nam I had gotten hit several times while I was sleeping and I had gotten into the habit of sleeping with a gun.

Dr. Bellak: By "hit" you mean attacked?

Patient: Yeah, while we were asleep. And I started dreaming about the day I was hit in Vietnam. For some reason, something made a noise in the house and I rolled out of bed and fired six times, blew six holes.

Dr. Bellak: In the dream?

Patient: No, really. And that was what scared me. I had rolled out of the bed. We were sleeping on cots in Vietnam and I always had an M16 there and here I had a .38 and when we got hit, I would roll out of the bed and start shooting. Before I really realized I was not still in Vietnam, I had rolled out of the bed and fired the gun six times till I flicked the trigger. And I blew six holes in the side door of my house. Luckily there was nobody there.

Dr. Bellak: OK, that was the night after you left your wife off with her parents in Pittsburgh.

Patient: Four years ago.

Dr. Bellak: And any others?

Patient: I had one while I was still in the hospital. Well, I had several of them that reoccurred as the same dream. It was the day we were hit, going through the minefield. The day I was hit I had 20 men on patrol . . . 20 men . . . seven of them were killed . . . and 12 of us came back amputees. Mutilated. One leg . . . both legs . . . both legs and arms. And the dream was about the same thing. About all the pain.

Dr. Bellak: Do you recall any dreams from your childhood?

Patient: When I was real young—about being attacked by a big gorilla. A bunch of gorillas.

Dr. Bellak: Gorillas?

Patient: Being attacked by a bunch of gorillas. I think I had a habit of watching a lot of Tarzan movies. That dream really stuck with me.

Dr. Bellak: OK, that tells me a little bit. You certainly have had a rough time. I just know a little bit about it. I'm still a consultant to West Point and I was during Vietnam so I saw quite a few people coming back and during World War II, I just had enough of a taste of it myself to know what you're talking about. Nothing quite that drastic.

Would you be kind enough and give me a very brief capsule of your life history?

Patient: I was born in 1948. I'm 30 years old. I lived in Philadelphia about until the time that I got drafted in the service.

Dr. Bellak: Your family?

Patient: I have an older brother, and an older sister, and a younger sister.

Dr. Bellak: How much older is your brother?

Patient: My brother is two years older than I am. My sister is six years older than I am, and my younger sister is six years younger than I am.

Dr. Bellak: And your parents? What kind of people are your parents?

Patient: They're basically, from anybody else's standpoint of view, very pleasant, easygoing people. Which my father is in reality. My mother likes to put on one face for everyone else and she really likes to bitch a lot.

Dr. Bellak: And what was her relation to you?

Patient: At times we had, or I had . . . problems growing up, where I had gotten into trouble doing certain things in school.

Dr. Bellak: Two terms that I don't understand. Problems growing up and getting into difficulties in school. What does that mean?

Patient: In school, I had always been passive, but twice I had gotten into trouble for fights.

Dr. Bellak: Passive meaning what?

Patient: Easygoing. I didn't like to fight, didn't want to fight. Didn't want to argue. Didn't want to be a bully. Didn't—I tried to get along with people.

Dr. Bellak: I'll remind you of that later, OK? But twice you got into fights?

Patient: And both times I felt that I was basically justified and then I was expelled from school.

Dr. Bellak: Did you hurt the guys?

Patient: Not so that they had to go to the hospital. Just two black eyes, that's all.

Dr. Bellak: OK (*Laughs*). What was the worst thing your mother ever did to you?

Patient: That fight—that time I felt I was justified in getting into that fight, when I got home my father agreed with me, but yet my mother gave me a whipping for it.

Dr. Bellak: How did she whip you?

Patient: With a belt.

Dr. Bellak: How old were you at the time?

Patient: The first time probably 13. The second time about 15.

Dr. Bellak: You were a pretty big guy.

Patient: Basically, it wasn't that she could hurt me by the whipping. Just so that she could hurt me inside. I leaned on her chair for her to do it. She didn't . . .

Dr. Bellak: She didn't what?

Patient: She didn't just whip me standing there. I basically . . .

Dr. Bellak: So you sort of agreed to it.

Patient: Yeah . . .

Dr. Bellak: Was it with your pants? You wore your pants?

Patient: Without my pants.

Dr. Bellak: If you would describe—if you would apply three descriptive words to your father, what woud you pick?

Patient: (*Silence*)

Dr. Bellak: The first ones that come to your mind. Don't make it too hard.

Patient: Passive, in terms of my mother. In comparison. Strong. Outgoing in terms of everybody else.

Dr. Bellak: What does he do?

Patient: He's retired now.

Dr. Bellak: What did he do?

Patient: We had a grocery store in Pittsburgh. Then when we moved to Philly, he and my brother opened a construction company, which I worked with.

Dr. Bellak: And your mother? If you would describe her? You already said she was bitchy. What else?

Patient: Two-faced. She was one way outside to everybody else and another way inside. Incredible! She expected everyone to live one way and she wanted to live another way.

Dr. Bellak: You got through high school?

Patient: Yes.

Dr. Bellak: And then what did you do between that and the Army?

Patient: The time between high school and the time I was drafted . . . Well, I left home about six months before I graduated high school. The reason I left was that I had a fight with my father and he slapped me. That was the first time that he had beaten me up in five or six years. And I left because I was afraid that I was going to hit him back. I wanted to hit him back . . . but I loved him. (*Starts to cry*) I loved him but I wanted to hit him. That's the reason I left.

Dr. Bellak: Why did he hit you?

Patient: We had that grocery store down there. We worked there together in the mornings. He had this habit of thinking that people were supermen. He'd tell you ten things that he wanted you to do, come back in five minutes, and think of two more things for you to do.

Dr. Bellak: I get the picture.

Patient: I think I was about 17. One day in the store I just finally told him that I couldn't take it anymore, that I only had two hands and not four hands. And that's the first time I think I ever talked back to him. And he slapped me.

Dr. Bellak: So that was a good time to get into the Army?

Patient: I worked for a year and a half for an oil company, after high school and then I got drafted.

Dr. Bellak: Let's just think over some of the things that you've been saying.

Patient: Well, basically, what I didn't like about the way I was living was that I had gotten totally passive.

Dr. Bellak: If I can interrupt, if I may, I really didn't ask you enough about your wife. Would you just give me a very brief capsule. What kind of a woman is she?

Patient: My wife is 28, attractive. She has a different notion of what love is.

Dr. Bellak: What's her background? Let's stick to simple things.

Patients: Her background? After she got out of high school, she worked in a bank.

Dr. Bellak: What kind of family?

Patient: Her father is German, mother is Italian. And a lot of our problems stem from them because they never showed any love of any kind to her. They totally refuse—they ignore that sex exists. According to them, they don't know how kids are born, they just hatched them. She did not understand that. Her parents would never kiss in public or kiss openly or show any affection of any kind. Totally closed, cold, no feeling.

Dr. Bellak: If you were to describe how her parents are different from each other, what would you say?

Patient: Her father basically dominating, overbearing. Very tight with money. To the point where I know there were times when I have seen her younger brothers and sisters ask him for money, like a quarter to get a coke or something, he would never let anybody see what he had, he'd turn around and hide it and just take out a quarter.

Dr. Bellak: And her mother?

Patient: Her mother is like the father, basically.

Dr. Bellak: And your wife? If you could describe her briefly?

Patient: When we first got married, she was not basically aggressive. She was not aggressive in any way. She was afraid of any kind of sex. She really didn't know how to show affection. Just blocks it away.

Dr. Bellak: And did sex remain a problem?

Patient: Yes.

Dr. Bellak: Ordinarily, I would go into it, but I don't think we need to under the circumstances.

But, now that you've rounded that out, did you mention children?

Patient: Yes, I have two girls.

Dr. Bellak: How old?

Patient: Five and almost two.

Dr. Bellak: How do you get along?

Patient: (*Sighs*) Both girls and me get along very well. I keep them every weekend—Friday and Saturday.

Dr. Bellak: OK, let's go back to what you think we might have learned from what you have told me so far. After all, my job is, among other things, to be of help you.

Patient: (*Silence*).

Dr. Bellak: Well, let me make it a little bit easier. After all, I have a bit more perspective. It's easier for someone standing away. Also, I'm supposed to know something about it. Let's see if we can agree on some things. Look, what you complain about most and what brought you here is a fear that your anger might get out of hand and that you might do violence. And you have some very good reasons for it. Vietnam was a terrible experience. A couple of times it almost got out of hand and you had some very disturbing dreams, one of being hit and another in which you actually shot your .38.

Patient: Yeah, and in the other dream—well they were the same dream but it was when I was in the hospital.

Dr. Bellak: OK. Now, well curiously enough, when you told me your earlier history, particularly with school, you started off by saying that most of the time you were passive. Then a couple of times you beat up guys pretty badly. Your whole concern now, and about the marriage, was that you were being too passive. Feeling a great deal of anger, and the more you sat on it because you were afraid that it might get out of hand, the more you felt relief. As a kid, you had dreams of a gorilla going after you. And it scared you.

Patient: Yeah, terribly!

Dr. Bellak: In a way, I see a little similarity between that anxiety dream of somebody big, like a gorilla, doing you violence and the dreams of being hit, being attacked.

Patient: Basically, they're both about being attacked.

Dr. Bellak: That's right.

Patient: They're both forms of being attacked. One by an animal and the other by a man.

Dr. Bellak: Yes. Whom did the gorilla look like, incidentally, in the dream? The first thing that comes to your mind.

Patient: A big ape.

Dr. Bellak: Is it anybody you know?

Patient: No.

Dr. Bellak: All right. (*Laughs*).

Patient: Just looked like a big furry gorilla.

Dr. Bellak: So there is a certain continuity. While Vietnam undoubtedly made things worse . . .

Patient: The fear of being attacked. The thought of it.

Dr. Bellak: And also, the whole axis turns around aggression, passivity. In school, you say that you were passive most of the time, which is a curious way of putting it. Not everybody would put it that way. And that continues through your marriage, the closest relationship you have. You started out by saying, if I remember correctly, that when your parents arranged it, you were passive about it and agreed to the arrangement. When you described your wife, you said that she was not aggressive. That seems to be very much on your mind. You mentioned that she was not aggressive and then that she got to be and bugged you with the constant changes about the blueprints and different things. But at any rate, the point I want to make is that to be aggressive or to be passive seems to be a thread that runs through your mind very readily. It's practically the main axis. Now, then, what did you tell me about your parents that might have a bearing on that?

Patients: Only that my father was passive with my mother.

Dr. Bellak: What effect might that have had on you? On your personality?

Patient: It made me where I almost did the same thing with my wife. Like the way my parents continuously argued.

Dr. Bellak: If I put it in my vulgar way, I would say that you might have said to yourself as a kid. "I'll be goddamed if I'm going to be a patsy to a woman the way my father has been." Is that right?

Patient: And I wound up doing the same thing. Either that, or I let myself get to the point of doing the same thing.

Dr. Bellak: Either that, or at least it felt that way to you.

Patient: Right.

Dr. Bellak: What conclusions would you draw?

Patient: That I'm afraid of being like my father. Afraid of being pushed.

Dr. Bellak: OK, could I push that just a bit? That you're afraid of being passive. One of the guys who got to you particularly was a homosexual in the bar.

Patient: Yeah. But I was only 21 at the time. I had never had relations with another man. Never wanted to. Never. . . .

Dr. Bellak: So, if I may stretch things a little by implication—the idea that he would think that you would be in any way interested in something not masculine got you sore. That's the point I want to make for right now. And how do you think we could fit in that other time that you nearly got at the guy's Adam's apple?

Patient: That was over a man striking a woman. I was brought up never to do that.

Dr. Bellak: Well, aside from the fact that . . . psychologically, what do you think it might be? Look, you saw somebody attacked. When you and I see a car accident on the highway, what do we do?

Patient: Stop and see if we can help.

Dr. Bellak: But if there is already an ambulance and a cop car there, what do we do anyhow?

Patient: Stop and see if anybody was hurt.

Dr. Bellak: Yes, but usually everyone slows down a bit because you feel that "Gee, this could happen to me. Maybe I shouldn't drive so fast." One identifies, as we psychiatrists say, with the other person. Could there have been something in that, when you saw the guy hit the woman?

Patient: Other than the actual fact?

Dr. Bellak: Well, I could be wrong, but what I wonder about in such a case, if one doesn't identify with the underdog. You don't want to see her hit, because you feel, "Damn, I don't want to be hit."

Patient: I don't want to be hurt, but I don't want to hurt anyone either.

Dr. Bellak: OK, let's see if we can agree on a couple of things. One is that Vietnam was a terrible experience. It might do all sorts of things to anybody's . . .

Patient: *(interrupts)* People have to do a lot of things that they shouldn't have to do.

Dr. Bellak: I know, but this might just have made more of an impression on *your* personality because you had already been concerned with a fear of being attacked, as witnessed in the dreams about the gorilla, a recurrent dream in your childhood. You felt that you had to stand up against your mother, about whom you had understandably mixed feelings. Mixed feelings. You bent over the chair and let her whip you, but at the same time you must have been full of a hell of a rage.

Patient: Anger, because I didn't understand why. I felt that I was justified in what I did.

Dr. Bellak: Well, among other things . . . So that you came with that pattern. Vietnam made it worse. Then you had the feeling that you let yourself be shoved into a marriage. You started out with a bit of a grudge and misgivings that you had let yourself be shoved. And then, very promptly, saw yourself in a situation and a relationship that seemed too much like the one you saw between your father and mother.

What does it add up to? If you and I would just change chairs mentally and you were the psychiatrist, what would you think of all the things you have heard today?

Patient: As far as the marriage?

Dr. Bellak: No, as far as understanding what is going on with you.

Patient: What's going on with me?

Dr. Bellak: Yes, and what we might do about it.

Patient: *(Silence)*

Dr. Bellak: Well, in view of the fact that we see that some of the same problems that trouble you now and troubled you in your marriage existed in some form in your youth, in your earlier life, what do you think you and your therapist might work on?

Patient: Getting me to the point that I can, basically, release enough of myself to feel.

Dr. Bellak: How do you propose to do that?

Patient: The only way I can do it is to learn not to be afraid of reaching out and of being hurt.

Dr. Bellak: Is there another way? Obviously, what ails you now has its origins in childhood. Getting to understand the fact that many of the things that happened to you as a kid make Vietnam much more difficult for you to absorb and digest and to deal with now—and they still have an effect on you today, the things that happened to you as a child. The better you can understand to a certain extent how you either overemphasize or even distort some of the things that happen to you now because you were already primed in childhood— the gorillas and all that—the less you are going to feel that rage. I think that rage has been there since childhood, and got an extra shove from all the things in Vietnam. I don't know if you could have married any woman . . .

Patient: At that point.

Dr. Bellak: At any time, and not come with the same set of expectations. "I better watch out that she is not a battle-axe who shoves me around." Because that is what you were accustomed to. So, the more you work on that, on understanding your current feelings in terms of your early past, with Vietnam just thrown in psychologically for good measure, the better able you will be to handle the tensions that you have, which just seem to be all along a matter of passivity, aggression—really, apparently, the axis around which your life revolves. Some people have that problem even without Vietnam if one has had that childhood. That's one thing. The more you can go into that, the better.

Would you like to hear my guess about who the gorilla was in the dream? I bet you can make a pretty good guess. Can you tell me? The first person who comes to your mind.

Patient: My mother.

Dr. Bellak: Oh, sure. And I bet if we could go into the dream in enough detail, we could find things that would identify her. And I think that she is even sometimes identified in your mind with some of the Vietnamese.* Well, it gets a bit complex. But those are some of the things that you two can continue to go into. Meanwhile, I'm sure you use whatever athletics you can to get rid of some of the tension. I think that's a very good short range measure. Like punching a bag.

You're right-handed, I take it.

Patient: Yes.

Dr. Bellak: Never were left-handed?**

Patient: No.

Dr. Bellak: Well, I think that's probably as much as we can go into now. I feel, having seen problems similar to yours before, that there is a good deal of hope that the two of you—you and your therapist—can really work this out.

You know, there's not anyone so tough that he doesn't have some passivity. I don't care how tough the guy is.

Patient: Basically, I'm not afraid of being passive. The problem is that usually I get too passive.

Dr. Bellak: Well, in part I guess you had to because with your mother . . . and then that made you feel like nothing and you had to get really angry. So, if you two can work it out so that you neither feel too passive nor the need to feel too aggressive, I think that things should work out very well.

---

* The ideal concise interpretation I should have made here is: "I think all you did was to replace the *gorillas* with *guerillas*."

** This was just a brief notion that the patient's problems with impulse control might be related to any aspect of minimal brain dysfunction. I discuss this more fully in another book (1).

Thank you very much again. I really appreciate that you were willing to discuss things.

Patient: Thank you very much.

REFERENCE

1. Bellak, L. Adult psychiatric states with MBD and their ego function assessment. In L. Bellak (Ed.), *Psychiatric Aspects of Minimal Brain Dysfunction in Adults.* New York: Grune & Stratton, 1979.

4

Enabling Conditions for the Ambulatory Psychotherapy of Acute Schizophrenics

LEOPOLD BELLAK, M.D.

The psychotherapy of acutely disturbed schizophrenics can be one of the most rewarding of therapeutic experiences. It is frequently possible to effect a dramatic loss of symptoms and general improvement of the acute manifestations of the disorder rather promptly. It often enough holds true that after the acute phase has been successfully dealt with, there remain the characterological features which are of complex nature and that often require prolonged and patient treatment. The present discussion, however, addresses itself only to the circumstances necessary for the treatment of the acute phase of a schizophrenic episode.

Certainly, the first question that must arise in the treatment of an acutely disturbed psychotic on an ambulatory basis, in the private office, social agency, or a clinic, must be whether a patient is suitable for this type of treatment.

Therefore, I want to address myself to the necessary conditions, the conditions that enable one to perform ambulatory psychotherapy with acute schizophrenics. If the enabling conditions outlined cannot be met, ambulatory psychotherapy may not be advisable, and an alternate mode of treatment may be indicated.

The author is greatly indebted to Helen Siegel, M.A. for her editorial assistance.

1) *A Reasonably Cooperative, Non-assaultive Patient*

One of the most obvious enabling conditions is that one has to have a *reasonably cooperative, non-assaultive patient*. By reasonably cooperative, I mean that he at least comes to the session or is willing to be brought by a third party. However, it may be possible to start psychotherapy with a patient who is unwilling to come to therapy. Sometimes it is necessary to visit the patient in his own home, at least to initiate therapy. When this is not possible or feasible, an effective means of getting an unwilling patient to the office is to instruct a family member to ask the patient to accompany him to see the psychotherapist for his—the relative's—own sake. It is usually true enough that the relative is deeply concerned and upset, and is being sincere when he tells the patient that he wants some help for dealing with some of his own problems. Often the patient is then willing to come along as a mute companion. The initial exchanges are all between the therapist and the patient's relative. It must be part of the therapist's skill to eventually engage the patient until he or she slowly becomes the main interactor and ultimately the sole one.

One other possibility of engaging a patient in treatment, if the above procedure is ineffectual, is to engage in *mediate interpretations*. If a patient refuses to come by himself or even with a companion, as described above, it may be possible to learn enough about the psychodynamics of the patient from the relative to suggest statements or interpretations which the relative can then relay back to the patient. If, in turn, the relative reports back to the therapist, he can be used to mediate the therapy in such a way that the patient might be affected beneficially enough to a point where he is willing to come for treatment with the relative as companion. Then the therapist can proceed as above.

The fact that many schizophrenics may start out mute or barely communicative is no contraindication to therapy. Even potential assaultiveness need not be a contraindication, provided one sets up certain conditions which I will discuss later, with regard to certain precautions and the possible concomitant use of drugs. Of course, I include patients in ambulatory psychotherapy who are often actively deluded and hallucinated. Most of us are aware of the fact that in many patients extensive delusions and hallucinations need not necessarily interfere in seemingly normal social behavior. There is many a patient who thinks he is Jesus Christ or believes he can understand what the birds are saying, but nevertheless may continue to hold a skilled job and arrive punctually for each of his appointments. Although some patients may not be well enough to come on their own by car or bus, they may still profit from ambulatory psychotherapy, if someone brings them to the therapist's office.

The premise is that, whenever possible, it is better to avoid hospitalization, provided the patient is not actively homicidal or suicidal or so disturbed as to do harm inadvertently. The fact is that very little competent psychotherapy is offered in any hospital. In university-affiliated institutions, residents are usually the ones directly treating the patient, even though under supervision. Though they may be competent, the fact is they are still at an early stage of their training. In private institutions, there are usually not enough psychotherapists available, or else the therapists available are of questionable competence. The cost of hospitalization often approaches $100,000 a year. In addition, regression and secondary gain from being cared for ("nursed") produce other problems. Very frequently, the patient's reentry into the community, if it is not extremely skillfully handled, starts a new flare-up.

2) *One Stable Relationship in the Patient's Life*

Less obvious and less generally considered is the almost absolute need for at least *one stable relationship in the patient's life situation*—at least one person, such as parent, spouse, child, close friend—anybody whom one might turn to if the circumstances should warrant it. The therapist must be able to talk to somebody who is willing to keep an eye on the patient at home, because of concerns about suicide, or other potentially harmful situations; someone who can take a helpful role if the patient should require hospitalization, or can otherwise serve as a constructive influence in the patient's life. Without at least a single stable person close to the patient, I have found through bitter experience that one may be left with almost impossible situations, more responsibility than one can reasonably handle, and with less safety than is essential for the treatment situation.

3) *A Close Relationship with a Nearby Hospital*

The third enabling condition for anybody who wants to treat rather acutely disturbed psychotics is that one have a *close relationship with a nearby hospital,* including a general hospital willing to take psychiatric patients. It is essential in treating acute psychotics that one be willing to take reasonable risks. Those reasonable risks include the possibility that some patients will become more disturbed in the course of treatment, either for adventitious reasons or for reasons intrinsic to the treatment.

The therapist can engage in psychotherapy with acutely disturbed people only if he feels safe enough. He needs an arrangement which permits almost instant hospitalization of the patient, should the need arise. At times, even only two or three days of hospitalization can make a crucial difference. This provision certainly helps to give one more therapeutic freedom with less anxiety for patient and therapist. The hospital provides some immediate protection for the patient and gives the therapist freedom to engage in interventions which might possibly be upsetting to the patient.

Though therapeutic freedom sometimes has to include interventions which might prove unnerving to the patient, I do not believe in inducing regressions intentionally: I am not certain that therapeutically induced regressions and dissociations may not lay the foundation for easier regression and dissociation at other times, and therefore do not consider them a desirable therapeutic modality.

However, I do believe in such active steps as cathartic interpretations, i.e. interpreting unconscious material directly à la John Rosen (3), without waiting until it becomes preconscious, as is more customary in the treatment of less disturbed people.

Aside from the importance of having easy access to a hospital, it is extremely desirable that it be a hospital setting in which one can continue to see and treat one's own patient while he is there. This type of situation is often difficult to attain because teaching hospitals always insist on having only their residents and staff treat patients. In view of this fact, proprietary hospitals, which may be otherwise less desirable, are to be preferred. While the patient is hospitalized for an acute disorder, actively deluded and hallucinated, one can make crucial interventions which will speed up the therapeutic process greatly. Of course, it is also essential that the patient has a sense of not being deserted, so it is extremely beneficial when there is continuity of contact. Therefore, anyone who wants to engage frequently in the treatment of acutely disturbed psychotics has to cultivate a close relationship with a hospital that will permit him quick hospitalization and continued care of his own patient, both psychotherapeutically as well as psychopharmacologically.

Another aspect which may be even more difficult than the first two with regard to hospitalization is that it must be possible to get one's patients released from the hospital as promptly as possible. Ordinarily, administrative procedures may make it difficult to remove a patient from the hospital speedily. Yet, those patients who are suitable for ambulatory psychotherapy could especially easily be harmed by excessively long hospitalization which induces passivity and secondary gains from the hot-house conditions of support and external controls.

4) *A Family Network*

This point is really an elaboration of the second one, namely the requirement that there be at least one person whom the therapist can address himself to, who will take some responsibility for the patient. If there is a whole *family network* available, this may play a crucial and beneficial role. Family network therapy has a definite and well-known place in treatment. Especially if inter-family pathology plays a marked role, it is essential to draw other family members into the therapeutic situation. This may be accomplished in different ways. Indeed, one may choose to engage in either conjoint therapy with one other family member, or in family therapy per se. Under certain circumstances, the original therapist may wish to work with the entire family himself. In other instances, it may be more suitable to have other family members, or even the entire family, seen by another psychiatrist or social worker or psychologist. The two therapists must have the privilege of conferring with each other, so as to work as a team, even if not necessarily under the same roof.

5) *An Auxiliary Therapist*

The above point brings me to one of the less well-known and less practiced techniques, and that is the desirability of utilizing an *auxiliary therapist*, i.e. having two therapists treating the same patient simultaneously. The auxiliary therapist may be drawn in only during particularly stormy episodes. These may be due to an especially acute transference psychosis, or at times to a particular countertransference problem on the part of the therapist. Then the role of the auxiliary therapist is to deal specifically with the transference psychotic phenomenon which may be too difficult for the patient, and maybe for the primary therapist, to handle directly. Meanwhile, the primary therapist continues to work on the problems that produced the acute transference psychosis.

Dyadic psychotherapy, especially in an office, can be a very lonely type of endeavor, fraught with all sorts of emotions, including anxiety for both therapist and patient. Therefore, it is often very useful to have, as a routine proviso, an auxiliary therapist who can dilute the transference and countertransference, if necessary. If one routinely works with acutely disturbed psychotics, it is often useful to introduce an auxiliary therapist early in the relationship, explaining to the patient that this colleague will be available should the primary therapist catch a cold, go on vacation, or otherwise be unavailable. Such availability, of course, is crucially important with the most highly disturbed people. This kind of arrangement is made more easily in a clinic or social agency than in private practice, but it is not impossible in the latter.

6) *Awareness of Family and Community Resources*

Especially for psychiatrists in private practice, it is important to be aware of all possible *resources in a patient's life* (relatives, friends, etc.) *and in the community.* Social workers and psychologists are more likely to be aware of these social support systems, such as social agencies, rehabilitation facilities, halfway houses, recreational facilities, and eventually vocational rehabilitation. It is important to make use of these facilities during treatment and certainly towards the end of treatment, when the patient needs a setting in which he can continue his improvement and recovery.

7) *Hot-lines and Emergency Centers*

A variation on the theme of having access to an auxiliary therapist is the need to have easy access to *hot-lines and emergency centers.* Most communities, at this point, do have such services available, as part of their community facilities. These emergency services are usually listed on the inside cover of the phone book and, when they are properly administered, are accessible 24 hours a day. The telephone contact should be backed up by an available psychiatric emergency center in a clinic or social agency and, if possible, a mobile team which can visit a patient in his home and, in an extreme situation, commit and hospitalize him.

8) *Do Not Be a Hero*

I consider it extremely important to have *easy access to an alarm system,* in case a patient should become acutely disturbed and possibly dangerous. The ability to treat acutely disturbed people depends as much on the relative security of the setting within which therapy takes place, as on the therapist's capacity to tolerate feelings of anxiety and discomfort. Under any circumstances, *it is essential not to be inappropriately heroic.* The therapist should never allow situations to exist which are unduly dangerous in terms of his own safety. An anxious therapist can certainly not function effectively. An unsecured setting also makes the patient uneasy, because he may well fear his own possible loss of impulse control. Especially in large and active emergency treatment centers, it is best to have security personnel available. In settings which are less likely to have extremely disturbed patients, it is advantageous to have an office which is not located in too isolated a setting. It may be helpful to leave the door slightly ajar, provided that reasonable privacy is still retained. Again, such a provision is often also of benefit to the patient, who feels less frightened of the therapist and of his own impulses, when he perceives the situation as relatively secure.

9) Housing Situations

This point deals with a very difficult problem—the *suitability of the patient's housing situation*: namely, where the patient lives and where he or she should live for optimal improvement. The family setting is often extremely unhealthy and it may be almost impossible to do constructive therapeutic work in two or three hours a week if the remainder of the time there are forces within the family setting which are regressive and pathogenic. Therefore, it is often essential, and certainly a major enabling condition, that if his present living situation is unsuitable then the patient must be moved to another setting. At first glance, this often appears to be impossible. I strongly suggest a very careful survey of all his relatives, friends and community resources, in an attempt to find a place for the patient to live and to sleep other than with his immediate family, if they are acutely pathogenic. If there are no appropriate relatives or friends, then foster homes or even half-way houses may be preferable, even though these facilities are often deleterious in their own way.

I cannot stress strongly enough the importance of proper living situation for the patient, in order not to have the therapeutic process be more difficult than is necessary, or even to be ineffective. I have found this factor, namely a healthy setting, to be so important, that if a patient of mine had a suitable family member living in another state, I was in favor of the patient moving to that other state, living with that family, and continuing with another therapist rather than myself.

10) Drugs

Finally, the use of *drugs* has to be mentioned as one very important enabling condition for engaging in psychotherapy with acutely disturbed psychotic patients. My favorite analogy of the role of medication in psychotherapy is that a drug plays the same role in facilitating the psychotherapeutic operation as an anesthetic does for a surgical intervention. It enables the doctor to engage in the often painful but necessary interventions, and still have a cooperative patient. Before general anesthetics were available, it was not only excessively traumatic, but often fatal, to perform an abdominal operation without properly relaxed musculature. A similar situation holds true for some psychotherapeutic interventions. Interpretations may be extremely painful and distressing for a patient—indeed, more than he can bear. This may provoke an episode of violence to himself or others, and lead to a more acute psychotic state. In other instances, without the benefit of psychotropic medication, the patient may be generally too anxious, too withdrawn, or too depressed to be either willing or able to communicate. Some patients may be terrified of approaching particular subject matters, material which it is crucial to air and analyze. In such instances, drugs can be used to decrease "approach anxiety" or, as in the case of antidepressants, provide the patient with the "energy" to relate.

Caution must be observed not to medicate a patient to a point where most ego functions are interfered with and reality testing and the sense of self have been unduly affected by the psychotropic drug (1). It is undesirable to have a patient who feels foggy or "spaced-out"—so lethargic as not to have any motivation for psychotherapeutic work. But it is, in fact, possible to choose one's drugs in such a way that some ego functions are improved, thereby facilitating the therapeutic process. Improvement of impulse control, e.g. of aggression, may be accomplished with lithium or phenothiazines. The latter may also improve thought processes, helping the patient to think logically and reason deductively—skills basic to his understanding therapeutic interpretations.

Summary

Before initiating therapy with acutely disturbed schizophrenics (and other psychotics), it is not only necessary to make a diagnosis in the narrow sense of the word, but also extremely important to evaluate all assets and liabilities in the patient's life situation. All difficulties which are likely to emerge in the process of treatment should be carefully assessed and planned for (2). Such accurate assessment and treatment design can serve to eliminate a great deal of trouble, waste and even tragedy.

However, if at least the minimal enabling conditions outlined above are met, the ambulatory treatment of acutely disturbed schizophrenics and other psychotics may be a truly rewarding experience for both patient and therapist. In most instances, after the acute condition has been dealt with, it is desirable to engage in extensive psychoanalytic psychotherapy in order to deal with the patient's subtle structural, dynamic and characterological problems.

REFERENCES

1. Bellak, L., Hurvich, M., and Gediman, H. *Ego Functions in Schizophrenics, Neurotics, and Normals. A Systematic Study of Conceptual, Diagnostic, and Therapeutic Aspects.* New York: John Wiley & Sons, 1973.
2. Bellak, L. and Meyers, B. Ego function assessment and analysability. *The International Review of Psycho-Analysis*, 1975, 2:413-427.
3. Rosen, J. *Direct Psychoanalytic Psychiatry.* New York: Grune & Stratton, 1962.

5

Psychotherapy with Borderline Patients: An Overview

OTTO F. KERNBERG, M.D.

REVIEW OF THE LITERATURE

The main question raised in the literature on intensive psychotherapy with borderline conditions is whether borderline patients can be treated by psychoanalysis or whether they require some form of psychotherapy. Intimately linked with this question is the delimitation of what is psychoanalysis and what is not.

Gill (13, 14) has clarified this issue in delimiting classical psychoanalysis from analytically oriented psychotherapies. He states that psychoanalysis, in a strict sense, involves consistent adherence by the analyst to a position of technical neutrality (and neutrality, he rightly states, does not mean mechanical rigidity of behavior with suppression of any spontaneous responses). He believes that psychoanalysis requires the development of a regressive transference neurosis and that the transference must be resolved by techniques of interpretation alone. In contrast, Gill further states, analytically oriented psychotherapies imply less strict adherence to neutrality; they imply recognition of transference phenomena and of transference resistance, but they use varying degrees of interpretation of these phenomena without permitting the development of a transference neurosis, and they do not imply resolution of the transference on the basis of interpretation alone.

Eissler (8) has further clarified this issue in his discussion of the "parameters of technique," which imply modifications of the analytic method usually necessary in patients with severe ego distortions. He suggests that the treatment still remains psychoanalysis if such parameters are introduced only when indispensable, not transgressing any unavoidable minimum, and when they are used only under circumstances which permit their self-elimination, their resolution through interpretation before termination of the analysis itself. Additional clarifications of the differences between psychoanalysis and other related psychotherapies can be found in papers by Stone (69), Bibring (3), Wallerstein and Robbins (78), and Wallerstein (75, 77).

From the viewpoint of Gill's delimitation of psychoanalysis, authors dealing with the problem of the treatment of borderline conditions may be placed on a continuum ranging from those who recommend psychoanalysis, to those who believe that psychotherapy rather than psychoanalysis, and especially a supportive form of psychotherapy, is the treatment of choice. Somewhere in the middle of this continuum there are those who believe that some patients presenting borderline personality organization may still be analyzed while others would require expressive psychoanalytic psychotherapy; also there are those who do not sharply differentiate between psychoanalysis and psychoanalytic psychotherapy.

The early references in the literature to the therapeutic problems with borderline patients were predominantly on the side of recommending modified psychotherapy with supportive implications, in contrast to classical psychoanalysis. Stern (67, 68) recommends an expressive approach, with the constant focus on the transference rather than on historical material, and with constant efforts to reduce the clinging, childlike dependency of these patients on the analyst. He feels that these patients need a new and realistic relationship, in contrast to the traumatic ones of their childhood; he believes that such patients can only gradually develop a capacity to establish a transference neurosis similar to that of the usual analytic patient. Schmideberg (63) recommends an approach probably best designated as psychoanalytic psychotherapy.

Knight's (39, 40) important contributions to the psychotherapeutic strategy with borderline cases lean definitely in the direction of the purely supportive approach, on one extreme of the continuum. He stresses the importance of strengthening the ego of these patients, and of respecting their neurotic defenses; he considers "deep interpretations dangerous because of the regressive pull that such interpretations have, and because the weak ego of these patients makes it hard enough for them to keep functioning on a secondary process level. He stresses the importance of structure, both within the psychotherapeutic setting and in the utilization of the hospital and day hospital, as part of the total treatment program for such patients.

At the other end of the spectrum are a number of analysts influenced to varying degrees by the so-called British school of psychoanalysis. These analysts believe that classical psychoanalytic treatment can indeed be attempted with many, if not all, borderline patients. Some of their contributions have been of crucial importance to the better understanding of the defensive organization, and the particular resistances characteristic of patients with borderline personality organization. Despite my disagreement with their assumption about the possibility of treating most borderline patients with psychoanalysis and with many of their theoretical assumptions in general, I believe that the findings of these analysts permit modifications of psychoanalytic psychotherapies specifically adapted to the transference complications of borderline patients. I am referring here especially to the work of Bion (4, 5, 6), Khan (37), Little (42, 43, 44), Rosenfeld (60, 61, 62), Segal (65), and Winnicott (79, 81).

In this country, Boyer and Giovacchini (7) also recommend a nonmodified psychoanalytic approach to schizophrenic and characterological disorders. Although Giovacchini, in chapters dedicated to character disorders, does not refer specifically to borderline conditions (in contrast to severe character pathology in general), his observations focus on the technical problems posed by what I think most authors would consider patients with borderline conditions.

Somewhere toward the middle of the spectrum are the approaches recommended by Stone (70) and Eissler (8). Stone feels that borderline patients may need preparatory psychotherapy, but that at least some of these patients may be treated with classical psychoanalysis either from the beginning of treatment or after some time to build up a working relationship with the therapist. Stone also agrees with Eissler that analysis can be attempted at later stages of treatment with such patients only if the previous psychotherapy has not created transference distortions of such magnitude that the parameters of technique involved cannot be resolved through interpretation. In following Eissler's and Stone's approaches, various authors in this country have recommended a modified psychoanalytic procedure or expressive psychotherapeutic approach to borderline patients that has influenced and is related to my own treatment recommendations that are outlined below.

Frosch (10, 11) has spelled out the clinical approach to borderline patients within a modified psychoanalytic procedure, and summarized his overall strategy of treatment with these patients. Greenson (17, 18, 19) proposes a similar approach, illustrating his modified psychoanalytic technique with clinical cases. Both Frosch and Greenson stress the importance of clarifying the patient's perceptions in the hours, and his attitude toward the therapist's interventions. Their approach (with which I basically agree) implies a neutral technical position of the therapist, and only a minimum deviation from such a position of neutrality as might be necessary.

In contrast, other psychoanalytically derived psychotherapeutic approaches to borderline conditions involve more modifications of technique. Thus, Masterson (49, 50, 51) designs a special psychotherapy as specifically geared to the resolution of the "abandonment depression" and the correction and repair of the ego defects that accompany the narcissistic oral fixation of these patients by encouraging growth through the stages of separation-individuation to autonomy. He proposes that psychotherapy with borderline patients start out as supportive psychotherapy and that intensive reconstructive psychoanalytically oriented psychotherapy is usually an expansion and outgrowth of supportive psychotherapy. He stresses the importance of the analysis of primitive transferences, and has expanded on the description of two mutually split off part object relations units (the rewarding or libidinal part object relations unit and the withdrawing or aggressive part object relations unit) thus combining an object relations viewpoint with a developmental model based upon the work of Margaret Mahler.

Rinsley (57) and Furer (12) are other authors among a growing group of psychoanalytically oriented therapists who are combining an ego psychological object relations theory with a developmental model stemming from Mahler's work (45, 46, 47, 48). Giovacchini (15), Bergeret (2), Green (16), Searles (64), and Volkan (74) have also been applying object relations theory derived models, and Searles, particularly, has focused on the understanding of the characteristics of transference and countertransference developments in the treatment of borderline and psychotic patients. Comprehensive overviews of some of these approaches can be found in Hartocollis (21) and Masterson's (51) recent book.

While the American authors just mentioned base their approach on an essentially ego psychological model that incorporates recent developmental findings and ego psychological object relations theories, the British school of psychoanalysis (that was originally identified with certain object relations theories) has continued to influence the technical approaches to borderline patients. Little's work (42, 43, 44) focuses mostly on technique. Although she assumes that the patients she describes are mostly borderline conditions, her implication that her patients presented a lack of differentiation between self and object, and her technical proposals for helping them develop a sense of uniqueness and separateness, seem to focus on the pathology of the early differentiation subphase of separation-individuation. Her views are somewhat related to those of Winnicott, but her patients seem to be more regressed than those described by him.

Winnicott (80) stresses the need to permit the patient to develop his "true self" by avoiding an "impingement" upon him at certain stages of therapeutic regression. Winnicott has described the optimal attitude of the therapist under these conditions as a "holding" object, a function akin to basic mothering for patients for whom, for whatever reason, normal mothering was lacking. At such moments, Winnicott suggests, a silent regression takes place to what amounts to a primitive form of dependency on the analyst experienced as a "holding mother." At such times, the analyst's intuitive, empathically understanding presence may be sufficient, in contrast to the disturbing, intrusively experienced effects of verbal interpretation.

This conception is related to Bion's theory that mother's intuitive daydreaming (or "reverie," in Bion's terms) permits her to incorporate the projected, dispersed, fragmented primitive experiences of the baby at points of frustration, and to integrate them by means of her intuitive understanding of the total predicament of the baby at that point. Mother's intuition, Bion says, thus acts as a "container" which organizes the projected "content." Similarly, Bion goes on, the dispersed, distorted, pathological elements of the regressed patient's experience are projected onto the analyst in order to use him as a "container," an organizer, one might say, of that which the patient cannot tolerate experiencing in himself.

In short, both Winnicott and Bion stress that it is very important for the therapist working with borderline patients to be able to integrate both cognitive and emotional aspects in his understanding of the therapeutic situation, and while Bion focuses on the cognitive ("containing") in contrast to Winnicott's emphasis on the emotional ("holding"), these seem closely related aspects of the analyst's attitude.

In recent years, there has been a gradual shift away from the recommendation that borderline patients should be treated with supportive psychotherapy, and Zetzel (83) and Grinker (20) seem to be the last proponents of the purely supportive approach to the psychotherapy of borderline conditions that was so predominant twenty years ago. Zetzel recommends regular but limited contact (very seldom more than once a week) with these patients in order to decrease the intensity of transference and countertransference manifestations, and a stress on reality issues and structuralization of treatment hours, all of which constitute jointly an essentially supportive approach. Zetzel acknowledges that, with that approach, it may be necessary for many borderline patients that the therapist remain at least potentially available over an indefinitely extended period. The implication is that this supportive approach, while effective in permitting the patient to adjust better to reality, may contribute to an interminable psychotherapeutic relationship. Zetzel and Grinker share the fear expressed in earlier literature regarding the presumed "frailty" of the defensive system, personality organization, and transferences of borderline conditions. Implicitly, this fear is also reflected in various psychoanalytically based but operationally manipulative approaches, such as those of Marie Nelson (53) and Arlene Wolberg (82).

In summary, a majority of clinicians who have worked intensively with borderline patients have been shifting in recent years from a supportive approach inspired by Knight's earlier work to modified psychoanalytic techniques or psychoanalytic psychotherapy for most patients, while still considering the possibility that some patients may be treated by nonmodified psychoanalysis from the beginning of treatment and others with a modified psychoanalytic procedure which might gradually evolve into a standard psychoanalytic situation at advanced stages of treatment (11, 19, 26, 70).

My own work in this area fits clearly within this overall approach (28, 30, 32, 33, 35). I think that, while some borderline patients may respond to a nonmodified psychoanalytic approach, the vast majority respond best to a modified psychoanalytic procedure or psychoanalytic psychotherapy which I shall describe in detail below. I believe that for some borderline patients a psychoanalytic approach—standard or modified—is contraindicated, and that these patients do require a supportive psychotherapy (that is, an approach based upon a psychoanalytic model for psychotherapy relying mostly on the supportive techniques outlined by Bibring (3); Gill (14); and Zetzel (83). I also think that psychoanalysis and psychotherapy should be most carefully differentiated, and I follow Gill (14) in this regard.

In addition, I think that much of what appears as "ego weakness," in the sense of a defect of these patients, turns out, under a psychoanalytically based exploration, to reflect conflictually determined issues. Obviously, this conviction underlies my stress on the value of an interpretive, in contrast to a supportive, approach with borderline patients. A major source for this conviction stems from the psychotherapy research project of The Menninger Foundation (36), which revealed, contrary to our initial expectations, that borderline patients did much better with an interpretive or expressive approach, and much more poorly with a purely supportive one.

OUTLINE OF PSYCHOANALYTIC PSYCHOTHERAPY WITH BORDERLINE PATIENTS

If psychoanalysis is defined by 1) a position of technical neutrality, 2) the predominant use of interpretation as a major psychotherapeutic tool, and 3) the systematic analysis of the transference, psychoanalytic psychotherapies may be defined in terms of changes or modification in any or all of the three technical paradigms. In fact, I think the definition of a spectrum of psychoanalytic psychotherapies, ranging from psychoanalysis, on the one extreme, to supportive psychotherapies, on the other, is possible in terms of these three basic paradigms.

Within an ego-psychological approach, psychoanalytic psychotherapy may be defined as a psychoanalytically based or oriented treatment that does not attempt, as its goal, a systematic resolution of unconscious conflicts and, therefore, of all impulse/defense configurations and the respective resistances; rather, it attempts a partial resolution of some, and a reinforcement of other resistances, with a subsequent, partial integration of previously repressed impulses into the adult ego. As a result, a partial increase of ego strength and flexibility may take place, which then permits a more effective repression of residual, dynamically unconscious impulses, and a modified impulse/defense configuration (that increases the adaptive—in contrast to maladaptive—aspects of character formation). This definition differentiates psychoanalysis from psychoanalytic psychotherapy, both in the goals and in the underlying theory of change reflected in these differential goals.

Regarding the techniques employed in psychoanalytic psychotherapy geared to the achievement of those goals, and the differences between such techniques and those of psychoanalysis proper, the ego-psychological approach defines two major modalities of treatment based upon the psychoanalytic framework: 1) exploratory, insight, uncovering, or, simply, expressive psychoanalytic psychotherapy, and 2) suppressive or supportive psychotherapy.

Expressive psychotherapy is characterized by the utilization of clarification and interpretation as major tools, and, in this context, also abreaction. Partial aspects of the transference are interpreted, and the therapist actively selects such transferences to be interpreted in the light of the particular goals of treatment, the predominant transference resistances, and the patient's external reality. Technical neutrality is usually maintained, but a systematic analysis of all transference paradigms or a systematic resolution of the transference neurosis by interpretation alone is definitely not attempted.

Supportive psychotherapy is characterized by partial use of clarification and abreaction and the predominance of the use of technical tools of suggestion and manipulation. Bibring (3) defined these techniques and illustrated their technical utilization. Insofar as supportive psychotherapy still implies an acute awareness and monitoring of the transference on the part of the psychotherapist, and a careful consideration of transference resistances as part of his overall technique in dealing with characterological problems and their connections with the patient's life difficulties, this is still a psychoanalytic psychotherapy in a broad sense. By definition, however, transference is not interpreted in purely supportive psychotherapy, and the utilization of technical tools such as suggestion and manipulation implicitly eliminates technical neutrality.

The major problem with this psychoanalytic theory and technique of psychoanalytic psychotherapy has been the contradiction between the theoretical model from which it stems and the structural intrapsychic organization of many patients with whom it has been used. The theoretical model underlying this approach holds remarkably well for patients with good ego strength. In contrast, however, the application of this psychoanalytic psychotherapy model to patients with severe psychopathologies—particularly the borderline conditions—has led to puzzling and contradictory findings.

First, these patients present a constellation of primitive defensive mechanisms centering around dissociation of contradictory ego states rather than on repression. Second, the transferences of these patients have peculiarities that are very different from the more usual transference developments in better functioning patients. Third, and most importantly, their primitive impulses are not unconscious but mutually dissociated in consciousness. In this connection, the evaluation of defense-impulse constellations often does not permit a clarification of what

agency within the tripartite structure (ego, superego, and id) is motivating and activating a defense against what impulse within what other
agency. In other words, the transference seems to reflect contradictory ego
states that incorporate contradictory, primitive internalized object relations within an overall psychic matrix that does not present a clear
differentiation of ego, superego, and id.

This leads to an additional, specialized psychoanalytic approach that
attempts to deal with the phenomena just described, namely, psychoanalytic object relations theory.

Within an object relations framework, intrapsychic conflicts are conceptualized as always involving self- and object representations, or, rather,
as conflicts between certain units of self- and object representations under
the impact of a determined drive derivative (clinically, a certain affect
disposition) and other, contradictory or opposite units of self- and object
representations under the impact of their respective affect dispositions.
Unconscious intrapsychic conflicts are never simply conflicts between
impulse and defense, but, rather, the drive derivative is represented by a
certain primitive object relation (a certain unit of self- and object representation), and the defense, as well, is reflected by a certain internalized
object relation. Thus, all character defenses really reflect the activation
of a defensive constellation of self- and object representations directed
against an opposite and dreaded, repressed self-object constellation. For
example, in obsessive, characterological submissiveness, a chronically submissive self-image in relating to a powerful and protective oedipal parental image may defend the patient against the repressed, violent rebellious self relating to a sadistic and controlling parental image. Thus,
clinically, both character defenses and repressed impulses involve mutually opposed internal object relations.

From the viewpoint of object relations theory, the consolidation of the
overall intrapsychic structures (ego, superego, and id) results in an
integration of internalized object relations that obscures the constituent
self representation-object representation-affect units within the overall
structural properties of the tripartite system (33); the psychopathology
of the symptomatic neuroses and less severe character neuroses is produced by intersystemic conflicts between such integrated ego, superego
and id systems. In contrast, in the psychopathology of borderline personality organization, such an integration of the major intrapsychic agencies is not achieved, and conflicts are, therefore, largely or mostly intra-
systemic (within an undifferentiated ego-id matrix). In severe psychopathologies—particularly the borderline conditions—early, primitive

units of internalized object relations are directly manifest in the transference, in the context of mutually conflictual drive derivatives reflected in contradictory ego states.

In these cases, the predominance of a constellation of early defense mechanisms centering around primitive dissociation or splitting immediately activates, in the transference, mutually contradictory, primitive but conscious intrapsychic conflicts (30). What appears on the surface as inappropriate, primitive, chaotic character traits and interpersonal interactions, impulsive behavior and affect storms actually reflect the fantastic, early object relations derived structures that are the building blocks of the later tripartite system. These object relations determine the characteristics of primitive transferences, that is, of highly fantastic, unreal precipitates of early object relations that do not reflect directly the real object relations of infancy and childhood, and that have to be interpreted integratively until, by reconstitution of total—in contrast to partial or split—object relations, the more real aspects of the developmental history emerge (31). In the treatment, structural integration through interpretation precedes genetic reconstructions.

Let me now spell out a proposal for an integration of ego psychological and object relations theory derived conceptualizations geared to outlining a theory of psychoanalytic psychotherapy for borderline conditions.

Because primitive transferences are immediately available, predominate as resistances, and, in fact, determine the severity of intrapsychic and interpersonal disturbances, they can and need to be focused upon immediately, starting out from their interpretation only in the "here and now," and leading into genetic reconstructions only at late stages of the treatment (when primitive transferences determined by part object relations have been transformed into advanced transferences or total object relations, thus approaching the more realistic experiences of childhood that lend themselves to genetic reconstruction). Interpretation of the transference requires that the therapist maintain a position of technical neutrality for the reason that there can be no interpretation of primitive transferences without a firm, consistent, stable maintenance of reality boundaries in the therapeutic situation, and without an active caution on the part of the therapist not to be "sucked into" the reactivation of pathological primitive object relations by the patient. Insofar as both transference interpretation and a position of technical neutrality require the use of clarification and interpretation and contraindicate the use of suggestive and manipulative techniques, clarification and interpretation are maintained as principal techniques.

However, in contrast to psychoanalysis proper, transference interpretation is not systematic. Because there is a need to focus on the severity of acting-out and on the disturbances in the patient's external reality (that may threaten the continuity of the treatment as well as the patient's psychosocial survival) and, also, because, as part of the acting-out of primitive transferences, the treatment easily comes to replace life, transference interpretation now has to be codetermined by: 1) the predominant transference paradigm, 2) the prevailing conflicts in immediate reality, and 3) the overall specific goals of treatment.

In addition, technical neutrality is limited by the need to establish parameters of technique, including, in certain cases, the structuring of the patient's external life and the establishment of a teamwork approach with patients who can not function autonomously during long stretches of their psychotherapy. Technical neutrality, therefore, is a theoretical baseline from which deviations occur again and again, to be reduced— again and again—by interpretation. One crucial aspect of psychoanalytic psychotherapy with patients presenting severe psychopathology is the systematic interpretation of defenses. In contrast to expressive psychotherapies in better functioning patients—where certain defenses are selectively interpreted while others are not touched—the systematic interpretation of defenses in severe psychopathology is crucial to improve ego functioning and to permit the transformation and resolution of primitive transferences.

Therefore, the similarity between expressive psychoanalytic psychotherapy and psychoanalysis is greater in the case of severe psychopathology than in the case of patients with milder psychological illness. One might say that, in psychoanalytic psychotherapy of borderline conditions, the tactical approach to each session may be almost indistinguishable from psychoanalysis proper, and that only from a long-term, strategic viewpoint do the differences between psychoanalysis proper and psychoanalytic psychotherapy emerge. By the same token, the cleavage between expressive psychotherapy and supportive psychotherapy is sharp and definite in the case of patients with borderline conditions, while it is more gradual and blurred in cases with less severe illness. In other words, it is not possible to bring about significant personality modifications by means of psychoanalytic psychotherapy in patients with severe psychopathology without exploration and resolution of primitive transferences, and this requires a purely expressive, meticulously analytic approach, although not psychoanalysis proper.

Manipulative or suggestive techniques destroy technical neutrality and interfere with the possibility of analyzing primitive transferences and resistances. Such analysis is the most important ego strengthening aspect of the psychoanalytic psychotherapy of borderline patients. Technical neutrality means equidistance from the forces codetermining the patient's intrapsychic conflicts, and not lack of warmth or empathy with him. One still hears comments implying that borderline patients need, first of all, empathic understanding rather than a precise theory and cognitively sharpened interpretations based on such a theory. All psychotherapy requires as a base line the therapist's capacity for authentic human warmth and empathy; these qualities are preconditions for any appropriate psychotherapeutic work.

Empathy, however, is not only the intuitive, emotional awareness in the therapist of the patient's central emotional experience at a certain point, but must also include the therapist's capacity to empathize with that which the patient can not tolerate within himself; therefore, therapeutic empathy transcends the empathy involved in ordinary human interactions, and includes the therapist's integration, on a cognitive and emotional level, of what is actively dissociated or split in borderline patients.

In addition, when serious distortions in the patient's reality testing in the psychotherapeutic hours evolve as part of the activation of primitive transferences and primitive defensive operations (particularly that of projective identification), it may be crucial for the therapist to start out his interpretive efforts by clarifying the reality of the therapeutic situation. Such initial interventions often require a great deal of active work on the part of the therapist, a direct dealing with what the reality is in the sessions or in the patient's external life, that may be misunderstood as a technically supportive, suggestive, or manipulative intervention.

STRATEGY AND TACTICS OF TRANSFERENCE INTERPRETATION

Perhaps the most striking characteristic of the transference manifestations of patients with borderline personality organization is the premature activation in the transference of very early conflict-laden object relationships in the context of ego states that are dissociated from each other. It is as if each of these ego states represents a full-fledged transference paradigm, a highly developed, regressive transference reaction within which a specific internalized object relationship is activated in the transference. This is in contrast to the more gradual unfolding of internalized object relationships as regression occurs in the typical neurotic patient.

The conflicts that typically emerge in connection with the reactivation of these early internalized object relations may be characterized as a particular pathological condensation of pregenital and genital aims under the overriding influence of pregenital aggression. Excessive pregenital, and especially oral, aggression tends to be projected and determines the paranoid distortion of the early parental images, particularly those of the mother. Through projection of predominantly oral-sadistic and also anal-sadistic impulses, the mother is seen as potentially dangerous, and hatred of the mother extends to a hatred of both parents when later they are experienced as a "united group" by the child. A "contamination" of the father image by aggression primarily projected onto mother and lack of differentiation between mother and father tend to produce a combined, dangerous father-mother image and a later conceptualization of all sexual relationships as dangerous and infiltrated by aggression. Concurrently, in an effort to escape from oral rage and fears, a "flight" into genital strivings occurs; this flight often miscarries because of the intensity of the pregenital aggression which contaminates the genital strivings (23).

The transference manifestations of patients with borderline personality organization may at first appear completely chaotic. Gradually, however, repetitive patterns emerge, reflecting primitive self-representations and related object-representations under the influence of the conflicts mentioned above, and appear in the treatment of predominantly negative transference paradigms. The defensive operations characteristic of borderline patients (splitting, projective identification, denial, primitive idealization, omnipotence) become the vehicle of the transference resistances. The fact that these defensive operations have, in themselves, ego-weakening effects is suggested as a crucial factor in the severe regression that soon complicates the premature transference developments.

Once a borderline patient embarks on treatment, the crucial decompensating force is the patient's increased effort to defend himself against the emergence of the threatening primitive, especially negative, transference reactions by intensified utilization of the very defensive operations which have contributed to ego weakness in the first place. One main "culprit" in this regard is probably the mechanism of projective identification, described by Melanie Klein (38) and others, namely, Heimann

(24), Money-Kryle (52), Rosenfeld (59), and Segal (65). Projective identification is a primitive form of projection, mainly called upon to externalize aggressive self- and object-images; empathy is maintained with real objects onto which the projection has occurred, and is linked with an effort to control the object now feared because of this projection.

In the transference this is typically manifest as intense distrust and fear of the therapist, who is experienced as attacking the patient, while the patient himself feels empathy with that projected intense aggression and tries to control the therapist in a sadistic, overpowering way. The patient may be partially aware of his own hostility but feel that he is simply responding to the therapist's aggression, and that he is justified in being angry and aggressive. It is as if the patient's life depended on his keeping the therapist under control. The patient's aggressive behavior, at the same time, tends to provoke from the therapist counteraggressive feelings and attitudes. It is as if the patient were pushing the aggressive part of his self onto the therapist and as if the countertransference represented the emergence of this part of the patient from within the therapist (52, 55).

It has to be stressed that what is projected in a very inefficient and self-defeating way is not pure aggression, but a self-representation or an object-representation linked with that drive derivative. Primitive self- and primitive object-representations are actually linked together as basic units of primitive object relationships (27), and what appears characteristic of borderline patients is that there is a rapid oscillation between moments of projection of a self-representation while the patient remains identified with the corresponding object-representation, and other moments in which it is the object-representation that is projected while the patient identifies with the corresponding self-representation. For example, a primitive, sadistic mother image may be projected onto the therapist while the patient experiences himself as the frightened, attacked, panic-stricken little child; moments later, the patient may experience himself as the stern, prohibitive, moralistic (and extremely sadistic) primitive mother image, while the therapist is seen as the guilty, defensive, frightened but rebellious little child. This situation is also an example of "complementary identification" (55).

The danger in this situation is that under the influence of the expression of intense aggression by the patient, the reality aspects of the transference-countertransferense situation may be such that it comes dangerously close to reconstituting the originally projected interaction between internalized self- and object-images. Under these circumstances, vicious circles may be created in which the patient projects his aggression onto the therapist and reintrojects a severely distorted image of the therapist under the influence of the projected aggressive drive derivatives, thus perpetuating the pathological early object relationship. Heimann (24) has illustrated these vicious circles of projective identification and distorted reintrojection of the therapist in discussing paranoid defenses. Strachey (71) has referred to the general issue of normal and pathological introjection of the analyst as an essential aspect of the effect of interpretation, especially in regard to modifying the superego.

Rapidly alternating projection of self-images and object-images representing early pathological internalized object relationships produces a confusion of what is inside and outside in the patient's experience of his interactions with the therapist. It is as if the patient maintained a sense of being different from the therapist at all times, but concurrently he and the therapist were interchanging their personalities. This is a frightening experience which reflects a breakdown of ego boundaries in that interaction, and as a consequence there is a loss of reality-testing in the transference. It is this loss of reality-testing in the transference which most powerfully interferes with the patient's capacity to distinguish fantasy from reality, and past from present in the transference, and also interferes with his capacity to distinguish his projected transference objects from the therapist as a real person. Under such circumstances, the possibility that a mutative interpretation will be effective is seriously threatened. Clinically, this appears as the patient experiencing something such as "Yes, you are right in thinking that I see you as I saw my mother, and that is because she and you are really identical." It is at this point that what has been referred to as a "transference psychosis" is reached.

"Transference psychosis" is a term which should be reserved for the loss of reality-testing and the appearance of delusional material within the transference that does not affect very noticeably the patient's functioning outside the treatment setting. Hospitalization may sometimes be necessary for such patients, and at times it is quite difficult to separate a transference-limited psychotic reaction from a broader one. Nevertheless, in many borderline patients this delimitation is quite easy, and it is often possible to resolve the transference psychosis within the psychotherapy (25, 41, 56, 58, and 76). Control of transference acting out within the therapeutic relationship becomes of central importance.

The acting out of the transference within the therapeutic relationship becomes the main resistance to further change in these patients, and parameters of technique required to control the acting out should be introduced in the treatment situation. There is a danger of entering the vicious circle of projection and reintrojection of sadistic self- and object-images of the patient as the therapist introduces parameters of technique. He may appear to the patient as prohibitive and sadistic. This danger can be counteracted if the therapist begins by interpreting the transference situation, then introduces structuring parameters of techniques as needed, and finally interprets the transference situation again without abandoning the parameters. Some aspects of this technique have been illustrated in a different context by Sharpe (66), who demonstrates how to deal with acute episodes of anxiety.

Because the acting out of the transference within the therapeutic relationship itself appears to be such a meaningful reproduction of past conflicts, fantasies, defensive operations, and internalized object relationships of the patients, one is tempted to interpret the repetitive acting out as evidence for a working through of these conflicts. The repetition compulsion expressed through transference acting out cannot be considered working through as long as the transference relationship provides these patients with instinctual gratification of their pathological, especially their aggressive, needs. Some of these patients obtain much more gratification of their pathological instinctual needs in the transference than would ever be possible in extratherapeutic interactions. The patient's acting out at the regressed level overruns the therapist's effort to maintain a climate of abstinence.

The question of insight in borderline patients deserves discussion. Unfortunately, one frequently finds that what at first looks like insight into deep layers of the mind and into unconscious dynamics on the part of some borderline patients is actually an expression of the ready availability of primary process functioning as part of the general regression of ego structures. Insight which comes without any effort, is not accompanied by any change in the patient's intrapsychic equilibrium, and, above all, is not accompanied by any concern on the patient's part for the pathological aspects of his behavior or experience, is questionable insight. Authentic insight is a combination of the intellectual and emotional understanding of deeper sources of one's psychic experience, accompanied by concern for and an urge to change the pathological aspects of that experience.

The following general principles summarize what has been said in this section.

1) The predominantly negative transference of these patients should

be systematically elaborated only in the here and now, without attempting to achieve full genetic reconstructions. The reason is that lack of differentiation of the self concept and lack of differentiation and individualization of objects interfere with the ability of these patients to differentiate present and past object relationships, resulting in their confusing transference and reality, and failing to differentiate the analyst from the transference object. Full genetic reconstructions, therefore, have to await advanced stages of the treatment. 2) The typical defensive constellations of these patients should be interpreted as they enter the transference; the implication is that the interpretation of the predominant, primitive defensive operations characteristic of borderline personality organization strengthens the patient's ego and brings about structural intrapsychic change which contributes to resolving this organization. 3) Limits should be set in order to block acting out of the transference, with as much structuring of the patient's life outside the hours as necessary to protect the neutrality of the therapist. The implications are that, although interventions in the patient's external life may sometimes be needed, the technical neutrality of the therapist is essential for the treatment; moreover, it is important to avoid allowing the therapeutic relationship, with its gratifying and sheltered nature, to replace ordinary life, lest primitive pathological needs be gratified in the acting out of the transference during and outside the hours. 4) The less primitively determined, modulated aspects of the positive transference should not be interpreted. This fosters the gradual development of the therapeutic alliance; however, the primitive idealizations that reflect the splitting of "all good" from "all bad" object relations need to be interpreted systematically as part of the effort to work through these primitive defenses. 5) Interpretations should be formulated so that the patient's distortions of the therapist's interventions and of present reality (especially of the patient's perceptions in the hour) can be systematically clarified: one implication is that the patient's magical utilization of the therapist's interpretations needs to be interpreted. 6) The highly distorted transference (at times, of an almost psychotic nature), reflecting fantastic internal object relations related to early ego disturbances, should be worked through first, in order to reach, later, the transferences related to actual childhood experiences. All transferences, of course, recapitulate childhood fantasies, actual experiences, and defensive formations against them, and it is often difficult to sort out fantasies from reality. However, the extreme nature of the fantasied relationships reflecting very early object relations gives the transference of borderline patients special characteristics, our next issue.

THE TRANSFORMATION OF PRIMITIVE INTO ADVANCED OR NEUROTIC TRANSFERENCES

The ordinary transference neurosis is characterized by the activation of the patient's infantile self, or aspects of that infantile self linked to or integrated with his infantile self in general, while the patient reenacts emotional conflicts of this infantile self with parental objects that are, in turn, integrated and reflect the parental figures as experienced in infancy and childhood. In contrast, the nonintegrated self- and object-representations of borderline patients are activated in the transference in ways that do not permit the reconstruction of infantile conflicts with the parental objects as perceived in reality, and rather, the transference reflects a multitude of internal object relations of dissociated or split-off self aspects with dissociated or split-off object-representations of a highly fantastic and distorted nature.

The basic cause of these developments in borderline patients is their failure to integrate the libidinally determined and the aggressively determined self- and object-representations (27, 29 and 36). Such a lack of integration derives from the pathological predominance of aggressively determined self- and object-representations and a related failure to establish a sufficiently strong ego core around the (originally nondifferentiated) good self- and object-representations. However, in contrast to the psychoses, in which self images have not been differentiated from object images, in borderline patients there has been at least sufficient differentiation between self- and object-representations for the establishment of firm ego boundaries. The problem with borderline patients is that the intensity of aggressively determined self- and object-representations, and of defensively idealized, all good self- and object-representations makes integration impossible. Because of the implicit threat to the good object relations, bringing together extremely opposite loving and hateful images of the self and of significant others would trigger unbearable anxiety and guilt; therefore, there is an active defensive separation of such contradictory self and object images: in other words, primitive dissociation or splitting becomes a major defensive operation.

The overall strategical aim in working through the transference developments of borderline patients is to resolve these primitive dissociations of the self and of internalized objects, and thus to transform primitive transferences—that is, the primitive level of internalized object relations activated in the transference—into the transference reactions of the higher level or integrated, more realistic type of internalized object relations related to real childhood experiences. Obviously, this requires intensive, long-term treatment along the lines I have suggested (31), usually not less than three sessions a week over years of treatment. The strategy of interpretation of the transference of borderline patients may be outlined into three consecutive steps. These three steps represent, in essence, the sequence involved in the working through of primitive transference developments in patients with borderline personality organization.

The first step consists in the psychotherapist's efforts to reconstruct, on the basis of his gradual understanding of what is emotionally predominant in the chaotic, meaningless, empty, distorted or suppressed material, the nature of the primitive or part-object relation that has become activated in the transference. He needs to evaluate what, at any point, in the contradictory bits of verbal and behavioral communication, in the confused and confusing thoughts and feelings and expressions of the patient, is of predominant emotional relevance in the patient's present relation with him, and how this predominant material can be understood in the context of the patient's total communications. In other words, the therapist, by means of his interpretive efforts, transforms the prevalent meaninglessness or futility in the transference—what literally amounts to a dehumanization of the therapeutic relationship—into an emotionally significant, although highly distorted, fantastic transference relationship.

As a second step, the therapist must evaluate this crystallizing predominant object relation in the transference in terms of the self image and the object image involved, and clarify the affect of the corresponding interaction of self and object. The therapist may represent one aspect of the patient's dissociated self and/or one aspect of the primitive object representation; and patient and therapist may interchange their enactment of, respectively, self or object image. These aspects of the self and of object representations need to be interpreted and the respective internal object relationship clarified in the transference.

As a third step, this particular "part-object" relation activated in the transference has to be integrated with other "part-object" relations reflecting other, related and opposite, defensively dissociated "part-object" relations until the patient's real self and his internal conception of objects can be integrated and consolidated.

Integration of self and objects, and thus of the entire world of internalized object relations, is a major strategic aim in the treatment of patients with borderline personality organization. Integration of affects with their related, fantasied or real, human relation involving the patient and the significant object is another aspect of this work. The patient's affect dispositions reflect the libidinal or aggressive investment of certain internalized object relations, and the integration of split-off, fragmented affect states is a corollary of the integration of split-off, fragmented internalized object relations. When such a resolution of primitive transferences has occurred, the integrative affect dispositions that now emerge reflect more coherent and differentiated drive derivatives. The integrative object images now reflect more realistic parental images as perceived in early childhood.

ARRANGEMENTS AND DIFFICULTIES IN THE EARLY STAGES OF TREATMENT

A major question in the early stages of treatment is to what extent an external structure is necessary to protect the patient and the treatment situation from premature, violent acting out that may threaten the patient's life or other people's lives or threaten the continuation of the treatment. When the treatment starts out right after a recent or still active psychotic episode (which borderline patients may experience under excessive emotional turmoil—under the effect of drugs, alcohol, or in the course of a transference psychosis), there may be indication for a few days to a few weeks of hospital treatment, with a well-structured hospital milieu program and clarification of the immediate reality and a combination of an understanding and clarifying and yet limit-setting milieu approach. A generally chaotic life situation, particularly when complicated by the patient's difficulty in providing meaningful information about his life to the psychotherapist, may represent another indication for short-term hospitalization. Severe suicidal threats or attempts, a deteriorating social situation, or severe acting out with involvements with the law, are all typical examples of situations which threaten the patient's life or the continuation of treatment. Under such circumstances, short-term hospitalization may be necessary, simultaneously with the beginning or continuation of intensive psychotherapeutic treatment along the lines mentioned before.

The most important objective regarding the degree of structuring required is to set up an overall treatment arrangement which permits the psychotherapist to remain in a position of technical neutrality, that is, equidistant from external reality, the patient's superego, his instinctual needs, and his acting (in contrast to observing) ego (9). This objective can sometimes be achieved with less than full hospitalization, by means of the utilization of part-hospitalization arrangements, foster home placement, the intervention of a social worker within the patient's environment, etc. There are borderline patients who do not have a sufficient degree of observing ego for intensive, outpatient psychoanalytic psychotherapy; for example, many borderline patients with extremely low motivation for treatment, severe lack of anxiety tolerance and of impulse control, and very poor object relationships may require a long-term environmental structuring of their lives in order to make an expressive psychotherapeutic approach possible. Such long-term structuralization of their life may be provided by many months of hospitalization or a part-hospitalization environment, or by extra-mural social services which provide the necessary limit-setting in the patient's life or support of his family for this purpose. Severe, chronic acting out, suicidal or general self-destructive trends which the patient cannot control, and some types of negative therapeutic reaction, may require such a long-term external structuralization.

Many borderline patients are able, without external structuring of their lives, to participate actively in setting limits to certain types of acting out which threaten their treatment or their safety. At times the psychotherapist has to spell out certain conditions which the patient must meet in order for outpatient psychoanalytic psychotherapy to proceed. The setting up of such conditions for treatment represents, of course, an abandonment of the position of technical neutrality on the part of the psychotherapist, and the setting up of parameters of technique. Such parameters of technique need to be kept at a minimum.

If a patient has a history of frequent suicidal attempts, or of utilizing threats of suicide to control his environment (including the psychotherapist), this situation needs to be discussed fully with him. The patient must either be able to assume full control over any active expression of his suicidal tendencies (in contrast to the freedom of verbally expressing his wishes and impulses in the treatment hours), or he must be willing to ask for external protection (in the form of hospitalization or part-hospitalization) if he feels he cannot control such suicidal impulses. In other words, several brief hospitalizations arranged by the patient himself, by his family or a social worker may provide an additional, external structure needed to maintain the treatment situation; this is preferable to the therapist changing his technique in the direction of relinquishing a primarily interpretive approach in the context of technical neutrality.

In contrast, many other potentially self-destructive symptoms may be left untouched for a long period of time, if they do not threaten the patient's life or treatment. For example, it may take years before a borderline patient with severe obesity may be able to control his obesity effectively; general failure in school or at work and interpersonal difficulties of all kinds may express the patient's psychopathology and a long time may elapse before they can be brought into the focus of the treatment.

When the patient consciously withholds information, or when he lies, the psychotherapist's first priority has to be to interpret fully and reduce this suppression of information by interpretive—in contrast to educational—means. This may take weeks or months, particularly in cases with antisocial features. However long it may take, full resolution of the reality and transferential implications of the patient's lying takes precedence over all other material, except life-threatening acting out. However, because lying interferes with the psychotherapeutic approach toward all other problems including acting out, it may be preferable, if the patient who habitually lies also shows evidence of life-threatening or other treatment-threatening acting out, to start his treatment with sufficient structuring in his life, such as long-term hospitalization. Patients who lie habitually, and, therefore, give evidence of serious superego deterioration, tend to project their own attitude regarding moral values onto the psychotherapist as well, and to conceive of him as being dishonest and corrupt. The interpretive approach to the transference functions of lying includes, therefore, focusing on the patient's projection of his own dishonesty onto the therapist, and on the transferential implications in the "here and now" of this development.

In some borderline paranoid patients conscious withholding of material is acknowledged by the patient as part of the expression of paranoid fantasies about the therapist; for example, one patient refused to give his real name over a period of several weeks. Whenever manifest paranoid ideation becomes predominant in the early hours of treatment, it is important for the therapist to evaluate carefully whether the patient is, indeed, a borderline patient, or whether the patient suffers from a paranoid psychosis. Since a psychotic paranoid patient might present serious aggressive acting out when transference psychosis develops, it is extremely important for the therapist to carry out an early, careful differential diagnosis, and not to initiate an intensive psychotherapeutic treatment without a clear understanding of all the implications of treating a psychotic patient. At times, when this diagnostic question cannot be clarified in the early treatment hours of a borderline paranoid patient, it may be preferable to start the psychotherapy with a concomitant period of brief hospitalization geared to evaluate the situation further. The long-range benefits of an early, brief hospitalization compensate for the increase of anxiety and transference distortions and other complications in these patients' daily life related to an early, brief hospitalization. In any case, it is important that the psychotherapist not permit the patient to control the treatment situation in a pathological way, as this would affect not only the psychotherapist's technical neutrality, but his very availability, on a simple human level, to the patient. Sometimes it is preferable not to treat a patient at all rather than to treat him under impossible conditions.

In the case of borderline patients whose treatment is carried out, either initially or during later phases of the treatment, in combination with hospitalization, it is important for the psychotherapist to keep in close relationship with the leader of the hospital management team. This raises such issues as confidentiality, danger of splitting of the transference, and general coordination of hospital treatment and psychotherapeutic work.

In my experience, I have found it helpful for the psychotherapist to receive routinely full information regarding the patient's interactions in the hospital, and for the patient to be told about this. Thus, the psychotherapist can share significant information regarding the patient's interactions in the hospital with the patient himself and integrate it into his analysis of the transference. At the same time, the psychotherapist should inform the patient that he will keep confidential all information given him by the patient, except for specific issues which the therapist might wish to explore with the hospital team. But, before doing so, he would ask the patient specifically for authorization. In other words, general confidentiality should be maintained unless specific authorization is given by the patient for the psychotherapist to share certain information with the hospital team. Finally, I explicitly inform patients that I would not feel bound by confidentiality under circumstances which would involve threats to the patient's or other people's lives; again, under these circumstances, I would first share with the patient the nature of the information I feel needs to be talked over with the hospital treatment team.

The general implication of this approach is that if hospitalization is needed and carried out during psychotherapeutic treatment, the total treatment should be integrated; in practice, this should help reduce or prevent splitting operations by which part of the transference is expressed to the hospital treatment team. In the case of outpatients where social complications, for example, pressures from the family, are expressed in the form of efforts of relatives or other persons related to the patient to establish direct contact with the psychotherapist, a social agency, or a psychiatric social worker might be asked to provide a structure which keeps the psychotherapist separate from the patient's external social environment, while still containing the overall treatment situation that has evolved. Again, under these circumstances the psychotherapist should maintain an open communication with the social worker who is seeing the family, but any information that the psychotherapist is planning to share with the social worker must be discussed with the patient.

THERAPEUTIC STALEMATES IN ADVANCED STAGES OF THE TREATMENT

Many borderline patients do not change significantly over years of treatment, despite the efforts of skilled therapists of various orientations. What follows are some general considerations regarding the issues frequently involved in lack of change in the treatment situation and some general requirements for the therapist which have seemed helpful to me in facilitating significant change in some of the more difficult cases.

The problem merges with that of the development of severe negative therapeutic reactions in the treatment of borderline cases. In fact, negative therapeutic reactions are a major cause of lack of significant change. However, in order to avoid an excessive broadening of the term negative therapeutic reaction, I think it preferable to discuss these issues in terms of lack of significant change.

I would restrict the meaning of negative therapeutic reaction to the worsening of the patient's condition, particularly as reflected in the transference, at times when he is consciously or unconsciously perceiving the therapist as a good object who is attempting to provide him with significant help. Such negative therapeutic reactions derive from 1) an unconscious sense of guilt (as in masochistic character structures); 2) the need to destroy what is received from the therapist because of unconscious envy of him (as is typical in narcissistic personalities); and 3) the need to destroy the therapist as a good object because of the patient's unconscious identification with a primitive, sadistic object which requires submission and suffering as a minimal precondition for maintaining any significant object relation (as in some borderline and many schizophrenic patients who severely confuse love and sadism (30)). My findings seem consonant with those of other recent contributions to the psychoanalytic study of negative therapeutic reaction (1, 54, 60, 61, 62, 73).

I would like to focus on some common features of chronic stalemates in treatment. The situations most frequently met with are: 1) Unchanged grandiosity in severe narcissistic structures. Dehumanization of the treatment situation, amounting to a complete denial of any emotional reality in the transference, may appear even in narcissistic patients who seem to be functioning at a nonborderline level. 2) Severe masochistic acting out, related to the submission to and triumphant identification with a relentless, sadistic superego formation. 3) The even more primitive identification with a sadistic, mad object which provides love only under the aegis of suffering and hatred. Any satisfactory relation is thus equivalent to killing—and being killed by—the needed parental image, and, therefore, losing it, while the triumph over all those who do not suffer from such a horrible human destiny is the only protection from a sense of total psychic disaster.

4) The need, derived from all these situations, to neutralize or defeat the therapist's efforts may evolve into a malignant vicious circle. As the therapist persists in helping the patient in the face of obvious lack of response or even worsening of the patient's condition, the patient's envy and resentment of the therapist's commitment and dedication may reinforce the need to escape from what would otherwise be unbearable guilt.

In the middle of chronic therapeutic stalemate, patients may formulate quite directly the angry, revengeful request that the therapist compensate them for their past suffering by dedicating his life totally to them. But, regardless of the extent to which the therapist might go out of his way to accommodate the patient's desires, eventually the following issues tend to become prominent. First, the patient may destroy time in the sense of losing his perspective on time; that is, he focuses on each session as if time had come to a halt in between the sessions, and, in a deeper sense, as if both patient and therapist would live forever.

Second, this destruction of time may be accompanied by a specific neglect and rejection of what otherwise would have to be perceived as manifestations of the therapist's concern for and dedication to the patient. It is as if the patient's suspiciousness and destructive disqualification of the therapist were geared to destroying love with cruelty, while projecting this cruelty on to the therapist. Relentless accusations implying that the therapist does not love the patient enough are the most frequent, but not the most severe, manifestation of this tendency. Uncannily, at times when the therapist may in fact be internally exhausted and withdraw passively from active attempts to work with the patient, the patient's accusations may decrease, and an eerie unconscious collusion fostering paralysis and emptiness in the psychotherapeutic situation ensues.

Third, the patient may attempt to convince the therapist that the patient is really not human, that ordinary psychological understanding and empathy have no place in this situation, and the therapist may be induced to replace his concrete understanding of the dynamics of the transference by more general formulations of ego arrests, lack of capacity for emotional understanding, cognitive deficits, and the like.

In short, something very active in the patient attempts to destroy time, love and concern, honesty, and cognitive understanding. I think that under these circumstances the therapist is facing the activation of the deepest levels of human aggression—sometimes hopelessly so. However, it is sometimes possible to resolve these severe treatment stalemates with an essentially analytic approach, and it seems to me that some of the therapist's general characteristics and attitudes now become crucial. I shall attempt to spell out these attitudes.

First of all, it is helpful to combine an attitude of patience over an extended period of time with an attitude of impatience, of not accepting passively the destruction of concrete psychotherapeutic work in each hour. This approach is in contrast to a gradual giving up reflected in a passive wait-and-see attitude in each hour, while the therapist actually becomes more and more impatient and discouraged as time passes; he may even reach a sudden explosion point. The implication is that the acting out of severe aggression needs to be actively countered by the therapist. Activity does not mean abandoning the position of technical neutrality, a point I have explored in detail before.

It hardly needs to be stressed that the therapist should intervene only when he is not under the sway of negative, hostile affects toward the patient. Such aggression toward the patient may be a normal reaction under such extreme circumstances, but it usually becomes condensed with whatever potential for aggressive countertransference reactions exist in the therapist, and the therapist must contain this reaction in terms of utilizing it for his understanding rather than transforming it into action.

A second major attitude of the therapist that might be helpful under conditions of therapeutic stalemate is to focus sharply on the patient's omnipotent destruction of time. The therapist needs to remind the patient of the lack of progress in treatment, to bring into focus again and again the overall treatment goals established at the initiation of treatment, and how the patient appears to neglect such goals completely while assuming an attitude that the treatment should and could go on forever. In this connection, the establishment of realistic treatment goals and their differentiation from the patient's life goals, as stressed by E. Ticho (72), become crucial.

The focus on the broad goals of the treatment needs to be complemented by a sharp focus on the patient's immediate reality. Usually, under conditions of extreme, prolonged stalemate, the patient also neglects his immediate reality situation and reveals what at times amounts to an almost conscious sense of triumph in defeating his own efforts; a triumph over the therpist, whose impotence is reconfirmed every day as impossible situations develop and disaster is courted. It is essential that the therapist interpret the unconscious (and sometimes conscious) rage at him expressed in the patient's playing Russian roulette in his daily life.

The patient will, in the process, have to reassume responsibility for his immediate life situation as well as for his long-range plans. This is a responsibility that I think we expect any patient who undergoes psychoanalytic psychotherapy on an outpatient basis to be able to assume, and it constitutes the reality baseline against which transference acting out can be evaluated and interpreted. In other words, acting out may take the form of burning all bridges with the present external life and with the future, with the implicit expectation that the therapist will assume full responsibility for these; this must be interpreted consistently.

COUNTERTRANSFERENCE

I have suggested elsewhere (30) that one can describe a continuum of countertransference reactions ranging from those related to the symptomatic neuroses at one extreme, to psychotic reactions at the other, a continuum in which the different reality and transference components of both patient and therapist vary in a significant way. When dealing with borderline or severely regressed patients, as contrasted to those presenting symptomatic neuroses and less severe character disorders, the therapist tends to experience, rather soon in the treatment, intensive emotional reactions having more to do with the patient's premature, intense and chaotic transference and with the therapist's capacity to withstand psychological stress and anxiety, than with any specific problem of the therapist's past. Thus, countertransference becomes an important diagnostic tool, giving information on the degree of regression in the patient, his predominant emotional position vis-à-vis the therapist, and the changes occurring in this position. The more intense and premature the therapist's emotional reaction to the patient, the more threatening it becomes to the therapist's technical neutrality, and the more it has a quickly changing, fluctuating, and chaotic nature—the more we can think the therapist is in the presence of severe regression in the patient.

The therapist normally responds to the patient's material with some affective reaction, which under optimal conditions, is subdued and minor, and has a "signal" quality rather than reflecting an intense emotional activation. At points of heightened transference reactions, or when countertransference reactions complicate the picture, the emotional intensity of the therapist's reaction increases and may interfere with his overall immediate understanding of, or internal freedom of reaction to, the patient's material. With borderline patient's not only is the intensity of the therapist's emotional reaction higher after relatively brief periods of treatment, it is also more fluctuating, and, at times, potentially chaotic. Obviously, rather than reacting to the patient under the sway of these affective reactions, the therapist has to be able to tolerate them and utilize them for his own understanding. Insofar as what the patient is reactivating in the transference and the analyst is perceiving in his affective response to it is not only a primitive affect, but a primitive object relation connected with an affect (that is, the therapist perceives a primitive self-image relating to a primitive object-image in the context of the particular activated affect) the therapist's diagnosis of his own emotional reaction implies the diagnosis of the patient's—often dissociated—primitive object relations in the transference.

Nowadays, the term countertransference is often used to refer to the therapist's total emotional reaction to the patient. For the most part, however, particularly for those with an ego-psychological approach, the term is still reserved to apply to the therapist's specific unconscious transference reactions to the patient. In other words, this latter, restricted definition of countertransference focuses on its pathological implications, while the former, broader one focuses on the intimate relationship between the general affective responses of the therapist with his specific countertransference potential.

From the viewpoint of treatment of borderline patients it is an advantage to consider the total emotional reaction of the therapist as a continuum of affective responses from mild, realistic "signal" affects to intense emotional reactions which may temporarily interfere with the therapist's neutrality, and which constitute a compromise formation determined by the transference and specific countertransference reactions. In any case, the therapist needs to be free to utilize this material both for resolving analytically his own excessive reactions to the patient, and for diagnosing primitive object relations activated in the transference.

One important force active in neutralizing and overcoming the effect of aggression and self-aggression in the countertransference is the capacity of the therapist to experience concern. Concern in this context involves awareness of the serious nature of destructive and self-destructive impulses in the patient, the potential development of such impulses in the analyst, and the awareness by the therapist of the limitation necessarily inherent in his therapeutic efforts with his patient. Concern also involves the authentic wish and a need to help the patient in spite of his transitory "badness." On a more abstract level, one might say that concern involves the recognition of the seriousness of destructiveness and self-destructiveness of human beings in general and the hope, but not the certainty, that the fight against these tendencies may be successful in individual cases.

Realistic treatment goals involve the acceptance not only of unresolved shortcomings but of the unavoidability of aggression in ordinary life. The therapist's tolerance of his own aggression and that of the people he loves may make it easier for him to interpret the patient's aggression without being sucked into the patient's conviction that his aggression is dangerous because it will inevitably destroy love, concern, meaning, and creativity. Therefore, the therapist's thoroughly understood awareness of the aggressive components of all love relations, of the essentially ambivalent quality of human interactions, may be a helpful asset in the treatment of extremely difficult cases.

The fact that the therapist can accept truths about himself and his own life may permit him to express in his behavior the conviction that the patient might also be able to accept truths about himself and his own life. Such uncompromising honesty in facing the most turbulent and painful of life's prospects may become part of very concrete interventions with patients having long-term stalemates in the treatment. The confidence that the patient can take and accept the truth about himself expresses at the same time a confidence in the patient's potential resources.

REFERENCES

1. Asch, S. S. Varieties of negative therapeutic reaction and problems of technique. *J. Amer. Psychoanal. Assn.*, 1976, 24:383-407.
2. Bergeret, J. *Les Etats Limites.* Revue Francaise de Psychoanalyse, 1970, 34:605-633.
3. Bibring, E. Psychoanalysis and the dynamic psychotherapies. *J. Amer. Psychoanal. Assoc.*, 1954, 2:745-770.
4. Bion, W. R. *Transformations.* London: Heinemann, 1965.
5. Bion, W. R. *Second Thoughts: Selected Papers on Psychoanalysis.* London: Heinemann, 1967, pp. 86-109.
6. Bion, W. R. *Attention and Interpretation.* London: Heinemann, 1970.
7. Boyer, L. B. and Giovacchini, P. *Psychoanalytic Treatment of Characterological and Schizophrenic Disorders.* New York: Jason Aronson, 1967.
8. Eissler, K. R. The effects of the structure of the ego on psychoanalytic technique. *J. Amer. Psychoanal. Assoc.*, 1953, 1:104-143.
9. Freud, A. *The Ego and the Mechanisms of Defense. The Writings of Anna Freud,* vol. 2. New York: International Universities Press, 1946, pp. 45-57, 117-131.
10. Frosch, J. Psychoanalytic consideration of the psychotic character. *J. Amer. Psychoanal. Assoc.*, 1970, 18:24-50.
11. Frosch, J. Technique in regard to some specific ego defects in the treatment of borderline patients. *Psychoanal. Quart.*, 1971, 45:216-220.
12. Furer, M. Personality organization during the recovery of a severely disturbed young child. In: P. Hartocollis (Ed.), *Borderline Personality Disorders.* New York: International Universities Press, 1977, pp. 457-473.
13. Gill, M. Ego psychology and psychotherapy. *Psychoanal. Quart.*, 1951, 20:62-71.
14. Gill, M. Psychoanalysis and exploratory psychotherapy. *J. Amer. Psychoanal. Assoc.*, 1954, 2:771-797.
15. Giovacchini, P. *Psychoanalysis of Character Disorders.* New York: Jason Aronson, 1975.
16. Green, A. The borderline concept. In: P. Hartocollis (Ed.), *Borderline Personality Disorders.* New York: International Universities Press, 1977, pp. 15-44.
17. Greenson, R. R. The struggle against identification. *J. Amer. Psychoanal. Assoc.*, 1954, 2:200-217.
18. Greenson, R. R. On screen defenses, screen hunger, and screen identity. *J. Amer. Psychoanal. Assoc.*, 1958, 6:242-262.
19. Greenson, R. R. The unique patient-therapist relationship in borderline patients. Presented at the Annual Meeting of the American Psychiatric Association. Unpublished, 1970.
20. Grinker, R. R. Neurosis, psychosis, and the borderline states. In: A. M. Freedman, H. I. Kaplan, and B. J. Sadock (Eds.), *Comprehensive Textbook of Psychiatry —II.* Baltimore: Williams & Wilkins, 1975, pp. 845-850.
21. Hartocollis, P. *Borderline Personality Disorders.* New York: International Universities Press, 1977.
22. Heimann, P. On counter-transference. *Int. J. Psychoanal.*, 1950, 31:81-84.
23. Heimann, P. A combination of defense mechanisms in paranoid states. In: M. Klein, P. Heimann, and R. E. Money-Kyrle (Eds.), *New Directions in Psycho-Anal.* London: Tavistock Publications, 1955a, pp. 240-265.
24. Heimann, P. A contribution to the re-evaluation of the oedipus-complex. The

early states. In: M. Klein, P. Heimann, and R. E. Money-Kyrle (Eds.), *New Directions in Psycho-Anal.* New York: Basic Books, 1955b, pp. 23-38.

25. Holzman, P. S. and Ekstein, R. Repetition-functions of transitory regressive thinking. *Psychoanal. Quart.*, 1959, 28:228-235.
26. Jacobson, E. *Depression.* New York: International Universities Press, 1971.
27. Kernberg, O. Structural derivatives of object relationships. *Int. J. Psychoanal.*, 1966, 47:236-253.
28. KERNBERG, O. (1968). General principles of treatment. In: O. Kernberg, *Borderline Conditions and Pathological Narcissism.* New York: Jason Aronson, 1975, pp. 69-109.
29. Kernberg, O. A psychoanalytic classification of character pathology. *J. Amer. Psychoanal. Assoc.*, 1970, 18:800-802.
30. Kernberg, O. *Borderline Conditions and Pathological Narcissism.* New York: Jason Aronson, 1975a.
31. Kernberg, O. Transference and countertransference in the treatment of borderline patients. *Strecker Monograph Series No. XII* of the Institute of Pennsylvania Hospital, 1975b. (Reprinted in: *J. Natl. Assoc. Priv. Psychiat. Hosp.*, 7:14-24.)
32. Kernberg, O. Technical considerations in the treatment of borderline personality organization. *J. Amer. Psychoanal. Assoc.*, 1976a, 24:795-829.
33. Kernberg, O. *Object Relations Theory and Clinical Psychoanalysis.* New York: Jason Aronson, 1976b.
34. Kernberg, O. Structural change and its impediments. In: P. Hartocollis, (Ed.), *Borderline Personality Disorders.* New York: International Universities Press, 1977, pp. 275-306.
35. Kernberg, O. Contrasting approaches to the psychotherapy of borderline conditions. In: J. F. Masterson (Ed.), *New Perspectives of Psychotherapy of the Borderline Adult.* New York: Brunner/Mazel, 1978, Chapter 3:78-119.
36. Kernberg, O., Burnstein, E., Coyne, L., Appelbaum, A., Horwitz, L., and Voth, H. Psychotherapy and psychoanalysis: Final report of the Menninger Foundation's psychotherapy research project. *Bull. Menninger Clinic*, 1972, 36:1-275.
37. Khan, M. *The Privacy of the Self—Papers on Psychoanalytic Theory and Technique.* New York: International Universities Press, 1974.
38. Klein, M. Notes on some schizoid mechanisms. *Int. J. Psychoanal.*, 1946, 27:99-110.
39. Knight, R. P. Borderline states. In: R. P. Knight and C. R. Friedman (Eds.), *Psychoanalytic Psychiatry and Psychology.* New York: International Universities Press, 1954, pp. 97-109.
40. Knight, R. P. Management and psychotherapy of the borderline schizophrenic patient. In: R. P. Knight and C. R. Friedman (Eds.), *Psychoanalytic Psychiatry and Psychology.* New York: International Universities Press, 1954, pp. 110-122.
41. Little, M. Countertransference and the patient's response to it. *Int. J. Psychoanal.*, 1951, 32:32-40.
42. Little, M. "R"—The analyst's total response to his patient's needs. *Int. J. Psychoanal.*, 1957, 38:240-254.
43. Little, M. On basic unity. *Int. J. Psychoanal*, 1960, 41:377-384; 637.
44. Little, M. Transference in borderline states. *Int. J. Psychoanal.*, 1966, 47:476-485.
45. Mahler, M. *On Human Symbiosis and the Vicissitudes of Individuation, Infantile Psychosis.* New York: International Universities Press, 1968.
46. Mahler, M. A study of the separation-individuation process and its possible application to borderline phenomena in the psychoanalytic situation. In: *Psychoanalytic Study of the Child*, vol. 26. New York/Chicago: Quadrangle Books, 1971, 403-424.
47. Mahler, M. Rapprochement subphase of the separation-individuation process. *Psychoanal. Quart.*, 1972, 41:487-506.

48. Mahler, M. and Kaplan, L. Developmental aspects in the assessment of narcissistic and so-called borderline personalities. In: P. Hartocollis (Ed.), *Borderline Personality Disorders*. New York: International Universities Press, 1977, pp. 71-85.

49. Masterson, J. *Treatment of the Borderline Adolescent: A Development Approach*. New York: Wiley-Interscience, 1972.

50. Masterson, J. *Psychotherapy of the Borderline Adult: A Developmental Approach*. New York: Brunner/Mazel, 1976.

51. Masterson, J. *New Perspectives on Psychotherapy of the Borderline Adult*. New York: Brunner/Mazel, 1978.

52. Money-Kyrle, R. E. Normal countertransference and some of its deviations. *Int. J. Psychoanal.*, 1956, 37:360-366.

53. Nelson, M. Effect of paradigmatic techniques on the pyschic economy of borderline patients. In: H. Greenwald (Ed.), *Active Psychotherapy*. New York: Atherton Press, 1967, pp. 63-89.

54. Olinick, S. L. The negative therapeutic reaction. *Int. J. Psychoanal.*, 1964, 45: 540-548.

55. Racker, H. The meanings and uses of countertransference. *Psychoanal. Quart.*, 1957, 26:303-357.

56. Reider, N. Transference psychosis. *J. Hillside Hosp.*, 1957, 6:131-149.

57. Rinsley, D. An object-relation view of borderline personality. In: P. Hartocollis (Ed.), *Borderline Personality Disorders*. New York: International Universities Press, 1977, pp. 47-70.

58. Romm, M. Transient psychotic episodes during psychoanalysis. *J. Amer. Psychoanal. Assoc.*, 1957, 5:325-341.

59. Rosenfeld, H. Notes on psychopathology and psychoanalytic treatment of schizophrenia. In: H. Azima and B. C. Glueck, Jr. (Eds.), *Psychotherapy of Schizophrenia and Manic-Depressive States* (Psychiatric Research Report #17). Washington, D.C.: American Psychiatric Association, 1963, pp. 61-72.

60. Rosenfeld, H. On the psychopathology of narcissism: A clinical approach. *Int. J. Psychoanal.*, 1964, 45:332-337.

61. Rosenfeld, H. A clinical approach to the psychoanalytic theory of the life and death instincts: An investigation into the aggressive aspects of narcissism. *Int. J. Psychoanal.*, 1971, 52:169-178.

62. Rosenfeld, H. Negative therapeutic reaction. In: P. L. Giovacchini (Ed.), *Tactics and Techniques in Psychoanalytic Therapy*, vol. II. *Countertransference*. New York: Jason Aronson, 1975, pp. 217-228.

63. Schmideberg, M. The treatment of psychopaths and borderline patients. *Amer. J. Psychother.*, 1947, 1:45-70.

64. Searles, H. Dual- and multi-identity processes in borderline ego functioning. In: P. Hartocollis (Ed.), *Borderline Personality Disorders*. New York: International Universities Press, 1977, pp. 441-455.

65. Segal, H. *Introduction to the Work of Melanie Klein*. New York: Basic Books, 1964.

66. Sharpe, E. F. Anxiety, outbreak and resolution. In: M. Brierly (Ed.), *Collected Papers on Psycho-Analysis*. London: Hogarth Press, 1931, pp. 67-80.

67. Stern, A. Psychoanalytic investigation of and therapy in the borderline group of neuroses. *Psychoanal. Quart.*, 1938, 7:467-489.

68. Stern, A. Psychoanalytic therapy in the borderline neuroses. *Psychoanal. Quart.*, 1945, 14:190-198.

69. Stone, L. Psychoanalysis and brief psychotherapy. *Psychoanal. Quart.*, 1951, 20:215-236.

70. Stone, L. The widening scope of indications for psychoanalysis. *J. Amer. Psychoanal. Assoc.*, 1954, 2:567-594.

71. Strachey, J. The nature of the therapeutic action for psycho-analysis. *Int. J. Psychoanal.*, 1934, 15:127-159.
72. Ticho, E. Termination of psychoanalysis: Treatment goals, life goals. *Psychoanal. Quart.*, 1972, 41:315-333.
73. Valenstein, A. F. On attachment to painful feelings and the negative therapeutic reaction. In: *The Psychoanalytic Study of the Child*, vol. 28. New Haven: Yale University Press, 1973, pp. 365-392.
74. Volkan, V. *Primitive Internalized Object Relations*. New York: International Universities Press, 1976, pp. xiii-xvii.
75. Wallerstein, R. S. The goals of psychoanalysis: A survey of analytic viewpoints. *J. Amer. Psychoanal. Assoc.*, 1965, 3:748-770.
76. Wallerstein, R. S. Reconstruction and mastery in the transference psychosis. *J. Amer. Psychoanal. Assoc.*, 1967, 15:551-583.
77. Wallerstein, R. S. Introduction to panel: Psychoanalysis and psychotherapy. *Int. J. Psychoanal.*, 1969, 50:117-126.
78. Wallerstein, R. S. and Robbins, L. L. The psychotherapy research project of The Menninger Foundation (Part IV: Concepts). *Bull. Menninger Clinic*, 1956, 20: 239-262.
79. Winnicott, D. W. *Collected Papers: Through Paediatrics to Psycho-Analysis*. New York: Basic Books, 1958.
80. Winnicott, D. W. Ego distortion in terms of true and false self. In: *The Maturational Process and the Facilitating Environment*. New York: International Universities Press, 1958, Chapter 12:140-152.
81. Winnicott, D. W. *The Maturational Process and the Facilitating Environment*. New York: International Universities Press, 1965.
82. Wolberg, A. R. *The Borderline Patient*. New York: Intercontinental Medical Book Corp., 1973.
83. Zetzel, E. R. A developmental approach to the borderline patient. *Amer. J. of Psych.*, 1971, 127:867-871.

6

The Treatment of Established
Pathological Mourners

VAMIK D. VOLKAN, M.D.

and

DANIEL JOSEPHTHAL, M.D.

There is much in the psychiatric literature about the similarities and differences between uncomplicated grief and the reactive depression that follows the death of someone close and important to the mourner. Freud (12) showed long ago how both "mourning and melancholia" may be initiated by such a loss, and how both include painful dejection, a loss of interest in the world outside the self, a decrease in the capacity to love, and the inhibition of any activity not connected with thoughts of the dead. What distinguishes mourning from neurotic depression is the disturbance in self-regard that appears in the latter state. In uncomplicated grief the mourner can loosen his ties to the representation of the dead through the work of mourning, or can form the kind of loving identification with it that promotes his growth. In depression, however, the mourner experiences disruptive identification with it, and the ambivalent relationship he had had with the one now dead becomes an internal process; the yearning to keep the representation and at the same time to destroy it is felt as an issue of one's own—a struggle between cherishing and doing away with one's self.

Further accounts of the complications of grief appear in the literature. For example, the initial absence of a grief reaction is mentioned by Deutsch (7), and the chronicity of what are generally thought of as "normal" grief manifestations by Wahl (48). However, differentiation between varieties of complicated grief and depression over loss by death is not always made, and these diagnostic terms are commonly used interchangeably. The study of adult mourners carried out at the University of Virginia has demonstrated the existence of a type of established pathological grief with a clinical picture and underlying psychodynamics which are unique, persistent, and different from those of either a normal but protracted grief reaction or a neurotic depression. It is, in fact, a common pyschiatric problem.

After the death of someone greatly valued, the grief-stricken relative or friend goes through consecutive phases of mourning. One might anticipate that when the process develops complications these might include fixation in any one of these phases, but clinical research shows that fixation usually occurs at one specific phase—that in which the mourner is in a limbo of uncertainty about the death and yearns to bring the dead to life. The situation is complex inasmuch as along with the longing to restore the dead is a dread of ever seeing him again. These conflicting emotions result in the picture of established pathological grief with its characteristic underlying psychodynamic processes. Once diagnosed, this condition may be successfully treated by a method of brief psychotherapy called re-grief work (39, 41, 46, 47).

THE PHASES OF GRIEVING

The psychological phenomenon involved in the process of grieving over the loss of someone who had been important to one's self is one, the course of which can be represented graphically as though it were the course of a physiologic process seen longitudinally. Indeed, Engel (8), in asking whether or not grief might be called a disease, suggested that it resembled the working-through of a healing wound. Just as a wound can become infected or form keloids, so can the course of grieving become complicated.

It begins when someone is lost, or when his loss is seen as imminent. This external event affects the internal milieu of the mourner, triggering a psychological process. Freud (12) described how this process runs its course over an interval of time. As the work of mourning goes on, memories and expectations connected with the one who died are brought to the mourner's mind one by one. When they are hypercathected and examined, it becomes possible to detach the libido that had been invested in the deceased, and when the mourning is completed the mourner's ego becomes "free and uninhibited again." However, a closer look suggests that the end of the grieving process is not so easy to identify, since the internal image of the lost one remains with us to a certain extent all our lives—and may sometimes be externalized with a degree of communication with that person continuing. When one is asked to recall a dead relative, for example, his image is usually readily available to the mind's eye; what is more important is that such an image may impress itself on the mourner in moments of need without conscious recall. For example, a woman who has completed the healing of the wound caused by her father's death may find herself preoccupied with his image at the approach of her wedding day, as she longs for his approval of this important step in her life. Nonetheless, the grieving process does terminate for all practical purposes when the image of the dead person is not required in any absolute and exaggerated way to maintain the mourner's internal equilibrium, although it may from time to time be reactivated, as in anniversary reactions (29, 30). The healed wound is, as it were, at least covered over by scar tissue, but it never altogether disappears; the feelings about an internal relationship to the one who is lost continue.

Once initiated, the phases through which mourning over the death of someone important proceeds are recognizable. Although these have been described somewhat differently by different writers, it is clear that they were all observing similar manifestations. Engel (9) divided grieving into three stages: a) shock and disbelief; b) a growing awareness of the loss; and c) restitution, the work of mourning. Schuster (34) focused further on the stage of shock and disbelief. Bowlby (4) also identified three phases of grieving, although he and Parkes (5) later worked out a schema with four. They describe the first phase as a brief phase of numbness that may last from a few hours to a week and be interrupted by outbursts of extremely intense anger and distress. The second phase is one "of learning and searching for the lost figure" that lasts for some months, even years. The third phase is one of disorganization and despair; and the fourth, one in which reorganization appears. Pollock (28, 31) made a special contribution to the psychoanalytic understanding of this reorganization (adaptation) when he went beyond Freud's original notion of the transformation into ego loss that occurs with the loss of a loved object—or even of an ideal—by showing that the ego uses the adaptational process of mourning for its own healing. "Mourning processing, like working through, is internal work to restore psychic balance (32, p. 16). Using the term *mourning* in a broad sense to include reaction to losses other than those occasioned by death, he holds that to be able to mourn is to be able to change. People also mourn their *own* impending death; people aware of having incurable cancer, for example, go through similar phases if time allows and they are psychologically capable (17).

This paper refers only to the mourning of *adults,* its complications and therapeutic management. Psychoanalysts debate the possibility that infants or small children faced with loss grieve in the manner of the adult. In his review of children's reactions to the death of someone important to them, Nagera (23) concludes that such losses interface with development. Our own experience suggests that Wolfenstein (50) was accurate in saying that adolescence constitutes a necessary precondition of the ability to mourn. A painful and gradual decathexis of the living parents is accomplished in adolescence and serves as a model for the adult type of grieving.

As noted, our clinical research (39, 40, 42, 43, 44, 45), which was conducted with a hundred patients during eight years, confirmed our belief that the fixation typical of established pathological mourning occurs mainly in the phase Bowlby and Parkes (5) describe as one of "the yearning to recover the dead" and, to use a term of Kübler-Ross (17), to "bargain" for his return. When such yearning is crystallized, it is inevitably accompanied by dread of such a return. Manifestations of earlier grief stages—denial, numbness, or angry outbursts—may appear also, as well as occasional periods of disorganization usually more typical of a later phase. If the fixation we describe is extended we are, however, justified in diagnosing "established pathological grief."

THE CLINICAL PICTURE OF ESTABLISHED PATHOLOGICAL GRIEF

Although the pathological mourner has intellectual appreciation of the historical fact of the death, he clings to chronic hope that the lost will return, even after the six months or a year that usually disabuses the normal mourner of any such notion. The pathological mourner's dread of such an eventuality is as strong as his hope. This situation can persist over time without alteration, or the picture may be overlaid by others.

Wistful longing is not abnormal; Parkes (25), for instance, speaks of how a widow yearning for her dead husband may imagine hearing his footfall at coming-home time for a year after his loss, and even "hallucinate" his appearance. In the established pathological mourner, however, longing becomes such a strong preoccupation that it dominates his daily life and keeps him ongoingly involved in the conflict produced by the ambivalence of deciding whether to bring the dead person back or to kill him, i.e. expunge him from consideration. Many pathological mourners become interested in reincarnation (40), the sophisticated sublimating this interest in a related hobby or scientific hypothesis. Some compulsively read obituary notices, betraying not only anxiety over their own death but trying to deny the one they mourn by finding no current mention of his death, while at the same time recalling how such mention as it appeared earlier had the finality of "killing" the lost one. This kind of preoccupation can become extremely morbid, as in the case of one patient who changed his dead wife's burial place three times in as many years, one move taking her coffin some distance away and another bringing her "nearer home." When he came to our attention he was planning a fourth move. His preoccupation with his dead wife's image was ambivalent, clearly reflecting the painful struggle that this religious man had had being faithful to his marriage vows over the many years in which she had been a suffering invalid. He had longed for liberation from her tragic situation, and after her death he went through cycles of trying to draw her close to him and then to put her away.

Some established pathological mourners think they recognize their lost one in someone they see alive. A son pathologically mourning a father dead for years may be struck by a resemblance perceived in some stranger passing by, and rush forward to peer at him over and over to see if this can indeed be his parent. This act represents an effort to return the dead to life; when the illusion is recognized as such it serves the wish to "kill" him. The mourner may make daily reference to death, tombs, and graveyards in ritual ways that obviate painful affect, but it is unusual for such a mourner actually to visit the grave. For example, a 20-year-old college student still, a year-and-a-half later, mourning the sudden death of a grandfather she described as "the most important person in my life" was surprised when she was asked if she had ever gone to his graveside. Like most people with established pathological mourning, she was quick to find an excuse. She doubted that she could find it in a cemetery as "big" as the one in her small town. Her preoccupation with her grandfather was nonetheless evident in her daydreams about him and her search for him in an affair with a married man 30 years her senior.

The therapist of such a patient gets the impression that the one being mourned is in a sense alive as far as the patient is concerned and still exerts his influence. The patient uses the present tense, stating confidently, "My father likes to go to the movies." One patient joked nervously during our first interviews, cautioning that, "You can't talk much against dead people because if you knock them down they come back."

Certain typical dreams can be expected. They have been classified (40, 41) as:

1) "Frozen" dreams, to use a term many patients use themselves to describe tableaux without motion. One tableau may follow another as though the dreamer were watching the projection of a slide series. One patient used the analogy of watching slices of bread fall out of a package. The patient's associations to each tableau indicate a connection with his complicated mourning and his fixation in the grieving process as though the process had congealed in its course.

2) Dreams in which the dead person is seen alive but engaged in a struggle between life and death. He may be lying in a hospital bed or under the rubble of a collapsed building, or sitting in a burning vehicle. The dreamer tries to save him—or to finish him off. Interestingly, both persons in the dream are usually undisguised. The situation's outcome remains indeterminate because the patient invariably awakens before it is resolved.

3) Dreams of the dead body in which something indicates that death is only an illusion. The body seen in its casket may be sweating, or one long buried may show no sign of decay. Such dreams are not unusual among normal mourners during the months immediately after the death, but these dreams either cease or the appearance of the body begins to change. However, the mourner in pathological grief will dream of the undecayed body many years after death.

Several investigators (28, 41) have spoken of the reporting of dream *series* appropriately parallel to phases of uncomplicated grief in persons either completing their grief work without incident or beginning to re-grieve in normal fashion as the therapy for pathological grief starts taking effect. For example, what is first reported is a view of grass-covered earth in which, in the following dream, there is a grave-like excavation. The next dream will include the half-alive body of the lost one lying nearby; the dreamer may next see himself pushing it into the grave. In the final dream of the series, the manifest content of which has been the dreamer's progress toward resolution of his grief, a grave, smoothed over and covered with grass, appears. The established pathological mourner is usually ready enough to disclose to the therapist, when asked about his dream life, the appearance of the kinds of dreams we cite as characteristic of this pathological state. These dreams are usually repeating dreams, and information about them is diagnostically helpful.

The person with established pathological grief can keep in touch with the image of the dead, over which he maintains absolute control. He is able to establish contact with the dead by forming a presence (introject) of the dead person within himself that is perceived, by the patient, as having definite boundaries separating it from the mourner. Most patients, when questioned about it, can give good descriptions of this phenomenon. Volkan (41, 42) and Volkan, Cillufo and Sarvay (46) tell of patients who, during the time of their treatment, would ask the inner presence to get out of their bodies and leave them alone. It is also not unusual for the person with established pathological grief to hold "inner conversations" with the image of the deceased that dwells within him. One patient would hold conversations with his dead brother while driving in his car, and ask business advice from him, feeling that the brother was somehow living within his own breast.

Another sort of contact with the dead, again one under the mourner's absolute control, is maintained by the use of some object contaminated with certain elements, some of which came from the dead while others come from the mourner himself. These have been named "linking objects" (43, 44, 45). They differ from the ordinary keepsake since the mourner invests them with magic capable of linking him with the one he has lost. Typically, he keeps his linking object locked away or located in some place where he can be in touch with it in a way that is consciously or unconsciously ritualized. One patient, still mourning the death of a son from an automobile accident many years earlier, kept his son's shoes, polished except where they were blood-stained, in his own clothes closet. There he could see them daily as he removed and put away his own garments, while all the time never touching them. When he went into full-blown pathological grief after the passage of many years, and was sent by his family physician for consultation, he wore the shoes to the first interview. He was greatly surprised and anxious when the therapist asked if he had kept any special object or objects that had belonged to his dead son, and only then realized what shoes he was wearing.

A great variety of objects may become linking objects. The mourner chooses such an object from among a) something once used routinely by the dead, perhaps something worn on the person, like a watch; b) something the dead person had employed to extend his senses, like a camera (an extension of seeing); c) a symbolic or realistic representation of the dead person, the simplest example of which is, of course, a photograph; or d) something at hand when the mourner first learned of the death or when he viewed the body. We have also known patients to cling to something less tangible, such as an elaborate fantasy. For example, the mourner might entertain a certain thought during the burial ceremony and regularly reactivate it to keep controlled contact with the image of the dead.

THE PSYCHODYNAMICS OF ESTABLISHED PATHOLOGICAL GRIEF

Three major intrapsychic processes underlie the clinical picture described here: splitting, internalization, and externalization. One must identify and understand the defensive use of these mechanisms in order to make definitive diagnosis.

Splitting

The adult patient with established pathological grief uses the mechanism of *splitting* extensively. The term *splitting* refers here not to the "primitive splitting" currently used widely in relation to borderline personality organization—that persistent separation of "all good" self- and object-representations from those seen as "all bad." Here we see splitting on a higher, neurotic level, as a splitting of the ego functions to protect the individual from any global break with reality. Thus the ego's denial of the death can coexist with the ego's knowledge that the death has, in fact, occurred. The pathological mourner's splitting of ego function is selective and concerned only with the issues of the death in question. Freud (13, 14) spoke of this type of splitting in connection with both grief and fetishism. The fetishist does not experience a global break with reality either; he understands that women do not have penises but behaves as though they did. Similarly, the established pathological mourner acknowledges the death but behaves as though it had not occurred. One particular function of his ego has become inconsistent with the rest. He is usually able to identify the point at which splitting began, as when he recalls gazing at the corpse in full knowledge that it was a dead body, and convincing himself that he saw perspiration appearing on its brow as an evidence that life continued in it. Such a notion is not outside the experience of the normal mourner, but he soon sets it aside, whereas it remains a powerful question in the mind of the pathological mourner, militating against the separation/castration anxiety triggered by the death. Two other cogent psychological processes inherent in this condition—internalization and externalization—foster the illusion of continuing contact with the dead and thus support the mechanism of splitting in its defense against anxiety. All three of these mechanisms contribute to the patient's continuing existence in a limbo of uncertainty.

Internalization

Such processes—including introjection and identification—which are involved in both grief and reactive depression, have been known since the original publication of the works of Abraham (1) and Freud (12). When his search for the lost one forces the mourner to test the reality of his disappearance, he uses hundreds of memories to bind him to the one he mourns, and becomes so preoccupied with doing so that he loses interest in the world around him. This painful longing must be worked through piecemeal. Tensions are discharged through weeping, for example. He regresses and resorts to "taking in" the deceased by introjection. Thus, the dead person's representation within the mourner's self becomes hypertrophied and is seen as an introject. As noted earlier, the introject may be perceived by the patient as an inner presence. Although the patient may describe this psychological phenomenon in such a realistic way as to call it "a foreign body in my bosom," it should be remembered that, in actuality, introjects are only code symbols of complicated affective-dynamic psychological processes. Fenichel (11) states that "introjections [introjects] act as a buffer by helping to preserve the relationship with the object while the gradual process of relinquishing it is going on." Our work with established pathological mourners indicates that the gradual process of relinquishing an introject fails to take place. Thus the introject's continued presence does not lead either to disruptive identification, as in reactive depression, or rewarding identification (19) for the enrichment of the patient's psychic system. He is obliged to retain it and, like the introjects of early life representations in psychotic patients, it never evolves further but remains chronically cathected and is continually a party in the yearning/dreading transactions of the patient.

Externalization

The child's transitional object (49), perhaps a teddy bear or a "security blanket," is vitally important to him. Its main function, one universally present, is to cause the infant to develop in response to the ministrations of the "good enough" mother. In it he has created his first "not-me" possession, which falls short nevertheless of being totally "not-me" since it links not-me with mother-me (15). The transitional object provides a bridge over the psychological chasm that opens when the mother and child are apart; the child may need it if he is to sleep, for example. Some children who experience defective child/mother interaction may have such extreme anxiety when separated from the mother that they concentrate unduly on this object and use it in bizarre ways. At this this level such objects are called childhood fetishes (37), psychotic fetishes (21), or instant mothers (36). Since the main function of these inanimate objects is to deal with separation anxiety, it is not surprising that the adult suffering a separation, to which he has responded with established pathological grief, may reactivate in his regression this archaic way of dealing with this stress. This would create in a linking object a locus for the meeting of part of his self-representation with the representation of the dead. Thus an externalization—a projection of self- and object-images—is crystallized (43, 45).

Jaffe's (16) emphasis on the dual role played by projection in object relations, and the ambivalence it facilitates, can be applied here. He wrote: "On the one hand of the continuum, the annihilation of the object is predominant, while on the other, the identification with and preservation of the object is paramount" (pp. 674-675).

The linking object is completely under the patient's control; he has the unconscious illusion that it makes it possible for him to kill the dead person or bring him back to life. It is contaminated with intense emotion, i.e., the urge to kill, and is nothing that can simply be put to use in the manner of a keepsake. It must be hidden away and perhaps even locked away, or have a ritual for relating to it. For example, one patient had a picture of his father as linking object and developed a ritual concerning it that persisted for many years until he had treatment. He could manage to remain in a room alone with it until, when lost in contemplating the picture, it seemed to him that his father began to move toward him out of the frame. Then he would be so overwhelmed by anxiety that he would rush from the room. He had a strong desire to know at all times where his linking object was. Many mourners are satisfied to keep theirs in a distant place, provided that it is safe and accessible. Another patient used the clothing of his dead brother as a linking object; he kept the garments locked away, but worried constantly that he would grow to "fit" them.

One young woman's psychotherapist committed suicide while she was in the middle of a transference neurosis. When she learned that he had been cremated and his ashes had been placed in an urn, she bought an urn-like vase which she established on the mantel in her living room, depositing her last appointment slip in it as a linking object. Although knowledge of its presence in the vase was necessary to her, she would neither look at it nor throw it away.

No patient we studied reactivated a transitional object in the form of the transitional object or childhood fetish used in his childhood, but patients did employ the same dynamic processes that foster in the infant his illusion of power over the environment. Put into the external world, the linking object also helps the patient externalize the work of mourning and helps him put the work aside for future attention which he keeps on postponing because of the pain it would cause.

DIFFERENTIAL DIAGNOSIS

There is no dearth of observation in psychiatric literature that recognizable mental illness, such as the different neuroses, psychoses, antisocial behavior patterns, psychosomatic conditions, etc., is precipitated by a loss by death (6, 10, 18, 20, 22, 24, 26, 27, 33, 38). In such conditions, while death and loss are precipitating events, these are distinctly different from established pathological grief, the latter state being, as we have stressed, unique in a number of ways. It should be differentiated with care from depression, fetishism, and psychosis.

Depression

Internalization processes are common to both depression and established pathological grief, but in the latter, the introject of the dead does not bring about identification. Thus, the introject does not blend into the patient's self-representation, but it is something he reacts to as an internal presence that has its own discrete boundaries. The mourner's tie to the introject does not loosen. In a reactive depression, however, introjection of the lost object leads to identification so that the mourner *is* the battleground on which the conflicts, formerly so lively between the patient and the one now dead, continue to be played out. Thus, we see the pathological guilt, and the self-reproachful and self-degrading features of the depression. We agree with Pollock (28) and Smith (35) that in depression, identification tends to be nearly total, with little difference being made between characteristics of the mourner and aspects of the dead he takes in. As Freud (12) indicated: ". . . if the love for the object—a love which cannot be given up— takes refuge in narcissistic identification, then the hate comes into operation on this substitute object, abusing it, debasing it, making it suffer and deriving sadistic satisfaction from its suffering" (p. 251). To be sure, there are grey areas between pathological grief and a depression that follows a death. One suffering from depression (total identification with the representation of the dead) after a death may, in fact, go into typical established pathological grief with an ambivalently related introject before he is able to respond appropriately to his loss. We have seen situations in which it was hard to determine whether the patient had an introject or identified totally with the dead; since the mourner's behavior resembled on the surface that known to have been characteristic of the deceased, careful scrutiny was required. In any case, the patient who can easily fluctuate psychodynamically between reactive depression and established pathological grief may be a suitable candidate for re-grief therapy. The *fusion* with the image of the deceased that is exhibited by the person in established pathological grief, and which comes and goes, contains manifestations of identification. However, the identification of the reactive depressive is usually different inasmuch as it follows the establishment of an introject before turning into something more clearly identification *per se.*

The pathological mourner may experience feelings of guilt, but with him such feelings are transient, since he maintains the unconscious illusion that he can bring the dead to life again (as well as kill him) if he chooses. Intense guilt is the earmark of depression, which is characterized also by the dominant ego feeling of helplessness (3). In established pathological grief there is *chronic* hope—and dread (40, 42).

Fetishism

High-level splitting occurs in both fetishism and established pathological grief, as does the use of certain objects in magical ways. The differences that distinguish the fetish, the linking object, and the transitional object are described elsewhere in some detail (43, 45). The linking object provides a means for external maintenance of object relationships with the dead. The ambivalence of the wish to annihilate the deceased and to keep him alive is condensed in it so that the painful work of mourning has an external reference and is thus not resolved. The linking object thus deals with separation anxiety, but the classical fetish used by adults serves primarily to deal with castration anxiety and only secondarily with separation anxiety. The literature (2) reports the development of fetishistic behavior in a classical sense after a loss by death, and in this circumstance a grey area between fetish and linking object is evident. If the therapist takes his patient's history with great care and is watchful for any historical loss that might have initiated the appearance of the clinical picture, he is usually able to find clues to the nature of the magical object being used by his patient. One of our patients discovered a pair of women's shoes in the desk of his father after his death, and kept them—primarily fetishistic objects for his father—for his own linking objects.

Psychosis

As noted, a break with reality does in one sense occur in established pathological grief through the use of high-level splitting, but it falls far short of being global, as it would be in a full-blown psychosis. For example, we would not over-diagnose as psychotic a widow who tells of hearing her dead husband's footsteps. If she is suffering from established pathological mourning her experience indicates no more than what might be called "mini-psychosis," since it is focused and reversible by the patient's own capacity for reality-testing.

The Suitability of Patients for Re-grief Therapy

There are a number of reasons why an adult may be caught up in established pathological grief. He may not have been prepared for a sudden death, for example, and fall victim to something like traumatic neurosis when a sudden death does occur. His situation may in this case be seen as one of established pathological grief that is a variation of traumatic neurosis, the most suitable variety of pathological grief for re-grief therapy. Or the mourner may have unfinished business with the one who died, and be unconsciously trying to keep him alive for this reason, while at the same time feeling anger toward the dead person that makes him want to "kill" him. Such unfinished business would include uncompleted intrapsychic processes. An example is provided by a young man whose father had died suddenly while the son was courting the girl who was to become his wife. During the boy's puberty his father, a physician, had had some reason to be concerned about his son's genital development and shared these misgivings about what a failure to develop properly might mean to the boy's manhood. So the son, who had a need to prove his virility to his father, accordingly impregnated his fiancee soon after the father died. He had to keep his father's image alive to convey this triumph to him (41).

It is significant whether the death being mourned came about from natural causes or involved violence, as in suicide, accident, or homicide. Violence, unconsciously connected with the mourner's aggressive feelings, fosters guilt that can preclude the expression of natural anger and aggressive reactions. This situation may involve the patient's fixation in established pathological mourning, so that he can avoid feeling aggression and guilt. Such fixation may in some cases be accomplished in the service of so-called secondary gain. When a death brings about such changes in the real world as the blow of losing the family home or having to face a sudden loss of income because of the wage-earner's death, the mourner is more apt to keep the dead one alive and struggle with the wish to "kill" him in order to complete the natural process of grieving.

Any loss, including the death itself, deals a narcissistic blow to the psyche of the one left behind. If the mourner has narcissistic character pathology, brief psychotherapy is unlikely to change this, however closely the clinical picture following the death may resemble that of established pathological grief. He may seem to go through re-grief therapy readily enough but still become symptomatic very easily whenever his narcissistic character organization is threatened. Such patients, while seemingly trying to deal with the lost object, are actually trying to deal, whether in hidden or open ways, with the narcissistic blow itself. For such people to become able to grieve genuinely usually requires more than re-grief therapy by itself can provide. We do not advise taking into re-grief therapy the patient with narcissistic personality organization.

The therapist should ascertain if the individual with the clinical picture indicative of established pathological grief has severe problems that stem from separation/individuation, and has extensively used such primitive defenses as internalization and externalization prior to the death he mourns. If he has low-level psychic organization—that is, if he has moderate-to-severe pathology in his internalized object relations—it is doubtful that he will benefit from "re-griefing." The most suitable patients are those with intact ego functions in all respects other than higher-level splitting, and who are psychologically-minded, motivated, and thus capable of forming a therapeutic alliance. Since "re-griefing" is a process leading to an inner structural change, it is not surprising that candidates suitable for it are those who would be suitable for classical psychoanalysis proper.

It has been demonstrated (46) that the Minnesota Multiphasic Personality Inventory is not only an effective self-rating measurement of change occurring during re-grief therapy, but a promising instrument for the selection of patients for this kind of treatment. It pointed to an underlying personality trait of hysteria and dependence in those patients who received great benefit from re-grief therapy with us. A pilot study suggested that established pathological mourners tended to have an elevation of scales 1, 2, 3, 7 and 8, and, to a lesser extent, of scales 4 and 6 also. Peaks came generally in scales 2 and 7. The data of the pilot study suggest that elevation of scales 2 and 7 to a point in excess of the showing on scale 8 is predictive of maximum benefit from "re-griefing."

A DESCRIPTION OF RE-GRIEF THERAPY

Once the patient has been seen in a diagnostic interview and found suitable for re-grief therapy, he is told that his psychological condition is due to his inability to complete the grieving process, which a brief course of therapy will help him to complete. One of the therapist's first tasks will be to develop a formulation as to the cause of his patient's being "frozen" in the course of his grieving. This requirement makes it necessary for him to have had adequate experience in psychodynamically oriented therapies, and to have developed a high degree of competence in formulating unconscious mental processes. If the patient is capable of really "hearing" at the outset what his reasons are for failing to complete the normal process of mourning, they can be shared with him; otherwise, the therapist may keep his formulation to himself for later use in interpretations when the patient is ready to hear them.

Since the established pathological mourner is in a state of chronic hope that the dead will return—and simultaneously wants to "kill" him in order to complete grieving—he is preoccupied with psychological contact with the introject. During the initial phase of re-grief therapy, after carefully taking a history, we help the patient to distinguish between what is his and what belongs to the representation of the one he has lost, using what have been called (47) demarcation exercises. Demarcating the introject, so to speak, will enable the therapist to help his patient see what he has taken in and thus what he feels about the introject, and which of its aspects he wants to retain in non-disruptive identification and which he wants to reject. It is important here to note again that although the patient employs the kind of physical terms we use in referring to his introject, it is, in actuality, an affective-dynamic *process.* The therapist of such patients should have sufficient experience to keep from engaging in intellectual gymnastics instead of bona fide therapy when he attempts the analytic formulations involved here. The manifest content of the patient's dreams may demonstrate to him how his grieving has been "frozen."

In the initial phase of demarcation, which lasts for several weeks, the therapist does not encourage an outpouring of intense emotions, but helps his patient into a state of *preparedness* for such an outpouring. If the patient senses emotion building up in himself and feels frustrated at being unable to allow himself yet to feel its full impact, the therapist may say, "What is your hurry? We are still trying to learn all about the circumstances of the death and the reasons why you cannot grieve. When the time comes you may allow yourself to grieve."

Following the demarcation exercises and exploration of the reasons why the patient was fixated and unable to work out his grief, the therapist will focus on the linking object. When the linking object is being dealt with, the therapist will make a formulation about its choice from among many possibilities. Meanings condensed in a linking object are discussed elsewhere (43, 45). Because it has physical existence with properties that reach the senses, it has greater impact as "magical" than the introject has. Once the patient grasps how he has been using it to maintain absolutely controlled contact with the image of the dead, as well as to postpone grieving and keep it frozen, he will use it to begin his "re-grieving," and this move will increase his dread. He is asked to bring the linking object to a therapy session, where it is at first avoided. With the patient's permission the therapist may lock it away somewhere in the therapy room, saying that its magical properties exist only in the patient's perception of it. Finally, introduced into therapy, it is placed between patient and therapist long enough for the patient to feel its spell. He is then asked to touch it and explain anything that comes to him from it. We are constantly surprised at what intense emotion is congealed in it, and caution others about this; such emotion serves to unlock the psychological processes contained until now in the linking object itself. Emotional storms so generated may continue for weeks; at first diffuse, they become differentiated, and the therapist, with his patient, can then identify anger, guilt, sadness, and so on. The linking object will then at last lose its power, whether the patient chooses to discard it altogether or not.

A graft of secondary process thought is needed to help heal the wound that this experience has torn open. During the weeks that follow, patient and therapist go over in piecemeal fashion memories of how news of the death came; recognition of when splitting began; the funeral; the attempts to keep the dead alive, etc. Although this review may make the patient highly emotional at some point, he can now observe what is happening to him, and disorganization no longer frightens him. Many patients spontaneously plan some kind of memorial ritual. For example, one went, without advice from us, to the synagogue from which his father had been buried and to the grave in which he lay, making a photographic record of it all. Many patients consult their priests, ministers, or rabbis for religious consolation as they begin to accept the death toward the conclusion of re-griefing. With suitable patients, we were successful in using, toward the end of their therapy, the manifest content of their serial dreams to indicate where they were in their re-griefing (41). Patients then have a sense of the introject's leaving them in peace, and they are often able to visit the grave to say "goodbye." They feel free, even excited with the lifting of their burden, and begin to look for new objects of their love. Re-griefing is over. Our experience has been that it can be completed in about four months, with sessions occurring at least three times a week.

TRANSFERENCE: THERAPEUTIC EFFICACY

In re-grief therapy the transference relationship becomes the vehicle whereby insight into ambivalence and the conflict between longing and dread may be gained, and resolution effected. A truly supportive approach is required, as in all other therapies whether psychoanalytic or not. The therapist must convey his non-exploitative desire to heal, and encourage his patient to express himself directly without any fear of hostile, punitive, engulfing, or abandoning responses. The therapist should actively, directly, and instructively oppose any initial shame or excessive control with which the patient may conceal the complications of his grief, and encourage his head-on exploration of feelings and fantasies about the person he has lost and the internal and external relationship he has with him. Through his activity the therapist offers himself as a new object for the patient's consideration, aiming, as in psychoanalytic therapy, to develop a therapeutic alliance without encouraging an *infantile* transference neurosis. Transference—but not transference neurosis—is inevitable, and may be therapeutic by providing close and intimate contact within the therapeutic setting as conflicts are understood. At times the patient may relate to his therapist as he had related to the one he mourns, and thus make it possible to work through in a focal way the conflicts he had had with him. The fresh grief caused by separation as therapy terminates can be put to appropriate use.

Although re-grief therapy is brief, lasting for some months rather than for years, it is intense, intimate, and certainly not superficial. It can be likened to a "mini-focal analysis" since it leads to the activating of certain areas of intrapsychic process, however focalized, and effects intrapsychic change in areas under treatment by means of "working-through." Thus, it is not recommended for therapists inexperienced in listening to the flow of unconscious process. It requires adherence to a therapeutic position and expert handling of transference and countertransference.

A CASE REPORT

A 30-year-old, well-respected, and highly competent female lawyer sought treatment from one of us (Josephthal) for the trouble she was having in resolving her grief reaction to her husband's death in an airplane accident six months earlier. Although she showed some manifestations of what could be understood as prolonged "normal grief," her case history revealed a basic picture of established pathological grief with typical psychodynamics underlying it. She continued unable to control the tears and weeping that came whenever she thought of him, and she was ashamed over so losing her self-control and dismayed that the situation seemed not to improve as time went on. Her tears were accompanied by sad and poignant longing for her husband and for her own death to come in order that they might be together again. She reported being especially upset on the tenth and twelfth of each month; she had had to identify the body on the tenth day of the month in which he died, and to make arrangements for the cremation two days after.

Her history indicated no significant psychological, developmental trauma, nor deprivation, overindulgence, or difficulties with object relations. She grew up in a farm family in which self-reliance was a virtue, and she rejected any sign of dependency within herself. Her social, educational, sexual, and vocational development progressed smoothly, and when she was 24 she married a dynamic, successful, and glamorous lawyer who was also a real-estate investor, and she spoke of having had a full and exciting life with him. The couple traveled extensively and had many friends. She felt that her relationship to her husband, which was deep, rich, and intimate, had only one flaw—his engagement in several transient extramarital affairs while on business trips. Although she tried to condone this as unimportant in the contemporary climate of openness and enlightenment, and felt that he did not, in fact, have any real emotional involvement with the women in question, she was inwardly upset and felt that her husband had shown less than total commitment to their marriage. She tried to feel accepting and liberated, and not to be controlling, but, however she questioned her objections intellectually, emotionally she continued to resent his affairs. This was an unresolved issue at the time of his death, but otherwise she felt hers had been a very happy marriage. The couple had chosen to delay having children, but the patient was making plans for a child when her husband lost his life in the crash of a private plane while on a business trip abroad.

In the first few sessions she recounted her experiences immediately after being notified of her husband's death. She had felt shock and disbelief at first, and continued to hope against hope that the news was in error until she identified the body two days after the accident in the country where the plane had crashed. The identification had been very traumatic for her; she saw to her horror that his face had suffered severe mutilation. Part of his jaw was gone, and the tissue that remained was bloated and discolored. His mutilated face kept appearing in her mind's eye in what she called a "flash," but it was interesting to hear that as time went on it began to return to its normal appearance without volition on her part; the missing area was filling in, and the swelling was subsiding. Such gradual fading of horror was reminiscent of what happens in the recurring dreams of traumatic neurosis.

The patient kept her husband's ashes in her bedroom in a wooden box. Although she had made plans to dispose of them in several places meaningful in terms of their shared experiences, she found that she kept procrastinating. She had never been able to open the box and examine the ashes, but she could not dispose of them. When she happened to see the Tutankhamen exhibit which was touring the country, she had what she described as a "weird experience." In reading the dates of the excavation of the Tutankhamen tomb and doing some mathematical calculations concerning her husband's birthdate, his age at death, his age at the excavation dates, etc., she had a sudden flash of insight that momentarily persuaded her that her husband had been the King's reincarnation. She quickly saw the absurdity of this and understood that it indicated a wish that her husband could return through reincarnation. This insight was replaced by a search for meaning. Being of a philosophical turn of mind and well-read in Eastern philosophy, she began trying to understand what lessons or meaning her husband's death would reveal to her.

She came weekly for therapy, except for one week during which the box of her husband's ashes was in the therapist's office, where she opened it in his presence; then she came on four consecutive days. She began treatment with a well-developed capacity for the alliance and unusual insight and psychological-mindedness, and she seemed at each session to bring in fresh and absorbing material, showing deep and appropriate affect. She had shared her grief response with no one and seemed eager to unburden herself and to work on some of her difficulties. She very quickly began to work through her problems while the therapist encouraged her and acted as an auxiliary superego to help her overcome her initial resistance based on shame and fear over being what she thought of as weak, dependent, and vulnerable. After the first few visits she had fewer episodes of crying; now they seemed to occur chiefly during her sessions in therapy. Shortly after beginning treatment she took a previously arranged trip which included a plane flight. This was preceded by a dream:

> Five pterodactyls fly over my property. I hide. One of them seems to have a man's body. He swoops down and carries me off. It felt pleasant.

Her immediate associations were that there had been five people in the plane crash, that the pterodactyl was her husband, and that this was a dream of reunion. The therapist offered that her husband has mastered what killed him by being able to fly, and she immediately added "and thus be immortal." She then reported a recurring thought, a quotation from T. S. Eliot's *Quartos*: "After all our searchings we return to the same place and see it for the first time."

She then suggested—as the therapist had been about to do—that it might be therapeutic to open the box of ashes in the therapist's office. Her wish for reunion, seen in the dream, along with the attendant dread, was experienced and worked through in the following way. She brought the box to her therapist's office and left it there in his safe-keeping while together they explored all her fantasies about it. These included what she called her "terrible imaginings"; she had not opened the box because she was afraid she would be impelled to smear the ashes over her face and hug herself if she did so. Although clearly pointing to images of merger, the opening of the box also meant the final separation from her fantasied reunion, and thus an act of "killing" her husband.

On the day she opened the box she was dressed completely in black without realizing the meaning of this, and wore a necklace of seashells. When she opened the box, trembling and with great trepidation, she gasped at unexpectedly seeing chips of bone. She likened these to sea-shells—she and her husband had enjoyed sailing and spent considerable time at the seashore. She sifted through the ashes in an almost caressing manner, then unconsciously patted the side of her jaw. When this gesture was called to her attention, she immediately realized that she was trying to "fix him." She then relaxed and examined the ashes with a more detached interest. After that session she took the ashes home with her and went on to dispose of most of them, keeping some in the box. She would occasionally pat it as she walked out of the room, and engage in fond reminiscence as she did so. The box of ashes continued to be a linking object, but further exploration disclosed that it no longer evoked anxiety and dread, but held a new meaning. At first she said, "I'd rather keep it and not think about it." She explained that if she thought about it she was afraid that she "would think angry thoughts and lose the fond memories." She also thought, "I'm keeping him in the box," and this came to mean that she was holding him as she had been unable to do completely when he was alive. She was somewhat ashamed to realize that she was acting this fantasy out, but her shame gave way to greater interest in her motivation. She began to work with more integration on the ambivalence she felt, trying to sort out and reconcile the anger she had been denying and the affectionate feelings that had contained an over-idealization of her husband. At this point, "further unfinished business" came up when she described in greater detail her experience of mourning the death of her father when she had been in her early twenties. He had died of metastatic cancer and until the end so used denial that she had been unable to discuss his impending death with him. Any approach to the subject disturbed him and with tears in her eyes she would begin talking of something more hopeful. She felt that she had never had "the chance to say goodbye," and she realized that this had been true also with her husband.

After six months, reference was made to terminating her treatment. She was reluctant to terminate, recognizing spontaneously that this would involve yet another separation and experience of grief that she would have to resolve. She recognized also that the positive feelings and the closeness and intimacy that she had invested in her treatment had served at some level as a replacement for the loss of closeness and sharing with her husband. She reported what she called a termination dream. In this she was a schoolgirl painting with great care and in considerable detail the portrait of a girl. She was unable to finish the portrait in the time allotted because when she applied the brush to one eye and one side of the mouth no color resulted although the rest of the face had been colored without difficulty. She thought, "Oh well, I can always come back and finish it later; besides, what I've done is beautiful." She saw the incomplete eye as evidence that there was more to see about herself, and the incomplete mouth as testimony that there was more to say.

The therapist offered the interpretation that the lack of color around the eye represented her tears, and wondered about the incomplete mouth as representing her husband's jaw. This made her tearful and she said, "I thought I had gotten over identifying with him." She went on to describe her feeling that a piece of her had died with him. Delineating a small square space with her hands, she spoke of "this space in me where he resides." However, there was now a boundary around her and the dream, and the dream face, although a fusion of herself with her husband, was also separate from her, the dreamer. The suggestion in the dream that she could "finish the portrait later" represented her thinking that she might like to be analyzed at some future time since some characterological issues—some obsessional and superego features, and her concerns about dependency—had come into discussion. Agreement had been reached that analysis might await fuller resolution of her grief. The feeling that the rest of the painting was beautiful had to do, she surmised, with her feeling of being otherwise fairly hopeful and optimistic about herself and her life. Thus a termination date was planned for a short time after the first anniversary of her husband's death.

During the termination period she presented what she called a "healing dream." It was introduced in association with her mention of a man she had been seeing toward whom she now felt it possible that she might come to respond deeply; she had until then been judging men as, first, not her husband, and then, not like him.

I was running in a marathon, a peculiar kind with a lot of obstacles, over a gorge. It was 26.2 miles. My husband was there encouraging me. In the first part of the dream it was as if I were running in a slow motion. I thought I'd never do it. It got dark. I didn't want to stop but I was afraid I'd trip in the dark. My husband went into a store, bought me a flashlight, and gave it to me.

> I was able to run easily. The next morning I had finished the race. Getting the light was a great relief. At the finish, where I placed or what my time was didn't matter—it was a notable finish.

She immediately connected this dream with her experience in therapy and the past year of dealing with her husband's death—how hard it had been, how slow and painful. In association to getting the light she felt that her husband's death had made her aware of troubles previously warded off, and that the therapist had given her the light of the therapeutic process to guide her way. She began that session with a radiant smile which reflected her relief and well-being—her delight at finishing the race after dreaming heretofore of incompleteness. She had not finished grieving, but the obstacles and complications of her grief were gone. The obstacle of the gorge or chasm with an unfathomable black bottom represented her wish for union with her husband in death. She had gotten over that obstacle, hand over hand, in therapy. The finish of the race, which came in the morning in the dream, transformed *mourning* into *morning;* she associated to this by saying that she had once again begun to enjoy the morning sunrise on her way to work. She wept as she said that although she had been eager to tell her therapist this dream, it also made her very sad because it was so evident that she was ready to leave him. He had appeared as her husband in the dream as she lived again through the loss of her husband with him. She felt that if she could set a date for terminating therapy she could prepare herself for losing the therapist, and feel some control over the loss as she had been unable to do when she lost her husband so unexpectedly. She was wearing a black dress, but a white blouse and grey jacket with it, and she commented that she realized after dressing so that she had finally become able to blend white and black.

REFERENCES

1. Abraham, K. (1924). A short study of the development of the libido, viewed in the light of mental disorders. In: *Selected Papers in Psycho-Analysis.* London: Hogarth Press, 1927, pp. 418-501.
2. Bak, R. C. Fetishism. *J. Amer. Psychoanal. Assoc.,* 1953, 1:285-298.
3. Bibring, E. The mechanism of depression. In: P. Greenacre (Ed.), *Affective Disorders.* New York: International Universities Press, 1953.
4. Bowlby, J. Process of mourning. *Int. J. Psycho-Anal.,* 1961, 42:317-340.
5. Bowlby, J. and Parkes, C. M. Separation and loss within the family. In: E. J. Anthony and Cyrille Koupernik (Eds.), *The Child in His Family,* vol. I. New York: Wiley Interscience, 1970.
6. Brown, F. and Epps, P. Childhood bereavement and subsequent crime. *Brit. J. Psychiat.,* 1966, 112:1043-1048.

7. Deutsch, H. Absence of grief. *Psychoanal. Quart.*, 1937, 6:12-23.
8. Engel, G. L. Is grief a disease? A challenge for medical research. *Psychosom. Med.*, 1961, 23:18-22.
9. Engel, G. L. *Psychological Development in Health and Disease*. Philadelphia: W. B. Saunders, 1962.
10. Evans, P. and Liggett, J. Loss and bereavement as factors in agoraphobia: Implications for therapy. *Brit. J. Med. Psychol.*, 1971, 44:149-154.
11. Fenichel, O. *The Psychoanalytic Theory of Neurosis*. New York: Norton, 1945.
12. Freud, S. (1917). *Mourning and Melancholia*. In: J. Strachey (Ed.), *The Complete Psychological Works of Sigmund Freud, Standard Edition*. London: Hogarth Press, 1957, 14:237-258.
13. Freud, S. (1927) *Fetishism*. In: J. Strachey (Ed.), *The Complete Psychological Works of Sigmund Freud, Standard Edition*. London: Hogarth Press, 1961, 21:149-157.
14. Freud, S. (1940). *Splitting of the Ego in the Process of Defense*. In: J. Strachey (Ed.), *The Complete Psychological Works of Sigmund Freud*. London: Hogarth Press, 1964, 23:271-278.
15. Greenacre, P. The fetish and the transitional object. *Psychoanal. Study Child*, 1969, 24:144-164.
16. Jaffe, D. S. The mechanism of projection: Its dual role in object relations. *Int. J. Psycho-Anal.*, 1968, 49:662-677.
17. Kübler-Ross, E. *On Death and Dying*. New York: The Macmillan Company, 1969.
18. Lehrman, S. R. Reactions to untimely death. *Psychiat. Quart.*, 1956, 30:565-579.
19. Loewald, H. Internalization, separation, mourning and the superego. *Psychoanal. Quart.*, 1962, 31:483-504.
20. Lidz, T. Emotional factors in the etiology of hyperthyroidism. *Psychosom. Med.*, 1949, 11:2-9.
21. Mahler, M. S. *On Human Symbolism and the Vicissitudes of Individuation*. New York: International Universities Press, 1968.
22. McDermott, N. T. and Cobb, S. A psychiatric survey of fifty cases of bronchial asthma. *Psychosom. Med.*, 1939, 1:203-245.
23. Nagera, H. Children's reactions to the death of important objects, a developmental approach. *Psychoanal. Study Child*, 1970, 25:360-400.
24. Parkes, C. M. Recent bereavement as a cause of mental illness. *Brit. J. Psychiat.*, 1964, 110:198-205.
25. Parkes, C. M. *Bereavement, Studies of Grief in Adult Life*. New York: International Universities Press, 1972.
26. Parkes, C. M. and Brown, R. J. Health after bereavement: A controlled study of young Boston widows and widowers. *Psychosom. Med.*, 1972, 34:449-461.
27. Peck, M. W. Notes on identification in a case of depressive reaction to the death of a love object. *Psychoanal. Quart.*, 1939, 8:1-18.
28. Pollock, G. Mourning and adaptation. *Int. J. Psycho-Anal.*, 1961, 42:341-361.
29. Pollock, G. Anniversary reactions, trauma and mourning. *Psychoanal. Quart.*, 1970, 39:347-371.
30. Pollock, G. Temporal anniversary manifestations: hour, day, holiday. *Psychoanal. Quart.*, 1971, 40:123-131.
31. Pollock, G. On mourning, immortality, and Utopia. *J. Amer. Psychoanal. Assoc.* 1975, 23:334-362.
32. Pollock, G. The mourning process and creative organization. *J. Amer. Psychoanal. Assoc.*, 1977, 25:3-34.
33. Schmale, A. H. Relationship of separation and depression to disease. I. A report on a hospitalized medical population. *Psychosom. Med.*, 1958, 20:259-275.

34. Schuster, D. B. A note on grief. *Bulletin of the Philadelphia Association for Psychoanalysis,* 1969, 19:87-90.
35. Smith, J. H. Identificatory styles in depression and grief. *Int. J. Psycho-Anal.,* 1971, 52:259-266.
36. Speers, R. W. and Lansing, C. *Group Therapy in Childhood Psychosis.* Chapel Hill, North Carolina: University of North Carolina Press, 1965.
37. Sperling, M. Fetishism in children. *Psychoanal. Quart.,* 1963, 32:374-392.
38. Volkan, V. D. The observation of the "little man" phenomenon in a case of anorexia nervosa. *Brit. J. Med. Psychol.,* 1965, 38:299-311.
39. Volkan, V. D. Normal and pathological grief reactions—A guide for the family physician. *Virginia Medical Monthly,* 1966, 93:651-656.
40. Volkan, V. D. Typical findings in pathological grief. *Psychiat. Quart.,* 1970, 44: 231-250.
41. Volkan, V. D. A study of a patient's re-grief work through dreams, psychological tests and psychoanalysis. *Psychiat. Quart.,* 1971, 45:255-273.
42. Volkan, V. D. The recognition and prevention of pathological grief. *Virginia Medical Monthly,* 1972a, 99:535-540.
43. Volkan, V.D. The linking objects of pathological mourners. *Arch. Gen. Psychiat.,* 1972b, 27:215-221.
44. Volkan, V. D. Death, divorce and the physician. In: D. W. Abse, E. M. Nash, and L. M. R. Louden (Eds.), *Marital and Sexual Counseling in Medical Practice.* Harper & Row, 1974, pp. 446-462.
45. Volkan, V. D. *Primitive Internalized Object Relations.* New York: International Universities Press, 1976.
46. Volkan, V. D., Cillufo, A. F., and Sarvay, T. L. Re-grief therapy and the function of the linking object as a key to stimulate emotionality. In: P. T. Olson (Ed.), *Emotional Flooding.* New York: Human Sciences Press, 1975, pp. 179-224.
47. Volkan, V. D. and Showalter, C. R. Known object loss, disturbances in reality testing, and "re-grief" work as a method of brief psychotherapy. *Psychiat. Quart.,* 1968, 42:358-374.
48. Wahl, C. W. The differential diagnosis of normal and neurotic grief following bereavement. *Psychosomatics,* 1970, 11:104-106.
49. Winnicott, D. W. Transitional objects and transitional phenomena. *Int. J. Psycho-Anal.,* 1953, 34:89-97.
50. Wolfenstein, M. How is mourning possible? *Psychoanal. Study Child.,* 93-123, 1966.

7

The Psychotherapy of the Depressed Patient

MYER MENDELSON, M.D.

CONCEPTUAL ASPECTS

Anyone engaged in the psychotherapy of the depressed patient must not overlook the ambiguities inherent in the term "depression." It has become increasingly clear that this term has been used to refer to a transient mood, to a symptom found in a number of clinical states and to any one of a variety of affective illnesses. Writers on depression often confusingly fail to distinguish between these various uses of the word. Consequently, it is often difficult to know which usage of the term depression their writing has reference to.

One of the most experienced and sophisticated of psychoanalytic writers on depression, Edith Jacobson (1), expresses herself solidly in favor of distinguishing clearly between depressive moods and depressive illness. She is very critical of any tendency to neglect differential diagnostic criteria. She impatiently points out the futility, for example, of doing research on "endogenous types of degression with a group of patients consisting of neurotic, manic-depressive and schizophrenic patients" (p. 170). This kind of research, she emphasizes, "cannot yield scientifically correct, acceptable results." She is critical of writers who fail to make these distinctions. Clearly separating psychodynamic and diagnostic con-

143

siderations, she disagrees with those who, like Beres (2), restrict the diagnosis of depression to those conditions which are characterized by guilt.

She also stands out for her insistence on differential diagnosis within the group of depressive illnesses. Jacobson points to what she regards as quite distinct differences between neurotic and psychotic depressions. She views this distinction as based on "constitutional neuro-physiological processes" (1, p. 183). She describes how differently the psychotic depressive experiences his depression compared with the neurotic depressive. She notes "an impoverishment of the ego" characterized by "feelings of blankness and detachment, inner weariness and apathy, a mental and physical inability to enjoy life and love, sexual impotence (or frigidity) and feelings of deep inferiority, inadequacy and general withdrawnness" (1, pp. 171-172). She refers not only to symptoms such as insomnia, anorexia, amenorrhea, weight loss and other "vegetative" symptoms, but also to the psychosomatic features in the retardation which affect the way that cyclothymics experience their inhibitions, a subjective experience quite different from that of neurotic depressives. Such patients may be unaware of depressed spirits or a depressed mood and may complain primarily about their fatigue and exhaustion. "They may compare the slowing up to a fog settling down in their brain, to a veil drawn over their thinking: to insurmountable walls blocking their feelings, their thinking and their actions" (1, p. 174).

I have referred to her description of the typical subjective experiences in a cyclothymic depression because I believe this is the best such description in the psychoanalytic literature on depression. It is a testimonial to her clinical as well as to her conceptual perspicacity. It corresponds in every detail to what I have observed myself in such patients. And I agree that these experiences are very different from those of the neurotic depressive, although I would label the difference between neurotic and other affective illnesses differently (3, Chapter 1).

Treatment in psychiatry, as well as in medicine generally, is based on some theory of etiology. Insofar as the psychotherapy of the depressed patient is concerned, it is based on an understanding of the particular patient. Before going on to the specifics of psychotherapy, it is, therefore, necessary to make explicit the underlying theoretical structure on which the treatment is based.

As we know, Freud (4) in "Mourning and Melancholia" pointed out that his melancholic patients' self-castigations were not, if one listened carefully, complaints, but rather accusations and could be best understood as accusations leveled not actually at the patient himself but rather at a disappointing love object at whose hands the patient had experienced a rejection. In other words, Freud discerned that the patient's hostility, engendered by the loss or injury that he had suffered, found itself directed by a circuitous route at the patient himself rather than at the appropriate target for his aggression, the rejecting love object.

It was this finding that, later, in the hands of inexperienced therapists, became transformed into a universal formula for the treatment of all depressed patients. In light of this, it is instructive to note Freud's description of the condition that he was discussing:

> The distinguishing mental features of melancholia are a profoundly painful dejection, cessation of interest in the outside world, loss of the capacity to love, inhibition of all activity, and a lowering of the self-regarding feelings to a degree that finds utterance in self-reproaches and self-revilings, and culminates in a delusional expectation of punishment (p. 244).

This is clearly the description of a psychotic depression, a fact which should obviously make one very cautious about applying the findings in "Mourning and Melancholia" too widely. And, in fact, Freud explicitly announced that "any claim to general validity for our conclusions shall be foregone at the outset" (p. 243).

Abraham (5) directed attention to what he considered to be constitutional factors predisposing to melancholia. From his observations of symptoms, fantasies and perversions centering around the mouth, he drew the conclusion that melancholics had a constitutionally determined over-accentuation of oral eroticism which predisposed to fixations at the oral level of psychosexual development. This fixation, he believed, led, as a consequence, to excessive needs and subsequently frequent frustrations associated with acts of eating, drinking, kissing and sucking.

He believed that the increased frequency and intensity of such frustrations made the potential melancholics more vulnerable to disappointments in their relations to their love objects and hence more prone to melancholia. He drew attention, in melancholics, to the frequency of repeated disappointments in parental affection (presumably related to these patients' intensely great oral needs) and their consequent vulnerability to deprivation and disappointment. He believed that the melancholic becomes ill when he experiences a repetition of these early disappointments.

Rado (6) in 1926 translated these concepts into psychological rather than semi-visceral language. He visualized the depressive as comparable to a small child whose self-esteem is dependent on external affection, appreciation, approval and love. He conceptualized the melancholic's vulnerability in terms of his "intensely strong craving for narcissistic gratification" and of his extreme "narcissistic intolerance." As he viewed it, the depressive derives his self-esteem not from his accomplishments and effectiveness but from external sources, a characteristic which constitutes his vulnerability.

He elaborated both on Freud's concept that melancholia occurs after the loss of a love object and on Abraham's emphasis on oral eroticism and the dangers of disappointments in the life of the depressive. He viewed the melancholic's self-derogation as "a great despairing cry for love," a manipulative device unconsciously designed to win back the love that was lost and to undo the disappointment. Rado, thus, in partial contrast to Abraham, viewed the melancholic's vulnerability more purely in psychological terms. He cast his formulation in the framework of external narcissistic supplies to emphasize the precarious self-esteem of the potentially depressed patient who is so dependent on these external supplies.

In 1936 Gero (7), with a more sophisticated grasp of the importance of object relations, expanded the concept of "orality" in a manner that represents the sense in which the term is currently understood—namely, as having to do not only with the sensual gratification of the mucous membrane of the mouth and alimentary canal but also with the emotional satisfactions inherent in the whole mother-child relationship. "The essentially oral pleasure is only one factor in the experience satisfying the infant's need for warmth, touch, love and care" (p. 457). Thus "orality" took on the current symbolic associations of this term, referring to the yearning for "shelter and love and for the warmth of the mother's protecting body," along with the more literal meaning that refers to the libidinal stimulation of the oral zone. It was in this widened sense of the need for dependency, gratification, love, and warmth that Gero agreed with Abraham and Rado in declaring that "oral erotism is the favorite fixation point in the depressive."

Other writers (e.g. 8) began to question the universality of Freud's formulation. They argued that not all depressions were similar to the ones that he had studied. Furthermore, they explained the process that Freud had observed in different ways. Fenichel (9), for example, pointed out that in depression, two distinct intrapsychic processes occurred, an "instinctual regression and a regression in the sphere of the ego." By "instinctual" regression, he referred, of course, to regression to the oral phase of psychosexual development which Freud, Abraham, Rado, and Gero had successively elaborated. He felt that this form of regression was common to both neurotic and psychotic depressions. But he considered that in a psychotic depression or "melancholia," there was, in addition, a regression in the sphere of the ego. As a result of this, the individual could not distinguish himself from the love-object. This led to the substitution of self-vilification for reproaches more appropriately directed at the disappointing love-object. He visualized this as regression to a stage of ego development before there was an awareness of objects as distinct from the self. Thus, accepting Freud's disclaimer to general validity for his formulation, he revised Freud's theory as indicated and restricted his revised version of Freud's formula to psychotic depression.

Furthermore, Fenichel stressed the role of self-esteem in depression by defining a depressive as a "person who is fixated on the state where his self-esteem is regulated by external supplies" (p. 387). He went so far as to state that the precipitating factors in depression "represent either a loss of self-esteem or a loss of supplies which the patient had hoped would secure or even enhance his self-estreem" (p. 390). Among these experiences he listed failures, monetary losses, remorse, a drop in prestige, or the loss by rejection or death of a love partner.

Bibring (10) and Jacobson (1, 11), in somewhat different ways, contributed valuable insights to the understanding of depression. The importance of self-esteem in depression had been particularly stressed by Rado and Fenichel. What Bibring and Jacobson did was to delineate the variety of determinants of self-esteem. In the views of previous writers, the loss of self-esteem in depression was related to the deprivation of oral supplies.

Bibring fully acknowledged the marked frequency of depressions related to the frustration of the "need to get affection, to be loved, to be taken care of, to get 'supplies' or by the opposite need to be independent, self-supporting." However, what represented a quite original contribution was Bibring's thesis that many patients experienced their loss of self-esteem because of the frustration of aspirations other than those associated with the oral level. In other words, he indicated that depressions could be precipitated by frustrations associated with either the anal or the phallic levels of development.

When frustration is associated with anal development, aspirations consist of "the wish to be good, not to be resentful, hostile, defiant, but to be loving, not to be dirty, but to be clean, etc." (p. 38). The failure to attain these goals could precipitate depressions colored by feelings of being too weak and helpless to control one's impulses or by guilt about this lack of control. Depression related to frustrated phallic aspirations such as "the wish to be strong superior, great, secure, not to be weak and insecure" (p. 24), might be characterized by feelings of inadequacy, inferiority and ineffectiveness.

He was aware that the three modes of being depressed often overlapped. However, he maintained that most depressions represented a loss of self-esteem characterized chiefly by feelings of helplessness associated with one or another of the levels of psychosexual development. Clinically, these depressions were characterized respectively by feelings of dependency, loneliness and the need for love, or by feelings of guilt and unworthiness or by feelings of inadequacy and ineffectiveness.

Edith Jacobson (1, 11, 12) considered the subject of depression from the perspective of Hartmann's (13) important contributions to ego psychology. Hartmann had introduced a number of useful refinements in psychoanalytic thinking and terminology. He had, for example, made a distinction between the terms "self" and "ego.' 'As he saw it, the "self" refers to one's own person as distinguished from others. The "ego," on the other hand, refers to a structure of the psychic apparatus which represents an integrated organization of psychic functions referred to as "ego functions." He did not think of the ego, as there is undoubtedly a tendency to do, as a reified part of the brain or as a homunculus directing operations.

He also adopted the terms self-representation or self-image by which he meant the endopsychic representations of our bodily and mental self. In addition, he introduced the analogous concepts of "object-representations" or "object-images" to stand for the endopsychic representations of person- or thing-objects.

Jacobson adopted and expanded this terminology. She, too, along with Rado, Fenichel, Bibring, and others, found that lowered self-esteem represented the core of depression. She, therefore, explored the determinants of this self-esteem that were of such central importance in depression and the multiplicity of depressive states that derived from these different determinants.

She conceptualized one's self-image as not being at first a firm unit but as representing a series of ever-changing transient self-representations derived from the infant's early fluctuating perceptions of himself and of those objects, or part-objects, such as the breast, to which he is exposed. Under optimal circumstances, the self-image gradually becomes integrated into a relatively enduring, consistent endopsychic representation of his self and becomes clearly distinguishable from the internal representations of objects.

In other words, the child begins to acquire a clear sense of his identity and becomes able to distinguish himself from other people. Furthermore, under ideal developmental circumstances, his self-image becomes optimally libidinally cathected. In the context of loving parents and of tolerable frustrations adequately managed, he develops a high level of self-esteem and self-confidence and a lesser likelihood of developing a depression.

When the desirable outcome described above does not occur, the child is burdened with a poorly integrated, aggressively cathected, and inadequately differentiated self-image. Expressed clinically, he is destined to experience problems of identity ("Who am I?") and of low self-esteem (with a predisposition to depression) or difficulties in distinguishing himself from others with possible psychotic troubles of a depressive, paranoid, or schizophrenic type, depending on the vicissitudes of his development.

In addition to this pathological development of the self-image (which essentially represents the reflected appraisal of the patient by his earliest love-objects), Jacobson also examines other determinants of self-esteem. His actual talents, capacity, and achievements also inevitably affect an individual's estimation of himself. Problems in this area may give rise to depressions characterized by feelings of inadequacy and ineffectiveness.

Another determinant of self-esteem is the character of the superego that the individual has developed. If developmental circumstances have endowed the person with a harshly critical superego retaining the unmodulated, exaggerated, fantasy-related version of parental expectations associated with the early years of childhood, then his self-esteem is proportionately vulnerable and his predisposition to depression increased. The type of depression resulting from such a superego may be characterized by feelings of guilt and "badness."

Jacobson also considers the ego-ideal an important determinant of self-esteem, since, of course, the more grandiose and unrealistic the individual's expectations of himself are, the more likely it is that his performance will not match this ego-ideal and the more probable it is that he will suffer a loss of self-esteem, with resultant depression. Depending on the specific characteristics of this ego-ideal and of the patient's expectations of himself, the depression may be characterized by feelings of inadequacy and inferiority or by feelings of guilt and weakness.

Thus, Jacobson makes room in her conceptual framework for a great variety of depressive reactions and does so primarily in the language of ego psychology, rather than in the more simplistic terminology of Bibring, who, while speaking of depression as an ego phenomenon, never-theless used psychosexual fixation points as his major explanatory device.

But what of Freud's formulation of the regressive identification in melancholia? Jacobson conceives of regressive identification as occurring when the boundaries between the self-image and the object-representation dissolve away and result in a fusion of self-and object-images. The target of the patient's hostility—the disappointing object-representation —thus becomes indistinguishable from the self-image; hence self-re-proaches and self-vilification occur. But this kind of dissolution of boundaries between self- and object-representations is by definition a psychotic process. Therefore, the depression resulting from this is, by definition, a psychotic depression, as indeed was the case in the melancholia that Freud described but which by a strange fate mistakenly became the model for all depressive illness.

To remind ourselves of why we have reviewed the psychoanalytic concepts of depression, I must point out again that the treatment of de-pressed patients is necessarily based on some theoretical model of the psychodynamics of depression. However, as we have become aware, the term depression covers a variety of affective states which differ not only overtly, but also subjectively. Many of the previous formulations of de-pression and of the depressive character structure are simply not com-prehensive enough to do justice to the variety of clinical types. Depressed patients are to be found not only among those who are excessively de-pendent for self-esteem on external narcissistic supplies, or only among rigid over-conscientious perfectionists who expect the impossible of them-selves; the spectrum is not nearly so narrow.

This relative multiplicity of depressed states—associated in some in-stances perhaps with private biases on the parts of the authors describing these states—has led to a variety of psychodynamic formulations and conceptualizations of the depressive illnesses, each with partial applica-tion. For different writers, depression has not only different components but also different purposes. For one author it is, in essence, emptiness and loneliness; for another it is rage and guilt. For one observer it is a passive consequence of having sustained a loss in self-esteem; for another it is an active, though distorted, attempt to undo this loss.

A more widespread awareness of the complexity and variety of the depressive reactions will perhaps give rise to less dogmatic and more sophisticated theoretical models.

Of course, how one regards the genetic, constitutional or physiological aspects of the depressive illnesses also affects one's view of the treatment of these conditions.

Although writer after writer has attempted to explain the etiology and mechanisms of depression in psychological terms, there has been evident a lingering feeling of discomfort and an underlying but varying degree of awareness that there was more to the depressive reaction than could be explained by environmental and experiential factors. Kraepelin (14) regarded depression in its various manifestations as essentially a constitutional disease process. Meyer (15) pointed out the therapeutic uselessness of such a focus and determinedly turned toward an examination of the potentially treatable factors in the reaction. Freud did not exclude the possibility that some types of melancholia were constitutional, while proclaiming his field of interest to be the psychologically understandable features of the condition. Yet, even in types of melancholia which he considered essentially psychogenic, he felt that some symptoms, such as diurnal variation, were basically somatic in nature. Abraham, in his effort to understand the choice of neurosis, postulated that in depressives there was an inherited constitutional increased oral eroticism, a heightened capacity of the mucosa of the mouth to experience pleasure with an accompanying increased need and a consequent greater possibility of frustration of this need. Gero broadened the meaning of the term "orality" to include all manifestations of the need for dependency, love and warmth, with the implication that in depressives a heightened constitutional need of this kind stood in greater danger of frustration. Melanie Klein postulated a constitutionally strengthened oral sadism as a possible factor in the most serious deficiencies of development and in psychic illnesses.

Jacobson (1), with her interest in the ego psychological apect of depression, considers the question of predisposition in a somewhat different light. First of all she clearly distinguishes neurotic from psychotic depression and feels that the latter represents not only a mental but an unknown psychosomatic process. She believes that psychotic patients are predisposed to total regressive processes by an arrested defective ego and superego development, the result of their inherited constitution and their infantile history.

Jacobson (1) contends that a psychodynamic approach to the understanding of depressive psychosis is insufficient. She takes issue with writers such as Bibring who reduce the diagnostic lines between the various types of depression to matters of "content." She argues for a qualitative rather than a quantitative difference between psychotic and neurotic depressions. She calls for what Bellak (16) refers to as a "multiple-factor . . . psychosomatic" (p. 5) approach to the affective disorders. Insofar as such an approach deals with the psychological aspects of neurotic or psychotic depression, however, she takes it for granted that it will use psychoanalytic theory.

This brief survey of the gradual evolution of the psychodynamic understanding of depression has been necessary in order to explain and to emphasize the undesirability of a too simplistic view of depressive dynamics. As was mentioned above, Freud's insightful observation of the presence of aggressive components in melancholia has given rise to a tendency to treat all depressives as if their conflicts were identical with those of the psychotic melancholics whom Freud had studied. Too often, even before the psychodynamic issues in a particular depressed patient have been identified, treatment is focused on making the patient aware of hostile feelings and on encouraging him to express these feelings.

As we have seen, the pathognomonic introjection that Freud described represents essentially a psychotic failure to maintain the boundaries of the self-representation rather than a typically depressive mechanism. It is the fusion of self-images and object-images that causes the melancholic to berate himself in terms that are more appropriate to the disappointing object.

Neurotic depressives do not undergo this psychotic regressive process. They do not confuse themselves with the object. And although the self-image may, in psychoanalytic terms, be aggressively cathected by the superego, the "aggression" here refers to instinctual energy, an entity belonging more in the realm of metapsychological conceptualizations than in the world of hostile feelings.

Nor is it universally agreed among psychoanalytic authorities that aggression, even in the form of tension between the superego and the self-image, plays a universal role in depression. Some analysts (e.g. 10) see depression entirely as an ego phenomenon, not involving aggressive cathexes at all. However, even analytic writers who do not question the role of aggression and the superego in depression visualize some types of depression as resulting from a defect in ego development secondary to early disturbed parental interactions. This ego defect results in a self-image inadequately endowed with libidinal cathexis. It results in an individual who chronically feels empty, lonely, and yearning for affection and closeness. Oversimplified, his problem is not that he is inadequately expressing his hatred of others; his problem is that he feels starved for love, closeness, and self-respect.

Even in those patients where seemingly unavoidable resentful and hostile feelings are not being expressed, it is often a therapeutic error to focus on these feelings too early. Frequently, the patient's inability to express or experience these feelings stems from his own sense of unworthiness. It requires a certain amount of self-respect before one can feel resentment at an injury. Before one can experience and express hostility, one's self-esteem must be restored.

Furthermore, not all endogenous depressives are characterized by guilt and by self-castigations. As Jacobson (1) has perceptively noted, they may experience their condition as an illness which robs them of the capacity to function rather than as a state of unworthiness. The balance of psychological and biological elements varies enormously from patient to patient.

Given all this, how does the literature—that is the most sophisticated literature—view the psychotherapy of non-neurotic depression? We found that the views expressed ranged across the spectrum from a determined optimism to a discouraged pessimism. In the early literature, Abraham set the tone with his resolute declaration (17) that psychoanalysis was the "only rational therapy to apply to the manic-depressive psychosis" (p. 154). Of the six patients in his series, two had already completed their analyses. One of these analyses had taken what seems now to have been the unusually short period of six months. Abraham acknowledged that "it is usually extraordinarily difficult to establish a transference in these patients who have turned away from all the world in their depression" (p. 153) and he advised that treatment should be begun during the free intervals between their attacks because he did not feel that analysis could be carried on with severely inhibited depressed patients.

In 1945 Fenichel (9) summarized the current views on the therapeutic analysis of manic-depressive conditions. He cited three special types of difficulties which must be overcome in the treatment of these patients. The first was the oral fixation, "the remoteness of crucial infantile experiences which the analysis must uncover" (p. 413). The second was the looseness and the ambivalence of the transference. And the third was the inaccessibility of the severely depressed patient. He recommended the free interval as the period of choice for treatment but drew attention to the observation which had also been made by Abraham and other workers that even inaccessible patients who do not appear to be in contact with the world are grateful and may sometimes derive benefit from a patient listener. Fenichel's tempered optimism about the treatment of manic-depressives is revealed in his remark that "even if the analysis fails, the patient is temporarily relieved through the opportunity of unburdening himself by talking" (p. 414). He was much more sanguine about the treatment of neurotic depressives. He felt that they needed no special techniques and presented no problems not found in other neurotic conditions.

Lampl-de Groot (18) felt that a deeply melancholic patient was not amenable to analytic therapy, while Kohut (19) feels that manic-depressive psychosis is not analyzable because of its very considerable psychosomatic component.

Jacobson (1), in her consideration of the efficacy of psychoanalysis and psychoanalytically oriented psychotherapy in the treatment of depressive illness, reveals a wary, discriminating optimism. She considers that treatment is least successful in chronic depressions and in patients who had had depressive episodes and suicidal ideas as far back as childhood. She feels that prognosis is best in patients with hypomanic and compulsive characteristics in their premorbid states, which seems to mean in patients who are most effective in the interpersonal and vocational spheres of their lives. She adheres firmly to the usefulness of making diagnostic distinctions between neurotic depressives and patients with endogenous or psychotic depressions. She notes that treatment goes best in the healthy intervals between depressive episodes but acknowledges that patients are least likely to come for treatment then. She acknowledges that it is often not possible to carry analyses with depressed patients to the point "where their pre-oedipal fantasies and impulses are produced and interpreted" (1, p. 300). Despite all this, Jacobson advocates the use of psychoanalysis or psychoanalytically oriented treatment for depressed patients.

TECHNICAL ASPECTS

Before the patient is accepted for treatment, a therapist's first encounters with a patient usually consist of a period of evaluation, brief or extended. This introductory period should be used not only to identify the dynamic issues that the patient may manifest but also to assess the degree of biological contribution to the depression. The higher the incidence of endogenous or physiological features (e.g., early morning awakening, diurnal variation of symptoms, impairment of concentration, loss of interest, appetite and libido, psychomotor retardation or agitation), the more likely it is that the patient will require antidepressant medications in addition to psychotherapy. The differential usefulness of antidepressants and psychotherapy in such instances is beyond the scope of this chapter and, indeed, is a subject that has not yet been adequately studied.

The therapist must estimate the depth and severity of the depression and the danger of suicide. If there is evidence of a serious suicidal risk, the patient should be hospitalized.

The criteria for the likelihood of a suicidal attempt include the depth of the mood disorder, feelings of hopelessness, and the presence and quality of suicidal thoughts, fantasies, or plans. A criterion that has more to do with the personality structure and the ego functions of the patient than the depression itself has to do with the patient's history of impulsivity or with the degree of control he has over his impulses.

The lifelong, empty, lonely kind of depressed patient may at some point decide that, unless something can be done to make his life seem worthwhile, he will commit suicide. Here the clinician is faced with the management not of a depressive episode but of a long, enduring, lonely or depressed state. A brief period of hospitalization will not abolish the danger of suicide. Unless the inner emptiness and desolation are relieved, the patient may at any point decide that he has had enough distress. And it is impractical to hospitalize a patient like this for the rest of his life.

An empathic, understanding and nonexhortatory attitude on the part of the therapist is a prerequisite in the treatment of depression. Needless to say, the clinician should avoid admonishing or advising the patient to cheer up, to try harder, to stop complaining, or to cease being so absorbed with himself. The probabilities are good that the patient's relatives and friends have been very generous with advice of this type, often to the patient's despair.

The clinician who treats depressives must be able to tolerate the intense dependency needs of many of these patients and the often monotonously recurring complaints. He must be sensitive to certain reactions in himself that may interfere with an effective therapeutic relationship. The patient's incessant complaining may eventually irritate or anger the therapist. If the patient does not seem to be improving, it may threaten his sense of effectiveness. It may then produce a defensive avoidance reaction on his part or perhaps an attitude of antagonism or blame, as if it were the patient's fault that he was not getting well despite all that the therapist was doing.

Jacobson (1) emphasizes the danger of seeming to offer these patients "seductive promises too great to be fulfilled" (1, p. 298). To avoid this she advises that early in treatment, in connection with interpretations regarding the illusory nature of the patients' expectations, one should utter warning about the future. She advocates deviations from the classical technique. For example, she advises only three or four sessions per week, because she believes that this tends to reduce rather than increase the ambivalence of these patients. She has noted that daily sessions are intrepreted by them either as unspoken and really unfulfillable promises or as intolerable obligations which must be masochistically submitted to. However, she acknowledges that more frequent or longer sessions may sometimes be necessary with very deeply depressed patients. Further, she notes that during periods of deep depression, the therapist may serve merely as a patient listener, providing the patient maybe for weeks or months "no more than support from a durable transference which may carry them through the depression" (1, p. 299).

One of the analyst's or therapist's difficult tasks is to adjust his responses and remarks to the patient's psychological rhythm. This is essentially an exercise in subtle empathy. "There must be a continuous, subtle, empathic tie between the analyst and his depressive patients; we must be very careful not to let empty silences grow or not to talk too long, too rapidly and too emphatically; that is, never to give too much or too little. . . . What those patients need is a . . . sufficient amount of spontaneity and flexible adjustment to their mood level, of warm understanding and especially of unwavering respect; attitudes which must not be confused with over-kindness, sympathy, reassurance, etc." (1, p. 280). Jacobson remarks that analysts who tend to be detached in temperament seem to have greater difficulty in treating these patients.

Jacobson takes up the matter of the apparently almost inevitable occasional spontaneous flash of anger on the part of the therapist. She believes that this is a most precarious event since it is, in a sense, a response to the patient's demandingness, for not only does he demand love and affection but, at times, he unconsciously demands a show of power from the analyst. As she observed, when the patient finds that the analyst is no longer able to live up to his expectations of love, he may, in his fear of the complete loss of his object, regress a step further. "The patient may now attempt to hold on at least to the reanimated image of an omnipotent, not loving, but primitive sadistic object" (1, p. 239).

He may try to bring down upon himself a show of strictness, anger and punishment. She feels that the patient prefers an angry therapist to a nonparticipating one, a punitive object to no object. This explosion of anger sometimes serves to carry the patient over a dangerous depressive stage, but, in view of the provocativeness of these patients, she advocates "the most careful self-scrutiny and self-control in the analyst" (1, p. 300).

The first phase of treatment, as Jacobson outlined it, may be marked by the establishment of prompt, intense rapport with the therapist, reflected in idealized fantasies about him and in marked enthusiasm for the treatment. Improvement may follow rapidly. But it is a deceptive improvement which depends on the unrealistic magical quality of the transference feelings and on the "exaggerated idealization and obstinate denial of possible or visible shortcomings of the analyst" (1, p. 288). No real change occurs in the patient but his mood is one of hope and optimism. Success seems certain to him, though perhaps not until a time long in the future.

This phase may then be followed by a period of growing disappointment, which is marked by sporadic doubts about the excellence, wisdom and kindness of the therapist, followed by immediate efforts to transform him again into the loving, idealized image of the patient's former fantasies. Feelings of hopelessness and self-doubt increase. Manifestations of ambivalence become more marked and may be displaced for a time to a third person, perhaps the spouse. Typically, a long period follows in which the patient becomes more and more involved in therapy and withdraws dangerously from other interpersonal relationships. Dependent, masochistic attitudes now characterize the transference, accompanied by demands for self-sacrificing devotion. The transference becomes more ambivalent and the patient, with his attempts to arouse guilt in the therapist for his alleged mistreatment of him, becomes more exhaustingly provocative.

Such a phase may be followed by a deepening of the depression, in which the patient may totally abandon the "bad" object and enter a stage of pathological introjective defenses and narcissistic withdrawal, i.e., his restitutive maneuvers may now be enacted entirely in the psychic plane. The danger of discontinuation of therapy in this phase is great.

Despite the unanswered questions that she freely raises, Jacobson is able to report some considerable success with these trying and difficult patients. She emphasizes the importance of a slow and careful analysis of their transference conflicts, their ego distortions and their superego defects.

A number of other helpful papers on the treatment of depression have recently appeared (e.g., 20, 21, 22). It is interesting that many topics which so exclusively preoccupied previous writers on depression—such as the depressive's self-reproaches, his hostile introjection of the abandoned object, the freeing of his hostility in treatment—now, in the broader perspective of the recent workers, find their place as mere phases in the interpersonal and transference conflicts of these very difficult patients.

Beck (23, 24) has introduced one major new note in the treatment of depressive illness, a technique which he refers to as the cognitive therapy of depression. In brief, his view is that the patient's depression is activated either by the effect of specific stresses or by the overwhelming accumulation of nonspecific stresses on his idiosyncratic cognitive patterns. When activated, these tend to dominate the patient's thinking and produce depressive affective and motivational phenomena.

He believes that cognitive psychotherapy may help the patient symptomatically during the depression by helping him gain objectivity and some control over his automatic pattern. When the patient is not depressed, the treatment is directed toward modifying his idiosyncratic patterns in order to reduce his vulnerability to future depression.

In this insight therapy, an important step is to identify the major maladaptive patterns through a study of the patient's life history. It is usually possible to demonstrate to him that he does not overreact indiscriminately to all situations but that he responds selectively to certain events and experiences. The therapist attempts to help the patient understand these overreactions as the consequences of early-life experiences which produced idiosyncratic sensitivities to certain kinds of stress. Thus the patient is enabled to understand his disturbances in terms of specific problems, rather than as an amorphous collection of symptoms. This in itself gives the patient a beginning sense of mastery over his problems. He may, for example, understand his reaction to an unusual slight by his spouse or by an employer as a stereotyped response dating back to an early feeling of being slighted or perhaps of not receiving preferential treatment.

Many of the techniques that Beck identifies and labels are part of our daily therapeutic work which we do not ordinarily label or identify with technical terms. But technical language of this kind does brings into clear awareness the nature of the therapeutic work that one does. To name, as even primitives know, is to acquire power over what is named.

One criticism that might be made of cognitive therapy is that there seems to be a special emphasis on cognitions having to do with success, failure or guilt. Cognitions having to do with loneliness, emptiness, and loss—not so much distortions as perceptions of painful states—would seem to lend themselves less well to cognitive techniques, except in those instances where negative self-concepts are largely responsible for the patient's inhibitions or lack of self-confidence in establishing satisfying relationships.

However, Beck (23, p. 319; 24, p. 130) acknowledges that the major usefulness of cognitive therapy during a depression is with those reactively depressed neurotic patients who are not severely ill, whose depressions are precipitated by identifiable events and who do not have the characteristics of endogenous depressions. "The depressed patient who is amenable to cognitive psychotherapy generally shows wide fluctuations during the course of a day and also from day to day. These fluctuations, moreover, are related to specific environmental events; positive experiences diminish and negative experiences increase the degree of depression" (23, p. 379, 24, p. 130). This seems to be the description of a neurotic depression rather than an endogenous depressive illness. Despite these reservations, however, it would appear that Beck considers cognitive insight therapy in the post-depressive period to be not limited in its usefulness by these diagnostic and phenomenological characteristics.

There is, as we have seen, widespread agreement that depression is essentially an affective state characterized by a loss of esteem. The therapeutic task, therefore, is to examine the circumstances of this loss and of the factors that predispose the patient to it. The goal of treatment is not only the alleviation or resolution of the depressive symptoms but also the development of the kind of insight that will give the patient greater immunity to subsequent recurrences and that will permit a more successful adaptation to life.

Therapy involves one or more of the following tasks.

1. Where the patient is empty and lonely, the therapeutic task may be to uncover the factors that prevent the patient from achieving the kind of object relationships that are necessary for adequate self-esteem. This may lead into the following areas: helping the patient identify his needs, for not every person is consciously aware of his interpersonal and affectional needs; examining defensive maneuvers that tend to isolate the

patient; identifying self-defeating patterns of relating to members of the opposite sex. To achieve these goals often requires a long period of intensive therapy, especially if the patient has evolved complex or stubborn defenses or personality patterns that interfere with the gratification of his needs.

2. Where the problem is one of guilt, the therapeutic task may involve the modification of an unrealistically harsh conscience, that is, of a superego retaining much of its early unmodulated punitiveness, somehow insufficiently affected by the usually softening influence of the developmental process. Although guilt is probably more characteristic of psychotic depressions, it is by no means unusual in the neurotic depressive reaction.

3. Where the patient's reduced self-esteem is a consequence of an unrealistic feeling of inadequacy, the therapeutic goal, whether accomplished by cognitive or other modes of treatment, will be to help the patient acquire a more realistic perspective on his abilities and talents. This usually includes the modification of an unrealistic ego-ideal in the direction of a more reasonable level of aspiration.

REFERENCES

1. Jacobson, E. *Depression*. New York: International Universities Press, 1971.
2. Beres, D. Superego and depression. In: R. M. Loewenstein, L. M. Newman, M. Schur, and A. J. Solnit (Eds.), *Psychoanalysis—A General Psychology*. New York: International Universities Press, 1966, pp. 479-498.
3. Mendelson, M. *Psychoanalytic Concepts of Depression*, 2nd ed. Flushing, New York: Spectrum, 1974.
4. Freud, S. *Mourning and Melancholia. Standard Edition*. London: Hogarth Press, 1957, 14:237-260, 1917.
5. Abraham, K. (1924). A short study of the development of the libido. In: *Selected Papers on Psycho-Analysis*. London: Hogarth Press and the Institute of Psycho-Analysis, 1927, pp. 418-501.
6. Rado, S. The problem of melancholia. *Int. J. Psychol-Anal.*, 1928, 9:420-438.
7. Gero, G. The construction of depression. *Int. J. Psycho-Anal*, 1936, 17:423-461.
8. Deutsch, H. *Psychoanalysis and the Neuroses*. London: Hogarth Press, and the Institute of Psycho-Analysis, 1932.
9. Fenichel, O. *The Psychoanalytic Theory of Neurosis*. New York: Norton, 1945.
10. Bibring E. The mechanism of depression. In: P. Greenacre (Ed.), *Affective Disorders*. New York: International Universities Press, 1953.
11. Jacobson, E. Contribution to the metapsychology of cyclothymic depression. In: P. Greenacre (Ed.), *Affective Disorders*. New York: International Universities Press, 1953.
12. Jacobson, E. *The Self and the Object World*. New York: International Universities Press, 1964.
13. Hartmann, H. *Ego Psychology and the Problem of Adaptation*. New York: International Universities Press, 1958.
14. Kraepelin, E. *Clinical Psychiatry*. New York: Macmillan, 1902.

15. Meyer, A. The problems of mental reaction types. In: *The Collected Papers of Adolf Meyer,* II. Baltimore: The Johns Hopkins Press, 1951.

16. Bellak, L. *Manic-Depressive Psychosis and Allied Conditions.* New York: Grune & Stratton, 1952.

17. Abraham, K. Notes on the psycho-analytic investigation and treatment of manic-depressive insanity and allied conditions. In: *Selected Papers on Psycho-Analysis.* London: Hogarth Press and The Institute of Psycho-Analysis, 1927, pp. 137-156.

18. Lampl-de Groot, J. Depression and aggression. In: Rudolph M. Loewenstein (Ed.), *Drives, Affects, Behavior.* New York: International Universities Press, 1953.

19. Kohut, H. *The Analysis of the Self.* New York: International Universities Press, 1971.

20. Gibson, R. W. Psychotherapy of manic-depressive states. *Psychiat. Res. Rep. Amer. Psychiat. Assoc.,* 1963, 17:91-102.

21. Levin, S. Some suggestions for treating the depressed patient. *Psychoanal. Quart.,* 1965, 34:37-65.

22. Lorand, S. Adolescent depression. *Int. J. Psycho-Anal.,* 1967, 48:53-60.

23. Beck, A. T. *Depression: Clinical, Experimental and Theoretical Aspects.* New York: Paul B. Hoeber, 1967.

24. Beck, A. T. *The Diagnosis and Management of Depression.* Philadelphia: University of Pennsylvania Press, 1973.

8

Brief Psychotherapy of Stress Response Syndromes

MARDI J. HOROWITZ, M.D.

and

NANCY B. KALTREIDER, M.D.

Stress response syndromes are neurotic reactions to serious life events such as loss or injury. The signs and symptoms include episodes characterized by intrusive ideas, feelings or behavior, as well as episodes which include periods or ideational denial, emotional numbing, and behavioral constriction (5). Preexisting sets of meaning, conflicts, and developmental problems are invariably incorporated into how a person responds to the life event in question. When indicated by the severity or per-

Research on which this article is based was supported by a Clinical Research Center grant from the National Institute of Mental Health (MH 30899-01) to the Center for the Study of Neuroses of the Langley Porter Institute, University of California, San Francisco. Staff and faculty members of the center include: Seymour Boorstein, Dennis Farrell, Eric Gann, Michael Hoyt, Nick Kanas, George Kaplan, Janice Krupnick, Richard Lieberman, Norman Mages, Charles Marmar, Alan Skolnikoff, John Starkweather, Robert Wallerstein, and Nancy Wilner, who also edited this manuscript. Their contribution to these ideas is gratefully acknowledged. Additional research grant support was given by the Fund for Psychoanalytic Research of the American Psychoanalytic Association, the Chapman Research Fund and the general fund of UCSF for bio-medical research (BRSG-05755).

sistence of the reaction, brief psychotherapy can provide both symptom relief and restoration of ongoing personal development. We plan to present here the goals of such brief therapy and several aspects of the related technique.

STRESS RESPONSE SYNDROMES

The word "stress" has connotations ranging from the aggravations of everyday life to the physiologic response states produced by acute and chronic trauma. Here, we discuss stress response syndromes as personal reactions when a sudden, serious life event triggers internal responses with characteristic symptomatic patterns. All persons would be expected to have some reaction to a disruptive event, such as the death of a loved one or a personal injury. Here we focus on responses that, because of intensity or special qualities, reach a level of painful neurotic symptomatology, that interfere with the integration of the event into the life schemata and thus lead the person to seek help. For several years, we have been evaluating and treating such patients in a special outpatient clinic at Langley Porter Institute, University of California at San Francisco. Our experience, theoretically drawing on the work of others (1, 9, 11, 12, 13) has led to formulation of a specific therapeutic strategy based on a pattern of phases and modified by individual character style.

Phases of Response

As reviewed elsewhere (5), a sudden, serious life event may evoke a predictable pattern of response. The affected person may react with an outcry, such as "Oh no, no. It can't be true," or appear stunned and unable to take in the meanings of the loss. Especially in situations where the person has sustained a physical injury and must get help, or has to carry out functions such as planning for a funeral, there is often a phase of effective, well-controlled behavior. Over time, the multiple painful meanings of the event and its disruption of the patient's homeostasis leads to other, less well controlled states of mind.

Particularly prominent is a state of mind characterized by intrusive symptomatology: unbidden thoughts, images, nightmares, pangs of emotion and compulsive behavior. The attempt to deflect such experiences may lead to avoidant symptoms such as conscious warding off of thoughts about the event, isolation of affect, overactivity and overt denial of the meaning and consequences of the loss. Eventually, the implications of the event are worked through, leading to relative completion of the stress response. This rough delineation of phases, with normal and pathological variations, is found in Figure 1. The typical signs and symptoms of the denial and intrusion phases are found in Table 1 and Table 2.

FIGURE 1

STRESS RESPONSE STATES AND PATHOLOGICAL INTENSIFICATION

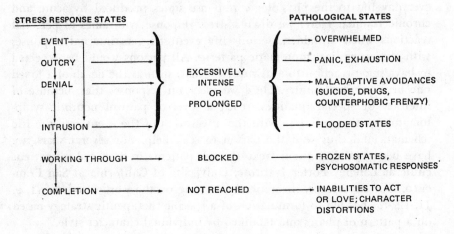

TABLE 1

Denial Phase

PERCEPTION and ATTENTION	Daze
	Selective inattention
	Inability to appreciate significance of stimuli
CONSCIOUSNESS	Amnesia (complete or partial)
	Non-experience
IDEATIONAL PROCESSING	Disavowal of meanings of stimuli
	Loss of reality appropriateness
	Constriction of associational width
	Inflexibility of organization of thought
	Fantasies to counteract reality
EMOTIONAL	Numbness
SOMATIC	Tension-inhibition type symptoms
ACTIONS	Frantic overactivity to withdrawal

TABLE 2

Intrusiveness Phase

PERCEPTION and ATTENTION	Hypervigilance, startle reactions Sleep and dream disturbance
CONSCIOUSNESS	Intrusive-repetitive thoughts and behaviors (illusions, pseudo-hallucinations, nightmares, ruminations and repetitions)
IDEATIONAL PROCESSING	Overgeneralization Inability to concentrate on other topics, preoccupation Confusion and disorganization
EMOTIONAL	Emotional attacks or "pangs"
SOMATIC	Symptomatic sequelae of chronic fight or flight readiness (or of exhaustion)
ACTIONS	Search for lost persons and situations, compulsive repetitions

Pathological Response

The pathological stress response syndrome is one that is prolonged, blocked, or exceeds a tolerable intensity. In other words, pathology is usually not the result of some qualitatively different response, but rather of responses that are of such magnitude that the person requires help, or they are responses that do not progress towards adaptive completion over an extended time. At this point, referral of the patient for psychotherapy is indicated.

A case vignette will be used as an example of a stress response syndrome.

The patient was a 21-year-old female Italian-American college student referred to the Stress Clinic from a local general hospital. Twelve days previously, she and her fiancé were shot by her father, who disapproved of their relationship. Before losing consciousness, the patient recalled watching her fiancé fall to the ground and remembered seeing her father shoot himself. She awoke in the hospital and was told that both her fiancé and her father were dead. She had had surgery for a bullet imbedded in her skull with no impairment remaining other than recurrent headaches and dizziness. She reacted with disbelief, felt "numb," and spent most of the next several days ignoring the event and focusing on physical sequelae from the shooting. Three days prior to discharge, she began having recurrent, unbidden images of the shooting and her life with her fiancé. She also experienced anxiety attacks, crying spells, difficulty falling asleep, and night terrors. These continued until the day after discharge, when she came to the Stress Clinic.

The patient was raised by her mother, whom she describes as hardworking but critical and sometimes emotionally distant. She had no siblings. Her father left the family when she was a few weeks old. The patient always believed he left because she wasn't born a male, an idea reinforced by her mother. She did not see her father until she was in high school, when he made a visit to her home city. She was immediately disappointed, describing him as "seedy-looking, crude, and macho." Although he sent her money and gifts and tried to visit her over the next few years, she managed to avoid him. After several months without communication, the father suddenly reappeared on the day of the shooting. The patient felt that he had learned about her and her relationship with her fiancé through "cronies" sent out to spy on her.

The patient met her fiancé during their first year in college. He was a pre-med student, and she described him as extremely bright, well-liked, kind, and understanding. His intellectual interests motivated her to do better in school; in time, his influence awakened her interest in medicine. The patient described their relationship as unique in her life, in that she had not generally attracted many men since she was always a "tomboy" and preferred to dress "like a boy." Her only other serious boyfriend was someone she had dated for a few months in high school until he left her for another girl (8).

The pattern of treatment of this case will be examined in more detail later on.

TREATMENT OF STRESS RESPONSE SYNDROMES

Goals

If we see the goal of brief therapy as working through a recent serious life event and all its related personal issues to a point of completion, then we can state three goals for therapy that are orienting ideals rather than generally achieved aims.

1. Despite the fact that a person may have experienced a loss or an injury, an ideal goal would allow him to retain a sense of his competence and self-worth. In doing so he would have to accept whatever unalterable limitations were placed on his life plans. This should be done without loss of hope or a sense of meaning in his life.

2. The person should continue realistic and adaptive action. This would include maintenance of available relationships and development of new, adaptively useful ones.

3. In terms of long-range experience and behavior, an ideal goal for completion of working-through reactions to a serious life event would be the use of that opportunity, even with its inevitable losses, for some type of growth.

The Pattern of Treatment

After a serious life event, persons usually reconsider the meanings and plans for response to that event in a manner that is systematic, step by step, and dosed. When emotional responses become excessive, or threaten flooding, the person initiates control operations. The intrinsic property of recollection of the unfinished processing of sets of meanings will tend to counteract these controls. When the person cannot handle both the repetition compulsion (3) and the defensive counters (2), he seeks help. The therapist, after establishing a working alliance, assists the person in working through his natural responses to the event and the overall situation. In addition, efforts may be directed at modification of pre-existing conflicts, developmental difficulties, and defensive styles that made the person unusually vulnerable to traumatization by this particular experience.

Therapy is dependent, in part, on establishing a safe relationship. Once this is done, work within the therapy alters the status of the patient's controls. With a safe relationship and gradual modification of controls, the patient can then proceed to reappraise the serious life event, as well as the meaning associated with it, and make the necessary revisions of his inner models of himself and the world. As reappraisal and revision take place, the person is in a position to make new decisions and to engage in adaptive actions. He can practice the altered models until they gradually become automatic. Overlapping with these processes is the necessity of working through reactions to the approaching loss of the therapist and the therapy.

As the person is able to accommodate to new levels of awareness, this process repeats itself. When he can relate in a still more mutual and intimate manner, he can examine himself more deeply, tnd controls can be modified further. Additional work of this sort may modify aspects of character structure.

Within the time limits of a brief psychotherapy, the therapist works to establish conditions which will be helpful to the processing of the painful event. There is an early testing by the patient both of the safety of the relationship and the therapist's ability to help him cope with symptoms. Most commonly, patients will seek help for intrusive symptoms. These symptoms can seem less overwhelming when the therapist provides support, suggests some immediate structuring of time and events, prescribes medication if anxiety or insomnia is too disruptive, and gives "permission" for the patient to work his feelings through one step at a time rather than as quickly as possible.

Patients who are more handicapped by their avoidance symptoms can be helped by encouragement from the therapist to recollect the stress event with associations and abreactions, while working towards changing attitudes that made the controls necessary.

Frequently, symptoms subside rapidly with the establishment of a good working alliance. Then therapy can focus on the relationship of the stress event to the patient's various self-concepts.

Introduction of the plans for termination several sessions before the final one leads to a reexperience of loss, often with a return of symptomatology. But this time loss can be faced gradually, actively rather than passively, and in a communicative, helping relationship. Specific interpretations of the link of the termination experience to the stress event are made and the final hours center on this theme. At termination, the patient will usually still have symptoms due, in part, to the time needed to process a major loss and to anxiety about the loss of the relationship with the therapist. Follow-up evaluations suggest to us that the therapy serves as a catalyst for both symptomatic and structural change over the ensuing year or more. This very global and generalized overview is diagrammed in Figure 2, for a modal 12-hour therapy.

Illustration of Treatment Course

The pattern of treatment in the case previously presented can now be considered, followed by a closer look at selected facets of the treatment process. The patient previously described was seen for 21 sessions over a period of about four months. No time limit was set at treatment onset, although there was a clear intent to complete a brief therapy. During the first three sessions, her symptoms gradually decreased as she regained control over her actions and thoughts. Following this, she avoided discussing the stress event. She also avoided encounter with angry feelings toward her father and any sense of loss of her fiancé. Instead, she focused on minor physical sequelae from her injuries and spoke idealistically of her fiancé as if he were still alive.

Although she began reexperiencing anxiety, anger, and intrusiveness

FIGURE 2

Examples of Timing in Brief Psychotherapy

Sessions	1.	2.	3.	4.	5.	6.	7. 8. 9. 10.	11. 12.
Relationship Issues	Initial positive feeling for helper	Lull as sense of pressure reduced	Patient tests therapist	Therapeutic alliance deepened			Transference reactions interpreted, when seen and indicated, and linked to other configurations	Working-through focus and termination
Patient Activity	Patient tells story of the event	Event related to life of patient	Patient adds associations		Work on avoidances			
Therapist Activity	Preliminary focus discussed	Therapist takes psychiatric history	Realignment of focus			Termination time discussed		Clarification of unfinished issues with recommendations

just prior to and during her therapist's two-week vacation, which occurred one month after she began treatment, these symptoms disappeared
on his return. The patient spent much of the next two sessions discussing
her plans to return to school in another city. The night before she was to
leave (two months after the stress event), she dramatically called her
therapist at home, saying she was fearful and anxious about returning
to the place where she and her fiancé had spent so many happy months.
She admitted that part of her motive in leaving was to prove to herself
she could "hack it." She calmed down as she spoke to her therapist and
reaffirmed her intent to leave. One week later, she again called
her therapist and stated she was experiencing anxiety and intrusive
thoughts of her fiancé, and had decided to return to continue therapy.

Over the next month and a half, the patient first denied and then
began dealing with feelings of anger and self-blame over the death of
her fiancé. She began making connections between the two separations
from her therapist, the permanent loss of her father and fiancé as a
result of the shooting, and the emotions that resulted from "causing"
her father to leave the family when she was an infant. She discussed her
feelings and viewed her fiancé's death in terms of its realistic meaning.
She expressed a desire to date other men, discussed feelings of guilt
at being unfaithful to the memory of her fiancé, and expressed warm
feelings for her therapist.

During the patient's intrusive stages, the therapist was supportive and
encouraged her to reduce external demands. For example, she was
encouraged to delay enrolling in school because it might activate painful
memories. An anti-anxiety agent was prescribed when needed for occasional symptomatic relief. The therapist often tried to help her organize
her thoughts. Once, when she felt she was "going crazy" because of intrusive thoughts, the therapist helped her put these thoughts into perspective by relating them to the severity of the stress event and to the universality of this type of response to stress. During the avoidance stages,
when the patient eluded discussion of the importance of the stress event,
the therapist focused on the event and encouraged her to be aware of
her emotions and make associations to past conflicts. It was sometimes
necessary to interpret her use of denial and relate it to its defensive
purposes.

The patient had several dynamic conflicts triggered by the stress
event. She had a long history of losses related to men, beginning with
her father's abandonment and continuing with her difficulty in maintaining relationships with boyfriends. She blamed herself for her father's

desertion and felt both angry and guilty at his leaving. The stress event caused her to lose the two significant men in her life, thus reactivating the theme of loss and its attendant unresolved conflicts. This theme was again demonstrated in the transference during the two separations from her therapist, and was reviewed for reality-fantasy comparison in that context.

In addition to these object loss issues, the bodily injury she suffered in the shooting also activated old themes. Her tomboyish dress and manner represented a reaction to the anxiety and insecurity she felt at being born a female. She had always been concerned with her body image. As a result of the stress event, she not only had real physical sequelae, but, after her hair was shaved off for skull surgery, she was often mistaken for a male. These old areas of conflict were explored during the course of therapy in relation to themes associated with the recent stress events.

The final two sessions were devoted to issues of termination. The patient exhibited some transient anxiety at leaving her therapist but was able to admit she was feeling much better and was "ready to go" (8).

Relationship Issues

If we think of a person as coming in after a loss: to the self (as in surgical removal of an organ); of another person (as in the response to the death of a loved one); or after a work situation (as in being fired), then it is obvious that he will test the therapist to see if the therapist will deplete, leave, or insult him. He consciously (and/or unconsciously) will also want to see not only if the therapist is competent to help, but if the therapist will go beyond helping him with this problem to personally replace that which has been lost.

We see the therapeutic alliance as a pathway, with other potential relationships falling to either side. On one side lies the social relationship used as a deflection from work; on the other side of the pathway lies the potential for various transference relationships.

Instead of beginning to communicate the kinds of ideas and feelings that he has been avoiding on his own, the patient may attempt to engage the therapist in ordinary levels of social discourse. He may do this by telling his story, by maintaining a kind of bantering manner, or by trying to find out details about the therapist's personal life and experience with similar life events.

When there is stress response syndrome where the person wears the badge of a recent serious loss, he may tend to do the social things naturally done at those times, such as requesting sympathy and advice on how to manage. To some extent, these requests are realistic, but they also may be tests to see if the therapist expects the relationship to go beyond ordinary social interchange. As the patient tests to see if he is going to be expected to deepen the relationship to the level of the therapeutic alliance, he is also alert and is testing to see if the therapist will do more than this.

In the mind of each person there are certain role relationships that contain feared self-images. The loss implied by most serious life events tends to reduce the stability of more developmentally advanced or compensatory self-images. He now may feel weak, bad, or worthless. Even though his goal is recompensation of a competent self-image, he will sometimes test to see if it is possible that the therapeutic alliance may, in a sense, go too far for him. That is, he may be concerned about reaching some excessive degree of exposure that would be threatening to him. The patient may fear falling in love or being enthralled with the therapist, becoming too needy, or becoming dependent upon exhibiting himself for the therapist. The patient may also fear, as he begins to establish a real attachment to the therapist, that the therapist might then desert him, scorn him, or use him.

In other words, even in a brief therapy focused on the patient's recent serious life event, there are all the various tests and trials that establish the network of communication in a long-term therapy. If the therapeutic alliance is like a pathway, then the patient and therapist can step to either side of the path. Stepping to one side would preserve an excessively social relationship and not deepen it to the usually open communication of a therapeutic alliance; stepping to the other side would intensify transference reactions.

Formation of a therapeutic alliance does not mean that transference reactions will not develop, nor does it mean that the patient and the therapist may not at times engage in social interchange. It does mean that there is a relatively secure and agreed upon model of the roles of each person and the ground rules they will follow. When a transference reaction occurs, it can be examined in contrast to this therapeutic alliance. The image that the patient has of the therapist in the transference can be contrasted with the image that the patient has of the therapist as his therapeutic ally. His self-image within the transference can be contrasted with his self-image in the working relationship. These contrasts and challenges allow the patient to revise or subordinate the self-images and role relationships that have been projected into the transference reaction.

As the therapy progresses, even if it is very brief, the safe relationship is deepened because both parties, but particularly the patient, learn that risks can be taken and result in good outcomes. The patient may work out new levels of awareness, especially about primitive self-images and role relationships activated in response to the life event. Through the therapeutic communication, he may learn new ways of thinking through immediate problems. He may learn these skills, not only directly by insight, but also by identification with the therapist. As in other therapies, the brief treatment of stress response syndromes often produces a period in therapy in which the patient reverses roles. After initial relief he tends to make the therapist feel helpless, just as he has been made to feel helpless by the stressful event. He then watches very carefully to see how the therapist handles helplessness. He copies the therapist's coping maneuvers. If the therapist appears intact he may then allow himself to experience the feelings he has warded off. For example, he may tell about the loss of a loved one in such a moving manner that the therapist feels sad. He watches this very carefully, and if the therapist can feel sad and can tolerate feeling sad, then the patient may allow himself to feel sad and to begin a mourning process.

Information Processing Issues

Let us assume now that the therapeutic alliance is established and within that safe relationship there is work on modifying the status of the patient's controls. Once again, talking particularly about stress response syndromes, one notices two common variations from the ideal path of naturally working through reactions to a serious life event. One is that the person is in a state of relative failure of controls; he feels and acts flooded and overwhelmed by ideas and emotions related to the stress event. The other is that he cannot permit contemplation of the event and its personal implications.

When the person experiences relative failures of control, the activities of the therapist are geared toward helping him to regain a sense of his ability to be self-regulating. This is done through the everyday methods of psychotherapy: by helping the patient to focus attention, by asking questions or repeating comments, and by clarifying statements. Most importantly, it is helped by reconstructive interpretations—interpretations that help the patient to order facts in a sequence of time (7), to make appropriate linkages, and to separate reality from fantasy in order to reduce the threats of reality by reducing the adherence to fantasy expectations. Even when a person is frightened by his own impending death, as when he has a serious and fatal illness, he can often courageously cope with the reality of this, if he is helped to dissociate the real loss, real sadness, and real tragedy from imagined, fearsome consequences such as being entombed while alive, being helpless and deserted by people, and endlessly falling away from life with continued panic-stricken consciousness.

One aspect of working-through a serious life event is review of the various self-images and role relationships that are associated with it. Because of the emotional pain aroused by this review, most patients will have interrupted some aspects of it. In therapy the controls used in that interruption are set aside in a sequential manner. Most of this is done automatically by the patient himself, once he has established a safe relationship with the therapist. When there is reluctance to do so, the therapist, using the repertoire of customary psychotherapeutic interventions, may alter the defensive deployment by interpreting defenses and the reasons for them, by increasing attention to warded-off material through interpretation and labeling, or by simply creating evocative situations into which the patient will bring the ideas and feelings that have been avoided.

The goal is to allow the patient to reappraise and revise his inner thoughts so that models of the world now accord with new realities. This may be reached by establishment of a safe relationship or by additional interventions to alter the status of the patient's control.

As he examines warded off ideas, the patient may find, even after a serious life event where he has sustained a loss, that he is not as vulnerable or as incapable of coping with this event as he had thought. He may also become aware of other real available resources.

Every life event will set in motion a process of analysis of the changes caused by that event, as the mind seeks to maintain a reasonably accurate inner model of the external reality. Therapy will deal with the themes or constellations of meaning that the person cannot process on his own. Certain themes are relatively universal, as indicated in Table 3. The person will examine many of these themes independently and without difficulty. One or another theme, however, will either be accompanied by flooding of emotions, be warded off by pathological defensive maneuvers, or a combination of both. These themes will be a primary focus in therapy.

TABLE 3

Common Concerns After Stressful Life Events

> Fear of repetition.
> Fear of merger with victims.
> Shame and rage over vulnerability.
> Rage at the source.
> Rage at those exempted.
> Fear of loss of control of aggressive impulses.
> Guilt or shame over aggressive impulses.
> Guilt or shame over surviving.
> Sadness over losses.

Realignment of the Therapeutic Focus

The patient will have presented a problem state as a chief complaint or motivation for seeking help. The first focus or agreement between patient and therapist will be to help attenuate this state, or avoid reentry into it. This state will be seen in relation to other states of experience and behavior. A broader analysis of the situation, with the patient, will include examination of the reasons for entry into problem states, as well as other even more threatening states that are warded off. A more detailed analysis of this issue, with a verbatim account of a brief therapy of a stress response syndrome is available in the literature (5).

As this process occurs, there is modification of the focus agreed upon by patient and therapist. At first the focus is a problem state, such as intrusive ideas and pangs of emotion which exceed tolerable limits. As these symptoms are resolved, the focus is on when and why the person enters such painful states. This revised focus often has to do with particular self-images and inner models of role relationships. If the focus is not modified, then the patient tends to move towards termination or avoidance of treatment when he achieves enough control to enter a relatively stable denial phase. We see separation from treatment at this time as an error because the patient has not worked through some of the most difficult issues of his response, and may not do so on his own.

A clinical example may illustrate this point.

> The patient was a young woman in her mid-twenties. She sought help because of feelings of confusion, intense sadness, and loss of initiative six weeks after the unexpected death of her father. Her

first aim was to regain a sense of self-control. This was accomplished within a few sessions, because she found a substitute for the idealized, positive relationship with her father in the relationship with the therapist, and experienced a realistic hope that she could understand and master her changed life circumstances.

As she regained control and could feel pangs of sadness without entering flooded, overwhelmed, or dazed states, she began to wonder what she might accomplish in the therapy and if therapy was worthwhile. The focus gradually shifted from recounting the story of his death, her responses, and the previous relationship with the father to understanding what her current inner relationship to her father was and how her view of that relationship affected her shifts among a variety of self-images. The focus of therapy became her vulnerability to entering states governed by defective, weak, and evil self-images.

Her defective self-images related to feelings that her father had scorned her in recent years because she had not lived up to the ideals that he valued both in himself and in her during an earlier, formative time. He died before she could accomplish her goal of reestablishing a mutual relationship of admiration and respect by convincing him that her modified career line could lead to its own worthwhile accomplishments.

This image of herself as defective was matched by a complementary image of him as scornful of her. Reacting to that interpretation of the relationship, she felt ashamed of herself and angry at him for not confirming her as worthwhile. In this role relationship model, she held him to be strong, even omnipotent, and in a magical way saw his death as his deliberate desertion of her. These ideas had been warded off because of the intense humiliation and rage that would occur if they were clearly represented. But contemplation of such ideas, in the therapeutic alliance, also allowed her to review and reappraise them, revising her view of herself and of him.

Every person has multiple self-images and role relationship models. In this patient, an additional important self-image of herself was as a person too weak to tolerate the loss of a strong father. As is common, no life event occurs in isolation from other life changes, but is almost invariably part of a cluster or domino effect. As she returned from the funeral for her father, she turned to her lover for consolation and sympathy. She had, however, selected a lover who, like her father, was superior, cool and remote. When she needed care and attention he was unable to comfort her, and they separated. Establishment of a therapeutic alliance provided needed support, but termination threatened her once again. In the mid-phase of therapy, it was also necessary to focus on these weak self-images in order to test them against reality and her other self-images as competent and capable of independence.

In addition, a focus was also established on her self-image as an evil, destructive person. It was her belief that persons of sound mind and psychological well-being did not fall physically ill. Her father had died suddenly of a cerebrovascular accident and was thought to be in perfect health until that time. Before his death she had indicated to her father that he was too cold and remote, and had detached himself from a relationship with her that ought to be warm and loving. She now felt as if she had caused him emotional conflicts that had contributed to his hopelessness, guilt, and self-punishment, as well as to his somatic reactions. Her anger with him for deserting her before his death was activated by rage responses at his deserting her by dying. Recognition of incipient hostile thoughts tended to bring forward her evil, destructive self-images. Confrontation with this theme allowed separation of reality from fantasy, reduced guilt, and enabled her to complete this aspect of reviewing implications of the death.

To recapitulate, early in therapy this patient rapidly established a therapeutic alliance, focused on relieving her of the acute distress of the intrusive phase of a stress response syndrome. This alliance led to rapid attentuation of the problem states. With symptom reduction, the focus shifted to the agreed upon aim of working through various aspects of her relationship with her father. In addition to the primary meanings around grief, that is, the loss of continued relationship with her father and hope for working further changes in it, she had to work through several additional themes: herself as scorned by her father, herself as too weak to survive without her father, and herself as evil and partly responsible for his death.

These important self-images, present before the death, were worked with during the mid-phase of therapy. They were related not only to her father, but to other past figures (mother and siblings), current social relationships, and transference themes. As she developed controlled ability to recognize and work with these themes, the focus shifted from past and current versions of these constellations to future issues. Were she to continue with these self-images and views of role relationships, she might either reject men altogether or continue with a neurotic repetition of efforts to regain her father and convert him into the ideal figure she remembered from early adolescence. This prospective work also included examination of her reaction to separation from the therapist and how she would in the future interpret that relationship.

The focus in the therapy shifted from her responses to the death, to four major themes connected associatively to the loss. One theme was the mourning itself: herself as bereaved and her father now as lost except to her memory. Exploration of this theme could not be completed in a brief therapy. The issue in therapy was to normalize the grief process so that she could continue on her own, feeling dejected and sad, but not uncontrollably overwhelmed by the process.

Another theme focused on her self-image as being too weak without the inner model of her strong father to sustain her. Active confrontation with this fantasy was enough to restabilize competent self-images which allowed her to enter and continue mourning.

A third problem image was herself as worthless and defective, in relation to scornful men. She held this preexistent self-image in check by having relationships with older, "superior" men. Their admiration for her was held as an effective but brittle rebuttal to the other premise she held that she was as worthless to them as she had been to her father. This was a core neurotic theme examined in the therapy and related to her future prospects. It was not worked through in the brief therapy. There was, however, the possibility that once she recognized the issue, she might be able to work it through herself in the course of her later life experiences, with resulting structural personality change.

A fourth self-image was herself as evil because she had experienced anger with her father and the associated premise that anger harms others physically. Once this idea was encountered with clear consciousness, it could be dissociated from magical thinking and lose its power to make her feel guilty.

Working with Control Operations

Every person has his own style for controlling the flow of ideas in order to avoid entry into painful states. The shifts in focus just discussed in the case evolved gradually because the person had warded off threatening ideas about herself as guilty for the death, as too weak to cope with it, and as too defective to have a future. Once she contemplated these ideas in the therapeutic alliance, which strengthened and stabilized her competent self-image, she could tolerate and deal with them. But en route to this position, various controls interrupted her associative processes.

Each person will exert different control patterns. While all persons may inhibit some ideas and feelings, switch between reversed ideas and feelings, or slide around the interpretation of an important idea or feeling, each person may favor certain avoidances and certain ways of representing ideas and feelings. Even in a focal therapy aimed at working through ideas and feelings responsive to a serious life event, the technique of the therapist should be sensitively geared to these habitual modes. It is beyond the scope of the present communication to go into detail on varied approaches to the facilitation of information processing. However, three tables (Tables 4, 5, and 6) summarize some of these issues. Relevant discussions may be found elsewhere (4, 5, 6).

TABLE 4

Some "Defects" of the Hysterical Style and Their Counteractants in Therapy

Function	Style as "Defect"	Therapeutic Counter
Perception	Global or selective inattention	Ask for details
Representation	Impressionistic rather than accurate	"Abreaction" and reconstruction
Translation of images and enactions to words	Limited	Encourage talk Provide verbal labels
Associations	Limited by inhibitions Misinterpretations based on schematic stereotypes, deflected from reality to wishes and fears	Encourage production Repetition Clarification
Problem solving	Short circuit to rapid but often erroneous conclusions Avoidance of topic when emotions are unbearable	Keep subject open Interpretations Support

TABLE 5

Some "Defects" of Obsessional Style and Their Counteractants in Therapy

Function	Style as "Defect"	Therapeutic Counter
Perception	Detailed and factual	Ask for overall impressions and statements about emotional experiences
Representation	Isolation of ideas from emotions	Link emotional meanings to ideational meanings
Translation of images to words	Misses emotional meaning in a rapid transition to partial word meanings	Focus attention on images and felt reactions to them
Associations	Shifts sets of meanings back and forth	Holding operations Interpretation of defense and of warded-off meanings
Problem solving	Endless rumination without reaching decisions	Interpretation of reasons for warding off clear decisions

TABLE 6

Some "Defects" of Narcissistic Style and
Their Counteractants in Therapy

Function	Style as "Defect"	Therapeutic Counter
Perception	Focused on praise and blame	Avoid being provoked into either praising or blaming
	Denial of "wounding" information	Tactful timing and wording to counteract denials
Representation	Dislocates attributes as to whether of the self or another person	Clarify who is who in terms of acts, motives, beliefs, and sensations
Translation of images into words	Slides meanings	Consistently define meanings, encourage decisions as to most relevant meanings or weightings
Associations	Overbalanced in terms of finding routes to self enhancement	Hold to other meanings; cautious deflation of grandiose meanings
Problem solving	Distortion of reality to maintain self esteem, obtain illusory gratifications, forgive selves too easily	Point out corruptions (tactfully), encourage and reward reality-fidelity
		Support of self esteem during period of surrender or illusory gratification (real interest of therapist and identification with therapist as non-corrupt person help)
		Help develop appropriate sense of responsibility
		Find out and discourage unrealistic gratification from therapy

Termination

Overlapping with these processes is the recognition by both patient and therapist, especially if a time limit is used, that they must work through detachment from each other. In our work, we now generally set a time limit of 12 sessions; the patient and therapist then know how to pace topics and can relate themes of termination to themes of loss involved in the prior stress event. For example, the approach of an agreed upon endpoint of therapy may be misinterpreted by the patient as a rejection because he is unworthy, as a separation that he is too weak to tolerate, or as a retaliation for his hostile ideas and feelings. Interpretations of transference reactions involved in such views can be related to reactions to the life event and configurations of the developmental past. In this linking work the focus on the stressful event is not lost, but intensified by meaningful linkages to recurrent patterns of self-image and role relationship. These patterns, especially during a termination period, can be examined from different points of view, from the "here and now" of therapy, the "there and now" outside of the therapy, and the "there and then" of the past as reviewed "here and now" in the therapy.

Towards What End?

While there has been general clinical agreement on the gains of working through a focal problem, there has not been agreement on the types of change in character structure that are possible through brief therapy. Some say that radical changes can be made in psychic structure as a result of processes initiated although not completed in brief therapy (10, 11). Others believe such changes in personality structure can only take place in the context of extended psychotherapy or analysis.

In our own treatment of stress response syndromes, we have not yet accumulated sufficient research data to say, on the basis of evaluations, what structural changes generally are possible. We have, however, seen some instances where some personality changes have been set in motion and then accomplished by the patient through life development in the ensuing year or two. We speculate here on some reasons for these observations.

In the previous discussion, we briefly described a process concerned with completing the reaction to a serious life event. This involved working through not only the meanings of the event itself, but its implications for one's relationships, self-images, and behavior in the world. Such work entailed not only reappraisal of the event and reappraisal of the self, but revision of core inner models of self, role relationships and future plans. During this process the person decides to make revisions, plans different types of actions and attitudes, and finally practices new attitudes until new models become as automatic as previous models. This practice continues after termination.

In the course of this work, the patient studies his own responses, not only to this event, but to a series of related life events in the past. Thus, the patient is learning something from the therapy that goes beyond the focal working-through of the specific event. When he is following the more directive interventions of the therapist, he is learning new skills such as the ability to use reflective awareness to think in new ways. When he is following the interpretive line suggested by the therapist, he is learning how to be insightful and how to modify habitual avoidances that usually operate preconsciously or unconsciously.

Patients sometimes become aware, in the course of these brief therapies, of a particular style they have of not thinking about events, and they are able to deliberately alter that situation. It may be possible for them, by continued work on their own after the therapy, to live out changes that may gradually be incremental in altering habitual controls.

When a person experiences the impact of a serious life event, such as a loss or injury, there is threat of undermining his most advanced, adaptive role relationships. There may be regression to earlier role relationships or the meaning of the event itself may tend to create some new role relationship, perhaps with unattractive, dangerous or undesirable characteristics. The person may then enter a series of painful, strongly affective states based on the altered self-images and the changed role relationship. As a consequence of therapeutic facilitation of normal processes, the disturbing role relationships or self-images can once again be subordinated to more adaptive, mature self-images and role relationships. Intensive work in a brief therapy model may both alter the symptomatic response to a stressful life event and facilitate further progress along developmental lines.

REFERENCES

1. Caplan, G. *Approach to Community Mental Health*. New York: Grune & Stratton, 1961.
2. Freud, A. *The Ego and the Mechanisms of Defense*. London: Hogarth Press, 1920, p. 7-64.
3. Freud, S. *Beyond the Pleasure Principle. Standard Edition*, Vol. 18. London: Hogarth Press, 1920, pp. 7-64.
4. Horowitz, M. J. Sliding meanings: A defense against threat in narcissistic personalities. *Int. J. Psychoanal. Psychother.*, 4:167-180. New York: Aronson, 1975.
5. Horowitz, M. J. *Stress Response Syndromes*. New York: Aronson, 1976.
6. Horowitz, M. J. Structure and the processes of change. In: M. J. Horowitz (Ed.), *Hysterical Personality*. New York: Aronson, 1977.

7. Jacobson, G. E. "The Crisis Interview" presented at symposium on "Comparative Psychotherapies," University of Southern California School of Medicine, Department of Psychiatry, Division of Continuing Education. San Diego, Ca.: June 1974, 24-28.
8. Kanas, N., Kaltreider, N. B., and Horowitz, M. J. Response to catastrophe: A case study. *Dis. Nerv. Syst.,* 1977, 37:99-112.
9. Lindemann, E. Symptomatology and management of acute grief. *Amer. J. Psychiat.,* 1944, 101:141-148.
10. Malan, D. *A Study of Brief Psychotherapy.* London: Tavistock, 1963.
11. Malan, D. *Frontier of Brief Psychotherapy.* New York: Plenum, 1976.
12. Mann, J. *Time Limited Psychotherapy.* Cambridge, Mass.: Harvard University Press, 1973.
13. Sifneos, P. E. *Short Term Psychotherapy and Emotional Crisis.* Cambridge, Mass.: Harvard University Press, 1972.

9

Psychotherapy with the Obsessive Personality

LEON SALZMAN, M.D.

PSYCHODYNAMIC CONCEPTION OF OBSESSIVE DISORDERS

The therapy of the obsessional states must bear some relationship to the psychodynamic concepts that underlie the etiology of these obsessive disorders. If one views the problem as a process of holding in check sexual or aggressive impulses, we can hypothesize that the patient is overwhelmed by angry, hostile or sexually exploitative feelings that, if unrestrained, would seriously endanger his existence. Our therapy would, therefore, be directed at helping the patient recognize that, in fact, he has such feelings that he is managing to control by displaced obsessional or compulsive symptoms which impair his functioning.

This notion would encourage the therapist to see the patient's behaviors, overt or subtle, conscious or unconscious, manifest or latent, as distortions, displacements, reaction formations, and the like, of hostile, aggressive or sexual feelings and interpret such feelings in this light. The focus would be on the patient's hostility and even his tender feelings would be viewed as defenses against his hostility. The content of his rituals, doubting, procrastinating, indecisiveness and perfectionistic drives would be visualized by the therapist and translated to the patient as evidence of his hostile designs and intentions towards the significant individuals in his life. The psychotherapeutic process would focus on exposing, interpreting and reviewing these activities to emphasize the hostilities and ultimately relate them to the original libidinal source in the anal psychosexual period of development. The expectation would be that after sufficient exposure of these regressed tendencies through a transference relationship the behavior would be abandoned as unnecessary.

This was the initial conception of these disorders. Freud saw the symptom as a device for dealing with unacceptable hostile or sexual impulses by using displacement, condensation, and symbolization as defenses against them. The symptom, he thought, was a compromise of "doing" the forbidden wish and at the same time "undoing" it. However, not only sexual or hostile impulses need to be controlled, but also the tender, friendly, or stupid and unworthy thoughts and feelings. In my view, *the obsessive-compulsive dynamism is a device for preventing any feeling or thought that might produce shame, loss of pride or status, or a feeling of weakness or deficiency—whether such feelings are hostile, sexual, or otherwise.* I see the obsessional maneuver as an adaptive technique to protect the person from the exposure of any thought or feeling that will endanger his physical or psychological existence. This extends Freud's views and does not require the postulate of an instinct theory or libido theory.

PSYCHOTHERAPY

A rational psychotherapy must include an understanding of the pervasive and persistent tendency to resist change in order to preserve the relative stability of the anxiety-reducing defensive structure. It is also necessary to have a knowledge of techniques of therapy which aid the process of illumination, insight and behavior alterations. Awareness of both the neurotic structure and the overpowering need of the obsessive individual to maintain it intact is crucial in the treatment of the obsessional states. Every tactic, gambit, maneuver, interpretation and clinical intervention must take into account the extraordinary capacity of the obsessional to evade, distract, obfuscate and displace in order to avoid confrontation and change. Tactics which reinforce or encourage those defenses must be avoided by the therapist who, more often than not, has many obsessional characteristics himself.

The essence of the obsessional defenses is antithetical and opposed to the essential requirements of the therapeutic process and militates agaist the exposure and discovery of the patient's deficits and deficiencies. The obsessional often views therapy as a challenge to his omniscience and omnipotence and steadfastly rejects any new awareness which would require him to admit to himself and others that there are matters about which he is unaware. Since he feels he must know it all, he frequently rejects an observation as invalid—only to present it later as his own discovery. The therapist's early tolerance of this tactic must give way to a later confrontation after a positive relationship has been established. This may be long in developing, since the requirements of trust and commitment needed to bind a therapeutic relationship are precisely what the patient fears and tries to avoid.

The overriding need to control one's inner and outer world requires orderly, manageable and guaranteed living. The adaptive devices, such as the ritual, the maintenance of doubts and the unwillingness to commit oneself, along with the attempts of omniscence, omnipotence and striving for perfection and superhuman performance, are all attempts to control one's safety, security and survival. This permits the obsessional to have an illusory feeling of being safe, secure and in control. Being in control means guaranteed certainty and an absolutely secure stance, which interferes with the growth of enough trust for a minimal commitment to therapy. The barrier to trust may never be overcome, regardless of the ostensible cooperative behavior and the willingness to be a patient in an interminable program. No wonder the treatment is long, uncertain and tediously unrewarding for both parties! The obsessional spends many therapy hours in distracting avoidances and contentious disagreements while he is intellectually astute and cognitively capable of clearer analysis. Affectively, however, he is totally unengaged until well into therapy.

To be absolutely safe and certain, it is necessary to know everything in order to predict the future and prepare for every eventuality. The obsessional needs to know everything and emphasizes intellectual attainments above all else. To maintain the fiction of perfection he must never make an error or admit any deficiency. It requires that he never risk being wrong by taking sides, making definite decisions or committing himself to a point of view or course of action, in case it turns out to be the wrong one. This, in turn, produces the classical behavior of the indecisive obsessional, who tries to avoid definitive actions of any kind lest he be wrong.

How do we deal with the indecision, and the unwillingness to make a commitment or express a point of view? We must encourage the patient to take the risk of being unsure and even making an error. He must see that this does not imply danger and total rejection. He must try to experience the reality of being human and uncertain. The therapeutic task, therefore, is to encourage action and decision even when all the facts are unavailable and the issue is in doubt. The therapist must also risk being criticized if the decision he encourages is not the best. This applies to only minor decisions and not to the major ones like marriage, change of job or the like. In cases such as those, the therapist must be very clear and cautious in not providing the patient with the rationalization for his decision and not allowing him to put the responsibility for failure on to the therapist. The patient must be encouraged to take a stand, but the therapist must be the neutral agitator who pushes for a solution without taking sides. In fact, decisions and closures are so difficult for the obsessional that he/she generally makes them by default rather than by committed intention. In any situation the therapist must not take the responsibility for being the decision maker.

The tendency towards procrastination is intimately related to the tendency to doubt as a way of guaranteeing one's omniscience when life forces a decision or a choice. It is the pervasive doubt that produces some of the most bizarre obsessive symptoms, such as trying a door dozens of times to make certain it is, indeed, locked. No sooner has the action been taken than the individual becomes uncertain that he has carried it out. It is also the doubting that produces the "yes-no" response we call ambivalence. One must entertain both feelings or support both sides of every issue in order to come out correct and in control of the situation. The ambivalent attitude in the obsessional is this aspect of playing both sides and promoting an ambiguity and uncertainty which allow him to maintain doubts and to avoid positive feelings and attitudes.

The rituals, whether they relate to hand-washing, checking the lights or door, keeping books in order, etc., are attempts to achieve certainty and control by magical gestures. At the same time, they shift the focus of the patient's interest onto issues not directly related to the main concern. The ritual activity becomes so pervasive and time-consuming that the original reason for engaging in this activity is forgotten.

Attempting to understand the precise meaning of the ritual may be an interesting intellectual exercise, but in general it will not advance the therapeutic process to any appreciable extent. The same problems which stem from investigating the origin of the doubting also apply in the instance of rituals. Further, while the symbolic meaning of the ritual can often be inferred from the various elements in it, an intellectual elucidation of the symbolic acts seldom, if ever, alters the ritual. The classical hand-washing ritual, for example, can be correctly interpreted as an attempt to guarantee safety and survival by eliminating dangerous germs or sexual contamination or wash away guilt. It could also be a device for keeping the person preoccupied and thereby prevent him from getting on with his living. The particular ritual employed may be entirely accidental or coincidental and may have significance only in terms of the setting in which a severe anxiety attack may have occurred. Since the real roots of the ritual lie in deep-seated feelings of uncertainty about one's safety and security, the proper interpretation of its meaning usually does not influence its continuation. The understanding of the purpose of the ritual may be easily and readily accepted by the patient, while at other times the ritual may be so autistic and complicated that its elucidation is impossible.

Generally, the search for the origin of the ritual is not worth the time spent, since one way of evading the therapeutic relationship is for the patient to become preoccupied with descriptions and detailed explanations of the ritual. The presence of many rituals in a patient is some indication of the severity of the obsessional illness and generally implies a poor prognosis, while a paucity of rituals suggests a less severe personality disorder. In either case, the fate of the ritual is tied to the overall treatment progress, and the patient must be so informed from the beginning.

The ritual will be abandoned when the patient's need for magic and ultimate control of himself and the universe is lessened. If the ritual is particularly incapacitating, the therapist might try to attack it directly and either eliminate it or alter it. In doing this, however, it must be clear that the basis for the development of the ritual has been unchanged even though its presence may have been eliminated.

Communication

The obsessional's need for perfection, which colors his communication, is especially complicated and difficult in a treatment situation, since verbal productions are an integral part of the process. In his effort to be precise and clear, the obsessional introduces more and more qualifications in his presentation to be certain the matter is presented in its fullest and most complete form. This adds confusion to the process and, instead of clarifying, tends only to cloud the issues. While it may appear that the patient is deliberately trying to confuse the therapist, the therapist must understand that the patient is trying to be more precise and avoid making errors; he is not trying to sabotage the treatment. The tendency to be distracted and to move off in tangents keeps the patient from getting to the point of his communication and makes exchanges with him seem like a never-ending succession of waves, with each idea setting off a multitude of ripples. Because of the obsessional's tendency to ramble and be distracted, the free association process often serves to defeat its purpose and may involve the therapy in endless trivia and irrelevancies. The therapist must be active and energetic to prevent this development by attempting to interrupt the irrelevancies and focus on the relevant whenever it is apparent to him.

The therapist must always be aware of the limits of his patient's capacities to tolerate certain interpretations or observations; he must stop short lest he increase the defenses which ordinarily protect the patient against anxiety. Anxiety will limit the patient's capacities to observe and acknowledge the therapist's interpretations. When interpretations are seen as criticisms or as deflating to the patient's esteem, the patient will react with even more elaborate defenses. On the other hand, the therapist's observations must not be too bland or they may be easily overlooked.

Activity

Activity on the part of the therapist is absolutely essential from the beginning of the therapy to the end. Even a meagre understanding of the dynamics of the obsessional state requires that the therapist not permit the techniques which defeat communication to continue for too long a time—although the therapist's activities must never be so intense as to overwhelm the patient or make him feel that the therapy is being dominated by the therapist. Free association, as well as the tendency to endless detail and circumstantiality in the obsessive accounts, must be controlled by the therapist. Therapist passivity can only lead to interminable analyses in an atmosphere that becomes more clouded and confused, which is often the reason for the long, fruitless analyses, which characterized an early stage in the development of the methodology of psychoanalytic treatment of the obsessional.

How do we determine what is relevant and what is irrelevant in the clarification of an obsessional problem? The notion that "everything is relevant" in a deterministic view of the mind often leads to endless and interminable inquiries which reinforce the obsessional pattern, while discouraging certain communications may imperil the unfolding of significant and illuminating details. Clinical judgment, based on the growing knowledge of the etiology and maintenance of an obsessional neurosis, permits us to make such decisions with reasonable expectation of success.

One must determine, from the abundance of issues presented, those details and matters which should be dealt with at once and those which can be left for a later date. What is selected depends on many factors, such as the therapist's theoretical orientation, the nature of the main theme currently being explored, the possibility of a potentially enlightening recollection being introduced, or the contradictions or substantiation of earlier material. Of all the possible determinants I would suggest that the most cogent issue is the therapist's treatment plan and the direction he is currently pursuing. He should pick the lead that is generally moving towards the goal.

Emotions

Difficulty in controlling one's feelings and emotions, which is ontogenetically more primitive than intellectual capacity, leads to the tendency to avoid, isolate and displace emotional responses. In addition, feelings may involve or commit one to a person or an idea. The need to control emotions prevents a commitment to the process of therapy, to a person, or to the therapist.

The obsessional exhibits great skill in avoiding any involvement with the therapist, although he may talk extensively about involvement and the problems of transference and countertransference. He will even talk about feelings and emotions. However, it will be a succession of words drawn from an intellectual comprehension of the issues involved, devoid of any real emotional response. It is, therefore, necessary to focus on real feelings and to limit, as much as possible, such intellectual discussions. Obviously, they cannot be avoided entirely, but they can and should be minimized and, whenever possible, the expression of feelings be encouraged with questions such as "How do you feel about that?" or "You must have been annoyed (pleased, etc.)."

Recent Events

Much of the therapeutic process comes from the examination of events that can be explored in the immediacy of the therapeutic hours, especially in the transference relationship. While this is true in any psychotherapeutic situation, whatever the disorder or personality style, it is crucial in the treatment of the obsessional, whose recollections are pervaded with doubts that limit conviction about the interpretations growing out of earlier reconstructions. The endless bickering, qualifying and uncertainty about past events make it much more convincing when the patient can see his distortions or other defensive activity under circumstances where doubts cannot be introduced or used to defeat insight. The most effective technique is the examination of recent events, here-and-now events, which allow for the least distortions. Even under these circumstances there are many complications. It is difficult to avoid getting involved in a "flypaper relationship" or a tug-of-war with the patient, who reacts to what he experiences as control and attempts to put down the therapist and minimize the value of the exploration.

Our desire to explore the emotions is also aided by the tactic of focusing on recent events. The patient can readily discuss the frustrations, disappointments and despairs of previous years. They are behind him and are open to explanations and justifications of many kinds. Past feelings can be described and experienced calmly, judiciously and intellectually, so that the value of their assessment in the therapeutic process is sharply reduced. However, present hostilities and frustrations, particularly as they involve ongoing relationships, are much more difficult to admit. For the patient they represent failures or deficiencies and expose too much of his feeling.

Sharing his feelings of distrust, dislike or liking for the therapist is very difficult, even though he attends to the formal requirements of the therapeutic contact. Anger is much more easily expressed because it is more actively encouraged and presumed to be therapeutic.

The obsessional is often visualized as having stored up hostilities, and the critical element in the resolution of the disorder is the expression of these aggressive feelings. The overriding tendency towards control blankets both tender and hostile feelings; consequently, the obsessional appears to be calm and controlled. However, his hostile feelings are more available to him than his tender feelings; they are invariably expressed in subtle, covert, but unmistakable ways in detracting, derogating, sniping, petty oversights and the like. Direct expressions are avoided but the presence of hostility is apparent to the patient and to others. The tender impulses and affectionate reactions, which are viewed as threatening and dangerous, are securely bound down and rarely exposed overtly or covertly, even in the subtleties of his behavior. The obsessional must learn to identify these feelings and be encouraged to express them. I believe the control over these tender and loving feelings constitutes the essence of the obsessional defenses. It is the failure to express these feelings, rather than his hostile behavior, that initiates retaliatory behavior from others, which in turn stirs up the obsessional's wrath and hostile rejoinders.

The emphasis on the "here and now" by many post-Freudian theorists finds its greatest reward in the treatment of obsessional disorders. The more recent conceptions of mental illness do not focus exclusively on the genesis of these disorders as libidinal deformations, nor do they conceive of the beginnings in relation to any specific trauma. The developments are seen as occurring in an atmosphere in which repeated experiences produce effects on the person in obvious or subtle ways. Therefore, discovering the actual origin or beginning of a symptom or personality characteristic seems of less value than a general recognition of the milieu or atmosphere of the household, or the general attitudes of the parents.

In the adult years, one deals with a problem, the origin of which is only a single element in its continuation; the persistence of the faulty pattern is related to the process of conditioning and habit. Therapy must unravel the detailed and widespread defensive techniques which develop and penetrate into every aspect of the obsessional's life, as well as search for the origins of the symptoms. This requires a knowledge of the patient's present living, in order that the therapist may see the subtleties and intricacies of his defensive processes. This is a most difficult task and comprises the bulk of the work in the therapeutic process. To achieve this the therapist must be prepared for a long and arduous job of repeating the same observations and interpretations frequently before they are truly recognized by the patient. It requires patience and understanding of the tenacious and persistent nature of the obsessional process.

Grandiosity

To deal with his feelings of powerlessness, and his assumption of omnipotence, the obsessional often develops attitudes which get expressed as belittling and condescending feelings towards others, as well as toward the therapist. The patient remains distant but proper in fulfilling his role. Secretly he feels superior and contemptuous of the therapist and feels he is "on" to all that is happening. He catalogues all the therapist's deficiencies, storing them up for use at a proper time. In this way he maintains a secret ammunition cache and an advantage over the therapist. The therapist therefore cannot take for granted that the patient, even though he appears to be pursuing the therapeutic process is, in fact, doing so. He may simply be doing the right thing. It is a long time before such patients can experience and express their doubts and concerns about the process. Their omniscient needs do not allow the recognition of deficiencies and, therefore, they resist interpretations which require them to admit they were ignorant about many things, especially interpersonal relationships.

In order for the patient to accept new insights, he must be encouraged to see how it will benefit him instead of visualizing the disasters that will confront him when he feels helpless and is not in total control of everything. This problem becomes acute when the patient is called upon to try out new insights in his living, and his needs for certainty and guarantees deter him from attempting new and untried pathways or solutions. Since the patient will report difficulties and failures in his attempts at change, this tendency must be clarified to avoid becoming entrenched in his neurotic, circumscribed existence which is experienced as safe because it is familiar.

The obsessional's grandiosity leads him to expect magical leaps and massive advances in therapy. He is impatient with small gains and expects every meaningful interpretation to be followed by great advances or total cure. There is often a profound disappointment when an illuminating exchange is followed by a repetition of the old pattern. When this happens, the patient criticizes the therapist and the psychotherapeutic theory as well as himself because he feels that he has failed to live up to his own grandiose expectations. As he can accept only total and complete restoration of his grandiose self through therapy, he cannot abide the slow, gradual process of learning and changing. This leads him to the frequent charge that the therapy is doing no good—"Nothing has changed; it's been a waste of time and money."

The therapist must avoid trying to justify his work or blaming events on the patient's lack of cooperation. When progress is slow or absent, the therapist should not put the blame on the patient's resistance or resort to the concept of the negative therapeutic response. While many factors may be at work in the negative therapeutic reaction, it is clear that many therapeutic impasses or failures are also caused by the therapist's inadequate handling of the obsessional defense. This the therapist must face and take responsibility for. Therefore, failure cannot be said to be the fault of either the patient or therapist exclusively.

It should be clear that understanding of undue expectation, a need for magical solutions, and feelings of despair and disappointment when immediate success is not forthcoming is of particular significance in the treatment of obsessionals.

Change

The process of therapy involves a tedious examination and exposure of a patient's patterns of behavior which he compulsively maintains and reluctantly alters. The therapist's task is to review and strengthen the patient's awareness of these patterns and assist him in overcoming his doubts about the validity of the view that they play a destructive role in his life. Before any moves can be made to change one's behavior, the individual must have a strong conviction about the need to change and a trust in the understanding derived in collaboration with the therapist. This is especially true with the obsessional who clings rigidly and tenaciously to his behavioral pattern and to his rationalizations and explanations for his behavior. The strength of his defenses demands strict, rigid, compulsive adherence, since the dangers which would unfold if he were to stop defending against anxiety would be severe and dramatic. The obsessional's stickiness, persistent intellectual defiance and resistance to seeing his behavior in alternative ways are intense and stubborn. His views and attitudes are firmly embedded and defended by barricades that must be slowly eroded piece by piece. This requires patience, tolerance and the ability to sustain a continual interest in the face of boring, repetitive behavior which seems to continue in spite of clarification and agreement about its destructive, negative quality. In fact, this is precisely the nature of the compulsive symptom, which is repeated with no alteration and no deviation in spite of the knowledge of its lack of validity.

Consequently, a large part of the therapeutic process is concerned with a review and reexamination of issues that are dealt with over and over again. The therapeutic skill lies in the therapist's ability to see the same issues in a new light, adding an additional piece of insight and reviving an additional recollection to strengthen and fortify the patient's conviction about the understanding so that it becomes such an intrinsic part of himself that he finally sees it as if he discovered it all alone. Familiar neurotic tendencies must be explored from the fresh perspective of different events, which include new pieces of data and additional insights. This also relieves the monotonous refrain of the patient, who says, "We went through that already," and the deadly dullness for the therapist, who must become reconciled to the awareness that a single clarification is rarely followed by a change in behavior. Working-through must be seen as a necessary ingredient in the process of change in providing conviction and trust to risk a new and untried approach that previously was considered dangerous by the patient. This is crucial to the resolution of an obsessional disorder.

Not every obsessional patient presents all of the obsessional characteristics. Some are more prominent than others. Some relate to the need to be in major control by bringing in lists or agendas to the session. Others will have to do with the presence of severe rituals or phobias that occupy the forefront of the communication process. Others are hampered mostly by their grandiosity and contempt for others and still others are overwhelmed by their need for guarantees and certainties that prevent them from taking any risks or accepting any new interpretations.

The particular elements which are most prominent in the patient being treated determine the general principles that need to be applied in each instance. Where intellectual discussions seem to be preeminent, the therapist must permit himself to be somewhat spontaneous in expressing some of his own feelings and perhaps encouraging the expression of feelings from his patient by allowing and fostering the communication of his doubts and certainties. Spontaneous behavior is so difficult for the obsessional that the therapist can encourage this by getting more involved with the patient, taking some risks in exposing some of his own weaknesses so that he can allow the patient to recognize that human fallibility is not a cause for total rejection by others. In this connection it is important for the therapist to be aware of how he is being controlled or manipulated by the obsessional's tactics. The inevitability of being drawn in and being unable to find one's way after being caught in the sticky mesh of obsessional communication need not be viewed as a failure or a weakness of a therapist's technical skill. A review of such entrapments by the therapist can be illuminating as an example of the enormous difficulties in seeing one's way into the process so that one can avoid being caught by the obsessional's tactics.

Each occasion in the development of the interaction with the therapist needs to be seen in the light of the obsessional mechanisms and the therapist's tendencies to be fallible. This allows the process of therapy to be one which is not autocratically determined by the expert and his helpless patient, but rather by two people attempting to explore an issue together in which one has skills the other does not.

Indecision

The indecision of the obsessional is closely related to his morbid doubts. As he requires certainty in every choice he must make and is unwilling to take any risks, it is understandable that he puts off making a decision until he can feel absolutely sure.

It is indecision which keeps the obsessive from coming into therapy early. Once in, however, he may remain endlessly and be unable to leave unless an adequate handling of the therapeutic situation forces a change. He must be very careful, since he presumes that every decision will tie him down permanently, with no way out. This accounts for his tentative acceptance of the exchanges in the therapeutic process; nothing is seen or experienced with any degree of closure, but remains open to alteration or reversal. Therefore, interpretations are rarely accepted with conviction or full agreement, but with a qualifying, uncertain uneasiness. The usual instructions to forego any decision during therapy and to postpone living until more valid decisions can be made play directly into his neurotic pattern. Many obsessionals who should benefit greatly from the psychotherapeutic process find a haven for their neurosis and a reinforcement of their defenses because of inadequate or inept therapeutic handling in this regard. The obsessional prefers to take no action. Thus, psychotherapy, under certain conditions, can become an ideal culture for the enhancement of obsessional doubts and indecisions.

It is only in recent years that psychoanalysts have begun to recognize that the routine therapeutic techniques are not suitable for all types of character structures and sometimes need to be adjusted to the particular characteristics of the personality involved. The obsessional should be encouraged to arrive at conclusions and to make decisions which are the product of a reasonable and adequate exploration of the relevant factors. The technique for dealing with the patient's indecisiveness involves the need to clarify his quest for absolutes and certainties.

Use of Dreams

The analysis of dreams in the therapy of the obsessional must take into account the tendencies to evade and obfuscate the therapeutic process, since such patients tend to either comply or resist suggestions. If the therapist puts undue emphasis on dreams or displays any special interest in them, he may be flooded with dream material, or else get no dreams at all.

There are no particular characteristics of the obsessional's dreams. They reflect the life problems and the emotional relationships of the patient with the therapist, friends, etc., as all dreams do. The patient also utilizes the particular techniques of defense in the dreams which are characteristic of his patient's waking life. As so much of the obsessional's life is preoccupied with problems of control, it is not surprising to find that much of the dream material concerns itself with control.

The dream content should be examined in terms of the "here and now," as it sheds light on the current living of the patient, and can be very illuminating with regard to sources and unacknowledged feelings and attitudes. The tendency to get deeply involved in understanding all the associations and every bit of detail can become a trap for the therapist. It can turn into an obsessional investigation in which the ultimate effect is to become distracted from the main pursuit. The dreams must be treated as simple data and dealt with in the same way as other productions of the patient.

Termination

When the patient comes to therapy, his goal is to achieve a state of anxiety-free living while retaining the same collection of personality traits that he had originally. During the course of therapy the patient must recognize the extreme nature of his demands and accept some limitations of his expectations. It is hoped that he will be able to achieve some balance and compromise; instead of having to be a superhuman, he will be able to function as a fallible human being. This simplified picture of the therapeutic goal of treatment of the obsessional provides some clues as to guidelines in determining a termination date.

What are the criteria for assessing termination? First, there must be a recognition that termination must be done gradually and experimentally, and rarely in an absolute way. To begin with, the number of interview hours can be cut down, or the frequency reduced over a reasonable period of time. Experimental reductions in therapy hours can begin when the patient becomes comfortable enough to accept some reverses in his living which heretofore stimulated panic or severe anxiety. There should also be a reduction of tension in many areas of his living, coupled with a greater emotional involvement in all his relationships. Another criterion is evidence of reduction in ritualistic behavior; also, many of the obsessions which plagued the patient when he came to treatment should have become less tenacious or no longer occur. There should be an increased capacity to enjoy life without having to fulfill certain demands all the time. But even these criteria should be flexible. The therapist must not get trapped into postponing or abandoning his plans to terminate because the patient gets a renewed anxiety attack when termination is under consideration. It must be clearly understood by both patient and therapist that anxiety attacks will occur throughout the life of the patient and that therapy is not a permanent guarantee against disturbed living.

The therapy of the obsessional involves illuminating and exposing the patient's extreme feelings of insecurity and uncertainty—which he tries to handle through the complicated patterns of defense already described in detail. As he comes to understand his neurotic structure as a defense against recognizing these weaknesses, he can then begin to build a new security system. At therapy's inception, the obsessional defense cannot be abandoned because the individual is afraid of the consequences. As his esteem grows and the awareness of his strength increases, he can slowly risk abandoning such patterns and be freed to function on a more productive level. The goal is to move from superhuman expectations to human productiveness—which can reach whatever limits the individual is capable of. When he recovers, his ambitions will no longer be sparked by his neurosis; rather, his achievements will be limited only by his capacities. The impossible goals which left him disappointed will be abandoned. An awareness of his valid capacities to produce may actually stimulate greater activity. In essence, the obsessional must learn that in abandoning rigid, inflexible patterns of behavior designed to control and protect himself, he can actually feel more secure and more capable—and be more productive as well.

10

Psychotherapy in Sexual Dysfunctions

JON K. MEYER, M.D.

Although sex and sexuality are often used synonymously, there are differences in what the words connote. Sex in its abruptness conveys a sense of mechanical acts. There is little subtlety about the word. Sexuality, on the other hand, conveys a sense of progression from sensual awakening to intimacy. Sex connotes what the genitals do; sexuality connotes integrated and highly personal responses including, but by no means limited to, genital involvement (11).

Sexual dissatisfactions are virtually universal among individuals who seek psychotherapy. Hesitation, fright, repugnance, anger, withdrawal, or disappointment infect sexual participation whether or not there is an accompanying incapacity in performance. In fact, the more substantial the ego strengths and the more compensated the neurosis or character disorder, the more likely there are to be failures of satisfaction or impairment of sexual creativity rather than loss of function. What varies is the prominence of sexual complaints, either in consultation or in treatment. Sexual complaints may serve as the principal motivation for treatment, or may be mentioned only in passing. In an analogous way, sexual issues may emerge in treatment as the major arena of conflict and resistance, or may be of little importance.

When the sexual problem is the primary complaint, consultation reveals that sex has replaced sexuality. The sexual efforts are not over-stimulating, unusual, or shocking, but stagnant and unimaginative. Manipulation of orifices has replaced passionate caress. There is fear of giving fantasy its play and intolerance of the tension and controlled aggression in sexual hunger. The sex acts have a concreteness, an anatomical preoccupation, a paucity of fantasy, and a denial of intense emotion, all of which exclude sensuality and intimacy and stultify passion.

In listening to the patient's history and associations, the spouse often fails to emerge three-dimensionally. There seems to be little in the way of shared elements of experience which allows identification and empathic sharing of eroticism. Romantic gestures have become stereotyped and, rather than being enjoyed in themselves, provide the merest pretext for coitus.

The inhibited, mechanical quality of the sexuality, however, does not indicate that the person is without feeling or insight. His sexual inhibitions and fears may seem quite unreasonable, but he is at a loss to be rid of them.

The usual patient with a primary sexual complaint is a young or middle-aged adult who is married or wishes to be. Occasionally, such a relationship is longed for, but feared. There is a sense that it is desirable and possible to have a relationship with another person—usually, though not necessarily, of the opposite sex. In other words, there is a hunger for intimacy, as well as sexual release, and the sense that another person would complement rather than complicate life. Thoughts about children generate mixed feelings. Although there is a concern that children would be an economic stress and a psychological burden, underneath there is the capacity to feel that a child is also a blessing. The patient can perceive, however dimly, that as a child himself he was welcomed and loved at least to the limits of his parents' capacities. Sufficient emotional sustenance was available to him that he can conceive of sharing warmth with a new generation of children.

Clearly, such a patient deserves an opportunity to unfetter his sexuality, and his life, through psychotherapy. The patient's sexuality is our central interest because it is an integral component of his personal and biological enjoyment. His sexuality, however, cannot be viewed or worked with in isolation from the remainder of his personality. Although the sexually handicapped individual may in certain ways be unique in the construction of his illness and in his requirements for psychotherapy, universal issues of individual development, symptom construction and treatment cannot be avoided.

PSYCHOTHERAPY

I have not met a psychiatrist, or practitioner from related psychological or humanistic fields, who did not claim to do psychotherapy. Yet, clearly, what is done and how it is conceptualized vary immensely. While this observation is inescapable in general, it is pointedly apt among those whose special interests are in the treatment of sexual disorders. In this subspeciality methods range from the most abstinent to the most intemperant.

I believe psychotherapy is defined by psychoanalysis by virtue of the elegant simplicity of its assumptions, methods, and observations, and its extended, intensive patient contact. The basic assumption of analysis is that what goes on inside the head, rather than what happens in the surroundings, is most germane to treatment. The patient's rules of thought —governing linkages of feeling, recollection, and anticipation—determine his strengths and pathology and provide the pathway to his recovery.

Fundamental psychoanalytic methodology consists of inviting verbal expression of thoughts and feelings, and then doing as little to impede and as much as possible to expedite the process without directing it. There is a repeatedly confirmed observation that, given a chance, the patient will do his best to manifest his difficulties in living form in treatment, and in the process hear, feel, and rework his conflicts. Frequent contact paves the way for the trust and security that bring guarded thoughts and feelings into the open and for the intense relationship that brings conflicts to life. For those patients, however, who would find the analytic combination of intensity with abstinence disorganizing, dynamic psychotherapy (the psychoanalytic derivative with the same fundamental assumptions) is the treatment of choice.

Other psychotherapies, in one way or another, most often constitute a retreat from the patient and from what is intrinsically emotional in his difficulties. Other methodologies, including those clinical efforts lumped together as "sex therapy," largely utilize counseling (i.e., giving advice or direction), direct education, or manipulation through suggestion. The difference between counseling or educative approaches and dynamic methods is, for example, that rather than giving counsel, we would be interested in what counsel the patient might give himself (and in what way he might be suspicious of it or reluctant to use it).

Sex therapy is the creation of Masters and Johnson, growing out of their laboratory observations (7) and their treatment procedures (8), although in recent years they have appeared unhappy about some extensions and applications of their work. Central to sex therapy is the notion of the uniqueness of sexual problems and their treatment, about which I have previously expressed my reservations (10). Sexual problems differ from other forms of psychiatric difficulty in terms of the manifest symptom, but there are very few differences in the makeup of the illness. To illustrate what I mean, impotence and agoraphobia are clearly different symptoms (and the dynamics behind such symptom choices are important), but there is the distinct possibility that unresolved castration anxiety lies behind both. The phobic state in one case shows up as a fear of leaving the house and in the other as a fear of entering the female genital. The critical factor in the two situations is not the difference in the symptoms, but whether the fear stems from castration anxiety or a more primitive separation anxiety, since the focus of interpretation and concern would be different in the two instances.

Efforts have been made to explain the phenomenal success claimed for sex therapy, but my impression is that such efforts are unnecessary. Recent series (5, 12) have not substantiated the results published by Masters and Johnson (8) and claimed by others (4). Time seems to have passed by sex therapy. The loss of popularity is related in part to the failure to replicate success rates and in part to the well-known phenomenon of therapeutic erosion once initial enthusiasm is exhausted. An additional factor among some sex therapy teams is that clinical success seems to vary directly (factors of patient selection and prognosis being equal) with the latent sexual excitement between the co-therapists. Mutual erotic interest investing the co-therapists' work seems to establish a libidinal field which temporarily fans patients' ardor. Once the work becomes routine and the co-therapists' interest in one another desexualized, success rates drop off (3).

If there has been a major benefit to the use of sex therapy it has been, almost paradoxically, in the education of the patients to the authentic nature of their difficulties. After a couple has been treated with the Masters and Johnson techniques, one partner or both may recognize for the first time the presence of internal resistances to working through a problem initially seen as educational and mechanical. In this sense, the techniques of sex therapy may occasionally be used as an introduction to treatment proper.

SEXUAL DEVELOPMENT AND SYMPTOM CHOICE

In the last decade, simplified assumptions about etiology and symptom maintenance have marked much of the psychiatric writing on sexuality. Some serious authors have justified this simplification on the grounds of data reduction, a commonly employed and useful scientific procedure.

Data reduction, however, is more applicable in systems that operate through mechanical, although not necessarily simple, rules. Biochemical and biomechanical systems, unlike the patient and his fellow human beings, do not defensively disguise, rationalize, deny, forget, negate, reverse or substitute objects or interactions. No matter how complex and marvelous the chemistry of substrate and enzyme, whimsy or perversity is not part of it. When systems follow cut and dried rules, no matter how complex, data reduction is a reasonable goal. When the system is not only as intricate as the human mind but also motivated and capable of synthetic functions, data reduction can become reductionism. Presently, one of the clearest examples of reductionism in the field of human sexuality is the assertion that "homosexuality is like left-handedness," in other words, purely a biological variant (11).

Sexuality is not simply biology. In addition to physical processes leading to arousal, tumescence, and release, sexuality involves the capacity to trust and feel trustworthy, to merge and separate without intolerable anxiety, and to experience the sexual partner as a consort rather than an incestuous parental substitute. Sexuality, physically and subjectively, flows so smoothly when properly integrated that it seems almost natural, yet it is the product of a long, complicated, and difficult developmental sequence.

Although there are elements that are singularly sexual in development, sexuality does not ripen in isolation from other aspects of the personality. Sexual gratification is a single aspect of a broader capacity to feel good about others and to get satisfactions from them. Sexual disorders may present monosymptomatically, but are always strongly and pervasively attached to hidden neurotic conflicts and character defenses. A sexual problem in this light is simply one manifestation, although an important one, of a more complex disorder.

The patient's sexual symptom is a creative, though uncomfortable, synthesis of early experiences, childhood fantasies, and biological needs. Except in incestuous households, sexual performance ordinarily is limited in childhood to masturbation and eroticized peer-level play. Nonetheless, the roots of intimacy, fantasy, and sensuality are put down in infancy.

The roots of emotions and behaviors are like the halting and stumbling first steps in learning how to walk that establish the base for future locomotion, no matter how skillful and sophisticated it may become. Similarly, halting and stumbling early formative experiences with intimacy and sensuality are the germs of later capacities for friendship, intimacy, sexual relations, procreation, and childrearing.

In sexuality, as in other essential components of the personality, there are developmental lines which may be traced through a convergent sequence from infantile emotional dependence to mature sexual and work relationships. In this progression there is an interplay among psyche, constitution, predisposition, and environment to achieve, in the healthy situation, more and more satisfactory levels of mastery and integration. Personality maturation, as distinct from the simple accumulation of years, is dependent upon a "good enough" experience at one stage to allow, seriatim, personality consolidation at succeeding levels. Interference with the normal sequence is usually brought about by a combination of unfortunate relationships, untoward coincidence, constitutional predispositions, and the seductiveness or fearfulness of fantasy.

Sexual development involves the drives, object relations, the psychic structures, and aspects of the self. Although it is known that all these personality components participate in sexual growth, I don't believe the interrelationships and contributions of these factors have been well worked out and so it is only possible to outline a few points.

In the first few months of life, during autistic and symbiotic phases, the essential substrate for psychological development is an empathic and stable relationship between mother and child, which helps the infant deal with his poorly controlled tensions. An empathic mother-infant relationship serves as the feeling basis for comfortable and trusting intimacy in later childhood and in adulthood. From this relationship comes the basic sense that biological needs and tensions are acceptable and appropriate and will call forth an intuitively sensitive response. Without this basic sense, all intimacy suffers, including sexual intimacy.

Sexuality trapped at this oral level is marred by an insatiable emptiness which gives rise to perpetual efforts to extract sustenance from other people. The hopeless inadequacy of any response from others leads to efforts to exact revenge. Emptiness, envy, and destructive rage are the uncomfortable bedfellows of sexual expression.

At five months, or somewhat later, the child normally hatches from the symbiotic shell, slowly at first and then with gathering speed independently moving away and dependently returning to mother in the process of establishing against her grid the capacity to relate as a separate and individual person (6). The child in difficulty at this stage will often manifest night terrors, chronic nightmares, phobias, fear of the dark, fear of being left alone, or a need for the touch of clothes, jewelry, and other items associated with mother. Relative failure at this stage causes separation to be experienced as abandonment and closeness to be feared as engulfment.

The father is important in the separation-individuation process, fostering the inquisitiveness and exploration that leads to separation and differentiation. He is a familiar and caring person, but outside of mother's immediate orbit. Where father is absent, uncaring, effeminate, devalued, or dominated by mother, he is also unable to help his sons disidentify from mother or his daughters shift object choice. Feminine identification or failure to shift object choice has a variety of pathological manifestations in sexual life.

In the pre-oedipal, separation-individuation phase, the drives are strongly tainted with oral and anal components and butt against a severe, primitive superego. The drives, along with self- and object-images, are split into aggressive and libidinal clusters. Internalized objects and identifications are primitive. Sexuality arrested at this level is characterized by perverse trends, being particularly infiltrated with sadomasochism. Coincidentally, there is exquisite sensitivity to engulfment or abandonment with an uneasy oscillation in the degree of intimate contact permitted. In an effort to cope, devices such as fetishes, which are simultaneously bridging and distancing part objects, may be adopted and incorporated into sexuality.

A pre-oedipal appreciation of anatomic, behavioral, and biological differences between males and females leads to a gender identity—a basic sense of maleness or femaleness. I believe that the psychological basis of reproduction—the concept of oneself as an individual who can ultimately bring forth children—is laid down at the same time as gender identity formation. Disorders of gender are associated with aberrations in the psychological fabric of maternity or paternity, with problems of abandonment and engulfment, with primitive internalized objects, and with severe splitting of self and object images along libidinal and aggressive lines. Developmentally, the gender identity disorders are closely linked with the perversions, but are intermediate between the perversions and the psychoses.

The incorporation of significant pre-oedipal psychopathology into a sexual dysfunction has effects in two directions. First, there may be severe impairment of sexuality to the point of lost function, or, second, in the effort to preserve sexual expression, sexuality may be modified by perversion or defensive externalization. In the more usual dysfunctions (e.g., premature ejaculation, impotence, and dyspareunia), dominance of pre-oedipal factors may lead to virtual loss of sexual performance. Pre-oedipal fixation, of course, is often evident in the perversions and the homosexual variants. Perhaps the most impressive defensive externalization I have seen was in a young man who requested sex reassignment. He showed the usual gender dysphoric detachment from his penis and, in fact, wanted it surgically removed. Nonetheless, he was sexually active with remarkable staying power and potency. He took pride in the admiration this elicited from his casual partners although he derived no pleasure and scarcely any physical sensation from the act itself. His penis was psychologically an external instrument. Although psychotherapy was strongly recommended, he did not allow through and, sadly, committed suicide a year or two following consultation.

The separation-individuation phase closes with the sufficient internalization and integration of the mother's caretaking and loving functions that the child can separate periodically without feeling abandoned or regressing in function. Following on its heels is the oedipal phase, during which relationships with parents become highly sexualized, complicated, and triangular. In the positive oedipal constellation girls become coquettish toward their fathers and irascible toward mother while boys are demonstrative, beguiling, or compelling toward their mothers and openly resentful or belligerent toward their fathers. Side by side with the positive oedipus is the negative with an attraction toward the parent of the same sex. An amalgam of positive and negative oedipal longings and identifications makes up the ultimate sexual identification and object preference. Although negative oedipal identifications and object choices predominate in homosexuality, there are opposite sex identifications and longings for intimacy with the same sex even in the most heterosexual individual.

Negotiation of the oedipal stage is a landmark for integrated, individualized sexuality. If all goes well there is an integration of bodily representations, sexual object choice, and masculine and feminine identifications. Sexuality is thoroughly woven into drive structure, identifications, ego ideal, superego, and self. Because of this integration, conflict cannot be defended against in any realm of the personality without compromising sexual interests. Unsatisfactory resolution of the childhood neurosis always compromises sexuality but most often in the direction of dissatisfactions without loss of function.

Latency is classically a time of relative quiet following oedipal storms, but I have never been impressed that boys or girls (particularly boys) were especially latent. They are simply less obvious about their sexual interests than oedipal youngsters or adolescents. Latency boys and girls don't like each other very much and frequently show their contempt. Contemptuous disinterest comes about, in part, as a result of the relative inadequacy of peers in comparison with the original parental object choices. Not only is the little boy licking his wounds after being rejected by his mother or muscled-out by his father, but he is upset about the inadequacy of the little girls to whom he must turn. The antagonism between boys and girls grows out of castration anxiety and penis envy to be sure, but is also designed to demonstrate how second best they feel each other to be. This process is reversed in adolescence with defiant overvaluation of peers, but the reversal is still part of the process of giving up parental objects. The more conflicted the attachment to parental objects, the more second best non-parental objects seem. In some adult couples there is a continuing, nagging, bitterness at the age-appropriate partner which seems very much related to latency-age disappointments.

Latency comes to a stormy end with a surge of biological and psychological development. Changes in physical, coital, and reproductive capacities are new factors to contend with. Any and all areas of conflict are worked through again at a more sophisticated level. Behavioral disorders, antisocial activity, psychosis, depression, homosexual experimentation, or perversion may emerge as signs of long-standing difficulty. In the happy situation, personality consolidation in later adolescence serves as a basis for intimacy. Where the outcome is less fortunate, problems that were acute and flagrant in early adolescence often show signs of settling into a more chronic and crippling form.

The early phase of psychosexual maturity is marked by intimacy and marriage, the prospect of children, and beginning life's work. Later the psychological potential for procreation laid down at the time of gender identity formation finds expression in parenthood and another developmental stage is entered. With conception, gestation, delivery, and child-rearing, the adult's own developmental milestones are reworked in identification with his child and with his parents. Conflicts in the new father or mother may show up as symptoms and distress in the offspring. Alternatively, residual parental conflicts may be catalyzed into symptoms by an offspring's entry into a particular developmental stage. A striking example of this phenomenon from the gender dysphorics, in whom almost everything stands out in bold relief, occurs among a group of men with more or less transvestite histories (9), who precipitously applied for sex reassignment when their sons reached the ages of three to five. Their headlong flight into sex reassignment represented a concrete expression of negative oedipal wishes (in addition to developmentally more primitive wishes for fusion with mother) precipitated by an oedipally-conflicted son. The correspondence between the child's oedipal flowering and the father's anxious quest for sex reassignment indicated a peculiar identification with the child and a special sensitivity to phallic and castration issues (15).

I have outlined some developmental issues related to clinical sexual dysfunctions. My purpose has been to emphasize the sexual symptom in a developmental context as a guide to meaningful diagnosis, prognosis, and treatment selection. The presenting symptom is a guide to treatment only when it is understood as being that outgrowth of a developmental sequence which is the most acceptable synthesis of unresolved conflicts. In sexual disorders as in other psychiatric problems treatment selection and prognosis turn on a determination of ego strength, patterns of defense, superego characteristics, level of drive maturation and the accomplishment of milestones in object relations.

In the clinical setting the commonest sexual symptoms are impotence in the male, anorgasmia in the female, and withdrawal from sexual activity on the part of either sex. Less common, although still prevalent, are premature ejaculation in the male and dyspareunia in the female. The perversions, homosexuality, and the gender identity disorders are of lesser frequency. Ejaculatory incompetence, the sexual anhedonias, and the sexual anesthesias are rare.

Certain sexual symptoms cluster preferentially with particular psychopathological states. For example, the full syndrome of the adult gender identity disorders is associated with pre-oedipal pathology showing up as severe borderline character problems. Similarly, the perversions show some borderline features, although the borderline pathology may be of a relatively mild degree in the well organized perversion. Ejaculatory incompetence is not a perversion, but it is a closely allied condition. Sado-masochistic practices, often of a severe degree, are a regular finding in individuals with retarded ejaculation and, not uncommonly, erection or intravaginal ejaculation requires antecedent sadistic activity.

The probable symptoms of a neurotic patient with a sexual disorder cannot be predicted with certainty. However, as I have mentioned previously, sexual dissatisfaction without loss of function is more likely to be found in neurotic individuals functioning at an oedipal level. On the other hand, dissatisfaction accompanied by frank loss of function or obligatory modification of practice is more likely to be found in borderline individuals functioning at a preoedipal level. Sexual dysfunction, of course, may serve as the visible peak of a psychosis and unwary pursuit of the sexual symptom may precipitate personality fragmentation.

The neurotic choice of a sexual symptom presents intriguing problems. In my experience the sexual dissatisfaction or dysfunction serves at one time or another each of the following secondary functions: As a means of avoiding sexuality and as a means of having at least some sex; as a means of avoiding intimacy and as a means of providing at least some intimacy; as a means of sustaining and as a means of breaking up a relationship; and as a motivation for treatment and as the most substantial resistance to it. The primary function of the sexual symptom varies in its specifics from patient to patient although there is no reason to doubt that it serves as a compromise formation expressing the drive in limited fashion while incorporating superego sanctions and keeping the true aim or object of the drive out of awareness.

THE CONSULTATION INTERVIEW

Consultation interviews are conducted with the outline of sexual development in mind. Since assessment takes time, I ordinarily schedule three evaluation sessions. This provides the opportunity to take a thorough history, during which I take pains to notice the linkages between history and symptom and observe the patient's capacity to hear and work with his own material.

I begin by inquiring after the patient's life and what he can tell me about it, expressing a hope that in the process he will tell me the details of his symptomatology. If the patient is inclined to be silent or vague, I may ask what he has noticed about the onset of his difficulties, its timing, the events associated with exacerbations or remissions, his best sexual experience, his worst, his fantasies, his theories of causation, and so forth. In terms of his life, I may ask him to tell me about his family, his hometown, his wife, etc. Although I may inquire about aspects of the patient's life, my inquiries are carefully framed as questions and not as veiled conclusions.

Inquiring after what the patient has noticed or can recall serves a number of purposes. It keeps descriptions in the patient's frame of reference and avoids hasty, often erroneous assumptions about the nature of his illness. Secondly, steadfast interest in the patient's observations assesses his curiosity about himself and powers of observations, both of which serve as measures of the capacity for self-explorative psychotherapy. Finally, in outlining his observations in detail the patient inevitably makes associations to developmentally significant events or people. The timing of the associations (i.e., their appearance in sequence with specific details of history or symptomatology) establishes presumptive links between history, symptom, and development. As associative points of contact between symptom and genetic history, such material serves to open the door to the meaningful parts of the developmental history.

A difficulty that inexperienced clinicians have with the developmental history is that they tend to administer it in the same way to every patient, almost as a standard interview. While the facts may be obtained in this manner, they are most often meaningless both to the psychiatrist and to the patient because they are not tied in to the patient's memories, affects, or associative linkages. Proceeding in the way I have suggested will uncover the same facts but the facts will come alive.

Extended, apparently unstructured history taking will also give the patient an opportunity to reveal his defensive operations. These essential ingredients of prognosis may show themselves in terms of what is missing from the history, as elements of character, and as reactions to the evaluator's questions or silence. It goes almost without saying that primitive defenses like denial, projection, and splitting portend a difficult therapeutic time, whereas repression, reaction formation, and dissociations are likely to be less formidable (although never easy to work through).

Two insights are prerequisites to restoration of sexual enjoyment and function through psychotherapy: The first is a sense that internal blocks preclude emotional freedom and the second is a hope that things really could be better. For the patient to work on his symptoms usefully, it is critical for him to feel that the sexual inhibitions come from within, however much he may overtly blame his sexual partner or external circumstance. Treatment has little to offer the patient who believes that sexual gratification will be accomplished by changing partners or altering circumstances, or for the patient who has no hope that things could ever be different. For example, although homosexuality is a developmental aberration, the homosexual may be comfortable in his deviancy and be without motivation for treatment. On the other hand, the homosexual may feel hopeless about ever being different even though the inversion's central generative disappointments and conflicts are intuitively grasped. In the one case, there is no motivation for treatment and, in the other, no hope for it.

Once assessment is complete, the decision regarding treatment may be made. Where interest is in remodeling and not renovation, the patient may best be aided by counseling or support. Where there is both the interest in and capacity for personal restoration, analysis or dynamic psychotherapy may be recommended.

TREATMENT

A multiplicity of difficulties may be reflected in sexual dysfunction. Sexuality is plastic and multifaceted, lending itself to the expression of conflicts, fantasies, and aggressive and libidinal drives in subtle and highly personal variations. Sexuality involves objects and their representations in fantasy, allowing the reenactment of unresolved attachments. Sexuality, unlike breathing or eating, is not essential for life itself and may be given up entirely, thereby serving as a vault for intolerable anxieties.

Sexuality is historically at the center of psychoanalytic theory. With the exception of the perversions, however, therapeutic specifics are scarce in the literature despite the ubiquity of sexual inhibitions and dissatisfactions. I believe the reason for the relative absence is that in any analysis sexual conflicts are always present and are dealt with as a matter of course. In other words, sexual problems are so universally dealt with that their very commonness has excluded them from attention. Since the early days of analysis they have attracted little technical commentary. In the following pages I will try to focus on a few issues which, if not unique to sexual difficulties, are more common or exaggerated in such conditions.

Although the general structure of analysis and dynamic psychotherapy is well known, I will outline some aspects that I believe are important. I establish from the beginning the fact that treatment will be open-ended, continuing until the patient is satisfied. Artificial time constraints, which are sometimes employed in sex therapy, focus the work but allow resistance to hold out long enough to cover embarrassing or conflictual material. I ask the patient to report recollections, thoughts, fantasies, bodily feelings, and affects as they come to mind even though the material may seem embarrassing, trivial, offensive, or in violation of some external confidence. It is my aim to aid in this self exploration through open-ended questions about the material at hand and through interpretation of roadblocks to free association and communication. I take special responsibility for maintaining the structure of the treatment situation. I am reliably present and punctual and free from telephones and administrative matters during sessions. I maintain an unwavering respect for the patient which I view as an integral component of the structure. Such respect is easy to sustain. The patient's sexual difficulties are a source of embarrassment, they are of immediate interest to him; treatment is a frightening experience, and a high degree of hope is riding on the outcome. He is also an extraordinary person. Rather than simply living with his problems or demanding to have them accommodated, he has set out on a course of self-exploration designed to remedy them.

Respect for the patient, regard for the structure of the psychotherapeutic situation, free association, interpretation of resistance, and abstinence from immediate gratification pave the way for the analyzable transference. (Transference will come in any event, but will not be analyzable unless the preconditions of analytic structure are met.) Transference brings conflicts and fantasies into the immediacy of the therapeutic relationship, allowing dynamically important affects, object relations, and defenses to be replicated and observed in a current time frame. The transference makes vivid both unsatisfied claims for love and sexual release and prohibited aggressive feelings (13). Transference comes in behavioral as well as in verbal form, showing up in repetitive behavior in the treatment hour and outside. The greater the resistance to remembering and reporting, the more likely the transference is to take the form of repetitive behavior.

Transference operates Janus-like, in two directions, not only as a means to understanding and moderation of psychopathology but also as a stubborn resistance to successful outcome. The phenomenon of transference, however, fundamentally provides an opportunity for real work since a neurotic construction cannot be dismantled purely in retrospect or, as Freud (1) put it, "in absentia." Demands for transference gratification are given up only grudgingly, after considerable effort to make the transference wishes come true. The end point of treatment, of course, is not freedom from all transference, but rather replacement of primitive, conflicted transferences with direct and satisfying eroticism and mature sublimations.

It is not unusual for the patient to fall in love as part of the transference, although "falling in love" is an inadequate and trite description of a powerful and complex phenomenon. As Freud (2) pointed out, falling in love is induced by the treatment situation rather than the charms of the psychiatrist, and its effects are in the service of resistance. Love seems to blossom just when the most difficult and painful material begins to emerge. Having a reputation as a "sex doctor" sometimes lends the erotic transference a more overt and concrete coloration. The demands may be for concrete and immediate alleviation of the sexual frustration. This tendency is more likely in borderline patients where the therapeutic alliance is tenuous and an observing ego difficult to sustain. In such patients the analytic or psychotherapeutic situation is often interpreted as an opportunity to achieve real satisfaction of transference longings, including sexual satisfactions. The assumption is that their difficult sexual situation could be corrected by accepting them as pupils or partners rather than as patients. The difficulties encountered are illustrated by a patient who, upon entering treatment, separated from her husband and made it clear that I was to function as her emotional support, companion, and regulator of her daily life. There were constant disappointed and vituperative attacks because I was insufficiently gallant and accommodating. The wish for immediate symptom relief is common among sexual patients. Other patients may have similar inclinations, but the tendency is more pronounced with sexual dysfunctions because of the publicity given rapid treatment. I deal with this unfounded hope for speedy cure by acknowledging the wish while pointing out the value of symptoms as markers of difficult areas. I assure the patient that he is always free to work on his problem by bringing up sexual associations.

It should go without saying that the patient is not taken up on his or her offer of love. However, since among sex therapists there are those who misunderstand the transference and prescribe their sexual attentions as medicine for the patient's frustrations, it may be necessary to make the point explicitly. Sexual intimacy with patients completely derails treatment. Treatment inevitably terminates without completion, although often not rapidly enough to prevent a great deal of wasted time, money, and therapeutic opportunity. The patient may at first feel elated at the attention or triumphant at toppling the psychiatrist from his pedestal. In the final analysis, however, he feels betrayed. Transference love must be allowed to flourish, but for purposes of understanding and resolution. The analysis of the detailed characteristics of being in love brings to light the infantile and conflicted roots of the patient's symptoms.

Issues of the structure of the treatment situations and the manifestation of transference are as important in the treatment of sexual problems as in other conditions. Issues specifically related to the treatment of sexual disorders, however, can best be approached by grouping the patients ac-

cording to the overall severity of their psychopathology. Although schizophrenic patients may have severe sexual pathology, it is often not
sufficiently organized to deserve consideration as a syndrome. Not infrequently, the sexual symptom serves as a shaky bolster against decompensation and it is ill-advised to remove it. Among severely borderline, less
severely borderline, and neurotic patients (including those with neurotic
characters), organized sexual symptoms may be dealt with profitably for
the patient.

The two more common organized sexual syndromes among patients
with severe borderline pathology are the perversions and the gender
identity disorders (gender dysphoria syndromes; "transsexualism"). There
is considerable pessimism about psychotherapy in the gender dysphoria
syndromes. In part, pessimism is warranted because of the severity of
the disorder, but it derives, in part, from an assumption that the gender
reversal is non-conflictual. If there were unconflicted core gender reversal,
pessimism would be doubly justified. It is axiomatic in psychiatry that
conflict heralds therapeutic opportunity; without conflict there is no
energy driving the therapeutic process. In the cases I have seen, however,
the apparent non-conflictual core gender reversal turns out to be a symptomatic compromise formation that is superficially ego syntonic as in the
perversions. Some patients readily respond to the suggestion for exploratory work so long as their major symptom, the gender dysphoria, is not
attacked head-on. The treatment of these patients is similar to that of
other severe borderline characters and requires the back-up of ready
hospitalization. Since such psychotherapy is in the patient's own best
interest, it should be a routine part of any evaluation for sex reassignment.

I proceed in a similar manner for the gender identity disorders and
for the perversions which have severe borderline personality disturbances.
In both clinical situations, head-on tackling of the perverse conviction
only increases the patient's counter-resistance immeasurably. It is useless for this reason to make giving up the perverse practices or the search
for sex reassignment the condition for treatment. The patient cannot
comply since the symptom protects against ego dissolution.

I set the task of treatment as the patient's reporting his thoughts, feelings, and observations as they come to mind. Although this is standard
analytic technique these patients are seldom, if ever, put in analysis
proper since they cannot tolerate the regression it fosters. Whenever possible I arrange for twice-weekly sessions. I keep the patient sitting up
and make myself more available as a "real person." What this means

is that I am more encouraging, more sympathetic regarding the difficulty of putting thoughts and feelings into words, more obvious in my concern about the serious problems in the patient's relationships with himself and others, and more available by phone and for special sessions than I ordinarily would be within the constraints of psychoanalytic abstinence.

I never deviate, however, from the fundamental position that the task of treatment is for the patient to understand himself through expressing and hearing his thoughts, feelings, recollections, and fantasies as they come to mind. This is the only procedure that will put the patient into contact with the desperate conflicts and all but overwhelming affects which have led him to embrace severe and crippling symptomatology as a preferable alternative. It is difficult to keep in mind that the patient's self-exploration is the essential task in treatment since the patient will resist coming face-to-face with his feelings. He will resist by attempting to have you guess (from the patient's point of view "explain") his thoughts and feelings, to have you endorse his perversion or quest for sex reassignment, or to have you take a stand against his practices. In a variety of ways he will attempt to make his manifest symptoms a battleground in order to completely eclipse the true work of treatment. Needless to say, when the patient's symptom may involve castration and penectomy (as in gender dysphoria) or other severe risk (as in eroticized hanging), it is difficult to resist the battle. It may be necessary to hospitalize the patient to protect his life and physical integrity; on the other hand, it is useless and counterproductive to decry the symptom. The situation is best handled by taking those steps which are necessary to protect the patient while at the same time being interested in the timing of the symptomatic eruption and the thoughts and feelings which accompanied it. Almost without exception, the eruption of the symptomatology will be due to unendurable tension unconsciously related to a loss, a separation, or envious rage at some perceived slight in the therapeutic or other meaningful relationships.

Interpretations of the transference are almost always directed toward loss, emptiness, feelings of personality dissolution, and rage rather than toward the developmentally more advanced concerns of castration anxiety, penis envy, homosexual attraction, or guilt. It is only toward the end of prolonged treatment that such higher order developmental issues may be the dynamics that are truly operative and therefore appropriately interpreted. In fact, as therapy proceeds and the relationship intensifies the transference may become psychotic in its intensity. Under these circumstances, I maintain a low threshold for hospitalization, particularly around times of separation.

The outcome of treatment with severe perversions and gender identity disorders may well not be the highest level of psychological integration. It is not uncommon for the severely crippling perversion which threatens life or physical integrity to be replaced by a more stable and less destructive paraphilia. For example, a stable homosexual state or transvestite depressive picture may be the outcome of treatment of the gender dysphorias.

Analysis and psychodynamic treatment of borderline patients is often many years in duration since the slow accrual of ego strengths through contact, analysis of crippling defenses, structure building, and partial replacement of highly pathological internalized parental objects is required to transform concrete demands for satisfaction into a transference neurosis which may be analyzed in collaboration with an observing ego. Neurotic patients, for whom the difficulties with separation and oral fixation are not so severe, tend to move more rapidly toward an analyzable transference. In either case my experience is that the transference neuroses of patients with sexual disorders contain exaggerations of certain familiar elements.

In women with prominent sexual dysfunctions, feelings of genital inferiority, penis envy, and penis-breast-feces-baby equivalencies are marked. This is associated with a singular competitiveness between mother and daughter. These mothers have pushed precociously mature attitudes toward anatomy and reproduction, while at the same time making it clear that independence or separation, let alone competition, was intolerable. The father deepens the conflict and the regressive pull by encouraging a little-girl sexuality while being clearly unable to handle his wife. The patient as a little girl was in a situation in which her father could not provide a frame of reference sufficiently independent from mother to help effect optimum separation. He stimulated her but could not establish limits on her infantile sexuality or help in her establishment of age-appropriate outlets and sublimations. Because of father's relative impotence, fantasies of mother's potency are extravagant, as are the fantasied consequences of competition with her. Fantasies of having been castrated or denied a penis by mother—who greedily appropriated all good things to herself (father, penis, breasts, and babies)—are unusually strong, the rivalry intense, and the guilt and anticipated punishment correspondingly severe. All drives are put under strong interdiction. Issues of control—including control of impulses, people, part objects, and events—reach proportions where the patient is frantic to avoid an unguarded moment which might let a dangerous impulse escape. In the nature of the symptom, of course, efforts at control provide ample opportunity for the unconscious expression of rivalry, sadism, and rage.

Such women are anorgasmic for many reasons. They have not effected a complete separation from mother, nor are they completely identified as female. Their orientation remains strongly bisexual. Although the desire for sexual fulfillment is strong, their objects remain confused. Furthermore, men and sexual congress with them is a prerogative of mother so that sexual desire becomes contaminated with intense rivalry and guilt. Constant wariness against an unguarded thought or act virtually eliminates the possibility of being swept away to orgasm.

Transference and the transference resistance revive and intensify the conflicts and defenses in the relationship with the internalized mother. Separation and control are the early issues in treatment and only later does frank penis envy emerge along with the paternal transference.

Among men who are sexually dysfunctional, the fabric of their disability is woven out of an impressive degree of feminine identification. In borderline men, an aspect of incomplete separation-individuation includes a partial failure to dis-identify after having formed the primary maternal identification. Neurotic men have resolved their primary identification with mother, but form a secondary identification with the frustrator. Their mothers are cold, withdrawn, and often chronically depressed. Although there is no question these women love their sons, the watchword is responsible rather than empathic parenthood. There is very little spontaneity or joy in these families and the people within the household may lead rather isolated lives despite the spatial contiguity of their existences. These mothers have an unresolved attachment to their own mothers which has left them with conflicts surrounding femininity and maternity. Their masculine strivings are reflected in their marriage to a man with strong maternal leanings and often more than the usual feminine identifications. Through his failure to provide a strong male object for identification and through the example of his rather feminine attachment to his wife, the father fosters feminine identification in his son.

The boys who grow up to be neurotic men with sexual problems are not usually effeminate or sissified to outward appearance. However, during the oedipal childhood neurosis the more than usual feminine identification materially intensifies castration anxiety. The fantasies of castration are all the more fearful because in some ways the boy must struggle with a longing to yield up his penis in order to express his feminine identifications.

As adults these men are usually premature ejaculators or impotent. The characteristics of their sexual lives most maddening to their partners, however, are the hesitation and passivity in their sexual approach. Their apparent timidity is not simply due to lack of confidence as a product of the erectile or ejaculatory dysfunction. The passivity continues even if the primary sexual symptom is relieved. The primary sexual symptom and the passivity independently serve multiple functions including to express feminine identification, to camouflage intrusive phallic strivings, to withhold satisfaction from the maternally-identified sexual partner, and to allay castration anxiety.

The transference usually develops with the patient being passive, dependent, and little-boy charming in an attempt to elicit encouragement, approval, and care. It is only later that the resentment, phallic strivings, and conflict around such strivings come into play.

I do not mean to suggest that either the dynamics or the transference of patients with sexual disorders is predictable. I do feel, however, that in women with sexual disorders issues of control, genital inferiority, and penis envy are especially prominent and in men with sexual disorders feminine identification is particularly problematic.

However the transference may be manifest, just as in the treatment of any other neurosis or character disorder the transference neurosis is resolved by small increments through mutative interpretations timed to coincide with the emergence of emotionally laden material which is tinged with archaic fantasy and directed toward the therapist as a transference object (14).

If the patient is appropriately selected for analysis, interpretations are likely to be directed toward castration anxiety, penis envy, perverse fantasies, forbidden sexual impulses, and other areas which, in whatever derivative form, are related to issues of sexuality. I always keep in mind the uselessness of *en bloc* interpretation. It does no good to suggest to a female patient that her difficulties are related to "penis envy." Instead, following the policy of small increments, it is fruitful to observe that her fantasies suggest uncertainty about whether her lover's penis is attached to her or separate from her. If it is there, the patient should be allowed to discover penis envy on her own. A similar sense of discretion and tact about the patient's anxieties should accompany the interpretation of homosexual interest, feminine or masculine identifications, and the other anxiety provoking material.

REFERENCES

1. Freud, S. (1912). The dynamics of the transference. In: J. Strachey (Ed.), *Standard Edition of the Complete Psychological Works of Sigmund Freud*, Vol. 12. London: Hogarth Press, 1958, pp. 99-108.
2. Freud, S. (1915). Observations on transference-love. In: J. Strachey (Ed.), *Standard Edition of the Complete Psychological Works of Sigmund Freud*, Vol. 12. London: Hogarth Press, 1958, pp. 159-171.
3. Halle, E. Personal communication with Mrs. Halle has suggested these observations, 1978.
4. Kaplan, E. *The New Sex Therapy*. New York: Brunner/Mazel, 1974.
5. Levay, A. N. and Kagle, A. A study of treatment needs following sex therapy. *Amer. J. Psychiat.*, 1977, 134 (9):970-973.
6. Mahler, M. *On Human Symbiosis and the Vicissitudes of Individuation*, Vol. 1. New York: International Universities Press, 1968.
7. Masters, W. and Johnson, V. *Human Sexual Response*. Boston: Little, Brown, 1966.
8. Masters, W. and Johnson, V. *Human Sexual Inadequacy*. Boston: Little, Brown, 1970.
9. Meyer, J. K. Clinical variants among applicants for sex reassignment. *Archives of Sexual Behavior*, 1974, 3:527-558.
10. Meyer, J. K. Training and accreditation for the treatment of sexual disorders. *Amer. J. Psychiat.*, 1976, 133:389-394.
11. Meyer, J. K. Sexual dysfunction. In: A. Freeman, R. Sack and P. Berger (Eds.), *Psychiatry for the Primary Care Physician*. Baltimore: Williams & Wilkins, 1979, pp. 381-399.
12. Meyer, J. K., Schmidt, C. W., Jr., Lucas, M. J., and Smith, E. Short-term treatment of sexual problems: Interim report. *Amer. J. Psychiat.*, 1975, 132:172-176.
13. Novey, S. *The Second Look: The Reconstruction of Personal History in Psychiatry and Psychoanalysis*. Baltimore: Johns Hopkins University Press, 1968.
14. Strachey, J. The nature of the therapeutic action of psycho-analysis. *Int. J. Psychoanal.*, 1934, 15:127-159.
15. Wise, T. Personal communication with Dr. Wise has led to the development of these ideas, 1978.

11

Psychotherapy of Ambulatory Patients with Severe Anxiety

STANLEY LESSE, M.D., Med. Sc.D.

Psychiatrists who treat ambulatory patients with severe anxiety reactions must have immediate, intermediate and long-range goals. Different therapeutic procedures may be more or less effective with regard to the attainment of one or another of these aims. Depending on the therapist's personality and earlier training, a broad spectrum of treatment modalities may be brought into play. Some psychiatrists who are purely organicists in their orientation will automatically administer tranquilizing drugs or electroshock therapy, and these treatment procedures will be the sum and substance of their planned therapy.

Other psychiatrists and psychologists will only employ purely psychotherapeutic techniques in the management of severely anxious patients whether the prime nosologic problem is psychoneurosis, schizophrenia, or sociopathy. These polarized therapeutic conceptualizations of the treatment of patients manifesting severe anxiety are anachronistic at our current level of psychiatric development (1). In my experience, psychoanalytically oriented psychotherapy, combined with properly chosen and administered tranquilizing drugs, is the optimum therapeutic technique for the effective management of the vast majority of patients in whom severe or even massive anxiety is a prominent clinical feature.

I will present a step-by-step description of the technical intricacies involved in the use of tranquilizers in combination with psychoanalytically

220

oriented psychotherapy. It is a digest of more than 20 years of experimentation and experience with this treatment procedure in the management of many hundreds of severely anxious patients who had a broad spectrum of psychiatric illnesses (2, 3).

The combined tranquilizer-psychotherapy procedure is a complicated method from a theoretic basis, because it involves the compounding of biodynamic, psychodynamic, and sociodynamic elements into a single unified treatment approach. At present, few psychiatrists use combined therapy in a planned, intended fashion. Dynamically oriented psychotherapy has not been purposefully combined with psychopharmacologic therapy, owing mainly to the lack of broad training that is necessary if one is to employ this technique. Psychiatrists, in order to utilize this combined procedure effectively, must have extensive experience with the organic therapies and with dynamically oriented psychotherapy, particularly brief analytically oriented psychotherapy. Unfortunately, most psychiatrists adhere either to the organic treatments or to the psychotherapies and use combined therapy only unintentionally.

COMBINED THERAPY IN A PATIENT WITH MARKED ANXIETY

The combined process can be introduced at any of three phases of the therapeutic procedure, namely, at the inception of therapy, during the course of treatment, or as maintenance therapy.

At the Inception of Treatment

Combined therapy logically should be instituted at the beginning of the therapeutic procedure in patients who are too overtly anxious to be amenable to psychotherapy alone or on an ambulatory basis. It is especially effective if the motor component of anxiety is extremely marked. At this phase of treatment, the therapist is primarily interested in short-term goals related to the amelioration or blunting of the initial level of anxiety and the symptoms and signs that are the secondary defenses against this anxiety.

Prior to the advent of the tranquilizers, when psychotherapeutic techniques were employed alone, weeks or months were often spent in ameliorating the level of anxiety to the point at which the patient had sufficient ego strength to cooperate effectively in a dynamically oriented psychotherapeutic relationship. In a great many instances, the early administration of tranquilizing drugs greatly shortens the period of anxiety decompression and thereby enables the patient to cooperate effectively and meaningfully more quickly. Since the advent of the combined technique, many patients who formerly would have required hospitalization can be managed on an ambulatory basis. The proper use of the combined technique prevents the necessity for hospitalizing many severely anxious schizophrenic patients and some patients with agitated depressions, who otherwise would have been exposed to the psychic trauma and economic drain that are often associated with institutionalization.

Combined therapy is particularly effective among those severely anxious patients who are commonly diagnosed as having schizophrenia, pseudo-neurotic type (2). I would go further and state that, from my point of view, the combined therapy technique is the treatment of choice for most pseudo-neurotic schizophrenics who overtly manifest a marked degree of anxiety. I have also found that many severely decompensated schizophrenic patients, whose illnesses were previously considered incompatible with ambulatory psychotherapy, often become suitable candidates for analytically oriented therapy when it is combined with tranquilizing drugs, particularly those of the phenothiazine group.

Combined therapy is a necessity in the management of many very anxious patients who have organic mental reactions. Prior to the advent of the tranquilizing drugs, outpatient electroshock therapy or hospitalization was mandatory for a very large group of these individuals. At the present time, a high percentage of those anxious patients with organic mental illnesses, particularly those that fluctuate in appearance and intensity, can be managed very effectively by a combination of tranquilizing drugs and supportive psychotherapy.

Though combined therapy has its most dramatic effects in the outpatient treatment of anxious psychotic patients, it is also indicated at the very inception of treatment with some extremely anxious psychoneurotic patients. Weeks and even months of painful anxiety that severely limits the benefits of all psychotherapeutic efforts may be greatly shortened if combined therapy is diligently employed.

The combined therapy approach is also indicated at the inception of treatment with very anxious, acting-out adolescents and some hyperactive children, where the acting-out or hyperactivity is a secondary defense mechanism against a marked increase in the degree of anxiety.

During the Course of Treatment

The tranquilizing drugs also may serve a purpose when introduced during the course of analytically oriented psychotherapy or even during the course of intensive, reconstructive, psychoanalytic psychotherapy. They should be considered when the level of anxiety escalates sharply or persistently secondary to an increase in environmental stress or psychotherapeutic events. The judicious introduction of the tranquilizers may often literally save psychotherapy. This is particularly so in the ambulatory management of anxious schizophrenic patients.

The insights unveiled during the course of dynamically oriented psychotherapy may precipitate a marked or even massive elevation in the intensity of anxiety in some neurotic patients, and most particularly in a large group of schizophrenic patients, no matter how diligent and careful the therapist may be. This marked increase in anxiety may be attended by the appearance of a strong negative transference and a decrease in effective free association. The tranquilizing drugs, when properly utilized, by rapidly reducing the level of anxiety not only may ameliorate the secondary signs and symptoms associated with the increased level of anxiety, but also may ameliorate the destructive effects of a strong negative transference and permit more significant free association.

As Maintenance Therapy

Many patients require intermittent psychiatric treatment throughout their lives. This is particularly true with schizophrenic patients. To a lesser degree it pertains also to a segment of the population of neurotic patients who have been chronically ill and to some with recurrent depressions.

An experienced therapist learns to recognize and appreciate which patients require scheduled visits and which patients may be permitted to use their judgment as to when they should seek help. As I have noted before, it is imperative that patients be taught to recognize the earliest evidences of mounting anxiety and the threshold beyond which they should return for further treatment.

The nature of maintenance therapy will differ depending on the patient, the therapist, and the environment. Some patients are unable to function successfully vocationally, socially, or sexually without maintenance drug therapy even in the face of routine, everyday responsibilities. Usually the required dose of a tranquilizer for maintenance purposes is far less than the amount needed to ameliorate the original anxiety. Indeed, a less potent tranquilizer than that originally required, one that may also have less severe side effects, may be sufficient during the maintenance period.

There are literally tens of thousands of patients who are on a continuous program of tranquilizing drugs. Very often, when they evidence psychic decompensation, the problem may be met by a simple increase in the dose of the prescribed drug. On occasions it may be necessary to change the drug with a different biochemical agent being substituted. The psychotherapeutic techniques utilized in combination with the drugs will differ depending on the intensity and rate of increase in the level of anxiety and the patient's immediate response to the tranquilizers (4, 5). If the level of anxiety is readily controllable, an analytically oriented psychotherapeutic approach, in which reeducation is continued, is feasible. If the level of anxiety is very pronounced, a return to a supportive psychotherapeutic approach will be necessary.

Certainly not all patients require maintenance drug therapy but instead can be managed with various types of psychotherapeutic techniques alone, the visits being scheduled periodically or as required by evidences of psychic decompensation. Usually, maintenance psychotherapy merely reinforces previously learned processes. Less frequently, the widely spaced maintenance visits may further the learning process by bringing to light insights that advance psychic maturation.

If the presenting level of anxiety is severe or if the rate of increase is pronounced, the therapeutic process will become more supportive until the overt manifestations of anxiety are significantly reduced. Very commonly it is advisable to supplement the psychotherapeutic regime by the addition of a tranquilizer, depending once again on the degree of manifest anxiety and the rate of acceleration in the degree of anxiety. If the level of anxiety is not marked, small amounts of the original drug or even a less potent tranquilizer usually are sufficient to block or ameliorate the presenting symptoms and signs. In any case, when employing any drug, one must use the appropriate preparation in sufficient amounts.

SELECTING THE PROPER TRANQUILIZER

My rules for the selection of a particular type of preparation are very simple. Wherever there is clear-cut evidence of marked or extreme, overt anxiety, usually accompanied by one or more secondary symptoms or signs, I select a neuroleptic, usually a phenothiazine preparation. If the patient has a history of an inadequate response or a sensitivity to drugs of the phenothiazine group, then one of the butyrophenones or thioxanthenes may be chosen. In patients in whom anxiety is obviously very pronounced I find that chlorpromazine, the first of the phenothiazines to be introduced, is still the most reliable and effective preparation. The initial soporific side effect commonly associated with chlorpromazine may be beneficial.

Where the level of anxiety is moderate, and the patient has not responded to psychotherapeutic procedures alone, drugs such as Librium (chlordiazepoxide) or Valium (diazepam) may be utilized.

If neurotic patients are extremely anxious, the so-called minor tranquilizers are of relatively little benefit and the major tranquilizers usually must be employed (1). Conversely, there are ambulatory schizophrenic patients, seen in private or clinic practice, who will respond to chlordiazepoxide or diazepam if the degree of manifest anxiety is not severe.

ANALYTICALLY ORIENTED PSYCHOTHERAPY IN COMBINATION WITH TRANQUILIZERS

Initial Phase

This combined technique is optimally suited to patients whose illnesses are characterized by marked or extreme overt anxiety, together with various secondary symptoms and signs. Indeed, it is the preferred technique for such patients. The primary purpose during the initial phase of treatment is to ameliorate the severe pathologic level of anxiety, this decrease being accompanied by a blunting or removal of the secondary clinical manifestations.

When this is accomplished, the therapist should not be deluded that he has caused a grand metamorphosis that will stand the ravages of time and stress. All that has been accomplished is the lessening of the patient's psychic pain, as evidenced by marked anxiety, and of those symptoms that are secondary defense mechanisms against this anxiety.

The initial process of the combined therapeutic procedure usually lasts from one to three weeks. It is rare for this phase to be of longer duration. The psychotherapeutic aspect is strongly supportive and is conducted in a face-to-face setting. Under no circumstances should the patient be placed on a couch at this point, for it is imperative that the therapist be sharply aware of all clinical changes, whether the information is transmitted to him by visual, auditory, or tactile means.

The recording of the anamnesis is an intimate part of the technique of anxiety reduction. The therapist should take great pains to reassure the patient as to a positive outcome. During the initial interview, the therapist must obtain a detailed qualitative and quantitative analysis of the anxiety that is present, together with a sharp awareness of the sequence of appearance of the secondary defense mechanisms. He must also evaluate as clearly as possible the sources of stress, both chronic and acute. In addition to being aware of the initial value or level of anxiety, the therapist must know prior to the institution of therapy whether the level of anxiety is increasing, has already plateaued, or is decreasing. The therapist may require a number of visits before he can accurately ascertain the direction and rate of change in the quantitative degree of anxiety. The therapist should be aware also as to whether the anxiety and secondary symptom formation are in a psychotic or neurotic framework. (Though this determination cannot be made in some instances during the initial interview, a tentative evaluation is a great aid.)

The patients should be seen two to three times during the first week of combined therapy. This permits the therapist to adjust the dosage of medication, obtain further history, and continue the supportive psychotherapy begun during the initial interview.

In very anxious patients the tranquilizers are prescribed at the time of the initial interview. The psychiatrist should have a thorough knowledge of the drug that he is employing, both from a therapeutic standpoint and with regard to possible side effects. He must be confident in his handling of the medication. It is also imperative that he be experienced in the technique of brief analytically oriented psychotherapy. He should understand the capacities, as well as the limitations, of both the organic and psychotherapeutic aspects of the procedure. The therapist should also understand the benefits and limitations of hospitalization, for with many of these patients, should their ailments worsen instead of improving, emergency hospitalization may be necessary. Finally, the therapist should be cognizant of the benefits of ambulatory electroshock therapy, for some of the psychotic patients who continue to regress or show no significant improvement may be excellent candidates for electroshock therapy as far as the amelioration of the initial levels of anxiety and secondary symptoms and signs is concerned.

Before the therapist prescribes a drug, its nature and purpose, especially its potential positive benefits, should be described to the patient in general terms. The mechanism by means of which the combined technique operates can best be described to the patient in terms of anxiety reduction, with symptomatic relief being secondary to this amelioration. Many patients come expecting medication. Indeed, many may request one particular "magic pill." Environment may exert a negative effect on the patient. Some patients come with great antipathy to drug therapy or psychotherapy or to a particular type of drug therapy or a particular type of psychotherapy. This is especially true if they have had any prior treatment. Such a situation may complicate the initial therapeutic situation to varying degrees.

The most common potential side effects that many occur secondary to a particular drug should be presented simply and honestly. The descriptions must take into account the patient's preconceived conceptualizations, correct or incorrect. Every therapist should be prepared for possible difficulties arising in anxious patients who have hypochrondriacal manifestations as part of their secondary defense mechanisms, should side effects occur. Finally, one should be aware of difficulties that may arise among severely anxious schizophrenic patients, particularly among those in whom there are evidences that a decrease in the level of consciousness may be followed by difficulties in reality contact. Some very anxious patients who have organic mental deficits also are prone to pose problems should the tranquilizers have a potent soporific side effect. Finally, patients with a very pronounced obsessive-compulsive matrix may pose a problem in the very initial phase of therapy as a manifestation of their fear of losing control secondary to the use of any drug.

One of the primary aims during the initial phase of treatment is to foster a very strong, positive transference reaction (2). The accomplishment of this aim is rendered relatively easy if the therapist's and patient's initial goals are in harmony and the prime basis for concomitancy at this point is an expectation of rapid amelioration of the presenting symptoms and signs. If the initial aims are divergent, therapy will be star-crossed from the very beginning. Unfortunately, a negative transference reaction is likely to occur if the therapist states, in effect, that "the main purpose of treatment is reeducation and this will take a long, long time." The severely anxious patient's prime desire at this point is symptomatic relief, and he should be approached overtly with the general idea that, "I will relieve you of your pain."

By the use of this combined tranquilizer-psychotherapeutic approach, a working relationship between doctor and patient that would have taken months to establish with psychotherapy alone may be accomplished in a matter of weeks. Many patients react to the rapid relief of painful anxiety with unquestioning gratitude and a desire, indeed an eagerness, to relate to the psychiatrist. This is quickly established and enhances the strong positive transference. It occurs at times as part of the magical expectancy, with the therapist being viewed as an all-powerful father who is infallible in the patient's judgment.

I cannot stress too forcefully that the initial phase of the combined technique produces rapid clinical changes that are ever-changing and that have a momentum far greater than that seen when psychotherapy is used alone. This puts greater demands on the therapist. Indeed, some therapists are poorly equipped psychologically to effectively handle this type of procedure.

During every visit, by direct questioning and careful observation, the degree of the patient's anxiety, the nature and status of the secondary symptoms, the vocational, social, and sexual behavior, and the dream material are reviewed in detail. Close contact is made, where possible, with the patient's family and friends. I appreciate the fact that relatives and friends may be poor informants, but the nature of the information to be gathered is simple and can be readily correlated with the data obtained from questioning and observing the patient.

In view of the rapid change in the patient's clinical status, the therapist may be prone to overestimate the patient's capacities for vocational and social adaptation. However, I must emphasize that at this point the improvement is primarily symptomatic in nature, with the patient having little or no understanding of the nature or origins of his problems. It is safer to be conservative in the estimation of a patient's ego capacities. At this point in treatment, overoptimism could result in anxiety to the point of panic if the patient is exposed prematurely to excessive vocational or social stress.

The rate of change that occurs as a result of the combined technique can be controlled. This pacemaker can take several forms. First, the dosage of the tranquilizer can be varied. A rapid buildup is often necessary during the first week with changes being made daily or every few days until the intensity of anxiety is very definitely ameliorated. After the level of anxiety is decreased, the total daily dosage of medication may be lessened. The total daily dosage has to be titrated against the degree of overt anxiety.

From a psychotherapeutic standpoint, the level of anxiety can be affected by the relative control or encouragement of the process of patient catharsis. In some patients, a free outpouring of affect-laden material may be an effective tool leading to anxiety decompression. However, at times it can cause a negative feedback reaction and actually increase the level of anxiety, leading to a new pananxiety state. In such instances the therapist may aid anxiety amelioration by limiting the nature and rate of catharsis. Systematic autorelaxation exercises, vigorous physical outlets, and occupational diversions are good temporary channels that may serve as braking mechanisms. It should be understood that this process is very fluid and depends entirely upon the rate and direction of the patient's clinical change. The rate of clinical change can also be affected by controlling the patient's activities relevant to work, socialization, and sexual relationships.

It can be affected to a lesser degree by interpretations. At this phase of treatment, interpretations should be made sparingly. The therapist must be careful not to precipitate insights that the patient is emotionally incapable of handling. Interpretations, when they are given, should deal with the here and now. When they involve situations from the patient's past they should be pertinently related to the patient's current behavior or life situation. Poorly timed and poorly conceived interpretations may precipitate a massive panic reaction.

The reporting of dreams is encouraged even in the initial phase of therapy. As the level of anxiety is rapidly decreased, there is a greater awareness of dream material. The therapist should be cautious and not overwhelmed by this seeming deluge of dream recall. Once again, at this point he should refrain from making profound interpretations that the patient may not be able to tolerate. *At this phase of treatment dreams should be viewed primarily as a source of psychodynamic information and secondarily as a means of anxiety decompression.* Interpretations, when deemed pertinent, should be related to the current scene and should be gauged according to the patient's capacities to tolerate an awareness of the latent content.

Dangers Associated with the Initial Phase

Many complications can occur during the initial phase of treatment. Most can be anticipated and avoided. Others can readily be corrected.

Excessive Tranquilizing. At times the dosage of the tranquilizers may be increased too rapidly or, as the overt level of anxiety is decreased, the drug level may be kept at levels more appropriate for the period when the overt level of anxiety was much greater. It is imperative that the dose of medication be optimally titrated according to the intensity of manifest anxiety. This titration should proceed gradually, never precipitously.

One must be particularly cautious in the reduction of drug dosage in schizophrenic patients, for at times an excessively rapid decrease in medication may precipitate a panic episode. On the other hand, overtranquilizing may cause a paradoxic, massive pananxiety state in schizophrenic patients if the soporific side effects of the drug lead to difficulties in reality control. On occasions this may be relieved by the addition of small amounts of amphetamine.

Excessive tranquilizing also may produce a degree of placidity and passivity that will block further effective treatment. The overly rapid amelioration of anxiety may lead some patients to minimize the severity of their illnesses. Indeed, in some, one can observe the unfolding of a complete scheme of denial or illness. Some will run from treatment. Others may remain purely to receive the medications. It was interesting that these patients are afraid, in many instances, to have other physicians take over the administration of drugs. This is an example of what I have called *drug transference,* in which the therapist becomes merely the purveyor of a "magic elixir" (6).

Insufficient Dosage of Tranquilizer. The danger of an insufficient dosage is self-evident. If the therapist utilizes the information that can be accumulated from an awareness of the basic mechanisms of anxiety reduction (4), he should have little difficulty in administering the amount of drug necessary for the amelioration of a certain quantum of anxiety. I repeat that the therapist must know his drug, its benefits and its limitations.

Side Effects of Medication. All drugs that have any potency may have adverse side effects. Fortunately, most that occur as a result of the administration of tranquilizers are mild and transient. The patients should be forewarned to minimize the anxiety that is associated with the appearance of side effects.

As side effects appear the therapist should interpret them clearly to the patient so that they are not falsely conceived by the patient as being an integral part of his illness. This is particularly important in patients who have hypochondriacal defense mechanisms. It is also important in patients who have an obsessive-compulsive personality matrix, for they may conceive that side effects are a further indication of their lack of control. Paranoid schizophrenics may interpret side effects as evidence of the therapist's malevolence toward them.

Excessive Positive Transference. In some instances the patients develop a degree of dependency that renders them affectively almost inert. In general, this is not a problem during the initial phase of treatment; it usually becomes a major concern during the second, or psychoanalytically oriented phase of treatment. Quite often this difficulty may be associated with overmedication and can be corrected by a reduction in the daily dose of tranquilizer.

Drug Transference. As mentioned earlier, drug transference pertains to situations in which patients will remain in therapy with a given psychiatrist because they associate him with the administration of a successful drug and are afraid that the same drug will not be so effective if administered by a different physician (6). In these instances, the therapist becomes merely the purveyor of a pill. At times drug transference may be confused by the therapist as representing a true, strong, positive transference. When such misinterpretations are marked, owing to the therapist's own emotional needs, effective treatment is bound to collapse. With the use of drugs, as with all types of treatment, accurate observations, undiluted by exaggeration due to immodesty and neurotic wishful thinking, are necessary for optimum benefits.

Premature or Excessive Environmental Commitments. The rapid amelioration of the initial level of anxiety and secondary symptoms and signs is interpreted by most patients as a sign of a "return to health." When this occurs, almost all patients, if left to their own design, immediately will attempt to resume full vocational and social activities. Indeed, many will strive to make up for lost time. They will try to compensate for that period of time in which their psychic difficulties limited effective activity.

I cannot emphasize too urgently that, following the initial symptomatic improvement secondary to drug therapy, premature resumption of routine responsibilities may lead to a massive psychic collapse. It is one of the main tasks of the psychotherapist, at this phase of treatment, to guide the patient's vocational and social performance with a firm hand until the patient demonstrates firm evidence of increased ego capacities. The failure on the part of psychiatrists to follow these suggestions is one of the commonest causes of failure in drug treatment.

Family Interference. The rapid amelioration of the presenting symptoms and signs is considered to be synonymous with a cure in the minds of most relatives and friends of patients, and they often become a negative influence with regard to the patient's remaining in therapy.

To a degree this can be forestalled by predicting for the patient and family at the first visit that symptoms and signs will probably disappear very quickly but that any cessation of treatment at that point would be fraught with danger. This admonition may now be repeated, if unintentionally malevolent advice from the family threatens to interfere with further treatment. Both the family and the patient should be warned in no uncertain terms of the dangers of premature termination of treatment.

Psychoanalytically Oriented Phase

There is no sharp demarcation between the initial and secondary, or psychoanalytically oriented, phase of treatment. Rather, the change takes place gradually, with the psychotherapeutic process becoming less and less supportive. The change usually begins from one to three weeks after the onset of treatment, after there has been definite evidence of a marked decrease in the quantitative degree of anxiety and a significant amelioration of secondary symptoms and signs. In some instances the secondary symptoms and signs may be completely gone. In other patients, one or even two of the symptoms may be present but only intermittently and without their pretherapeutic level of affect.

Aberrations such as delusions, illusions, and hallucinations should be ameliorated completely before the analytically oriented phase of the treatment begins.

The primary aims of the psychoanalytically oriented phase of treatment are 1) reinforcement of anxiety decompression begun in the initial phase of treatment and 2) reeducation with the aim of increasing the patient's psychosocial maturation.

As treatment progresses, the first goal becomes less and less important as the second goal becomes increasingly realized. I would like to reaffirm that at the onset of this second phase of treatment the patient has little or no insight as to the sources or pyschodynamics of his difficulties. Improvement, thus far, has resulted from the tranquilizer, the supportive psychotherapy, and various placebo effects.

This is a dangerous point for a therapist to become overwhelmingly enthusiastic and undercautious, particularly if he becomes enamored with his own magical powers. Poor judgment, in this regard, may lead to a precipitous collapse of all that has been attained. At this point, the patient still has relatively fragile ego capacities.

The psychotherapeutic support that characterized the initial phase of therapy can be gradually relaxed when there is adequate indication of increasing ego strength. This is measured to a great extent by the degree of overt anxiety and the patient's vocational, social, and sexual adaptation. Therapy remains ego supportive in nature but to a gradually lessening extent. Free association is encouraged but in a guided fashion.

The clinging positive transference relationship is given active attention. As noted before, if it continues in an undiluted form, therapy will become paralyzed. The positive transference is actively interpreted and dissipated, for its existence is a constant threat to the effective continuation of the psychoanalytically oriented phase of treatment. Its presence is a residue of magical expectations and is antithetical to any psychotherapy that has emotional maturation as a goal.

As mentioned before, in the presence of a very strong positive transference reaction there is often a marked inhibition of any negative or hostile responses. I do not mean that repressed hostility is completely inhibited. To the contrary, marked anxiety has a hostility-inhibiting effect in many patients, and during the initial phase of therapy, as the level of anxiety is rapidly reduced, anger directed toward persons other than the therapist may come forth.

The decompression of anxiety during the initial phase of treatment is often followed by a free flow of repressed hostility, but this hostility is rarely directed toward the therapist in the form of a strong negative transference reaction. This situation poses a therapeutic problem in a number of instances if it persists in the psychoanalytically oriented phase of treatment. Manifestations of negative transference, when kept within reasonable bounds, afford an excellent means for the controlled discharge of hostility and at that same time serve as a valuable medium by means of which the patient obtains significant insights.

As the excessively positive transference is reduced in intensity, the therapist usually can expect the appearance of a negative reaction. However, it will usually not be so intense as it might have been if a tranquilizer had not been used in the initial phase of treatment. This poses an active task for the psychotherapist to guide the release of hostility in such a manner as to benefit the patient, while at the same time avoiding an indiscriminate and inappropriate outburst of rage against family and friends. I have noted only a few instances, in my studies, in which the released hostility could not be managed by diligent guidance even with schizophrenic patients.

Communication Zone

The term *communication zone* refers to a quantitative degree of anxiety in which the patient appears to communicate most freely (6). In some patients the range appears rather broad, whereas in other patients, it is relatively narrow. Psychotherapists, beginning with the classical psychoanalysts, correctly warned that, if the patient's level of anxiety is depressed to too great a degree, the patient will not communicate efficiently. Relatively few psychotherapists have drawn attention to the fact that when patients are extremely anxious there is also relatively little effective communication.

Though the pattern is highly individualized, in many instances I find that there is a certain threshold of anxiety below which the patient will communicate with greater freedom. The rate of change in the quantitative degree of anxiety also appears to affect communication. The level of communication is greatly enhanced as an excessive level of anxiety is decreased and is less evident as anxiety establishes a plateau effect. Similarly, as the quantitative degree of anxiety is increased in patients who present a flat affect, a zone of anxiety will appear characterized by relatively free communication that may disappear if an excessively high level of anxiety is attained. I repeat, once again, that this is a highly individualized process that requires greater study.

With regard to interpretations made by the psychotherapist during the combined therapy technique, the same general rules pertain as in any other brief psychoanalytically oriented procedure. It should be remembered, once again, that the process of change is much more rapid here than in the usual psychotherapeutic process. The therapist must be very cautious lest he permit the development of a free-floating pananxiety state secondary to interpretations that the patient is unable to accept at a particular state of emotional maturation. As in dream interpretation, the interpretation of other material should focus on the here and now, with past events and associations being related as much as possible to current processes. At all times, evidence of increasing anxiety should be probed.

Vocational and social adaptation, with pride and pleasure in relationship to past and present relationships, is stressed, with primary emphasis on current processes. The necessity to function within one's current psychic capacities is prominently emphasized throughout this analytically oriented phase of treatment. The patient is conditioned, so to speak, to an awareness of the earliest evidences of increased anxiety secondary to any type of environmental stress. As the patient attains a more mature level of awareness, he learns to anticipate situations more positively. Usually, at this point, the amount of anxiety precipitated by a particular situation is relatively slight. The final attainment of maturity with regard to a particular situation is attained when the patient is automatically able to manage a situation without significant anxiety.

If the tranquilizing drugs are introduced during the psychoanalytically oriented phase of treatment for the first time, or if they are reintroduced after having been discontinued, the degree of the positive transference that occurs is not so profound as noted when drugs are introduced in the initial stage of the combined therapy program. Similarly, in such instances it is rare for a strong drug transference to occur. The patients in this situation usually maintain a realistic attitude toward the medications, and they merely credit the therapist with good judgment for having employed the tranquilizers.

REFERENCES

1. Lesse, S. Drugs in the treatment of neurotic anxiety and tension. In: P. Solomon (Ed.), *Clinical Studies in Psychiatric Drugs.* New York: Grune & Stratton, 1966, pp. 221-224.
2. Lesse, S. Psychotherapy and ataraxics. *Amer. J. Psychother.,* 1956, 10:448.
3. Lesse, S. Combined use of psychotherapy with ataractic drugs. *Dis. Nerv. Syst.,* 1957, 18:334.
4. Lesse, S. Psychodynamic relationships between the degree of anxiety and other clinical symptoms. *J. Nerv. Ment. Dis.,* 1958, 127:124.
5. Lesse, S. *Anxiety—Its Components, Development and Treatment.* New York: Grune & Stratton, 1970.
6. Lesse, S. Psychotherapy in combination with ataractic drugs—A six-year study with 350 patients. *Amer. J. Psychother.,* 1960, 14:491.

12

Psychotherapy with Violent Patients

Robert Weinstock, M.D.

Psychotherapy with violent patients can best be regarded as psychotherapy with patients having a variety of diagnoses who present with the symptom of violence. One definition of a violent patient is an individual who is physically assaultive toward other people or things (1). Except for the fact that the symptom can be so frightening and potentially dangerous, it is not really that different in kind from other symptoms, such as suicidal behavior. A suicide attempt, violence directed against the self, can also occur in a variety of different conditions. However, since violent patients present special problems, institutions often set themselves up in ways in which they are unable to deal with such patients. They are passed from institution to institution until often they end up in a punitively oriented criminal justice system, which can exacerbate the person's problem. Alternatively, the patient can find himself in an open community hospital setting which has no locked facility or capacity to deal with violent patients. Staff become frightened and can try to extrude the patient and put him into the criminal justice system.

I believe that the only constructive solution is to approach the problem as a multifaceted one. First, a unit capable of dealing with the violent patient in a manner such that both staff and patient can feel secure that no harm will come to anyone is needed. Second, one must evaluate what the immediate cause of the violent behavior is with a particular patient. Third, the underlying psychiatric problem must be diagnosed and treated according to standard techniques. Fourth, the reactions of the staff towards the patient must be handled in a way which will enable the patient to be treated in a rational manner. Last, a follow-up plan must be instituted which will help prevent future instances of the problem.

Because of the potential severity of the danger in dealing with such patients and because of the complex reactions of staff and society towards them, it is impossible to discuss treatment without also examining some of the ethical issues involved. Violent patients are seen both in mental health and criminal justice systems. They probably produce stronger feelings, usually of a negative kind, than any other patient group. Where a particular patient is seen may depend on the seriousness of his violence, his socioeconomic status, the prevailing views of the community and social era, facilities available and many purely fortuitous factors. The violence can range from throwing something against a wall, to assaulting someone, to murder. It can be a result of many different causes, such as paranoid schizophrenia, homosexual panic, temporal lobe epilepsy, alcoholism, explosive and impulsive personalities, depression, pseudopsychopathic schizophrenia, narcissistic injury, a reflection of staff conflict, and organized criminal behavior. Each of these causes needs to be treated differently.

We also have to cope with our own tendencies to stereotype and scapegoat. Undue therapeutic pessimism can result from fears of such patients and disappointments or failure of previous unrealistic optimism. In recent years we have seen a paradoxical incarceration of violent patients in correctional facilities because mental health districts have often not even had one locked facility. Instead, a unit where one can safely examine and evaluate such patients, with adequate well-trained support staff, is required to come up with rational nonpunitive therapeutic plans on an individual basis. One should have a secure facility and a nonvindictive staff. Unfortunately, such a combination is all too rare in our current mental health-criminal justice system.

SPECIAL FACTORS IN TREATMENT OF VIOLENT PATIENTS

Halleck (2) has discussed some of the ethical problems in treating violent patients. When the patient is seen in an institution, the psychiatrist must decide to what degree he should follow the goals of the treated subject or those of the treating agency. Treatment goals can range all the way from controlling behavior, with total disregard for the psychological state of the offender, such as prolonged restraint, seclusion, or incarceration, to the more desirable development of internalized controls accompanied by greater personal comfort and awareness. Alternatively, one could aim towards development of internalized controls, without external restraint, with no regard whether the person became more withdrawn, nonproductive, passive or even mentally ill. Hopefully, treating personnel will show respect for individual rights and values and not be hypocritical and call anything, even punishment, treatment. It is important to be honest to patients and realize that when an institutional psychiatrist acts for the good of the institution he is not necessarily acting in the patient's interest. Often, preventing a patient from doing harm is in the patient's long-term interest also, but there are times when an institutional psychiatrist's loyalties conflict and he must be honest to the patient about the conflict and to what use a potential report will be made. Reasonable risk-taking, which will allow the patient whatever responsibility he can handle, is necessary. An appropriate balance between security and ego-strengthening activities must be found.

Violent patients additionally present problems because of society's needs to have a scapegoat for its problems. Ryan (3) has stated the important symbolic role of prisoners is that they symbolize crime that has been contained and this makes the citizens feel safe. Menninger (4) has described the cops-catch-robbers ritual as a morality play which is not totally without redeeming social value, but with scapegoats necessary for the spectacle. According to Menninger (5), as long as the spirit of vengeance and a punitive attitude persists, and as long as we seek to inflict retaliatory pain, we will neither be able to assess appropriate and effective penalties nor make headway in the attempt to control crime.

Most murders are committed as isolated acts by people closely acquainted with the victim. Mass murderers, the ones who stir up the most hatred and fear, and the least sympathy, are, according to Lunde (6), almost always insane. Contrary to the view that the United States goes too easy on murderers with insanity pleas, Lunde reports that the United States has insanity verdicts in only 2% of the cases, compared with 25% in England.

Unfortunately, scapegoating is an issue from which even mental health professionals are not immune, particularly when people are overburdened. A sort of projective identification with the violent patient can occur. The therapist can project his own violent impulses into the patient, and see the patient as much more dangerous than he really is.

Kernberg (7) describes some of the problems a therapist struggling with his own aggressive impulses can have, where he can project the impulse into the patient whom he then sees as the bad dangerous side of himself. Violent patients can bring up extreme reactions in the therapist. One must guard against either being excessively punitive or alternatively masochistically submissive to the patient's control efforts, while excessively denying the real dangerousness of a patient. Moreover, the openness of aggressivity, sexuality, and dependency in such patients can lead to countertransference problems for the therapist (2, p. 330).

Involuntary commitment of such patients raises questions of dangerousness. Stone (8) has criticized the criteria of dangerousness for civil commitment because of the impossibility of accurately predicting it. Even Kozol's study (9), which succeeded to some degree in predicting dangerousness, had 61.3% false positives. The Baxstrom decision (10), which released a large number of so-called dangerous people from maximum security prison hospital in New York into the community, showed that there had been a severe overprediction of violence. The overwhelming majority of the released prisoners were, in reality, not dangerous. This natural experiment shows that psychiatrists can be overconservative in their judgments. There can be problems with so-called indeterminate sentences where a psychiatrist must guarantee that a patient will not be dangerous in order to discharge him. I believe a better model is one in which there are yearly reviews of any long-term commitments and where a judge makes a final decision rather than putting the full burden for retention or release on the psychiatrist. The public seems better able to accept a court making a mistake than a psychiatrist making a mistake. Recidivism is acceptable from prison, but psychiatrists are often under pressure to be infallible.

Monahan (11) makes the point, though, that the difficulty with most predictions of dangerousness is that the context of prediction is a locked facility, while the context of validation is the community. In an emergency room setting, the context of prediction and validation is almost the same; the patient has been living in the community, and will likely be returning there. The time interval between prediction and validation is short, so one should be able to do a much better job at this sort of prediction. Skodol and Karasu (12) found in a study of emergency room patients, however, that most acts of violence are spontaneously occurring and unpredictable. They did find, though, that a statement of intent to do harm and a family member being the target both indicate serious situations. I believe that there can be some meaningful assessment of imminent dangerousness (2) and that, Szasz notwithstanding (13), such patients should be hospitalized even involuntarily.

The problem is not, in my opinion, so different from the suicidal patient (14), where one can monitor and assess his suicide potential even if one does overpredict it. More serious ethical problems arise because, while almost no one would seriously argue for hospitalizing or incarcerating a suicidal patient for years or even life because he might regress and become suicidal again, one does hear such proposals for potentially violent patients. It is very difficult to disentangle feelings about a patient and values of a particular psychiatrist from any long-term assessment of a patient's dangerousness. However, it is unrealistic to think that the criminal justice system always handles these situations reasonably, or that psychiatrists could even agree about the treatability of such patients, should treatability become the prime criterion as some have proposed. I believe reasonable assessments of imminent danger to others can be made, as well as danger to oneself. Longer-term assessments of potential danger are possible but much more questionable.

It is also important to be aware of the social factors that contribute to law-breaking. Law-breaking (2, p. 322) can have many different meanings. Undoubtedly, not every law is correct and moral. Certainly, there are differences between the professional criminal, civil rights demonstrators, American Revolutionary leaders and a poverty-stricken adolescent who steals. Some of the abuses of Soviet psychiatry stem from psychiatrists' being willing to see all law-breakers as mentally ill. Obviously, the treatment of violent patients can be fraught with many political implications. Psychiatrists must watch not to become an agent for political and social repression.

Kernberg (7, p. 115), in assessing the meaning of antisocial behavior, suggests assessing whether the behavior is antisocial from the viewpoint of a conventional social prejudice, reflects a normal adaptation to a pathological environment, is an adjustment reaction of adolescence, is reflective of other character pathology such as a narcissistic or infantile personality, or is reflective of an antisocial personality proper. He feels factors other than pure antisocial personality improve the prognosis.

The diagnosis of antisocial personality itself can often obscure more than it enlightens. Many workers have been impressed by the similarities of so-called antisocial personalities to psychotic patients. Schizoid elements, such as poor interpersonal relationships, are a part of most diagnostic criteria for the diagnosis. Lewis and Balla (15) feel it may be a forme fruste of a psychotic disorder. Cleckley (16) believes the central disorder may not only be similar in degree to schizophrenia but more similar in quality that is generally realized. Menninger (5, pp. 178-180) believes many individuals perform criminal acts in order not to go crazy. Violence and crime may be attempts to escape from madness, and mental illness may be a flight from violence. Murder can be used to avert suicide or can even be a form of suicide attempt.

Lewis and Balla (15, p. 39) suggest that many of the symptoms used to define sociopathy, such as poor school performance, discipline problems, cruelty to animals, fire-setting, and multiple delinquent acts, are found in children with many types of psychiatric disorders. Guze (17) diagnoses antisocial personality, if in addition to a criminal record the person has two of the following five in their history: excessive fighting, school delinquency, poor job record, a period of wanderlust, and running away from home. It is not clear that the list says much more than the lay judgment of a prior criminal record, the first of the criteria, and a long-term history of behavior problems. The danger of such diagnoses is that they may lead to premature closure attempts to find underlying psychopathology and lend themselves to hidden moral judgments disguised as medical science. As Lewis and Balla (15, pp. 41-42) indicate, DSM II uses terms like selfish, callous, irresponsible, and impulsive to describe antisocial personalities, giving an indication of the feelings of the psychiatrist towards a patient whom he gives such a diagnosis.

These issues are not academic matters; a diagnosis for a patient involved with the legal system can have profound consequences for the patient. In some states it can make the difference between six months in a psychiatric hospital and a life sentence in a maximum security prison. The American Law Institute (118) criteria for criminal responsibility exclude conditions manifested solely by repeated criminal or otherwise antisocial conduct, although this exclusion, if applied meaningfully instead of being equivalent to a personality disorder as it has been defined by case law, would apply more properly to dyssocial behavior, such as organized crime, rather than to antisocial personalities or personality disorders, to whom the exclusion is generally applied. Appropriate diagnoses of underlying psychopathology can lead to proper treatment, both psychopharmacologically and psychotherapeutically. It is important, though, that mental illness not be used as an excuse for indefinite incarceration.

Kernberg (7, p. 13) states that all antisocial personality structures he examined present a typical borderline personality organization. Borderline patients (7, p. 24) seldom give evidence of formal thought disorder in clinical mental status examinations, but on projective testing with un-structured stimuli, primary process thinking shows itself with primitive fantasies, peculiar verbalizations and a deficient capacity to adapt to the formal givens of the test material. These indications show the patient's tendencies to become psychotic for brief intervals and implicate that he could have been psychotic at the time of a crime. It is rare, however, that projective tests are given in forensic evaluations and rarer still that the patient has either the trust or the time to reveal his psychosis to an examining psychiatrist in an unfriendly setting. The diagnosis of border-line personality at least calls attention to the potential for psychosis though this possibility must be stressed since DSM III lists borderline personality as a personality disorder potentially obscuring a patient's propensity to have brief psychotic episodes. In contrast, antisocial per-sonality, in most people's minds, implies the absence of psychosis, cer-tainly a matter with potentially grave implications for a patient.

Guttmacher (19) coined the term "pseudopsychopathic schizophrenia," a condition which in my experience occurs frequently. Lewis and Balla (15) have called attention to the presence of all types of psychopathology in people with antisocial behavior. My own experience in a maximum security hospital setting in the corrections system confirms these observa-tions by showing numerous instances of frank psychosis in people whom correctional staff saw as merely antisocial. Psychosis and violent or even antisocial behavior are by no means mutually exclusive and are, not un-commonly, coexistent.

It is important to realize that antisocial behavior, as well as violence, can be found in people with all types of psychiatric disorders, and can have diverse etiologies. The danger of antisocial personality as a diag-nosis, however, is that it can foreclose all further attempts to look for underlying psychopathology which can be treated by standard procedures. Too often the diagnosis of antisocial personality leads to therapeutic nihilism and nontreatment in a prison facility, or to discharge of danger-ously mentally ill people into the community. At least in some places, a diagnosis of mental illness can lead to appropriate treatment.

As I have indicated earlier, the best approach to violent patients is, first, to contain the violent behavior, then to accurately diagnose the cause of the behavior, next to determine the extent of underlying psycho-pathology, and finally, to institute appropriate treatment procedures. It is important to remember that violence can be a symptom of many dif-ferent conditions and that lesser forms of violent behavior may even be appropriate responses to certain situations. One must also remember that the violent patient is a person and be careful not to use him as a projection of our own unwanted impulses or our own stereotypes. One must examine the patient in a setting where both staff and patient can feel secure, and institute appropriate treatment procedures for whatever underlying psychopathology the patient is found to have.

The initial problem one may need to confront is how to contain the violent behavior. This containment may entail restraint and appropriate pharmacotherapy. Redl (20), writing about children, says patients can exhibit fits of rage which remind us of total abandon and constitute a real state of emergency. The situation can also occur with violent adult patients. One may have to hold the patient physically, remove him from the scene of danger and involvement, and prevent the patient from doing physical damage to others or himself. Since psychiatrists are ordinarily not skilled at handling physical violence, it is necessary to have members of the staff who are able to subdue the patient sufficiently without becoming overly punitive. Redl and Wineman (20, pp. 211-212) describe the ideal approach as one in which no more counterforce is used than is necessary to achieve the goal of restraint. Ideally, the therapist should remain calm, friendly, and affectionate, neither threatening nor blaming the patient. Patients in a fit of rage can sometimes be totally irrational, and a show of force can often be reassuring. It can be a face-saving device for a patient, allowing him to feel that it is not shameful to stop fighting in the presence of an opposing army. It is important to realize that the underlying theme in the lives of such patients is helplessless, which leads to feelings of inadequacy and terror (1, p. 14). It is crucial to approach patients in ways which are reassuring and do not increase the panic.

Lion (1, pp. 3-4) writes that the psychiatrist must be comfortable with a violent patient in order to convey a sense of security. Often, the presence of ancillary personnel can help lessen the physician's own anxieties and later allow him to work better individually with the patient. The patient's underlying fears of loss of control can be accentuated by panic-like states in personnel. Most violent patients are afraid of their impulses and want controls furnished so that they will not hurt or kill. After the patient is subdued, he may be put in restraints, and may be given barbiturates such as sodium amobarbital intramuscularly or intravenously, benzodiazepines such as diazepam administered slowly intravenously, phenothiazines, or other antipsychotics (21). Haloperidol, intramuscularly, is especially useful and has less of a hypotensive effect than chlorpromazine. On a longer-term basis, one should prescribe medications, but not overmedicate with the idea that large dose will help a dangerous patient. Sometimes paranoid patients can be made worse by drowsy side effects which feel like a loss of control. Antipsychotic medications with frequent side effects of sexual inhibition, such as thioridazine, should probably be avoided in patients with conflicts about their sexual identity.

It is also crucial to accurately assess the patient diagnostically. The patient should be tested neurologically and an EEG performed to rule out temporal lobe epilepsy (22, 23). In addition, it is important to evaluate for the episodic dyscontrol syndrome (24). One must try to understand what social situation triggered the violent behavior to attempt to make certain the patient does not return into exactly the same situation which initially set off the behavior. Family intervention may be essential in this process.

It is useful to further determine whether the violent person has been what Lion (1, pp. 29-30) describes as an obsessive compulsive and schizoid individual who doesn't ordinarily express anger, and who one day loses control in a fleeting violent psychotic episode. Alternatively, the person can be an individual with labile mood swings who is immature, explosive with low tolerance for stress, and impulsive with poor judgment. Megargee (25) has referred to overcontrolled and undercontrolled patterns of aggression.

The underlying psychopathology must be assessed. One should ascertain whether there is an underlying situational disorder, which psychosocial interventions in the community can affect; whether the violence is due to a schizophrenic episode, which antipsychotic medications can alleviate; whether a psychotic affective disorder is the problem, which appropriate medications can help and control; whether the problem is alcoholism, and an alcoholic abstinence program like Alcoholics Anonymous is indicated; or whether drug use, such as amphetamine use, is the problem and appropriate treatment needed. Lithium has been found helpful in emotionally unstable patients who have problems with frustration and who are impulsively violent. Anticonvulsants can be helpful in people with seizure disorders. Additionally, the problem can be a long-standing characterological one which would require long-term treatment in facilities that are unfortunately rarely available to lower socioeconomic level patients. Also of use is the assessment of the person's childhood, since child abuse and the triad of enuresis, fire-setting, and cruelty to animals have been associated with violent behavior (26).

Havens (27) has described an interpersonal technique of displacement and resultant reduction of projection, which can be helpful in the acute management of such patients, especially when the patient is either building up to a violent outburst or is recovering from one. "Counterprojection" is a technique used to displace aggression towards other people and, at the same time, have the therapist on the side of the patient. During the acute phase one should not talk of introjection and projection. So-called reality interventions may often just lead to the therapist's being included in the patient's projection and the patient's becoming violent toward the therapist. Such clarifications can be offered later on if needed. During the phase where the patient is building up his projections, the therapist must do everything he can to separate himself from the patient's projections. Moralistic statements at such times can be dangerous as well as untherapeutic. Some reality-testing about the doctor can sometimes be useful. If the doctor has reason to believe that the patient is favorably disposed toward the medical profession, he might emphasize that he is a doctor and there to help. Pinderhughes (28) has stated that violence toward another can't occur in a moment of introjective relationship, while the victim is seen as an acknowledged and valued part of the self. Violence can occur only in moments of projective relationship against a renounced part of the self, which in the moment of violence is perceived as evil. The victim is seen as deserving and needing the violent act to bring about justice. This dynamic operates both in individual violence and in group violence, where there are shared projections.

In counterprojection, one might speak negatively about the introject, thereby giving the patient permission to do likewise. Since speaking too negatively about introjects can terrify some schizophrenics, one might have to use ambiguous and double remarks like "Mother wasn't an unmitigated blessing." By expressing such feelings, the therapist helps the patient to bear what he cannot bear alone and has previously had to project because he could not take responsibility for it. As the therapist takes over the feeling, the patient can give up the feelings he really didn't want anyway—which was why he projected them in the first place. In dangerously conflictual situations, ambiguous and double statements can help. Double statements explore the other side; for example, the therapist might say, "She is a pain but she has, I suppose, a good side." By techniques of successive approximations, the truth eventually comes out. The use of the counterprojection technique can sometimes be difficult; other people can become upset if they feel the doctor is taking the patient's side against them. This situation can be especially difficult when the other people are police or correction officials, or even other hospital officials. In my experience, one sometimes has to direct counterprojective devices toward other staff when referring to violent patients, such as exaggerating how dangerous or difficult a patient may be.

Another frequent error in dealing with violent patients is premature confrontation motivated out of the therapist's own hostilities. The borderline patient's narcissism may be the healthiest part of him. Buie and Adler (29) describe the fear of abandonment and aloneness of the borderline. It can feel like annihilation, and lead to destructive rage in a desperate effort to obtain the needed person permanently. The patient may not be experiencing the neurotic narcissistic entitlement described by Murray (30), but more of what Buie describes as an entitlement to survive. An overlay of megalomania may help the patient keep from facing the painful belief that he is devoid of all significance. The struggle can be perceived as a life or death matter. Confrontation may be used by the therapist to express his own fury and resentment (31). It can be disastrous to ask a patient to prematurely give up narcissistic demands when that patient is struggling with an entitlement to survive.

Countertransference problems (used in the total sense defined by Kernberg (7) as conscious and unconscious reactions to the patient's reality as well as his transference) can be difficult when treating such patients. The therapist, according to Adler (31, p. 157), may have to deal with a sense of helplessness and hopelessness in a patient who seems to remain unresponsive for long periods. Glover (32) writes that the therapist must handle repeated disappointments and assaults on his most cherished possession, his capacity to heal. The psychopathic patient begins treatment in a state of negative transference and tests the therapist with a series of relapses or crises, repeating his lifelong tendency to exploit, hurt, and disappoint people. Unfortunately, too often therapists give up on patients at such junctures, confirming the patient's view of the world. In order to withstand, in any long-term work with such patients, the pain and suffering psychopathic patients can cause the therapist, he must basically like the patient, and accept the patient as he is, much as Day and Semrad (33) have described with schizophrenics. He should also be hopeful, but realistic, and aware of the patient's tendencies to appear much more healthy and motivated than is real in an "as-if" manner. Both therapist and patient can sometimes avoid facing the real problems and can engage in a shared denial. The patient can put on a charming façade to appease the therapist, and can then suddenly regress and disappoint him in order to keep what he believes will be an inevitable rejection under his control. Sometimes interpretations of such maneuvers, particularly when they have been previously predicted by the therapist to the patient, can be helpful.

Lion (1, p. 62) warns of the importance of monitoring the transference since negative feelings about the therapist can be converted into destructive behavior outside of sessions. With potentially violent patients, neglect of negative transference feelings can be disastrous. If the patient is allowed to get too close too soon and then the therapist becomes frightened of the patient, this can lead to an accentuation of the patient's panic and potential violence towards the therapist. Usually, however, in an inpatient setting the transference will be diffused, and in an outpatient setting the patient's avoidance defenses will lead to the patient's taking off rather than seriously hurting the therapist. It can be helpful for a therapist to tell a patient when the patient's behavior frightens him, so that the patient doesn't misinterpret and, by means of projective identification, see the therapist as frightening and attack him. Therapists can at times also experience what Kernberg (7, p. 59) describes as complementary identification, where the therapist is identified with the transference objects of the patient. The therapist experiences the feeling the patient is putting into his transference object, and the patient experiences the feeling he had in the past with that particular parental image. Commonly, the therapist can feel angry at the patient and the patient wary and suspicious of the therapist.

On occasion, work with such patients can lead to an additional potential problem described by Kernberg (7, p. 62), whereby the therapist has unrealistic ideas of being able to help a patient in spite of all reality factors and approaches the patient with total dedication. Unfortunately, the unrealistic views of the therapist can break down in a sudden way and lead to an abrupt termination of treatment. MacVicar (34) writes about a not uncommon problem of masochistic submission by a staff member, with attempts to gratify every whim of a patient to avoid an explosion. It can be a problem to overly submit to a patient, and it can deprive a patient of an opportunity to learn how to handle small amounts of unpleasant affect, with resulting strengthening of the patient's ego. Interpretations to the patient can be helpful at such junctures. Either overpunitiveness or oversubmission can be counterproductive. Timing is also important, since underlying character pathology should not be confronted too soon.

Helplessness (1, p. 15) is an important underlying dynamic with violent patients, and should be kept in mind in determining how to approach them. They have reaction formations against helplessness and dependency. They pretend to be tough and independent to cope with helplessness, and are threatened by any insults to their masculinity or

potency. Menninger (5, p. 183) describes bravado crimes done with bru-
tality and ruthlessness which seek to prove to the doer that he is no
weakling but a tough man who fears nothing. Nazi storm troopers were
often mere boys trained to stiffle all tender emotions and behave heart-
lessly brutal and ruthless. Halleck (2, p. 317) says that men who have
serious doubts about their masculinity and a need to constantly reassure
themselves and others are more prone to violent behavior. People driven
to prove their masculinity can ignore the consequences of their actions.

Homosexual panic can lead to violence. Ovesey (35) has referred to
pseudohomosexual concerns, motivated by strivings for dependency and
power, which can develop in men not meeting societal standards for masculine performance. The man tries to dissipate his weakness in compensatory fashion through competition about anything and everything and
a show of strength (35, pp. 56-58). He exaggerates so-called masculine
traits with care to look manly, be overaggressive (with a hypersensitivity
to any slight that connotes feminine behavior), the power motivation
being predominant (35, p. 111). He tries to have men submit to him,
sometimes sexually, and denies his own dependency at the expense of
the weaker man whom he makes into a woman. It is a fragile adaptation;
the homosexual act is ego-alien and is often felt to be a confession of
masculine failure.

Sometimes, a male patient who becomes afraid of dependency feelings
on a male therapist will become afraid that he is a homosexual, and can
become violent in a homosexual panic. It can help to discuss the patient's
fears of and wishes for dependency and define the issue as fear of closeness and fusion, with feared annihilation of the self. It often can relieve
the patient to see the conflict as a pseudohomosexual one, rather than a
homosexual one which can imply to a patient loss of his identity as a
man, with resulting destruction as an individual. Other times, desires
for dependency in and of themselves can make a patient believe he is not
a man and lead to his becoming aggressively violent in a panic-like attempt to prove to himself that he is a man and that he is not afraid. He
can project his feelings onto a therapist and can become violent if the
therapist does, in fact, become afraid and not explain to the patient that
it is the patient's threatening behavior that is making the therapist
uneasy. Woods (36) has described instances of pseudohomosexual panic
leading to violence. Sometimes a patient needs to be able to discuss homosexual feelings with a therapist in order to feel comfortable enough
with them not to project them onto the therapist. It can be an error for
the therapist to avoid discussing the issue with a patient at such times.

When hypermasculine behavior is exhibited in relation to women, the patient becomes a Don Juan. He has a need to "score" with women to prove his masculinity, often in a compulsive and, on occasion, desperate manner. Sometimes sex and aggression can become fused or, in instances of rape, sex can be used in the service of aggression (37).

Patients with an underlying dynamic of helplessness and a need for hypermasculine behavior often seem to be the male counterparts of the female hysteric, and might appropriately be called male hysterics as described by Blacker and Tupin (50). They exhibit masculine sexual behavior in contrast to the feminine sexual behavior of women hysterics. In addition, the aim is often not really sexual, in spite of the overt behavior; their behavior is an exaggeration of the culturally defined male stereotype, often accompanied by sexual anxieties and inhibitions. The patient can function at a relatively high narcissistic level or at a low borderline level. Similar to the so-called good hysteric of Zetzel (38), such a patient can use masculine behavior as part of proving his entitlement to survive, proving his adequacy as an individual, or even satisfying dependency needs at the hands of nurturant women or men. Alternatively, he can struggle in a reaction formation way against all feelings of dependency or passivity.

Guze (17, p. 97) finds an interesting association between sociopathy and hysteria, giving added credence to the suggestion that some sociopaths may be the male equivalent of the primitive borderline hysteric, each using exaggerations of the culturally defined sexual stereotypes. Guze, in studying female felons, found sociopathy or hysteria in 80 percent of them, suggesting a possible relationship between the two disorders. Hysteria and sociopathy are the two psychiatric disorders he found to be most often associated with classical conversion symptoms. It is possible that the two disorders are related, but hysteria tends to manifest itself most often in women and sociopathy manifests itself most often in men. Women's liberation, perhaps, may lead to more sociopathic behavior previously reserved for males. Women with behavior problems frequently show signs of sexual promiscuity and running away from home (2, p. 138). However, it is possible that they will now turn to more violent behavior. Women hysterics, according to Chodoff and Lyons (39), can use exaggerated femininity and passivity in a controlling way; men tend to be more directly aggressive. It is important to realize that the hypermasculine behavior of what has been labeled male hysterics, or what Oversey calls pseudohomosexual anxiety, covers over feelings of helplessness. A challenge to the patient by a staff member who also needs to prove his masculinity can precipitate violent behavior.

Yochelson and Samenow (40) use a reality-moralistic approach which can, I believe, be helpful for those patients who need a male authority figure for identification. However, I believe the approach only can work with significant numbers of patients in an atmosphere of warmth, and that Yochelson and Samenow (41) are too pessimistic about more standard approaches. I believe their approach is not immune from being vulnerable to the possibility they fear of patients' giving the therapist merely what he wants to hear. Yochelson, in my opinion, is too ready to confirm the patient's own already low opinion of himself, which society also already has confirmed.

The patient may initially feel understood if the therapist believes he is bad. However, I believe it is more effective not to confirm the patient's notion but merely to convey to the patient that the therapist understands that the patient himself believes he is bad but that the opinion is not necessarily correct. I believe Yochelson's approach leads to overly rigid bad-good dichotomies and, even when successful, can lead to patients' becoming narrow, conventional people who lead lives almost the opposite of the chaotic ones they led before. Too often people feel that an overly hard, tough, authoritarian approach is needed for such patients, who at least on the surface present a tough, hard exterior. It can be important to realize the patient's underlying insecurity; often, a non-threatening, sympathetic, though aware and incorruptible, approach can be much more effective.

Secondary gain issues can be prominent in the treatment of patients with a more sociopathic picture. Some patients have advantages to be gained by feigning mental illness; however, at least an equal number will probably try to conceal mental illness, even from themselves, because it is more acceptable in their subculture to be considered criminal rather than crazy. It can be difficult, at times, to establish a real therapeutic alliance, and the therapist can often be "taken in" and believe a more meaningful alliance has been established than is really the case. Patients may be more mistrustful than is at first evident, and participate in therapy in more of an "as-if" manner. A therapeutic alliance can often eventually be established around issues of concern to the patient himself, such as his self-defeating behavior or his loneliness. The alliance is fragile and tested on many occasions. However, ambivalent motivation occurs with many types of patients. Some patients even need to be "forced" into therapy, such as by a probation condition, in order to "save face." The danger with the treatment of more sociopathic patients is that a naive therapist can be led to falsely believe he has "cured" the patient, and react in an overly rejecting, punitive manner, when he discovers he has been deceived. Disappointments such as these lead, in my opinion, to many therapists' becoming disillusioned and giving up on working with such patients incorrectly at crucial junctures. The therapist must set realistic goals for his work and expect regressions and disappointments.

Longer-term intensive treatment, in my opinion, though rarely available, can help a number of violent patients with characterological disorders. However, one needs a setting which can cope with the patient's behavior and regressions, and the patient needs at least the potential for both a locked setting and more independence when he can handle it. The setting can be a locked hospital setting, or a therapeutically oriented correctional setting with a nonpunitive atmosphere (a rarity). Motivation is important, and therapy is most necessary and useful when the patient is aware of how unreasonable his behavior is and wishes to do something about it (2). Many patients also need things like vocational rehabilitation, and group therapy can be of value.

The psychotherapy study of the Menninger Foundation (42) indicated intensive psychotherapy, combined with hospitalization, to be useful for borderline patients. Therapists who worked on undoing the manifest and latent negative transferences were the most successful. This study contrasts with many prevailing views regarding treatment of borderlines, and notions about their untreatability. Kernberg (7) sees a continuum between the narcissistic personality and antisocial personality, which he sees as an extreme form of pathological narcissism with absence of an integrated superego.

Treatment of such patients requires consideration of other dynamics which are sometimes present and can require intervention. Johnson and Szurek (43) have described superego lacunae in antisocial patients, who act out their parents' unconscious conflicts. Family intervention may be required in such cases. Also, as stated earlier, it is important to interpret projective identification when it occurs, whereby the bad part of the self is projected into another person with lack of self-object differentiation. The patient continues to experience the impulse as well as the fear of it and this dynamic can sometimes lead to violence (7).

Treatment of narcissistic personalities requires consideration of the idealizing and mirror transferences, described by Kohut (44), which narcissistic patients develop about their therapists. Therapists can find such transferences difficult to accept and reject them by prematurely given, though correct, genetic or dynamic interpretations. The therapist may experience embarrassment, self-consciousness, and shame at the narcissistic tensions generated by his own repressed fantasies of his grandiose self being stimulated by the patient's idealization. Accepting the admiration would be a more correct response when an idealizing transference starts to germinate. In the mirror transference, the patient wants the therapist to reflect, echo, approve, and admire his exhibitionism and greatness. For a long time, the therapist should encourage the patient to reveal his grandiosity; it would be a mistake to prematurely emphasize the irrationality of the grandiose fantasies or stress that it is realistically necessary to curb his exhibitionistic demands. The therapist must accept a limited role. In settings which allow for long-term treatment of patients with characterological disorders, or even in brief, limited insight therapy, issues of narcissism and techniques for treating borderline personalities become especially relevant.

It is useful to realize the importance of narcissism and its connection with aggression. Rochlin (45) says that aggression always issues as a reaction to threatened or actually damaged narcissism. Narcissism, moreover, is in double jeopardy; when threatened it becomes intensified and more brittle. We deal with aggressiveness easiest (45, p. 164) when we are, or believe we are, the victim of another's hostility. Aggression, and identification with the aggressor (45, p. 213), can enhance self-esteem and fend off fears and uncertainty. Social and other factors influence the development of narcissistic personalities. Upper-class narcissistic personalities can become businessmen and political leaders; lower-class narcissistic people may feel that their only resort is antisocial behavior.

Rochlin (45, p. 157) suggests that the value we accord another person acts as the most effective deterrent to violence. I have seen (46) several examples of Capgras' syndrome, where patients insist that an important figure has been replaced by an impostor, as a delusional way of coping with unacceptable hostility and as an excuse for violent action. The patient seems to need to deny that the individual is a valued other person in order to cope with his hostility; however, this denial unfortunately can enable the person to become violent towards an individual he would otherwise not harm.

I believe, like Halleck (2, pp. 324-327), that one should not be moralistic but should approach the patient in a manner that suggests that the patient's behavior is not bringing the patient what he is looking for and can lead to even more discomfort. Since this behavior can result in loss of liberty, one should suggest that there are better ways for the patient to achieve his own goals. Insight can lead to the discovery of alternative adaptations which can be chosen by a patient. It is also relevant to look for instances of what Alexander (47) called the neurotic character, describing a person who commits crimes in order to be punished for things about which he feels unconsciously guilty. Halleck (2) describes a close linkage of masochism and paranoia, with the criminal denying that he brought his difficulties on himself and projecting all his problems to the outside. The sociopath has conflicts with dependency and searches for a painless freedom from object relations—an ideal which is never achieved. He says he doesn't need people, in a way to ensure a return to dependency. Moreover, it is important to work with whatever elements of a positive transference exist, as Aichhorn (48) did in his work with delinquent youth.

CONCLUSIONS

I have suggested that violent behavior is a symptom. It is important to keep one's countertransference feelings under control; violent patients, probably more than any others, lead to all types of countertransference difficulties usually related to the therapist's difficulties with his own hostility towards the patient. Mental health people should try not to engage in scapegoating but realize that violent patients are people who have problems with violent behavior. They are not inherently different from other patients or members of a different species.

It is important to contain the violence on an emergency basis and then try to assess its causes. Certain types of problems, such as situational difficulties, acute psychosis, or unresolved hospital staff conflicts, such as described by Stanton and Schwartz (49), lend themselves to emergency, crisis-oriented interventions. Antipsychotic medications can have dramatic results, if the violence is a result of a psychosis. Assessment and treatment must be done in settings where both patient and therapist can feel realistically safe and dangerous acting-out by the patient can be prevented. Attempts should be made not to become confused with the patient's projections. Structure and limit-setting are necessary.

A further assessment of the patient's characterological difficulties should be made and treatment instituted if suitable facilities exist. Otherwise, one is often forced to settle for incarceration or release of the patient to the streets. Issues regarding commitment of dangerous patients can produce problems and must be considered. Motivation of patients is an important factor for successful psychotherapeutic endeavors. Many patients with characterological difficulties will probably be found on careful examination to have borderline personality organizations and/or narcissistic personalities and should be treated appropriately. Issues relating to object splitting and trouble integrating good and bad introjects are encountered.

Depending on the nature of the patient's problem and the severity of the pathology, the patients can be difficult or relatively routine to treat. I believe it is important, however, that mental health personnel not shun their responsibilities and neglect treating such patients. Such neglect leads to violent behavior in the streets and paradoxical incarceration of such patients in prisons. The majority of violent patients are treatable by one of the approaches I have described and it is important that neglect of the problem not be rationalized by the myth of their untreatability. While it is true that some patients have been so badly scarred and are so suspicious, mistrustful and unmotivated that they may be untreatable, the majority are, in my opinion, treatable by appropriate personnel in appropriate settings. It is essential that facilities be available where therapists and patients can feel secure. Therapists, moreover, must be aware of and constantly examine the complex ethical problems which the treatment of such patients represents and try to not let their own moral values or their own political beliefs overly influence treatment decisions made for patients. Patients should not be forced to adopt the therapist's life style in the name of treatment. We can also be overconcerned with a patient's rights instead of treating him, and the result can sometimes lead to his being incarcerated in an antitherapeutic prison paradoxically.

It is also crucial to remember that emergency crisis intervention approaches may be all that is needed for many violent patients, but such patients should not be prematurely discharged, without any psycho-social intervention, right back into the problematical or crisis situation which originally led to the violent behavior. It is ironic that large amounts of money are often spent to keep someone incarcerated in prison, but sufficient funds and personnel are often not available to treat someone less expensively for shorter periods of time in mental health facilities. Some judges are reluctant to send clearly mentally ill violent patients to treatment facilities because they do not have confidence that mental health personnel will keep the patient hospitalized for adequate periods of time or follow him persistently in the community. Instead, such patients can be sent to expensive, often antitherapeutic, penal facilities which encourage regression, dependency, and stifle any constructive, ego-developing efforts by their inmates. Prisons generally have inadequate follow-up resources with poor recidivism rates. Hopefully, psychiatrists will continue to be actively involved in the treatment of violent patients and will keep in mind specialized techniques such as the ones I have described. Moreover, serious attempts should be made to organize treatment programs in an individualized manner and not require that patients have the right psychopathology to fit in with someone's idea of what a program should be. Careful attention to some of the techniques I have discussed will help in treating patients who have already become violent or who have a great potential for becoming violent.

REFERENCES

1. Lion, J. *Evaluation and Management of the Violent Patient*. Springfield: Charles C Thomas, 1972.
2. Halleck, S. *Psychiatry and the Dilemmas of Crime*. Berkeley: Univ. of California Press, 1967.
3. Ryan, W. *Blaming the Victim*. New York: Vintage Books, 1976, p. 322.
4. Menninger, K. *Whatever Became of Sin*. New York: Hawthorn Books, Inc., 1973, p. 56.
5. Menninger, K. *The Crime of Punishment*. New York: Penguin Books, 1968, p. 218.
6. Lunde, D. *Murder and Madness*. San Francisco: San Francisco Book Company, Inc., 1976, pp. 48, 107.
7. Kernberg, O. *Borderline Conditions and Pathological Narcissism*. New York: Jason Aronson Inc., 1975, pp. 31-62.
8. Stone, A. *Mental Health and Law*. Washington, D.C.: U.S. Government Printing Office, 1975.
9. Kozol, H., Boucher, R., and Garofalo R. The diagnosis and treatment of dangerousness. *Crime and Delinquency*, 1972, 18:371-392.
10. Baxstrom V. Herold, 383, U.S., 107, Feb., 1966.
11. Monahan, J. Prediction, research and the emergency commitment of mentally ill persons: A reconsideration. *Amer. J. Psychiat.*, 1978, 135:198-201.
12. Skodol, A. and Karasu, T. Emergency psychiatry and the assaultive patient. *Amer. J. Psychiat.*, 1978, 135:202-205.
13. Szasz, T. *Law, Liberty and Psychiatry*. New York: Collier Books, 1963.
14. Stone, A. and Shein, H. Psychotherapy of the hospitalized suicidal patient. *Amer. J. Psychother.*, 1968, 22:15.
15. Lewis, D. and Balla, D. *Delinquency and Psychopathology*. New York: Grune & Stratton, 1976, p. 120.
16. Cleckley, H. *The Mask of Sanity*, (Ed. 5). St. Louis: The C. V. Mosby Company, 1976, p. 255.
17. Guze, S. *Criminality and Psychiatric Disorders*. New York: Oxford University Press, 1976.
18. American Law Institute Model Penal Code, Sec. 201.3, Tent. Draft No. 9, 1959.
19. Guttmacher, M. Pseudopsychopathic Schizophrenia. *Arch. Criminal Psychodynamics* (Special Psychopathy Issue), 1961, 502-508.
20. Redl, F. and Wineman, D. *Controls from Within*. New York: The Free Press, 1952, p. 209.
21. Tupin, J. Management of violent patients. In: R. Shader (Ed.), *Manual of Psychiatric Therapeutics*. Boston: Little Brown and Company, 1975, pp. 125-136.

22. Blumer, D. Epilepsy and violence. In: D. Madden and J. Lion (Eds.), *Rage, Hate, Assault and Other Forms of Violence.* New York: Spectrum Publications, 1976.
23. Mark, V. and Ervin, F. *Violence and the Brain.* Hagerstown, Maryland: Harper & Row, 1970.
24. Monroe, R. *Episodic Behavioral Disorders.* Cambridge, Mass.: Harvard Univ. Press, 1970.
25. Megargee, E. The prediction of violence with psychological tests. In: C. Spielberger (Ed.), *Current Topics in Clinical and Community Psychology.* New York: Academic Press, 1970, p. 98.
26. Hellman, D. and Blackman, N. Enuresis, firesetting and cruelty to animals: A triad predictive of adult crime. *Amer. J. Psychiat.*, 1966, 122:1431-1435.
27. Havens, L. *Participant Observation.* New York: Jason Aronson Inc., 1976.
28. Pinderhughes, C. Managing paranoia in violent relationships. In G. Usdin (Ed.), *Perspectives on Violence.* New York: Brunner/Mazel, 1972, pp. 111-112.
29. Buie, D. and Adler, G. The uses of confrontation in the psychotherapy of borderline cases. In: G. Adler and P. Myerson (Eds.), *Confrontation in Psychotherapy.* New York: Science House, 1973, pp. 123-147.
30. Murray, J. Narcissism and the ego ideal. *J. Amer. Psychoanal. Assn.*, 1964, 12:477-528.
31. Adler, G. and Buie, D. The misuses of confrontation in the psychotherapy of borderline cases. In: G. Adler and P. Myerson (Eds.), *Confrontation in Psychotherapy.* New York: Science House, 1973, p. 154.
32. Glover, E. *The Roots of Crime.* New York: International Universities Press, 1960, p. 149.
33. Day, M. and Semrad, E. Schizophrenic reactions. In: A. Nicholi (Ed.), *The Harvard Guide to Modern Psychiatry.* Cambridge, Mass.: Harvard Univ. Press, 1978, p. 227.
34. MacVicar, K. Splitting and identification with the aggressor in assaultive borderline patients. *Amer. J. Psychiat.*, 1978, 135:229-231.
35. Ovesey, L. *Homosexuality and Pseudohomosexuality.* New York: Science House, 1969, p. 31.
36. Woods, S. Violence: Psychotherapy of pseudohomosexual panic. *Arch. Gen. Psychiatry*, 1972, 27:255-258.
37. Sadoff, R. Other sexual deviations. In: A. Friedman, H. Kaplan, and B. Sadock (Eds.), *Comprehensive Textbook of Psychiatry* (Second Edition). Baltimore: The Williams and Wilkins Company, 1975, p. 1541.
38. Zetzel, E. The so-called good hysteric. In: E. Zetzel (Ed.), *The Capacity for Emotional Growth.* New York: International Universities Press, 1970, pp. 229-245.
39. Chodoff, P. and Lyons, H. Hysteria, the hysterical personality and hysterical conversion. *Amer. J. Psychiat.*, 1958, 114:734-740.
40. Yochelson, S. and Samenow, S. *The Criminal Personality,* Vol. 2. New York: Jason Aronson, 1977.
41. Yochelson, S. and Samenow, S. *The Criminal Personality,* Vol. 1. New York: Jason Aronson, 1976.
42. Kernberg, O., Burstein, E., Coyne, L., et al. Psychotherapy and Psychoanalysis. Final report of the Menninger Foundation's Psychotherapy Research Project. *Bull. Menninger Clinic*, 1972, 36:1-275.
43. Johnson, A. and Szurek, S. The genesis of antisocial acting out in children and adults. *Psychoanal. Quart.*, 1952, 21:323-343.
44. Kohut, H. *The Analysis of the Self.* New York: International Universities Press, 1971.
45. Rochlin, G. *Man's Aggression.* New York: Dell Publishing, 1973, p. 130.

46. Weinstock, R. Capgras' syndrome, a case involving violence. *Amer. J. Psychiat.,* 1976, 135:855.
47. Alexander, F. *The Criminal, The Judge and The Public.* New York: Macmillan, 1931.
48. Aichhorn, A. *Wayward Youth.* New York: The Viking Press, 1935.
49. Stanton, A. and Schwartz, M. *The Mental Hospital.* New York: Basic Books, 1954.
50. Blacker, K. and Tupin, J. Hysteria and hysterical structure: Developmental and social theories. In: M. Horowitz (Ed.), *Hysterical Personality.* New York: Jason Aronson, 1977, pp. 122-123.

13

Psychotherapy with Physically Ill Patients

TOKSOZ B. KARASU, M.D.

CONCEPTUAL AND CLINICAL FOUNDATIONS

Psychotherapy with patients who are afflicted with so-called psychosomatic disease is one of the most challenging areas in our profession. Not only the knowledge and the technique of the therapist, but also his personal resources, face the greatest test in dealing with these patients. "Psychosomatherapists" have limited theoretical concepts and frames of reference in dealing with these patients, in comparison to those available in the treatment of neurotics, character disorders or borderline patients, and even psychotics. Craddock (1) has noted how the therapist's limited knowledge and experience make work with somatic patients discouraging.

The most striking influence in the field of psychotherapy with psychosomatic patients has undoubtedly been the application of psychoanalytical principles to the study of the so-called "holy seven"—bronchial asthma, dermatitis, hypertension, thyrotoxicosis, peptic ulcer, rheumatoid arthritis, and ulcerative colitis. While Dunbar (2) investigated the correlation between particular personality dimensions and different diseases, Alexander (3, 4) examined the relationship of specific intrapsychic conflicts to specific psychosomatic disorders. These types of theoretical models still constitute the core of working hypotheses for practitioners who are engaged in the treatment of such patients. Later work of Wolff (5, 6), Rahe (7, 8, 9) and others has addressed itself to social and environmental crises in the lives of patients, thereby initiating an era of stress-oriented, short-term approaches and the extension beyond orthodox psychosomatic disorders to encompass the recently renamed "psychophysiological" reactions (10), as well as diseases such as myocardial infarction, migraine headaches, anorexia nervosa, etc.

The conceptual foundations and application of psychoanalytic theory and psychodynamic principles to the treatment of psychosomatic disorders are well reflected in the case studies of Sperling (11, 12), Jessner (13), and Castelnuovo-Tedesco (14, 15). The basic psychodynamic thesis of Sperling, for example, is based on her work with children who have severe psychosomatic disorders, especially ulcerative colitis and bronchial asthma. She has concluded that "every case of psychosomatic disorder has its origin in the mother-child relation of dependency." That is, "no matter how independent and self-sufficient a patient's life may appear to be, we find on closer inspection in every psychosomatic case . . . that the patient lives in an emotional symbiosis with one object in his environment, who does not have to be the actual mother but who somehow, in the patient's unconscious, serves the dynamic function of a mother figure. The psychosomatic patient cannot consciously tolerate his pregenital impulses . . . he, therefore, denies them completely and they are converted into somatic symptoms and in this way gratified" (11, p. 286). Castelnuovo-Tedesco (14, 15), who worked with adult patients, has emphasized the roles of fantasized or real alterations (i.e., real or threatened separation, coercion or intrusiveness in significant object relationships of the patient) which play a major part in the exacerbation of illness.

Although some success with psychoanalytic techniques has been reported by individual therapists, research findings have been nonconfirmatory (16, 17, 18). The application of analytical approaches in the therapy of psychosomatic disorders has not synchronized with the wide acceptance of its theory. Thus, few therapists still continue to treat these patients in a traditional psychoanalytical manner. Their reluctance is compounded by the general opinion of the public and the resistance of referring physicians, whose view of psychotherapy for psychosomatic patients has been less than favorable (19).

Moreover, not much support has come from within the profession itself. Sperling (11) stressed the uneconomic aspect of therapy with these patients. Sifneos (20) suggested that some patients actually get worse from the psychodynamic process, and that, for the majority of patients with psychosomatic disorders, dynamic psychotherapy is contraindicated.

Similar statements could be made about any group of patients. Certainly, analysis of neurotic patients is no less uneconomic, and one may comfortably state that, for the majority of the patient population at large, an analytical approach would be contraindicated. One should not forget, however, the heuristic value of working with these individuals, as well as the contribution that psychotherapy could make to the health of such individuals who are suffering from intractable chronic illnesses, no matter how few they are and how expensive it might be.

The above attitudes certainly have not encouraged psychosomatherapists to continue the arduous task of working with these patients. Most psychiatrists in the field have therefore confined their work to consultation-liaison services and brief intervention approaches. Alexander's (21) "platonic ideal" of teamwork between the psychiatrist, the medical specialist and others on the wards is not necessarily an unachievable goal. In fact, relative success has been gained in such collaborative efforts on liaison services. Rather, a major difficulty is the lack of accepted theory and a working hypothesis that one is relatively sure about and can share with others. The latter, I believe, is the main source of therapist countertransference in working with these patients, as discussed in the writings of Fain and Marty (22) and Wolff (19).

Nonetheless, research work in this area has continued to explore the efficacy of psychotherapy. Lazarus and Hagens (23) have utilized brief psychotherapy in their attempt to decrease postoperative delirium in cardiotomy patients. Layne and Yudofsky (24) have reported positive results with even single interviews, and Surman et al. (25) have replicated these favorable findings. These brief approaches utilized supportive as well as educational techniques, including rectifying possible misconceptions about forthcoming procedures, teaching patients a simple autohypnotic technique, etc.

The aim of this chapter, however, is to delineate some of the specific practices of long-term individual psychotherapy with patients who have a medical illness, addressing psychological components in initiation, maintenance, or etiology of the disease.

It may be hypothesized that all medical diseases have psychological components. The earlier theories, that there are specific factors in the psychological makeup of the patients which make them susceptible to certain somatic diseases, have not been confirmed by research findings. But controversy on the matter is still quite alive, as exemplified in theories of the dependency struggle of ulcer patients, or the hard-driven personalities of patients with cardiac disorders. Others have focused their attention upon more generalized factors, such as the patients' cognitive organization, defense mechanisms, and attitudes, e.g., inability to verbalize emotions, denial of psychic conflicts, and a major manifestation—profound resistance to therapy. Reckless and Fauntleroy (26) viewed such denial as an archaic defense against feelings of anxiety, and emphasized the difficulty of these patients in expressing emotions, especially their aggressive feelings against others. O'Connor (27) pointed out the psychosomatic patient's need to have his physical symptoms for the very purpose of warding off psychological insights. Wolff (19), in fact, believes that somatic disorders often develop because emotional conflicts and impulses are not allowed direct expression. In addition, most somatically distressed patients are usually unaware of their being under stress (28). Thus, they will consciously deny the psychological contributions to their illnesses with a façade of emotional strength, regarding the show of emotional problems as signs of weakness, or as synonomous with malingering (29). Others have focused on the fundamental character problems of patients with psychosomatic disorders. A so-called "psychosomatic character pattern" has been formulated with the following manifestations: lack of libidinal affect, impoverished use of language, operational thinking, inability to regress, and lack of neurotic behavior (30). Sifneos (31) observed these patients' poverty of fantasy life, constriction of emotional functioning, inability to find appropriate words to verbalize feelings, and absence of ability and motivation for self-examination, which occurred within the therapeutic situation. He termed this composite of characteristics, "alexithymic." McDougall (28) recognized a "psychological hardiness" in these patients, a need to refuse to reveal or give in to their dependency, disappointment, anger or despair. Castelnuovo-Tedesco (14) spoke of the ulcerative colitis patient's aloofness, detachment, and contentious demandingness, which tends to come to the fore in the analytic situation. Reckless and Fauntleroy (26) described this overall posture of psychosomatic patients in treatment as "a negative attitudinal set."

Nevertheless, these hypotheses and observations have not been sufficiently translated into the language of practice so that they might be applied to the actual treatment of patients. In describing this, I will focus my discussion on the treatment of patients with peptic ulcer or myocardial infarction, with whom I have had the most contact, although I believe that the following generalized principles are clinically applicable to most somatically disturbed patients.

THE TREATMENT PROCESS

Treatment of illnesses like acute ulcers and myocardial infarctions in an inpatient hospital setting relies upon the therapeutic benefits of a great deal of physical and psychological rest and, to a great extent, the actual removal of the patient from his life situation and its stresses. The role of the psychiatrist at this time is usually limited to identifying the sources of stress in the life of the patient. Most patients may not volunteer such material for discussion with the therapist. In general, the therapist's support and availability are needed, but only tolerated by the patient, his family and physicians. Unfortunately, after treatment of the acute phase of their illness, patients are usually discharged to the same situation from which they came. But these illnesses are usually chronic, and stresses in the life of an individual everlasting. It would be unwise for the therapist to promote the fantasy of a nonstressful existence; however, if the therapist's relationship with the patient can be established, the therapist may temper the situation by neither indulging nor totally denying the stress. These efforts by the therapist, unfortunately, are often of little avail, since a large proportion of patients tend to drop out at this early stage of treatment.

In a moderately longer-term treatment, where a manageable stress situation can be maintained, the therapist may attempt to make the patient aware of some of his unconscious needs and defenses, and try to modify his coping mechanisms to life stresses. Here, lack of success in simple reduction of stresses, or rejection by the patient of suggestions of alternative coping mechanisms, may lead to the therapist's becoming discouraged. In such instances, the therapist may revert back to the typical analytical model with which he is most comfortable.

The psychodynamic working theory for long-term treatment of somatic patients is based on certain assumptions: a) that unconscious impulses are manifesting themselves in pathology of the organs; b) that affective experience is inhibited or repressed and/or somatically manifested; and c) that developmental stages of the individual are arrested and have never reached their symbolic, verbal, expressive stage. Regardless of the validity of these theoretical formulations, such generalizations are of little practical use as such. Moreover, they may actually interfere with the clinician's careful evaluation of the patient, since they provide ready-made explanations. Such categorical approaches only help to comfort the therapist. Therefore, firstly, the psychotherapist treating psychosomatic illnesses should get away from any generalized formula that may be applicable to all diseases or patients; rather, he needs to explore with the individual patient the role of his symptoms in his life, their conscious and unconscious meanings, and whether there are stresses that initiate them, or conflicts that maintain the patient's disease. Individual patterns of somatization, the patient's coping mechanisms and defense structures, instinctual patterns, and his total character organization require careful individual attention prior to assessing the specific patient's suitability for psychotherapy. Criteria used to assess the suitability for psychotherapy of neurotic patients and those with character disorders are quite applicable to medically ill patients, that is, ability to establish an interpersonal relationship, insightfulness, psychological mindedness, ability to sustain motivation, etc. Yet, the relative lack of these desirable qualities should not deter the therapist from attempting to treat the patient because it may mean altering his approach. Practitioners modify their approaches all the time to accommodate psychotic populations, less intelligent patients, severe borderlines, etc.

At the end of the initial evaluation of the person, the patient and therapist should share a sense that either the patient's medical illness is reactive to external stresses, or is the result of his failing coping mechanisms (with or without primary or secondary gains associated with illness). It is then possible to formulate a treatment approach that can be acceptable to both parties. Such a negotiation is quite an important aspect of working with somatic patients.

On the other hand, if the therapist does not find external stresses or failure of coping mechanisms, but identifies certain characterological structures of the patient as either causing or participating in the initiation or maintenance of the illness, he may still attempt to do psychotherapy, recognizing that such assumptions are only inferential. Whether the primary goal of psychotherapy is addressed to the maturation of the individual or a resolution of psychodynamic conflicts, it must be understood that the therapist may state only that the patient's illness be secondarily helped by such a process. It is important that the patient agree to a working relationship on this basis at the beginning; otherwise, the question of "what has all this got to do with my illness?" will become a major obstacle in therapy, and the patient will drop out of treatment sooner or later.

The difficulty of keeping these patients in treatment is well-known. This might be due partly to factors relating to the patient per se, such as defensiveness and the characterological aspects discussed earlier, but it is also a result of the psychiatrist's inability to present convincing evidence to the patient that he might be of help. This is partly related to the fact that we are not ourselves convinced about the nature of these diseases and their psychological treatment, and we certainly do not have enough experience or confidence. There is a lack of a consistent body of knowledge in the field, especially in the application of psychotherapy and its techniques in the treatment of these patients. Therefore, the therapist is very much without adequate tools. Unfortunately, most training programs fail to provide experience in the treatment of psychosomatic illnesses. This, compounded with insecurities from limited knowledge in the field itself, creates an unfavorable condition from the beginning. These uncertainties are consciously and unconsciously conveyed to the patient in the earlier stages of treatment, possibly resulting in disruption of the therapeutic relationship. This is not to say that the therapist ought not have scientific skepticism about what he does and its effects in clinical practice, but the balance has to favor the basic premise of the importance of the therapist's confidence in his work. That is, he must be relatively sure of his theoretical frame of reference, his goals to be accomplished, their feasibility, as well as how he will go about performing his therapeutic tasks, i.e., his techniques.

Unfortunately, psychosomatherapists are handicapped in all of these areas. Moreover, medically ill patients constantly challenge the therapist, his knowledge, the relevancy of the psychological material to their illnesses, etc. Since the therapist is under such attack when working, these patients typically pose a threat to his self-esteem and self-confidence, and tax his patience. Very few therapists are willing or able to survive such an experience. The typical neurotic patient may confront the therapist similarly, but usually responds favorably when the therapist makes explicit the patient's implicit doubts and questions about his ability. Also, he is more accepting of the therapist when he interprets the negative transference. But generally such approaches have not proven to be successful in dealing with psychosomatic patients. Rather, the clarification or interpretation of the patient's doubt of the psychotherapist and psychotherapy in the treatment of his illness tends to lead to confirmation of the patient's doubt; most attempts at the searching into the negative transference only serve to exacerbate the situation by precipitating termination.

In practice, a reasonable therapist would suggest at this stage that he is not sure that the patient's medical illness would be ameliorated by psychotherapy. But there are probably certain problems in the individual's life, which may be identified during the sessions, which he would be glad to work on with the patient in the hope that somatic symptoms of the patient might benefit from such treatment. However, most patients are not likely to be favorably disposed to such a proposal and will demand either a greater promise or a more concrete statement from the therapist that symptoms will be helped by psychotherapy. That is usually the end of the relationship. A therapist who overpromises with the hope of keeping the patient in treatment will suffer through each session again and again answering the same questions, but will end up with the patient terminating anyway.

CASE ILLUSTRATIONS

A typical case demonstrates some of the difficulties confronting the therapist in the initial interview: A 49-year-old male patient, owner of a large manufacturing company, was referred to me after having his first myocardial infarction. His physician was familiar with the studies of type A personality and felt that his patient belonged to this category and might benefit from psychotherapy.

The patient was a largely built man, weighed about 300 pounds and was 5 feet, 9 inches tall. He was well-dressed, self-confident, aggressive and verbal. He had been married for 20 years to his high school sweetheart and had two children, ages 18 and 16. Both girls were doing well in school and their social lives. His wife was a maternal, somewhat demanding woman, but dedicated and loyal to him. The family situation was relatively stable. The patient was the youngest of three children, with a sister five years older and a brother 14 years older than himself. His father died when he was 15 years old and left a large business to his brother, himself and his brother-in-law. His mother was living in a nursing home. His older brother had taken charge of the operation of the business since the death of the father, but the patient himself was quite active and successful, especially in a special part of the business. He smoked one pack of cigarettes a day, drank two to three cocktails every night, was sexually active with his wife at least three times a week, and also was seeing other women, mostly call girls, at least once a week while entertaining his out-of-town customers. The patient had no history of other medical illnesses or psychiatric problems. He was put on a diet and anticoagulants by his medical doctor, but he was not complying with these orders.

In his relationship with me, he reluctantly gave responses to my questions in trying to explore his psychological world. He looked annoyed and asked what all this had to do with his heart problems. I told him I did not know, but perhaps he felt there were areas in his life about which he felt distressed. He said that he would like to smoke less and eat less, and asked whether I could hypnotize him for that purpose. He was clearly interested in a quick and effortless result. I told him that I agreed that smoking and eating were certainly important areas for him to modify, that hypnosis might be one of the possibilities to explore in getting help, and asked if that was the only area he considered problematic. He said that there was nothing else that might be helped by a psychiatrist. It was clear that the communication between me and the patient was leading towards a typical ending. I decided to tap some of the other areas mentioned at the risk of further alienating the patient. I asked him whether he was conflicted about sleeping with other women. He said, "No," that this had been his pattern throughout his marriage and had never interfered with his life. In relation to business, he said it was all okay—he was making a lot of money, though his brother sometimes was too domineering, but he had learned to bear with him.

As far as his medical illness (myocardial infarction), he said, "I guess I could have died," recognizing some degree of fear, but bragged about his flirting with the nurse the second day of his admission to the hospital. I asked him whether that was his way of dealing with his fears. His answer was "No, I always like women." About dying, he said that one day he will die, but he cannot stop and worry about it, and that he is determined to enjoy his life. He had no other interest in matters such as art, music, etc., although he had finished college. He said that he did not fantasize, that his dreams were very realistic. He did say he had some preoccupations, but when I asked whether he could tell me about them he replied, "You would be bored with what's on my mind." When I persisted he responded by saying that his mind was blank at the moment.

I asked him why he agreed to come to see me even though he felt that psychologically there was nothing wrong with him. He said that he came because his physician insisted. He apologetically added that he didn't want to insult me, but thought he was wasting his time and money with me. There was a long silence while I was thinking that he might be right. We looked into each other's eyes, searching for a graceful way of terminating the session. I asked him what he was thinking while looking at me. He said that he was wondering whether it would be difficult to find a cab at 5:00 p.m. in this neighborhood. Our time was up for the day. When I then told him that we should set up another appointment for the next week, he looked rather surprised.

This case illustrates how my attempts to find an area of intrapsychic conflict were responded to with denial, even though his resentful relationship with the brother, his sexual acting out, and his concern about dying were rather easy to identify. Although he did so reluctantly, he responded to the questions enough for me to formulate some understanding of the patient. However, he was completely unaware of the pathological aspect of his own behavior. In contrast to psychopathic persons who would likely make some attempt to justify or rationalize their behavior or manipulatively may express some pseudo-guilt, my patient was quite comfortable with himself, and only annoyed by my search for an ego-alien aspect of his behaviors, feelings or tendencies towards acting out. His feelings toward his dominating brother were kept out of his consciousness, and my attempts to unearth them created further solidification of his defensive attitude; this was the beginning of his disengagement with me during the interview. His "operational thinking" (30) was almost caricatured in his wondering whether, "he would find a cab at that hour," at a moment of search for insight, feelings or comments about our interaction. Of course, at the end one could have terminated the session without further appointment. But I have learned with these patients not to take the *no* for an answer. Yet the therapist who takes such a risk must be ready to deal with sarcasm, further questioning, or outright rejection.

This patient illustrates several initial difficulties in working with these patients—reluctance to become engaged with the therapist; lack of suitable material for psychological work; lack of motivation or incentive for the therapy; lack of introspectiveness; apparent absence of ego-alien psychological symptoms; absence of seeds for transference; pensée opératoire par excellence; affective distancing; strong denial and other pathological defenses; and frustrating, challenging and other non-accepting postures towards the therapist. But one should not be discouraged by this conglomerate of negative factors because these are related parts of the overall defensive structure of the patient, and potentially amenable to therapy. These can become workable patients.

A negative attitude or set as initial resistance to becoming engaged with the therapist is typical of many patients with psychosomatic disorders. Basically, they are loners who will maintain their self-image and the relative stability of their psychological order, internally, by using a great deal of denial, and externally, by constantly reshaping their environment to secure their stability. Any threats directed towards these external factors may create disorganization for the patient, whose defense mechanism of denial may no longer be successfully operative. In some patients, the somatic symptoms are manifestations of this particular stage of failure of coping mechanism, the latter precariously kept in balance between the denial and the private order of the external world. Here, these patients' reluctance to engage with the therapist is a resistance to a real, as well as to a transferential, relationship. I call this avoidance the "resistance to transference" because, in contrast to psychotic patients, these patients' potential for transference does exist. Therefore, the first task of the therapist is to keep the patient in treatment, which is an inherently difficult task. One cannot expect a typical positive attitude from these patients, as compared to those who are experiencing psychic pain, because of their lack of ego-alien symptoms such as depression, anxiety, etc. As such, there are no given incentives to keep the patient in treatment, nor enough motivation generated during the interview to maintain the patient's initial interest in treatment (which is usually meager to begin with).

In this regard, I have found certain similarities between somatic patients and adolescents, who are also somewhat reluctant to talk about their psychological problems at the initial stage of treatment. In the latter instances, the therapist has to engage the adolescent actively in the discussion of a subject that is to his interest, i.e. football, jazz, etc. With the patients who have somatic disorders, a common initial ground for patient and therapist is the patient's daily life, which is his major preoccupation even though he may be reluctant to talk about it. Therefore, in order to engage the somatic patient in a relationship, the therapist has to, at times, learn a great deal about the person's business life or other daily life, almost as much as about the childhood and interpersonal relationships of the patient. What may appear to be a trivial matter that preoccupies the patient's mind and a seemingly unimportant detail to the therapist in his attempt to understand the patient may lead to a great deal of information, if the therapist is willing to listen with patience. Interpersonal and work behaviors are always worth exploring because they may give clues to the psychological makeup of the individual as well as his conflicts.

The psychosomatherapist should not make any attempt to replicate traditional psychotherapy by keeping silent and encouraging development of the classical transference. If he is successful at all in his attempts, he will only create a negative transference, which will not be undone by interpretations, and the patient will end up dropping out of therapy. The fact that the patient is not forming transferences is a manifestation of his object relations in life. Patients that I have treated never had a good object relationship in their lives. Most of the objects in the past have been extremely ambivalently incorporated; therefore, every effort is being made by these patients against the development of transference.

Another feature, lack of affective experiencing, which is commonly mentioned in the literature, is related either to the overpowering aspect of the affect, which is usually negative, or to the fact that the affect is associated with certain somatic experiences and therefore to be avoided. The therapist should not insist upon inquiring into the absence of affects or keep prodding the patient, "tell me how you feel"; rather, he should understand the defensive purpose of the affective block as one of the characteristics of these personalities.

Even during the initial interviews, there are usually longer silences than psychotherapists are accustomed to. This is related to a particular inability of the patient to engage in free associations, verbalization of his feelings, spontaneity, etc. This is consistent with the findings of Marty, M'Uzan and David (30), in their studies of psychosomatic patients. They observed a type of inertia which threatened to bring discussion to an end; the investigator had to make vigorous efforts to stimulate associative material concerning the patient's relationships, life experience and illness; also, significant or painful events were absent unless directly solicited. In such instances, therapists should not stay silent as they might in typical psychotherapeutic situations with neurotic patients.

Mushatt's (32) work with ulcerative colitis patients confirms that these patients cannot tolerate therapists' silences. Therefore, therapists should be as encouraging as possible and actively try to engage the patient to speak. Sifneos (20) also noted that psychosomatic patients find little to talk about. In fact, most of these patients will respond by saying "nothing" to the question, "What are you thinking?" On further inspection, they usually are thinking about minor matters and details in their lives, and are embarrassed to mention them unless the therapist insists and also reassures them that such realities are important to talk about.

Since material that is necessary for psychotherapy is so difficult to elicit, one is often tempted to talk to the patient about his defensive posture and his avoidance of the therapeutic situation. Again, such an approach generally proves to be rather useless and even further alienates the patient. As a result, the countertransference of the therapist to these patients is a very significant matter to consider; it commonly manifests itself in annoyance, boredom, or belittling statements of an aggressive nature, either in the guise of attacking their defenses or of interpreting the affective distance, which further eliminate the potential for a therapeutic alliance. Since the traditional therapeutic frame of reference is not operative, the typical therapist tends to become defensive. Feelings of impotence, rejection, self-doubt, and defeat emerge. Such unsettling conditions in the therapist are not conducive to creating any confidence in the patient; therefore, the vicious cycle will continue, with a typical statement on the part of the therapist that the patient is not motivated or suitable for psychotherapy. Fain and Marty (22) have pointed out the countertransferential lack of interest that develops from the patient's character and constitutes a chronic narcissistic blow to the therapist's interpretive powers because the patient appears impervious to his special skills. The truth is that the patient has come to at least explore the possibilities, but the working hypothesis of the therapist may not be suitable for that particular patient.

Four years later, the patient I discussed earlier in a case study is still with me. Recently we are in the process of discussing termination of therapy. He does not have any symptoms of MI, has lost 100 pounds over the past two years, stopped smoking and acting out, is complying with his medical doctor's food and activities regimen, has taken up a hobby of his father (photography) upon my suggestion, and has become a more active partner in the business. There are many relatively unresolved issues related to his character structure, such as his fear of aggression and his strong dependency needs, but he acknowledges them with a sense of humor, expressing his disappointment that he has to lose childhood forever. In summary, I do not want to overestimate what has been accomplished. The patient's characterological problems by and large remain unchanged or mildly modified. But he has gained a perspective over his life and his problems, has learned to think psychologically, and has begun to enjoy himself and to laugh at times at his "craziness." He has explored the other simple pleasures of life, and stopped the sexual acting out which was guilt provoking (though previously denied). He has become less anxious and made contingency plans in case of death; a reasonable fear of death has begun to emerge. Whether these changes have contributed to his not having any signs of MI, I cannot answer. But if he does have one in the future, I know he will be able to cope with it.

TREATMENT RECOMMENDATIONS

In considering the totality of treatment, there are many stages of the relationship between the psychiatrist and the patient. Initially, the therapist may have to be involved with the physician, the family of the patient, and the other staff involved in his care. During this stage, the psychiatrist's main focus is diagnosis and management. He will continue to explore the psychological makeup of the patient, but basically treatment is limited to recommendation of medication, changes in the environment, and facilitating the communication between the parties involved. This first phase is applicable not only to psychosomatic disorders, but to all medical illnesses. The therapist is basically a supportive person who is available to deal with the stresses in the person's life, family, job, etc. He may explore the patient's psychological contribution to his illness as well as his psychological reaction to it, i.e., fears of dying, shattering of omnipotence, guilt, frustration, and issues such as money, confinement, etc. The therapist may provide an alternative to the patient's pathological and nonadaptive defenses.

In a chronic phase, the therapist may repeat the issues of the acute phase in a modified way, especially if it is his first contact with the patient. Otherwise, the therapist's role would be one of focusing more on establishment of the working alliance with the patient and engaging with him in the areas where mutual work could be done. Chronic patients are more reluctant than acute ones in establishing a relationship with the psychiatrist. Initially, a session once a week is the best frequency that a patient can tolerate. This allows the patient to be distant enough not to force premature intimacy, but also it will provide sufficient continuity of contact with the therapist. Towards the resolution of the dependency phase, one may increase the sessions to more than once a week. This stage usually corresponds to development of freer associations and the presence of dream material and is, therefore, appropriate in its intensity.

During the initial phase of the treatment, then, the therapist must:

1) take an active role during the sessions in creating an atmosphere of easier interchange;

2) receive initial trust of the patient by a display of acceptance and knowledge of his medical illness;

3) create a working alliance by taking an interest and learning about the daily life of the individual, and tolerating his operational thinking while gradually educating him to psychological introspection;

4) recognize and tolerate the patient's major defenses, which are: splitting, avoidance, manipulating, distancing; and

5) resist the temptation for premature interpretations.

After a successful first phase of therapy, the patient may begin to recognize the therapist as a teacher, ally, supporter, etc. The second phase may be described as the "phase of experiencing." This is the time when the patient develops dependency on the therapist. He will begin to open up about his well-kept secrets in his daily life, testing the acceptance of the therapist, and also making an attempt to deal with the guilts and fears associated with it. Even at this stage, psychological elements of early child-hood are rarely present, and the focus of therapy is basically here-and-now. Any attempt on the part of the therapist to interpret increasing dependency is ill-advised, because it usually leads to denial of it by the patient, and very commonly, to a reexperiencing of the somatic symptoms. Stevens (33) noted that the transference interpretations in therapy mobilize enormous anxiety in these patients. Most patients mistakenly view the therapist's comments about their dependency as a threat of termination. Such fear will not dissipate with interpretation or reassurance, which the patient may perceive as confirmation of his dependency, a weak position that he has defended against all his life. The rate of drop-outs among these patients is probably higher during this phase than at any other time, except the initial phase of treatment. The therapist is usually blamed for having aggravated the patient's condition. However, in a well-managed second stage, the patient should be able to experience the first positive feelings towards the therapist—affection, dependency, protective friendliness, etc. These feelings usually do not create any somatic symptoms, much to the amazement of the patient, who had with-held all these feelings for a lifetime. With the pleasure of these new sensations, the patient may indulge himself by going into a positive expressive stage, not only with the therapist, but also with some members of the family and friends alike. The therapist should allow this somewhat superficial stage of experiencing positive feelings to go on for a long time. Of course, one cannot necessarily avoid the unpleasantness in a person's life, but experiencing negative feelings should not be encouraged during the therapy sessions. Rage, anger and similar affects should not be explored prior to establishing some somatic comfort along with positive feelings.

Affect has been said to be non-existent in the patient, that is, the patient usually makes every effort not to experience the feelings associated with unpleasant bodily sensations. In the past, headaches, stomach acid, pain in the chest, etc. are experienced with feelings such as anger, anxiety, fear, and later on generalized to include the positive feelings as well, i.e. warmth, intimacy, love, affection, dependency, yearnings. All affect is to be avoided if one wants to stay somatically well. Therefore, for the patient to express his positive feelings without experiencing bodily discomfort is an important step in the treatment.

The earlier objects of the patient are commonly remembered as undependable. Therefore, the therapist should avoid any behavior, i.e., cancellations, lateness, in order to prevent development of negative feelings during the initial phase of the treatment. During this time, the initial doctor/patient relationship will gradually shift towards more of a friend/friend relationship. Later on, a teacher/student type of relationship may begin to develop. The typical analytical therapist/patient relationship, which has been likened to a father/child relationship, may eventually be established, approximately six to twelve months after the onset of treatment. Only when a reliable dependency relationship has been established will some early material start to emerge. At such time, the affect that is experienced may be positive or negative; at this point the therapist has to monitor the somatic symptoms before he can encourage further regression, freer associations, or the reporting of dream material. The conduct of treatment during this phase is no different from the traditional approach, that is, insight-oriented dynamic psychotherapy. At the same time, the patient may be encouraged to do certain homework in the form of behavioral exercises, i.e., controlled aggression and assertion, sexual intimacy, and the expression of dependency needs to other individuals.

Conclusion

The following guidelines are recommended in the treatment of physically ill patients:

1) First and foremost, the therapist has to create a climate of therapeutic acceptance, warmth, understanding, and empathy in the therapeutic situation, as well as provide all the other nonspecific conditions for a supportive environment. Specific techniques have to be flexible enough to accommodate a range of psychosomatic concepts, such as the psychogenesis of the illness, one's psychological contribution or psychological reaction to life stress and illness, maintenance of the disease and symptoms and/or specific psychological predisposition to them, psychodynamic configurations and character structures related to particular somatic disorders, etc. In some instances, none of these elements may be represented; in others, one or more of these possibilities may exist. Therefore, a highly individualized approach to each patient, with specific assessment of his respective psychological picture, is important prior to initiating or formulating the therapeutic plan.

2) A thorough medical and psychological history should be taken on intake. This requires that the therapist must be familiar not only with the disease in question, but with its medical treatment.

3) At the beginning, the therapist should address himself to the patient's understanding of the psychiatric referral itself, about which there

are fears and concerns as well as expectations. Most patients do show up for the first interview to pass the test of sanity, but not necessarily to be helped by a psychiatrist. Halsted and Weinberg (34), for example, had observed that the ulcer patient would ultimately agree to pyschiatric investigation not because of a recognition of his own needs, but because he was convinced he was doing it for someone else. It is important to recognize this phenomenon at an early session, which has an educational value for the patient as well as helping to create positive relations with the therapist.

4) Therapeutic intervention should be carefully paced. Initially, the patient should not be seen more than once or twice a week because any more intensive involvement can generate excessive anxiety and exacerbation of symptoms. At this time, he should be able to discuss the questions of the patient with regard to his illness without competing with the internist. This interaction will serve to increase the confidence of the patient in the therapist, and will also serve an educative function of clarifying those questions of the patient that the internist may not have answered. For example, Bilodeau and Hackett's (35) study of cardiac patients in group therapy revealed several questions and concerns of their patients, including issues of diminished libido and fear of death during intercourse; yet, no group member had discussed these concerns with his medical doctor, and none of the internists ventured to bring up these subjects with their patients. The patient's misconceptions and misunderstandings about his illness need to be corrected first as a way of dealing with his anxieties, fears, and concerns about himself. Such discussions usually include the vulnerability and mortality of the patient, his or her fear of dying, issues of separation, etc. On one level, medical illness and its medical treatment are discussed, and on the other, psychological parameters of the illness are explored.

5) In terms of therapeutic technique and its timing, the therapist has to engage the patient initially in reality issues, which may be trivial daily affairs, in order to establish a common ground between patient and therapist. It must be emphasized that, as Sperling (11) has pointed out, interpretation of maladaptive defenses in psychosomatic patients at an early stage of the treatment may aggravate the patient's somatic condition. It is common, too, that the patient's psychological condition may also deteriorate. However, precipitation of a pyschotic breakdown, however feared by therapists, has been reported as unlikely in actual practice (19).

6) In general, the therapist should recognize that it is not his role to treat medical illness, but that he must be concerned with identifying

psychosocial contributors in patients' lives to their illness. He must help patients to recognize their adaptive and nonadaptive responses to their medical illness and help them to modify their responses where necessary, identify secondary gains associated with the illness in order to prevent maintenance of the symptoms, and anticipate and prevent psychological conflicts which might exacerbate somatic symptomatology.

7) Finally, although I suggest that the therapist establish an authentic object relationship with the patient and try to closely monitor the patient in experiencing affect within the therapeutic context, he must at the same time be *flexible* enough to utilize all potential therapeutic agents which might be suitable to his patient. In this way he will be able to establish an approach that might be not only therapeutic as conceptualized by the therapist, but also acceptable to his patient.

REFERENCES

1. Craddock, C. Chronic ulcerative colitis: Effect of a specific psychotherapeutic measure. *Psychosom. Med.*, Sept-Oct 1953, 15 (5):513-522.
2. Dunbar, F. *Emotions and Bodily Changes.* New York: Columbia University Press, 1938.
3. Alexander, F. Emotional factors in essential hypertension. *Psychosom. Med.*, 1939, 1:173-179.
4. Alexander, F. *Psychosomatic Medicine: Its Principles and Applications.* New York: Norton, 1950.
5. Wolff, H. *Stress and Disease.* Springfield: Charles C Thomas, 1953.
6. Hinkle, L. and Wolff, H. Ecologic investigations of the relationship between illness, life experiences and social environment. *Ann. Int. Med.*, 1958, 49:1373-1378.
7. Rahe, R., McKean, J., and Arthur, R. A longitudinal study of life-change and illness patterns. *J. Psychosom. Res.*, 1967, 10:355-366.
8. Rahe, and Arthur, R. Life change patterns surrounding illness experience. *J. Psychosom. Res.*, 1968, 11:341-345.
9. Rahe, R. Subjects' recent life changes and their near-future illness susceptibility. In: Z. Lipowsky (Ed.), *Advances in Psychosomatic Medicine, Volume 8: Psychosocial Aspects of Physical Illness.* Basel: Karger, 1972, pp. 2-19.
10. DSM II. *Diagnostic and Statistical Manual of Mental Disorders.* Washington, D.C.: American Psychiatric Association, 1968.
11. Sperling, M. Psychotherapeutic techniques in psychosomatic medicine. In: G. Bychowski and J. L. Despert (Eds.), *Specialized Techniques in Psychotherapy.* New York: Basic Books, 1952, pp. 279-301.
12. Sperling, M. A psychoanalytic study of bronchial asthma in children. In: H. J. Schneer (Ed.), *The Asthmatic Child: Psychosomatic Approach to Problems and Treatment.* New York: Harper & Row, 1963, pp. 139-165.
13. Jessner, L. Psychoanalysis of an eight-year-old boy with asthma. In: H. I. Schneer (Ed.), *The Asthmatic Child: Psychosomatic Approach to Problems and Treatment.* New York: Harper & Row, 1963.
14. Castelnuovo-Tedesco, P. Ulcerative colitis in an adolescent boy subjected to homosexual assault. *Psychosom. Med.*, 1962, 24 (2):148-155.
15. Castelnuovo-Tedesco, P. Psychiatric observations on attacks of gout in a patient with ulcerative colitis. *Psychosom. Med.*, 1966, 28 (6):781-788.

16. Gildea, E. Special features of personality which are common to certain psychosomatic disorders. *Psychosom. Med.*, 1949, 11:273-279.
17. Chalke, F. Effect of psychotherapy for psychosomatic disorders. *Psychosom.*, May-June, 1965, 6 (3):125-131.
18. Kellner, R. Psychotherapy in psychosomatic disorders: A survey of controlled studies. *Arch. Gen. Psychiat.*, Aug., 1975, 32:1021-1028.
19. Wolff, H. H. The psychotherapeutic approach. In: P. Hopkins and H. H. Wolff (Eds.), *Principles of Treatment of Psychosomatic Disorders*. London: Pergamon Press, 1965, pp. 83-94.
20. Sifneos, P. Is dynamic psychotherapy contraindicated for a large number of patients with psychosomatic diseases? *Psychother. and Psychosom.*, 1972-73, 21:133-136.
21. Alexander, F. The development of psychosomatic medicine. *Psychosom Med.*, 1962, 24 (1):13-24.
22. Fain, M. and Marty, P. A propos du narcissisme et de sa genese. *Rev. Franc. Psychoanal.*, 1965, 29:561-572.
23. Lazarus, H. and Hagens, J. Prevention of psychosis following open-heart surgery. *Amer. J. Psychiat.*, 1968, 124:1190-1195.
24. Layne, O. and Yudofsky, S. Postoperative psychosis in cardiotomy patients: The role of organic and psychiatric factors. *New Engl. J. Med.*, 1971, 284:518-520.
25. Surman, O., Hackett, T., Silverberg, E., and Behrendt, D. Usefulness of psychiatric intervention in patients undergoing cardiac surgery. *Arch. Gen. Psychiat.*, June 1974, 30:830-835.
26. Reckless, J. and Fauntleroy, A. Groups, spouses, and hospitalization as a trial of treatment in psychosomatic illness. *Psychosom.*, 1972, 13 (6):353-357.
27. O'Connor, J. A comprehensive approach to the treatment of ulcerative colitis. In: O. W. Hill (Ed.), *Modern Trends in Psychosomatic Medicine*, Vol. 2. New York: Appleton Century Crofts, 1970, pp. 172-187.
28. McDougall, J. The psychosoma and psychoanalytic process. *Int. Rev. Psychoanal.*, 1974, 1:437-459.
29. Raft, D., Tucker, L., Toomey, T., and Spencer, R.: Use of conjoint interview with patients who somatize. *Psychosomatics*, 1974, 15 (4):164-165.
30. Marty, P., M'Uzan, M., and David, C. *L'Investigation Psychosomatique*. Paris: Presses University de France, 1963.
31. Sifneos, P. The prevalence of "Alexithymic" characteristics in psychosomatic patients. *Psychother. and Psychosom.*, 1973, 22 (2-6):255-262.
32. Mushatt, C. Psychological aspects of non-specific ulcerative colitis. In: E. D. Wittkower and R. A. Cleghorn (Eds.), *Recent Development in Psychosomatic Medicine*. Philadelphia: Lippincott, 1954, pp. 345-363.
33. Stevens, A. The role of psychotherapy in psychosomatic disorders. *Behav. Neuropsychiat.*, 1972, 4 (7-8):2-5.
34. Halsted, J. and Weinberg, H. Peptic ulcer among soldiers in the Mediterranean theater of operations. *New Engl. J. Med.*, 1946, 234:313-318.
35. Bilodeau, C. and Hackett, T. Issues raised in a group setting by patients recovering from myocardial infarction. *Amer. J. Psychiat.*, 1971, 128 (1):23-78.

14

Psychotherapy with Dying Patients

ARTHUR M. SCHWARTZ, M.D.

and

TOKSOZ B. KARASU, M.D.

Edith Weigert said, "The exclusion of death deprives life of its meaning, the personality of its wholeness and human relations of the depth of mutuality" (1, p. 192). Death is an existential fact, and it is more than likely the model for all human feelings of abandonment and separation. Is it, then, so difficult to understand why one should not feel anxious when faced with leaving the life he finds so rewarding and enriching? What we have in mind is the shared denial of death, in both the patient and the psychotherapist, and that the current thinking is overwhelming on the passionate, pleasurable, and sexual aspects of the human experience. After all, if we actually believe in the reality-principle, death is, or should be, as much a part of our discussions as life, else we deny something vital to our patients and, of course, to ourselves. If we are going to be able to offer a therapy for the dying person, then the psychotherapist must examine his own attitudes towards his very own death. It is the countertransference aspects that must first be understood. It has been our impression that psychotherapists are especially reluctant to face up to death in their personal lives and in their professional fields. For the most,

This is a modified version of the paper that was published in the *American Journal of Psychotherapy*, Volume XXXI, No. 1, pp. 19-35, January, 1977.

the psychotherapist relegates matters of dying to other specialties or para-medical professions. It is only within the last decade that the psycho-therapist has allowed himself some closeness with the dying person.

All professions, and especially the health sciences, have a very neces-sary mythology which helps and allows one to get on with more disagree-able portions of the work. It may be that the others, particularly theology, have a better myth. For the clergyman, his myth does not see death as necessarily an end. For the psychotherapist, this is not true. For him dead is dead and irrevocable, and consequently we can anticipate some of his resistances in dealing with a dying person. The selection of the material that the patient brings to the "talking-treatment" is not always as random as we would have ourselves imagine. There exists a "patient empathy" whereby the patient tells us what he thinks we would like to hear. And, if his input senses our reluctance to deal with death, then it is very likely that we will not hear about his fears of death. There exists a discomfort in both parties in talking about death and, in a sense, that is the way it should be. It is no easy matter to tell a patient of his fatal illness, and even more difficult to tell of his coming death. We know that there are physicians for whom this represents no problem. Inured to death and untouched by it, they, of course, are no help for the suffering of the dying person. They might, conceivably, give rise to more suffering, psychosis or stimulation for a massive self-destructive act.

In the past, it was felt that one must not talk with patients about any-thing that might disturb or excite them; they had to be treated like chil-dren. Phrases like, "be brave and everything will be all right," were most commonplace. While we would not deny that in many instances this "suggestion"—a popular albeit frequently misunderstood word—had a magical feeling and did prove helpful, we must admit that the results were, at best, temporary and short-lived, requiring frequent reassurance. In this "psychotherapy," there are also elements of the confessional which tended to hide rather than reveal. While these methods restrict the func-tion of secondary process reasoning and obtain their cure by attaching primary process thinking, there remain some individuals for whom this could be thought of as the method of choice. This is, and should be, an assessment that the psychotherapist would be making during the early phases of his relationship with the dying person.

The gratification for the psychotherapist in his work with patients is seeing and taking part in the resolution of intrapsychic conflict, reducing anxiety and consequently freeing energy for additional libidinal cathexis. There is no doubt of the gratification when we are dealing with a young person who comes to treatment in good physical health, who brings as his chief complaint a desire to establish more loving relationships and in whose growth and maturity we can play a part. But, what are the gratifications for the therapist when the patient's life ends in death? For the therapist, the rewards, in part, can be in terms of trying to bring about a "euthanasia" (2, 3), which literally means the art of dying easily and without pain.

There would be little difficulty if the pain were restricted only to the physical. However, the mental anguish and fear of death, menaces from a punitive superego, are what we have to deal with. Also, as stated earlier, the pitfalls of the manifold countertransference feelings present difficulties. When faced with a hopelessly ill, dying person, the therapist is struggling with many conflicts. For example, is it really harder to die or witness death? The question has a justification when the relationship with the dying person has a closeness. Likewise, there exists a strong sense of embarrassment as one attempts to talk with encouragement when the future is death. Especially at those times when the patient's denial becomes so massive that it goes beyond that of the therapist, and is consequently so unrealistic that the therapist feels removed from reality, a failure of the treatment could be a possibility. At those moments, if the therapist chooses to remain silent, his silence could be understood as accepting the patient's denial as truth. Still another opportunity for failure exists if the therapist permits himself to become part of the real family-situation with all the feelings of guilt and hostility, as if he were really a family member.

More specifically, when working with the dying person, affective empathy is the most effective—where it is understood that there exists an honesty, with very direct communications and without any semblance of value judgments. There must also be present an acceptance, without reservation, of the other person's life story, at least for transitory moments. The empathizer must be able to allow himself to share in the reliving and living through of the dying person's experiences. From this, the dying person gains a sense of this experience and becomes aware of a fusion, which is brief but certainly realized. There seems to be much more difficulty for an observer to be aware of this state in the usual therapeutic situation; at times, however, the dying person's response will make the affective empathy known.

In our personal experience of treatments with dying persons, there have been moments when the patient reversed the roles and became the comforter or caregiver. The fusion permitted and allowed identification and empathy with the therapist, thereby diminishing the sense of extreme loss for both. It is this state of feeling which removes the alone-ness for all of us. The aversion to empathize with the dying person, to feel his helplessness and terror, can be most uncomfortable with our own built-in needs to avoid pain and anxiety. This affective empathy senses the person's real needs rather than waits until it is expressed in uncompromising terms. It is not just emotional closeness or identifica-tion with its narcissistic implications and possible failure of any real support but, rather, allowing oneself to enter into another's life experi-ence fully and without reservation.

The affect of empathy does not mean to imply a mutual suffering along with the person. Olden (4) remarked that it is the interplay be-tween mother and child with mutual sensitivity to the other's feelings that should be regarded as the starting point of empathy. She also stated that the mother needs satisfaction from the infant in order to accomplish the transition from physical gratification to mature empathy. She feels it may begin with the infant's searching of his mother's face. Beres (5) separated the process of identification from empathy. The feeling of identification is transitory and implies a temporary fusion with the ob-ject. Beres and Arlow (6) stated that empathy is not merely feeling with the patient or the object, but about him. Frequently, in the caring for and about the dying person, a bodily contact, i.e., holding or touching an arm or hand, will be meaningful and supportive.

The quality of empathy is the most significant affect a therapist can bring to the treatment of the dying person. It is a quality that requires a substantial degree of ego development, namely, memory, thinking, and good conceptualization; it is likewise much enhanced with age and ex-perience. Greenson (7) also separates identification from empathy by virtue of its permanence and unconsciousness. It is meaningful in the therapy with the dying person because its aim, as in childhood, is to over-come anxiety, guilt, and object loss. Our ubiquitous conscious fears of death are felt in the everyday life as fears of helplessness, injury or aban-donment which, in turn, have their origins in the infantile anxiety due to separation from the protecting mother and in situations where the ego feels powerless. In this state of consciousness with which we are con-fronted in the interaction with the dying person, it will be the degree of affective empathy which will aid in removing the terror of death, and still permit us, as therapists, to maintain our individuality and perspec-tive. At the conclusion of Greenson's paper, he suggests that "people with a tendency to depression make the best empathizers" (p. 422).

The problems of bringing the necessary degree of empathy to the treatment of the dying person are manifold: firstly, because we seem to live our lives deliberately ignoring the anticipation of our own death as well as the deaths of those we love; additionally, the confrontation with the dying person forces us to deny the truth of death to the point of aversion. Painters' and writers' works frequently confront us with the dirty, ugly realities of our existence, perhaps saving great energies which we often expend in avoiding and facing death. In his "Thoughts for the Times on War and Death," Freud (8) stated it thus: "Si vis vitam, para mortem"—"if you would endure life, be prepared for death" (p. 317).

We would like to report the treatment of two persons who came to "thanato-therapy" via two different routes.

CASE 1

The first patient, a 26-year-old, moderately attractive, bright, keen, and mistrusting woman, developed a fatal illness during the course of analysis. When entering treatment, she was married and sought help because of difficulties within the marriage and obsessive thoughts of death and illness with accompanying anxiety. Also, she had an honest desire to spare her one-and-a-half-year-old adopted son her neurotic problems and conflicts. She had felt that her problems were destructive to herself and the family.

Following the summer vacation, she returned to analysis and reported that she had been able to enjoy being with her son and husband on brief holidays at beach resorts and on short trips. However, in keeping with her basic character structure, which was predominantly masochistic, she had sought out a situation during the vacation that would make for guilt and anxiety by entering into an extramarital affair. The material following her return was occupied with efforts to understand the meaning of the acting out. It was during this time that she began to complain of intermenstrual bleeding with painful gums and teeth, all of which she viewed as punishment for her indiscretions.

She had consultations with a dentist and her gynecologist; her dentist encouraged her to have more extensive blood examinations. At this point, she contacted her uncle, a physician, who had functioned as the family doctor through most of the early years. Following a preliminary examination, he phoned the therapist without knowledge of the patient, informing him that everything pointed to acute myelogenous leukemia. He did not comply with the therapist's demand to discontinue the telephone conversation, stating that the emotional shock—a feeling shared by the therapist—made him incapable of providing any further help. He implored the therapist to take over and make any arrangements that he felt necessary.

The therapist informed the patient of the uncle's phone call, but did not disclose the exact nature of the findings other than to say that the uncle would like the therapist to suggest an internist. The patient was most willing to accept the recommendation of the internist who suggested hospitalization for a more complete examination. While hospitalized, she phoned the therapist's office asking if he would be coming to the hospital, since she knew that it was the hospital where the therapist taught psychiatric residents. Her phone call was regarded as a request and the therapist visited her.

There was a quietness about her mood; she was seemingly satisfied with the diagnosis which was said to be infectious mononucleosis. She was free from anxiety and did not appear depressed. There was a distinct sense of well-being about her affect. She was free of symptoms and it was the feeling of the therapist that the illness represented the fulfillment of some unconscious childhood wishes that had the effect of appeasing an underlying harsh and critical conscience, thus causing the neurosis seemingly to vanish.

After this visit, the therapist was button-holed by various family members—the physician-uncle, mother, and husband. The father was present, but chose to remain out of the conversation. The mother and uncle immediately raised the issue of the diagnosis, and both agreed that, at all costs, the truth would be kept from the patient. The husband was not as firm that this should be the course of action, as he would be the one with the patient most often, and having to fend off her ever-present suspicions would be nothing less than formidable. The family, following the patterns of her early childhood, exerted great pressure that the truth be hidden.

Bowing reluctantly to family pressure, the therapist agreed to continue in the deception for the time being. However, he insisted on reserving the right to disclose the nature of her illness to the patient, should he feel that this would alleviate her anxiety, guilt, and despair, when assured at the same time that she would never be abandoned, but rather that the therapist would try to share her experience. He explained to the family that the denial would foster mistrust and the feeling of being set apart, both of which should be avoided if the patient were to have any real opportunity for an "easy death."

The patient returned to the "analysis," where no changes were suggested in the way treatment was to be conducted. The manifest content of her first dream had themes of punishment and death. For the most part, the time that followed was filled with similar material. She would talk about death, diagnosis, punishment and guilt. At no time did she directly question the diagnosis of her illness. The game of hiding the reality and reinforcing the denial continued. She wondered how one goes about explaining death to a child and said that her own mother always shielded her from the realistic details of death. Then she added, "When you die, you are put out of the house and separated from the family." The therapist's formulation, in part, was that it was this separation anxiety with which she had struggled most of her life. She developed an interest in, and fascination with, perpetual motion machines and would fantasize about inventing one.

About two weeks before her death, she decided to write her will, mentioning that she had somewhat less money than when she first married. Four days before her death, she called, saying that she felt too weak to keep her appointment. She had fever, a sore throat and a cough, and asked directly what she should do. The recommendation was that she call her internist and follow his advice. She was hospitalized, but it could not be certain whether this episode represented an upper respiratory infection or perhaps the terminal part of her illness. The following day she called the therapist from the hospital, saying that she did not want to see him, and if he had made plans to visit, it would not be necessary. He was quite aware of her rage, her disappointment with him and his magic. She was experiencing the most intense despair and helplessness, so the therapist decided to visit in spite of her conscious contrary verbalizations. He was cognizant that his insistence on the visit could confirm the seriousness of the illness and give additional proof that he would never abandon her. His formulation and attitude would be reality testing dependent on the assessment of her ego strengths with preserved hope and magical thinking.

The laboratory reports were very unfavorable, disclosing an overwhelming process. Upon first seeing her, there was little doubt in the therapist's mind that she was nearing the end of her life. She was outspoken towards him with her rage, wished for enough strength to toss the water pitcher at him, and advised him that he was lucky she was so weak. But, the ambivalence quickly revealed itself when she thanked him for coming to see her and for sensing that this was really what she wanted. After a while, her father came into the room. She introduced the therapist, asking her father to leave and return later. The remainder of the visit concerned the new medication, her fever, and the weakness she felt. As the therapist was leaving, she repeated that it would not be necessary for him to return the next day, since it was Saturday and should be spent with his family. He said he would return, because he felt she needed him more.

Departing from the hospital, the therapist reviewed the hour just spent in the hope of gleaning what, perhaps, was uppermost in her unconscious. The intuitive response was that she felt he was failing her in the moments of her greatest need. In reality, she felt his performance was very similar to all others in her past and present life. He was making a pretense, keeping secret the truth and not acknowledging that she was dying. He was, for all purposes, allowing her to die alone (9), without comfort, without expression of his grief or compassion, merely continuing a hoax, the nature of which had long since been known to her.

For the following visit, the therapist formulated a tentative plan: to listen, wait for the appropriate moment and disclose the nature of the illness. His hope was to allay or appease the conflict of ambivalence by giving her the feeling that somehow that part of him was dying with her. In his paper, "Dying Together," Ernest Jones (10) pointed to this fantasy and noted that it also contained the wish to be impregnated by, or fused with, the partner. The previous material gave strong evidence for this feeling. At one point during the past months, her desire to adopt another child was so strong that she brought her husband to the office specifically to discuss this possibility. In this psychotherapy, the therapist would be accepting her on one level as a mature woman, giving her the feeling of intense sublimated love or, better called, fondness, and at another level accepting her as a helpless child, but being truthful and refusing to be caught up in the performance of her past family experience.

The next morning the clinical state was somewhat improved, giving hope that a remission might possibly be in the offing. Of course, the therapist's own ambivalence was revived. If this were to be true remission, perhaps the course now would be to withhold the facts and continue the game of making strong the ever-present archaic belief of her own immortality. His decision had to be guided by the expression of her overt anxiety and what he felt she was asking to know. Her greeting was friendlier than the previous day, and she reiterated that this visit was undoubtedly inconveniencing him additionally as, for the most part, she did not feel it was necessary. Her denial was still active and her testing the transference was manifest. She was anxious, tearful and mildly agitated. At the moment the hematologist was preparing to leave the room, and upon his leaving, she expressed relief that the "clown" was gone. She could no longer stand his silly jokes and the talk about infectious mononucleosis; certainly now, she was more aware than at any other time of her impending death.

The therapist sat at her bedside and she continued to talk. She was clear and lucid, giving no evidence of any alteration in her state of consciousness. She spoke about the illness—her doubts about the diagnosis, the trouble she was putting the family through. She was bothered by the loneliness her young son must be feeling; just talking with him by telephone must have helped some. "Why is it taking me so long to get well? Why don't they tell me the truth?"

The therapist reminded her that in all the previous months she never once asked him the diagnosis. She continued to talk, generally performing like a person without the benefit of hearing. After a silence, she turned toward him and asked, "What do I have?" With knowing hesitation, he told her. For the first time in many days, she sat up in bed, reached for his arm, held it tightly, and rested backwards on the pillow. She looked for his hand and clasped it in hers. Speaking softly, haltingly, and with a seriousness of which more would be heard, she asked, "What will I do now?" He replied that they would continue as they had during the past months and that he would give all possible help. She admitted that she had suspected this for a long time, but would never ask him, knowing that he, of all people, would tell her the truth. She remarked that she felt strange and that things appeared unreal to her. She thought and spoke of suicide but felt that there is a difference to a child as to how a parent dies, and she would not leave her son with this other burden.

She began crying, and the intensity of her emotional response brought tears to the therapist's eyes. His first impulse was to attempt to conceal this from her. Would his crying forfeit the omnipotent role she so heavily demanded? His own feelings of compassion and sorrow were uppermost. No one else previously had permitted himself the freedom of crying with her, and his behavior might give additional strength to the formulation that he was empathic with her feelings and that perhaps he, too, was "dying." For the most part, others were bent on playing the game of denial without truly acknowledging her illness. She said, "I'm feeling a little better now. I think it took a lot of guts for you to tell me. Aren't you afraid that I might go crazy? Maybe I'll have a delayed reaction?" The therapist was beginning to feel reassured and his own doubts were assuaged. There was the feeling of a shift in their roles, with her identifying herself as the therapist. Realistically, it was a "gift situation," giving her part of his life—like "dying together." Her unconsciously incorporating the therapist thereby insured the mutual death. This fantasy of mutual death has been called "Liebestod Fantasies" by J. C. Flugel (12) and is further documented and elaborated on in a recent paper by Bernard Brodsky (11).

She spoke about her pregnancy that had occurred during the second year of treatment and, in spite of the fact that it had ended in a spontaneous abortion, she said, "I was happy to know that I could at least almost have a baby." Soon after, her husband arrived. She promptly informed him that there was no longer any need for pretense. It appeared that this knowledge of her illness made her unique and imparted a feeling of strength. Her affect became more elated and she phoned the hematologist, informing him that he, too, could stop playing the hoax. She asked for a drink of liquor—this had been restricted during the past four months—quickly assuring the therapist that it was not to be dead drunk, because she loved life too much, but merely to feel somewhat mellow. At her invitation, the therapist joined her and her husband with a drink. Leaving her with her husband, the therapist mentioned that he would return later that day. She replied that she would be looking forward to the visit, and to talking more. This last verbalization gave dramatic proof that in some way her ambivalence had gained some resolution.

The therapist's second visit that same day was shorter, and for most of it her husband was present. She was quite eager to relate her fantasies, especially about the future. She had a great interest in travel and wanted to go to far-off lands, but only by airplane. Her husband, who owned a small plane, joined in by saying that he would fly all of us to Europe. It appeared that he, too, had entered the fantasy of "dying together," since his plane had a very limited range and would carry all of us to a watery grave. In this fantasy, the therapist was to be her personal physician, again giving affirmation, I felt, of the theme of "dying together." Before leaving, he suggested that arrangements could be made to bring an extra bed in the room so that the husband, who was most eager to be of honest help, might spend the night at her bedside. Their marriage had been estranged and his guilts were being rather strongly felt. Her final words to the therapist, when leaving, were, "I want to see you for many more hours, and I hope you make lots of money from us."

The therapist visited the following morning to find the patient unconscious, breathing in a labored manner, and moribund. Her husband related the events of the evening leading to the coma. She began to feel anxious, and became talkative, having concern about the enlarged nodes in her neck. The resident physician was called and ordered a mild sedative for the night. Shortly thereafter, quietly and without a struggle, she lapsed into a deep coma. Most fitting, and quite appropriate at this point, are the words of Lewin (13): "In the desired sleep state related to ecstasy, we meet the quality of immortality, the unending heavenly bliss . . . union with the immortal superego forms a prominent feature and the sense of immortality is a function of the fusion"—as he emphasizes, "the good death with the good sleep" (pp. 1551-1552). She fulfilled a long sought goal. There was some harmony, some lessening of fear and trepidation, with little mention of resentment about her coming death.

At various moments since her death, the therapist's speculations concerning the specific event itself, and the time it occurred have been most provocative. One cannot help but feel that what we call the human person represents a tremendous interaction of many various and diversified psychobiological forces, and that when we refer to the realities of life giving the appearance of being the only dynamic forces, perhaps we might be putting aside the totality of the human organism. It is suggested that her death, this most decisive event, final and ultimate, may very well have come by her own choice. Without anxiety or despair, she saw her death as a solution to her problem rather than as a source of conflict.

CASE 2

The second case presents some different problems related to the psychotherapy with the dying person. This patient made a request to the internist for psychiatric assistance after she had been told of the discovery of an abdominal malignancy. The discovery of two metastic lesions in her lungs was not revealed to her. The therapist visited her in the hospital six days following her surgery, and the remainder of his visits occurred within the hospital. They met for a total of ten sessions during a three-week period. As the course of illness came closer to her death, the visits were more frequent. Several unexpected and unannounced visits were made at what might be thought of as "odd" times, for which she expressed great pleasure. Their first meeting had been seven years earlier at the funeral of her older son whom the therapist had seen for five months of psychotherapy before his sudden and, in a sense, unexpected death. The son had had a session with the therapist at the office two days before he suffered a massive intracerebral hemorrhage.

Though at the first meeting with the mother in the hospital, neither she nor the therapist recognized each other, the transference had a "ready-made" component, as did the therapist's feelings about this patient. Her son had been a talented and distinguished scholar with an international reputation, about whose early life the therapist was very curious. To have the opportunity to meet his mother was an added dimension for the therapist.

At the time of the first session, the room was bright and cheerful, with full sunshine streaming through the blinds. The patient was out of bed, standing in front of the wall mirror, grooming herself with care. She looked her age of 77, but certainly not like a woman who was preparing for her death. After the introduction, there was little necessity for him to ask questions. She mentioned how much she had enjoyed the changes in her son during his visits with the therapist, and hoped the same could be done for her. "I know that I have a malignancy and that I probably will die from it," she said, touching the area of her wound as she talked. She added, "I have made out a 'living-will' (4), so please see that the other doctors do not use any heroic measures." He said that he understood these feelings and would try to see that her wishes were respected.

After this prologue—this contract between them—she launched into a list of complaints about the nursing staff and some physicians. Getting enough medication for her pain and for sleeping was uppermost in her mind. She felt that medication for pain should be given before the pain returned—"it makes it more difficult, and then I have to wait almost 45 minutes before there's help." She was unhappy about the fact that the staff did not reveal to her the names of the various medications as well as her temperature. This woman had been a scientist, working at a full-time job until before the surgery, and had been independent since her husband's death two years previously. It was difficult for her to accept a position of passivity in merely being a patient. She spoke quite openly about her death, but found it most difficult really to accept the idea. She did not express any feelings of "why me?" or any significant anger other than the complaints about staff. She wanted to have more talks with the therapist and hoped he could help her arrange her life.

The therapist was taken by this woman, and there was no difficulty in his mind about his full commitment for the remainder of her life. He completely enjoyed her stories about her early education in a small Central European town and her later university studies. When she spoke in scientific jargon about her field of interest, there was complete seduction. She was a most extraordinary and unforgettable person, and now he also had some additional documentation for her son's character. Tentatively, he felt that the current evidence led toward thinking of her coming death as a most peaceful, if not a happy one.

During the next visit, it appeared that much had changed. She was more disturbed about the staff and blamed the breakdown in her wound on faulty technique. The wound drainage became the reality which did not allow adequate denial to take place, as did the continued pain. The therapist felt that she "knew" more of her was dying, but did not really understand that she would be dead. It was made clear that he would improve the arrangements for the medication, both for pain and sleeping. The nursing staff was instructed to tell her the names of all drugs, to give her some sense of control. This was done, of course, with the realization that this desire to know might represent some feeling that the staff was being less than honest. She was encouraged to feel that the therapist's position was to be utilized for her welfare.

The draining wound prevented the denial and the symbolic displacement from incurable illness to curable. The focus on the wound was an expression of the symbolic fear of death for her. Her trusted "friend," her body, was beginning to fail and desert her; she was feeling "attacked" and becoming somewhat more angry and depressed. Nine days following the first visit, she was eating less, and she was beginning to permit some assistance from the therapist at mealtime (some visits were especially made to coincide with meals).

The 47th birthday of her deceased son was close at hand. She spoke again about his untimely death, and also about her mother's grave remaining unmarked. She made a request that her mother's name be inscribed along with her own on the new tombstone. Here the therapist felt that the material revealed some sense of guilt towards her mother and that the knowledge of her impending death was an atonement for same; likewise, there was the theme of "dying together" (16) and fusion. In other words, freedom from guilt is derived from the conscious recognition of death. During this visit, she spoke somewhat about the difficulty of being alone at night. The therapist's next visit, unscheduled, was on a Sunday morning, and she questioned the reason for his coming to see her unannounced. He responded that on Friday he had sensed a feeling that she was fearful of being left alone. Then she said, "I'm pleased to have a chance to talk more with you."

Four days before her death, she requested that her phone be turned off; she no longer had the patience to speak, even with old friends. This was the first striking evidence of a desire for the beginning of cutting her ties and decathecting old subjects. The odor from the wound was a continuous concern and source of much displeasure. She was embarrassed, and said that her death would be easier if she did not have that added burden. She requested that the therapist prescribe a tranquilizer for her anxiety, and mentioned her regret that she had not brought her own medication. He agreed to order the additional medication.

On the same day, her younger son came from another city and, during his visit, told her that, when discharged from the hospital, she would come and live at his home. She spoke of dying in this other city. Then, by administrative decision, and unbeknown to the therapist, she was transferred to another part of the hospital. Briefly, she was moved from an acute active service to the more chronic part of the hospital where beds are also utilized for convalescence. From this point on, her course was rapidly downhill. The therapist sensed and felt that she regarded the move as a signal that staff had despaired of her recovery. She stopped eating completely, talked little and left her bed only for bathroom needs. The nights, with darkness and the quietness about the hospital, became more frightening. She accepted fluids from the therapist in the form of ice water and tea.

Visiting with her about 12 hours before her death, he found her silent, lying in bed staring straight ahead, but not actually acknowledging his presence. The silence was complete without any verbal response even to colloquial questions. She did not appear to be in any severe pain; her face was not tense, but she was perspiring. After about half an hour, when asked whether she might wish him to leave, she shook her head negatively. He remained longer, but they never spoke again. Some relatives who came received the same silence; her only responses were displayed by head-nodding. The silence possibly was part of an acceptance and her way of saying, "Nothing more need be said." She died the following morning.

In this psychotherapy, there was no conspiracy which would have tended to isolate the patient. None of her questions were ever considered irrelevant and all were answered in a very direct manner. However, she was never told directly that she was dying, nor was she told about the metastases. The therapist felt honest with her, despite his withholding some of the truth. They talked about death often and she was aware of her diagnosis. In their first visit, she informed him that she was in fact dying—it was after she knew the diagnosis that she requested his visit. In addition, there existed this "ready-made" transference as the person who had treated her son before his death, and the transference had the appearance that the therapist was the bridge for her to the dead son and mother. But even this "reconciliation" was not sufficient to make her death positively a happy one. The transfer to the more chronic division of the hospital seemed to hasten the course of her death. Her ego must have felt that the "game" was up. There was no way out except through a flight into "psychosis," manifesting itself in withdrawal, feelings of unreality, negativism, and becoming completely mute. When the body was threatened—and with this patient the constant draining wound was felt as a continuous threat—there was the gradual withdrawal from objects and great intensification of her feeling of narcissistic injury. This aggression against her was felt, perhaps, as a punishment. Early in the treatment she fought back and directed complaints against the staff. During the last few days the therapist speculated that there existed some, perhaps masochistic, albeit pleasurable, suffering. All visiting relatives were made to feel guilty and helpless by her negativism. The guilt was especially strong with her former daughter-in-law, who was a constant and devoted visitor at her bedside, and who found it difficult to accept the patient's behavior in spite of the therapist's explanations.

The dynamics in this case, indeed, are complicated further with the time of her dead son's birthday and her wish that her mother's name be inscribed on her tombstone. We are all quite familiar with the anxiety that many women suffer before parturition, and how this often becomes fear of death. While there is no actual strong data to support the speculation that the thought of being in childbirth was active within her (i.e., abdominal mass), it remains a thought for consideration. Also, perhaps, the wish for reunion with her mother might have been another possibility—the headlines of the material were present. Additional support for these speculations centers on the meaning of the mass growing within her. Candidly, the therapist could not say that her death was a complete euthanasia (2) in spite of his original feelings following the first meeting. Perhaps the death might have been happier, if the transfer had not occurred, but that will remain her secret. However, the case does show the investment of time and torment that the physician who commits himself to the treatment of the dying person must be prepared to make. In such instances, he must sustain some sense of medical failure and, not least of all, at times a poor psychological death. No matter the degree of honesty, each person has his death in his appropriate setting, based on the concept that all of us will have our own private style of dying, an outgrowth of our previous life cycle.

An Approach to Helping a Dying Person

The material presented from the history and course of treatment of these two particular dying people can be helpful in delineating various essential psychotherapeutic tools which could be comforting for the dying person. However, in both these situations there was a "ready-made" transference, an advantage that does not exist in all instances. In the first case, the fatal illness became part of an ongoing treatment. With the second case, it was clear at the first session that the therapist was to be the bridge between her dead son and her death (2). In numerous situations of consultation the goals, of necessity, will have imposed limitations, and the time needed does not exist. Often, the assessment must be quite rapid and, hopefully, gets to the heart of the matter. Consequently, the considerations should be 1) to help the patient; 2) to give assistance to the staff, including paramedical helpers; 3) to provide time to be spent with the family. In dealing with these categories, the matter of the individual and collective *grief* must be realized and treated. Most usually, this involves management of their guilt and feelings of *helplessness* referable to themselves and towards the dying person as well. The referring physician, with his sense of medical *failure* and damage to his *narcissism,* cannot be forgotten or neglected.

The therapist who decides to involve himself in the treatment of a dying person must commit himself 1) to utilize all his efforts in behalf of the patient's welfare. The patient must understand this clearly, and also know that the therapist will be a constant, available, and reliable figure for the patient. The psychodynamic evidence is that the fear of abandonment occupies a central position in the mind of the dying person. The therapist should have knowledge of the various pharmacological agents that can allay anxiety, counter depression and, at times, handle more malignant symptoms, namely paranoid thinking. Superficial optimism is usually opposed, since it can encourage suspicion and mistrust. However, in certain instances of persons with character traits of being chronic optimists, the denial should not be challenged; it should be viewed as homeostatic and as ego-syntonic for maintaining self-esteem; 2) to try to respond appropriately to the patient's needs by listening carefully to the complaints and the words used to express them. It is especially important to watch for *displacements* of the symbolic representation of the fear of death, namely, "the room is dark, please open the blinds," . . . "the room is stuffy." Making minor, or seemingly minor, physical changes often has a remarkable way of making the patient more comfortable, reducing anxiety and lifting depression; 3) to be fully prepared to accept his own countertransference, as *doubts, guilts* and *damage* to his narcissism are encountered. He must be fully prepared to have his own death *wishes* from earlier years reactivated and, of course, to be reminded constantly of his own *death* and *mortality*.

From this, it remains an easy step to see why we have left in the past and continue now to leave the dying person alone. We know that the pain of death is made more intense, if the journey is embarked upon alone. Without a partner, the fear quickly escalates to panic and dread. Here, then, is the role for the therapist—an empathy—an affective one which provides a fusion with the patient's unconscious and transmits the feeling that a part of the therapist will die with that person. Superficial optimism which is so removed from the reality can oppose this fusion and empathy.

The ability to transmit this feeling quite naturally transgresses individual capacities in therapists and is not accessible to all. The therapist must be aware that his own defenses cannot be rigidly adhered to, since they tend only to widen the gap in communication between himself and the patient. The treatment must permit a guilt-free regression in the patient; this will go a long way to preclude object-loss.

It is not too difficult to know and realize a "bad" death, but to be able to sort out a "good" death presents more difficulty. The therapist must work for relief of pain, and counter the arguments of "addiction" as often, reflecting, in part, some of the staff's inability to give up control, even though they require that the patient do so. It may also express their denial and false hope or, at best, indicate an example of awkward thinking. Above all, the therapist must understand that this personal presence remains all that is available against the fear of abandonment (15)—the journey to death remains an illusion that must have some allies. The struggle and torment for the therapist with the dying person is always the battle of David and Goliath, but we must recognize beforehand that Goliath, in all instances, will be the winner.

REFERENCES

1. Weigert, E. The nature of sympathy in the art of psychotherapy. *Psychiatry*, 1961, 24:187.

2. Deutsch, F. Euthanasia: A clinical study. *Psychoanal. Quart.*, 1936, 5:347-368.
3. Eissler, K. R. *The Psychiatrist and the Dying Patient.* New York: International Universities Press, 1955.
4. Olden, C. On adult empathy with children. In: *The Psychoanalytic Study of the Child.* Vol. 8, New York: International Universities Press, 1953, pp. 111-126.
5. Beres, D. The role of empathy in psychotherapy and psychoanalysis. *J. Hillside Hosp.*, 1968, 17:362.
6. Beres, D. and Arlow, J. Fantasy and identification in empathy. *Psychoanal. Quart.*, 1974, 43:26.
7. Greenson, R. Empathy and its vicissitudes. *Int. J. Psychoanal.*, 1960, 41:418.
8. Freud, S. Thoughts for the times on war and death. In: J. Strachey (Ed.), *Collected Papers*, Vol. 4. London: Hogarth Press, 1925, pp. 288-319.
9. Saunders, C. The moment of truth. In: L. Pearson (Ed.), *Death and Dying.* Cleveland: Press of Case Western Reserve University, 1969, pp. 49-78.
10. Jones, E. Dying together. In: E. Jones (Ed.), *Essays in Applied Psychoanalysis.* London: Hogarth Press, 1951, pp. 9-21.
11. Brodsky, B. Liebestod fantasies in a patient faced with an illness. *Int. J. Psychoanal.*, 1959, 40:13.
12. Flugel, J. C. Death instinct homeostasis and allied concept. *Int. J. Psychoanal. Suppl.,* 1953, 34:43.
13. Lewin, B. D. *Psychoanalysis of Elation.* London: Hogarth, 1950.
14. Hendin, D. *Death: A Fact of Life.* New York: W. W. Norton, 1973.
15. Kübler-Ross, E. *On Death and Dying.* London: The Macmillan Publishing Co., 1969.

15

The Behavioral Psychotherapy of Anorexia Nervosa

MICHEL HERSEN, PH.D.

and

THOMAS DETRE, M.D.

PREAMBLE

The label of anorexia nervosa is misleading on two accounts: 1) *anorexia*—far from being anorectic, these patients are starved and periodically engorge themselves; 2) *nervosa*—this implies that the ailment is psychological in origin, but apart from change in dietary habits consistent with the patient's belief system that she is too fat, the majority of the cases exhibit no changes in mood or cognition typically found in psychiatric disorders. The situation is not unlike the one found in transsexuals, who are convinced that their "soul" has been mistakenly placed in a body shell displaying sexual characteristics that are inconsistent with their internal convictions about their sexual assignment. Both have, as has been pointed out, an obsessoid personality structure.

Although the biological symptoms and signs thus far reported in anorexia nervosa also are scarce, inconsistent, and mostly secondary to weight loss, it is by now generally recognized that a significant percentage of patients becomes amenorrheic before developing symptoms of anorexia.

295

Minimally, this finding should suggest that at least one subgroup of patients suffers from some sort of disorder involving neuroendocrine regulation.

Irrespective of the etiology, all evidence points to the effectiveness of psychological rather than biological treatment, though the latter has been used as co-adjuvant in the management of patients. It also is reasonably clear, but by no means surprising, that the success or failure of treatment depends largely on the consistency of the family environment, given that the majority of patients are preadolescent or adolescent and thereby still dependent on the parents or parent-substitutes when first brought to medical attention.

The major difficulties encountered in the management of anorexia nervosa, however, have less to do with the failure on the part of the parents to acknowledge their child's need for treatment than with the failure of mental health professionals to recognize a fatal error in their own reasoning: namely, that the success of psychological therapies per se does not prove that the disorder should be regarded as a psychiatric disorder. Yet, the view that anorexia nervosa is a "mental disorder" and the insistence that patient and family endorse and enthusiastically participate with the staff in a "fishing expedition" aimed to uncover some sort of psychological problem (or at least come to an agreement about one), even when the evidence is unconvincing, do turn family members off, and rightly so. The collaboration between treatment staff, the patient, and the family should be based on an honest understanding of what we know and do not know about this disorder. Accordingly, and given the considerable short- and long-term risks, it is perfectly appropriate to present the need for psychological management convincingly. On the other hand, the fact that psychological treatment seems effective is insufficient reason for persuading the patient and the family that the psychiatric disorder exists, or worse yet, that in some mysterious manner it has been produced by them. Indeed, statistically just the opposite is true. In those instances where symptoms and signs of an affective, obsessive, or schizophrenic disorder are observable, the chances are very high that patients suffer from a secondary rather than a primary or idiopathic type of anorexia nervosa.

GENERAL PSYCHOTHERAPEUTIC CONSIDERATIONS

When we speak of anorexia nervosa, the generic label not only is misleading, as already noted in our Preamble, but it subsumes a wide variety of specific signs and symptoms in any given individual so afflicted. Recent comprehensive reviews of the literature by Van Buskirk (1) and Bemis (2) clearly suggest, however, that individuals who eventually receive the diagnosis of anorexia nervosa do not necessarily share *all* of the same signs and symptoms. For example, although many anorectics have lost at least 25% of their "normal" body weight, all do not typically induce vomiting as a means to maintain diminished weight. Some anorectics exhibit certain characterological difficulties such as a "passive-aggressive" life-style, but that does not hold true for many others who are quite obsessive in their orientation. While in some cases there may be an alternation of anorexia and periods of bulimia, in still others, particularly when the disorder remains untreated for many years, anorexia predominates, leading to a dramatic linear reduction in weight.

Given that specific symptomatology *does* vary considerably across patients labeled anorexia nervosa, there can be no uniform psychotherapeutic approach that will deal effectively, at one time, with all the manifestations of the disorder. Indeed, a very careful diagnostic appraisal of each aspect of the disorder is warranted. Then, for each aspect of the disorder so identified, the appropriate treatment strategy must be specifically tailored (3). In light of the specificity of treatment required and in consideration of the unique problems posed by each of the individual symptoms subsumed under anorexia nervosa, we submit that, for the most part, the behavior therapy approach should prove parsimonious and expedient (4, 5).

Although the behavioral approach for treating anorexia nervosa has received some sharp criticism by Bruch (6), as astutely pointed out by Wolpe (7), failures of behavioral treatment can easily be traced to an incomplete behavioral assessment and attention to only one facet of the disorder (e.g., attention to weight gain but no attempt to deal with the "weight" phobia leading to the original weight loss). Thus, in the succeeding sections, we will outline specific treatment strategies that may be applied to each of the identified facets of the disorder. Undoubtedly, future research should confirm that a multifaceted approach to treatment will prove superior to the more naive behavioral treatment approach that only deals with one facet (i.e., weight gain) or the nonspecific psychotherapy that is not at all tailored to the patient's unique presenting problems. Even more important, we will argue that for maintaining gains initially accrued during inpatient treatment, programmed booster therapy sessions over a period of many years will probably be required.

WEIGHT LOSS

Treatment of the weight loss, which at times may be of life-threatening proportions, is best accomplished in a well-controlled environment such as the inpatient psychiatric ward. Although when medical complications arise (e.g., viral infection), forced feeding via a naso-gastric tube may become a necessity, under ordinary circumstances a less invasive procedure for inducing weight gain is recommended.

Experience in a wide variety of centers over the last decade indicates that the use of operant conditioning procedures is the behavioral treatment of choice for obtaining "rapid weight restoration at times of nutritional crisis" (8, p. 171). In essence, *a somewhat one-sided contract* is drawn up between the treating agent and the patient, stating that the patient will be given access to reinforcers (e.g., physical activity, television, reading material, other privileges) contingent on a specific weight gain in a designated time period. For example, Halmi, Powers, and Cunningham (9) maintained patients in relative isolation unless they gained 0.5 kg per five-day period. Naturally, the specific weight gain required per time period should be realistic and determined by the extent of the weight loss. Also, to maximize the efficacy of the behavioral contingency, it is of paramount importance that the patient be given access to her (only 15% of reported cases are males) favorite reinforcers. Moreover, Agras, Barlow, Chapin et al. (10) found that informational feedback about caloric intake and weight gain given to the patient as well as presenting her with four high caloric meals (1500 calories each) per day further promoted rapid weight gain.

To summarize, the patient should be restricted to her room, privileges are to be given contingently on increased caloric intake and weight gain, informational feedback about caloric consumption and weight gain are to be provided, and large as opposed to small meals are to be presented to the patient at least four times a day. No comments should be made to the patient prior to or while eating. That is, the therapist need not engage in a prolongation of the verbal struggle with the patient. In addition, the patient should be weighed daily under standardized conditions (i.e., after urinating, in hospital gown only, at precisely the same time each day). It is widely known that anorectics attempt to falsify their weight and, of consequence, need to be carefully examined for foreign objects in or on their bodies and garments when being weighed.

Although making privileges strictly contingent on weight gain first requires the withdrawal of non-contingent reinforcement and has been described by some as coercive and furthering the "power struggle" with the patient (6), it is no more coercive and certainly less invasive than forced feeding by tube. Also, considering that weight loss in anorexia nervosa has led to eventual death in up to 15% of documented cases, the polemical nature of such an argument is nonsensical. Indeed, the first order of business in treating the anorexia nervosa patient is to restore her weight to a level that is reasonable and medically safe.

ATTITUDES TOWARD FOOD AND WEIGHT

We fully agree with Bruch's (6) contention that the concern with weight gain alone in anorexia nervosa constitutes only a partial and surface treatment of the problem. A very careful interview of the anorectic patient clearly reveals that she invariably has a most negative attitude about gaining weight, which often has an historical antecedent (i.e., at one point she actually may have been overweight). However, what also becomes readily apparent is that her current perception of how she looks and what she weighs is highly inaccurate. Thus, even though in reality rather thin (at times emaciated), the patient continues to think of herself as if she were still "fat." Therefore, one might conceptualize the problem as a cognitive distortion with a resultant phobia for gaining weight.

Several single case reports have appeared in the literature illustrating the use of systematic desensitization in the treatment of anorexia nervosa (11-13). In these case studies the patients were treated as if they were suffering from a "weight" phobia. Generally, following training in deep muscle relaxation, separate hierarchies involving consumption of food and gaining weight were constructed. Then, in standard fashion, systematic desensitization treatment proceeded until all items in the two hierarchies were successfully completed under conditions of minimal anxiety. Of the cases reported, follow-ups were brief with the exception of the patient treated by Ollendick (13). But, although Ollendick's (13) patient has a five-year follow-up and the controlling effects of systematic desensitization on weight gain are documented, additional strategies (e.g., cognitive restructuring) were required to reinstate weight gain and maintain the patient's improvement during follow-up.

Thus, while systematic desensitization or some form of cognitive behavior therapy appears to make sense in dealing with the anorectic's faulty cognitions and perceptions, it would be essential to obtain empirical documentation of the long-range effects in a large number of cases. Nonetheless, irrespective of the therapist's specific choice of technique at this point, a direct intervention aimed at modifying the patient's cognitive distortion about her body image should complement the operant approach directed to increasing weight. In practice, application of systematic desensitization could be accomplished concurrently with contingency management after some of the patient's weight has been restored.

BULIMIA

Surprisingly, little attention has been accorded to the direct treatment of episodes of bulimia even though it is well documented that many anorectics (contradicting their diagnostic label) periodically engorge themselves with fattening foods during the course of binges. Some of these binges may last for several hours or days at a time and are usually followed by the patient's feeling of disgust or remorse, leading to self-induced vomiting. When interviewed about their binge behavior, anorectics describe the antecedent as an irresistible impulse (associated with high levels of anxiety) which must be fulfilled. Once eating behavior has actually begun, the patient feels totally helpless, cannot stop, and continues consumption well past the state of normal satiation, even though the act of eating at that point no longer is enjoyable. Often it is reported that various food cues in the environment trigger off the entire chain of behaviors: impulse—bulimia—remorse—self-induced vomiting.

Although bulimia in anorexia nervosa may subside after lost weight has been regained and "normal" eating patterns have been established, it is quite possible that extinction of the phenomenon *may not automatically take place.* This being the case, it also is conceivable that with the appropriate stimulus conditions bulimia may recur, thereby leading to a return of self-induced vomiting after appropriate food consumption has taken place, once again eliciting the dramatic weight loss that brought the anorexia nervosa patient to our attention in the first place.

Considering the phenomenon of bulimia as anxiety-based and the resulting chain of events as anxiety-reducing, we recently have dealt with bulimia using anxiety-reducing techniques of flooding and response-prevention (14). In a few cases of anorexia nervosa, where bulimia was a prominent feature, we have placed the patient in a laboratory situation surrounded by her favorite foods (e.g., candy bars, cakes, chocolates, etc.). Upon presentation of food cues the patient appears physiologically aroused (increased heart and pulse rate). She is instructed to take a few bites of food and then told to stop eating. At that point physiological arousal is further enhanced (confirmed by the patient's self-reports of heightened anxiety). The patient is then maintained in this environment (with the salient food cues), prevented from binge eating, and also prevented from inducing vomiting after "normal" food consumption. Such flooding and response prevention are continued (2-4 hours at a time) until physiological responses return to normal resting levels and the patient reports no further impulse to engage in binge eating. After several sessions of combined flooding and response prevention, a "temptation" test is given the patient to assess the effects of treatment. In spite of a few successes employing this strategy, obviously further confirmation would be needed to determine whether generalization of treatment gains extend to the patient's natural environment.

FAMILY THERAPY

Although it is most tempting to speculate what role the family has in producing anorexia nervosa, any such speculation must take into account that such patients, apart from bizarre food habits and eating patterns, appear psychologically quite well. The contrast between the patient's peculiar views on food intake and her otherwise "normal" behavior also is the reason why referral to treatment occurs usually late in the course of the disorder, when the patient is already emaciated and the family is no longer able to cope with the situation. It should come as no surprise that by the time the patient comes to medical attention, the power struggle which almost inevitably ensues when family members attempt (albeit ineffectively) to deal with the patient's attitude causes considerable dissension as well as inconsistencies which inadvertently reinforce the patient's weight loss and bizarre eating habits. Indeed, the situation parallels that of the family's reaction to severe obsessive-compulsive ritualistic actions and his/her increasing demand for family participation. Thus, even though we find the etiologic role assigned to the family by some theoreticians unconvincing, we agree that a comprehensive approach to treating anorexia nervosa must include family therapy (15). Our preference for family therapy is one that is educative, non-punitive, and focused on the presenting problems unless, of course, there is evidence of conflicts unrelated to the patient's eating problems. Since the relief which hospitalization provides to the immediate family tends to be very temporary, we believe the anorectic's inpatient stay presents an excellent opportunity to teach the family how to manage her when she returns to the home setting. In essence, the goal is to teach family members those strategies that were successful in dealing with the patient while she was hospitalized. Formal behavioral contracts (specifying behavior, privileges, and punishments) are helpful, as are treatment sessions done in a semi-naturalistic fashion during the course of meals in the hospital (15). It is, in our experience, always preferable to reinforce the patient's positive behavior while ignoring her negative initiatives. However, as with most aspects of the contemporary treatment of anorexia nervosa, confirmation of the successes reported will have to await the outcome of well-controlled clinical trials.

LONG-TERM MAINTENANCE

We already have potent psychotherapeutic techniques in our arma-mentarium to improve the condition of anorectics during the course of their hospital stay. The often dramatic gains achieved during the in-patient phase of treatment, however, are misleading, for it is clear that in the absence of maintenance therapy following discharge, long-term results will be disappointing (6, 7, 13, 16). While the multi-faceted ap-proach to anorexia nervosa suggested by us should facilitate long-term maintenance, it is very difficult to predict what stresses the anorectic and her family may encounter that would lead to the recrudescence of the disorder even after a prolonged and well-organized aftercare program.

Given the chronicity and acute exacerbations, there is every reason to believe that psychiatric care should continue regardless as to how success-ful inpatient therapy has been. Looking at the natural history of anorexia nervosa and consistent with the medical model of treatment for chronic disorders, it would seem logical to recommend long-term maintenance treatment for at least five years.

Thus, the follow-up care of such patients should not be confined to the periodic reassessment of the situation, but consist of an active booster treatment program in which individual and family therapies are sched-uled at regular intervals, minimally six to twelve times per year. Further-more, since relapses with severe weight loss are common and since, in our experience, neither the patient nor the family show less reluctance than the first time around to consider hospitalization, it is always advisable to spell out under what conditions the clinician is willing to assume responsibility for continuing care as well as to explain the rules which will prompt the clinician to recommend rehospitalization. Although some clinicians are willing to treat such individuals as outpatients even in the face of severe and progressive weight loss, it is our practice to insist on readmitting the patient whenever there is 15% weight loss, using weight at discharge as a baseline. Should the patient (or family) refuse readmission, the alternative of transferring the patient into another clinician's care should be offered.

CONCLUSION

In conclusion, we view anorexia nervosa as a disorder of uncertain etiology which responds to psychological treatments. Because of the diversity of symptoms, not all of which may be prominent or even present in a particular case, rather than recommending a single form of therapy, a highly individualized treatment program using techniques of behavior therapy is indicated. Given that the majority of such patients are preadolescents or adolescents and still dependent on the parents or parent-substitutes, we consider family therapy essential both in the immediate and long-term management of patients. Our approach calls for family therapy that is educative rather than punitive and teaches the family how to manage the patient when she returns to the home setting. Since anorexia nervosa is a chronic disorder with periodic exacerbations, we consider it essential to provide maintenance therapy for at least five years consisting of an active booster treatment program administered at regularly scheduled intervals.

REFERENCES

1. Van Buskirk, S. W. A two-phase perspective in the treatment of anorexia nervosa. *Psychol. Bull.*, 1977, 84:529-538.
2. Bemis, K. M. Current approaches to the etiology and treatment of anorexia nervosa. *Psychol. Bull.*, 1978, 85:593-617.
3. Hersen, M. and Bellack, A. S. *Behavioral Assessment: A Practical Handbook.* New York: Pergamon Press, 1976.
4. Stunkard, A. J. New therapies for the eating disorders: Behavior modification of obesity and anorexia nervosa. *Arch. Gen. Psychiat.*, 1972, 26:391-398.
5. Kellerman, J. Anorexia nervosa: The efficacy of behavior therapy. *J. Behav. Ther. & Exp. Psychiat.*, 1977, 8:387-390.
6. Bruch, H. Perils of behavior modification in treatment of anorexia nervosa. *J.A.M.A.*, 1974, 230:1419-1422.
7. Wolpe, J. Behavior therapy in anorexia nervosa. *J.A.M.A.*, 1975, 133:317-318.
8. Bhanji, S. and Thompson, J. Operant conditioning in the treatment of anorexia nervosa: A review and retrospective study of 11 cases. *Brit. J. Psychiat.*, 1974, 124:166-172.
9. Halmi, K. A., Powers, P., and Cunningham, S. Treatment of anorexia nervosa with behavior modification: Effectiveness of formula feeding and isolation. *Arch. Gen. Psychiat.*, 1975, 32:93-96.
10. Agras, W. S., Barlow, D. H., Chapin, H. N., et al. Behavior modification of anorexia nervosa. *Arch. Gen. Psychiat.*, 1974, 30:279-286.

11. Hallsten, E. A. Adolescent anorexia nervosa treated by desensitization. *Behav. Res. & Ther.*, 1965, 3:87-91.
12. Schnurer, A. T., Rubin, R. R., and Roy, A. Systematic desensitization of anorexia nervosa seen as a weight phobia. *J. Behav. Ther. & Exp. Psychiat.*, 1973, 4:149-153.
13. Ollendick, T. H. Behavioral treatment of anorexia nervosa: A five-year study. *Behav. Mod.* 1979, 3:124-135.
14. Marks, I. M. Behavioral treatments of phobic and obsessive-compulsive disorders: A critical appraisal. In: M. Hersen, R. M. Eisler, and P. M. Miller (Eds.), *Progress in Behavior Modification*, Vol. 1. New York: Academic Press, 1975, pp. 65-158.
15. Liebman, R., Minuchin, S., and Baker, L. An integrated treatment program for anorexia nervosa. *Amer. J. Psychiat.*, 1974, 131:432-436.
16. Erwin, W. J. A 16-year follow-up of a case of severe anorexia nervosa. *J. Behav. Ther. & Exp. Psychiat.*, 1977, 8:157-160.

16

Psychotherapy with Suicidal Patients

EDWIN S. SHNEIDMAN, PH.D.

It seems logical that before we consider what the psychotherapy of a suicidal person ought to be that we have some common understanding of the suicidal state itself. Of course, everybody agrees that suicide is an enormously complicated term, encompassing a wide variety (and different ranges) of dysphoria, disturbance, self-abnegation, resignation, terror-cum-pain—to mention but a few inner states that are involved. But perhaps nowhere is there as insightful a description of suicide in as few words as that found in the opening paragraph of Melville's *Moby-Dick*: "a damp and drizzly November in my soul." For that is what, metaphorically, most suicide is: a dreary and dismal wintry gale within the mind, where the vital issue that is being debated is whether to try to stay afloat in a stormy life or willfully to go under to nothingness.

Suicide is the human act of self-inflicted, self-intended cessation (i.e., the permanent stopping of consciousness). It is best understood as a bio-socio-psychologico-existential state of malaise. It is obviously not a disease and just as obviously a number of kinds of trained individuals other than physicians can help individuals who are in a suicidal state.

If we are to escape many of the current somewhat simplistic notions of suicide (especially those which totally equate a disease called suicide with a disease called depression), then we need to explicate what the suicidal state of mind is like. Our key source in this can be the ordinary

305

dictionary—eschewing any nomenclature of technical and, especially, technically diagnostic terms. In the dictionary there are words, e.g., angered, anguished, cornered, dependent, frustrated, guilty, helpless, hopeless, hostile, rageful, shamed, that will help us in our understanding. For us, in this chapter, two less common (but ordinary) dictionary words—*perturbation* and *lethality*—will be the keystone words of our understanding.

Perturbation refers to how upset (disturbed, agitated, sane-insane, discomposed) the individual is—rated, let's say, on a 1 to 9 scale. Lethality refers to how lethal the individual is, i.e., how likely it is that he will take his own life—also rated on a 1 to 9 scale.

At the outset, I need to indicate what kinds of suicidal states I am talking about in order to indicate what kinds of psychotherapy are appropriate for them. We can arbitrarily divide the seriousness (or risk, or lethality, or suicidality) of all suicidal efforts (actions, deeds, events, episodes)—whether verbalizations (ordinarily called threats) or behaviors (ordinarily called attempts)—into three rough commonsense groupings: low, medium and high. In this chapter, I shall focus on the suicidal events or deeds of *high* lethality, where the danger of self-inflicted death is realistically large and imminent; what one might ordinarily call high suicide risks. Of course, a suicide act (deed, occurrence, event, threat, attempt) *of whatever lethality* is always a genuine psychiatric situation and should be treated without any iatrogenic elements. Thus, in the treatment of the suicidal person there is almost never any place for the therapist's hostility, anger, sardonic attitudes, daring the patient, or pseudo-democratic indifference.

By focusing solely on the *psycho*therapeutic approaches to high suicide risks, it should be obvious at the beginning that this chapter is a moiety —omitting entirely (and advertently) the lively areas of treatment suicidal individuals receive by means of chemical, electrical or institutional modalities.

Theoretically, the treatment of an acutely highly suicidal person is quite simple: It consists, almost by definition, of lowering his lethality level; in practice, this is usually done by decreasing or mollifying his level of perturbation. In short, we defuse the situation (like getting the gun), we create activity of support and care around the person, and we make that person's temporarily unbearable life just enough better so that he or she can stop to think and reconsider. The way to decrease lethality is by dramatically decreasing the felt perturbation.

Working intensively with a highly suicidal person—someone who might be assessed as 7, 8 or 9 on a 1 to 9 scale of lethality—as distinguished from someone of moderate or low lethality, is different from almost any other human encounter, with the possible exception of that of working intensively with a dying person—but that is another story. Psychotherapy with an intensely suicidal person is a special task; it demands a different kind of involvement. The goal is different—not that of increasing comfort, which is the goal of most ordinary psychotherapy, but the more primitive goal of simply keeping the person alive. The rules are therefore different, and it follows (or rather precedes) that the theoretical rationale is different.

At this juncture, I wish to make a distinction among *four* psychologically different kinds of human encounters: conversation (or "ordinary talk"); an hierarchical exchange; psychotherapy or a "professional exchange"; and, finally, clinical suicidology or working psychologically with a highly lethal person.

In ordinary talk or conversation, the focus is on the surface content (concrete events, specific dates, culinary details); on what is actually being said; on the obviously stated meanings; on the ordinary interesting (or uninteresting) details of life. Further, the social role between the two speakers is one in which the two participants are essentially equal. Each participant has the social right to ask the other the same questions which he or she has been asked by the other. The best example of ordinary talk is two friends conversing with one another.

In a hierarchical verbal exchange the two participants are socially, and hence psychologically, unequal. This difference may be imposed by the situation, such as the exchange between a military officer and an enlisted person, or it may be agreed to by the two involved parties, such as between a physician and a patient. In either instance, the two are not psychologically equal. For example, an officer or a physician can ask an enlisted person or a patient, respectively, certain personal questions to which a rational response is expected, that the person of "lower status" could not ask the other person in return without appearing impertinent or aberrant. Yet most of the talk is still on the surface, concerning the real details of everyday life.

In a professional psychotherapeutic exchange the focus is on feelings, emotional content and unconscious meanings, rather than on what is apparently being said. The emphasis is on the latent (between-the-lines) significance of what is being said more than on the manifest and obvious content; on the unconscious meanings, including double-entendres, puns, and slips-of-the-tongue; on themes that run as common threads through the content, rather than on the concrete details for their own sake. Perhaps the most distinguishing aspect of the professional exchange (as opposed to ordinary talk) is the occurrence of transference, wherein the patient projects onto the therapist certain deep expectations and feelings. These transference reactions often stem from the patient's childhood and reflect neurotic patterns of reaction (of love, hate, dependency, suspicion, etc.) to whatever the therapist may or may not be doing. The therapist is often invested by the patient with almost magical healing powers, which, in fact, can serve as a self-fulfilling prophecy and thus help the interaction become therapeutic for the patient. In this paragraph, the use of the words therapist and patient already implies that, of the two parties, one has tacitly agreed to seek assistance and the other has agreed to try to give it. The roles of the two participants, unlike those in a conversation, are, in this respect, not co-equal. A therapist and a patient could not simply exchange roles.

In working as a clinical suicidologist with an individual who is highly suicidal, the focus is again different. In this situaton, the attention is primarily on the lethality. Most importantly, what differentiates this modality of therapy from any other psychotherapy is the handling of the transference feelings. Specifically, the tranference (from the patient to the therapist) and the countertransference (from the therapist to the patient)—especially those positive feelings of affection and concern—can legitimately be much more intense and more deep than would be seemly or appropriate (or even ethical) in ordinary psychotherapy where time is assumed to be endless and where it is taken for granted that the patient will continue functioning in life.

Working with a highly suicidal person demands a different kind of involvement. There may be as important a conceptual difference between ordinary psychotherapy (with individuals where dying or living is not *the* issue) and psychotherapy with acutely suicidal persons as there is between ordinary psychotherapy and ordinary talk.

The main point of working with a lethally-oriented person—in the give-and-take of talk, the advice, the interpretations, the listening—is to increase that individual's psychological sense of possible choices and sense of being emotionally supported. Relatives, friends and colleagues should, after they are assessed to be on the life-side of the individual's ambivalence, be closely involved in the total treatment process. Suicide prevention is not best done as a solo practice. A combination of consultation, ancillary therapists and the use of all the interpersonal and community resources that one can involve is, in general, the best way of proceeding.

Recall that we are talking about psychotherapy with the highly suicidal persons—not one of low or even medium lethality. With this in mind—and keeping in mind also the four psychological components of the suicidal state of mind (heightened inimicality, elevated perturbation, conspicuous constriction of intellectual focus, and the idea of cessation as a solution)—then a relatively simple formula for treatment can be stated. That formulation concentrates on two of the four psychological components, specifically on the constriction and the perturbation. Simply put, the way to save a highly suicidal person is to decrease the constriction, that is, to widen the range of possible thoughts and fantasies (*from* the dichotomous two—either one specific outcome or death —*to* at least three or more possibilities for admittedly less-than-perfect solution), and, most importantly—without which the attempt to broaden the constriction will not work—to decrease the individual's perturbation.

How does a psychotherapist decrease the elevated perturbation of a highly suicidal person? Answer: by doing anything and almost everything possible to cater to the infantile idiosyncrasies, the dependency needs, the sense of pressure and futility, the feelings of hopelessness and helplessness that the individual is experiencing. In order to help a highly lethal person, one should involve others; create activity around the person; do what he or she wants done—and, if that cannot be accomplished, at least move in the direction of the desired goals to some substitute goals that approximate those which have been lost. Remember that life— and remind the patient of this fact (in a kindly but oracular way)—is often the choice among lousy alternatives. The key to functioning, to wisdom and to life itself is often to choose the least lousy alternative that is practicably attainable.

Taken down to its bare roots, the principle is: To decrease lethality one puts a hook on perturbation and, doing what needs to be done, pulls the level of perturbation down—and with that action brings down the active level of lethality. Then, when the person is no longer highly suicidal—then the usual methods of psychotherapy (which are not the subject for this chapter) can be usefully employed.

As to how to help a suicidal individual, it is best to look upon any suicidal act, whatever its lethality, as an effort by an individual to stop unbearable anguish or intolerable pain by "doing something." Knowing this usually guides us as to what the treatment should be. In the same sense, the way to save a person's life is also to "do something."

Those "somethings" include putting that information (that the person is in trouble with himself) into the stream of communication, letting others know about it, breaking what could be a fatal secret, talking to the person, talking to others, proferring help, getting loved ones interested and responsive, creating action around the person, showing response, indicating concern, and, if possible, offering love.

I conclude with an example—actually a composite of several actual highly suicidal persons I have known.

CASE STUDY

A young woman in her 20s, a nurse at the hospital where I worked, asked me pleadingly if I would see her teenage sister whom she considered to be highly suicidal. The attractive, younger woman—agitated and tearful but coherent—told me (in the privacy of my office) that she was single, pregnant and determined to kill herself. She showed me a small automatic pistol she had in her purse. Her being pregnant was such a mortal shame to her, combined with strong feelings of rage and guilt, that she simply could not "bear to live" (or live to bear?). Suicide was the *only* alternative, and shooting herself was the *only* way to do it. Either she had to be unpregnant (the way she was before she conceived) or she had to be dead.

I did several things. For one, I took out a sheet of paper and—to begin to "widen her blinders"—said something like, "Now, let's see: You could have an abortion here locally." ("I couldn't do that.") It is precisely the "can'ts" and the "won'ts" and "have to's" and "nevers" and "always" and "onlys" that are to be negotiated in psychotherapy. "You could go away and have an abortion." ("I couldn't do that.") "You could bring the baby to term and keep the baby." ("I couldn't do that.") "You could have the baby and adopt it out." ("I couldn't do that.") "We could get in touch with the young man involved." ("I couldn't do that.") "We could involve the help of your parents." ("I couldn't do that.") and "You can always commit suicide, but there is obviously no need to do that today." (No response.) "Now first, let me take that gun, and then let's look at this *list* and rank them in order and see what their advantages, disadvantages and implications are, remembering that none of them may be perfect."

The very making of this list, my fairly calm and nonhortatory and nonjudgmental approach already had a calming influence on her. Within 15 minutes her lethality had begun to deescalate. She actually rank-ordered the list, commenting negatively on each item, but what was of critical importance was that suicide, which I included in the total realistic list, was now ranked third—no longer first or second.

She decided that she would, reluctantly, want to talk to the father of her child. Not only had they never discussed the "issue," but he did not even know about it. But there was a formidable obstacle: He lived in another city, almost across the country and that involved (what seemed to be a big item in the patient's mind) a long distance call. It was a matter of literally seconds to ascertain the area code from the long distance operator, to obtain his telephone number from information, and then—obviously with some trepidation and keen ambivalence for her—to dial his number (at university expense), with the support of my presence to speak to him directly.

The point is not how the issue was practically resolved, without an excessive number of deep or shallow interpretations as to why she permitted herself to become pregnant and other aspects of her relationships with men, etc. What is important is that it was possible to achieve the assignment of that day: to lower her lethality.

In general, any suicidal state is characterized by its transient quality, its pervasive ambivalence, and its dyadic nature. Psychiatrists and other health professionals are well advised to minimize, if not totally to disregard, those probably well-intentioned but shrill writings in this field which naively speak of an individual's "right to commit suicide"—a right which, in actuality, cannot be denied—as though the suicidal person were a chronic univalently self-destructive hermit.

A number of special features in the management of a highly lethal patient can be mentioned. Some of these special therapeutic stratagems or orientations with a highly lethal patient attend to or reflect the *transient, ambivalent* and *dyadic* aspects of almost all suicidal acts.

1) A continuous, preferably daily, monitoring of the patient's lethality rating.
2) An active out-reach; being willing to deal with some of the reality problems of the patient openly, where advisable; giving direction (sans exhortation) to the patient; actively taking the side of life. It relates to befriending and caring.
3) Use of community resources including employment, Veterans Administration (when applicable), social agencies, and psychiatric social work assistance.
4) Consultation. There is almost no instance in a psychiatrist's professional life when consultation with a peer is as important as when he is dealing with a highly suicidal patient. The items to

be discussed might include the therapist's treatment of the case; his own feelings of frustration, helplessness or even anger; his countertransference reactions generally; the advisability of hospitalization for the patient, etc.

5) Hospitalization. Hospitalization is always a complicating event in the treatment of a suicidal patient but it should not, on those grounds, be eschewed. Obviously, the quality of care—from doctors, nurses and attendants—is crucial. Stoller (1), discussing one of his complex long-range cases, says: ". . . there were several other factors without which the therapy might not have succeeded. First, the hospital. The patient's life could not have been saved if a hospital had not been immediately available *and a few of the personnel familiar with me and the patient.* (Italics added).

6) Transference. As in almost no other situation and at almost no other time, the successful treatment of a highly suicidal person depends heavily on the transference. The therapist can be active, show his personal concern, increase the frequency of the sessions, invoke the "magic" of the unique therapist-patient relationship, be less of a *tabula rasa,* give "transfusions" of (realistic) hope and succorance. In a figurative sense, I believe that Eros can work wonders against Thanatos.

7) The involvement of significant others. Suicide is most often a highly charged dyadic crisis. It follows from this that the therapist, unlike his usual practice of dealing almost exclusively with his patient (and even fending off the spouse, the lover, parents, grown children), should consider the advisability of working directly with the significant other. For example, if the individual is male and married, it is important to meet his wife. The therapist must assess whether, in fact, she is suicidogenic; whether they ought to be separated; whether there are misunderstandings which the therapist can help resolve; or whether she is insightful and concerned and can be used by the therapist as his ally and co-therapist. The same is true for homosexual lovers, for patient and parent, etc. It is not suggested that the significant other be seen as often as the patient is seen, but that other real people in the suicidal patient's life be directly involved and, at the minimum, their role as hinderer or helper in the treatment process be assessed.

8) Careful modification of the usual canons of confidentiality. Admittedly, this is a touchy and complicated point, but the therapist should not ally himself with death. Statements given during the therapy session relating to the patient's overt suicidal (or homicidal) plans obviously cannot be treated as a "secret" between two collusive partners. In the previous example of the patient who opened her purse and showed me a small automatic pistol with which she said she was going, that day, to kill herself, two obvious interpretations would be that she obviously wanted me to take the weapon from her, or that she was threatening me. In

any event, I told her that she could not leave my office with the gun and insisted that she hand her purse to me. She countered by saying that I had abrogated the basic rule of therapy, namely that she could tell me anything. I pointed out that "anything" did not mean committing suicide and that she must know that I could not be a partner in that kind of enterprise. For a moment she seemed angered and then relieved; she gave me the gun. The rule is to "defuse" the potentially lethal situation. To have left her with a loaded gun would also leave her with a latent message.

9) Limitation of one's own practice to a very few highly lethal patients. It is possible to see a fairly large number of moderate and low-rated lethal patients in one's patient load, but one or two *highly* lethal patients seem to be the superhuman limit for most therapists at any given time. Such patients demand a great deal of investment of psychic energy and one must beware of spreading oneself too thin in his or her own professional life.

Working with highly suicidal persons borrows from the goals of crisis intervention: not to take on and ameliorate the individual's entire personality structure and to cure all the neuroses, but simply to keep him or her alive. That is the *sine qua non* without which all the other expert psychotherapists represented in this volume could not function.

REFERENCE

1. Stoller, R. J. *Splitting*. New York: Quadrangle Books, 1973.

BIBLIOGRAPHY

Below I have listed a half-dozen references of my own.

Shneidman, E. S. Lethality and perturbation as precursors of suicide in a gifted group. *Life-Threatening Behavior*, 1971, 1:23-45.
Shneidman, E. S. Suicide. In: *Encyclopaedia Britannica*, 1973 edition, Vol. 21, 383 *et seq* to 385.
Shneidman, E. S. Suicide notes reconsidered. *Psychiatry*, 1973, 36:379-394.
Shneidman, E. S. Psychiatric emergencies: Suicide. In: A. M. Freedman, H. I. Kaplan, and B. J. Sadock (Eds.), *Comprehensive Textbook of Psychiatry*, Second Edition. Baltimore: Williams & Wilkins, 1975. Vol. II, Chap. 29, pp. 1774-1784.
Shneidman, E. S. (Ed.). *Suicidology: Contemporary Developments*. New York: Grune & Stratton, 1975.
Shneidman, E. S. Some aspects of psychotherapy with dying persons. In: C. A. Garfield (Ed.), *Psychosocial Aspects of Terminal Patient Care*. New York: McGraw-Hill Book Co., 1978.

17

Psychotherapy with the Elderly

RALPH J. KAHANA, M.D.

What is special about psychotherapeutic work with older people? When we try to answer this question we may err in two opposite ways: by equating aging with extreme, *debilitated* or senile old age, thus accentuating the differences from earlier years, but taking a narrow, pessimistic view of the nature and value of therapy; or by overemphasizing the psychological similarities between older and younger adults and, in effect, *denying* and failing to take into account the impact of aging. These common errors have a history.

Until recently, interest in the mental and emotional problems of later life centered almost exclusively upon the most disabled segment of older people, the confused, demented, psychotic, institutionalized, physically ill or dying. Excluded was the larger, more vigorous segment of aging persons. Contributions to geriatric psychotherapy tended to be limited to approaches to the special problems of the disabled minority of elders, and they were often put forth as if they applied generally to the entire population of older people. On the other hand, dynamic psychotherapy, growing out of psychoanalysis, found its application and sources of knowledge first among young adults and then among children and adolescents. As interest extended to encompass the later years it was logical to stress continuities in psychological development over the entire life span. Early psychoanalytic discoveries pointed to the lasting importance of formative experiences in infancy and childhood. The excitement of these findings led to overvaluation of the idea that personality is established in all its essentials during childhood, so that later development merely repeats and reworks these foundations. It followed that the inner life of older people was only the continuation of post-adolescent existence without essential differences in normal personality or psychopathology except for organic brain diseases. The unique qualities of older persons and the special experiences and problems of later life were neglected.

DIFFICULTIES IN APPLYING PSYCHOTHERAPY WITH OTHER PEOPLE

Although today psychoanalytic psychotherapy is an established method for younger adults and even children and adolescents, when we try to apply it to aging or elderly patients we encounter special difficulties in defining when a person is "old," in approaching the topic objectively, in gauging whether patients are flexible enough to benefit from treatment, and in making useful generalizations.

While psychological aging, like physical aging, is correlated with adaptability, it defies simple definition. Although related to chronological age, senescence of body and brain, and accumulation of experience, aging cannot be equated with any of these. An 80-year-old, despite physical infirmities, may be more responsive, adaptive and forward-looking than a healthy 50-year-old. The only clearly established age-related change in the functioning of the central nervous system in the healthy older person is a slowing down of perceptual processes, with prolongation of the time spent in recovery between mental or physical actions that call for accurate perception and adjustment to changing stimuli; this decline is not uniform or specifically predictable. Some people are wise and experienced when quite young, while others remain relatively naive and simple through their late years. The complexity and ambiguity in defining "old" facilitate the errors of denying aging or equating it with senility. This may impede diagnosis of manifestations of illness which vary with age, or lead to misunderstanding of the motives, values and adaptive tasks of the older patient or to setting of too ambitious or too limited therapeutic goals.

A vigorous woman of 79, still able to run her own business, was observed to distinguish herself from her contemporaries and even somewhat younger friends who showed diminished energy, dwelled upon their physical illnesses and complaints, or displayed an accentuation of characterological stinginess, as if *they* were the *old* people. Thus, she agreed implicitly with those who define old age as physical infirmity and she had a pejorative attitude toward old age.

Disparagement and denial of aging are prevalent in our youth-oriented culture where youthful appearance, activity and achievement are overvalued. When aging is recognized, it may be pictured as unduly bleak, or it may be caricatured or treated with patronizing praise. Psychotherapists may unconsciously reflect gerontophobia and prejudice against older people through stereotyped attitudes in which the aging are regarded a priori as burdensome, demented, psychologically rigid or untreatable (1). A number of common circumstances, especially with the debilitated older group, play a part in evoking and rationalizing these attitudes and in inducing countertransferences. Older patients frequently show increased needs for encouragement, appreciation, and even admiration. They express depressive helplessness, or demand advice, assistance and magical help, thus placing particular strain upon their therapists. Unpleasant regressive character manifestations may appear or intensify in later life. Often, attention must be paid to the needs and sometimes interfering behavior of family members. There may be difficulties in communication, as with patients who show the early indications of organic brain disease. Younger therapists may have insufficient empathy with the perspective, physical limitations and traumatic experiences of older persons. They must draw upon whatever analogous personal events are available to them, such as periods of intensified physical and mental change and development, illnesses, family crises, raising their own children and, especially, dealing with their own aging parents.

Regarding psychoanalysis, the most intensive form of psychological treatment, analysts, following Freud (2, 3, 4), have been reluctant to treat persons over 45 by classical psychoanalysis. Even though his own later discoveries regarding narcissism and the structural point of view (id, ego and superego) increased the scope and the effectiveness of analysis, and despite the cautiously optimistic findings of other pioneering analysts, Freud apparently never revised his early opinion that by age 50 the mental processes are too rigid for favorable treatment results. As we know, Freud himself made major revisions and additions to his theories when he was near 70 and continued his scientific contributions into his 80's. His view may have impeded study of the psychodynamics of aging and application of dynamic psychotherapy in older people. Today many psychotherapists would agree with Berezin (5) that rigidity and flexibility are not functions of age but rather of personality structure throughout life. The impact of Freud's pessimism was mitigated by the initial successes of other analysts, such as Abraham (6) and Jelliffe (7). It was their point of view that chronological age did not of necessity involve deterioration of those intellectual and emotional capacities required for analysis, and hence *some* older persons could successfully undergo orthodox treatment. Kaufman (8) applied psychoanalytic principles in the treatment of two hospitalized patients with psychotic depressions, aged 56 and 60, achieving significant improvement. More recently, Hanna Segal (9) reported the 18-month treatment of a man in his late 70's with a chronic psychotic state of depression, paranoia and hypochondriasis, unresponsive to electroconvulsive therapy; and Anne-Marie Sandler (10) described the analysis of a man with narcissistic oversensitivity, treated between the ages of 58 and 65. These latter cases attest further to the possibilities for analysis, but also to the difficulties and limitations.

In a useful review of the literature on psychotherapy with geriatric patients, Rechtschaffen (11) evaluated psychoanalytic studies as well as some other contributions ranging from idiosyncratic efforts of talented therapists through Jungian, Meyerian, general psychiatric and social casework approaches. He noted that psychotherapy with the aged had a slow, pessimistic beginning followed by a wave of optimism and then a more considered attitude. Although almost 20 years have passed, the papers reviewed have much to offer that is useful today.

Starting in the 1940s, Grotjahn, Alexander, G. Lawton, J. Weinberg, G. J. Wayne, M. H. Hollender, and Meerloo used modified analytic approaches which stressed support and the active participation of the therapist. For example, Wayne (12, 13) suggested that the treatment begin with the elicitation of enough historical material to permit a psychodynamic formulation and an understanding of transference; that limited goals be set; and that a focus be kept upon a current problem that the patient consciously recognizes. He also made the following points: The patient should be given a readily perceivable part in solving his own problems; without deliberately avoiding material, no attempt should be made to rekindle old conflicts; the therapist should be active in providing guidance, reassurance and environmental manipulation; some educational techniques may be used, such as discussions of the cultural attitudes toward the elderly; scheduling should be flexible, with an effort to progressively decrease the number of weekly sessions; therapy need not be finally terminated; and tranquility, the goal of old age living, can be accepted and expressed tacitly in the therapeutic atmosphere. One may raise all sorts of questions, not easily resolved, about this advice: What is the nature of transferences in older people? Who or what limits the goals and how is this done? What is "activity" on the therapist's part? Is there a unitary "goal" of old age living? Yet, from a sufficiently broad and general standpoint, these and similar technical recommendations seem clear and sensible enough. But to which patients and in which conditions do they apply?

It is difficult to make accurate generalizations about older persons as a group, since they present the greatest diversity and individuality in life experiences, personality styles and current circumstances. In order to help clarify the aims and technical approaches in psychotherapy of older people, and at risk of making another procrustean overgeneralization, the distinction will be made between those past middle life who are *aging* and the smaller group of *debilitated aged*. There are, of course, many gradations and various combinations between these polarized extremes. Those in the group of the *aging* are experiencing: physical changes in appearance, attractiveness, strength, agility and reaction time; physical illnesses which are manageable rather than critical; some fluctuation and recession of instinctual drives; conflict over and reassessment of the balance between ideal aspirations and actual achievement, whether in personal development, social relationships, community activities, work or creative efforts; the prospect of retirement from work; awareness of limitation of time and of the eventual reality of dying; the deaths of people who are significant to them; and changes in their relationships with spouses, children, friends and co-workers.

An *intermediate group* of people experience states of crisis stemming from severe physical and mental illnesses, losses by death, divorce or radical change in personal relationships, or failures in their work.

The *debilitated aged* show in varying combinations and degrees: the limiting and burdening effects of chronic, multiple or dangerous illnesses, with diminished functional reserves of organ systems; manifestations of brain damage; constriction of activities; inability to maintain themselves without considerable assistance from their families, community resources or institutional facilities; a dominance of pregenital drives; and the depletion of stimulation, affection and satisfaction, the recurrence of grief reactions, and the strengthening of defenses against painful affects resulting from repeated, cumulative losses of significant people.

If we distinguish these groups, we can see that much of the literature on psychotherapy with older people appears directed to the debilitated group. This is explicit in Alvin Goldfarb's (14) special application of psychoanalytic thinking in brief therapy for the very old, mainly brain-damaged, residents of a home for the aged. His major point of departure was the overdependence of the aged, which he attributed to somatic changes, intellectual impairment, and socioeconomic and personal losses. Instead of responding as previous writers had with discouragement or promoting acceptance of dependency and providing dependent gratification, he attempted to utilize the patient's misperception of the therapist as a powerful parental authority. This illusion enables gratification of needs for affection, respect, protection and punishment. Patients were seen for five to 15 minutes weekly or less frequently. With those who have never been able to accept a dependent position he attempted, e.g. by granting small concessions, to create the feeling of having triumphed and gained control over the "parent"/therapist.

The kind of behavior that Goldfarb refers to was seen in a married woman in her mid 70's with an agitated depression, hypochondriasis and a definite degree of loss of recent memory. She came to the psychiatrist's office accompanied by family members, usually by her husband and one or more children. Initially fearful of the interviews and urgently requesting relief, she cast her younger therapist in the role of a savior or at least a superior court judge. He demurred and cautioned her overvaluation but could not entirely escape this omnipotent role. In a later session, when she felt better, she clasped him in her arms, said that she loved him—teasing that he mustn't tell his wife—and at the end of the session gave him a kiss. He was, of course, pleased with her improvement and he accepted her positive expression as he might from any affectionate older relative.

THE AIMS AND TECHNIQUES OF INDIVIDUAL PSYCHOTHERAPY

The purpose of any treatment is, of course, to relieve suffering, to allow normal functioning and, if possible, to "cure" and prevent difficulties. With these goals in mind, in psychotherapy we may place emphasis upon one of three intermediate treatment aims or strategies. We may try to bring about structural change, a further development and integration of drive derivatives, ego and superego functions, the self and other components of the personality. Alternatively, we seek to reinstate the best level of functioning that the patient has ever attained. Or we direct our attention primarily to assisting the patient's responsive and caretaking environment, usually the family. As shown by Grete and

Edward Bibring (15, 16), our techniques for accomplishing these aims include the promoting of insight, adaptive intervention (manipulation), and basic supportive methods. Insight occurs at two levels. The form employed most often is clarification, the giving of understanding of what is preconscious, that is, "fit to be conscious" but outside of immediate attention and comprehension. The other form of insight involves bringing to consciousness well-defended unconscious mental contents. The possibility of achieving insight depends upon the patient's tolerating an optimum intensity of conscious exposure to distressing conflicts that were preconscious or unconscious.

Gradual increase in self awareness was observed in a woman treated in her late 50's and early 60's for depression precipitated by grief at the death of her aged mother (17). Mrs. A's depression was marked by sadness, psychomotor retardation, and excessive concern with the distress that her condition produced in her family members. When most depressed, she repeatedly asked for reassurance and wanted change to occur without her understanding anything. When depression lifted, persistent clarification of her covered-over feelings sometimes led to appropriate weeping and the recall of events and emotions, particularly during the period of her mother's terminal illness. Her mother had died of a slow-growing gastrointestinal tumor after a two-and-one-half-year terminal illness in which she had little pain, but weakened, lost weight, and went through several crises. She lived by herself in a city 400 miles away, and although a married son lived in the same town, it was the patient, her only daughter, who assumed the burden of looking after her. Mrs. A, who had not been away from her husband for more than a day in over 30 years, spent long periods with her mother and observed her deterioration. When she returned home she constantly expected a telephone call announcing a further crisis. When the question of palliative surgery came up, she felt that the decision was placed in her lap even though another brother, living 2000 miles away from her, was a physician.

It became apparent that her mother had been phobic, overdependent and self-sacrificing. Moreover, the patient herself had struggled since childhood against similar fears, dependent feelings and masochistic tendencies. She spoke of having been somewhat depressed for many years. She dated this to the time when one of her children developd a school phobia, reactivating conflictual, repressed memories of her own struggle with her phobic mother who had tried to keep her at home. Psychotherapy, assisted by antidepressant medication, was usually scheduled at weekly intervals and was intermittent. The patient came when distressed and at times, later on, when she wanted to work on her problems. Movement in therapy proceeded as follows.

She recalled more of the events preceding her mother's death, particularly the deaths of two other close relatives, one by suicide. Also, two of the patient's grown children had experienced significant emotional crises then. Her awareness of the precipitating causes of recurrent depressive episodes increased. These causes included experiences which reminded her of her mother, anniversaries, the prospect of vacations and other separations, the deaths of relatives and acquaintances, and, increasingly, her children's problems and her husband's approaching retirement. Clearly, she had difficulty in achieving objectivity based on sufficient psychological differentiation from her children. She recognized that she was oversensitive, particularly to boastful and overbearing attitudes of others. This became focused upon important family members. Eventually she experienced strong resentment of the humble and sacrificing role assumed by her husband and, she felt, forced upon her as well in relation to his family. As she expressed these feelings, over a period of time, she gained courage and became purposefully and appropriately more assertive in these family relationships. She received added support from one of her children who coincidentally had also started therapy. Her husband made an effort to be more understanding and she became more perceptive of his depressive symptoms. Her intermittent depressions were painful, but her affective expressions were freer. When well, she felt better than she had in years, her imaginative community activities blossomed, and she renewed old friendships. Her transference was generally positive and her husband was the one who expressed displeasure, at times quite strongly, with the long, slow course of treatment.

In this case a childhood neurosis, phobic and depressive, was covered over by reaction formations, though at the price of overdependence and masochistic attitudes. Her defenses broke down under the impact of problems of aging, i.e., her mother's death, the independence of her children, and her husband's retirement. A new equilibrium had to be found based upon better resolution of her early conflicts. Prevention of the recurrence of depression was one of the treatment goals.

Where insight plays a major role in achieving structural improvement, therapeutic manipulation or adaptive intervention (15, 16) is the technical principle most useful in reinstatement of optimum functioning within the existing personality structure. Particularly suitable for brief therapy of psychological emergencies and crises and for medical psychotherapy, it utilizes the patient's defenses and adaptive methods, enabling him to find and follow ways in which he can function more satisfactorily and gain increasing security without having to go through a major psychological reorganization. Goldfarb's approach, noted above, can be characterized as a form of adaptive intervention.

In the case of Mr. B, a 60-year-old, single man seen in a surgical ward consultation, we can see how both his character type and his age characteristics were taken into account in a therapeutic intervention (18). He was referred for psychiatric evaluation because he repeatedly postponed necessary surgical treatment. Almost seven months before, on a private surgical service, he had been operated for gallstones which obstructed his bile duct. The complication of acute pancreatitis necessitated drainage of an abdominal abscess. Because of his financial situation in the face of his long illness, the patient was transferred to the ward service. Subsequently, a third operation for revision of the sinus was performed. Although it appeared that a fourth procedure to assist drainage would shorten his hospital stay, he had become anxious and talked of signing out of the hospital. The patient had discussed this important decision with his sister who lived in another city. Greatly concerned, she had contacted his private surgeon and also the chief of surgery. This added to the house doctors' determination to treat him very successfully; the difficulties which they encountered then led to feelings of frustration and to definite tension between them and their patient.

When interviewed, Mr. B was friendly and polite, had a very neat appearance, and showed great consideration of others on the ward. He knew that he was upset and thought that the psychiatrist might help him to feel better. As he spoke of his grave fears about the proposed operation and then described his life and work, a picture of him emerged as a steady, reliable, responsible, planful, conscientious person, who approached decisions gradually. He had run his own business for many years with great resiliency in the face of setbacks, and had then taken over direction of a section of a larger enterprise, strongly identifying himself with the management. His positive appreciation of his former private surgeon contrasted with his feeling that the younger ward physicians were inconsiderate and "walked away" from him at rounds. The psychiatric discussion and formulation centered upon the patient's compulsive personality structure and his seniority.

It was emphasized to the surgical staff that Mr. B felt disappointed and anxious because of the stress of his prolonged illness and reacted to pressure with indecisiveness and obstinacy, characteristic for the compulsive personality under stress. Accordingly, it was important to approach him in such a way as to permit him to use his careful, planful method of proceeding in order to deal with his anxieties adequately. He should not be pushed but rather be allowed further time to make up his mind about the operation. His questions were to be answered carefully, thoroughly, as often as necessary, and as unhurriedly as possible. With regard to his seniority and self-esteem, it was apparent that his transfer to the ward service had deprived him of the direct care of his private surgeon and he had found it difficult to establish a close relationship with the ward "management" in his accustomed manner. To correct this, it was to be suggested to the patient that if he felt anyone avoided answering his questions he did not have to accept this as final. In such circumstances he could make an appointment with the doctor to see him at a convenient time, e.g., after the rounds were completed. The doctors would try to establish clearly that the patient took an appropriate amount of responsibility in accepting or rejecting surgical recommendations.

As it turned out, following discussion along these lines between the consultant, the surgeons, the patient and his sister, Mr. B decided to permit the operation. Afterwards, he expressed appreciation of the talks with the psychiatrist and the surgeons because they had shown him how he could be strong. He was now functioning as an active, self-disciplined, effective compulsive type of personality, utilizing his rational and systematic abilities. The only clear elements of clarification and support (directed to his self-esteem) were expressed in acknowledging to him that his present anxiety at the prospect of a relatively minor surgical procedure could be understood in light of the strain and discomfort of the long illness (which he had actually borne in a good spirit).

The method of basic support is sometimes denigrated as being limited to a kind of unskilled, mindless handholding, demeaning to both holder and holdee—as if it required little therapeutic judgment, and as if one could not have a legitimate need to have one's hand held. In the hope of countering this prejudice, my illustration of this technique concerns a highly intelligent and insightful university professor with a national reputation in his field. He had been married for many years and was pleased with the way his children had turned out.

At 65, Professor C was facing the pressure of imposed partial retirement, with loss of the security of tenure, the recent appearance of symptoms suspected to be heart disease, and his wife's anxiety in response to these developments. He questioned whether her current anxieties and some related tensions between them were at least partly his fault. Both he and his wife had benefitted from psychotherapy directed toward structural change in the past, before middle age. Interestingly, he had recently discontinued psychotherapy after a brief trial, because he felt his former therapist had been too talkative and too supportive, that is, too directive. He was concerned that his cardiologist tended to see the diagnostic possibilities and treatment indications in an all or nothing fashion. His impressions were accurate but also reflected his personal needs and sensitivities. He understood that these feelings were related to his experience with his parents. His father had set an example of effective, professional, hard work, had encouraged his talent, had given him reams of advice and pressured him to be outstanding, was very stern, and had episodes of rage. The patient had identified strongly with his father's ways and values but reacted to his pressure at times by becoming stubbornly overcautious. His relationship with his mother had been very close and loving, and he took care of her in her late years until her death. This attitude of responsibility was continued with his young and admiring wife.

Although he did not specify how he thought psychotherapy could help, it was clear that advice was the last thing he needed. He utilized the sessions to air his concerns and get his bearings. One of the leading issues was the challenge to his self-esteem posed by the threats of illness (he had been quite athletic) and financial insecurity. He had strong feelings about the administrative opposition he encountered at the university where he believed that his contribution, which represented a special tradition of teaching in his discipline, was not well recognized. Here his insight and mature strength of personality proved useful. He said that he had recognized long ago that he was not the most celebrated living individual in his field. He was aware that when the urge to become famous was compelling he tended to overwork and to criticize himself. This awareness helped him to ease up and to regain his objectivity. In relatively few sessions he outlined his problems, expressed many feelings, remastered his revived conflicts, and then dealt with the realistic pressure that he faced. The therapist responded by indicating his understanding and trying to understand more, and by acknowledging the patient's expressions of feelings, attempted solutions, and frustrations and gains. These were supportive elements, gaining their effectiveness largely from a maternal transference. The therapist responded explicitly to Professor C's competence and experience, evident not only in his professional activities but in many of the ways in which he managed his life. This was an adaptive intervention. The therapist clarified issues which seemed most important, such as those bearing on the patient's self-esteem. Finally, the therapist accepted certain limitations of their therapeutic effort, for example, when his tension with his wife required joint sessions which were undertaken with his wife's therapist. It is significant that, despite persisting conflicts, the patient saw himself appropriately within his age group with regard to issues of achievement and prestige. He told a charming anecdote in which one distinguished man reminds another that, unlike younger people, the latter no longer has to struggle to establish his position in the world.

A COMPARISON OF AGING AND DEBILITATED PATIENTS

Among 16 patients treated in my practice, 11 women and five men ranging in age from late middle life to mid 70's, half were in the aging group, three intermediate, and five in the debilitated aged category. None was permanently institutionalized in hospitals, nursing homes or special residences. Almost all suffered some form of depression. In the aging group depression ranged from reactive (neurotic) to psychotic and paranoid. The intermediate group included one psychotic, paranoid depression and one of moderate severity, between neurosis and psychosis. All five of the debilitated patients had depressions, in two cases associated with senile brain disease. Three of these were anaclitic depressions associated with depletion of functions and satisfactions, while one was an agitated depression and another a deepening of chronic depression. With regard to diagnoses other than depression, two patients in the aging group had states of tension, another proved to have normal grief and a fourth was phobic. One of the patients in the intermediate category presented the surgical management problem cited above.

The precipitating causes of these problems were mainly personal losses and physical disorders. The aging patients were reacting to losses of mother, husband or brother, to physical or mental illness of a close relative, or to retirement from work. In the intermediate group two had physical illnesses and one was widowed. Brain damage and physical aging were the leading precipitants among the debilitated, followed by illness of a close relative, death of a spouse or retirement from work. A range of personality types was found in all groups, but in this small series the only hysterical types were among the aging, while the debilitated showed more oral behavior.

In keeping with the findings of others, structural change as the principal therapeutic aim was found only in the aging group. The aim of reinstatement of optimum functioning was important in all three groups and was the only aim in the intermediate or crisis sample. Offering basic support was a major aim in the treatment of the debilitated, but it was also employed significantly with the aging. Assistance to and through the family was a treatment aim in most of the debilitated patients. Prevention of future suffering, maladaptation or breakdown was a principal consideration in the aging and intermediate groups in relation to widowhood, preparation for retirement, the regression promoting threat of physical illness, and changes in a marital relationship. Regarding duration of treatment, there was no clear pattern among the three categories, whether brief (under three months), average (up to three years) or long-term (over three years). I was surprised to find that half of my aging patients were in the brief category and that most of the patients in the debilitated group were seen for an average length of time. In the aging group, one of my long-term patients had subsequent unterminated maintenance therapy at monthly intervals, while one of the intermediate category patients was treated for an average duration and then seen in follow-up twice a year until her death 15 years later.

To recapitulate and highlight these observations according to each group, psychotherapy of the *aging* was aimed at structural change, restitution of personality functioning or basic support. These patients had neurotic or psychotic depressions, other neuroses or adjustment reactions, often precipitated by personal losses or retirement. They represented a full range of personality types. Prevention of future disturbance was an important consideration. In the *intermediate* group, the aim of treatment was restitution of optimum functioning. Illnesses were of crisis proportions in reaction to physical diseases or personal losses, and prevention was a common goal. The *debilitated aged* responded to measures of basic support for treatment of anaclitic depressions set off by brain damage, physical aging or multiple personal losses. They often showed oral personality traits. Their families had a significant role in their treatment.

THE MANAGEMENT OF CRISES

Zinberg (19) observed how frequently a psychiatric referral of an older patient involved an emergency. Psychiatric emergencies at any age may require considerable involvement with members of the patient's family, time spent in telephoning, and pressures for immediate help, with insight taking second place to dealing with problems of the moment. The number of emergencies one sees in practice is, naturally, a function of where and how one practices. However, it is my impression that these circumstances often prevail with older people and especially with the debilitated aged.

The fundamental therapeutic injunctions to safeguard life and functioning, and to do no harm, as they are followed in geriatric psychiatry, have certain implications which are highlighted in crisis situations. On the one hand, emergencies, whether of confusion, anxious agitation, incipient or acute psychosis, or suicidal despair, call for rapid, concentrated intervention. At the same time, the limited adaptability, poor tolerance of painful affects, and potential for ego regression shown by elderly, and especially by debilitated patients, dictate that we intervene in ways that are the least disruptive of the individual's familiar life-style. The threat of suicide requires, of course, stringent protective measures— we are reminded of the high incidence of completed suicide in older men. States of confusion call for thorough medical investigation, often in the hospital. Acute psychoses may only be manageable in an institution. Otherwise, if possible, we try to keep the patient at home and treat him or her in the office. We help mobilize the support of close relatives whom the patient trusts, and we communicate and present ourselves in ways that are familiar and understandable to the patient.

A 75-year-old woman who became confused after an operation for cataracts was managed entirely by restructuring her environment. It was her first hospitalization, and separation from her home and family played a major role in her postoperative reaction. The surgeon had gained her cooperation by a preparatory discussion of the procedure, and he prevented more serious delirium by avoiding any blindfolding. When she became frightened and noisy she was moved to a private room away from gravely ill patients. A small night light and side rails on her bed were provided. Restraints were not used. Her daughters took turns staying with her during the day and sleeping overnight, while other visitors were restricted. The patient had been a mildly anxious, slightly over-devoted mother and now her children, in turn, found it easy to be protective, even a little overprotective, toward her. Under this regime she calmed down, believing that she was in her eldest daughter's home. She was discharged with a clearing sensorium after the minimum of hospitalization.

The principle of keeping interventions to a necessary minimum has its parallel at the physiological level where medications for anxiety and mood disorders are prescribed cautiously, in small initial doses, while we monitor carefully for any side effects to which these older patients may be sensitive. Psychotherapy, resting upon the patient's consent and collaboration, is the least interfering form of treatment. The use of psychotherapy is almost indispensable, even when the principal treatment is medication or electroconvulsive therapy. At a minimum, it constitutes the basic support necessary to have patients accept and continue with other methods. When communication with the patient is severely limited due to brain disorder or psychosis, then psychologically correct measures of environmental support are necessary, as we saw in the preceding example.

The combination of drug treatment and psychotherapy is often employed in the management of emergencies. A 65-year-old woman with an intense, worsening depression had the kind of symptoms that often respond to medication. She suffered from insomnia, tenseness and lack of enjoyment, was slowed down in speech and action, and felt ashamed of her condition. These complaints had begun a year before and had become more severe. Despite all this she was well-groomed and attractive in appearance. She lacked insight into any predisposing or precipitating causes of her depression. For example, she did not connect it with the death of her mother three years before. Mother, she said, was a nice person, who died in her old age after an illnes of a few days, and "I got over my grief." Referral came through a former therapist of her oldest son, and this son accompanied her on the first two visits. Her husband, in his late 70's and retired from work, came in with her each time. She had had a thorough medical workup and had taken on prescription a number of standard antidepressants and tranquilizers. Despite the apparently correct indications for these medications, they had not brought relief. The patient was seen six times in all, twice in the first week, then at two-week and finally one-month intervals, with a telephone follow-up.

In the interviews she quickly expressed an intense preoccupation with an elderly woman relative. They had had a misunderstanding dating back several years over a wedding gift given by the patient to this relative's grandson. The patient had meant to send a check but had accidentally mailed an empty envelope, and had then corrected this error. The relative's response, as the patient saw it, was to avoid attending the funeral of the patient's mother. Also, she had not sent gifts when the patient's grandchildren were born. The patient felt terribly guilty that she had, in turn, reacted by avoiding a baby shower for this relative's great grandson. Subsequent efforts by the patient at reconciliation had been rebuffed. Moreover, this woman's daughter, in her 40's and recently widowed, had also refused to see her. The patient could not answer why this troubled relationship was having such a drastic, lasting impact upon her.

She had grown up in a strictly regulated home as part of a small, stable ethnic community. She believed that, of all her siblings, she had been closest to her mother. Her marriage at 17 was arranged by a matchmaker. For the next 15 years her mother-in-law had lived out her life with her. The patient's existence had centered around raising her sons, visits with nearby relatives, attending a women's group of her church, and enjoying some handicrafts. Her mother, in the same city, was very demanding of attention by her children. The patient remarked that she has tried not to be this way with her children. However, it is lonely without a daughter. Her oldest son's wife is rather independent and the patient has to telephone before she goes over.

At 15, when her mother became ill and unable to work outside the home, the patient left school to take a job in a factory where she contracted a severe case of skin disorder, an eczema that involved her hands and was believed due to contact with an industrial chemical. After her last son was born, she had two miscarriages and then, following her doctor's recommendation, had tubal ligations. This had saddened her; she wondered if one of the miscarriages had been a daughter. Completing the relevant medical history, at 38 she had had a previous depression but snapped out of it after two shock treatments. It was not clear whether this was related to the loss of pregnancies and the sterilization.

At the end of the first hour the therapist prescribed antidepressant and sleep medication, employing drugs that had been given her before. Five days later she reported feeling calmer and sleeping well except for one night. She continued to speak about her elderly relative, and it was learned that this woman carried grudges and had avoided other funerals of family members. The patient's son provided additional information tending to confirm the therapist's hunch that this elderly woman relative was seriously ill physically and probably had a severe personality disorder; both she and her daughter wanted the patient to stay away. The therapist recommended strongly to the patient that she stop pursuing a reconciliation, suggesting that she had done all the proper things and that this was a kind of misunderstanding which could not be resolved in a reasonable fashion at this time. In the absence of side effects, the dosage of medication was increased.

A week later she was more alert and cheerful. She read some notes that she had made regarding her attempts to make up with her relative. The therapist reinforced his recommendation that she put aside this effort. On her fourth visit, two weeks later, she reported herself as back to normal. She complained that her husband doesn't go out of the house very much, implying that this limited her own mobility. The therapist suggested that she may need more outside activities and contact with friends, particularly women. He spoke with her about the death of her mother, putting forward the suggestion that she had reacted as most people do with feelings of loss, need, disappointment and even anger, and with an attempt at symbolic replacement of her mother. He said that he thought this was behind the pressure of her efforts to reconcile with the older woman relative. She listened but did not confirm or deny this.

A month later she had maintained her gains, and she described having had an enjoyable Christmas celebration. During the previous hour she had inquired about the therapist's name and its origins. Now, in a friendly way, she asked whether he had enjoyed the Jewish celebration of Hannukah. The pressure to see her relative had abated. It was agreed to meet again in a month and then, if she had maintained her improvement, to terminate therapy and discontinue the medication.

At the final meeting she was looking and feeling well. The therapist complimented her on her appearance. She reported memories of her mother which had come back, accompanied by tears, during the Christmas and New Year holidays. Then she told more about the stresses which she had experienced in the preceding years. Two of her sons had divorced nine or ten years before. She had had good relations with these daughters-in-law and still kept in touch with one and with a grandson. However, she had lost touch completely with the other daughter-in-law and with a granddaughter.

In her late 40's she had taken a factory job and had held it until three or four years ago, when she gave it up with the plan of enjoying traveling with her husband. Then mother died and her husband became "too old" and sedentary for this recreation. Now he is "her job" but she feels lonely. She was encouraged again to resume outside activities. The dosage of her medication was reduced and a date set to discontinue it. A week later she telephoned and said that she would like to stop all medication. It was agreed that she should. She was most appreciative of the help that she had received.

In this case, rapid intervention using psychotherapy and medication relieved an incipient crisis of worsening depression. It was essential to understand that the dynamic basis of her reaction was an unresolved grief reaction with attempted restitution of her loss through a current relationship. The relationship with her elderly relative was burdened with displaced ambivalent feelings, and was doubly unsuitable because of the relative's own personality disorder. The support for undertaking therapy given by the patient's son and the information that he supplied were essential. Suggestion, guidance, manipulation, and some clarification were utilized in the psychotherapy. The patient's son reinforced her belief in the expert power of the therapist, a basis of suggestion. Intervention to help her calm down and distance the relationship with her relative may be considered a form of guidance. The therapist approached her severe superego reaction manipulatively by giving her credit for her good intentions toward her relative. The patient's experience of grief during therapy tended to confirm the dynamic formulation and indicated some response to clarification. Previously medication alone had not been sufficient, but together with this psychotherapeutic approach it became effective.

VARIOUS DIMENSIONS OF PSYCHOTHERAPY WITH THE AGING AND ELDERLY

In recent years a number of reviews and detailed reports of psychotherapy with older persons have enriched our understanding of the process and its applications.

M. P. Lawton (20) notes some frequent characteristics of older patients that may signal the desirability of particular approaches to therapy. Older people tend to be relatively low in educational attainment as compared with younger ones, unfamiliar with psychological concepts, resistant to the idea of psychological assistance, and rejecting of moral liberalism. This suggests that the therapist must be careful in his choice of words, cautious in inviting older patients to explore tabooed feelings, and not too ready to assume that psychological explanations will be comprehensible. It may be better not to generalize too abstractly or to rely upon analogies and metaphors. Poorly structured interviews and the use of ambiguity may elicit anxiety and overcautiousness. Support may be necessary to maximize the older patient's ability to pursue problem solutions in his own way. The pace of therapy will often be slower than with younger persons. The therapist must tread between acknowledgment of the patient's limitations and succumbing to overgeneralized, ageistic devaluation of his patient. It appears that Lawton's observations are especially applicable to the debilitated aged.

Berezin and Fern (21) described a 70-year-old woman with a hysterical character disorder who was admitted to a mental hospital because of increasing alcoholism. She was seen initially because she had become a management problem. Psychotherapy twice weekly for 15 months enabled her to partially work through some early, persistent conflicts, so that she could function in less regressive ways and eventually make a satisfactory adjustment in a nursing home. During psychotherapy the availability of conflictual material, in the form of early memories and fantasies with their corresponding affects, was striking. As the discussants of this paper note, therapy enabled her to accept her age, i.e., that she was no longer adolescent. There is an interesting discussion of the use of transference in psychotherapy of older persons.

A beautifully written depiction of an eight-month treatment of a 66-year-old woman with a hysterical neurosis by Gitelson (22) highlights her transference reactions and the therapist's responses.

Hauser (23) details the treatment of a 78-year-old woman, utilizing psychotherapy and ECT. She had her first paranoid depression at age 59. Among important issues in her life and therapy were her fear of being abandoned and left helpless, her overdependence and the need to be in control of personal relationships, her suppressed anger, a strongly sexualized transference, and her enormous effort to deny aging.

Zarsky and Blau (24) describe the response to two brief periods of therapy of a woman with a lifelong narcissistic character neurosis, reacting to the death of her favorite son. During periods of regression she showed clinging dependence, insatiable overentitlement, and endless rage and blamefulness. When functioning better, she was dominating, bright, charming and entertaining, with a capacity for making and losing friends. Treatment was at ages 60 and 70 with a five-year follow-up. The paper and discussions consider the psychotherapeutic measures that helped reverse the process of regression. Differential diagnosis and therapeutic aspects are taken up.

Ronch and Maizler (25) agree that insight-oriented, dynamically based individual psychotherapy is an effective treatment modality with the institutionalized elderly. A crucial area in such psychotherapy is the heightened resurgence of dependency conflicts because of the institutionalization itself. One must deal with increased manifestations of ambivalence and anger toward the staff, and the correlated fear of abandonment. The treatment of a paranoid, suicidal depression in a man with Alzheimer's disease is cited. After about a year the patient moved from a protected psychiatric facility up to the second highest level of self-care of eleven levels of progressive care in the institution. The technique of reality orientation was also used to solidify his gains in judgment, memory, intellect and orientation. Another example is of a 69-year-old woman with overdemanding behavior, depression, pain and anxiety following a spinal operation. She perceived therapy as a magical rescue. Environmental measures, adaptive intervention and clarification met with considerable success.

Hasenbush (26) reported the successful brief therapy of a retired elderly man with intractable pain, depression, and drug and alcohol dependence. I think of this case as belonging to a category of patients who seem impossible to treat, but turn out, unexpectedly, to have some capacity for improvement. In some instances their psychopathology appears longstanding and deeply fixed. I have seen such patients whose chronic anaclitic depressions have worsened, increasing their suffering and distressing their families or others in their environment. Supportive psychotherapy and medication gave enough relief to make their condition tolerable. In other cases, life circumstances are the principal burdening and limiting factors. A woman in this group, with a reactive depression stemming from taking care of her husband who had Alzheimer's disease, was able to find some relief by ventilating her feelings of frustration. A man attached to his wife, despite her refusal of sexual intercourse, was able to manage by returning to a previous extramarital relationship. Dr. Hasenbush's patient seemed to belong to the first group with serious psychopathology. This 72-year-old man with lifelong character problems had retired from work seven years previously. Since then, he had suffered severe burning pain in a foot for six years, had not improved with two peripheral nerve operations, spinal blocks and 30 electric shock treatments, and had withdrawn to a bed and chair existence, depending upon increasing amounts of codeine, tranquilizers and alcohol. Despite all of this, there were some hopeful indications. The interdependence of needs and the matching of personality styles between the patient and his wife could be approached in concurrent therapy of both. Treatment in later life was facilitated by the psychoanalysis of each partner approximately 30 years before, even though the results of analysis had been limited.

Hypochondriasis is one of the typical disturbing symptoms of older people, and in its most common form reflects neurosis or borderline disorder rather than psychosis. It is often resistant to treatment. Busse and Pfeiffer (27) outline an approach to the treatment of this symptom by the family doctor or internist. They point out the limitations and drawbacks of giving the patient a full medical explanation or an organic diagnosis, of offering a psychiatric formulation of his condition, or of doing surgical procedures. Effective techniques include listening, respecting defenses, and conveying recognition that the patient is indeed sick and the assurance that he will be cared for. The use of medication, handling of relatives, and the conduct and spacing of interviews are discussed.

Da Silva (28) describes the treatment of a man with manic-depressive illness, seen in a state hospital between the ages of 81 and 84. The paper, which should be read together with the discussions that follow it, gives a moving and impressive picture of the patient's deep, longstanding loneliness, the correlation of his life history with his personality and psychopathology in old age, the ways in which he related himself to his therapist, and the strong feelings he evoked in his therapist. His images and concepts of death are of particular interest. Treatment moved from a phase in which he denied his oncoming death to one in which he gave up the denial, reviewed and examined his life, and in effect prepared for dying. Psychotherapy appears as a means of prolonging and enriching life.

Myerson (29) discusses two cases of psychotherapeutic management of terminal illness, one involving an 85-year-old woman (30). He concentrates upon the personal hazards for the therapist of intense involvement with a dying person. He observes that we have come to believe that, in general, the dying patient is better off if he has the opportunity to talk about his impending death, and can be supported by the caring presence of people who respect his dignity. In dynamic psychotherapy, the patient's desire for explicit reciprocation of transference love felt for the therapist cannot be gratified. The borderline patient has poor tolerance for this frustration. Intense therapeutic relationships with dying patients run the risk of creating a borderline situation. It is often not possible to analyze and work out the patient's transference feelings under these circumstances. The therapist senses that the patient wants more from him than he can provide. This is the level of distress that is peculiar to professionals. We are forced to frustrate people who have needs that cannot be met, and we feel guilty—in part because we recognize that we have implicitly promised that we would give what is desired of us.

REFERENCES

1. Blau, D. and Berezin, M. A. Neuroses and character disorders. In: J. G. Howells (Ed.), *Modern Perspectives in the Psychiatry of Old Age.* New York: Brunner/ Mazel, 1975, pp. 201-233.
2. Freud, S. Sexuality in the etiology of the neuroses (1898). In: *Standard Edition, Vol. 3.* London: Hogarth Press, 1962, pp. 263-285.
3. Freud, S. Freud's psychoanalytic procedure (1904). In: *Standard Edition, Vol. 7.* London: Hogarth Press, 1953, pp. 249-254.
4. Freud, S. On psychotherapy (1905). In: *Standard Edition, Vol. 7.* London: Hogarth Press, 1953, pp. 257-268.
5. Berezin, M. A. Psychodynamic considerations of aging and the aged: An overview. *Amer. J. Psychiat.,* 1972, 128:1483-1491.
6. Abraham, K. The applicability of psychoanalytic treatment to patients at an advanced age (1919). In: *Selected Papers on Psycho-Analysis.* London: Hogarth Press, 1927, pp. 312-317.
7. Jelliffe, S. E. The old age factor in psycho-analytic therapy. *Med. J. Rec.,* 1925, 121:7-12.
8. Kaufman, M. R. Psychoanalysis in late life depressions. *Psychoanal. Quart.,* 1937, 6:308-335.
9. Segal, H. Fear of death: Notes on the analysis of an old man. *Int. J. Psychoanal.,* 1958, 39:178-181.
10. Sandler, A. M. Problems in the psycho-analysis of an aging narcissistic patient. *J. Geriat. Psychiat.,* 1978, 11:5-36.
11. Rechtschaffen, A. Psychotherapy with geriatric patients: A review of the literature. *J. Geront.,* 1959, 14:73-84.
12. Wayne, G. J. Psychotherapy in senescence. *Ann. West. Med. Surg.,* 1952, 6:88-91.
13. Wayne, G. J. Modified psychoanalytic therapy in senescence. *Psychoanal. Rev.,* 1953, 40:99-116.
14. Goldfarb, A. L. One aspect of the psychodynamics of the therapeutic situation with aged patients. *Psychoanal. Rev.,* 1955, 42:180-187.
15. Bibring, G. L. Psychiatry and social work. *J. Soc. Casework.,* 1947, 28:203-211.
16. Bibring, E. Psychoanalysis and the dynamic psychotherapies. *J. Amer. Psychoanal. Assoc.,* 1954, 2:745-770.
17. Kahana, R. J. The concept and phenomenology of depression with special reference to the aged: Grief and depression. *J. Geriat. Psychiat.,* 1974, 7:26-47.
18. Kahana, R. J. Teaching medical psychology through psychiatric consultation. *J. Med. Educ.,* 1959, 34:1003-1009.
19. Zinberg, N. E. Special problems of gerontologic psychiatry. In: M. A. Berezin and S. H. Cath (Eds.), *Geriatric Psychiatry: Grief, Loss and Emotional Disorders in the Aging Process.* New York: International Universities Press, Inc., 1965, pp. 147-159.
20. Lawton, M. P. Geropsychological knowledge as a background for psychotherapy with older people. *J. Geriat. Psychiat.,* 1976, 9:221-233.
21. Berezin, M. A. and Fern, D. J. Persistence of early emotional problems in a 70-year-old woman. *J. Geriat. Psychiat.,* 1967, 1:45-60.
22. Gitelson, M. A transference reaction in a 66-year-old woman. In: M. A. Berezin and S. H. Cath (Eds.), *Geriatric Psychiatry: Grief, Loss, and Emotional Disorders in the Aging Process.* New York: International Universities Press, Inc., 1965, pp. 160-186.
23. Hauser, S. T. The psychotherapy of a depressed aged woman. *J. Geriat. Psychiat.,* 1968, 2:62-87.

24. Zarsky, E. L. and Blau, D. The understanding and management of narcissistic regression and dependency in an elderly woman observed over an extended period of time. *J. Geriat. Psychiat.*, 1970, 3:160-176.
25. Ronch, J. L. and Maizler, J. S. Individual psychotherapy with the institutionalized aged. *Amer. J. Orthopsychiat.*, 1977, 47:275-283.
26. Hasenbush, L. L. Successful brief therapy of a retired elderly man with intractable pain, depression, and drug and alcohol dependence. *J. Geriat. Psychiat.*, 1977, 10:71-88.
27. Busse, E. W. and Pfeiffer, E. *Behavior and Adaptation in Late Life.* Boston: Little, Brown and Co., 1969, pp. 202-209.
28. Da Silva, G. The loneliness and death of an old man: Three years' psychotherapy of an 81-year-old depressed patient. *J. Geriat. Psychiat.*, 1967, 1:5-27.
29. Myerson, P. G. To die young, to die old, management of terminal illness at age 20 and at age 85: Case reports, discussion. *J. Geriat. Psychiat.*, 1975, 8:137-145.
30. Morris, L. L. To die young, to die old, management of terminal illness at age 20 and at age 85: Case reports, death and dying in an 85-year-old woman. *J. Geriat. Psychiat.*, 1975, 8:127-135.

18

Psychotherapy with Bilingual Patients

VICTOR BERNAL Y DEL RIO, M.D.

Let us go down, and there confuse their language so that they will not understand one another's speech. For this reason the tower was called Babel, because there the Lord confused the speech of all the earth. GENESIS 11:7-9

I shall be sharing with you experiences with patients of multiple cultural backgrounds and of different languages whom I have encountered in more than 25 years of psychotherapeutic practice in Puerto Rico. Although the English-speaking population in Puerto Rico is small, 30% of my patients are English-speaking and 50% of the 70% who are Hispanic or of other origins have, at one time or another, lived in an English-speaking culture. All of my patients are bilingual to some degree.

Bilinguality in psychotherapeutic practice is not new. Freud recognized bilinguality and sometimes multilinguality in the analytic situation. What is unique, however, is that my patients live in a bilingual society that has a continuous bilingual input: in the streets, over the radio, in the newspapers, etc. Most of my patients are able to start treatment with equal facility in one language or in another.

The birth of language is the dawn of humanity. We are born into a world of sounds. The sound changes to language, the language to communication. If psychotherapy is defined as the intent of changing behavior, feelings, and emotions by psychological means, language is the core of that transference. In the *General Introduction to Psycho-Analysis*, Freud states that: ". . . in psychotherapy nothing happens but an exchange of words between the patient and the physician. The patient talks, tells of his past experiences and presents impressions, complaints, and expresses his wishes and his emotions. The physician listens, attempts to direct the patient's thought processes, reminds him, forces his attention in certain directions, gives him explanations and observes the reactions of understanding or denial thus evoked" (11, p. 61).

Thus, Freud establishes that psychotherapy is structured on verbal intercommunication. It is through language that the patient reveals himself to the physician who, in turn, exerts his therapeutic influence upon the patient by the same media. The work of Felix Deutsch on analytic posturology (6), of Sullivan on body language (24), of Jackson, Bateson and Haley on nonverbal communication, and of Weakland on double bind (2) has added significant dimensions to the understanding of communication. Yet, in the final analysis, the psychotherapist and the patient rely on the security of the spoken word.

The security of the verbal arena is not without complexity. Words have both an intellectual and emotional meaning: Few words are devoid of any emotional meaning. The individual's history of the acquisition of a word gives the matrix for the emotional response that is evoked by its use. Words may actually be repressed as concepts disassociated from their meaning.

Differences in the patient's emotional reaction to the recollection of even the most hypercathected objects or events in the environment are revealed by either his use of semi-technical/transitional terms that he has newly acquired or by his use of words that he had early in life—with their personal or family oriented particularities. It is within the realms of sexual, micturative, and evacuative behavior that such highly cathected words appear. At all stages of development the spoken word is cathected differently depending on whether it is said or heard, read or written.

I was treating a professional of Spanish parentage. He was raised in a Spanish-speaking country but had lived in the United States for a few years. He kept talking about *axilas* or arm pits, and gave recollections of an extremely personal nature regarding his early interest in this part of the human anatomy. He related it to a symptom of anxiety that he experienced while riding in the subway where women stood with their arms on the railing exposing their *axilas*. He went into early recollec-

tions of smell, meaning of hair, etc., and seemed to exhaust the possibilities of exploration without any change in his anxiety. After what
appeared an exhaustion of the theme, it became apparent that he was
always using the technical term *axila* (arm pit), undoubtedly of later
acquisition. I asked him if he knew any other word for *axila;* his brusque
answer was that there was no other word in Spanish for arm pit. He left
it at that. Upon insistence, he reacted with bitter, half concealed rage. I
finally asked him if he ever knew the word *sobaco* which is *axila* in
autochthonus Spanish. He was silent for a moment, recognized the word,
then continued to talk at length about the same recollection that he had
brought to previous sessions, now accompanied by body motion and
voice fluctuation. The recognition of a personal word and the continual
discussion allowed him, in time, to subdue his anxieties in regards to
the subway.

I also had a female patient who would use exactly the same word
fundillo, which in Spanish is a jovial term for the buttocks, interchangeably for female genitalia and anal region. I became aware of this double
meaning and its ensuing confusion. She finally recognized that she had
never established the word distinction for these parts of the anatomy
and further claimed that in her household, even as a child, this "confusion" was familiar. This patient suffered from severe menstrual pains
and very severe constipation. After word clarification and therapy, both
problems disappeared. With these examples in mind, and the complexity of language nuances, you may wonder how I dared to treat patients
in languages which were not mine from the cradle. I was not particularly
brave, but was sustained by the knowledge that more than 90% of the
psychotherapeutic work done in this country from the thirties to the
fifties was practiced in very similar circumstances and with the thickest
of mid-European accents. This interest in linguistic studies had a glori-
ous start, yet faded rapidly from the psychiatric literature, as pointed
out by Spitz, Rosen, Ekstein, and others.

Freud's linguistic observations were recorded in "The Psychopathology of Everyday Life" (12). He illustrated mistakes, slips of the tongue
and pen, memory lapses, etc. His examples were primarily from slips in a
foreign language, as the cases of "Signorelli" or the quotes from Latin
verse, etc. He generated the idea that slips of the tongue occurred more
in a foreign language. He analyzed many foreign patients, was extremely
interested in the translation of his own work, and personally supervised
some of his own translations. With such an auspicious start, it is strange

indeed that the psychotherapeutic literature is particularly undeveloped in comparative linguistic studies.

After 25 years of experience, I can assess that the therapist practicing in a foreign language can produce very rapid transferential cures which are seldom seen when dealing with the native tongue. After all, God does speak in a foreign tongue. Patients of different cultures and languages are difficult to categorize under sweeping generalities. Yet, residents treating exclusively Spanish-speaking patients on a face-to-face psychotherapeutic situation do not report occurrences of silence. On the other hand, in many classical books, the generality that silences are more frequent in Latin people is expressed. This can be seriously questioned. By analogy, if Latins are loquacious at a social level, they should be garrulous in therapy. Silences, although not frequent in psychotherapy, are very frequent in psychoanalysis and maintain a very profound type of resistance in the Spanish-speaking population. Silences are prolonged and resistive to interpretation or intervention.

Language, on the whole, can be seen as the principal characteristic of the ego in its performance of communication. When the ego cannot perform well in the role of communication, anxiety results. We have cases of neurotic depression, compensatory overreaction and transitional paranoid reactions, mostly from wives of English-speaking executives who are catapulted both geographically and hierarchically from the mainland into a Spanish-speaking situation. The psychodynamics of such a situation is very complicated indeed and could include competition with their husbands, anger reactions, etc., but the sudden language change is an added stress in the appearance of the pathology. Strangely enough, complaints are not voiced along the lines of language difficulties. Instead, many complaints reveal an intolerance towards differences of non-human physical surroundings. These complaints do not pertain to the man-made physical environment which would, indeed, be pertinent (breakdown of appliances, lack of adequate services, etc.). Rather, most complaints are noncontrollable areas such as rain, heat, light and lack of non-inhabited spaces.

Some people come into the country with a rationalization regarding the acquisition of the new language. These people keep alive the fantasy of eventually becoming very knowledgeable and efficient in the new language and its literature. Yet, they stress the differences in pronunciation and the usual use of localisms. Their fantasy is that some day they will learn "pure" Castillian, like Oxford English—it is as if a Spaniard going to Minnesota would decide not to learn English until he could go to Oxford, or at least to Boston.

Another example of ego conflict with language difficulties was a patient referred to me from the mainland, who presented, during a short period of treatment, particular language characteristics and ego confrontations. He was a tall, good-looking, amiable, 37-year-old, single, engineer, born and raised in Berlin. He had served in the German Army during World War II, after which he had migrated to the United States, where he had learned English and worked for two years. He had then been transferred by his company to Puerto Rico, and given the customary raise in salary. Although he was unhappy about the transfer, he accepted it because of the raise.

He had been seeing a psychiatrist on the East Coast, who had referred him to us because of insomnia, anxiety, and indecision regarding getting married. The patient started his treatment completely in English, four times a week. After a short period, he abandoned the island in a state of panic and returned to the United States. Later, when I looked over the protocol, I found two striking things: 1) His regressive behavior at the beginning of treatment was greater than any I have seen in such cases; 2) He immediately started dreaming in German exclusively, his dreams dealing with his previous experience in the German Army. There was no direct day residue, to speak of, detectable in the dreams.

It seems that having only recently carried through such a formidable job of adaptation into the English culture and language, the capacity of his ego was depleted for further adaptive compensation. Upon being faced too rapidly with a second new situation, in both language and culture, he suffered deep regression at a clinical level, and defensively went back to his original familiar grounds every night in his dreams, in an attempt to ease his tensions.

Language preference in psychotherapy is a commanding phenomenon. Many factors influence the acquisition of a foreign language. Studies have been made on preferences of second generation emigrees, identification difficulties, and tendencies to protest the parental figures. Many Puerto Ricans, by reasons of their multiple geographical and cultural upbringings, come very close to binguality—a perfect command of both languagse.

In Puerto Rican émigrés, rarely does language identification become so clearly and completely categorized as in this case quoted by Greenson,

"I would like to cite some material from the analysis of a young woman who developed a great aversion to speaking her mother tongue, German. She described her predicament as follows: 'In German, I am a scared dirty child; in English I am a nervous, refined woman.' As long as she spoke English, her picture of herself was the English-speaking refined lady. The moment she spoke German, her self-image changed, and she became a 'scared dirty child.' The English identity was a screen against the German identity. It served the purpose of maintaining in repression the painful German self-image, as well as offering an opportunity to exhibit a more pleasing aspect of the self" (14, p. 247).

Puerto Rican émigrés, especially the teenagers, go through intense language shifts. In general, I can say that most teenagers, as partial émigrés, would accept only a therapist who was fluent in both languages. The preference shifts at different stages in the therapy. Sometimes it is by deference to the therapist that a language is chosen. In only two cases of prolonged treatment have I seen a definite sequence which sharply demonstrates an analogy with their genetic development. Both cases were females in their late twenties, with social and sexual maladjustments, who had been transplanted to the mainland at around the age of 4½ years. Both had been raised on the mainland up to age 25, and had experienced sharp increases in their socioeconomic position. Both returned to the island from highly paid jobs. Both started consultation and undertook the initial phase of analysis in Spanish, with occasional shifts into English. In both cases, at about the fourth month, they shifted to English completely, remaining thereafter in that language, with very few mixtures. By the end of the third year, they both used English and Spanish interchangeably, and then made a final definite reintegration to the Spanish language.

Language tendencies are selected by patients. Some express their thoughts in what can be called a "progressive insecurity." Example: "It was Monday, no, Tuesday, no, Wednesday," or: "A hundred, two hundred and fifty, three hundred. . . ." This is in contrast to the patient who will express the same idea in a decreasing type of dialogue. "It was the 23rd, no, the 22nd, no, the 21st. . . ." Whether this gives some inkling into the emotional matrix "progressive or depressed" as characterological aspects should be the subject of further studies.

During a chance encounter, a friend reporting failure in his attempt to establish telephone communication could verbalize this in many different ways, as follows:

I called your house and there was no answer.
" " " " " they did not answer.
" " " " " there was nobody in.
" " " " " you did not answer.
" " " " " the telephone did not answer.
" " " " " the phone seemed to be out of order.

The choice seems to depend on the *emotional* state involved in the selection.

Strange and complex language usages were revealed by a patient who did not exhibit neologism proper, but who showed new logistics in language usages and word meanings. On a consultation at a V.A. facility, I saw a 22-year-old, single Korean War veteran with a diagnosis of paranoid schizophrenia. This patient's education was up to the second year of public high school in Puerto Rico; he was exposed to very little teaching of English which was followed by a two-year period in the Army, mostly in a Spanish-speaking milieu. Among his many complaints, he mentioned a "pressure on the right side of his head." He had a history of having painted his room totally black where he secluded himself for long periods. He stated that all his troubles were due to the fact that both his father and his brother, who were truck drivers, had their trucks painted red. Now, every time they drove their trucks, he could detect it from afar, which produced feelings of unpleasantness and discomfort. He claimed that if his father and brother would paint their trucks another color, preferably blue, his feelings of unpleasantness would subside. Not knowing really how to proceed, I asked him, I think by intuition, why was it that the right side of his head bothered him (right in Spanish is *derecho*). Immediately he answered, without hesitancy, that right (derecho) was made out of *der* and *echo*—that *der* was really the letters rearranged to spell RED, which was the color of the trucks. At his command was rapidity of both translation, word division, and letter rearrangement, meaning link of the phoneme from one language to another in the middle of a psychotic state. The opposite phenomenon of retranslation of visual stimuli into reconstructed words also occurred.

A Latin female patient* in the third year of her treatment revealed a

---

* Due to the limited geographical reality in Puerto Rico if you disqualify for treatment every person that you have met or that knows about you, your practice would become nonexistent. Therefore, because of this reality factor and possible feedback, great liberties have been taken with the rearrangment of personal data. On the other hand the geographical limitation and social inevitability provide us with a built-in follow-up system which proves a deterrent in self-aggrandizement and provides humble and cautious evaluation of therapeutic results.

dream. She was married to an English-speaking European and had previously been in treatment for two years in the United States during which she spoke English. The dream was: "I am standing on a balcony in a house by the seashore. The sea has receded, leaving a big empty beach. As I was preparing to investigate this dream, she exposed a linguistic association that made the meaning of the dream very plain. She said—"sea gone" (marido), *marido* means husband in Spanish. Her husband and her former therapist were both English-speaking, thus the dream in English would be nearly impossible for them to understand. Translated into Spanish, the clarity of the word play is transparent. Her present therapist is Spanish-speaking and, thus, she makes this direct gift of establishing understanding that would be foreign to her former therapist and to her husband. Her father was also Spanish-speaking. Her English world is gone and is being substituted by a Spanish-speaking world.

"Sound language" in the sense of awareness of grammar and syntax is more evident to the child than to the adult. Sometimes, apparently, the foreign word acquires sound meanings which are more feasibly explored in the bilingual situation. Children can imitate foreign utterances more readily than adults. This represents more "sound meanings" than actual meanings. A four-year-old English-speaking girl living in Puerto Rico in a bilingual household was asked what name she wanted to give her newly acquired puppy. She answered rapidly, *"Jayuya,"* which sounds like "hau hau" in Spanish, or the English equivalent of "bow-wow." This is the name of a small town in the interior part of the island, which in all probability this little girl may have heard mentioned a couple of times. It seems to be evident that she was struck by the sound of a barking dog, which is present in the word Jayuya.

While treating patients in different languages and adjusting my ear from one language to another at least four or five times a day, I became aware of an impossibility. I was unable to follow if the patient shifted suddenly from one language to another in a word or perhaps a phrase. This is not prominent when "tuned in free floating awareness," "listening with the third ear," or as Sullivan states, "deep in selective inattention" (24, p. 12). The sudden shift left me completely unaware of the meaning of the word or phrase. Usually I could not remember the word or phrase even though it was a completely familiar term. The sound was completely alien as if I had never encountered it before. After a number of observations of this sort, and certain tribulations regarding my own countertransference in these particular situations, I received personal communication from another therapist in town which corroborated my observations. At the time, I also wondered whether I was subjected to special pronunciations on the part of the patient which would have made it difficult to detect the meaning of the pronounced word. This was not the case at all; such "language unawareness" happens even when treating completely bilingual patients whose pronounciations are perfect in both languages. This phenomenon appears whether the word is a name, title, a familiar phrase, or even a verse. The key to the matter is the fact that verbalization is the message from the preconscious into the conscious and such processes happen within the framework of grammar, syntax, etc., which is particular to each language. Pick states, "grammar and syntax are not something added to the words chosen, but a matrix into which the words are embedded." It follows that one is, so to speak, tuned in to a certain grammar and syntax; the falling of a communication from a foreign language into such a matrix would be lost to understanding. "Deverbalization precedes verbalization," as stated by Rosen (21, p. 471). The same thing happens in the patient when faced with the task of free association: "the patient regresses to earlier stages of communication." The therapist on his own, when faced with the task of listening with his "third ear," regresses also and his deverbalization processes happen in a subconscious state of mind. If we see a patient or meet a person who by physical characteristics we expect to speak in one language and who does the opposite of what we expect, we suffer a similar sense of disorientation. I want to point out that the same feeling of loss does not happen in social conversations when our interlocutor shifts suddenly to a different language. Somehow the selective "third ear" never emerges in the nonprofessional situation and thus this particular idiosyncracy never occurs.

The matrix of continual verbalization is characteristic of mothers taking care of infants in a Spanish-speaking culture. They accompany their child-rearing practices with a continuous verbalization during the process of food preparation, diaper changing, etc. This is in contrast with the historical case quoted by Edelheit, "Salimbene, in his twelfth-century chronicles. He describes a linguistic experiment that has been made by the Emperor Frederick III: . . . he wanted to find out what kind of speech and what manner of speech children would have when they grew up, if they spoke to no one beforehand. So he bade foster mothers and nurses to suckle their children, to bathe and wash them, but in no way to prattle with them or to speak to them, for he wanted to learn whether they would speak the Hebrew language, which was the oldest, or Greek, or Latin, or Arabic, or perhaps the language of their parents, of whom they had been born. But he labored in vain, because the children all died. For they could not live without the petting and the joyful faces and loving words of their foster mothers" (7, p. 409). Continual verbalization is also necessary in taking care of catatonic regressed mute negativistic patients. If the nurse or attendant keeps communicating during the minutiae of their activities around the patient, it is an observed fact that the patient's response is better.

The child, not only imitates the mother's tongue, gestures, etc., in the prestages of language, whether in the first stage of echolalic repetition or in the second stage of naming, really communicating conceptual language. He also imitates all the other noises in the house, animals, cars, wind, seashore, etc. With the advent of popularity of radio, TV, phonographs, and tapes, sometimes on during the whole day and part of the night, children of today are subjected to a barrage of noises that at some level constitute an example of overstimulation or "emotional overload," according to Spitz.

Dream phenomena, whether in one language or another, have, in my experience, not presented themselves readily to cultural distinctions. Their composition of elaboration, symbol formation, and the aspects of the day residue are similar. I have been unable to assess the much valued and expressed idea of dreaming in Spanish, dreaming in English, or dreaming in German. Except for a few exceptions, verbal utterances are usually indistinguishable and confused. When thoroughly explored, the patient is seldom sure about the language of utterances, thus pointing out the power of secondary elaboration and to the presence of perhaps some functions of the consciousness mind which seems to be very resistant to any influence by the subconscious. As I expect some arguments on this observation, I want to make it clear that if I were to quote dreams from my protocols, I do not see how anybody could appoint them to English or Spanish patients except by guessing.

There is, in my experience, examples that show a difference in the culture but because of the lack of statistical value I am hesitant to communicate them. I do so only in the hope that it will stir some discussions and observations from other sources. In a few instances, some Spanish-speaking patients discussed what I call "mini-dreams," which were uttered in the shortest way possible. There does not seem to be a counterpart in English. The smallest meaningful word, almost a phoneme, constituted a whole dream. I am purposely avoiding the word condensed as there is a question in my own mind as to whether these particular dreams are the product of hypercondensation. Do these dreams pertain to the interminable as far as dream exploration and analysis are concerned or do they represent a special direct utterance from the unconscious with very little elaboration or dreamwork? These "mini-dreams," or psychotherapeutic snapshots, usually were revealed in the second year of treatment. Dreams such as a name, a word, a neologism, were reported as "night," or "raining." The best example was a patient in his second year of treatment who had a dream of "ants." He was, by then, well oriented in reporting dreams, developing associations, and analyzing them. In his particular dream he could say very little—just "ants." He did not know whether he had seen or felt the ants. As an association, he said, "crablice." He then proceeded to talk at length of the significance of this in his sexual development. This same patient had had another dream with an "ear" which I again consider within the range of a "mini-dream." Mini-dreams have also been in sequence repeated with a change in only one word. A patient in his second year of treatment had, within a span of two weeks, dreamt of the following sequence: first dream, "I was walking with an erect penis"; second dream, "I was walking with an 'inspoon' (ponzoña)"; third dream, "I was walking with a small knife."

I come at last to perhaps one of my most controversial statements. It has been my experience that bilingual patients, though not particularly loquacious, do present a great avoidance of the expression of verbal aggression in the therapeutic situation. Direct verbal expressions of anger are practically nonexistent. Even the raising of the voice is rare. The panting, raving patient is an infrequent occurrence. Patients are usually extremely polite. Even indirect verbal expressions of anger, long tirades against psychiatry, commentaries on adverse publicity, etc., are unusual. The use of foul language, even when encouraged, proves a formidable barricade. Quoting disparaging remarks about the therapist is done with extreme hesitancy. Nevertheless, indirect expressions of anger are evident: wanting more time, delaying payment of bills, accidentally throwing ashes on the rug, stumbling on chairs, banging doors when leaving, etc., are indeed to be found. What is worthy of consideration is that, upon very careful evaluation, it is evident that English-speaking Anglo-Saxon patients who have lived in the local milieu for some time acquire similar characteristics.

Rothenberg (22), Fernandez Marina, Mehlman, Ramirez de Arellano, et al., (10), Maldonado Sierra and Trent (19), have commented on aggression in Puerto Ricans, hyperkinetic-like seizures, muscoloskeletal expression of anger, rage, etc.—the so-called Puerto Rican syndrome. It seems to me that these superficial differences in dealing with aggression (I consider them "self" characteristics rather than ego characteristics) can be better explained by the smallness of the local geographical situation and population characteristics, the immediacy of the relationships (by familiar groups) and the inevitability of neighbors. A verbal insult could realistically establish an eventual vendetta. It is easy to insult a neighbor whom you do not see often or will never encounter again. But to do that with somebody whom you are sure you are going to meet twice a day, 365 times a year, is different. This would lead to tremendous amounts of pent up rage and could only be released by the musculo-skeletal expression, always of a psychotic-like flavor.

Rosen states that, "the prestages of language are seen as a development of a systems of signals between parent and infant," and later, "in the gestural system, the development of forefinger pointing is said to be a milestone in human evolution" (21, p. 479). It would seem to follow then that the increase of gestural language or its reappearance in psychotherapy could be either a sign of regression and a deeply embedded type of defense or an actual part of the self. The perseverance of sign language, gesture language, pointing, etc., could be interpreted as a lack in command of exclusively verbal communication. We know that verbal communication is always accompanied by certain aspects of gesture language, modulation, pitch, accent, etc., which form the core of the communicative process. Again, patients submitted to the bilingual situation, but more frequently Spanish-speaking patients, have a tendency to keep their hands occupied during the therapeutic session with toothpicks, lighters, pieces of paper, bags, etc., which are kept in their hands, caressed, played with, etc. This method of keeping their hands occupied makes gesturing difficult and complicated to assess. The patient submitted to the bilingual situation has a tendency not to express verbal hostility easily. He tends to be too courteous or correct. Keeping his hands occupied assures him that even in extreme bouts of anger, the hands will never be used for the expression of anger.

Patient behavior in Puerto Rico is markedly distinctive. The tendency of patients to use language proper as a resistance—almost as a weapon— is evident. Some resistances are of content, and others are of form. By the latter, I mean that patients tend to talk in the plural or in the present tense when recollecting, or they use crutch words like "then" and "and" to start every sentence with a phrase such as "I am thinking," or "it comes to my mind," etc. These resistances are sometimes impervious to exploration or interpretation. In a few cases, this resistance is maintained through the entire process of treatment. This occurs in English and Spanish speaking patients under treatment who are intensely subjected to a barrage of bilingual stimulation of radio, TV, newspapers, billboards, directions. Then, the question arises, if their mother tongue is continually subjected to the continuous attack by the bilingual milieu, could defensive maneuvers be raised inadvertently in the native tongue, which appear as resistances of form in the psychotherapeutic process? I am particularly impressed by the imperviousness, the duration and the almost complete opaqueness to interpretation of these real strongholds of defense.

Patients tend to use incognitos such as "my friend" persistently. Proper names are rarely use. Without consistent insistence by the therapist, identification of places, persons, and sources of opinions are rarely given. Patients express themselves in such terms as: "people say," "one does," "we do," "we want," "we think," "I am thinking," "I think," or "what comes to my mind." These phrases are repeated cacophonically by patients for months as an introduction to every paragraph. The usage of the past tense, "I was thinking" or "I thought," precedes the appearance of the "I think." Starting sentences with prepositions is a type of verbal defense of great consistency. Patients also use "I don't remember" as a form of defense. Ironically, "I don't remember" is a formidable denial of recollections and yet it is expressed as if it were a positive attempt at recollection. Patients also tend to start a paragraph with "for example"—examples are not the product of free association.

I find, in borderline Spanish-speaking cases and in narcissistic personalities, the presence of a type of verbal resistance that is extremely difficult to overcome. The patient will repeat in an echolalic form every intervention of the therapist before responding to it. I am talking specifically of material presented to stimulate association. Before the patient gives any association to the stimulus, he repeats it, usually slowly—whether it is a word, a phrase, part of a dream, or part of a sentence. The therapist must be aware that this is a resistance that can be interpreted as a very positive identification with the therapist. When encountered at the beginning of treatment, it seems a manifestation of a budding positive transference. It seems like an expression of interest, eagerness, and responsiveness. Yet it is a resistance and becomes even more evident when dealing with dream material or even when the therapist's intervention is a repetition of the last word or phrase of the patient. In some cases, the resistance is totally impervious to interpretation and demonstration. I have not seen it in neurotic patients in therapy except at the very beginning. We can theorize that this resistance is a demonstration of an ego defect. The word pronounced by the therapist cannot be received or accepted as a representation of an object or even as a transitional object to respond to. As long as it remains "in the voice of the therapist," it is a strange object to which the ego cannot respond. As the patient pronounces it with his own voice, he makes it his own by placing it in his mouth. The word or phrase as a representation of an object becomes part of the patient's ego or is at least positively cathected. It becomes less menacing and thus his own thoughts and words can come forth and be linked to the ego sound, ego word, and ego phrase. I have seen this happen in some neurotic patients on the couch but it disappears when pointed out and interpreted.

In borderline patients this resistance to words of the therapist is impervious and I have seen it persist in patients who have been in treatment for two to three years. In general, verbal resistances, even when carefully pointed out and analyzed, reappear in the course of the treatment. They become good means of judging the awareness of the transference situation or the stage of the therapeutic alliance.

Sharing experiences is to start the dialogue. I consider dialogue to be both a "hope" and an "end." Purposely then, our dialogue has its beginning.

REFERENCES

1. Appelbaum, S. A. Evocativeness. *J. Amer. Psychoanal. Assoc.*, July 1966, 14:3.
2. Bateson, G., Jackson, D. D., et al. A note on the double bind. *Family Process*, 1962, 2:154-164.
3. Bateson, G., Jackson, D. D., Haley, J., and Weakland, J. Toward a theory of schizophrenia. *Behavioral Science*, 1956, 1:251-264.
4. Bernal y del Rio, V. On psychotherapy. *Puerto Rico Med. Assoc. Bull.*, November 1968, 60:11.
5. Deutsch, F. Thus speaks the body. *Acta Medica Orientalia*, March-April 1951, 10: 3-4.
6. Deutsch, F. Analytic posturology. *Psychoanal. Quart.*, April 1952, 21:2.
7. Edelheit, H. Speech and psychic structure: The vocal auditory organization of the ego. *J. Amer. Psychoanal. Assoc.*, April 1969, 17 (2):381-412.
8. Ekstein, R. Historical notes concerning psychoanalysis and early language development. *J. Amer. Psychoanal. Assoc.*, 1965, 13 (4):707-729.
9. Fernandez Marina, R. The Puerto Rican syndrome: Its dynamics and cultural determinants. *Journal for the Study of Interpersonal Processes*, Feburary 1961, 24:1.
10. Fernandez Marina, R., et al. Psychiatry. *U.S. Armed Forces Med. J.* 1767-1955, 1961, 22-79.
11. Freud, S. *Introducción al Psicoanalisis*, Vol. II, Chap. 2. Madrid: Editorial Biblioteca Nueva, 1948a.

12. Freud, S. *Psicopathología de la Vida Cotidiana, Obras Completas,* Vol. I. Madrid: Editorial Biblioteca Nueva, 1948b, pp. 635-756.
13. Froeschels, E. Grammar, a basic function of language speech. *Amer. J. Psychother.,* January 1955, 9 (1).
14. Greenson, R. R. On screen defenses, screen hunger and screen identity. *J. Amer. Psychoanal. Assoc.,* 1958, 5 (2):242-261.
15. Jackson, D. D. Psychoanalytic education in the communication processes. *Science and Psychoanalysis,* Vol. V. Grune & Stratton, Inc., 1962.
16. Kohut, H. Clinical and theoretical aspects of resistance. (Scientific Proceedings Panel Report Midwinter Meeting 1956). *J. Amer. Psychoanal. Assoc.,* 1957, 5 (3): pp. 548-555.
17. Langer, S. K. The phenomenon of language. In: I. J. Lee (Ed.), *The Language of Language and Folly.* New York: Harper & Bros., 1949.
18. Lee, L. *Language Habits in Human Affairs.* New York: Harper & Bros., 1941.
19. Maldonado Sierra, E. D. and Trent, R. D. *Amer. J. of Psychiat.,* 1960, 117-241.
20. Ramirez de Arellano, R. et al. Attack, hyperkenetic type: The so-called Puerto Rican syndrome and its medical psychological and social implications. San Juan, Puerto Rico Veterans Administration Report, 1956.
21. Rosen, V. H. Disorders of communication in psychoanalysis. *J. of Amer. Psychoanal. Assoc.,* 1967, 15 (3):467-490.
22. Rothenberg, A. Puerto Rico and aggression. *Amer. J. Psychiat.,* April 1964, 120 (10).
23. Spitz, R. A. The derailment of dialogue: Stimulus overload, action cycles, and the completion gradient. *J. Amer. Psychoanal. Assoc.,* 1964, 12 (4): 752-775.
24. Sullivan, H. Stack. *The Psychiatric Interview.* New York: W. W. Norton & Co., Inc., 1954.

19

Racial Issues in Psychotherapy

Hugh F. Butts, M.D.

The appeal that psychotherapy and racism hold for me emanates from the confluence of several parameters: psychoanalysis, anthropology, sociology, politics, history, literature, mythology, economics, and racism.

As one attempts to tease out, examine and synthesize our treatment approaches to the interracial therapeutic situation, all of these parameters must be considered. Some of the frustrations experienced by those who have attempted to shed light on the topic may relate to the difficulty in assessing and weighting the several parameters, as well as a tendency to resort to oversimplistic theoretical formulations. Only by adopting a "multifactorial open systems approach" with respect to the subject of interracial psychotherapy, may we emerge in some rational, systematic manner with a holistic, meaningful and applicable theory. With this approach in mind, I would like to briefly summarize some of what we currently know by reviewing some of the literature, then explicate some of the lacunae in our knowledge, and highlight some future directions.

REVIEW OF THE LITERATURE

The majority of the works on interracial analyses have appeared within the past three decades. Early formulations during the fifties, such as those by Bernard (1), Kardiner and Ovesey (2), and Kennedy (3),

352

described both the problematic nature of such treatments and the nature of the resistances encountered. Some practitioners such as Oberndorf (4) expressed cynicism concerning the feasibility of the black-white treatment encounter. White behavioral scientists contributed the majority of the articles during the fifties. The formulations and writings of black practitioners emerged during the sixties and seventies. This fact may be significant for several reasons:

1) A significant increase began to take place in the numbers of black behavioral scientists during the fifties and sixties.
2) A significant increase began to take place in the numbers of black and other minority patients seeking help for psychological problems during the same period.
3) This was the tumultuous period of the civil rights and black power movements, both having profound effects upon all of our institutions, as well as upon the conduct of psychotherapy.
4) Socioeconomic and interpersonal factors and societal stresses impacted upon blacks in such a manner as to necessitate increased seeking of professional help.

Black professionals initially began writing not about interracial psychotherapy but about the psychological effects of institutionalized and individualized racism. Examples are: Pinderhughes' "Understanding Black Power: Processes and Proposals," Comer's "White Racism: Its Root, Form and Function," in addition to papers by Palmer (7), Butts (8), Harrison (9), and many others, such as Canon, Davis, Elam, Pierce, Poussaint, Spurlock, Tompkins, Wilkinson, Youngue and Calhoun (10).

One of the landmarks in terms of papers on interracial analysis was the Schachter and Butts work, "Transference and Countertransference in Interracial Analyses." It marked one of the first collaborative efforts between a black psychoanalyst and a white psychoanalyst, in an effort to come to grips with the salient issues in such treatments and to define some of the therapeutic issues. One aspect worthy of emphasis in this paper, that has been overlooked in many others, is the emphasis on countertransference issues that played a prominent role in these analytic situations. Both authors, with absolute professionalism and candor, admitted to their countertransference "problems" with contra-racial patients. In a sense, the black analyst was describing his pro-white, anti-black paranoia, as was the white analyst. In addition, both analysts made serious efforts to resolve these difficulties. Many of the papers on interracial analyses and therapies have been from the vantage point of the white therapist describing "Problems Posed in the Analysis of Negro

Patients" (3), whereas, papers by black therapists have focused on the unconscious racism (and its therapeutic vicissitudes) extant in white analysands, as well as emphasizing the manner in which the therapist's blackness often served to catalyze the treatment situation. Both approaches are extreme, and serve to reinforce the unconscious attitudes, myths, and racist notions that make the working-through process more difficult than it might be otherwise. Pinderhughes (11) has made a very salient observation:

> All individuals who highly value their groups encourage restriction or repression of those body parts, body products, and thoughts, feelings, and behavior that threaten, disrupt, or heighten conflicts in the group. Activity with the head is encouraged in the social relationship with one's group members while perineal activity is discouraged in the social context of one's group. "Racism" beginning pragmatically in the behavior of group members with fellow group members inadvertently produces racism within the mental functions of each individual as certain exciting, disruptive, "dark," "evil," threatening components are segregated. This internal "racism" is then externalized and projected into the behavior of each individual.
>
> . . . Each individual can resolve the ambivalence about the goodness or badness of one object by relating to two objects. One of these objects can be perceived as good, and one as bad, one can be loved and the other hated (p. 8).

In describing the group-related paranoias (of which racism is a subgroup), Pinderhughes regards as ubiquitous the tendency toward aggrandizing one's group and of projecting to other groups unacceptable, "dark," and "evil" characteristics. He concludes on a somewhat pessimistic or equivocal note:

> It seems quite likely that failure to recognize the primitive origins and dynamics of racism may lead to faulty, inadequate, or oversimplified diagnosis and treatment . . . ambivalence and the use of paranoid mechanisms in its resolution may be as ubiquitous as conflict is among and within humans. As with conflict emphasis upon management of paranoia may be more realistic than attempts to eradicate it. Some racism is a group-related paranoia having to do with exclusive groups, it may be eliminated by converting exclusive groups into inclusive ones (p. 8).

The white analyst-black patient, and black analyst-white patient represent pairings that exemplify many of the dynamics cited, as one observes and charts the vicissitudes of transference-countertransference during the progress of treatment.

We have no reason to expect that the conflicts, ambivalences, paranoid defenses, self-denigrations, and aggrandizements that occur in black-white extra-analytic or social encounters would not also be present in the professional treatment situation.

The white patient with the black analyst will often project his unacceptable "bad," "evil" self onto the analyst, whom he will then depict in his dreams as a threatening, malevolent, "father-devil" type. The black analyst may at times (12, p. 806), because of his unconscious need for acceptance into the "exclusive group," respond to references in accord with this need, and thereby miss the opportunity to interpret his patient's behavior. Sensitivity to racial epithets uttered by a white patient, may also indicate an unconscious wish for inclusion into the group. The black patient with the white analyst will often use race in the service of resistance. This often betokens a lack of trust, implicit in which is a conviction that his blackness is a barrier to admission to the white exclusive group. The white analyst in this duo will often react as did Schachter with an overdetermined response to apparent threats and menacing descriptions of former behavior by her analysand. This may have indicated her unconscious acceptance of the myths regarding the aggressive and threatening stereotype of blacks.

If black and white individuals are participating members of the exclusiveness of one and the concurrent rejection of the other, groups and institutions function similarly. "Some persons we understand by taking them in or by taking in what they offer while we understand others by dumping upon them things we do not want within ourselves with the claim that what we renounce belongs to them, and not to us (5, p. 11). Wherever a white and black experience conflict in "white racist" structure, the white is understood by projection and is presumed to be wrong and unacceptable. Several recommendations are appropriate at this point:

1) Any significant understanding and working-through of the interracial analytic situation must be based on a precise definition as to the manner in which both parties utilize projective as well as introjective mechanisms as means of dealing with unacceptable impulses (projective), or by "taking in" their virtues and aggrandizing them (introjection).

2) Any significant understanding of the working-through involving

blacks and whites in *group situations* should require the same process as in the first point.
3) Both the above points are difficult to attain unless there is adequate black and other minority representation among the candidates and supervising/training staffs of our analytic institutes and other training institutions. This is not merely a plea for psychoanalytic affirmative action, but represents an approach aimed at the elimination of the elitism of psychoanalysis and psychotherapy and a reduction of the *group-related paranoia* that has severely crippled the analytic movement.

Many of the interracial transference and countertransference manifestations we observe may be artifacts related to the practical nonexistence of black training analysts, and the miniscule numbers of blacks involved in analytic training. In the survey reported on by Harrison and Butts (13), the same 50% of white psychiatrists who did not refer to black psychiatrists reported having few or no black friends.

Black and White Characterization in Literature

Melville, Mark Twain, Fenimore Cooper, as well as contemporary white and black literary figures, have shed a great deal of enlightenment on the issues of whiteness and blackness as reflected in their literary characters. Melville, in his chapter entitled "On the Whiteness of the Whale" (*Moby Dick*), attempts to dissipate the myth equating whiteness with purity and blackness with evil:

This elusive quality it is, which causes the thought of whiteness when divorced from more kindly associations and coupled with any object terrible in itself, to heighten that terror to the furthest bounds. Witness the white bear of the poles, the white shark (requin) of the tropics: what but their smooth, flaky whiteness makes them the transcendent horrors they are?" . . . "and though in other mortal sympathies and symbolizings, this same hue (whiteness) is made the emblem of many touching noble things—the innocence of brides, the benignity of age; though among the Red men of America the giving of the white belt of wampun was the deepest pledge of honor; though, in many climes, whiteness typifies the majesty of justice in the ermine of the Judge, and contributes to the daily state of kings and queens drawn by milk-white steeds; though even in the higher mysteries of the most august religions it has been made the symbol of the divine spotlessness and power; by the Persian fire worshippers, the white forked flame being held by the holiest on the altar; and in the Greek mythologies, Great Jove himself being made incarnate in a snow-white bull . . . yet for all these accumulated associations, with whatever is sweet, honorable, and sublime, there yet lurks an elusive something in the innermost idea of this hue, which strikes more of panic to the soul than that redness which affrights in blood (14).

James Fenimore Cooper in *The Last of the Mohicans* described the red-white relationship. "The Indian represents to Cooper whatever in the American psyche has been starved to death, whatever genteel Anglo-Saxondom has most ferociously repressed, whatever he himself has stifled to be worthy of his wife and daughters." "Cora and Alice (the heroines) the passionate brunette and sinless blonde, made once and for all the pattern of female dark and light that is to become the standard form in which American writers project their ambivalence toward women" (15, p. 190).

Writers and literary critics have been aware for many years of the unconscious significance of blackness and whiteness. Huck Finn's relationship with Nigger Jim contains transferential overtones. "It is an impossible society which they constitute, the outcast boy and the Negro, who even for Huck, does not really exist as a person: a society in which momentarily, the irreparable breach between black and white seems healed by love . . . and through it all, Jim plays the role of Uncle Tom, enduring everything, suffering everything, forgiving everything. . . . It is the southerner's dream, the American dream of guilt remitted by the abused Negro, who, like the abused mother, opens his arms crying, 'Lawsy, I's mighty glad to git you back agin honey' " (15, p. 20).

Melville, Twain, Poe, Cooper, Hawthorne and others were utilizing fiction in order to demonstrate the American national character responses (conscious and unconscious) to blackness and whiteness. The black-white duo occurs frequently in American fiction, and is frequently utilized to represent the redemptive love of man for man.

There is no more precise explication of aspects of the American experience and of the American national character than that furnished us by Melville in *Moby Dick*. In what is probably the greatest love story in American fiction (15), Herman Melville describes a number of relationships in which the redemptive love of man for man is repersented. One of the several romantic duos in *Moby Dick* is Ahab and Pip, the black cabin boy. Pip, abandoned at sea, is blatantly psychotic when finally rescued. "He saw God's foot upon the treadle of the loom, and spoke out: and therefore his shipmates called him mad. So man's insanity is heaven's sense; and wandering from all mortal reason, man comes at last to that celestial thought, which, to reason, is absurd and frantic; and weal or woe, feels then uncompromised." Pip's "insanity" has resulted from abandonment, and his consequent sense of isolation. Ahab adopts Pip, with whom he shares his cabin. Dr. Jose Barchilon (16, pp. 22-23) states, "Ahab understands the depth and wisdom of Pip's craziness, identifies with him, and takes him to his cabin as a son. Not in an attempt to make amends for the harm done to Pip . . . but to find company in his misery, because Ahab knows that he and Pip are different sides of the same crazed coin. He also knew that, were he to like and grow too tender towards Pip, it would soften his hatred and make him give up his pursuit of white hooded phantoms." Ahab is in a sense doing that for Pip which was never done for him (he had been "doubly-orphaned" by 12 months of age). "This is his attempt at restitution, at recapturing by projective identification, the parents he didn't really have.

Thus, Melville, nearly 128 years ago, comprehended the genesis of psychotic decompensation, the therapeutic effectiveness of relatedness to another human, the nature of projective identification, the nature of the type of developmental arrest that follows parental loss, the nature of primary process thinking, and the unconscious meanings of blackness and whiteness.

A major and recurring psychological pattern of the "American national character" has been well stated by the literary critic Leslie Fiedler: "To express this 'blackness ten times black' (original sin) and to live by it in a society in which, since the decline of orthodox Puritanism, optimism has become the chief effective religion" (19, p. xxii). This pattern is reflected in the American literature, which is a literature of "darkness and the grotesque in a land of light and affirmation" (19, p. xxii). The major literary concerns from Cooper to Baldwin are with death, incest, and homosexuality. The child's world, in literature, is asexual, terrible, and a world of fear and loneliness. The companion of the lonely, frightened, "man-child" who ventures forth into the unexplored world is "pagan and unashamed," but the companion is described as both a dream and nightmare simultaneously. This literary, metaphoric companion (Chingachgook, Nigger Jim, Babo, Pip) is concretized in the form of the black American. One could at this point expatiate on the psychodynamics of unconscious racism. The "pagan" companion possessed of both material and demonic features permeates all of American literature. Splitting of the imagery in this way attests to and evokes ambivalent responses, in addition to allowing for or facilitating projection of unacceptable feelings and thoughts ("Racism-pro white, and anti-black paranoia").

> The colonial world is a world cut in two. The dividing line, the frontiers are shown by barracks and police stations. In the colonies it is the policeman and the soldier who are the official, instituted go-betweens, the spokesmen of the settler and his rule of oppression. In the capitalist societies the structure of moral reflexes handed down from father to son, the exemplary honesty of workers who are given a medal after fifty years of good and loyal service, and the affection which springs from harmonious relations and good behavior—all these esthetic expressions of respect for the established order serve to create around the exploited person an atmosphere of submission and of inhibition which lightens the task of policing considerably. In the capitalist countries a multitude of moral teachers, counsellors and bewilderers separate the exploited from those in power. . . .
> This world divided into compartments, this world out in two is inhabited by two different species. The originality of the colonial context is that economic reality, inequality and the immense difference of ways of life never come to mark the human realities. When you examine at close quarters the colonial context, it is evident that what parcels out the world is to begin with the fact of belonging to or not belonging to a given race. . . . The cause is the consequence; you are rich because you are white, you are white because you are rich (17, p. 32).

CASE STUDIES

Having laid down some of the theoretical and literary underpinnings for a better understanding of ethnicity and psychotherapy, a few case examples may be helpful. Some of these case are incorporated into papers already referred to. Other cases will represent brief vignettes drawn from my clinical practice.

Case #1: White Female Patient, Black Male Analyst

An attractive 32-year-old Jewish school teacher entered biweekly psychotherapy after having three years of analysis with a white analyst. She had sought help initially because of frigidity, vocational dissatisfaction, depression, and anxiety. In the course of that analysis, her vocational adaptation improved, her depression disappeared, and her anxiety diminished. She remained frigid, however, and unmarried. The major difficulty remaining after the three-year analysis was her fear of giving up the child's role in relation to men.

She was born and reared in New York, the oldest of three girls. Her father was a somewhat cynical, successful lawyer; her mother was described as a cold, frigid, materialistic matron. The patient was cared for by a succession of maids until the age of eight. Between the ages of eight and 15, she was cared for by one black maid with whom she established a warm and meaningful relationship and to whom she turned for warmth and dependency because of her mother's inaccessibility. In general, as a child, she did not express anger openly, and her parents were constantly critical of her inability to be openly affectionate. She and her mother perpetually quarrelled over her grooming and deportment, with her father supporting her mother in these disputes. She had no memories of the birth of her sister when she was seven years old. Her reactions of rage at the time of her second sister's birth, when she was 10, were displaced onto her other sister.

As a child she wanted to be a boy, and felt that menarche made her "dirty." She was always concerned about the value and importance of money. She was a pudgy adolescent who read voraciously, had few friends, and did not date. Throughout adolescence, she felt that her parents were dissatisfied with her physical appearance and her inadequate social adjustment.

After graduation from college, she attended and graduated from law school. At the age of 20, she married precipitously. Her dissatisfaction with her marital sexual adjustment caused her to seek brief psychotherapy after she had been married for one year. Two years later she obtained a divorce. Her vocational, social and sexual behavior deteriorated; she became progressively more depressed and sought therapy again at the psychoanalytic clinic.

Key among her dynamics, when she entered treatment with me, was her perception of men as destructive because of her projected rage. Rejection by the therapist was perceived by her as safer than dependency upon him. Vocational success was viewed as a renunciation of her femininity. Again, the most striking feature of her life adjustment was her failure in virtually every area of behavior: vocational, social, sexual, and family life. She felt disliked and rejected by everyone, and her hostile, provocative behavior tended to bring about rejection. The closer she approached adult womanhood, the more frightened she became of the consequences, namely a destructive sexual assault by a man. She rejected her feminine feelings and became aware of and anxious about sexual interest in women.

The analyst's anticipation of the development of a strongly erotic transference accompanied by intense anxiety was soon borne out, but her initial gambit consisted of applauding the therapist's empathic ability with the statement, "Negroes have guts." She had wound up the previous three-year analysis as she was beginning to express affection and to get closer to people. There, the oedipal implications of being "number one" were frightening, and she had created obstacles to block her awareness of the positive-affectionate tie to her father.

The selection of a black analyst was multidetermined In part it reflected a need to select a person whom she regarded as being the antithesis of her cold, distant father, thereby avoiding the anxiety of the oedipal strivings for her father. The early parent-child power disparity was also reflected in her choice, in that she saw herself in association with an "underdog," who she felt would understand her disenfranchised position in the family. The selection of a black analyst was motivated by a wish to utilize a counterphobic defense to deal with her sexual anxieties. She was overtly seductive, while expressing anxiety lest her sexual wishes be realized. In one session she reported this dream: "I was at an isolated house in the country with a man. Nobody was there, but then a maid came down and motioned upstairs. I was frightened to be there alone with him."

She placed her hand over her pubic area as she related the dream and asssociated to the isolation of the analytic situation. A series of dreams followed in which she depicted herself as deprived and losing in the oedipal struggle. For example: "A doctor was getting ready for a skiing trip. He was on the porch with his children and wife. She had dark hair."

The therapist utilized the transference to demonstrate her renunciation of her femininity lest she be damaged sexuality; her ability to function independently without dependency on her mother; and her ability to form a therapeutic relation not predicated on the exchange of sexual favors or on her parentifying the analyst. Her pain-dependent, self-defeating behavior was interpreted repeatedly. The therapist's genuine interest in her welfare was questioned by her from the outset of treatment; she identified him with her presumably indifferent, unaffectionate mother.

The two years of treatment resulted in a modification of her affective symptoms, and an increase in her self-esteem, with a consequent diminution of her self-defeating behavior. She was married six months after termination of her treatment.

Case #2: White Male Patient, Black Male Analyst

A 35-year-old, white, professional man of Jewish extraction, who was referred by his cousin, a former patient of the analyst, sought analysis because of his inability to get married. During each of two engagements he had become progressively depressed and anxious and in each instance had broken off the relationship. A second complaint, premature ejaculation, had begun a year before the patient sought help. Vocationally, he was insecure. despite the fact that he worked in an executive capacity. He was ingratiating with fellow employees and fearful that he might not be able to control his anger in work situations.

His most vivid memories of early childhood dated back to age six, with recollections of visits to his Jewish aunt and grandmother in Harlem. He took pride in making the subway trips alone, but recalled mixed feelings of anxiety and excitement. The Harlem community of that period was racially integrated. His anxiety was predicated upon his fear of physical attack, and his excitement seemed rooted in sexual fantasies which utilized racial stereotypes and myths.

An intense fear of losing his parents pervaded his childhood. He was a good student and active in athletics, but frequently needed his mother's intervention on his behalf during altercations with other children. At home, his mother was a severely critical, domineering, anxious woman, who subjugated her husband and chided him for being weak, inadequate, and a poor provider. She lamented her difficult lot in life and confided the intimacies of her marital dissatisfaction to the patient. The father was physically and emotionally inaccessible.

Castration anxiety increased at age 14 when his parents' concern about the size of his penis led them to consult a physician. He was embarrassed to shower with schoolmates for fear that they would discover that his penis was small. Adolescence brought sexual interest and exploration; he dated, but was always inhibited and anxious. During this period he shared his sister's bedroom but recalls only one instance of embarrassment, when she giggled on overhearing him masturbate.

Concern about the size of his penis persisted into adulthood. After completion of Army service and college, he worked in an executive position, continuing to live with his parents. He perceived phallic women as castrators, and used prematurity and impotence to defend against castration. With men, his nonassertiveness socially, sexually, and vocationally derived from his need to control his rage.

Early dreams gave form to the negative transference of the first six months and heightened one of the patient's key problems: The black man was presented as physically assaultive, drunk, and debased, and the patient feared his analyst's aggression and sexual exploitation.

In his association he dwelt on the theme of the menacing black, juxtaposing his sexual inadequacy, fear of women, and his perception of women as castrating, humiliating creatures. Soon after beginning the analysis he moved from his parents' home, magically utilizing the therapist's strength as a buffer against his mother. The move was accompanied by a great deal of anxiety, represented in dreams as a fear of starving to death. He began to date and to attempt sex, expressing his lack of assertiveness and his dependency orientation in dreams such as the following: "I was in my aparement with C; we were necking. I had her breasts in my hand. There were many women around. They were exposing their breasts. I was completely fascinated and felt pressure."

The therapist challenged his fragmented view of women and its emotional counterpart, his affective isolation and his wish to present himself as dead emotionally. His dreams and associations were replete with his wish to be regarded as a helpless infant, which was interpreted at that time as a defensive retreat to a position of dependent safety designed to avoid castration. The patient was then able to associate this with his difficulty in separating from his mother to attend kindergarten.

Ten months after the beginning of the analysis, he triumphantly reported that he was able to penetrate a woman sexually despite intense anxiety and fear of impregnating her. He plied the analyst with questions about contraception, in actually seeking approval for his sexual accomplishments. The analyst's mild disbelief in the therapeutic significance of the patient's achievement in part reinforced the patient's stereotyped perception of the Negro as a virtual sexual superman, thus widening the gulf between analyst and analysand.

Another source of difficulty during this period was the analyst's need to disclaim his therapeutic power to achieve such a great effect with the patient. This problem was rooted in the analyst's insecurity about his effectiveness which was combined, however, with a need to assert his greater power over the patient.

With continued attempts at intercourse, a pseudo-homosexual theme emerged in a dream: "I was in bed with S. She got on top of me. We were having intercourse. But it was not S's face. It was a man's face. I was frightened." He discussed the anxiety in the dream, adding, "I'm afraid of women so a man is safer. But why am I afraid of women? My mother is a woman."

The second year of analysis was concerned with his efforts to separate emotionally from his parents, to improve his sexual adaptation, and to deal with his chronic anxiety. During this period he maintained a relationship with one woman, advanced vocationally, and began to see himself as having an existence separate from that of his parents, with lessening anxiety about their death. References to the therapist's race were minimal, although when the patient's fear of the therapist mounted, the menacing black would reappear in his dream life: "A Negro trooper strikes a white policeman in the stomach. The white man beats him up."

Increased separation from his family brought mounting anxiety about his relationship with the analyst, and he reconsidered his childhood visits to his aunt's home in Harlem, which were marked by a mixture of pleasurable excitement and fear. The omission of his father's role in the family, previously justified by his father's absence at work during the patient's childhood, became a therapeutic focus, particularly since any information about his father had been transmitted by his mother. During the latter part of the second year of analysis, material emerged indicating that his father had protected him against the mother and against destructive women in general. His dreams became less frighteningly destructive and he dreamed of father and therapist in terms of helping figures. He was married in the third year of analysis and terminated six months later. His functioning had improved considerably in all areas.

Case #3: Black Male Patient, White Female Analyst

An unmarried man with one black parent and one white parent entered analysis because of his inability to form a stable relationship with a woman and increasing awareness of his inability to face marriage. He was also troubled by difficulties at work, particularly with a woman supervisor, which had contributed to his recent loss of a job. He was unable to express his feelings or to tolerate the expression of feelings by others, and appeared passive, isolated, and dependent upon his mother.

Early childhood was spent in a white commercial neighborhood in a northern city, living in the maternal grandfather's home with his light-skinned mother and father. During the depression, the family moved to Harlem. Thus, at six, he believed that it was his dark color that necessitated the family's choice of home. At 12 to 13 years, he was the successful vice-president of a gang because of his boxing skills, and two years later he was caught in his first serious delinquency, pilfering from the mail. After high school graduation, he got a construction job and began passive homosexual activities in toilets, apparently after his mother arranged for his girlfriend's abortion. On the job he suffered a minor injury, and during the subsequent hospitalization he applied to and was accepted by a large Negro college out of town.

Once there, he lived with an older woman off campus and avoided both school contacts and fraternities, which were divided on color lines. He associated only with men who were appreciably darker than himself. After graduation, he returned to his mother and sporadic employment until he was encouraged by a supervisor to take up his work seriously. In his first year he was successful and well liked and, after applying for analysis, finally moved into his own apartment, distant from employment and Harlem. He subsequently noted tenseness, frequent masturbation, difficulty with his girlfriends, work, and his woman supervisor. He had lost that job before his analysis had begun.

During the historical recounting in the opening phase of treatment, the patient used Negro stereotypes to fend off the analyst. For example, he described how he had been asleep at the wheel during an accident in which a male friend had been killed and a girl injured. He sought to impress the analyst that his subsequent behavior toward the injured girl passenger involved minimal guilt and maximal undependability. During this period of treatment, he also acted-out by attempting intercourse with his stepmother's sister, related several incidents in which he presumably had gotten girls pregnant, and recounted several "rape attempts." He was finally able to recognize his desire to scare the analyst by exaggerating the material, "You won't like me as much . . . do I want to be rejected and construct a situation?" At the same time, he directly verbalized anxieties about rejection related only to the building doormen and his feeling that he might be stopped on entering the lobby.

Dreams of the possibility, as well as the dangers, of a real concern for an attachment to a woman occurred shortly before he verbally recognized the analyst's pregnancy. Not only feelings of loss, but also those of considerateness were mobilized for the first time. When treatment resumed, he dreamed he was attempting in vain to find his Spanish Class, which he identified with passing as white. He felt that the analyst accepted the self-stereotyped rejected part of himself that he characterized as Negro. He later asked, "I wonder if my coming to treatment would tend to make me feel equal to white." He became increasingly involved with color and in a dream indicated that Negro children and white women, including his mother, could be assertive because they had rights, while he, as an adult Negro man, had none.

He insisted that he was basically ill-equipped for life, that the burdens of color and a poor cultural heritage increased his vulnerability, and that the analyst's attitude that he could make it only indicated how little she understood. At the same time, trust and mutuality developed through a discussion of *The Invisible Man,* which served as a vehicle for expression of his fears that the analyst would be paternalistic in setting his fee. For the first time he contemplated working in Harlem and enlarged upon the Negro stereotype. "I've never worked around many colored people. I have stereotyped ideas of what the people would be like . . . more impulsive, physically impulsive, likely to hit out . . . I see whites as having more controls over themselves."

Near the end of the second year of analysis, he began an affair with a blonde, white, woman co-worker, and during the analyst's second pregnancy he verbalized his feelings more meaningfully, and began to use insight to control himself. "What kind of woman do I want . . . someone like you. I'm not going to get it while I'm doing all the taking." The analyst demanded that he recognize and not give in to his impulse to change all his relationships with women into sexual affairs, despite his increased awareness of anxiety and anger. He made an abortive attempt to escape into marriage, then returned to examine his feeling that he lacked the equipment to explore reality and his stereotypes. Months of angry resistance followed, during which he repeatedly enunciated his desire to get what he wanted as a gift. Finally, however, he accepted the overtures of his white employer, who became the first woman outside analysis with whom he had a friendly, nonsexual relationship. This brought color specifically back into the analysis, and after he invited her out to dinner he dreamed that he was castrated and had his penis in his hand.

At the beginning of the fourth year of his analysis he met the young Negro professional woman whom he married two years later. When he met this woman, she was, presumably, engaged to a very light-skinned Negro man in a position of social importance, and he both acted-out his oedipal anxieties and became aware of them in the transference. The use of color as a barrier to sexual impulses to mother was further explored since it included his picture of father, the Negro, as neither gratifying mother nor able to serve as a model for control of impulses, thereby exposing the patient to his sexual desire for mother. At the same time, he felt that he had to lose out to a light-skinned man and could win only if he associated with darker people. "I get angry at all white people and have to think a second time." His attempt to exempt the Jewish analyst because of similarity in minority status was confronted by the distinction between mutual social problems as well as his need to obliterate differences. As he grappled to understand the nature of the sexual barrier between himself and his therapist, and between himself and his mother, he repeatedly came back to color. In a dream, the slow analytic train was held up by white barriers, which represented the analyst, who would cause the crash and hurt the driver. Furthermore, associations were to the analyst's open and free attitude toward color in comparison to his own feelings of prejudice against dark women. His angry self-justification was: "You've had a better life than I. . . . You can afford to be more liberal, freer of prejudice than I. How can you understand what it is to be a Negro in America . . . a bitter thought . . . it's one thing to see something from the outside and another to live within it."

During the last year of treatment he reexamined why the analyst was not afraid of his impulses or of him. "The only reason I can think of your being scared is because of color; it's the way I separated myself from my mother. I associate all my failures with color. My uncle drove a coal truck and was dirty and I identify him with color."

Setting his wedding date precipitated more anxiety, focused now on fears of having a dark child. He was forced again to face his prejudices and his feeling that his child would make him more identifiable, as did his fiancée, who was approximately his color and had a "pug" nose. At the same time, the realities of his life made him more aware of his opportunities. The pleasures ahead of him and guilt at leaving the analyst, as well as his parents, behind became the final theme of the analysis.

Follow-up has shown that the patient has consolidated the gains made in analysis. The opening up of his ambitions, particularly in the beginning of the sixth year of analysis, has expanded to active and successful work. He sees himself as a leader in his profession and of his race. His marriage appears stable and successful. Although he was momentarily upset at the birth of a child lighter than either he or his wife, he recognized and coped with these feelings, identified the child as his own, and made plans for another.

Case #4: Black Male Patient, Black Male Analyst

Although accorded scant clinical attention, the therapeutic situation in which both therapist and analysand are black contains both positive as well as resistant features. A 28-year-old black social worker sought professional help because of feelings of professional and personal inadequacy, periods of depression and anxiety, and marital discord. His past history, in brief, was characterized by an ambitious drive to achieve and gain recognition, combined with a self-defeating sense of inferiority which, during childhood, had been reinforced by the negative responses of his siblings, as well as by covert rejection by his parents. He approached the therapeutic situation with an optimism which was enhanced by his therapist's blackness and the unconscious, but later stated, impression that he would be immediately understood and his difficulties would be resolved without the need for his active participation in the therapeutic process. In transferential form, he soon began to express feelings of inadequacy and inferiority vis-à-vis the therapist and to experience a rapid and malignant pseudo-homosexual anxiety with respect to his therapist, based on his resort to myths and stereotypes about the supermasculinity of black men. What began as a quasi-alliance aimed at his personality reconstruction soon evolved into marked resistance, panic and feelings of distrust bordering on paranoid behavior. It was virtually impossible to examine and resolve these conflicts, and the treatment was terminated by mutual consent.

Maynard Calnek expresses the view that the black therapist/black patient therapeutic situation, while promising much, is threatened by difficulties because of the traditional American racial climate. Calnek cites instances in which the therapist's denial of identification/over-identification leads to a failure to appropriately assess the impact of class differences and/or similarities. He concludes, "I have attempted to state that because of the American racial situation there are some difficulties involved but not necessarily total roadblocks to working successfully with black clients. One of my major points is that the black family and the black community, not the white family and the white community, should be the reference points for diagnosis and therapy with any black person" (18).

I made an earlier reference to the confluence of psychoanalysis, literature, mythology, sociology, anthropology, politics, economics, as important parameters in the interracial therapeutic situation. While the focus of this paper has been on interracial psychotherapy, it would be a gross omission to make no mention of unconscious racist manifestations in the white-white therapeutic encounter.

Every black person has a "white mind" and a "black mind" and every white person has a "white mind" and a "black mind." "The white mind constitutes the elements which are uniting and not disruptive to one's groups and are therefore socially acceptable. The black mind constitutes those elements which are disruptive to one's groups and are therefore excluded from society. Racism prevails in every personality since the white mind is permitted free play in personality and behavior, whereas the black mind is carefully censored and excluded from the mainstream of social experience. Disruptive sexual, aggressive, or other emotions, sudden loud noises, and exciting or annoying body parts or body products are associated with the black mind and must be repressed" (19).

Case #5: White Patient, White Male Analyst

Myers (20) is one of the few white behavioral scientists to focus on the significance and utilization of blackness in the dreams and other unconscious manifestations of white patients. His formulation is consistent with those of Pinderhughes, Butts, and others. "These 'dirty' wishes are initially represented in the dream via the projection onto the black 'mammy' and then onto the real mother. As the color defense was broken down in the session, the feelings toward the father analyst emerged in more undiluted form" (p. 10). In the patient under discussion, a 25-year-old white man with obsessional doubts, the dream was reported in a session in which he was discussing his fear of the therapist's anger because of a missed session. He then related the following dream: "My father visited me with a black girl friend, not my mother. He said he'd separated from mother because she was seeing other men. I got upset but he seemed right in doing so. I felt I should live with him but I cried and said, 'I love mommy more and I want to live with her,' and he understood. Then my mother walked in and there was a man in a wheelchair who was having ideas of my mother naked and of having sex with her. I got anxious then and awoke."

Myers continues, "He associated to his sense of strangeness at seeing his father with a black girl. She reminded him of an attractive black patient of mine he had had sexual fantasies about and who he felt interested me more than he did. He perceived his competition with my black patient as paralleling his earlier competition with his sisters for his mother's love."

Myers reports on another patient, a white woman in analysis for anorexia nervosa. She dreamt frequently of swimming through seas of black feces, struggling to reach some pure white object. "In such dreams, the color black was seen as the representation of her sexual and aggressive wishes, which she had to keep hidden and under control, and the color white was conceptualized as the asexual, nonaggressive exterior she wished to present to the world, especially to her mother."

In his summary, Myers states, "The emphasis in the paper is placed on the defensive and resistance aspects these colors seem to serve against the emergence of the affectual aspects of the transference nenurosis . . . wishful self-representations and idealized object-represntations utilizing the colors black and white are seen in both inter- and intra-racial analyses . . ." (p. 17).

I have cited Myers' references because I believe they have limited applicability to the issue at hand. It is abundantly clear that white patients make use of blackness with white therapists in much the same way that white patients do with black therapists. In my discussion of Myers' paper at its presentation in 1975, I debated what I regarded as a limited view of the issues. "Since, however, both black and white patients have introjected both the positive and negative black stereotypes, it is surprising that only the negative transference or resistance aspect was evidenced in Dr. Myers' analyses. There were in my opinion several instances in which the analytic data rather easily lent themselves to interpreting blackness as being an expression of the positive transference."

Terry Rodgers (21), a white psychoanalyst, reports on the therapeutic vicissitudes, development of unconscious racism and then overt rabid anti-black sentiments in a white analysand. The treatment occurred in the South. The patient, a 43-year-old, single, white man, sought analysis for a variety of neurasthenic symptoms that had begun when his father died 12 years prior to the analysis. His symptoms were, for the most part, obsessional, and he tended to dichotomize everything as either good or bad, clean or dirty, acceptable or unacceptable. Both his parents also exemplified obsessional character traits. He was cared for by a black nurse. Early in the course of therapy it became apparent that "a common denominator running through all his obsessive symptoms was a struggle with authority" (p. 240). An early dream made reference to a "black cane," and to the sexual freedom of adolescents. The confluence of the two themes resided in his unconscious view of blacks as sexually lascivious. As his defenses began to yield to analytic uncovering, he made repeated references to the integration-segregation issue, finally reporting the following dream: "My mother is by me on the ground about to be gored by a huge bull with black horns. I feel momentarily paralyzed as in the other dream, but by an enormous act of will I overcome it. Then with a feeling of almost unlimited strength I leap at the bull and rip its horns off with my bare hands. I feel an indescribable sense of triumph and exhilaration."

There were obvious transferential references in the dream (father/ a black cane, therapist's black horn-rimmed glasses, and the association between black horns and black people). He terminated shortly thereafter and became intensely involved in anti-black political activities. Rodgers summarizes: "Thus, by the wholesale use of the defense mechanisms of projection and identification with the aggressor, he protects himself against eruption into awareness of (a) his unconscious homosexual wishes, (b) his incestuous desires, and (c) his patricidal impulses—and in so doing wards off a potential psychotic breakdown. Instead of being the white female who will be attacked by the Negro male (father, analyst) or the Negro male who commits the unpardonable crime of sexual union with the white female (mother), he becomes the powerful white male who protects the white female from the fantasied lust and aggression of the Negro male."

Rodgers draws heavily upon Sterba (22) in his psychodynamic formulation as to the significance and utilizations of blackness by white patients:

> . . . our negative feelings against God the Father have to be displaced onto a substitute figure which is created for this purpose, and that is the devil. Psychologically God and Satan were originally one and the same. The myth of the fall of the angels betrays that originally the two belonged to the same locality; Satan wears horns which are attributes of gods in many other religions . . . Satan is therefore the substitute for God as the object of our negative feelings, which derive from our original ambivalence toward our father in childhood. The devil has one significant feature in common with the Negro: Both are black. In the unconscious of many people the two are identical, both being substitutes for the father insofar as he is hated and feared (22).

Case #6: White Female Patient, Black Male Analyst

The transference/countertransference issues that have been described have occurred in the context of the treatment of patients who presented neurotic conflicts. The utilization of race either in the service of resistance to treatment or as an expression of the positive transference is rendered infinitely more complicated in patients with integrative pathology or borderline pathology. In such patients the pathology, transference and countertransference constitute a rather tangled skein requiring extreme sensitivity, careful timing, selectivity and skill, in those instances in which patient and therapist differ racially. The presentation of a patient illustrating the aforementioned issues is extremely salient because both black and white therapists have treated and will treat a significant number of borderline patients and patients with integrative pathology.

In this case the patient, a 53-year-old Jewish woman, was readmitted to a psychiatric hospital after having attempted to cope as an outpatient for approximately a month. Her most pronounced symptomatology on admission consisted of a fixed delusion that ultrasonic rays were being transmitted into her body, resulting in her physical discomfort and inability to remain in her apartment. Her symptom had existed for several months, but had become more intense just prior to admission. Other problems elicited by the therapist early in the course of this patient's therapy consisted of (a) an incapacity for close, intimate interpersonal relationships; (b) internal object splitting according to the pleasurable or unpleasurable nature of the affect associated with the object; (c) an inability to perceive others as separate from herself, but a tendency to identify others in terms of projected parts of herself; (d) cyclic alterations in thinking, feeling, and behavior; (e) vacillation between an erotic-dependent transference relationship and a hostile, vindictive, demanding one with marked fear accompanying the former reaction and intense guilt-fear accompanying the latter; (f) a tendency in the direction of over-intellectualization; (g) a general weakening of ego boundaries, reality testing and a lessened tendency to engage in secondary process thinking.

Some aspects of her history will be described. She was born and raised in New York City. Her parents were a merchant and a homemaker. She was the last of three girls and recalls that her father constantly stated he was disappointed that she was not a boy. She regards herself as rejected and physically abused by her parents and sisters Irene and Anna but actually received some degree of support and solace from her mother. She characterized herself as a brilliant but erratic student. Her rebelliousness resulted in her dismissal from two high schools. She ran away from home on several occasions during adolescence. At age 15 she "lost interest in school" and began playing the piano in night clubs. The next ten years were a chaotic period with periodic unemployment, periods of prostituting and use of opiates. She married a fellow musician at age 26 and after seven years of mental strife they separated. The next several years were characterized by a series of ungratifying affairs, diminished use of opiates, and gradual withdrawal from interpersonal contacts. Contact with her family decreased and painful verbal altercations occurred with each encounter.

Her withdrawal continued until her admission to the hospital. Her diagnosis was "borderline personality" and she exemplified the object-splitting, ambivalence, lability of affect and other symptoms consonant with that disorder. She was, at times, extremely hostile, and at other times quite seductive.

Approximately three months after admission she reported several dreams. The first was as follows: "In a huge meeting hall filled with people, a young woman was selling tickets. She was busy. I didn't like her face. It was ugly. I saw my sister smiling. It was a Communist party function and she wanted me to join. I pretended not to see her. She tried to make me notice her. I saw my psychiatrist. He was young, white and handsome. I accused him of plotting with her. He replied that he had nothing to do with it. I begged him to keep her away. He put a black umbrella between the two of us. I wanted him to take me home and fuck me."

Therapist interpreted patient's wish that he "protect" her from her sister.

The patient then reported this dream: "A postman in uniform. Fear. The middle of the night. He said he had come to deliver something. He had a large package from Irene that contained two puppies and three kittens. They were beautiful. I was annoyed. The puppy peed on the floor. I began fondling them. One pup should be a protector when it grows up. I was in the street naked. A woman permitted me to wear her jacket. The animals were starving. They were skinny and looked ugly. One kitten died. One was Persian white. Another was black and white (spotted). One cat grew vicious and clawed my arm, looked like a rat. I tore it off my arm."

She associated: "My sister was the cat that turned into a rat. The three kittens were me and my two sisters. One puppy was you (would protect me when it grew up). I wish you would see me objectively. I'm disturbed by the staff on the 4-12 shift. The vibrations are happening in my bed."

Therapist interpreted her wish to separate from her sister Irene and move toward therapist and the fact that this represented a source of anxiety.

She began the next session by presenting me with a gift, additional thoughts about the dream: "Coming in the middle of the night. This boy on his shoulder (transference?). You were being made a member of the family. I always wished for a brother. I really wished for *two brothers*. I should have been a brother. My father is fair, my mother is dark skinned (used to call her a gypsy). Anna got mother's love. I didn't get anybody's love. I was relieved to have the rat off my arm." She had an altercation with staff the night before.

She was obviously making several references to the transference: "The black umbrella," the two puppies, one of which was dark, the "black and white" cat, the reference to her "dark skinned" mother. The racial transference both facilitated and served as a resistance to treatment. Her object splitting was facilitated by references to blackness and its antithesis, whiteness.

The following dream and its associations further exemplify her unconscious utilization of blackness: "Anna and I were in a secondhand bookshop. I pulled out a handsome volume and we leafed through it. It seemed to have something to do with the history of ancient warfare. We decided to steal the book at my suggestions and as we approached the door the owner was looking straight at us so I motioned for her to slip it to me; she did so and we got out all right. Then outside it was dark, there was no landscape and it was windy; we were alone (no people). As we walked, I turned toward her and said (but not exactly in so many words) that we must love and trust each other. An embrace was attempted but not consummated, our bodies seemed to go awry. Then I held her away from me a bit to study the expression on her face, to see if she was in sympathy or crying. Instead, I observed her puzzlement that the side of her face turned toward me was black. I believed that this was a theatrical makeup and that the other side was white; I wondered why she had put on the makeup, then I wondered whether it really was her skin. At some point earlier in the dream, on leaving the bookstore, we looked at an illustration in the book and it depicted male exultation in warfare. I wanted to learn why men took such fierce pride in destruction. But I learned that the book was a sham; at the very opening there was a reference to Kitty Carlisle and early days of movie making with particular reference to her costume jewelry."

She associated the secondhand bookstore to "things written down," "as opposed to intellectualized"; "warfare with my sister." The handsome volume may have represented her past (anamnestic material). Stealing the book represented her taking that which was not freely granted (love?). She equated the shop owner with the therapist (= father). She was relieved to be out of the store, "we seemed to move to an emotional plain" (although barren and windswept). She compared the dark barren exterior with the treatment room. Made efforts to be loving toward "I" but to no avail. "She was cold." "Is a sham." She got all involved in the Angela Davis case, pretending to be pro-black while acting anti-semitic. "Anna's face was half-white, half-black."

"I still wonder if there's something secret going on between the two of you. Like you're in league with each other. Men want to win all the time. Like you." She equated the book to sessions and referred back to the theme of trust in the last session. "If I trust you, you will destroy me?"

The dream was an obvious transference dream in which her sister was substituted for therapist and an effort made to reconcile their warlike differences and substitute a more loving relationship. The dream indicated a wish to be involved in therapy, but a marked ambivalence and fear related to her perception of therapist's power-orientation. The theme was optimistic, in that the dream represented therapeutic engagement and a willingness to begin trusting her therapist.

RACISM AND PSYCHOTHERAPY

Schachter and Butts (12) underscore the fact that:

1) Racial differences may have little or no effect on the course of the analysis.
2) Racial differences may have catalytic effect upon the analytic process, and lead to a more rapid unfolding of core problems.
3) Stereotypes of race and color occasionally induce both analyst and patient to delay the analytic process, either by obscuring reality or by overestimating its importance.
4) Subculturally acceptable pathology or acting-out may evoke overreactions in the analyst while material fitting racial stereotypes may be ignored.
5) Countertransference may coincide with stereotypes and delay the analytic process.

In addition to underscoring the efficacy of interracial therapy and emphasizing the issues (both transferential and countertransferential as well as realistic) that catalyze or impede the therapeutic process, one cannot ignore the fact that unconscious racism and lack of awareness and sensitivity to the black (and other minority) experiences are crucial factors in the treatment accorded to blacks by whites.

Harrison and Butts (9) recommended that "one should tell patients honestly that their racial stereotypes do not get them doctors who are appropriate for them, and that stereotyped thinking only leads to more psychological troubles, particularly when it degrades or gives super-powers to someone based on racial characteristics" (p. 281). If psychoanalysts and psychotherapists are to advocate healthy and adaptive behavior on the part of their clients, it would behoove the mental health professionals to look to their own unconscious racism.

Based on this survey (9), destructive racial attitudes among psychiatrists manifested themselves in the following ways:

1) A fear that the black psychiatrist would not be able to cope with the racial attitudes of the patient, leading, in some cases, to: (a) failure to make referrals at all; and (b) failure to utilize the therapeutic effect of the positive aspects of the syndrome of the "liberal white patient" who is pleased with referral to a black psychiatrist.

2) Failure to refer patients because of overconcern that racist attitudes from these patients will "humiliate" and "hurt" the black psychiatrist.

3) Feelings that black psychiatrists are better able to treat children, adolescents, hippies, and super-liberals, which explicitly assumes a better communication between black psychiatrists and these anti-establishment patients. This unfortunately parallels in psychiatry the national policy of lumping together those groups that are seeking to change society as it is today.

4) Feelings that the black psychiatrist is better able to treat working-class patients, particularly black patients who use color as a defense. Working black patients pay lower fees. This has led to the misconception that competency in this area is due to the color of the psychiatrist rather than due to the talents of a skillful professional. Further, lack of skill or failure to learn techniques utilizable with this group of people was then excused on the basis of lack of color. Because there are so few black psychiatrists, these patients receive minimal psychiatric services at best. This exemplifies institutional racist practices.

5) Low-fee or free clinics without religious affiliations are remarkably free of any consideration of race when servicing clients. Only as fees increase, or in private practice, does racial differentiation in the selection of a therapist become an important issue. Fortunately, these low-fee or free clinical experiences allow us to see the irrelevance of race as an issue in a therapeutic relationship.

6) There is overconcern for the preference for a black therapist by

the black patients which in reality can never be met, and subsequently leads to no treatment at all for many of these patients.

7) Some of the white psychiatrists expressed their own initial reactions at being taught and interviewed by black psychiatrists, i.e., anxiety around feelings that the black psychiatrist was unable to teach or evaluate them. They reported that their anxiety decreased and that they were relieved to discover his competence.

8) White psychiatrists do not appear to accept the fact, or point out explicitly to patients with racist attitudes, that racial prejudice is a crippling symptom. They merely ask, "Why the feeling?" When a person has to use degradation of a group of people to maintain his own self-esteem, he is sick in this area and should have treatment around this issue, beginning with identification of the symptom as indication of illness. The failure to identify the symptom as evidence of illness may result in diminished referrals of white patients to black psychiatrists. The white psychiatrist may often feel that this symptom is an impossible one to treat, because of his failure to establish modifiability.

9) Both black and white psychiatrists report reactions of white patients to black therapists. White psychiatrists tend to report such reactions of white patients to black therapists as "shocking," "jolting," "dismaying," "disorienting." Black psychiatrists use words like "surprise." There seems to be evidence here then that patients' reactions to a black psychiatrist are perceived as more intense by the white psychiatrist.

10) Defined explicitly as their own stereotypic thinking by the white psychiatrists is that the black psychiatrists: (a) "have a natural sense of rhythm"; (b) are tied up in exploring and exploiting black/white situations; (c) are trying to work out past problems and change them a bit; and (d) are a little whiter than most blacks.

11) Only half of the psychiatrists polled have close black friends. This lack of social opportunity for modifying racial stereotypes contributes to the ineffectiveness of white psychiatrists, not only with black patients, but in the referral of white patients to black psychiatrists. Black psychiatrists encompass the greater part of the white culture, in contrast to white psychiatrists, who make no efforts to move into the black world.

Harrison and Butts made the following recommendations:

1) One should tell patients honestly that their racial stereotypes do not fit doctors who are appropriate for the patient and that stereotypic thinking only leads to more psychological troubles, particularly when it degrades or gives super-powers to someone based on racial

characteristics. Patients with questions or ambivalence about black psychiatrists need a definitive, reassuring statement by the white psychiatrist, not just an exploration of their feelings. Black psychiatrists are much clearer about this with their patients than white psychiatrists.

2) It is educational and ego-broadening to intimately know people of other ethnic groups. All psychiatrists should have this experience and get to know black people. They will then be able to deal more effectively with prejudice as a sickness in patients and society. A broadening of professional and social relationship increases the knowledge of others and self-knowledge.

CONCLUSIONS

In a multi-racial society such as ours, unconscious myths and stereotypes are ubiquitous, are maintained by both minority and majority members, and impact not only upon social relationships, but upon the processes of psychotherapy and psychoanalysis. There is no doubt that analysis or psychotherapy between blacks and whites can be effective, but the therapists involved in these treatments must be mindful of the resistances, catalytic effects of racial differences, and, in addition, must be aware of the fact that both black and white patients have incorporated the unconscious notions extant throughout the society.

The author draws heavily upon literature for examples as to the meanings and utilizations of blackness and whiteness. It is somewhat disconcerting and perplexing that white therapists and analysts have made so few references to "black thoughts" and "black deeds" surfacing in their treatment of white patients. It is also strange that only 4% of our nation's psychiatrists today belong to minority groups, even though the admission rate of non-whites to public mental hospitals is double what it is for whites. Equally amazing, only 7% of the research awards made by the National Institute of Mental Health are of major relevance to minorities, despite the stresses of prejudice and racism they must suffer. In addition, there are three black medical training analysts in the United States. Rather than a bid for behavioral science affirmative action, these statements are intended to put into a more comprehensive context the clinical issues referred to earlier.

This paper is an effort to examine pro-white, anti-black paranoia as it evidences itself in every therapeutic situation. For too long the focus has been on the white therapist/black patient duo. The vistas of this presentation have expanded to include the black therapist/white patient, black therapist/black patient, and white therapist/white patient. In each pairing, with varying degrees of intensity and frequency, references are made to blackness, "black thought and feelings," "black deeds." The unique background of each therapist and patient will undoubtedly influence the timing, form, frequency and intensity of the reference(s) to "blackness." Transference and countertransference manifestations that utilize blackness may occur in therapeutic and analytic situations. Although the main thrust of this paper has been a clinical one, since the focus is on emphasizing certain clinical issues (unconscious racism) that generally tend to be minimized or overlooked, one might, in broad terms, regard aspects of this presentation as "political" in nature (see Henry Stillman's (24) definition of politics as the science of how who gets what when and where). It would be naive to discuss clinical issues in isolation from institutional training practices, institutional racism and reality issues that have an impact on the treatment and therapists that effect patients.

Pinderhughes (19) concludes:

> The data on human beings from all sources overwhelmingly support the conclusion that man is more paranoid than wise. This paranoia is not accessible to reason, and attempts to alter it lead to confrontations and often to violence. The paranoia is especially oppressive and deadly when it has been frozen into culture and when it has molded institutions.
>
> When enough influential men in important institutions decided to humanize the structures over which they have power, then dissent, revolt, and revolution cease, the leaders are embraced with appreciation and affectionate bonds. However, there must be a sizeable numbre of such leaders, enough to constitute a movement among influential men.
>
> In essence, to eliminate racism, it would be necessary to develop a rededication to democratic and humanitarian values, a shift from the ethics of competition to those of sharing and a new order of priorities in major institutions.
>
> Factors like these determine, to a considerable degree, needs for psychotherapy, the nature of it, and who receives it. Factors like these determine the philosophies, the rationales, and the ethics with which psychotherapy is practiced and must be considered relevant in any discussion of racism and psychotherapy.

The author could not agree more wholeheartedly. In an unpublished article (23), the author expresses a view comparable to that of Pinderhughes. The American educational system is criticized for its lack of humanism and for its emphasis on technology. Such a value system lends itself to the type of dehumanization exemplified by pro-white/anti-black paranoia.

POSTLUDE

I sit on a man's back, choking him and making him carry me, and yet assure myself and others that I am very sorry for him and wish to lighten his load by all possible means—except by getting off his back.

LEO TOLSTOY

Both individuals are victims and both bear the emotional scars of the slave-master relationship.

REFERENCES

1. Bernard, V. W. Psychoanalysis and members of minority groups. *J. Amer. Psychoanal. Assoc.,* 1953, 1:256-26.
2. Kardiner, A. and Ovesey, L. *The Mark of Oppression.* Cleveland: World Publishing Co., 1951.
3. Kennedy, J. A. Problems posed in the analysis of Negro patients. *Psychiatry,* 1952, 15:313-327.
4. Oberndorf, C. P. Selectivity and option for psychotherapy. *Amer. J. Psychiat.,* 1954, 110:754-758.
5. Pinderhughes, C. Understanding black power—processes and proposals. *Amer. J. Psychiat.,* 1969, 125-11.
6. Comer, J. White racism: Its root, form, and function. *J. Amer. Psychoanal. Assoc.,* Dec. 1969, 126:6.
7. Palmer, Don. White training institutions. The Black Psychiatric Resident—The Encounter (unpublished).
8. Butts, H. F. White racism: Its origins, institutions, and the implications for professional mental health practice. *Int. J. Psychiat.,* December 1969, 8 (6).
9. Harrison, P. and Butts, H. F. White psychiatrist racism in referral practices to black psychiatrists. *J. National Med. Assoc.,* July 1970, 62 (4).
10. Cannon, Davis, Elam, et al. Personal communication.
11. Pinderhughes, C. Discussion of white racism: Its origins, institutions, and the implications for professional mental health practice. *Int. J. Psychiat.,* December 1969, 8 (6).
12. Schachter, J. and Butts, H. F. Transference and countertransference in interracial analyses. *J. Amer. Psychoanal. Assoc.,* October 1968, 16 (4).
13. Butts, H. F. Psychoanalysis and unconscious racism. *J. of Contemp. Psychother.,* Spring 1971, 3 (2):67-81.
14. Melville, Herman. *Moby Dick.* New York: The Bobbs-Merrill Co., Inc., 1961, pp. 252-264.
15. Fiedler, L. A. *Love and Death in the American Novel.* New York: Criterion Books, 1960, p. 190.
16. Barchilon, J. The uncircumcisable whale—a psychoanalytic study of Moby Dick. 1977, unpublished.
17. Fanon, F. *The Wretched of the Earth.* New York: Grove Press, 1963, p. 32.

18. Calnek, M. Racial factors in the countertransference: The black therapist and the black client. *Amer. J. Orthopsychiat.*, January 1970, 40 (1).
19. Pinderhughes, C. Racism and psychotherapy. In: Willie, Kramer and Brown (Eds.), *Racism and Mental Health.* Contemporary Community Health Series. University of Pittsburg Press, 1973.
20. Myers, W. A. The significance of the colors black and white in the dreams of black and white patients. American Psychoanalytic Association meeting. December 20, 1975.
21. Rodgers, T. C. The evolution of an active anti-Negro racist. *The Psychoanalytic Study of Society,* 1960, 1:237-247.
22. Sterba, R. Some psychological factors in Negro race hatred and in anti-Negro riots. *Psychoanalysis and the Social Sciences,* Vol. 1. New York: International Universities Press, 1947, pp. 411-427.
23. Butts, H. F. Education for humanism. Pending publication.
24. Hellman, S. Partial primer for all Americans. 1944.

20

Psychotherapy with Alcoholics

SHELDON ZIMBERG, M.D.

INTRODUCTION

Psychiatry has in general not been very effective in treating alcoholics. Most psychiatrists have little interest or experience in this field. Since most psychiatric residencies at the present time do not offer clinical training in the addictive disorders, psychiatrists are ill equipped to diagnose and treat alcoholism. Therefore, with a few exceptions, psychiatry has left the field of alcoholism largely to Alcoholics Anonymous, a few interested internists and general practitioners, and paraprofessional alcoholism counselors. However, psychiatry with its understanding of psychodynamics and the sociopsychological factors relating to human behavior can make important contributions to this field.

It is generally accepted that psychological factors alone are not sufficient to produce alcoholism in an individual. Sociocultural and physiological factors (possibly of genetic origin) along with psychological mechanisms are the *necessary* and *sufficient contributors* that produce the clinical state of alcoholism. How these factors interrelate to produce alcoholism in a particular individual is unknown. In some individuals one of the three factors may predominate. However, alcoholism shares with many other mental health related disorders a lack of etiological knowledge along with some fairly effective treatment approaches.

This chapter will present a psychiatrist's understanding of sociopsychological factors relating to alcoholism and the approaches for successful psychotherapy of this condition in a significant number of alcoholics. The experience and views presented are based on the author's work

382

with many alcoholics in urban ghetto alcoholism programs, in a suburban community mental health center, and in private psychiatric practice. There will also be a discussion of results obtained in the treatment of alcoholics during a two-year period in the author's private psychiatric practice.

PSYCHODYNAMICS OF THE PRIMARY ALCOHOLIC

There is considerable literature on psychoanalytic theories of alcoholism. Much of this literature was reviewed by Blum (1). Blum indicates that psychoanalytic concepts can be applied to the psychodynamic understanding of alcoholism and that oral fixation is the arrested stage of development for the primary alcoholic. This fixation accounts for the infantile and dependent characteristics noted in alcoholics, including excessive narcissism, demanding behavior, passivity, and dependence. This fixation occurred in the development of the primary alcoholic due to a significant degree of deprivation during early childhood development. Other types of alcoholics are described as being fixated at the anal level or the phallic oedipal stage. There is considerable evidence to support the view that alcoholics had been exposed to rejection by one or both parents and that dependency needs are among the major psychological factors that contribute along with other etiologic factors to the development of alcoholism (2, 3, 4, 5, 6).

The dependency needs of many of the alcoholics the author has treated have been profoundly repressed and there was often little evidence of overt passivity or dependent traits when the patients were sober. Such dependent and passive traits were apparent, however, when they were under the influence of alcohol. Alcoholics who were sober in many cases had obsessive-compulsive personality traits. They were often perfectionistic and in need of maintaining control over their feelings and their lives, and were often completely unaware of the most intense feelings, particularly anger. Therefore, it is not appropriate to look for or to characterize an "alcoholic personality." The psychological conflict that is discussed below forms a psychodynamic constellation which is the key psychological factor in alcoholism and is the core conflict that must be dealt with in therapy. This psychodynamic constellation is a common problem among alcoholics, but does *not* produce a common personality.

The psychodynamic conflict that the author found in the alcoholics he has treated has been lack of self esteem, feelings of worthlessness, and inadequacy. These feelings are denied and repressed and lead to unconscious needs to be taken care of and accepted (dependent needs). Since these dependent needs cannot be met in reality to compensate for the profound feelings of worthlessness, they lead to anxiety and compensatory needs for control, power, and achievement. These excessive needs are often doomed to failure, resulting in the use of alcohol which tranquilizes the anxiety felt in the face of failure and, more importantly, produces, pharmacologically, feelings of power, omnipotence, invulnerability. When the alcoholic wakes up after a drinking episode, he is full of guilt and despair because he hasn't achieved anything more than before he drank and his problems remain. Thus, his feelings of worthlessness are intensified and the conflict continues in a vicious circle fashion, often with a progressive downward spiral.

McClelland et al. (7) conducted extensive research with male alcoholics on the effects of alcohol on feelings and imagery. They noted that alcohol produces "ego-enhancing" effects and thoughts of power and strength. They hypothesized that "drinking serves to increase power fantasies and that heavy liquor drinking characterizes those whose personal power needs are strong and whose level of inhibition is low." They rejected the theory that alcoholism is related to dependent needs since they were unable to demonstrate increased fantasies regarding warmth and dependency during drinking. Similar studies conducted among women alcoholics by Wilsnack (8) suggest that alcohol enhances feelings of womanliness.

The psychological mechanisms presented above are basically not in conflict with McClelland's or Wilsnack's theories, since the male alcoholic can be viewed as striving for power and control consciously and the woman alcoholic as striving for womanliness as compensations for unconscious feelings of worthlessness, a poor self image, and the need to be nurtured. Alcohol provides an artificial feeling state of power and control in men and increased feelings of womanliness in women that cannot be achieved in reality for very long. The very act of producing such feeling states at will feeds the alcoholic's conscious grandiose self image. This intense need for grandiosity can be called a *reactive grandiosity*.

McCord and McCord (9) conducted longitudinal studies of families. Some of the boys in the families under study later became alcoholics. They noted that alcoholics were often raised in homes that could be characterized as conflict-ridden, and in which there was an extremely erratic, unstable mother and a rejecting, punitive father. They noted the alcoholics had evidence of heightened dependency needs which were unacceptable and had feelings of being victimized by society and compensatory feelings of grandiosity. Feelings of fearlessness, self-sufficiency and aggression that were noted in prealcoholic boys were felt to be a facade erected in place of feelings of rejection and a heightened desire for dependency.

The observation that the core psychodynamic problem in the treatment of alcoholism is *reactive grandiosity* and a need to feel omnipotent was discussed in Tiebout's paper describing the psychological process by which an alcoholic becomes involved in Alcoholics Anonymous (10). The conversion process was described as occurring in four steps: 1) the need to hit bottom; 2) the need to be humble; 3) the need to surrender; and 4) the need for ego reduction. These steps were based on Tiebout's observation of an excessive amount of narcissism in the alcoholic's ego which gives rise to feelings of omnipotence. The steps in the conversion process are necessary to produce a reduction in this narcissism which perpetrates the self-destructive drinking behavior and the coexisting denial of this behavior. Tiebout did not indicate in this paper what happens to the excessive narcissism of the alcoholic's ego. Clearly, the narcissism is sublimated toward the goal of A.A. to rescue other alcoholics. Thus, the grandiosity becomes fulfilled and socially useful in the rescuing of other alcoholics. A.A. members recognize that their help of other alcoholics is a way that they keep themselves sober. The first step in the 12 steps of A.A. is the recognition of the alcoholic's inhability to control alcohol. With this recognition, there is also the beginning of recognition of one's inability to control other aspects of one's life. Thus, the beginnings of humility appear in an alcoholic, with a crack developing in the wall of denial built by the need for omnipotence as the alcoholic becomes involved in A.A.

Therefore, the central problem in rehabilitating an alcoholic is breaking through the *reactive grandiosity* that produces the massive denial of profound feelings of inferiority and dependency and perpetuates the pattern of self-destructive and family destructive drinking. The alcoholic not only destroys himself but his loved ones as well, without really perceiving his lack of control of this behavior pattern. The typical response of an alcoholic without insight into this behavior is, "I can stop drinking any time I want to." This occurs in spite of overwhelming evidence to the contrary. This self-deception must be penetrated if rehabilitation is to succeed.

Sociopsychological Factors Affecting Treatment

In addition to recognizing the psychodynamics of the alcoholic in treatment, one must recognize the social circumstances of the alcoholic. It is necessary to evaluate the family and marital relationships that exist or existed in the past, as well as the employment situation. In addition, information should be obtained regarding the cultural attitudes toward drinking and drunkenness that existed in the individual's family while he was growing up and how he integrated these attitudes into his present drinking behavior.

There must be a determination as to how the individual has handled crises and stress, and whether he has been able to modify or stop destructive drinking behavior spontaneously in the past, and for how long. One must determine at what level the individual is psychologically, socially, and developmentally and how he reached these levels historically.

The social, family, and cultural contexts in which problem drinking occurs are significant factors in determining what treatment approaches can be most effective with the individual, and to determine what influences can be brought to bear to convince the alcoholic of his need for help. Coercion is often necessary because of the massive denial and self-deception that exist. Industrial alcoholism programs often use the implied threat of losing one's job unless the individual enters a treatment program for his alcoholism. Such programs report relatively high rates of success in rehabilitating their alcoholic employees. Such coercion can be viewed as *therapeutic leverage* in which a small degree of self-awareness is forced upon the alcoholic. Such therapeutic leverage can be useful; however, it cannot in and of itself produce recovery, which can occur only in the treatment process which will be described below. Therefore, looking for possible sources of therapeutic leverage should be a part of the initial evaluation of an alcoholic.

All alcoholics are not the same, even though most share the common psychodynamic conflict with dependency and the need for compensatory power and control. Alcoholics exist in differing age groups, socioeconomic circumstances, and cultural groups. Approaches with the skid-row homeless alcoholic cannot be the same as with the so-called "high-bottom" executive, or with the individual living in poverty in an urban ghetto. The skid-row homeless person is at the bottom of the barrel socially. He reached this depth after a prolonged history of alcoholism and has developed an adaptation, although a very tenuous one, to this state. The social, physical, and psychological consequences of this state require differing approaches aimed at physical, social, and vocational rehabilitation requiring years to accomplish. The executive who is still employed requires approaches dealing with his drinking, education about alcoholism, and psychotherapy and/or involvement in A.A., since social, vocational, and physical deterioration have not progressed to a severe degree.

One must make a distinction among various populations of alcoholics —for example, people living in poverty. In this case drinking problems are often a reaction to the depression and stress of poverty. Alcoholism treatment for this group is necessary, but not sufficient to produce recovery. Socioeconomic incentives are needed to provide a motivating force to remain sober once sobriety has been produced through treatment (11).

It has been noted by several studies that different subpopulations of alcoholics respond differentially to various treatment modalities (12, 13, 14). Varying social and psychological factors in the alcoholic subpopulation will affect outcome. Therefore, programs that offer the widest range of treatment alternatives will have the greatest success for mixed populations, as well as those programs that provide the most effective specific approaches to a relatively homogeneous subpopulation.

The elderly alcoholic facing the stress of aging uses alcohol to cope with these problems (15). Treatment in such cases can be effective by dealing with the depression and social isolation of the individual with socialization activities and antidepressant medication best carried out in a setting serving the elderly.

Therefore, treatment approaches must be based on knowledge of the sociocultural norms, attitudes and needs of the patients under treatment. Sociocultural influences are often major contributing factors in the etiology of alcoholism, and such influences must be understood if the alcoholism is to be successfully treated.

It should be noted that alcoholism does not occur as an all or none phenomenon, but rather as a degree which will vary in severity from time to time in the same individual. Table 1 shows a scale (16) which approximately defines varying levels of severity of alcohol abuse from no problem to the skid-row alcoholic at level six. Improvement in treatment can be determined by movement upward in this scale, although the goal of abstinence with improvement in social functioning and greater awareness of and insight into one's behavior should be the end point of rehabilitation.

THE TREATMENT PROCESS

The treatment of the alcoholic is a long-term process. Alcoholism is a chronic illness with a high potential for relapse. As in other such chronic disorders, continuous care is required in some cases for the duration of

TABLE 1

Alcohol Abuse Scale

Level	Characteristics
1. None	Drinks only on occasion, if at all.
2. Minimal	Drinking is not conspicuous, occasional intoxications (up to 4 per year). No social, family, occupational, health, or legal problems related to drinking.
3. Mild	Intoxication occurring up to once a month, although generally limited to evening or weekends, and/or some impairment in social, family relations, or occupational functioning related to drinking. No physical or legal problems related to drinking.
4. Moderate	Frequent intoxications, up to one or two times per week and/or significant impairment in social, family or occupational functioning. Some suggestive evidence of physical impairment related to drinking, such as tremors, frequent accidents, epigastric distress, loss of appetite at times. No history of delirium tremens, cirrhosis, nutritional deficiency, hospitalizations or arrests related to drinking.
5. Severe	Almost constantly drinking (practically every day). History of delirium tremens, liver cirrhosis, chronic brain syndrome, neuritis, nutritional deficiency, or severe disruption in social or family relations. Unable to hold a steady job but able to maintain himself on public assistance. One or more arrests related to drinking (drunk and disorderly).
6. Extreme	All the characteristics of severe impairment plus homelessness and/or inability to maintain himself on public assistance.

the individuals' lives. Alcoholics Anonymous is particularly well suited to provide this supportive treatment for an indefinite duration. All an individual has to do is to attend meetings and follow through with their "12 Step" procedures. However, professional intervention during the beginning stages of treatment is necessary to provide detoxification from alcohol and a thorough psychosocial evaluation. The psychotherapeutic process described is best suited for middle-class alcoholics who have family ties and a reasonable amount of socioeconomic resources.

Directive counseling during the process of detoxification can enhance the motivation of an alcoholic to continue the treatment after detoxification has been completed. Detoxification from alcohol can be accomplished in many cases on an ambulatory basis (17) using diazepam (Valium) 5 mg. 3-4 times a day progressively reduced over 1-2 weeks. Patients are seen in the office 2-3 times per week during the detoxification, but not maintained on Valium after detoxification. Patients who cannot be detoxified on an ambulatory basis should be hospitalized.

Counseling or more intensive psychotherapeutic approaches are often necessary after detoxification has been accomplished. Acquainting the alcoholic with the physical effects of alcohol on his body and the effects on his ability to perform his necessary functions should be part of this effort. The use of disulfiram (Antabuse) in maintenance doses of 250 mg. per day to produce a deterrent effect in regard to drinking is also an effective approach.

Several principles are important in the treatment of an alcoholic individual. The first principle is that the drinking itself must be terminated if therapy is to be at all effective in achieving rehabilitation. A common mistake mental health professionals make is viewing alcoholism as a symptom of underlying psychopathology or personality disorder and attempting to treat the underlying disorder. This approach to alcoholism psychotherapy has resulted in many failures and a reluctance of psychiatrists to treat alcoholics in spite of an occasional paper describing some success with psychoanalytic psychotherapy of alcoholism (18).

Psychological conflict does exist as indicated, but efforts must first be directed to achieve sobriety for the patient through detoxification and the maintenance of sobriety through intensive directive psychotherapy, and the use of Antabuse. A patient who is continuing to drink will not be responsive to counseling or psychotherapeutic approaches and a power struggle often develops between the therapist and the drinking patient.

The second principle in treating the alcoholic is the understanding of the transference the alcoholic will often establish with a therapist. This transference will be very intensive and be characterized by a great amount of dependence coupled with hostile, manipulating, and testing behavior. Thus, a great deal of ambivalence will be noted in the transference relationship. The alcoholic will be dependent, but at times act in a grandiose way, believing he can control his drinking as well as his life when the evidence is obviously to the contrary. Thus, massive denial is utilized by alcoholics to avoid facing their problems and their inability to handle alcohol. The therapist should encourage a dependent relationship with the patient by the use of support, acceptance, and directive counseling to permit the patient to change his dependence on alcohol, which can be considered an object relationship, to dependence on the therapist.

The third principle in the treatment of the alcoholic is understanding the countertransference that may develop in a therapist in response to the provocative behavior and drinking of the patient as testing of his continued interest. Because of this type of testing behavior, the treatment of an alcoholic can be felt to be frustrating and unrewarding. However, the therapist must recognize that he is not omnipotent in regard to the alcoholic's drinking. He cannot, nor can anyone, stop an alcoholic determined to drink. A therapist can only provide the means to assist the alcoholic in achieving sobriety and cannot force him for long into refraining from drinking. Only the patient's conscious efforts can achieve this for himself. Recognizing this reality, the therapist must impose limits on the behavior of the patient and conditions under which treatment can continue. If the patient cannot meet these conditions at a particular point in time, treatment should be discontinued. The door, however, should be left open to renew the efforts to achieve sobriety as the first step in the treatment process.

The treatment of an alcoholic has been observed to progress through several stages. Although the stages can be observed in group therapy, they are more apparent in individual therapy. The first stage involves the situation where the alcoholic "cannot drink." This situation exists when there is external pressure on the patient to stop drinking, such as the threat of loss of job, or his wife leaving, or deteriorating physical health. In a sense, the alcoholic is forced to stop drinking, at least for a short time. Most alcoholics are pushed into treatment because of such external pressure. Attitudes toward drinking and the denial of drinking as a serious problem have not changed. The alcoholic has stopped drinking not because he sees it as necessary, but because someone else does. Often during this stage after the alcoholic has stopped drinking, he feels extremely confident about his newly acquired sobriety and experiences a "glow" of euphoria. This behavior is a reaction formation to his unconscious lack of control over his drinking which is now experienced as a certainty of control over his not drinking as well as control over the other aspects of his life. This situation is by its nature very unstable since there has been no significant change in his attitude about drinking or an ego reduction as described by Tiebout (10). It can easily lead to a return to drinking or can lead through psychotherapy and/or further Alcoholics Anonymous involvement to a second stage where the alcoholic "won't drink." The use of Antabuse as an external control over the impulse to drink is particularly valuable during the beginning stage of treatment. All patients should be encouraged to attend A.A. meetings as an adjunct to the psychotherapy. Not all patients will be willing to attend, but those who do will learn a great deal about alcoholism and obtain a considerable amount of hope and support for their own recovery.

Involving the spouse in conjoint therapy and a referral to Al-Anon can also greatly enhance the therapeutic process by changing destructive attitudes and behavior in the spouse and tangibly demonstrating to the patient the spouse's active participation in the recovery effort.

The second stage is where the controls on the compulsion to drink have become internalized and there is no longer a serious conscious conflict about whether to drink or not. At this stage, the individual's attitude toward the necessity of drinking and the deleterious consequences in resuming drinking are apparent. He has experienced a considerable attitudinal change toward drinking. The conflict about drinking is still present, but at an unconscious level. Evidence of the continued existence of this conflict is present in terms of fantasies of the patient and in dreams. This stage is the level many Alcoholics Anonymous members have achieved. It is a reasonably good stage of recovery and is fairly stable, only occasionally leading to a "slip" after years of sobriety. This stage requires at least six months to one year of treatment and sobriety to achieve. A decision regarding the stopping of Antabuse can be considered at this time because there has been established a good set of internalized controls over the impulse to drink.

During the first two stages of therapy, most of the defenses of the alcoholic should not be analyzed but redirected, particularly the grandiosity, through A.A. involvement. Patients who do not attend A.A. but are able to achieve sobriety have the grandiosity turned into an ego enhancing feeling of being able to control a problem that was extremely difficult. A paper by Wallace (19) discusses in detail how defenses of alcoholics can be redirected rather than removed to facilitate the therapeutic process.

The third stage of recovery involves the situation where the alcoholic "does not have to drink." This stage can only be achieved through insight into the individual's personality problems and conflicts and their resolution to a major degree. The habitual use of alcohol at this stage can be understood as a way of dealing with the individual's conflicts and as a reaction to stress. With the resolution of the conflicts, the individual can achieve more adaptive ways of coping with problems, internal and external. This stage can be achieved only through psychotherapy and self understanding. It is a stable stage so long as the alcoholic refrains from drinking. The ability to refrain from drinking is relatively easy to maintain at this stage.

The fourth stage of recovery is a theoretical stage and involves the situation where "I can return to social drinking." Probably a small percentage of alcoholics can achieve this stage (20), but at our present level of knowledge, it is impossible to predict which alcoholic this might be. All alcoholics believe during the initial stages of recovery that they can return to controlled drinking. Therefore, for all practical purposes *abstinence* should be a necessary goal in the treatment of all alcoholics. Alcohol is not necessary to life and it is quite possible to live and even be happy without consuming alcohol. This fact should be part of the attitudinal change an alcoholic experiences during the process of recovery.

The termination of treatment with an alcoholic is a critical point. If the treatment process has been successful, the alcoholic will have established a dependent, trusting relationship with the therapist and, therefore, termination will produce anxiety and the possibility of return to drinking. This termination should be based on mutual agreement between the therapist and patient, a termination date in the future determined, and the final months of therapy involved with the issue of termination.

Termination can occur at stage II or III since both are relatively stable stages regarding control of drinking. A decision has to be made, however, when a patient reaches stage II as to whether further treatment to achieve insight into the psychological conflict related to his drinking problem and, therefore, moving to reach stage III are considered important to the patient. As far as control of drinking is concerned, it is not essential to reach stage III in treatment. Therefore, this option should be left to the patient.

Regardless of whether the patient terminates in stage II or III, the door to return to therapy at any time should be left open. A patient who stops treatment after stage II may determine after a while that not drinking is not enough to help him deal with his feelings and conflicts and, therefore, might wish to return to treatment to try to achieve insight into his personality conflicts. A patient terminated after stage III may have a slip; therefore, a return to treatment should be available. However, this slip should not be viewed as a treatment failure, but as part of a rehabilitation process that is not yet complete. Patients who slip in stages II and III generally do not return to continuous uncontrolled drinking because their awareness of their problem and control mechanisms are such that controls can be quickly reinstated. The slip can be analyzed as a psychological maladaptation to conflict and anxiety or as a transference reaction.

REPORT OF AN OUTCOME STUDY

The author analyzed data on 23 alcoholic patients treated in individual psychotherapy during a two-year period in a private psychiatric office setting where the methods described above were utilized. The patients were seen in most cases on a once-a-week basis. In some cases where marital problems were major aspects of the patient's difficulties, joint sessions were held periodically. All patients received a physical examination and laboratory studies from an internist.

The data obtained for this study came from a review of the charts kept on the patients and follow-up telephone calls to patients who were no longer in treatment.

The results of the study can be seen in Table 2. This table indicates

TABLE 2

Characteristics of Treated Patients

	Successes* 14*** (61%)	Early** Drop-Outs 5 (22%)	Failures 4 (17%)
A. SEX			
Male	8	4	2
Female	6	1	2
B. AGE			
Average	43	38	41
Range	33-54	22-52	30-51
C. RELIGION			
Catholic	3	1	1
Protestant	6	2	3
Jewish	4	1	0
Other	1	1	0
D. MARITAL STATUS			
Married	7	3	1
Divorced	3	1	1
Single	3	1	1
Separated	0	0	1
Widowed	1	0	0
E. EMPLOYMENT			
Employed	11	5	3
Student	1	0	0
Housewife	2	0	1
F. SOCIAL CLASS			
Lower Middle	1	2	1
Middle	7	1	1
Upper Middle	6	2	2

TABLE 2 (*continued*)

	Successes* 14*** (61%)	Early** Drop-Outs 5 (22%)	Failures 4 (17%)
G. DURATION OF ALCOHOL ABUSE (YEARS)			
Average	7	6	5
Range	3-17	2-12	2-10
H. LEVEL OF ALCOHOL ABUSE			
4	8	3	2
5	6	2	2
I. USE OF ANTABUSE			
Yes	13	2	4
No	1	3	0
Complications	2	0	0
J. TYPE OF DETOXIFICATION			
Hospital	3	0	1
Ambulatory	9	5	3
None	2	0	0
K. USE OF ALCOHOLICS ANONYMOUS			
Yes	10	2	1
No	4	3	3
L. PREVIOUS TREATMENT			
None	6	3	2
Psychiatric	7	2	2
Alcoholism	1	0	0

* One year or more of abstinence with improvement in other aspects of their lives.
** Six sessions or less.
*** Stage II—10; Stage III—4.

that 14 of the 23 patients treated (61%) were successes. An outcome was considered successful when there was at least 1 year of abstinence from alcohol with functional improvement in other aspects of their lives. Of the 14 patients who achieved a successful outcome, 10 patients achieved a stage II level of recovery (internalized controls over the impulse to drink) and 4 achieved a stage III level of recovery (conflict resolution).

In the study, 5 (22%) patients dropped out of therapy early (6 sessions or less) and 4 (17%) were failures. If we consider the outcome of the 18 patients who remained in therapy, 14 (78%) had successful results.

There were 14 males and 9 females. The average age was 44 with a range of 22-54. The average duration of their alcoholism was 8 years with a range of 2-17 years. The severity of their alcoholism placed 13 of the patients at level 4 of the Alcohol Abuse Scale (see Table 1) and 10 at level 5.

Additional demographic characteristics of this treatment population indicated that 11 patients were married, 6 divorced or separated, 5 single and 1 widowed; 5 were Catholic, 11 Protestant, 5 Jewish, 1 Moslem, and another with no religious affiliation; all of the patients were middle-class individuals, with 19 employed, 1 student and 3 housewives.

History of the treatment population indicated that 11 had no previous treatment for their alcoholism, 11 had previous psychiatric treatment which was unsuccessful, and 1 had previous alcoholism treatment which was unsuccessful.

When first seen for treatment, most of the patients required detoxification from alcohol, with only 2 being sober on initial contact. Of the 21 requiring detoxification, 17 (81%) were successfully detoxified on an ambulatory basis; 4 (19%) required in-hospital detoxification after failure of ambulatory detoxification.

Regarding Alcoholics Anonymous attendance, 13 participated in A.A. and 10 did not. Among the 14 patients who had successful outcomes, 10 used A.A. and 4 did not. Among the patients who dropped out and those who failed in therapy, 3 used A.A. and 6 did not. Although the numbers are too small to determine statistical significance, it is suggested that attendance at A.A. is associated with a successful outcome.

Antabuse was used with 19 of the 23 patients and with 13 of the 14 patients who had successful outcomes. There were 2 patients who had complications from the use of Antabuse which required its discontinuation. One patient developed a toxic hepatitis and another developed an organic brain syndrome. These conditions cleared up after the Antabuse was stopped.

CASE REPORTS

Case 1

Patient is a 44-year-old married, Jewish lawyer. He had a 17-year history of alcoholism with several hospitalizations, an episode of delirium tremens about 10 years ago and several attempts at alcoholism treatment including A.A. attendance, Antabuse, group therapy with a psychiatrist who specialized in alcoholism treatment, and most recently an internist who specialized in alcoholism treatment.

In recent years his drinking pattern had changed from daily drinking to abstinence of 1-2 months' duration and then going on binges of several days' to a week's duration. He came into treatment at a point when he appeared to be losing control of his periods of abstinence and his binges were becoming more frequent. He always planned his drinking to occur at times when it would least interfere with his work, but his more frequent binges were beginning to affect his work performance and create marital problems.

The patient was started in individual psychotherapy, Antabuse, and referred to A.A. He refused to go to A.A., however.

During the beginning stages of treatment he would stop taking Antabuse, wait a few days, and start a binge. This continued for several months until he was told he couldn't continue in treatment if he continued to drink. He came to one session drunk, at which time he was extremely depressed and full of anger at his father.

Prior to this session, the patient had denied any feelings about his father or, in fact, any disturbing feelings or thoughts of any kind. A joint session with his wife after this session confirmed his depression when he was drunk and his angry feelings at his father. He realized for the first time that he drank not only because he wanted to do so, but also as a way of coping with a great deal of emotional conflict.

The author's acceptance of him when he was drunk and the beginning awareness of his having repressed a great deal of feelings that were liberated by intoxication enabled him to accept the need for sobriety. He took the Antabuse on a regular basis and began attending A.A. meetings. He was able to identify with some of the members for the first time. He went on to achieve continuous sobriety.

The use of the dependent relationship he had established with the author in the transference was threatened by the possibility of discontinuing therapy and was enhanced by his being accepted when he came to a session drunk. This represents a breakthrough in the treatment. The transference was not interpreted. He achieved a stage II recovery level because once his drinking ceased, his defenses in relation to his underlying conflicts were strongly reinstituted. He was able to achieve more than a year of continuous sobriety.

Case 2

Patient is a 44-year-old divorced, Protestant man who was the controller and treasurer of a financial corporation. He had a 4-year history of alcoholism which had contributed to his recent divorce.

He came to treatment just before his divorce was finalized because his wife had indicated that his drinking was the major reason for her leaving him. He was started on individual psychotherapy, but at first refused to take Antabuse or attend A.A., saying that he could stop drinking on his own. He was told that if he had a drinking episode it would prove that he couldn't abstain without help and at that time Antabuse would be necessary for his continued treatment. He agreed to this suggestion.

After about 3 weeks of sobriety he began drinking heavily again. He said he really wanted to drink socially and that he wasn't an alcoholic. When reminded of the agreement, he reluctantly agreed to take Antabuse. He also went to an A.A. meeting. He continued taking Antabuse for several months; at that time he was told that he was going to lose his job because of an economy move of his company. He became very upset and would have begun drinking again except that he was still taking the Antabuse. He realized that without the Antabuse he couldn't control his impulse to drink.

His problem with his loss of his job was worked through and he began looking for another job. He had begun attending A.A. meetings and found them helpful. After about 6 months of therapy, he began to develop signs of organic mental impairment. The Antabuse was discontinued and his organic mental symptoms cleared up. He had changed his attitude significantly about the need to drink and he was able to maintain his sobriety when the Antabuse was discontinued.

He was referred to an organization called Parents Without Partners to help him meet women since he had problems making such social contacts. He met a woman whom he fell in love with and after 6 months of seeing each other they became engaged.

He was given a year to find another job by his present company. He had obtained some good prospects of another job and after about 14 months of treatment, with 1 year of sobriety, he was discharged from therapy.

SUMMARY

The approach to psychotherapy of alcoholics that has been presented in terms of stages of progression of treatment in relation to varying levels of ability to control the impulse to drink provides a framework that structures a complex and often amorphous treatment process. It provides a goal-directed approach to achievable levels of improvement. Complex therapeutic decisions regarding involvement of the family in treatment, starting or stopping of Antabuse, attendance at A.A. meetings, use of uncovering techniques, discontinuation of therapy, and others can be considered in relationship to these fairly predictable stages in the recovery process. It is possible to make predictions of outcome of therapeutic intervention or lack of intervention based on knowledge of the stage of recovery the patient has entered. Therefore, such an awareness can make the complex psychotherapeutic process with alcoholics potentially understandable and subject to a certain degree of predictability.

Data have been presented that analyzed the results of private psychiatric office treatment of alcoholics according to the approaches described in this chapter. A significant number of the 23 patients treated improved (61%). Patients who remained in therapy beyond 6 visits had a 78% successful outcome. Such results suggest that alcoholism can be successfully treated with individual psychotherapy with the modified approaches indicated.

Although group therapy had been considered the treatment of choice by many specialists in alcoholism, the author's experience with individual therapy suggests that it can be quite useful in the treatment of alcoholism. Individual therapy facilitates a profound transference relationship which, if effectively managed, can lead even very resistant alcoholics to recovery.

REFERENCES

1. Blum, E. M. Psychoanalytic views of alcoholism: A review. *Quart. J. Stud. Alc.*, 1966, 27:259-299.
2. Knight, R. P. The psychodynamics of chronic alcoholism. *J. Nerv. Ment. Dis.*, 1937, 8:538-543.
3. McCord, W. and McCord, W. *Origins of Alcoholism.* Stanford: Stanford University Press, 1960.
4. Bacon, M. K., Barry, H., and Child, I. L. A cross-cultural study of drinking. II: Relation to other features of culture. *Quart. J. Stud. Alc.*, 1965, 3:29-48.
5. Tahlka, V. *The Alcoholic Personality.* Helsinki: Finnish Foundation for Alcohol Studies, 1966.
6. Blane, H. T. *The Personality of the Alcoholic: Guises of Dependency.* New York: Harper & Row, 1968.
7. McClelland, D. C., Davis, W. N., Kalin, R., et al. *The Drinking Man.* New York: Free Press, 1972.
8. Wilsnack, S. C. The impact of sex roles and women's alcohol use and abuse. In: M. Greenblatt and M. A. Schuckit (Eds.), *Alcoholism Problems in Women and Children.* New York: Grune & Stratton, 1976.
9. McCord, W. and McCord, J. A longitudinal study of the personality of alcoholics. In: N. J. Pittson and C. R. Snyder, (Eds.), *Society Culture and Drinking Patterns.* New York: Wiley, 1962.
10. Tiebout, H. M. Alcoholics Anonymous—an experiment of nature. *Quart. J. Stud. Alc.*, 1961, 22:52-68.

11. Zimberg, S. Evaluation of alcoholism treatment in Harlem. *Quart. J. Stud. Alc.*, 1974, 35:550-557.
12. Pattison, E. M., Coe, R., and Rhodes, R. J. Evaluation of alcoholism treatment: A comparison of three facilities. *Arch. Gen. Psychiat.*, 1969, 20:478-499.
13. Kissin, B., Platz, A., and Su, W. H. Social and psychological factors in the treatment of chronic alcoholism. *J. Psychiat. Res.*, 1970, 8:13-27.
14. Mindlin, D. F. The characteristics of alcoholics as related to therapeutic outcome. *Quart. J. Stud. Alc.*, 1959, 20:604-619.
15. Zimberg, S. The elderly alcoholic. *The Gerontologist*, 1974, 14:221-224.
16. Zimberg, S., Lipscomb, H., and Davis, E. B. Sociopsychiatric treatment of alcoholism in an urban ghetto. *Amer. J. Psychiat.*, 1971, 127:1670-1674.
17. Feldman, D. J., Pattison, E. M., Sobell, L. C., et al. Outpatient alcohol detoxification: Initial findings on 564 patients. *Amer. J. Psychiat.*, 1975, 407-412.
18. Silber, A. An addendum to the technique of psychotherapy with alcoholics. *J. Nerv. Ment. Dis.*, 1970, 150:423-437.
19. Wallace, J. Tactical and strategic use of the preferred defense structure of the recovering alcoholic. *National Council on Alcoholism*, 1976.
20. Pattison, E. M. Abstinence criteria: A critique of abstinence criteria in the treatment of alcoholism. *Int. J. Soc. Psych.*, 1968, 14:268-276.

21

Hypnotherapy Combined with Psychotherapy

JAMES R. HODGE, M.D.

INTRODUCTION

Hypnosis is a very powerful tool in psychotherapy, with a wide range of application: from the superficial treatment of volitional disorders, such as smoking and overeating, through the treatment of specific symptoms, such as phobias; from intermittent use in psychotherapy programs, to being the basic treatment modality in psychotherapy; and finally to hypnoanalysis. It has been used effectively with individuals, with couples, and with groups.

Hypnosis is of least value in conditions in which there is a brief attention span, such as the organic brain syndrome and the acute psychotic episode, because attention is required for trance induction. The effective use of hypnosis depends upon a positive therapeutic relationship; failure to develop this relationship is the primary contraindication to the use of hypnosis as well as the primary reason for its failure.

The use of hypnosis in psychotherapy requires three attributes in the therapist: experience in hypnosis and in psychotherapy, imagination, and courage to try both accepted and innovative techniques. Also, he should always practice within his area of competence—that is, he should use hypnosis only for conditions he would be willing and able to treat without the use of hypnosis.

Inducing a hypnotic trance is the easiest part of hypnosis; more important is the therapeutic use of the hypnotic trance phenomena. The goal of this chapter is to demonstrate how a basic knowledge of psychotherapy and of hypnotic trance phenomena can be integrated into a total treatment program.

Fundamental Concepts of Hypnotherapy

When hypnosis is considered in the treatment program for any condition, the therapist must first make an adequate evaluation of the patient —his life history, his illness, and his psychological state—and then develop at least the beginnings of a positive doctor-patient relationship. The therapist should keep several basic questions in mind:

1. What is the therapeutic goal, regardless of hypnosis, and why?
2. At what point in the process of the illness is therapeutic intervention planned?
3. How can hypnosis help, that is, what are the strategies and tactics available and appropriate for the treatment of this specific patient?

To answer these questions appropriately, the therapist needs a basic understanding and awareness of: 1) the natural history of psychiatric illness in general and the history of the patient's illness in particular, 2) the nature of psychotherapy and the strategies available, and 3) the nature of hypnosis and the strategies and tactics available.

Advantages of Hypnosis

If the therapist is to use hypnosis only in the treatment of conditions which he would otherwise treat without hypnosis, then what are the advantages of hypnosis? There are several:

1. The use of hypnosis can shorten the duration of therapy without interfering with the permanence of results.
2. When used appropriately, it elicits the patient's awareness of his own participation in the treatment process.
3. Even more than the analysis of dreams and the process of free association, hypnosis is truly "the royal road to the unconscious"; it is certainly a more incisive and direct road to the "relevant unconscious." A hazard here is that it is also a royal road to the *therapist's* unconscious, and he must be constantly aware of the process of countertransference.
4. Hypnosis is a powerful tranquilizing agent. It can directly effect relief from some symptoms; it can lead to the moderation of others, thus

permitting their investigation without undue anxiety and without altering their dynamic meaning.

5. Hypnsois can facilitate the interpretation of symbolic material.

6. Hypnosis can promote the affective and relevant recollection of past events for connection with present life experiences.

7. Hypnosis strengthens the doctor-patient relationship. As a result, the patient is more willing to study himself in greater depth, more able to do it at greater speed, and less fearful of attempting new behaviors.

However, in spite of all these advantages, just because you can use hypnosis does not mean that you *should* use it; if you can do as well or better without it, you should do so.

The Nature of Hypnosis and the Hypnotic Relationship

Although no fully satisfactory theory of the nature of hypnosis has been generally accepted, it is essential that the therapist constantly bear in mind that the responsibility for the trance and for what happens during the trance always rests with the *patient*. The therapist does not actually "hypnotize"; instead, he helps the patient to enter a trance. The primary role of the therapist is that of a catalyst, a medium, a guide, a helper, a protector, and someone who can suggest ideas and techniques which the patient is not likely to think of by himself. Essentially, the therapist is a person who can teach the patient how to use the trance.

I assume that the reader has a basic familiarity with trance induction techniques and I will not address this topic here. For those wishing to study it in more detail; the books by Wolberg (1), Chertok (2), Weitzenhoffer (3), and Brenman and Gill (4) are recommended. Most important is that the therapist learn one or two basic techniques which he can use effectively and which he can modify as indicated by the patient's needs. Current concepts of trance induction and deepening are in terms of developing the patient's "talent for hypnosis" or "trance capacity" so that he can be taught to utilize the phenomena of hypnosis at all levels of trance from the very light to the very deep. For many therapeutic purposes the light trance is quite effective, and the therapist should not be deterred by a patient's apparent mediocre talent, for this may be all that is required and it may be improved with practice.

BASIC STRATEGIES OF PSYCHOTHERAPY

Though every therapist has his own concepts of the nature of psychotherapy, I will briefly review the basic types of psychotherapy in terms of strategies and tactics. Knowing and selecting the strategies and tactics that are available are two of the greatest skills in psychotherapy.

Psychotherapy by Promoting Rational Understanding

In the use of this strategy, the primary goal is to promote an understanding of the process of illness: "Now that you *know* the reason for your symptom, you can decide for yourself whether to keep it." It is basically exploratory and explanatory: 1) to find "the reason," or at least an *acceptable* reason, for the illness; 2) to make the irrational rational; and 3) to promote an understanding and acceptance of the acceptable reason.

The strategy of analytically oriented insight psychotherapy is the one in which the techniques of clarification, interpretation, paradoxical intention, and utilization of transference are used more than in any other.

Psychotherapy by the Direct Modification of Behavior

Here, the primary goal is the relief of symptoms and anxiety; however, interpersonal relationships and problem-solving in current life situations are also studied, and although an understanding of the cause is not sought, it may develop. What is being sought is that the patient develop a sense of personal mastery of the symptom and of his life situation: "Now that you are no longer afraid, you can do whatever you wish." The specific tactics of this strategy involve: 1) the behavior therapies, especially assertive training, systematic desensitization, reciprocal inhibition, implosion (flooding) therapy, and aversive conditioning; 2) education and instruction; 3) counseling and exhortation; and 4) paradoxical intention.

Psychotherapy by the Release of Energy

Many symptoms and problems of life situations can be relieved by the release of energy which has been dammed up, blocked, suppressed, or repressed. The primary goal of this strategy is the release of this energy: "Now that you have this out of your system, understand it, and do not fear a recurrence, you no longer need it." This is most often accomplished by: 1) ventilation; 2) abreaction; 3) connecting a feeling with an idea or an event; 4) seeking the barrier to the release of energy and removing it by promoting rational understanding; 5) confrontation through one of the various types of group psychotherapy.

Supportive Psychotherapy

In this strategy, it is acknowledged that no major changes are necessary nor are they likely to occur. The basic goal, then, is to help the patient live with his symptoms either by controlling, modifying, or accepting them or by modifying his life-style: "You are doing a good job. You see how situations like this can be handled. Keep up the good work. Your next appointment will be on. . . ." With transitory problems, such as grief or divorce, the goal is to support the patient through the adjustment period. A program of supportive therapy does not preclude the use of any other therapeutic strategy which may be indicated by the specific situation. The basic tactics in this strategy are support, reassurance, encouragement, promotion of a good therapist-patient relationship, "modeling" or the promotion of identification with the therapist, and the use of medicines appropriate to the condition.

Psychotherapy by the Direct Relief of Symptoms

In selecting this strategy, the therapist assumes that the direct relief of symptoms may be all that is necessary: "Now that your symptom is gone, is there anything else you would like?" This strategy is most helpful in habit pattern disorders (enuresis, tics, nailbiting) or volitional disorders (smoking, overeating, alcoholism). It is acknowledged that direct symptom relief may be followed by the release or substitution of another symptom; this is not necessarily "bad" if the therapist is prepared to continue treatment, possibly selecting another strategy.

The basic tactics in this strategy are those of instruction, exhortation, "planning a program," behavior therapy, direct or indirect suggestions such as may be given with hypnosis, and the use of appropriate medicines.

Psychotherapy by Paradoxical Intention

This particularly interesting strategy is sometimes used as a tactic within other strategies. It takes advantage of the paradoxical nature of human behavior; it stresses the need to confront fears in order to overcome them. Having selected this strategy, the therapist requires the patient not to avoid the symptoms, but actually to confront them, create them, study them, and become an expert on them. By using these tactics, the patient can learn when the symptoms come, how he keeps them going, and what makes them go away; seeking them out, he is no longer embarrassed by them and comes to learn how irrational they are: "Now that you can look at your symptoms without fear, you can understand them better and see how your fear and avoidance have perpetuated them. Now that you know that you are in charge of them, you may either keep them or let them go."

BASIC STRATEGIES OF HYPNOTHERAPY

There are three basic hypnotherapeutic strategies. These are (1) the projective strategy, (2) the strategy of direct and indirect suggestion, and (3) the strategy of behavior modification.

The Projective Strategy of Hypnotherapy

This strategy is similar to the use of projective psychological tests in that the hypnotized subject is requested to project himself into a situation different from that which exists in reality at the moment. Doing this with hypnosis permits him to be simultaneously both the observed and the observer. Some of the numerous tactics within this strategy are given below:

TACTIC 1: *Time distortion*. The subjective experience of time can be changed in many ways. Among these are:

> 1.1 *Age regression*. The basic concept here is to connect the past with the present in terms of memories, symptoms, and affects by having the hypnotized patient regress to an earlier period when an event occurred that is relevant to the current problem. Some techniques are: 1) using the "affect bridge" (6) from the present to the past by intensifying a present affect through hypnotic suggestion and then having the patient go back in time to a previous event where he experienced the same feeling, and then relating the two events; 2) using the "symptom bridge" from the present to the past over which the patient traces his symptom to its beginning and to the circumstances surrounding it; and 3) using the rational selection of a previous event which is chosen to induce abreaction or to study the circumstances around the event or to produce desensitization to that event.
>
> The purposes of age regression are several: 1) to explore the patient's past and to relate his past experiences to the present, especially on an affective basis; 2) to release the patient's dammed up energies associated with past experiences and present anxieties; and 3) to help the patient master the feelings of helplessness associated with his past experiences.
>
> 1.2 *Time compression and time expansion*. The subjective experience of the passage of time is changed by suggestion so that time can

be perceived as passing more rapidly, for example, when the patient is in pain, or more slowly, as when the patient is feeling well.

1.3   *Age progression.* In a sense, this involves forecasting the future by getting the patient to perceive how he may appear or behave at some future time.

TACTIC 2. *The production of hallucinations or dreams.* The dreams of a hypnotized patient can be analyzed in the same way that normally occurring dreams are analyzed in analytically oriented psychotherapy, but with the added advantage that the dream can be suggested to occur not only during normal sleep but also during the therapy session. Dreams can even be projected as hallucinations in which the patient can participate and then analyze. Even more, hallucinations and dreams whose meanings are not obvious can be reexperienced, or can be caused to recur with the use of different symbols, until the meaning becomes clear.

TACTIC 3. *Hypnoanalysis.* Hypnoanalysis is the procedure of analytically oriented psychotherapy taking place while the patient is in a hypnotic trance. Although this is rarely done *in toto,* during any given session or series of sessions most of the analytic therapy may occur while the patient is in a trance. This tactic is particularly helpful when the patient cannot confront the discussion of repressed material in the unhypnotized state but can discuss it relatively easily while in a trance knowing that he does not have to remember it upon awakening until he is ready to do so.

TACTIC 4. *Connecting affect and experience in the present.* This technique is especially helpful when the patient has physical or psychosomatic problems and denies the presence or relevance of his emotions. The symptom is intensified by suggestion, and while he is experiencing this he is requested to develop some affect of equal intensity which he will be able to recognize and express both behaviorally and verbally. This is a powerful method of producing insight.

TACTIC 5. *The mini-vacation.* The patient may briefly escape an intolerable situation by going on a 10- or 15-minute vacation to a place of his own choosing so that he may return refreshed. Since the ability for only a light trance is required, this tactic is most suitable for a person who has learned self-hypnosis and can use it between sessions.

TACTIC 6. *Behavior therapy.* Here, all the basic behavior therapy techniques can be accentuated and facilitated, especially the technique of relaxation by hypnotic suggestion. Particularly helpful is the method of psychodynamic desensitization in which the patient is asked to take "one step beyond" his expressed fear and to imagine what would happen if he were actually in the anxiety evoking situation. He will almost always find some fear of being out of control, and treatment of this fear is often of more value than treatment of the expressed fear.

TACTIC 7. *Ego state therapy.* The patient is asked to identify various aspects of his personality and to act out these states in the session, much as is done in Transactional Analysis.

The Strategy of Direct and Indirect Suggestion

Because it has often been said that one of the reasons Freud stopped using hypnosis was that his direct suggestions did not work, it has become almost axiomatic that hypnotherapists should not use direct suggestions to remove symptoms. As good an axiom as this may be, there are exceptions. The direct confrontation-challenge to the symptom is almost always bound to fail unless 1) the doctor-patient relationship is such that the patient can accept the suggestion and its results, and 2) a face-saving way out can be left for both the patient and the symptom. It is accepted that direct symptom removal may result in either the liberation or the substitution of another symptom by the patient for psychodynamic reasons, and that this is not necessarily undesirable if the therapist is prepared to make use of this experience in further treatment. Because of this phenomenon, however, most suggestive therapies have now turned from the simple directive, "Your pain (or other symptom) will disappear now," to indirect suggestions such as, "Here is a way to handle your pain (symptom) until we can get rid of it permanently," or, "If you are ready now to start giving up your symptom, here are some ways to do it." Sometimes a direct interpretation to the receptive patient will result in removal of symptoms as in the case of the woman who had had a constant headache for 26 years and who was told while hypnotized, "You have been carrying a heavy burden," and the symptom disappeared. The direct suggestion is imposed upon the patient; the indirect suggestion enlists the patient's aid.

Indirect suggestion is almost always accompanied by a great many direct suggestions; however, the indirect nature of these suggestions for symptom relief should be emphasized. The symptom is rarely attacked directly. Instead, some aspect of the symptom is modified while it is permitted to continue temporarily so that it may be studied analytically, removed gradually by desensitization or other behavior therapy methods, or allowed to die out by attrition. Self-hypnosis is a very effective technique which patients can use with only a small amount of training, but part of that training is learning not to attempt to remove the symptom directly. It may take longer to teach this than it takes to teach self-hypnosis itself. This hypnotherapeutic strategy, one of the most versatile, effective, and frequently used, involves what I like to call "emotional judo" in which the therapist uses the patient's momentum and problems for therapeutic purposes. Some of the tactics within this strategy are:

TACTIC 1. *Symptom substitution.* This involves the planned and purposeful replacement of one symptom with another. A classical way of doing this is to move the symptom from one part of the body to another, preferably within the same organ system; e.g. if a person is having a muscular pain, it is desirable to substitute some other form of muscular pain or muscular activity. When this tactic is chosen, it is important for the therapist to remember that it is the patient who substitutes the symptom, not the therapist. The therapist only takes advantage of the patient's own abilities, and helps him to change the symptoms in a controlled way for therapeutic purposes.

TACTIC 2. *Hypnosis as a deterrent.* Hypnosis can be used as a deterrent to almost any kind of acting-out behavior, e.g. suicide. When used as a direct confrontation-challenge to *prevent* such behavior, it may actually compel the patient to respond to the challenge. However, a suggestion such as, "You will not be able to carry out a serious suicidal act without first discussing it with me in my office very clearly," serves to enlist the patient's aid by giving him a task to perform before he can carry out his suicide attempt. It also gives the therapist a chance to work with the patient and not be caught by surprise.

TACTIC 3. *Promoting personal mastery.* General ego strengthening through promoting personal mastery is a valid, effective, and often undefined tactic of therapy. Many neuroses, especially the traumatic neurosis, are precipitated by the patient's having been caught by surprise as a helpless victim of circumstances beyond his control; this feeling of helplessness also often occurs as a characterological state. When this tactic is used, the goal is to promote feelings of strength, competence, and "copability." Sometimes this can be accomplished by direct suggestion, though more often it is promoted through the use of projective techniques, such as age regression with abreaction, or through the behavior therapy techniques. Another useful technique here is to have the patient visualize himself the way he was as a small helpless child ("Little Billy") and then to have him visualize himself with all the assets that he has as an adult ("Big Bill"). Visualizing this contrast lessens the sense of helplessness and increases the patient's awareness that he is no longer the helpless "Little Billy."

During the process of trance induction, I repeatedly state to the patient that as he enters and deepens the trance he will feel progressively more "relaxed, comfortable, pleasant, strong, and secure." These sensations serve as a baseline experience of the trance state, alleviate many unspoken fears, and cause the patient to expect that the trance will always be a pleasant and secure experience. As he proves through repeated experiences that this is true, he develops confidence in his ability to use hypnosis. Thus, he is better able to tolerate his symptoms and to confront them in a therapeutic manner.

TACTIC 4. *Direct and indirect control of symptoms.* For the use of this tactic the imagination of the therapist and his knowledge of hypnosis are particularly valuable.

In the treatment of pain, for example, sometimes all that is required for relief is for the hypnotized patient to be told that he will have no pain or that the pain will be of a different nature, as every dentist knows. Sometimes merely entering the trance will bring relief. Sometimes more specific techniques are chosen. One method is to give a psychological injection of novocaine to an affected trigger area. Another is to teach the patient to develop a glove anesthesia of one hand and to transfer that anesthesia to any part of the body that is painful. Another method is to teach the patient to take the pain from wherever it is into his hand and then to drop it into the nearest wastebacket. Still another, more physiological, method is to create a feeling of either heat or cold in an inert object, or in the therapist's hand, or in the patient's hand, and then to transfer that sensation to the affected area; this is particularly helpful for muscular types of pain, as is applying a psychological splint or brace.

Chronic and recurrent symptoms of many types can be aborted or attenuated by these techniques, such as episodes of anxiety or even of schizophrenia. The patient can be taught, for example, to recognize the earliest symptoms of the illness and then to use self-hypnosis with relaxation or taking a "mini-vacation" until the precipitating event can be analyzed and the problem brought under control.

TACTIC 5. *Creating physiological changes.* In the hypnotic state, it is possible to create physiological changes which can be used for diagnostic purposes, for a symptom bridge to connect affect with symptoms, and for direct treatment purposes. Biofeedback studies have demonstrated what practitioners of hypnosis have known for many years, namely, that the autonomic nervous system is not entirely beyond conscious control.

It is well known not only that sensations can be changed by hypnotic suggestion, but that heart rate can be altered, blood pressure changed, some bleeding controlled, and muscle spasm relieved. Hypnotic suggestion has both produced and relieved asthma attacks and has given temporary relief of bronchitis. It has been successfully used as a diuretic ("Each one of your body cells will squeeze out the excess fluid"), has relieved menstrual cramps by suggestions of relaxation and by hypnodiathermy, and has also altered the duration but not the occurrence of menstrual periods. Injections of "psychological cortisone" have been effective in treating some skin conditions. A very simple and effective suggestion is that the desired effects of any medicine, from a tranquilizer to an antibiotic, will be doubled while the undesirable effects will be halved.

The Behavior Modification Strategy of Hypnotherapy

The basic theory of behavior modification is that persistent maladaptive anxiety responses to stress are the nucleus of most neuroses, that anxiety is conditioned, and that it can be deconditioned. Almost all forms of behavior modification involve: (a) teaching the patient to relax even in the presence of stress; (b) creating visual and other sensory images, either of pleasant or of feared situations; and (c) presenting these images to the patient in a systematic manner in his imagination before exposing him to the anxiety-evoking situation in real life.

TACTIC 1. *Intensification of behavior modification techniques.* For the patient with a talent for hypnosis, all of the techniques described above can be facilitated and intensified, making therapy more effective and often shorter. The effect of hypnotically induced hallucinations, for example, is much more profound and realistic to the patient than is the simple use of his imagination in the unhypnotized state.

TACTIC 2. *Biofeedback.* Hypnosis is a natural and valuable adjunct to instrumental biofeedback training in which the patient is trained by a process of operant conditioning to achieve both specific and generalized relaxation and to produce other bodily changes. Further, the patient who can use hypnosis can bring about the changes sought in biofeedback training much more rapidly, regularly, and intensively than can other patients. Even more, since the ultimate goal of biofeedback training is for the patient to learn to produce the desired effects without the instrument, which does no more than to feed back information to the patient about how he is doing, hypnosis is of particular value in that it is always available. Merely entering a light trance for self-hypnosis can produce a recognizable state of general relaxation, and self-suggestion about specific changes may then be given if desired. Hypnosis, then, not only is an effective adjunct to instrumental biofeedback training, but can be used by itself as a form of subjective or non-instrumental biofeedback training.

TACTIC 3. *IRD*. The "IRD," or the "internal regulatory device," is a specific supportive, ego-strengthening, and quasi-instrumental biofeedback technique which has been found particularly helpful for patients who have fluctuating or unstable symptoms or anxieties. This concept occurred to me during the treatment of a patient suffering from cyclical bipolar affective disease before lithium became available. Searching for a method to control her mood swings from mania to depression, I gave the following suggestions: "I would like you to look into my right eye while I put one finger on each side of your head. At the spot where these two lines intersect you will soon feel a tingling sensation. We are creating an internal regulatory device in your brain which will work just like a thermostat. We can now put your euphoria on a scale of 0 to +10 and your depression on a scale of 0 to —10 and we can set this thermostat so that it will start to function at either +7 or —7 and your symptoms will not be able to go beyond these levels." As soon as we established that this technique was effective, we were gradually able to reduce the number-settings of what came to be called the "Psychestat" until the range of the mood swings was essentially within normal limits, where they have remained for many years. A refinement of this technique developed following the exclamation of a patient: "I feel that there is a part of *you* in my head!" Every experienced therapist is aware that over a period of time the patient tends to introject various aspects of the therapist; i.e. the patient gets to know the therapist just as the therapist gets to know the patient. For appropriate patients, then, this process can be utilized in a supportive way by "lending" the patient a "part of the therapist" along with the internal regulatory device. With this, the patient can then utilize the therapist even though the therapist is not physically present. Naturally, this technique should not be used early in therapy because a good doctor-patient relationship must first be established. When I use this technique, I specify that the situation may continue to exist for a defined period of time such as a week or a month, though it may be renewable as often as necessary.

THE COMBINATION OF PSYCHOTHERAPY STRATEGIES WITH HYPNOTHERAPY STRATEGIES

Hypnosis is used most effectively when it is used systematically, taking into account 1) the natural history of psychiatric illness, 2) how the patient's illness fits into that natural history, 3) the psychotherapy strategies available, and 4) the hypnotherapy strategies available. Hypnosis and psychotherapy are not the same thing. Hypnosis is merely a method of facilitating the overall program as a part of the treatment process. It may be used during most of every session, during part of every session, intermittently during the course of therapy, or regularly until a specific goal is accomplished. When the therapist elects to use hypnosis, he should keep in mind what he wants to accomplish, how he can accomplish it, and why hypnosis will be of value. Just because he *can* use hypnosis does not mean that he *should* use it.

The following rationale for using hypnotherapeutic strategies assumes that there is a natural course of psychiatric illness just as there is a natural history of physical illness and that in this natural history certain identifiable factors are involved, viz. a predisposing personality, a current conflict, an external precipitating stress, the development of anxiety, a primary gain or symptom-forming factor, the symptom complex itself, and a secondary gain or symptom-fixing factor. It further assumes the formulation of a total treatment program in which the therapeutic goal and sites of intervention are selected on the basis of this natural history. In choosing the site of intervention in accord with this formulation, the therapist should consider 1) the purpose of intervention at that site, 2) the psychotherapy strategies available and applicable, and 3) the hypnotherapy strategies available and appropriate. Further, the selection of the hypnotherapy strategies always depends upon the preselection of the psychotherapy strategies.

Predisposing Personality

The predisposing personality refers to all the genetic, constitutional, developmental, educational, and experiential factors which constitute the basic personality of the individual.

1. *Purpose.* The basic goal is to promote insight into the nature of the personality and understanding of it by demonstrating recurring patterns of behavior, the relationship between the past and the present, and the process of repetition compulsion or how present behavior is an extension of or a repetition of past behavior which may or may not be appropriate to the current life situation of the patient. Awareness of the self as an individual in the process of development is stimulated, and the patient becomes aware of the difference between himself as a child and himself as an adult; he learns the difference between "Little Billy" and "Big

Bill." Unconscious memories and experiences become conscious and are analyzed as part of the developmental pattern so that the patient may develop more of a free choice about what his further development will be.

Treatment designed to make changes in this area must be considered as long-term therapy. However, information obtained *about* the predisposing personality may be very useful in brief therapy and in therapy focused in other areas of the process of illness.

2. *Psychotherapy strategies.* The basic psychotherapy strategy chosen for work in this area is that of promoting rational understanding. During this process, psychotherapy by the release of energy may occur spontaneously or by rational selection. Sometimes, especially if a discrete symptom exists, behavior modification techniques may precede the development of rational understanding, for change may produce insight as frequently as insight will produce change. This is particularly noticeable when a strategy such as the use of paradoxical intention is introduced early in the therapy process, for it enables the patient to focus on exactly what he is doing, thinking, and feeling; it compels change which produces insight which may be followed by a more fundamental change.

3. *Hypnotherapy strategies.* When the psychotherapy strategy of promoting rational understanding is selected, the projective hypnotherapeutic techniques are most helpful, though any of the methods of hypnotherapy may be used as the developing situations might indicate. The therapist must be particularly careful, however, of providing too much relief of anxiety through direct suggestion, for otherwise this will increase the dependency of the patient on the therapist and will interfere with the progress of the analysis. It must be remembered that the goal of the therapy is insight and understanding, and that to accomplish this it may be necessary to confront anxiety or to liberate the anxiety that is bound in the production of symptoms. The therapist must be prepared to help the patient with this anxiety.

Current Conflict

Just before and at the time of onset of an illness, a person almost invariably experiences a conflict in his life. This conflict is continuous, troublesome, and disturbing the equilibrium of his life; and it usually involves his feelings about himself, his activities, or his relationship with some other significant person.

1. *Purpose.* The basic goal is to relate the presenting symptom to the current problems of living, and clarification of this relationship may be

all that is necessary for the patient. This may not be easy, however. It should be recalled that part of the function of the symptom is to conceal these current problems, yet it must also reveal them, especially when the symptom is carefully analyzed. Here again, insight may precede change or may follow it. For many patients a personality change is not necessary, though the patient may obtain self-knowledge which he can put to effective use if later episodes should develop. It is in this area of intervention that most of the useful short-term psychotherapy is done.

2. *Psychotherapy strategies.* The basic strategy here, also, is that of promoting rational understanding. Intervention in depth is not usually necessary, though it is often helpful to relate the new insights to the predisposing personality and patterns of behavior.

3. *Hypnotherapy strategies.* When therapy by promoting rational understanding is selected, the projective hypnotherapy techniques are of most value, especially those involving age regression using the affect bridge or the symptom bridge from the present to the past. Hypnotherapeutic techniques of the direct and indirect suggestion type may be necessary or helpful to give support to the patient while the basic therapy is proceeding.

External Precipitating Stress

A person with an appropriate predisposing personality and current conflict can be said to be waiting, even hoping, for something to happen which will solve his problem; and this "something" is often inaccurately called "the cause" of the illness when it is only a triggering factor or a permissive event. It may be a severe trauma or it may be an innocuous event which is seized upon as the solution to the current conflict.

1. *Purpose.* The primary goal is to relieve the stress or its sequelae whenever possible by the use of medicinal or psychotherapeutic methods. It is necessary to demonstrate the effect of the stress to the patient while relating the stress to the ever-present current conflict and the predisposing personality by promoting recall of the circumstances surrounding the external precipitating event. Desensitization of the patient to the stress or its memories is essential, as in a traumatic neurosis or a grief reaction. If the external precipitating stress consists of a series of minor stresses, relief of this input overload is important.

When early intervention is possible, therapy focused in this area is most effective; and sometimes only a few sessions may be necessary, especially when the external precipitating stress is quickly related to the current conflict. When early intervention is not possible, therapy may not be able to be limited to this area and will therefore take longer.

2. *Psychotherapy strategies.* Any or all of the psychotherapy strategies can be used during intervention at the level of the external precipitating stress as long as the therapist follows the basic principle that the patient must confront the stressful situation and recognize its effects. Psychotherapy by promoting rational understanding is effective in helping the patient to understand how the stress developed and how it is related to the current conflict and the predisposing personality. Psychotherapy by the modification of behavior using systematic desensitization and rehearsal techniques can be particularly helpful, especially as the patient is taught to relax while he recalls and contemplates the stressful situation. Aversive conditioning can sometimes be of value here. Repeated ventilation and abreaction can be especially helpful for releasing the dammed up energy and emotion associated with the stress. The direct relief or alleviation of symptoms through medicinal and/or psychotherapeutic methods, when possible, can be very helpful and supportive to the patient as he works through his problems, but it should not allow him to avoid working on them. Paradoxical intention helps the patient to confront the stressful situation, its memories, and its effects by compelling him to think about it in minute detail.

3. *Hypnotherapy strategies.* Any of the hypnotherapy techniques can be effective as long as they fit in with the psychotherapy strategies already selected. The most appropriate of the projective strategies are those of time distortion, abreaction, and the production of dreams and hallucinations. Hypnotherapy by direct and indirect suggestion is helpful when used to control symptoms and to give psychological support as the patient develops personal mastery of the situation and strengthens his personality. Accentuation of the behavior modification techniques by hypnotic suggestion will improve their effectiveness.

The Development of Anxiety

Whenever a stressful situation occurs, anxiety accompanies it or follows it. Anxiety is an essential ingredient in almost all psychiatric symptoms; but even more than this, the basic anxiety stimulates the personality defenses to attempt to control it, and these defenses will characteristically create symptoms in this attempt. The symptom, then, is an unsuccessful attempt of the personality to control anxiety.

1. *Purpose.* The main goal is to encourage the patient to become aware

of and to confront the primary anxiety related to the external precipitating stress, the current conflict, and the predisposing personality. The patient is to learn that the anxiety is either irrational, unnecessary, maladaptive, or simply not currently helpful to him. He is to learn to handle both current and future anxiety in a healthy, productive manner instead of in a pathological manner.

This is another point at which early intervention in the process of illness is not only helpful in relieving present symptoms but also in preventing future ones. Short-term therapy is often quite effective here.

2. *Psychotherapy strategies.* Any one or all of the psychotherapy strategies can be used in treating the problem of anxiety; but whatever strategy is chosen, the anxiety must first be admitted and confronted, and the patient must learn that fear is perfectly normal. When the strategy is to promote rational understanding, the current anxiety should be related to both past and future anxieties, for anxiety by its very nature is future-oriented in terms that "this could happen to me again." In this sense, dynamic desensitization is particularly helpful as the patient is asked to fantasize what would happen if he were in the anxiety-evoking situation. The key question here is "What if . . . ?" Promoting the release of energy will also be facilitated by connecting the present with the past. If the anxiety is considered maladaptive, it can be attacked directly by using one of the behavior therapy approaches, such as systematic desensitization or reciprocal inhibition. Supportive therapy, including the appropriate use of psychiatric medicines, can demonstrate that the anxiety can be relieved or modified so that it is not too intense for the patient to confront. Confronting the anxiety by taking charge of it, as taught by paradoxical intention, is effective in relieving the anxiety and developing an understanding of it.

3. *Hypnotherapy strategies.* The choice of hypnotherapy strategies depends upon the choice of psychotherapy strategies. Projective techniques are particularly helpful, especially with time distortion tactics such as age regression to recent and remote past anxiety situations, time compression to demonstrate a method of controlling anxiety and time progression to forecast how the patient can become in the future. The release of energy is promoted by age regression and abreaction. While this may be unpleasant for the patient, it is also supportive in that it shows that he can survive the anxiety and that it can be controlled. Direct suggestions about controlling the degree and duration of anxiety are supportive and promote mastery of the fear of anxiety. Accentuation of behavior therapy techniques with hypnosis aids the development of

a sense of mastery, and the installation of the "internal regulatory device" can be very supportive.

Primary Gain or Symptom-Forming Factor

Anxiety, like pain, is an unpleasant sensation, and the patient attempts to relieve it at all costs. The primary gain or symptom-forming factor is the process by which the patient attempts to do this; it is the process by which the defense mechanisms bind the anxiety by attaching it to a symptom or by creating a symptom.

1. *Purpose.* The primary goal here is to help the patient see and understand how symptom formation occurs and that it is not necessary for him to develop or maintain symptoms. It is important that he understand that he causes the symptoms himself in order to escape a sense of intolerable anxiety, that he "owns" them, and that he is not merely their victim. He should be helped to understand how he has handled stress in the past, continues to use the same techniques in the present, and can be expected to continue this way in the future unless he understands these processes better.

Treatment designed to make changes in this area must be considered as long-term therapy; however, information obtained *about* these processes may be very useful in briefer therapy and in working in other treatment areas.

2. *Psychotherapy strategies.* Only one basic psychotherapy strategy is appropriate here and that is the analytically-oriented strategy of promoting rational understanding through studying defenses, resistances, and transference. Gestalt methods and paradoxical intention may be helpful adjunctive techniques.

3. *Hypnotherapy strategies.* When analytically-oriented therapy is chosen, the most frequently indicated hypnotherapeutic techniques are the projective ones, especially the hypnotic analysis of natural dreams and the production of hypnotic dreams for analysis, and age regression using the affect bridge and the symptom bridge. Creating substitute symptoms by direct suggestion and then analyzing them is, in effect, creating a "parallel neurosis" much like that of a transference neurosis; and analysis of the substitute symptom makes the original symptom easier to analyze. Supportive suggestions should be given only with care so as not to distort the processes which are being analyzed. Observation and analysis of the patient's behavior during trance induction may be very enlightening, as may failure to dehypnotize if it should occur.

The Symptom Complex

The symptom is almost invariably the patient's presenting complaint, but it is important for the therapist to remember that the symptom is really only a stage in the development of the overall illness. It represents an unsuccessful attempt of the psychological defense mechanisms to control the primary anxiety and therefore involves elements of the primary anxiety as well as elements of the secondary anxiety about the presence of the symptom itself. The symptom, with its anxiety, represents a "cry for help" and is a "ticket of admission" to therapy.

1. *Purpose.* The primary goal here is the relief of symptoms while preventing their recurrence or replacement by other symptoms. This is accomplished by 1) relating the symptom to the basic anxiety, the current conflict, and the predisposing personality; 2) providing insight that the symptoms are not really necessary, are unadaptive or maladaptive, and do not truly solve the underlying problem; and 3) identifying the underlying problem by "getting behind the symptoms."

The symptom complex is the point at which all of the patient's problems come to a focus. It is a good place to intervene, perhaps the best; but intervention here is usually only the beginning of therapy. With the symptom as the focal point, therapy may spread out to all aspects of the process of illness.

2. *Psychotherapy strategies.* Any of the therapeutic modalities can be used here, either alone, in combination, or in sequence. The decisions must be made by the therapist according to his own continuing evaluation of the patient's needs, assets, liabilities, and progress in treatment. The strategy of choice is psychotherapy by promoting rational understanding; but this may be neither necessary nor possible, depending on the nature of the problem and the capacity of the patient for psychotherapy. Sometimes all that is necessary for a given patient is the relief of his presenting symptom with or without some degree of insight, as exemplified by the patient with a 26-year-old headache which was relieved in two appointments with the simple interpretation that she had been carrying a heavy burden. It is predictable that the mere relief of such a prolonged symptom without taking a history and providing insight through interpretation would have had little lasting value, but the combination did.

3. *Hypnotherapy strategies.* When the psychotherapy strategies of promoting rational understanding and/or of promoting the release of energy have been chosen, any or all of the hypnotherapeutic projective tactics

are especially indicated. Direct or indirect suggestion therapy may be effective either for temporary symptom relief while the analysis is proceeding or for long-term supportive therapy. The production of substitute symptoms by hypnotic suggestion is analogous to the production of substitute dreams, and they can be analyzed in the same way. Behavior modification may be a primary hypnotherapy strategy at this level of intervention, or it may be chosen as an adjunctive technique for the other strategies.

Secondary Gain or Symptom-Fixing Factor

The secondary gain is what keeps the established illness, the symptom complex, from going away like a self-limiting condition such as the common cold. Since the primary anxiety is not totally relieved by the creation of the symptom complex, the symptom must continue because of the danger of releasing the primary anxiety. Often, however, by the time the patient comes for therapy, the primary anxiety has essentially been dissipated, and the symptom continues almost as a habit or as a new life-style; it has become ego-syntonic. Further, the patient may not only adapt to the symptom itself, but may consciously or unconsciously learn that there are secondary advantages to having it; and if this occurs, he will hold on to it at all costs.

1. *Purpose.* The primary goal of treatment in this area is to break up the continuing development of the process of illness and to prevent the illness from becoming ego-syntonic. It can be very difficult, but the patient should be helped to develop insight into how he "uses" his illness as he has learned in the past to use other situations, how he must remain ill to do so, how the cost to him is high in terms of discomfort and dissatisfaction, and how there may be different and better ways to accomplish what he really wants to accomplish.

This is one of the most difficult areas to work in, partly because of the confusion between secondary gain and malingering, and partly because the patient has acquired a vested interest in maintaining his symptom. It is also one of the most important areas to work in, for therapy here, especially early in the illness, is true preventive medicine in the best sense of the word. It may prevent the need for rehabilitative therapy later. This is one of the areas in which other special techniques such as environmental manipulation and/or family therapy may be used effectively. Intervention in this area may be either preventive or therapeutic.

2. *Psychotherapy strategies.* Direct symptom relief, especially when early

intervention is possible, prevents the development of secondary gain. After the secondary gain is entrenched, however, a direct relief of symptoms may be almost impossible because such relief could threaten the patient's entire life-style. Any psychotherapy strategy, however, can be effective if it modifies the symptom, interferes with the development of the process of illness, or disrupts the equilibrium of the established illness. Environmental manipulation can be effective not only in preventing the development of any secondary gains, but also in eliminating their effectiveness and their desirability for the patient. None of the psychotherapy strategies are likely to be successful here, however, unless *the therapist* 1) can develop a rational understanding of the nature of the process of illness and the value of the secondary gains for his particular patient, and 2) can impart this same understanding to the patient through the strategy of promoting rational understanding, including analysis of how the illness affects the patient's environment and the other people in it. This process almost always involves the laborious procedure of identifying, analyzing, and interpreting the patient's conscious and unconscious resistance. It is in working in this area that the therapist and the patient are most likely to become adversaries, and thus both transference and countertransference phenomena abound. These must be handled by the therapist, whether or not they are interpreted.

3. *Hypnotherapy strategies.* When the psychotherapy strategy of promoting rational understanding is employed, the projective techniques directed toward cure, relief, and understanding of the symptoms are of most value. A combination of age regression and age progression can enable the patient to see himself as he was, as he is, and as he would like to become. Hypnoanalysis can be particularly helpful in that the patient, while in a trance, may be able to discuss things which he would not be able to discuss otherwise. Hypnotherapy using direct and indirect suggestions to give some degree of control of discomfort, or to produce substitute symptoms for analysis, can help to keep the patient stable enough yet in a sufficient state of disequilibrium that he will keep working on his problems and his "cure." Ego state therapy may assist the patient to become aware of the different parts of his personality, some of which may be working for cure while others are working to maintain the illness. The behavior modification strategy, especially with the special tactics such as biofeedback and the internal regulatory device, may alleviate the symptoms and maintain the patient's interest in treatment while those persons in his environment who are influenced by his symp-

toms are taking the opportunity to change their own behaviors, thus having an indirect positive effect upon the patient.

SUMMARY

Hypnosis has a wide range of application in the field of psychotherapy, but it is only a part of the overall psychotherapeutic program for any patient. It can be of value in the treatment of almost any condition. Hypnosis is of most value when it is used according to a rationale involving the concept of intervention at various sites of the natural history of the illness. Hypnotherapeutic strategies should be selected on the bases of 1) the purpose of intervention, and 2) the psychotherapeutic strategies already selected.

EXAMPLES OF HYPNOTHERAPEUTIC INTERVENTION

Dream analysis (7). A woman had a recurring dream of being in a closed room with thousands of spiders. While in a deep trance, she was asked to repeat the dream. She did, but it produced extreme anxiety. She was then asked to put distance between herself and the dream by watching it on a hallucinated television set. She noted that the spiders had features like those of her mother. She then recalled a current conflict with her mother and related this to childhood experiences with mother and father, then to her relationship with her husband. Again repeating the dream, she felt a desire to step on the spiders; she also visualized my presence in the background, and as I came to the foreground the spiders disappeared and she felt well. Interpretation is left to the reader.

Control of symptoms and age progression (8). A young marine had recurrent dissociative episodes in which his body was "taken over" by his dead dog. The episodes were unpredictable, and dangerous in that he would attempt to gouge out his eyes; so he had to remain under observation in the hospital and to be restrained during the attack. He was given the post-hypnotic suggestions that he could not have an attack without also being in a trance and that while having the experience he could not bring his hands within two inches of his eyes. Communication was established with "Brownie" by a ouija board technique, and "Brownie" could tell us when the next attack would occur. The patient was released from the hospital with post-hypnotic suggestions that at the scheduled time nothing could prevent him from returning to the hospital and that he could not have the attack without being in the psychiatric unit.

The suggestions protected the patient and permitted definitive therapy to proceed.

Hypnosis as a deterrent (9). A recurrently suicidal patient was given the suggestion that she could not make a serious suicide attempt without first discussing it with me in the office and that I would see her as an emergency if necessary. She became suicidal, called, and was seen. Her thought processes were severely suicidal, and she revealed that she had a gun in her purse. She readily entered a trance, revealed the nature of her current conflict with her husband, was given a face-saving way out, traded her gun to me for two sleeping pills, and returned the next day for conjoint therapy with her husband.

Age regression and hallucination production. A middle-aged man had severe pain and disability of his left arm as the result of an industrial accident. Part of his treatment involved age regression with abreaction of the incident. This was so anxiety-inducing that we reproduced it on a hallucinated television set. This was still too intense, so we speeded up the projection. When he was able to tolerate this, we slowed it down and ultimately he abreacted the episode repeatedly. In doing this he became aware of his anger and resentment at the company and also of his sense of being a cripple and losing his masculinity. This made the significant difference in his overall treatment program.

Producing physiological change. The patient mentioned previously had received many surgical forms of treatment, including nerve blocks. During one episode of pain, I touched a pencil to his neck and had him experience receiving a stellate ganglion block. He developed a typical Horner's syndrome, and his pain was relieved.

The mini-vacation. A woman, experienced in the use of hypnosis, reported that between sessions she had gone to the dentist, requested no novocaine for the first time ever, and had taken a vacation in the mountains while the dentist did his work. After several sessions like this, the dentist remarked, "Your hypnosis is the best thing that ever happened to me."

Aborting a psychotic episode. A woman had had episodes of schizophrenia requiring hospitalization and ECT about twice yearly for five years. She learned to use hypnosis, to recognize her earliest symptoms, and to call me when these occurred. If I could not see her immediately in the office, I would have her enter a trance by a prearranged signal and tell her to relax until I could see her and to analyze her current life situation. The episodes were aborted, became less frequent, and required less intervention by me. Following an emergency hysterectomy, she became catatonic at night. Using a telephone held to her ear by the house physician, I gave her the prearranged signal. She entered the trance, spoke calmly with me, accepted my supportive suggestions, slept well that night, and had no residuals the next day.

Hypnoanalysis involving secondary gain. A young woman was making great progress with her claustrophobia, but had reached an impasse. One day she entered a trance more deeply than ever and said, "Doctor, I don't want to remember this when I come out of the trance. I need my symptom. Please don't take it away from me." She did not remember saying this and left me with the difficult decision as to whether to attempt to continue her treatment. Using my best judgment under the circumstances, I arranged to gracefully terminate her treatment as "improved."

REFERENCES AND RECOMMENDED READING

1. Wolberg, L. *Medical Hypnosis, Vol. 1: The Principles of Hypnotherapy, Vol. II: The Practice of Hypnotherapy.* New York: Grune & Stratton, 1948.
2. Chertok, L. *Hypnosis.* New York: Pergamon Press, 1966.
3. Weitzenhoffer, A. M. *General Techniques of Hypnotism.* New York: Grune & Stratton, 1957.
4. Brenman, M. and Gill, M. *Hypnotherapy: A Survey of the Literature.* New York: Wiley, 1964.
5. Kroger, W. and Fezler, W. *Hypnosis and Behavior Modification: Imagery Conditioning.* Philadelphia: J. B. Lippincott, 1976.
6. Watkins, J. The affect bridge: A hypnoanalytic technique. *Int. J. Clin. Exper. Hyp.,* 1971, 19 (1):21-27.
7. Hodge, J. An exploration of psychodynamics with hypnosis. *Amer. J. Clin. Hyp.,* 1969, 12 (2):91-94.
8. Hodge, J. The management of dissociative reactions with hypnosis. *Int. J. Clin. Exper. Hyp.,* 1959, 7 (4):217-221
9. Hodge, J. Hypnosis as a deterrent to suicide. *Amer. J. Clin. Hyp.,* 1972, 15 (1): 20-24.
10. Hodge, J. Contractual aspects of hypnosis. *Inter. J. Clin. Exper. Hyp.,* 1976, 14 (4): 391-399.
11. Frankel, F. H. *Hypnosis: Trance as a Coping Mechanism.* New York: Plenum Press, 1978.

APPENDIX

THE SELECTION OF PSYCHOTHERAPY AND HYPNOTHERAPY STRATEGIES

Site of Intervention in Process of Illness	Purpose	Psychotherapy Strategies and Tactics of Most Value	Hypnotherapy Strategies and Tactics of Most Value
Predisposing Personality	1. Understand patterns of behavior 2. Relate past to present 3. Promote growth and development	1. Promoting Rational Understanding 2. Release of Energy 3. Direct Modification of Behavior	1. Projective
Current Conflict	1. Relate symptom to current problems of living 2. Prevent secondary gain 3. Brief therapy possible	1. Promoting Rational Understanding	1. Projective a. Age regression 2. Direct and Indirect Suggestion
External Precipitating Stress	1. Relieve stress 2. Relate stress to current conflict and predisposing personality 3. Prevent secondary gain 4. Brief therapy possible	1. Promoting Rational Understanding 2. Direct Modification of Behavior 3. Release of Energy 4. Direct Relief of Symptoms 5. Supportive Psychotherapy 6. Paradoxical Intention	1. Projective a. Time distortion b. Dreams and Hallucinations 2. Direct and Indirect Suggestion 3. Behavior Modification
Development of Anxiety	1. Promote awareness of anxiety and confront it 2. Relate to external precipitating stress and current conflict 3. Brief therapy possible	1. Promoting Rational Understanding 2. Direct Modification of Behavior 3. Supportive Therapy 4. Release of Energy 5. Paradoxical Intention 6. Direct Relief of Symptoms	1. Projective a. Time distortion Age regression and age progression 2. Direct and Indirect Suggestion 3. Behavior Modification (with or without IRD)

THE SELECTION OF PSYCHOTHERAPY AND HYPNOTHERAPY STRATEGIES (*continued*)

Site of Intervention in Process of Illness	Purpose	Psychotherapy Strategies and Tactics of Most Value	Hypnotherapy Strategies and Tactics of Most Value

Primary Gain or Symptom Forming Factor	1. Insight into psychodynamics
	2. Long term therapy
	3. May be useful in short-term therapy
		1. Promoting Rational Understanding
		2. Paradoxical Intention
			1. Projective
			  a. Dream analysis
			  b. Age regression
			  c. Symptom substitution

The Symptom Complex	1. Relief of symptoms
	2. Relate symptom to predisposing personality, current conflict, external precipitating stress, and basic anxiety
	3. Promote insight and understanding of symptoms
		1. Promote Rational Understanding
		2. Direct Modification of Behavior
		3. Release of Energy
		4. Supportive Therapy
		5. Direct Relief of Symptoms
		6. Paradoxical Intention
			1. Projective
			  a. Time distortion
			2. Direct and Indirect Suggestion
			  a. Production of substitute symptoms
			3. Behavior Modification

Secondary Gain or Symptom-Fixing Factor	1. Prevention
	  Promote insight and understanding
	2. Therapeutic
	  Promote insight and understanding
	  Promote disequilibrium
		1. Promote Rational Understanding
		2. Direct Modification of Behavior
		3. Supportive Therapy
		4. Direct Relief (or alleviation) of Symptoms
		5. Paradoxical Intention
		6. (Also, Family Therapy and Environmental Manipulation)
			1. Projective
			  a. Time distortion
			    Age regression and progression
			    Symptom substitution
			  b. Hypnoanalysis
			  c. Behavior Therapy
			  d. Ego State Therapy
			2. Direct and Indirect Suggestion
			3. Behavior Modification

22

Group Therapy Combined with Individual Psychotherapy

SAUL SCHEIDLINGER, PH.D.

and

KENNETH PORTER, M.D.

In view of the confusing ways in which therapeutic group approaches have been depicted in the mental health field, the term *group psychotherapy* will be employed in this chapter in its strictest sense, as connoting an intervention modality wherein a specially trained professional practitioner ". . . utilizes the interaction in a small, carefully planned group to effect 'repair' of personality malfunctioning in individuals specifically selected for this purpose. A clinical orientation, which includes a diagnostic assessment of each group member's problems, is part of this picture. Furthermore, each patient is cognizant of the psychotherapeutic purpose and accepts the group as a means to obtain help in modifying his pathological mode of functioning" (1).

The group psychotherapy field distinguishes between two distinct patterns of utilizing group psychotherapy for a patient who is concurrently receiving individual treatment. The first pattern, employed with the greatest frequency, involves the "combined" use of individual and group treatment by the same therapist. The second. termed "conjoint" therapy, calls for the cooperative utilization of the two treatment modalities for a given patient by two different therapists. The respective technical issues posed by these two similar, yet distinct approaches will be delineated at a later point.

It must be stated here that while we share the belief of most clinicians that both individual and group psychotherapy have their respective places in the clinical realm and that there are many specific circumstances where individual psychotherapy alone is not enough for certain kinds of patients, this view is not necessarily shared by others. In fact, as we will note in the review of the literature, there are a number of authorities in the group psychotherapy field, especially from the so-called "British School," who conversely advocate the *exclusive* use of group treatment for most patients and who are principally opposed to simultaneous dyadic interventions in any form. These latter group therapists frequently view the introduction of individual sessions as a dilution of the potent group transferences and as a resistance to the group treatment medium.

While combined therapy has been also employed with children and with adolescents, our chosen focus here will be on the treatment of adults only.

REVIEW OF THE LITERATURE

It is noteworthy that well over 50 contributions dealing with combined individual and group psychotherapy appeared during the fifties and sixties. The virtual absence of more recent publications on this subject is probably due to the fact that, like group psychotherapy employed exclusively, these once new and controversial modalities have by now become an accepted part of the mental health scene.

Beginning with a 1949 paper by Wender and Stein (2) there were a number of articles during the fifties by Fried (3), Sager (4), Papanek (5) and Lipschutz (6) dealing with the general subject of combined psychotherapy. The stress was on how the two approaches can be afforded equal importance in an overall treatment strategy or, in Wilder's (7) case, how he utilized the group sessions to facilitate his primary reliance on dyadic psychoanalysis. The most recent comprehensive review of the entire subject of combined therapy by Bieber (8) was published in 1971.

There were many publications which depicted the use of combined therapy for patients with specific diagnostic categories. These range from an early paper by Baruch and Miller on the treatment of allergic conditions (9), through the use of combined therapy in inpatient settings by such writers as Klapman (10) and Hill and Armitage (11), to a number of articles on the advantage of such treatment for oral characters by Jackson and Grotjahn (12), by Rosenbaum (13), and Tabachnick (14). Wolberg (15) discussed the use of combined therapy for borderline patients, while Glatzer (16) and Durkin (17), among many others, emphasized the special value of such an approach for narcissistic and other preoedipal character disorder. Some authors, among them Graham (18) and Shecter (19), employed combined therapy successfully with psychoneurotic patients.

As might be expected, the technical questions pertaining to the differential uses of individual and group sessions raised by Sager (20) and Spotnitz (21), as well as to transference and resistance in these concurrently used modalities, evoked most interest and controversy in the literature. Thus, Stein (22) subjected the broader issue of transference in combined therapy to special scrutiny, while Beukenkamp (23) depicted the ways in which this approach could facilitate the resolution of transference problems. Berger (24), among others, paid particular attention to the subject of resistance.

Other technical issues such as the handling of confidentiality, when and how to introduce the group medium, and countertransference in combined individual and group treatment were discussed by Aronson (25) and Sager (26). Some authors such as Ormont (27) and Teicher (28) reviewed the relative advantages of combined versus conjoint group psychotherapy.

As we mentioned earlier, some authorities in the group therapy field view combined group therapy with disfavor, advocating instead an exclusive emphasis on group therapy alone. Wolf and Schwartz (29) for example, asserted that individual therapy would interfere with the establishment and resolution of the transference neurosis characteristic of what they termed "Group Psychoanalysis." Whitaker and Lieberman (30), Foulkes and Anthony (31), and Ezriel (32) are also against the use of combined therapy, claiming that the group medium is markedly powerful in its own right and that individual interventions would be counterproductive.

THE UNIQUE POTENTIAL OF THE PSYCHOANALYTIC THERAPY GROUP

When a clinician decides to add group therapy to the individual treatment of his patients, he is likely to be influenced by certain assumptions regarding the special therapeutic ingredients inherent in the therapeutic group process. These have been spelled out in much detail in the voluminous group therapy literature and will accordingly be reviewed here in brief outline only:

1. *The Group as a Real Social Experience*

The co-presence of a number of people fosters multiple interpersonal relationships revealing to everyone's full view each individual's coping and defensive patterns. As a group member's characteristic ways of relating emerge and evoke reactions from others, the stage is thus set for non-verbal as well as verbal interventions by other group members as well as the therapist. This is especially advantageous for those patients who in their massive employment of denial, projection, silences and withdrawal are difficult to engage in the one-to-one setting.

2. *Multiple Transferences*

In addition to the above-noted largely conscious interpersonal relationships, the unconscious group level is characterized by transference manifestations to other members and to the therapist, as well as to the group as an entity. These transferences frequently assume the representations of siblings, of parental figures, and of the family as a whole. The shifting character of these "neurotic" transferences—coupled with the emergence of more primitive, defensive transference manifestations such as "splitting," identifications and part-object relationships—allow for significant diagnostic observations and for appropriate therapeutic interventions both in the group and in the individual sessions.

In this connection, the group psychotherapy literature is replete with discussions of the regressive perceptions and relationships which characterize the unconscious levels of group processes. These primitive emotional themes are believed by some writers such as Bion (33) to be of even greater "depth" than those elicited in the dyadic psychoanalytic setting. Such fleeting group manifestations pertaining to the reactivation of early relationship patterns and especially of primitive perceptions of the therapist, of the other members and of the group entity can be subjected to a more planned and controlled scrutiny in the context of combined therapy. Breen (34) provided a poignant illustration of some of the differences in the unconscious object relationship themes evoked by the group therapy and individual analytic settings, respectively.

3. *Opportunity for Reality Testing*

In contrast to the relatively unstructured dyadic setting which tends to promote only a regressive climate, the group, with its accompanying reality component of an open circle and the co-presence of a number of people, facilitates the testing of reality. Imagined fears, hurts and retaliations, as well as transference distortions, are thus subject to easier exploration and correction.

4. *Support of Peers*

While ego support offered in the context of individual psychotherapy is likely to reinforce dependency on the therapist, this is more readily avoided in the supportive climate of the group. Here, the frequently disheartened and demoralized patient is soon helped to realize that he is not alone nor necessarily the worst off. Furthermore, vivid examples of change for the better on the part of others promote hope for one's own improvement. The group's code of acceptance and of honesty, which is consciously fostered, tends to reduce irrational feelings of shame and guilt, to correct biases and cultural misinformation. Being afforded the role of helper to others enhances each patient's self-esteem besides serving as a motivation to take personal risks on the road to newer behaviors.

MAXIMIZING THE EFFECTS OF INDIVIDUAL THERAPY

The above-noted unique motivational factors for change and growth inherent in the group setting tend to enhance the effectiveness of the patient's simultaneous one-to-one treatment. In addition, other more experienced group members can serve as role models in the acceptance of irrational feelings and anxiety, as well as of the need for self-exploration, as a necessary ingredient of therapy. Furthermore, confrontations and interpretations by peers are often more readily accepted than those from the authority figure. The motivational reinforcement of the group's commitment to work toward therapeutic progress also helps to overcome resistances. While the earlier mentioned regressive group transactions are likely to facilitate the expression of deeply repressed ideations, the necessary lengthy, detailed and individualized working-through of such material is usually not possible in a group because the coexisting needs of so many others interfere with this process. It is here, as noted by Scheidlinger (35), where the individual sessions serve to complement the group situation, allowing for the repetitive and necessarily slow process of "working-through" to occur. The patient's observing ego is thus enabled to master the new insights at its own pace, with due regard to the inevitable resistances reinforced by early traumas.

SPECIFIC INDICATIONS FOR COMBINED THERAPY

There is considerable agreement in the literature that combined therapy, while potentially useful with most ambulatory patients, is the treatment of choice for character disorders and borderline personalities. The integrated use of the two modalities lends itself especially well to working with primitive, pre-oedipal transferences and related rigid character defenses which, as noted by Kernberg (36), are frequently coupled with schizoid behavior and deep fears of intimacy. (Some of these same problems are encountered in severe psychoneuroses.)

As we mentioned earlier, the group's aid in the evocation and resolution of complex transferences and resistances is likely to hasten the pace of individual treatment and its reconstructive nature. This is especially true under prevailing conditions of practice where financial limitations constrain many patients to a less intensive schedule of individual therapy than is clinically indicated. Under such circumstances, a single group session can often be combined with even a single individual session to marked advantage.

Following are some of the major therapeutic problems of patients with character pathology, including "borderline" conditions, which were found to be specially responsive to combined individual and group treatment.

1. *Difficult Transferences*

The varied complexities in the resolution of primitive transference themes encountered in pre-oedipal character problems in the dyadic treatment context are well known and do not require repetition. By introducing simultaneous group treatment, the patient's rigid narcissistic, paranoid, withdrawing or dependent transference patterns become subject to the group's scrutiny and confrontation. The therapist may at first need to use the individual sessions to support the patient in view of the group's undermining of his tenaciously defended perceptions. Subsequently, the inevitable negative transference reactions to other group members (siblings) are likely to be displaced onto the therapist, where they belong. At the same time, the positive transference ties to some of the group peers and the perception of the group entity in a positive maternal vein can serve as support on the painful road to the analysis of the patient's distorted angry perceptions of early objects in both the individual and group encounters. Individual sessions can be used flexibly—at times to offer ego support when the group's confrontations promote too much anxiety, at other times for analytic exploration and working through. Group meetings as well are likely to serve varied functions at different stages of treatment. These include experiential frustrations or gratifications of transference wishes and direct verbal expressions and confrontations of transference feelings coupled with reality-testing and resolution.

2. *Analysis of Rigid Character Defenses*

We referred earlier to the unequalled value of the group setting for portraying interpersonal behavior patterns and defenses. In fact, group therapists have often noted with amazement how different their patients appear in the group when compared to their behavior in the dyadic sessions. Thus when the new group member's narcissistic defenses of grandiosity, aloofness and arrogance persist over a period of time, the other members are bound to confront and later undertake concerted efforts to demand relevant self-scrutiny and modification of the unacceptable conduct. Similarly, a cohesive therapy group imbued with a spirit of self-examination coupled with genuine emotional support when called for will not tolerate persistent patterns of projection, denial, withdrawal, withholding or intellectualization. The frequently painful sequelae of such transactions are likely to involve the therapist in both the group and individual sessions as supporter, confronter and interpreter, as the situation may demand.

Clinical reports are unanimous about the special value of a group setting as a way station for patients to work through problems of relating to members of the opposite sex or of schizoid withdrawal. Somehow, these issues are better *lived out* in at least a microcosm of the real world—the group—rather than being merely talked about in the individual session.

THE DIFFERENTIAL USES OF INDIVIDUAL AND GROUP SESSIONS

During combined therapy, group sessions tend to be generally used to elicit and resolve resistances and to promote the expression of the earlier-noted deep affects and phantasies. The individual sessions can then serve as the calmer "laboratory" to analyze these therapeutic productions, especially of primitive transference perceptions, in greater detail and comprehensiveness. In either session, the stress may need occasionally to be placed on the provision of ego support. As part of the working through process, group meetings are more likely to offer opportunities for experimenting with new behaviors while the individual sessions would stress the integration of deeper intrapsychic themes.

Needless to say, all therapists do not necessarily operate in accordance with this scheme. The unique needs of different patients, the variability in the character of therapy groups, and the therapist-style may dictate different ways in which the two media are harmonized to enhance the task of therapy.

TECHNICAL ISSUES IN THE INITIATION AND SCHEDULING OF COMBINED THERAPY

It is almost universal practice among therapists employing combined therapy to initiate treatment with a period of individual psychoanalytic psychotherapy, and to add group therapy at a later point. A common view is that group therapy may be introduced once the patient has developed a strong working alliance with the therapist and after a transference has been clearly established and at least partially understood. If the patient is introduced to group therapy too soon, transference patterns may become confused or repressed and therapeutic progress halted. In fact, some patients may flee treatment altogether should they fail to be fully prepared for the group and feel that they are being "thrown to the wolves" or abandoned.

Similarly, patients in individual treatment should probably not be brought into a group until the acute problems that led to the treatment have been at least partially resolved and the patient's self-esteem is sufficiently strong to withstand the inevitable stresses entailed in group belonging.

In practice, there is considerable variation in the timing of combined therapy, ranging from a wait of only a few weeks at one extreme to a preceding stretch of several years of individual psychotherapy, at the other.

Although the pattern of commencing treatment with individual psychotherapy and later adding group therapy is the most common approach, there is no reason why the reverse procedure cannot be employed. Thus, some clinicians begin combined therapy with exclusive group psychotherapy, and only after a period of months or years do they add individual analytic sessions. This scheme may be best suited to patients with previous psychoanalytic experience, or to those who are extremely frightened of their transference reactions in the individual treatment setting.

As for the therapy groups in combined therapy, these may consist of a mixture of patients, including some in exclusive group therapy and others in combined or in conjoint therapy. While this might seem to create formidable problems of transference complexity and of rivalry reactions within the psychotherapy group, most workers have actually found such an approach quite workable. Given sufficient sensitivity and experience in the employment of combined therapy on the part of the therapist, the use of a flexible approach permits a truly rich variety of therapeutic transactions.

As can be expected, raising the issue of joining a group with a patient is likely to provoke a number of concerns. Most common are feelings of rejection, narcissistic injury, separation anxiety and sibling rivalry. These feelings invariably provide significant themes for the ongoing treatment program.

Combined treatment is usually initiated either by adding a group therapy session to the patient's pre-existing schedule of individual sessions or by substituting a group meeting for an individual session. The decision is made on clinical grounds, depending on the optimal intensity of individual psychotherapy sessions and the availability of time and financial resources. Naturally, the issues posed by the planning for combined therapy will differ in the two circumstances and the therapist must be prepared to deal with the relevant therapeutic material which is bound to arise.

The most common pattern of combined therapy appears to be one group therapy session per week combined with one or two individual sessions. Fewer therapists employ a twice-weekly group therapy schedule.

Whether it is feasible to combine a more intensive individual psychoanalytic schedule of sessions with group therapy has been extensively debated. Some writers maintain that the deep regressive transference of a classical individual psychoanalysis is incompatible with concurrent group therapy, while others believe that a schedule of three, four, or even five times a week for individual psychoanalytic sessions, including the use of the couch, can go hand in hand with group therapy. These therapists report that patients exhibit a variety of transference reactions in both group and individual analytic sessions. Although the anonymity of the clinician is obviously not preserved, the essential nature of the analytic development and resolution of the transference is believed not to be disturbed.

The most prevalent point of view at this time among practitioners of combined therapy is that intensive, three to five times weekly individual psychoanalytic sessions may be combined with group therapy. While this probably alters the nature of the transference relationship within the individual analytic treatment, the total process of this type of combined therapy is nevertheless considered as being compatible with the overall reconstructive goals of the psychoanalytic treatment process.

CONFIDENTIALITY IN COMBINED THERAPY

The use of concurrent individual and group psychoanalytic sessions offers the therapist a range of possibilities in exploiting therapeutic material which exceeds what is possible through the use of either therapeutic modality alone. To restrict the use of themes which emerged in either modality to subsequent sessions within the same modality only would deprive combined therapy of some of its greatest potential. For example, individual sessions may be utilized to permit the patient to discuss the defensive or transference patterns of fellow group members. These discussions may be a source of considerable insight for the patient and often facilitate his deeper understanding of similar aspects of his own psychopathology. Similarly, with the patient's permission, material from individual sessions may be productively employed to further understanding of this topic within the group transactions.

Considerations of clinical judgment and personal tact, are of course critical in the flexible use of therapeutic data emanating from combined therapy.

COMBINED THERAPY AND CONJOINT THERAPY

As we noted at the outset, "conjoint therapy" refers to combined treatment in which group and individual therapy of a patient are conducted by two different therapists. It is similar to traditional, shared treatment in most respects, and offers most of the same advantages.

The main issue which distinguishes combined from conjoint therapy is the effect of such a divided treatment structure on the working alliance and on transference. Conjoint therapy fosters the development of multiple transferences and of transference-splitting even more than the use of combined group and individual therapy. Some clinicians have claimed that this allows for clearer delineation, and hence for easier resolution, of some patients' transference patterns. Many others believe that the use of two therapists unnecessarily confuses the picture and invites complicated countertransference issues, plus the conscious and unconscious manipulation of the treatment situation by the patient to such a degree as to inhibit the successful resolution of basic pathology. At this time, it is probably fair to say that both treatment approaches appear to be effective, that their uses are similar, and that a clear preference for one or the other is up to the therapist. However, the fact that conjoint therapy is used with much lesser frequency suggests some doubt among most clinicians regarding its efficacy in deeper, reconstructive psychotherapy. Further experimentation will reveal the specific ways in which combined and conjoint therapy, respectively, have their proper place in the therapeutic armamentarium according to the varying needs of different patients, psychopathologies and treatment situations.

CONTRAINDICATIONS TO COMBINED THERAPY

There was a time when both group therapists and individual psychotherapists were wary of combined therapy. Individual therapists felt that the addition of group therapy to dyadic treatment would dilute it to the point where the attainment of analytic goals would be made more difficult, if not impossible.

As for clinicians who employ group therapy as the treatment of choice for most patients, they feared that the addition of individual sessions would drain off energy and material from the group.

It is our belief that to date neither side in this dialogue has been proven correct. We think that individual psychoanalytic treatment can essentially proceed with the attainment of its goals when group therapy sessions are added to the treatment regimen, and that, if anything, the work of character reconstruction may occur with greater alacrity and depth. Similarly, psychoanalytic group therapy is most often enhanced by the addition of individual sessions as patients are provided with the opportunity to work through issues in greater genetic and intrapsychic depth. The only two major clinical contraindications for combined therapy appear to be:

A) *Classical psychoneuroses,* which probably are still best treated with the technique of intensive individual psychoanalysis. For these patients, the addition of group therapy is probably unnecessary, since the latter's virtue is to facilitate the resolution of the character problems and severe transference patterns which are not characteristic of the neuroses.

B) *Some borderline, psychotic and masochistic patients,* whose ego structure is such that they respond to the addition of group therapy with enhanced anxiety, regressed behavior or depression when exposed to the group's psychological forces of regression and contagion.

Clinical Examples

Case #1

Joe is a 32-year-old, public utility repairman from a poor working-class background. He spends his free time as part of a group of motor-cycle riders who use a variety of non-addictive drugs. He is bright, up-wardly mobile and committed to psychotherapy. His childhood was characterized by a severely dominating mother and the almost total absence of a father. He is overweight, fierce-looking, and filled with rage toward women, coupled with a strong desire to overcome it. He was married for five years to a woman whom he described as in many ways a carbon copy of his mother. He said that he did not love her, but nevertheless could not get himself to leave her and his five-year-old daughter.

Joe began once-weekly individual psychotherapy and a year later was invited to join a psychoanalytic therapy group led by the same male therapist. At first, the therapeutic work in individual sessions was largely supportive, aiming to help Joe deal more competently with his wife and child as well as with a variety of work-related practical conflicts. Joe related to the therapist in a friendly and submissive fashion.

In the group, Joe was initially withdrawn and silent, and was often depressed. His occasional talk consisted of sarcastic comments to the women members and deferentially friendly remarks to the males. He usually came dressed in his torn, greasy work clothes.

Over a period of two years, the other group members, at first gently then more firmly, confronted Joe with his tendency to withdraw into depressions instead of dealing with his problems. The defensive aspects of his "Macho" denial of dependency, of his dress, appearance and aggressiveness, were repeatedly emphasized.

In time, several significant changes were noted. In the group, Joe began to talk spontaneously during every session, emerging also as being concerned and involved with all group members. He could now acknowledge pain, inadequacy, and vulnerability in front of the others, including the women. In fact, he began to use the group to practice new ways of relating to women as equals whom he might care about. In addition, there were the beginnings of a kind of transference rage toward women, as well as, for the first time, towards his male group therapist.

At this point, the nature of Joe's individual therapy sessions gradually also underwent a change. Dreams began to appear and the sessions became less reality-oriented and supportive and more concerned with genetic and intrapsychic material. The heart of this work settled for a time on homosexual fears and wishes involving male friends, Joe's father, and the therapist.

After three years of combined therapy, Joe was enabled to separate from his wife, to lose a significant amount of weight, to alter his style of dress, reduce his involvement with motorcycles and drugs, and begin to date women for the first time in his adult life.

This case illustrates the following points concerning combined therapy: 1) The value of the group to reveal and resolve character defenses; 2) the use of the group to explore and begin to resolve patterns of transference rage; 3) the group's availability as a testing-ground for more adaptive behavior during the working-through process; 4) the opportunity to focus in the individual sessions on genuine reconstructive psychotherapy.

Case #2

Rose is a 28-year-old nurse who is married and has a nine-month-old son. Rose's mother is schizophrenic; one of her psychotic episodes followed Rose's birth. Her father beat the patient when she was young. Rose was in individual psychoanalytically-oriented psychotherapy for five years with a female therapist whom she described as "very supportive and maternal." She felt that she had benefited greatly from this period of treatment, but she and her therapist believed that a span of analytic group therapy accompanying the individual work would be helpful to work on issues related to her anger and need for more self-assertion.

Rose entered a therapy group led by a male therapist. At first, she was quiet and shy. She rarely spoke, even when she appeared to be obviously upset. The group therapist suggested that she experienced the entire group as her schizophrenic mother and that she felt that if she asserted herself by asking for help, the group would not be emotionally available to her, just as her own mother had not been. Subsequently, with continued encouragement from the others, she began to verbalize her feelings, requests and needs to an ever greater extent.

Following this, the other members began to consider Rose's shyness, hesitancy, and soft voice as relating to difficulties with self-assertion and anger. Her timidity and marked friendliness were repeatedly interpreted as reaction-formations to underlying feelings of anger. Soon, Rose began to oppose others in the group, starting with the females but then going on to challenge also the male members and the therapist. She reported a concurrent increased ability to confront her husband when she felt he was treating her unfairly. Recently, she gave birth to a girl and went through the postpartum and infancy periods without significant symptomatology. She is now making plans to return to part-time work over the mild objections of her husband.

Needless to say, the two therapists communicated with each other on occasion, with Rose's knowledge.

This case illustrates the following: 1) The conjoint use of individual and group therapy sessions with differing therapists, in which the individual sessions served a mixed supportive-reconstructive function and the group sessions came to take on a primarily reconstructive quality; 2) The resolution of transference patterns in the group; 3) The use of group sessions to reveal and resolve character defenses; 4) The opportunity offered by the group to serve as an arena for the practice of new, adaptive patterns of behavior.

REFERENCES

1. Scheidlinger, S. Symposium on the relationship of group psychotherapy to other group modalities in mental health. *Int. J. Group Psychother.*, 1970, 20:470-472.
2. Wender, L. and Stein, A. Group psychotherapy as an aid to out-patient treatment in a psychiatric clinic. *Psychiat. Quart.*, 1949, 23:415-424.
3. Fried, E. The effect of combined therapy on the productivity of patients. *Int. J. Group Psychother.*, 1954, 4:42-55.
4. Sager, C. J. The effects of group psychotherapy on individual psychoanalysis. *Int. J. Group Psychother.*, 1959, 9:403-419.
5. Papanek, H. Combined group and individual therapy in private practice. *Amer. J. Psychother.*, 1954, 8:679-686.
6. Lipschutz, D. M. Combined group and individual psychotherapy. *Amer. J. Psychother.*, 1957, 11:336-344.
7. Wilder, J. Group analysis and the insights of the analyst. In: S. De Schill (Ed.), *The Challenge for Group Psychotherapy—Present and Future.* New York: International Universities Press, 1974.
8. Bieber, T. B. Combined individual and group psychotherapy. In: H. I. Kaplan and B. J. Sadock (Eds.), *Comprehensive Group Psychotherapy.* Baltimore: Williams & Wilkins, 1971, pp. 153-169.
9. Baruch, D. and Miller, H. Group and individual psychotherapy as an adjunct in the treatment of allergy. *J. Cons. Psychol.*, 1946, 10:281-284.
10. Klapman, J. W. Observations on the "shuttle" process in individual-group psychotherapy. *Psychiat. Quart.*, 1950, 23:124-129.
11. Hill, G. and Armitage, S. Analysis of combined therapy—individual and group—in patients with schizoid, obsessive-compulsive, or aggressive defenses. *J. Nerv. Ment. Dis.*, 1954, 119:113-134.
12. Jackson, J. and Grotjahn, M. The treatment of oral defenses by combined individual and group psychotherapy. *Int. J. Group Psychother.*, 1958, 8:373-382.
13. Rosenbaum, M. What is the place of combined psychotherapy? A comment and critique. *Top. Probl. Psychother.*, 1960, 2:86-96.
14. Tabachnick, N. Isolation, transference splitting, and combined therapy. *Compreh. Psychiat.*, 1965, 6:336-346.

15. Wolberg, A. The psychoanalytic treatment of the borderline patient in the individual and group setting. *Top. Probl. Psychother.*, 1960, 2:174-197.
16. Glatzer, H. Discussion of symposium on combined individual and group psychoanalysis. *Amer. J. Orthopsychiat.*, 1960, 30:243-246.
17. Durkin, H. Discussion of symposium on combined individual and group psychotherapy. *Int. J. Group Psychother.*, 1964, 14:445-449.
18. Graham, E. W. A case treated by psychoanalysis and analytic group therapy. *Int. J. Group Psychother.*, 1964, 14:267-290.
19. Shecter, D. E. Integration of group therapy with individual psychoanalysis. *Psychiatry*, 1959, 22:267-276.
20. Sager, C. J. Concurrent individual and group analytic therapy. *Amer. J. Orthopsychiat.*, 1960, 30:225-241.
21. Spotnitz, H. Comments on combined therapy for the hostile personality. *Amer. J. Orthopsychiat.*, 1954, 24:535-537.
22. Stein, A. The nature of transference in combined therapy. *Int. J. Group Psychother.*, 1964, 14:413-424.
23. Beukenkamp, C. The multi-dimensional orientation in analytic group therapy. *Amer. J. Psychother.*, 1955, 9:477-483.
24. Berger, I. L. Modifications of the transference as observed in combined individual and group psychotherapy. *Int. J. Group Psychother.*, 1960, 10:456-470.
25. Aronson, M. L. Technical problems in combined psychotherapy. *Int. J. Group Psychother.*, 1964, 14:425-432.
26. Sager, C. J. Insight and interaction in combined therapy. *Int. J. Group Psychother.*, 1964, 14:403-412.
27. Ormont, L. The resolution of resistance by conjoint psychoanalysis. *Psychoanal. Rev.*, 1964, 51:425-437.
28. Teicher, A. The use of conflicting loyalties in combined individual and group psychotherapy with separate therapists. *Int. J. Group Psychother.*, 1962, 12:75-81.
29. Wolf, A. and Schwartz, E. K. *Psychoanalysis in Groups.* New York: Grune & Stratton, 1962.
30. Whitaker, D. S. and Lieberman, M. A. *Psychotherapy Through the Group Process.* New York: Atherton Press, 1970.
31. Foulkes, S. H. and Anthony, E. J. *Group Psychotherapy: The Psychoanalytic Approach.* London: Penguin Books, 1957.
32. Ezriel, H. The role of transference in psychoanalytical and other approaches to group treatment. *Acta. Psychother.*, 1957, 7:101-116.
33. Bion, W. R. Group dynamics—A review. *Int. J. Psychoanal.*, 1952, 33:235-247.
34. Breen, D. Some differences between group and individual therapy in connection with the therapist's pregnancy. *Int. J. Group Psychother.*, 1977, 27:499-510.
35. Scheidlinger, S. The concept of regression in group psychotherapy. *Int. J. Group Psychother.*, 1968, 18:3-20.
36. Kernberg, O. F. *Object Relations Theory and Clinical Psychoanalysis.* New York: Aronson, 1976.

23

Family and Marital Therapy Combined with Individual Psychotherapy

STEPHEN FLECK, M.D.

INTRODUCTION

Family therapy, i.e. conjoint treatment of the family unit by one or more therapists, is of quite recent origin. Although Midelfort (1) treated families of schizophrenic patients some forty years ago, this was an isolated experiment until some fifteen years later, when studies of the family environment of schizophrenic patients at several different centers rendered treatment of these families a necessity. Seeing such troubled families routinely over time could not be accomplished without having a therapeutic impact (2-5).

Somewhat earlier Ackerman began treating families with disturbed children as units instead of having different clinic staff members see individual family members in the then traditional pattern (6). Although marital counseling has a long history, marital therapy along psychoanalytic concepts has been practiced only for the past few decades (6, 7).

Before presentation of indications and techniques of family therapy with or without simultaneous psychotherapy for one or more individuals

The editorial assistance of Ms. L. H. Fleck and Ms. K. Molloy is gratefully acknowledged.

in the group, some principal differences of families compared with other groups, and consequently differences between family treatment and other psychotherapies, must be understood.

Because the family as a human group and institution is ubiquitous and a part of everybody's experience, it has been difficult to conceptualize and formulate what the essential nature, characteristics and functions of this group are.

The family is the link between every individual and the larger society. Therefore, physicians and psychiatrists must consider this unit not only for therapeutic reasons, but also because social and preventive medicine and psychiatry must focus on the family as the relevant basic system (8-10).

Individual therapy, actually a dyadic system, is rooted in the ancient doctor/patient relationship, with a long tradition of confidential, private and privileged communication. Sigmund Freud, clearly the central figure in the development of psychotherapy, came to his discoveries as a physician by working with individual patients, and decided to exploit this dyadic field for investigation and therapeutic intervention centered on the evolving relationship of the patient to his or her physician. Although much of what he discovered was about familial experiences, and early in his venture into psychoanalysis he seemed to feel no compunction about having all sorts of contacts with family members or friends and, in one instance, treating a child by advising the father, he increasingly eschewed such contacts (11, 12). Apparently he never sought to confirm his findings or influence patients' clinical course by meeting with their families. Furthermore, despite his appreciation of the complexities of the human mind and the over-determination of all behaviors, he remained steeped in an essentially cause-and-effect-philosophy characteristic of his era and reinforced by the concurrent "single cause" discoveries in infectious disease medicine.

Group therapy is also rooted in medical tradition in that an inventive physician, Joseph H. Pratt, discovered that patients with like diseases, e.g. tuberculosis, have sufficiently similar problems to make it therapeutically effective to converse about these problems in groups (13). Although group therapy has long since been used primarily with psychiatric patients or even non-patient groups, incorporating psychoanalytic principles and formulations, it remains a technique for help-seeking persons who come to a therapist to join with strangers in such a group for therapy (14, 15).

The family has existed as a group long before help is sought, often help for one particular member, and the remainder of the family may not consider themselves in need of help or therapy or may even resist such involvement. Yet, as Richardson (16) pointed out many years ago, treating a patient as if he or she had no family is like treating an organ as if there were no body. In other words, the existence of a sick family member affects the entire group, has consequences for the entire group, and the sickness may have roots in the previous behavior and functioning of the family.

THE FAMILY AS A SYSTEM

A systems view obviates the phenomenological specification of deviance or abnormality as such because it addresses relationships and energy transformation within the system, thereby specifying the nature and effectiveness of relevant functions regardless of whether or not they will be found abnormal, deficient or excessive. But considering only energy transformation and making diagrams of relationships are abstractions useful to mathematical systems analysts, but hardly to a clinician. We propose, therefore, to examine this system, the family—or other human organizations, according to five system sectors or parameters which have clinical and managerial relevance. These five are: Governance or leadership; Boundary management; Affectivity or sentient forces; Communication; and Task performance or system mission. The family is minimally a two-generation system, with the children usually biologically related, but can be multi-generational and include collateral nuclear families in so-called extended family systems. We shall confine our discussion mostly to the nuclear family consisting of two generations, that is, one or two parents and a child or children living as a unit.

Unlike other human systems, the family lives through an extraneously given bio-psychosocial cycle which determines its internal individual and collective needs and tasks, while serving society by providing it with new adult members prepared to participate in the life of the community. Implicit in society's expectation is that the family produce adults who will not only participate in the community's work, but also adhere to and preserve its culture and values.

MARRIAGE

The family begins as a sub-system—the marriage or marital coalition, a relationship undertaken by two adults, by their choice or by inter-familial arrangement, in which latter case the spouses may still be quite young. These two people who join or are joined for a lifetime must establish life as a dyad for their mutual satisfactions and care and prepare themselves to function as parents, that is, leaders in the family system if this is created. Until they produce children or become parents through adoption of a child, their marital task is to serve each other, establish effective communication and a sense of belonging to each other in special ways, thus creating at least an eidetic boundary as a couple and a basically positive-feeling atmosphere toward each other. These issues entail respect for personal divergencies and a willingness to reconcile negative feelings instead of one demanding submission of the other or allowing conflicts to fester and produce a significant rupture in the relationship, be that overt or covert.

A special sub-system relationship of this couple with regard to intimacy and sex must be preserved throughout the family's life cycle and, eventually, in Western societies must serve again for them to live as a couple when children have left the nuclear family system.

Among the important leadership functions in established families are the role and task divisions parents work out for each other, basic arrangements for rearing and guiding their children, representing each other, i.e. the other parent, to children positively but realistically, and serving as gender- and culture-typical models for their offspring.

MARITAL THERAPY

Indications for therapeutic intervention in the marital sub-system derive from the foregoing outline of the nature and function of marriage and parenthood. Regardless of what indications there may be for individual psychotherapeutic treatment of one spouse based on clear formulation and understanding of an intrapsychic problem or mal-development related to a complaint or complaints, such treatment should not be recommended and undertaken without some consideration of its effect upon the marital and family systems. Nor can we any longer forego considering to what extent and in what way the marital relationship or the entire family situation may have contributed to the distress or may have ameliorated or delayed symptomatic expression. Such delay may have occurred at the expense of other system functions or because the marital or family systems had achieved a relatively comfortable equilibrium because of the disturbed and possibly disturbing behavior of one member, be that parent or child (17, 18).

Because marriages are undertaken at a certain stage of personality development and because further growth or change is a personal and family life cycle necessity, it is as possible that people will continue their personal development in a direction that fosters greater closeness, mutual understanding and empathy enhancing familial task sharing as it is that they grow apart, becoming increasingly estranged with the likelihood that whatever neurotic traits they brought into the marriage will become increasingly fixed in their interaction and relationship, resulting in disharmony, strife and defective leadership within the family.

If one partner had a stake in the spouse's immaturity or lack of full personal independence, then that spouse's development must either not occur or if it occurs the marriage may no longer be satisfactory to the other spouse. This is particularly cogent if such development is furthered or brought about (as it should be) by psychotherapy of the immature spouse. The therapist, therefore, has a clinical responsibility in all instances to evaluate whether the marital system can tolerate this change and, if not, at least to see to it that the "more mature spouse" receives some help in accepting the change, be that in individual treatment or marital therapy. On the whole, if a discrepancy of this type is ascertained in clinical investigation, it is preferable to undertake marital therapy first and individual therapy subsequently, if at all.

This preference is based on the experience that one relatively minor change in a human system can have consequences of a much more incisive nature than a simple and brief intervention would lead one to expect. The case of an elderly diabetic patient living with his wife may illustrate this. He had been in good metabolic control for quite a number of years, although he had slowly lost his eyesight. Yet he had managed to carry on his job as furnace supervisor with the help of special glasses and lighting. Over a period of several months his diabetes was repeatedly out of control, which led to some altercations with the clinic staff, who had been very proud of this model patient. Then he quit his job, although there had been no clear indication of any significant change in his eyesight or basic physical condition; he was therefore referred for psychiatric consultation while hospitalized to regulate his diabetes. Upon examination, it appeared that the reason for his diabetic discontrol was that his wife had stopped preparing lunches for him as she had done for many years. He claimed he had no explanation for the change, but it meant that he had to either forego lunch and adjust his insulin accordingly or eat lunch out, which he could not do very well within the limits of his diet near or at his place of work. The wife was then contacted, and she had little trouble explaining her dissatisfaction and her refusal to prepare his lunches, which she found a nuisance at best. She was suspicious, if not convinced, that he was unfaithful because he had "claimed" that he had become impotent. Even though this had not developed sud-denly, she was preoccupied in her own mind that he had some other woman. After it was explained to her and subsequently to both of them that impotence is a common symptom of long-standing diabetes, both felt relieved, she reassured and he less guilty and ashamed about this prob-lem, and they could resume their previous more cooperative equilibrium and he his job.

Marital therapy is indicated whenever clinical investigation reveals sig-nificant disturbance in the system. It is not possible to present an exhaus-tive list of such indications, but the following should include the more common system problems.

In the course of family investigation or therapy the original problem of a disturbed or disturbing child can often be traced to a significant, if not primary, marital conflict or maladjustment. In such instances, marital therapy may be instituted either in addition to or instead of therapeutic work with the family. For instance, in one family the initial contact be-tween the family and the mental health system occurred because of the elopement of a teenage daughter, the older of two children in this family. In the course of family work it became apparent that although every-body in the family was suffering to some extent, the basic problem re-sided in the parents' marriage. Although the mother had originally sought psychotherapeutic help on her own and had worked effectively in this situation, it resulted in a deterioration of the marital relationship in that the husband became more withdrawn and depressed as his wife became less dependent and more assertive. However, none of the family recognized this consciously or overtly until work with the entire group was begun following the elopement. The parents were then taken into marital treatment, with considerable improvement and a reasonable hope for eventual resolution of their difficulties and the father's depression.

In younger couples, especially before children have been born, one of the common symptoms and problems is insufficient emotional if not psy-chosocial emancipation from one or the other spouse's family of origin. In some instances, marriage is carried on as if it were a continued court-ship rather than the establishment of a fully adult and therefore rela-tively independent life situation (at least in Western societies) and the opportunity, if not desire, to create a new generation. But pregnancy and the birth of a child in and of themselves do not automatically change motivation or capacity for parenthood, nor necessarily influence a con-flictual marital bond for the better. Some marriages are undertaken to "regain" a family, one of the spouses having been either rejected by his or her own family or having lost them through death.

Any clinical investigation, therefore, must include information about how spouses got together, what sort of coalition they established for themselves, and how they decided to reproduce, if indeed such a decision was ever made. Over half first-ever pregnancies are conceived without clear intention to assume parenthood, however this responsibility may be perceived or understood. Such data have relevance to treatment indications, as do data derived from observing interspousal and familial interactions and transactions.

Incomplete emancipation of spouses from their respective parents interferes not only with the marital relationship, but even more with parenthood and family leadership. Moreover, guilt over leaving a needy parent or unresolved mourning over a deceased parent or even transmission of such unresolved guilt or mourning across the generation boundary is a common source of family difficulties and requires marital or family therapy with or without individual treatment for the directly affected spouse (19, 20). Sexual difficulties are common and probably indicate marital therapy more often than so-called sex therapy despite the current vogue for the latter.

Couples in severe chronic conflict are often referred for treatment by lawyers in an attempt to prevent, or ascertain the necessity for, a divorce. In some states, such referrals for counseling are mandated by law prior to the implementation of a legal separation. Such referrals can constitute a treatment indication, but more often they result from the effort of one spouse to save or repair a relationship in which the other spouse no longer has any investment and indeed may already have made an emotional commitment to another prospective spouse.

If divorce occurs or is imminent in the context of an established family, children will suffer and family treatment may be indicated to minimize suffering and its consequences. Such ameliorative and preventive treatments have been well presented by J. Wallerstein et al. (21, 22).

FAMILY PATHOLOGY

1. System deficiencies other than primarily marital ones, which require treatment, almost always also reflect leadership deficiencies. Such is the interdependency of system vectors and functions.

2. Boundaries may be drawn either too rigidly and narrowly or too loosely. The evolvement of ego boundaries for each child is difficult to

trace because it normally is a subtle, discrete and essentially intrapsychic process. Yet interferences with this normative development of the self-sense can be gross and the resultant defects are well known to psychotherapists as constituting indications for treatment. The severe boundary defects seen in schizophrenic patients have been described in detail by Lidz et al. (2, 8), Stierlin (23), Wynne et al. (24), and others. Such patients often have experienced both intrusive penetrations and impervious distance perpetrated by one or both parents instead of consistent boundary contiguity. Certain patients with severe psychosomatic problems may have experienced similar boundary violations especially, on the part of their mothers (25).

Violations of the generation boundary can produce or prolong incestuous proclivities, fears and conflicts (26). These pathological situations call for individual as well as family therapy.

The family-community boundary can be mismanaged, although this is usually not as devastating in itself to young children's personality formation as interferences with ego boundary development.

Overly rigid family boundaries will interfere with children's experiences and relationship opportunities in the community. School phobias are an early manifestation of such mismanagement, often rooted in parental anxiety and deficient separation mastery. At later stages, insufficiently permeable boundaries are often found in families with disturbed adolescents for whom increasing independence and emancipation then becomes problematic, a common family treatment indication.

Unduly loose family-group boundaries interfere with both personal and familial development. Children may feel uncared for if not unwanted, and this latter sense may even be a realistic appraisal of parental attitudes involved in such uncaring boundary management, e.g. not telling and expecting children when they are to return from playgrounds, visiting neighbors, dates, etc. Such children become dependent on peers and substitute parents in the neighborhood, if they are available, and a sense of family unity and belonging is stunted. Although there is an indication for family treatment for such families, lacking a sense of unity they often are not available for conjoint treatment.

3. Aberrations in familial affects are probably involved in all personal and family pathology. Even if primary, these also cannot exist without some functional decrement in other system parameters. Symptomatically, the outstanding example is probably the scapegoated member described in detail first by Ackerman (27). This occurrence constitutes a clear indication for family treatment, especially because it has been frequently

observed that if the "scapegoat" is treated alone, or removed, the family may scapegoat another member to re-establish the earlier equilibrium (27). Other manifestations of affect disturbance and family treatment indications are misuse of power to further parental or sibling hostility, or the reverse: failure to set limits or enforce any discipline. These may be two sides of the same hostile coin.

4. Communication difficulties characterize all disturbed families to some extent, and have been studied and analyzed more than other system sectors (28, 29). Communication itself is not usually presented as the problem or complaint, but it is very important in clinical assessment and in arriving at treatment indications. The nature of the aberrant communication may reveal quite specific clues as to individual pathology, e.g. Wynne and Singer's family Rorschach method. In and of itself, communicative disturbance in the family does not indicate what form treatment should take, because that decision must be based on considerations of all system functions. Yet a finding of amorphous or fragmented communication styles, usually in families with a schizophrenic member, requires family treatment as it is not likely that the patient can be helped with his thought disorder without some shift and improvement in the familial communication style.

Communication in the broadest sense provides an essentially crosssectional view of the family, as it does in any therapeutic situation, but may also reveal many clues about antecedent events and problems, gleaned and inferable in family interviews.

There may be culture-deviant language, for instance, when parents have persisted in and insisted on familial communication in a foreign language. This need not be a problem; in fact, growing up as a bilingual child can be advantageous, provided there is tolerance for both languages. However, some immigrants consciously or unconsciously resist integration into their new environment and denigrate the language of the surrounding community and also its values. In such families, children may be handicapped because they may feel guilty and constrained with regard to the language of their peers; indeed they may not easily think and conceptualize in that language.

However, even without adhering to a foreign language, parents' thinking and verbal expression may be so disordered that children do not, in fact cannot, acquire the syntax and the symbolic meanings of the language of the outside world. Such children not only are handicapped in formal learning, especially when they are expected to move from concrete to abstract forms of thinking, but will also be handicapped in interpersonal relationships and will find themselves distant and estranged from peers and other persons in their community. In reverse, if such offspring do manage to identify with extra-familial figures, they may be in serious conflicts with their own family and thus feel extremely threatened by such disloyalty. This type of situation is now known as a seedbed for schizophrenic disturbances. In addition to verbal communication aberrations, there may also be in such families a striking deviance between non-verbal and verbal communication, as well as frequent use of double-binding (30).

There are families in which communication is extremely sparse, although not particularly deviant. Their communication is not practiced as a means of expressing feelings or sharing feelings, and if children attempt expressiveness they may feel thwarted by non-response or even negative responses. In particular, in some families the expression of hostility or angry feelings is suppressed or denied, creating an atmosphere of pseudo-pleasantry and harmony. Such suppression and eventual repression of anger and hostility are, of course, well known in individual psychopathology as an important component of depression—not only a communication impediment, but also an affect disorder. Whether seen in one form or another, i.e. as depression or communicative blockage, it is an important indication for family therapy to break up such circularity of depression in one member leading to inhibition and repression in another or to destructive behavior in children. Children who have grown up in such an atmosphere often are seen later clinically as severely neurotic or so-called borderline patients who more likely need individual therapy even though the family roots of their difficulties may be striking. For example, a suicidal college student drop-out could not discuss with either of her parents or other family members the fatal metastatic illness of her father. She had to be hospitalized and treated individually, as the family could not be engaged as a unit, which would have been preferable.

Another type of communication aberration usually seen in families of sociopathic patients is the striking use of communication as an instrument to influence others regardless of truth or facts, and an absence of any expressive use of communication. Although there may be an assertion of strong feelings by such patients and their families, especially contrition early in treatment contacts, it is probably a contrived expression designed to influence others, e.g., the therapist. Such problems are probably best dealt with in a combination of family treatment and group treatment for the patient, possibly in a group-home for patients of this type, although not infrequently by the time these individuals come for treatment, often through court or police referral, regular contact among the family has been broken. It has also been our experience that such families often continue to aid and abet the asocial behavior for homeostatic reasons, as already discussed, resisting or interfering with therapy. Even treatment appointments are "forgotten" or cancelled with barely an excuse.

FAMILY TASK PERFORMANCE AND DEFICIENCIES

Family tasks are determined by the life cycle and therefore must be assessed by obtaining historical data for the period of family life prior to the initial contact with a clinician. Only the present state of family functioning can be observed directly. Aside from the task to establish a marital coalition and parenthood readiness, already discussed at the beginning of this chapter, the life-cycle-related task can be divided, albeit somewhat arbitrarily, according to the phases outlined by Erikson (31). The first stage is that of nurturance, which includes weaning and teaching infants and young children body mastery. This is followed by the era of enculturation, during which the child learns to speak and how to behave in the family, as well as with peers in nursery school or similar play experiences, play being the child's work. The child and family then enter a period of ordering their relationships, passing through the oedipal phase in individual development terms or from a systems view establishing equi-distant and comfortable relationships with both parents and with siblings, if there are any.

With the beginning of school, children should be ready for more significant peer relationships and friendships outside the family, and also should participate in family life during the next five years or so in increasingly reciprocal ways, assuming some responsibilities or chores. This is also the period of maximal harmony in the family, a period in which the family can move, work and play as a unit, celebrate and mourn together, and engage as a unit with other families with children of comparable ages.

When children reach adolescence, family harmony is hardly the order of the day. Looming ahead is the ultimate emancipation of late adolescents or young adults from their families. Adolescents initiate this eventual separation by challenging family life and values, by testing and probing the limits of parental leadership, while almost simultaneously also expecting, even demanding, dependency gratification from the family.

As children leave the family, the parental generation eventually returns to dyadic living in mid-life or later, and issues of non-familial creativity and effectiveness for both parents become important. They must also shift to accepting their children as equals, and the latter must be ready to be equals in their relationships with parents. Only thus can a sense of familiness continue without undue conflict or interfering with the formation of children's own nuclear families.

As the life cycle continues and parents, likely grandparents by then, begin to age and withdraw from productive life, infirmity may also require a role reversal between parents and children, the latter becoming the leaders and decision-makers even though they may not actually live together.

Therapy indications can arise at all these stages, but must be considered in the context of the total system and not only in terms of a particular family task deficiency. Elderly people should be helped to live as couples or even with one of their children's families for as long as this can be reconciled with caring for each other and them without any significant handicap for anyone concerned.

Treatment indications stem from performance defects of the family or any sub-system. Probably the most common and clearest recommendations to seek help, not necessarily in the form of family treatment, often arise from outside the system. General physicians, pediatricians, school staffs and recreation workers, e.g. scout leaders, are all concerned with children's behaviors and performance—indirect or direct indices of family system functioning. Lags in physical development, underachievement in school, or conspicuous behavior on the playground, all these can be manifestations of family disturbance and often are that. R. Beavers (32) speaks of therapy as growth; in general this is what therapy is about regardless of specific technique or diagnosis. J. C. Whitehorn, many years ago, also referred to people seeking or being referred for help from us as "unfinished people" (33). As we examine and increasingly understand family functioning and family failures and their connection with and reflection in individual functioning and failures and vice versa, treatment techniques and formats and their combinations become less important than is our competence to think in terms of systems. Typhoid fever can be prevented by removing the agent from our environment and from food and water, or by raising specific body defenses to interfere with the agent's invasion of and spread in tissues, or by introducing chemicals into our bodies which neutralize or destroy the agent. In other words, through knowledge and understanding of the systems and subsystems involved in a problem, we can determine which of several points of attack or intervention is the most efficient, appropriate and applicable. Thus we can and should explore with a single patient, or a family, or a group the nature of pain and difficulties and consider ways and means of relief and resolution. Often this step or process entails removal of growth obstacles or barriers, or, in systems terms, converting stagnating energy—homeostasis—to movement and change. Initiating such change from stagnation to mobility can occur on a cellular level, i.e. with drug treatment, in the personality system, e.g. through some special relationship, identification with or transference to a therapist or leader, or on an interpersonal plane. Whichever is chosen for the first step, if change occurs in one system there will be correlated or reactive changes in the others.

It must also be appreciated that observations and study in one context, e.g. the traditional dyadic treatment system, may obscure or hide other systems processes. The reverse is equally possible—some significant intrapersonal malfunction may be covered up or hidden in the family context.

For instance, the family of a young, single, art student who became psychotic when her boyfriend of long standing involved himself with another woman, on initial contact gave enough information to constitute

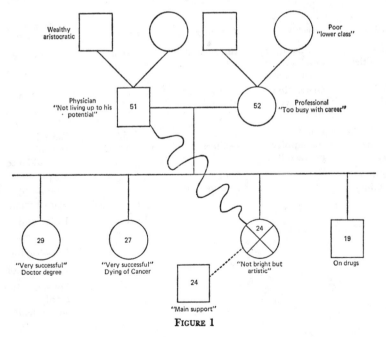

FIGURE 1

the genogram in Figure 1, confirmed subsequently despite increasing resistance to any form of therapy by all concerned. The patient initially convincingly denied any significant family events or involvement in her difficulties. The epithets are quotes from family members about each other.

One can glean from this diagram an ambitious mother, likely in need of improving herself, and an effective transmission of such values to two daughters, but not to the third (patient), who breaks down when her "main support" leaves her. She had never felt appreciated as her sisters were and thus felt unable to replace the dying sister. In addition, the father felt very close to the patient and overprotected her, trying to mend the rift with her boyfriend.

A summary list of clinical judgments about the five major family system components has been found useful in arriving at treatment indications. However, establishing the need for remedial measures in this way does not necessarily indicate what form or combination of treatments may be most suitable in any particular clinical situation. Assessments can be plotted along a continuum ranging from good or optimal, to mixed, to abnormal or deficient functioning, or for example from (1-Good) to (5-Aberrant). The following tentative list has been and is being tested in our center and its reliability among different clinicians validated.

Leadership	Boundaries	Affectivity	Communication	Task/Goal Performance
Parental personalities	Ego boundary development in children	Inter-parental intimacy	Clarity as to form and syntax	Nurturance and weaning
Marital coalition	Generation boundary	Equivalence of family triads	Responsiveness	Separation mastery
Parental role complementarities	Family-community permeability	Tolerance for feelings	Verbal/non-verbal consistency	Behavior control and guidance
Use of power (discipline)		Unit emotionality	Expressivity	Peer relationship management
			Abstract thinking	Unit leisure
				Crisis coping
				Emancipation
				Post-nuclear family adjustments

TECHNIQUES

We do not advocate a stereotype technique for family treatment. There are some ground rules we believe to be sound, but special technical maneuvers like "getting into the system" (34) or "reciprocal suggestions or tasks" (35), etc. are very successful if carried out by sensitive, experienced masters of the art, but are not necessarily so if attempted by others, even if there is conviction as to the soundness of a particular intervention.

We would advocate that a leader/therapist meet with the family, establish him- or herself as a helper and the person to set boundaries and rules if necessary. The therapist should use the first session or two to obtain a marital and family history, in addition to allowing for some relatively unstructured family interaction. The family should be invited to state the problem, and agreement or disagreement on this statement should be established. This may encompass much of the first session. The therapist should avoid special or intensive involvement with any one member, but in an initial interview should invite some activity from each member (36).

After the initial sessions—perhaps up to four or five—the therapist should put into writing his or her formulation of the problem and how it is to be treated, not necessarily only through family therapy. The recommendation should be communicated to the family in language useful to them and with appropriate proposals for subsequent sessions and schedules.

Unless two therapists intend to work together as a team indefinitely and are willing to work at becoming a team, we recommend against co-therapists. If there is a problem of data overload with a very active family, especially for a beginning therapist, it is preferable to have a non-participant observer either in the room or behind a one-way mirror instead of crowding a beginner by coupling him or her with an experienced therapist who probably would and should dominate the therapeutic interaction.

HOSPITALIZATION

Because of the system's interdependence, the hospitalization of any family member for whatever reasons constitutes a family crisis requiring minimally sympathetic and supportive interaction between family and hospital staff. If the hospitalization is for psychiatric reasons, such a crisis is particularly severe because of the probable prior efforts on the part of the family to contain the problem within its midst. Furthermore, it is possible, if not likely, that that containment served to maintain system equilibrium and also that such homeostasis has been maintained by virtue of the patient's symptoms and maladaptive or aberrant behavior. In this case, considerable resistance to hospitalization or to its continuance may be encountered. Lastly, the hospitalization can also represent the family's need and effort to extrude the identified patient either after or without prolonged efforts to maintain him or her within the system (37).

Whichever of these contingencies may be particularly valid, system upheaval is very likely at the time of hospitalization, including a sense of conflict, guilt, shame and anger in the individuals and in the group. A sense of failure may be unavoidable under such circumstances as it is in any situation where system dysfunction and discomfort cannot be corrected from within the system; with that sense of failure, reactive and defensive stances are likely to be manifest. In the case of psychiatric illness, this most often is expressed in an effort to find blame outside the system, or results in a magic belief in and frantic search for some causative biological factor beyond human control. Therefore, the family of any newly hospitalized psychiatric patient deserves professional attention and help with the immediate crisis by being informed as much as possible about the nature of the hospital program, about the likely duration of the institutional care, and about whatever therapeutic program is planned for the patient and for the family respectively. Often families and patients attempt to collude for a time in blaming the hospitalization and hospital procedures for the patient's difficulties, instead of exploring with the therapist(s) antecedents of the illness and the family's functioning and history.

Further treatment indications essentially parallel those listed for family treatment in general, but obviously with a hospitalized patient, individual and other forms of treatment for the patient are also indicated.

From the earliest possible time in the hospitalization, the family should be helped with the admission crisis. A minimal program for working with patients' families should be arranged to keep the family abreast of the patient's development and his or her clinical course, and to prepare and work with the family for the eventual disposition and discharge of the patient. Even when such plans can be formulated only tentatively, one of the major decisions to be made early is whether it is envisioned, if not planned, that the patient join the family to continue living with them or whether the assessment of the family system and of the patient's age-appropriate needs will point to the patient's living apart from the family in the future. The reverse can, of course, also be a necessary consideration, i.e. whether patients who have attempted to live apart from their families of origin or procreation should return to living with them, at least temporarily if not permanently.

A common constellation is a breakdown in personal functioning of a young adult at the time of expected emancipation from his or her family of origin, either while facing this step or after a relatively brief period of having attempted to implement it. These considerations must also determine whether therapeutic work planned with the family is to be done with the entire family as a group, the patient included, or whether the parents or the parents and siblings should be treated in sessions without the patient. Often it is indicated that one proceed from one format to another, but the ultimate aim is to enable the family to accept and live with whatever disposition is considered optimal. Without therapeutic work and some essential change in the family equilibrium, for instance a rapprochement between the parents so that one or the other parent can forego the close bind to a child or delegating a particular role to this child as described in detail by Stierlin (38, 39), pathogenic forces will continue and re-hospitalization is likely to occur.

It is also important that the family not reestablish a similar equilibrium without the hospitalized patient, thereby creating a new "patient" in their midst. It is not an infrequent experience that following hospitalization of one child and amelioration of the immediate crisis, another child will develop symptoms. Therefore, family therapy can have immediate preventive impact; it should also have a more long-range, but possibly less obvious, preventive result for the entire system.

Indications for more formal family treatment exist if there is a clear assessment that it is not only the family stressed by the mental illness of one member, but also the established type of family system that contributes significantly to the development of the illness. We can point out four types of such etiological movement.

1) We have indicated in the foregoing section that the patient may serve as a kind of messenger for family disturbance. However, if this messenger "status" is not reached until the particular family member becomes so disturbed that he or she has to be hospitalized, there are obvious indications for individual therapy as well as family treatment. Most likely in such families, there is severe leadership aberration aside

from other system defects pointing to marital conflict or some unresolved interpersonal or neurotic condition in one or both parents.

2) The identified patient may have served as a significant homeostabilizing element in the system. This phenomenon seems to occur in two ways (40):

a) One is in a family equilibrium where much concern and attention and emotional force are directed toward and attached to a problem-member, be it a delinquent child, an ailing possibly hypochondriacal parent, or a child with eating problems. As long as the overt problem continues as a daily preoccupation and concern, other more basic system deficits can be ignored, or indeed may exist and smolder because the "noisy" problem leaves no time or energy for more basic issues. Such a family pattern is often seen in patients identified as anorexia nervosa, and their treatment has been described in detail by Minuchin and Selvini (34,41). In such instances, family therapy is a must and often very effective in addition to the possibly lifesaving treatment of a hospitalized patient of this type. Even in less pathological systems, homeostasis may be based on infantilizing growing children so that just by virtue of biopsychological development an impasse is reached when one or the other child is expected and needs for the sake of his or her personal growth to move increasingly outside the family.

b) The other hidden homeostatic maintenance role we have observed at a time of acute psychiatric illness or deterioration in a chronic psychiatric condition concerns families in which parents are contemplating separation or dissolution of the marriage. The illness then provides a focus for both parents; unless the basic conflict between the parents is resolved in whatever direction, the patient will retain a stake in remaining ill so as to keep his or her parents together, or at least to remain involved with both of them in significant ways. This does not mean that the treatment goal must be in the direction of maintaining the marriage as such, but rather that the problems be treated as indicated regardless of ultimate reconstitution or dissolution of the system (42).

3) A related, but also different problem leading to hospitalization arises when emancipation of a child from the family is resisted by the system, also a common finding. In such instances, there may have been relatively little psychiatric disturbance in the clinical sense on the part of any individual, but the system, especially in its boundary management, is overly rigid and parents may be unable to face the prospect of living as a dyad again. There may be more pathological themes, such as that a child may have been used to avoid confrontations between

the spouses or between the parents and another child, or that one or the other parent, or both of them, will permit emancipation only in a constrained fashion—for instance, insisting on a career choice which may be anathema to the particular child. The hospitalization may, therefore, actually constitute for such a patient a step toward emancipation and separation, albeit a very circuitous and painful one. Again, this is a clear indication for family therapy in addition to whatever individual treatment may be indicated for the patient, but probably a family therapy plan that soon will move to working with the family without the hospitalized patient.

4) Lastly, there is extrusion of the patient by a family that cannot accept or work out within its system a particular member's handicap, career choice, personality change, etc. Extrusion can be perpetrated upon either parent, siblings or children, and may have beneficial effects for the entire family, as for instance in the case of the hospitalization of an alcoholic parent with a stance that he or she will not be acceptable into the system unless the drinking stops. It may indeed be realistic in that the family system can function better with one parent than with a severely disturbed and disturbing second parent. It is, of course, well known that often only such a step inflicts sufficient pain on an addictive person for him to accept treatment and rehabilitation.

REFERENCES

1. Midelfort, C. F. *The Family in Psychotherapy.* New York: McGraw-Hill, 1957.
2. Lidz, T., Fleck, S., and Cornelison, A. *Schizophrenia and the Family.* New York: International Universities Press, 1965.
3. Alanen, Y. O. Some thoughts on schizophrenia and ego development in the light of family investigation. *Arch. Gen. Psychiat.,* 1960, 3:650-656.
4. Bowen, M. The family as the unit of study and treatment: 1. Family psychotherapy. *Amer. J. Orthopsychiat.,* 1961, 31:40-60.
5. Jackson, D. D. and Weakland, J. Schizophrenic symptoms and family interaction. *Arch. Gen. Psychiat.,* 1959, 1:618-621.
6. Ackerman, N. W. Interpersonal disturbances in the family: Some unsolved problems in psychotherapy. *Psychiatry,* 1954, 17:359-368.
7. Dicks, H. F. *Marital Tensions: Clinical Studies Toward a Psychological Theory of Interaction.* New York: Basic Books, 1967.
8. Lidz, T. *The Person* (Revised ed.). New York: Basic Books, 1976.
9. Fleck, S. The Family and Psychiatry. In: A. Freedman, H. Kaplan, and B. Sadock (Eds.), *Comprehensive Textbook of Psychiatry—II.* Baltimore: Williams & Wilkins (Second ed.), 1976.
10. Fleck, S. Unified health services and family-focused primary care. *Int. J. Psychiat. Med.,* 1975, 6:501-515.
11. Freud, S. 1905 Fragment of an analysis of a case of hysteria. In: *Standard Edition of the Complete Psychological Works of Sigmund Freud, Vol. 7.* London: Hogarth Press, 1953.

12. Freud, S. Analyse der phobie eines funfjahrigen knaben. In: *Sigmund Freud Gesammelte Werke, Chronologisch Geordnet VII, Werke Aus Den Jahren 1906-1909*. London: Imago Publishing Co., Ltd., 1941.
13. Pratt, J. H. The influence of emotions in the causation and cure of psychoneuroses. *Int. Clinics*, 1934, 4:1.
14. Bion, W. R. *Experiences in Groups*. New York: Basic Books, 1961.
15. Skynner, A. C. R. *Family and Marital Psychotherapy*. New York: Brunner/Mazel, 1976.
16. Richardson, H. B. *Patients Have Families*. New York: Commonwealth Fund, 1948.
17. Oberndorf, C. P. Psychoanalysis of married couples. *Psychoanal. Rev.*, 1938, 25: 453-475.
18. Martin, P. A. *A Marital Therapy Manual*. New York: Brunner/Mazel, 1976.
19. Kreitman, N. The patient's spouse. *Brit. J. Psychiat.*, 1964, 110:159-173.
20. Paul, N. and Grossner, G. H. Operational mourning and its role in conjoint family therapy. *Community Mental Health Journal*, 1965, 1:339-345.
21. Wallerstein, J. S. and Kelly, J. B. Divorce counseling: A community service for families in the midst of divorce. *Amer. J. Orthopsychiat.*, 1977, 47:4-22.
22. Goldstein, J., Freud, A., and Solnit, A. *Beyond the Best Interests of the Child*. New York: Free Press (Macmillan), 1973.
23. Stierlin, H. Family dynamics and separation patterns of potential schizophrenics. In: Proceedings 4th Symposium of Psychotherapy of Schizophrenia, Amsterdam. *Excerpta Med.*, 1972, 56:166.
24. Wynne, L. C., Ryckoff, I., et al. Pseudo-mutuality in the family relations of schizophrenics. *Psychiatry*, 1958, 21:205-220.
25. Bruch, H. Falsification of body needs and body concepts in schizophrenics. *Arch. Gen. Psychiat.*, 1962, 126:85-90.
26. Fleck, S., Lidz, T., et al. The intrafamilial environment of the schizophrenic patient: Incestuous and homosexual problems. In: J. H. Masserman (Ed.), *Individual and Familial Dynamics*. New York: Grune & Stratton, 1959.
27. Ackerman, N. W. *Treating the Troubled Family*. New York: Basic Books, 1966.
28. Scheflen, A. *Body Language and Social Order: Communication as Behavior Control*. New Jersey: Prentice-Hall, 1972.
29. Watzlawick, P., Beavin, J. H., and Jackson, D. D. *Pragmatics of Human Communication*. New York: W. W. Norton & Co., Inc., 1967.
30. Bateson, G., Jackson, D., Haley, J., and Weakland, J. Toward a theory of schizophrenia. *Behav. Sci.*, 1956, 1:251-264.
31. Erikson, E. H. *Childhood and Society*. New York: W. W. Norton, 1950.
32. Beavers, W. R. *Psychotherapy and Growth: A Family Systems Perspective*. New York: Brunner/Mazel, 1977.
33. Whitehorn, J. C. and Betz, B. *Effective Psychotherapy With the Schizophrenic Patient*. New York: J. Aronson, Inc., 1975.
34. Minuchin, S. *Families and Family Therapy*. Cambridge, Massachusetts: Harvard University Press, 1974.
35. Selvini, P., Boscoto, G., et al. *Paradoxon und Gegenparadoxon*. Stuttgart: Klett-Cotta, 1977.
36. Stierlin, H. Rücker-Embden, I., et al. *Das erste Familien gespräch*. Stuttgart: Klett-Cotta, 1977.
37. Fleck, S., Cornelison, A., Norton, N., and Lidz, T. Interaction between hospital staff and families. *Psychiatry*, 1957, 20:343-350.
38. Stierlin, H. The adaptation of the "stronger" person's reality: Some aspects of the symbolic relationship of the schizophrenic. *Psychiatry*, 1959, 22:143-152.

39. Boszormenyi-Nagy, I. Loyalty implications of the transference model in psychotherapy. *Arch. Gen. Psychiat.*, 1972, 27:373-380.
40. Jackson, D. D. *The Question of Family Homeostasis. Psychiat. Quart.*, 1957, 31:79-90.
41. Selvini, P. *Self-Starvation.* London: Chaucer Publ., 1974.
42. Fleck, S. Psychiatric hospitalization as a family experience. *Acta Psychiatrica Scand. Suppl.*, 1963, 169 (39):1-24.

24

Behavioral Techniques in
Conjunction with Individual
Psychoanalytic Therapy

ALLAN COOPER, PH.D.

Psychoanalytic psychotherapy conducted by a competent therapist and an apparently motivated patient sometimes develops an impasse. Much time and thought have been devoted in the literature to dealing with various forms of therapeutic stalemates. Problems in the transference/countertransference relationship have been discussed; intrapsychic motivations to remain under psychological distress have long been considered part of such problems. In the treatment situation, the analytic therapist and patient look for unconscious motivations that may represent the resistance to change. After extensive exploration, the therapeutic stalemate sometimes remains. The therapist may have no alternative but to stop treatment, or do more of what he has been doing.

When certain impasses present a stalemate in psychoanalytic psychotherapy, the use of certain behavior therapy techniques may be of help. What makes this suggestion startling and unusual is that psychoanalytic theory and behavioristic theory appear to have very different views about the nature or source of symptoms and psychological difficulties. However, a therapist does not have to resolve issues of theoretical difference in order to utilize these procedures. The clinician has to see if a procedure will be of help to his patient. For instance, a therapist may feel that an antidepressant medication would be helpful during psychoanalytic psychotherapy without subscribing to the notion that all neuroses are biochemical in nature. If new procedures are successful. the clinician may modify his theory and find a way to reconceptualize the procedures so that they fit into his slightly altered theoretical position.

There have been a few authors who have attempted to integrate behavior therapy techniques with psychoanalytic psychotherapy (1, 2, 3). For the most part, however, psychoanalytic therapists have viewed behavioral approaches with alarm, fear, or disbelief. For the most part, analytic therapists are not acquainted with the procedures used in behavior therapy. They often react to what they imagine the procedures consist of and tend to regard these procedures as authoritarian in nature. Wachtel has discussed this issue at several points in his book (2) on the integration of psychoanalysis and behavior therapy.

The number of techniques that can be included under the rubric of behavior therapy is great. It is not possible to discuss all these techniques in the present discussion. This discussion will include only those techniques introduced by Wolpe, which probably represent the major techniques used in outpatient practice.

The techniques include desensitization, assertive training, and sexual retraining. These procedures have in common a gradual approach to a situation that produces anxiety. Be the problem an actual phobia or a fear of direct expression to others, the desired goal is approached in a series of incremental steps. These steps have been discussed with the patient, and the patient actively participates in bringing in material and evaluating how much anxiety would be produced if the patient were actually in the situation in question. The therapist also takes an active role in inquiring about situations related to the problem in question.

When ten to twelve situations related to the problem have been collected and rank-ordered for degree of difficulty, they are presented to the patient. In the desensitization procedure, the patient is taught muscle relaxation and trained to be able to enter a state of extreme body relaxation. In this state the patient is asked to visualize the scenes that were worked out earlier. Each scene is presented a few times, with a rest period between presentations. The scenes are presented in rank order, moving from least anxiety-provoking up the scale until the most frightening scene is finally visualized without anxiety. As each scene is desensitized so that it no longer evokes anxiety, the succeeding scene appears to be less frightening than it was before the procedure was begun. Thus, when the fifth item is presented for imagination, it does not evoke as much anxiety as it would have if it had been presented at the beginning of procedure. However, the imagined situation still does evoke some anxiety until it is desensitized by being imagined several times in the state of extreme body relaxation.

A typical hierarchy presented by Wolpe (4) contained the following items in a claustrophobic series: the lowest item—reading of miners trapped underground; a middle scene—on a journey by train (the longer the journey, the more disturbing); the highest anxiety scene— being stuck in an elevator (the longer the time, the more disturbing). At the conclusion of the hierarchy in imagination, the patient is expected to be able to confront the actual situations without anxiety.

In the case of assertive training, situations are discussed in the manner outlined above. The capacity of the situation to evoke anxiety is discussed, and the situations are rank-ordered. In ease of assertion it might be easier for the patient to express annoyance to a waiter who brings the wrong order than to ask his boss for a raise or a vacation. The types of situations that create interpersonal anxiety will vary with each individual, as will the order of difficulty different situations produce. The patient is then asked to express himself in the actual situations, moving from least to most anxiety-provoking. If the situations, despite their being rank-ordered, still evoke too much anxiety for the patient to express himself, desensitization of the situation in imagination may be added as a prior step. After desensitization in imagination, the patient may then be able to express himself successfully in the actual situation.

In sexual retraining for a problem with impotence, the patient would be asked to avoid attempting intercourse until less anxiety-provoking sexual activities are accomplished without anxiety. The order of activities might be: lying in bed naked with the sexual partner; caressing in a pleasurable, non-erotic way; erotic stimulation without intercourse; and, finally, intercourse. As in the case of assertive training, sexual retraining may be combined with desensitization.

The above descriptions of the procedures are necessarily sketchy in this short a space. A more complete description of the procedures, variations in techniques, and other behavior therapy techniques can be obtained from the literature (5, 6).

It is the use of the procedures of systematic desensitization, assertive training, and sexual retraining that will be discussed as techniques that might loosen some of the stalemates that develop in psychoanalytic psychotherapy.

One area of impasse is that in which specific troublesome symptoms do not abate during the analytic inquiry. This may cause continuous pain, anxiety, and/or embarrassment to the patient. It may also interfere with the patient's ability to talk about anything other than his symptoms and their ramifications. From an analytic perspective, the continuous discussion in therapy of problems with symptoms can be viewed as a resistance. However, if the resistance does not yield to interpretation, confrontation, etc., the therapist and patient are left in a painful stalemate. The introduction of behavior therapy techniques may alleviate the symptoms and may allow the psychoanalytic therapy to continue when the symptom is alleviated. Contrary to the thinking of a few years ago, the alleviation of symptoms does not necessarily reduce the patient's motivation for treatment, but may actually increase motivation for further change. It should also be added that symptom substitution has rarely been reported with treatment by behavioral techniques.

A man came to therapy with a primary complaint of impotence. He had been living with a woman for two years. He was clear about the positive quailties of this woman, who was a few years younger than he. She was bright, verbal, lively, exciting, successful in her career, and very attractive. He had had a good sexual relationship with her for over a year when the problem with impotence began. He could not trace his reaction to any difficulty in his interaction with his partner, nor could she identify any interpersonal difficulty that precipitated the lack of sexual response. Several other potential precipitants were explored in the course of early interviews. The death of a close friend from a lingering illness had occurred around the time of onset of the impotence, but precise relationship in time was vague. Business worries and successes had fluctuated during the past several years. His developmental history indicated both deprivation and a rather strict upbringing, with rather harsh punishments for minor infractions of conduct. However, he was not aware of any resentment, anger, or depression related to parental treatment in the past or present. He was aware that he did not feel very close to anyone in his family, but he remained on pleasant terms with family members and tried to fulfill what he considered his obligations to them.

During sessions he appeared to be cooperative and motivated, but his thoughts did not range far afield from his symptoms. After a few months of twice-a-week psychoanalytically-oriented psychotherapy, I suggested a behavioral approach to the problems of impotence in the form of a graded approach to sexual intimacy. The patient and I discussed the stages of intimacy that would lead finally to sexual intercourse. They ranged from lying naked together, to non-erotic but pleasurable caressing, to several levels of erotic intimacy, and, finally, to intercourse. I explained that he should not shift stages of sexual intimacy too rapidly, so that he could feel pleasure and enjoyment without the anxiety of having to perform. He explained the procedure to his friend, who was agreeable to following the plan. Within a month he was able to have erections and to have intercourse.

At first the patient and his girlfriend were delighted with the change. However, the patient soon began to complain that, although he could perform adequately, he did not enjoy it very much. This led the patient to a more careful evaluation of his relationship with his partner. He began to recognize a pattern in which most ideas about what they should do came from her. He began to be aware that he was both resentful at always pleasing her and chagrined at himself for not having many desires about what he, himself, would like to do. These issues led to further investigation in therapy.

The point of this vignette is to indicate that the use of a behavioral approach to a symptom is not incompatible with analytic therapy and may facilitate the analytic process. In the above instance, the alleviation of a disturbing symptom led to a closer investigation of the patient's character problems and how these problems affected his relationships.

We cannot know how things would have worked out if I had not employed the behavioral procedures. However, I am indicating that if one's clinical judgment suggests the use of other techniques, behavior therapy techniques may be useful both in alleviating a symptom and in facilitating analytic therapy.

Obviously, there is no guarantee that an attempt to alleviate a symptom by behavioral techniques will be successful. In one case of a married man with a problem of impotence alternating with premature ejaculation, a program similar to the one outlined above was suggested. In that case the patient reported that, atlhough his wife agreed to follow the procedure, she seemed to do everything wrong. The procedure failed to alleviate the symptom, and the analytic therapy continued. However, some information about this patient's capacity to cooperate with his wife and others was obtained and questions about his ability to accept help were raised for the analytic therapy. It did not appear that much was gained in the way of symptom alleviation from the procedure in this instance, but it did not appear that much was lost in the process and some increased awareness of character problems was obtained. Many analytic therapists who are not familiar with behavioral procedures regard them as authoritarian, controlling, and therefore dangerous and stifling of the patient's independence. However, anyone who has actually worked with the more common behavioral techniques is aware that they are quite benign and tend to be simply ineffective when they do not succeed.

An obvious area of concern by therapists would be how the introduction of behavioral techniques affects the therapeutic relationship. If a therapist takes as his exclusive model a psychoanalytic technique in which the therapist tries to remain neutral and vague in order to facilitate the expression of phantasy material in the transference, the introduction of any parameter is obviously incompatible with the procedure.

If, however, one accepts the concepts of psychodynamics and the transference, but is willing to interact with the patient, then the introduction of behavioral techniques should not alter the basic nature of inquiry into the relationship between the patient and therapist.

During the introduction of behavioral techniques, the therapist assumes a more active role of educator and expert. This may be especially helpful where the patient has difficulty in the process of working through certain issues of a long-standing characterological nature. When analytic therapy is working well, the patient recognizes and discusses patterns of interaction with people. Often the patient will attempt to change certain patterns to produce more effective and satisfying relationships. Much of this work is done spontaneously by the patient and may only be mentioned incidentally in the therapy sessions. For instance, a man began to observe in greater detail how he held back at meetings and in initial interactions with other professionals. He began to realize that he automatically expected that, if he appeared confident and competent, people would have excessive and unrealistic expectations of him. His phantasies and dreams indicated that not being able to fulfill these expectations would lead to severe disappointment and anger from others. When further inquiry in this area was pursued in succeeding months, his own competitive feelings began to emerge. The analytic inquiry and discussion led the patient to resonate within himself to the therapy discussions. This led to dreams, phantasies, new observations, recollections, and attempts at new behavior. Although he had employed a variety of defenses over the years to deal with his anxiety over angry, competitive feelings, he could recall having the feelings, and in some cases acting on these feelings, as a young boy. As he began to differentiate between appropriate and inappropriate reactions within himself, he was able to experiment with new behaviors on his own, with no prompting from the therapist. The patient's activity in his own behalf was of obvious help in changing his patterns of interaction with people and facilitated the working through.

With this type of patient no modification of technique seems to be required.

One of the serious problems in analytic therapy arises when the patient talks over and over about some pattern of interaction with people but makes no attempts at changing these patterns. Often the patient appears to search for new insights which will lead to his understanding why he doesn't change his behavior. The therapist may continue to explore, inquire, and analyze. He may continue to search for the meaning of the patient's resistance to change and hope that a more precise interpretation will lead to a significant insight that will move the patient towards change. However, as a number of therapists have observed, insight often follows change rather than being the cause of change. The search for understanding oneself is the important process of analytic therapy. However, at times the search for understanding can be put in the service of a subtle form of passivity in which the patient secretly hopes that the therapist will provide the correct insight that will magically change the patient. The patient hopes he can be spared the anxiety and struggle that often accompany attempts at change. The therapist's attempts at further understanding and interpretations may collude with the patient's passive orientation. The patient may even derive some gratification from the therapist's attempts to help or may enjoy seeing the therapist frustrated in his attempts to be helpful. In any event, the patient may ultimately be left with the frustrations and anxieties inherent in the types of interactions he has been unable to change. The therapist may be forced to conclude that the patient's resistances were too powerful, that the patient really needed this type of interaction, and that the patient had a powerful masochistic need to remain the same.

However, it may be that therapists with psychoanalytic orientation are at times oversold on the concept that the unconscious processes control all change. They therefore make an *a priori* assumption that attempts to achieve change by methods that do not deal with the unconscious are doomed to failure. However, this assumption does not agree with data that patients present to us.

One patient who came for treatment of depression with feelings of anxiety and sadness had on the occasion of the outbreak of her symptoms also developed a phobia of heights. She had on her own initiative developed a form of desensitization technique in which she gradually moved herself to looking out windows in her house at greater and greater heights. When she came to feel comfortable at one height, she would move on to the next. She continued this spontaneously developed procedure until she was able to endure the various heights without anxiety.

A man who came to therapy with problems centering around his difficulty in communicating and feeling close to a woman reported that a few years before he came to therapy he had developed a severe claustrophobic reaction. He was unable to sit in any small confined area. He was unable to have dinner in a restaurant because of the claustrophobic sensation of being trapped, with ensuing waves of panic. However, when he told one girlfriend about this problem, she suggested that they go to a restaurant and assured him that if he felt anxious she would be willing to leave immediately without finishing the meal. He reported that this produced a sense of security within him, so that when he went to the restaurant he did not feel the anxiety; the claustrophobia abated and had not returned since.

One can certainly wonder about what factors produced the change in this man; in fact, they were profitably explored in therapy. However, the point I am focusing on is that important change takes place without first making unconscious material conscious. In fact, previously dissociated material may become conscious as the patient begins to make changes, especially in his interaction with others. Under ideal conditions, discussion with the therapist may lead to pointing out of patterns that were not previously noted in a focused way by the patient. This may stir recollections of earlier patterns of interactions and clarification of feelings. The patient may then, spontaneously and without urging from the therapist, begin to behave and interact differently with others, which will lead to the surfacing of other conflicts and dissociated material. However, when this pattern does not occur and when the patient does not put into action any of the insight gained in therapy, the therapist may feel that his only recourse is to try to provide more insight into the unconscious processes. At some point of exasperation or frustration the therapist may ask, "What would be so terrible if you told your mother . . . father . . . child . . . that you didn't feel like doing what they ask?"

The problem with this indirect urging of the patient to action is that the therapist is forced to react to a situation that the patient has spontaneously brought to the therapist's attention. I think it is especially true, where patients have difficulty in asserting themselves and being direct and straightforward, that what they discuss in therapy is only a fragment of the total problem they have with assertion.

There are several problems that are often encountered by people who have serious difficulty in learning to assert themselves. They have often come from homes in which any form of assertion was strongly discouraged. Their families often equated assertion with aggression or hostility. The patients were threatened with loss of love and with being viewed in a negative way if they attempted to assert their feelings and opinions. If this pattern were not modified through interactions with peers, a total state of inhibition of assertion may have developed and been maintained until the patient entered therapy. The patient has become used to rationalizing his lack of assertion. In many, many small incidents he will tell himself that it would be unimportant to say what he felt, or that it might even be petty. There is nothing wrong with the judgment as it is applied to any given incident. However, if many incidents are observed, it could be seen that there is a compulsive quality to the lack of assertion and that the choice is not voluntary. The patient lacks the option to assert himself. This freedom of choice becomes the goal of the behavioral change. The goal should not be to make the patient an assertive individual. To decide what kind of person the patient should be is clearly a countertransference problem of the worst order and does indicate an authoritarian orientation. The patient who is used to rationalizing his lack of assertion will dismiss incident after incident until a situation develops in which his lack of assertion embarrasses him or causes him a severe problem, such as not asking for a raise.

This type of patient raises the issue only on the rare occasions in which an embarrassing situation has suddenly developed. He does not have the resources to handle such an extreme situation. He may continue to avoid assertions in the milder everyday encounters and probably will have a blind spot regarding these events. His self-image may be dependent on his being a saint. His initial discussion of difficulty in assertion probably will not be followed up spontaneously until a new humiliating incident develops. As in most learning or relearning situations, it is best to progress from the simple to the difficult. However, life's events, especially as observed by the patient with selective inattention, do not present themselves in a way that is orderly enough to be optimal for learning. Events may appear to pop up in a willy-nilly fashion, and it is especially the more difficult ones that capture the patient's attention.

It can be helpful to the patient if the therapist takes a more active behavioral approach with such a patient. In order to do this, the therapist must actively explore situations in which assertion is a possible response. He can use some stock situations requiring assertion that have been compiled in the literature and can use his imagination to raise questions about other situations. He can then rank-order these situations with the patient. The patient can then practice new behaviors in a way that is within his grasp and is conducive to learning. This is not to say that various problems and unexpected issues may not develop. They probably will, and this is all to the good as it probably represents other characterological issues that are related to the issue of assertion.

I am suggesting that it may be of more therapeutic benefit to develop a detailed analysis of the patient's capacity to assert himself with different people and in different situations than simply to explore his phantasies about assertion. Especially when the therapy is at an impasse, it would seem that the therapist should not do more of the same thing when that procedure has not yielded results. Furthermore, when a therapist addresses an issue as potent as being able to be direct with other people (strangers, friends, family), change in this area is bound to resonate with the total personality and produce new material in the patient's observation of self and others, in his dream life, and in his production of phantasies. This ripple effect, especially as it has its effect on intrapsychic processes, has not been reported in the literature because behavioral techniques are used primarily by behavior therapists and the production of dreams and phantasies is not used much in their work. It has been my observation that, when behavioral techniques are added to the analytic therapy, significant material develops in dreams and phantasies which can be used at the therapist's discretion for further analytic work.

One of the few reports of the interaction between behavior therapy techniques and psychoanalytic therapy is provided by Weitzman (3). In a detailed and thoughtful examination of the relationship between behavior therapy and psychoanalytic psychotherapy, he reports the use of desensitization to be of help in working with dreams. He states that when a patient reported a dream in which he had sparse associations, the patient was asked to use the muscle relaxation used in desensitization. The patient was then instructed to imagine either the last image of the dream or an image in the dream that seemed particularly disturbing. The author reports that the procedure greatly enhanced the patient's capacity to produce further images, free associations, and interpretations of their dreams.

Another example of the interaction between behavior therapy techniques and psychoanalytic psychotherapy is provided by Rhodes and Feather (1). They distinguish between symptoms that yield directly to systematic desensitization and those that are resistant to this procedure. These latter symptoms are hypothesized to be related to an active current intrapsychic conflict. The symptoms that yield easily are seen as once having been related to intrapsychic conflict but currently not tied to conflict. The symptom is seen as a vestige of the former conflict. The symptoms that do not yield easily to systematic desensitization are hypothesized to be related to a current intrapsychic conflict. The authors describe using a form of desensitization procedure, but the scenes that the patient is asked to imagine are made up of phantasies based on the therapist's hypothesis of the underlying intrapsychic conflict. For instance, in the case of a young man with a problem of transvestism, they hypothesized underlying unconscious sadistic phantasies towards women. They constructed phantasies to match their hypothesis and asked the patient to imagine these scenes in the desensitization procedure. They report rapid alleviation of the symptom in 29 sessions; five months later in follow-up the patient reported no further desire to dress in women's clothing.

This report presents an interesting amalgam of psychoanalytic and behavioral approaches in which psychoanalytic hypotheses are brought in to help the behavioral technique.

Having stated that use of behavioral techniques not only may produce desired change in some behavior or symptom, but will likely have strong reverberations in the rest of the personality, I would like to return to the question of symptom substitution and why it does not seem to occur when a symptom is alleviated by behavioral techniques.

From the analytic perspective, one would have predicted symptom substitution with the rapid alleviation by behavioral procedures. Since the symptom is seen as a result of an unconscious process, then the alleviation of the symptom leaves the unconscious process intact and it would be anticipated that a new symptom would take the place of the old. On empirical grounds, one would have expected the substitution from early observations of work in hypnosis. However, in early hypnotic technique, direct suggestion using the authority of the therapist and the passive obedience of the patient appear to have been the key factors in symptom alleviation. In using behavioral techniques, the *active* cooperation and participation of the patient are required. He must not only agree to the procedure but must actively help in developing hierarchies, bringing in relevant material and discussing with the therapist his assessment of what is being done. If at any point in the procedure the patient feels that the procedure does not suit him, he can break off the process directly or can sabotage the proceedings unconsciously. I suspect that if the process of change is felt to be threatening, the patient has enough latitude to interfere with the procedure so that change does not take place; therefore, symptom substitution is not an issue.

Viewing behavioral techniques from a psychoanalytic perspective, there has probably been too much emphasis on the older Id psychology. That is, where the unconscious motivations, drives, and conflicts are seen as the powerful, important forces and the primary focus of analytic attention. However, if one thinks more about the newer Ego psychology, much of what is accomplished could be viewed as a strengthening of the ego and the providing of procedures that allow greater adaptation and flexibility. Certainly, if one keeps focused on the patient's relatedness to others, as opposed to a narrow focus on primitive impulses, the learning situation provided by the behavioral techniques will seem more compatible with analytic therapy.

Whenever there is change in one significant area of personality, it is likely that the ripple effect will produce change or the desire for change in other areas. A young woman was afraid to ride in elevators. A new job required that she visit different businesses, requiring that she ride in elevators, which she was unable to do. She had previously been in psychotherapy, which had helped her. Desensitization was considered the technique of choice. She was taught muscle relaxation, and different types of elevators were rank-ordered in terms of the capacity to produce fear or terror. A large, open-grill elevator in a metal shaft where she could both see and communicate with the world outside the elevator was much less frightening than a small, old, slow-moving elevator. A modern, quick-moving elevator with a telephone that connected to the lobby was somewhere between the other two in ability to produce fear. About ten variations in elevators were developed. With her eyes closed and under muscle relaxation, she visualized being in the elevators. She imagined the least frightening elevator first and moved to the next most frightening when the preceding visualization ceased to produce anxiety. As this desensitization procedure was completed, she was able to ride most elevators without anxiety, or with minimal anxiety.

The sessions had not been devoted exclusively to the desensitization procedure. We spoke about her relationships with her husband, her family, her friends, business associates. We spoke somewhat about her daydreams and I listened to her dreams, making a few comments and observations. I had gotten to know her during the desensitization sessions. As she became more able to get around in elevators, she began to talk about her difficulties in relating to others on her job. She explored these relationships, as well as her relationship with her family. She made connections between the familial patterns and her relationships on the job. She began to sort out what she was entitled to and what she was responsible for.

The alleviation of the symptom gave her motivation for making further change. I think that, at the simplest level, it indicated to her that change was possible. The alleviation of the symptom gave her more energy to deal with other issues. The alleviation of the symptom, I think, also changed her self image. I think it made her feel much less like a frightened little girl and allowed her to see herself as a young adult who was entitled to share and interact in the world of other adults. As a result, she felt more motivated and more entitled to work out her relationships and to solidify her image of herself as a grownup.

It used to be said in analytic circles that the symptoms provided the motivation for self-exploration and change. It was feared that, if there were rapid symptom alleviation, the patient would lose his motivation for analytic therapy. I supposed that this might still be the case where the patient enters analytic therapy, becomes frightened, makes a rapid but illusory recovery, and leaves treatment. This type of flight into health is short-lived, and the symptoms usually return. With the use of behavioral techniques, the patient has not been frightened, but has been cooperating with the therapist in working to alleviate the symptom. Under the latter circumstances, when the system is alleviated, the patient feels he has achieved something that is positive for himself and may want to change other aspects of his life. However, it is possible that with the alleviation of the symptom the patient would feel that life is satisfactory and would not want further treatment. I feel that the patient should be entitled to leave with the option to return if life does not run as smoothly as he anticipates. If the therapist decides how much and what kind of change a person should make (albeit for humane reasons based on psychoanalytic understanding of character structure), the therapist will, nevertheless, begin to play Pygmalion. The therapist has the obligation to state what further change he feels might be indicated and to raise questions about stopping if he feels it is unwise to do. However, to insist on further change, exploration, and treatment is at best to play the role of the parent in deciding what is best for the patient and what type of person he should become. To take things a step further, when the analytic therapy bogs down because the patient becomes focused on a debilitating symptom, it may be an injustice to the patient to avoid the use of new techniques on theoretical grounds or on an aesthetic distaste for some other form of treatment, such as the behavior techniques.

It is often possible for the therapist practicing analytic therapy to refer the patient for behavioral techniques while continuing the analytic therapy. A man was in analytic therapy and had a severe elevator phobia. After two years of therapy, the phobia had gotten slightly worse and the patient spent a great deal of time talking about his problem of having to walk thirty flights of stairs to work. In addition to this unwanted exercise, the man lived in dread that someone would discover his fear. In therapy he spent more and more time discussing strategies for how to avoid elevators without anyone's discovering his phobia. The analytic therapy became bogged down in endless discussions of his fear, his strategies to avoid detection, and his search for the cause of the phobia. Both he and the therapist became increasingly frustrated and annoyed with each other.

At this point in the treatment the therapist might think of doing something to alleviate the fears. However, reasoning from an analytic point of view, the therapist might have some serious concerns. The increased focus on the troubling symptom could be viewed as a resistance. As such, the resistance should be analyzed. The therapist might fear that the addition of techniques to deal with the symptom would alter the transference and countertransference so that future analytic therapy would not be possible. However, the therapist referred the patient for behavioral treatment of the phobia. Desensitization of the phobia was successful in alleviating the intensity of the symptom; while it did not eliminate the fear entirely, the patient was able to ride the elevator to work. The patient had continued the analytic therapy while going to a second therapist for behavioral treatment. As soon as the behavioral therapy was added, the patient was able to talk to the analytic therapist about other things, feeling that the behavioral therapist would be dealing with the symptom. When the behavioral therapy was concluded, the patient continued to work with the analytic therapist on other analytic issues.

Analytic therapists who feel that they might like to add parameters when therapy is at an impasse often express concern about what the addition of behavioral techniques will do to the transference/countertransference.

If one is committed to remaining neutral and vague as a technique in order to promote and not interfere with the emergence of transference, then no parameter may be introduced without violating the technique. If one is willing to introduce modifications, then one does have to be alert to the effect on the therapeutic relationship, which includes transference and countertransference. However, if the therapist truly has respect for the powerful force that transference has, then he will not fear that the transference reaction will disappear because he takes a more active role. His activity as an expert who can work in cooperation with the patient in designing approaches to alleviate symptoms or working on procedures that will facilitate the learning of new interactions with others will undoubtedly produce reactions in the patient. Some of these reactions will be distortions based on the patient's prior interpersonal experiences. In working with these procedures, the patient could feel anything from undue gratitude to resentment that he couldn't do it himself. These reactions are worthy of further analysis in treatment, as they would be if the new techniques were not introduced. If transference is the powerful reaction we think it is, it will manifest itself without the special technique of neutrality. More active analytic techniques include working with transference, and analysts who are active, confronting, and spontaneous report a great deal of transference material developing in their work with patients. If the therapeutic atmosphere is open to hearing about these reactions, they will occur and be stated.

In describing what the therapist does when he uses behavioral techniques, there is a tendency to borrow the language of the behaviorists. This can actually be misleading in that the behavioral description is not only operational but includes behavioristic concepts. In behavioristic language, one could say that in desensitization the therapist, through discussion with the patient, develops a series of stimulus situations dealing with whatever the patient is anxious about. These stimuli are presented in rank order, from least to most frightening, while the patient is in a state of extreme relaxation. The presentation is made by asking the patient to imagine the stimulus situations. However, as in any complex activity, there are many things taking place simultaneously. Each therapist is alert to those aspects that his theory suggests are the important and crucial ones. If non-behaviorists used some of the behavioral techniques, they might be alert to the following phenomena: While imagining the frightening scenes, the patient is in a state of muscle relaxation. Does this effect a change in the character armor of the patient, as discussed by Reik?

In working with a patient who has anxiety reactions or multiple phobias, the therapist accepts that the patient has fears without questioning underlying motivations, wishes, impulses and the like. Is this a form of unconditional positive regard for the patient, as described by Rogers? In desensitization, the patient is asked to imagine a frightening scene that is judged to be at a level that will produce minimal anxiety. He is then asked by the therapist to relax. After relaxing, he is asked to face the next, slightly more anxiety-provoking scene and then asked to relax again. In this situation, is the therapist recreating the situation of the good mother, who encourages the child to face an age-appropriate level of anxiety with the reassurance that the child can return to the mother and feel protected and relaxed? Is the process of desensitization a way of correcting a developmental flaw that psychoanalysts have discussed but have no direct way of treating through analysis? The process of relaxation tends to promote an increase in visual imagery. When patients are asked to visualize a scene, they may visualize the scene for a time but may also visualize other images, while stray thoughts and feelings enter their awareness (3). I have had patients describe that, although they could visualize the scene they were asked to, they also had thoughts and images that they could not remember but that were like images they had in dreams, or while falling asleep. Are these stray thoughts and images free associations that are connected to the fear, and are these associations also being desensitized?

I raise these questions to indicate that there are many phenomena taking place that might be worthy of study in their own right. I do not raise these notions to refute the behavioral theory that a special kind of learning, called conditioning, is taking place. A theory is a model for understanding and predicting. I am suggesting that when therapists of other theoretical viewpoints use the behavioral techniques they may refine their observations and thinking about their own theoretical point of view.

At a practical level, the introduction of behavioral techniques into analytic therapy may be of help to the patient's problems and may facilitate further therapy. The use of behavioral techniques in analytic therapy may also broaden theoretical considerations.

REFERENCES

1. Rhodes, J. M. and Feather, B. W. The application of psychodynamics to behavior therapy. *Amer. J. Psychiat.*, 1974, 131:17-20.
2. Wachtel, P. L. *Psychoanalysis and Behavior Therapy*. New York: Basic Books, 1977.
3. Weitzman, B. Behavior therapy and psychotherapy. *Psychol. Rev.*, 1967, 74:300-317.
4. Wolpe, J. The systematic desensitization treatment of neurosis. *J. Nerv. Ment. Dis.*, 1961, 132:189-203.
5. Wolpe, J. *Psychotherapy by Reciprocal Inhibition*. Stanford: Stanford University Press, 1958.
6. Lazarus, A. A. *Multimodal Behavior Therapy*. New York: Springer, 1976.

25

Combined Psychotherapy and Pharmacotherapy

GERALD J. SARWER-FONER, M.D.

In discussing combined psychotherapy and psychopharmacology, several basic assumptions will be summarized to lay the groundwork for a discussion of the principles involved.

PSYCHOTHERAPY AND THE DOCTOR-PATIENT RELATIONSHIP

The assumption is that the patient is able to participate in psychotherapy and is able to make significant efforts to help himself master those of his problems which at the moment in time are partially or totally unmastered, thus producing symptoms. The patient has to have the attitude that he/she is to work, as an active participant in the process, while the doctor is helping him/her do this, using the therapeutic alliance that exists between doctor and patient for this purpose. This "psychotherapeutic doctor-patient relationship" differs from the "classic doctor-patient relationship." In the latter, the patient has done his duty when he has presented his body and his problems to the doctor for the physician's ministrations. The doctor in this "classic" doctor-patient relationship does the work, the patient being the passively-active recipient of the physician's acts.

In combined psychotherapy and pharmacotherapy, it is a basic assumption that the physician has a therapeutic alliance with the patient for dealing with the patient's problems. The patient discusses with the physician the problems that come to his or her mind. This is true for supportive or relationship psychotherapy in which the doctor is steady, present, friendly but objective, in relating to the patient, who develops a feeling of being cared for and strengthened.

TARGET SYMPTOM APPROACH TO PHARMACOTHERAPY

A medication is given to obtain the particular effects of the medication (4, 7, 11, 12, 22, 24, 25). With both neuroleptics and antidepressant drugs given in adequate dosage, the patients will show the characteristic "clinical pharmacological profile of the drug concerned" (15). This characteristic pharmacological effect is not "specific" for the therapy of a particular psychiatric disease, even though it reliably produces its typical pharmacological action. This is a complicated way of saying that the characteristic clinical pharmacological action of the drug does not necessarily "cure" the psychiatric illness. This author has published studies (1, 12-18, 20) indicating that the establishment of a neuroleptic effect or an "antidepressant" effect influences different patients in different ways, even though the same characteristic clinical pharmacological profile of the drug is present. Some patients, whose major symptoms are controlled or partially controlled by the drug, can improve remarkably quickly. Some improve initially and explore with their significant entourage whether they are indeed better, since they feel better or are beginning to feel better. If their entourage of significant individuals responds with, "Yes, you have changed," the patient continues to integrate his defences in progression towards relative health (17). In some patients, the typical clinical pharmacological profile of a drug may not control symptoms or signs, which are to the patients *the* significant landmarks proving that they are ill or out of their own control. When this occurs, these patients remain essentially clinically unimproved despite the presence of the pharmacological action of the drug. Other patients begin to improve when the drug controls significant symptoms, but if their significant people signal that they are unchanged, or that they are seen as inadequate, they rapidly relapse despite the continuing effects of the drug.

Both Freyhan (2) and Sarwer-Foner (15) advocated a "Target Symptom" approach to psychopharmacology in which the physiological action of the drug given in adequate dosage is used to control specific symptom complexes. For example, if one wants to stop agitation, to control the amount of energy available to striated muscle and the locomotive systems for aggressive, or energetic display, to lower the blood pressure, make a patient feel tired, sleepy, and make him feel held down and need to lie in bed, then a straight-chain phenothiazine having all the above mentioned actions would be used. If instead one wants a patient to be ambulatory despite a neuroleptic dampening effect, i.e. dopaminergic blockade, reducing capacity for muscular energetic action and reducing the feeling of wishing to act while permitting the patient to be up and about, then one of the piperazine substituted phenothiazines would be used. Here the patient's energy is reduced, but there is less tendency to produce a significant fall in blood pressure. The patient therefore finds it easier to be up and around even though he feels chemically held down, and under better control in terms of aggression and energy use.

The patient reacts to the physiological effects of a drug, its side effects, and the neuroleptically determined reactions such as akathisia, dyskinetic reactions, parkinsonism, etc. with either feelings of, "Yes, this is unpleasant, but it is good for me and I can take it," or "It is a hostile brutal attack on me, why are you doing this—you're like everyone else and I won't let you do this to me." If he feels in the last described way, the patient can become more disturbed. This latter often produces (in all varieties of patients, not just schizophrenic patients) the psychodynamically determined "paradoxical" drug reaction which we have previously reported (13). We have elsewhere published the psychodynamic principles governing this type of patient in relationship to drugs and established criteria for selection and for contraindications.

One must at this point introduce the problem of countertransference (16). If the doctor does not like, or fears, the patient (and many patients have excellent reality-testing mechanisms in this sense), and does not wish to become involved psychotherapeutically, he can give drugs as an "excellent" excuse to keep distance between himself and the patient. We have seen physicians trigger panic reactions in patients, not because of anything necessarily specific in that patient, but because the patient sensed all too well the deep rejection of himself by the authoritarian treating figure. This rejection was implied precisely when the physician gave the patient the drug in the first place; therefore, the physiological effects of the drug were interpreted by the patient as a rejecting, hostile, and threatening thing.

Dopaminergic Blockade

It is likely that dopaminergic blockade action by the neuroleptic drugs affects the buildup of the impulse to act at a motor level (9) in the central nervous system by lessening it, and that this is useful in dampening down the energetic tendencies of many schizophrenic patients. However, this is not specifically curative of schizophrenia. It lessens the quantity of action-oriented symptoms in schizophrenic patients, which can have a beneficial effect, once the neuroleptic effect is established, on secondary psychopathological constructs such as the capacity to have hallucinations, delusions, and ideas of reference. The latter actions are, however, secondary phenomena and are not seen in all patients.

COMBINING PSYCHOTHERAPY AND CHEMOTHERAPY

If the above principles are understood, we can then turn to the use of combined psychotherapy and chemotherapy in acute schizophrenic reactions in the hands of the skilled psychiatrist who understands both psychotherapy and pharmacotherapy. In the supportive relationship with an acutely psychotic patient, the doctor would have the basic therapeutic attitude that the patient was potentially capable of pulling himself together and of taking responsibility at some level for his potential improvement even while grossly psychotic. The physician would explain the need for neuroleptic medication after exploring this with the patient. Neuroleptic medication could be given to an involuntary patient, the action of the drug explained, and the patient encouraged to use this action to collaborate with the physician and improve his state.

The drug effect is subjectively perceived by the patient (8, 23). In the midst of an acute psychosis, if the patient sees the doctor as someone with whom he could form a therapeutic alliance, this sets the stage for the patient to begin to test out the doctor's reliability as a potentially trusted person even around crisis intervention in the emergency room or receiving hospital. In other words, this experience can be the beginning of a "bonding" relationship between that patient and that particular physician or other therapeutic staff who participate in helping the patient in acute crisis. As the patient settles down, the fact (because it is then a fact) that the doctor understands enough to give the patient what is needed while encouraging the patient's active collaboration in getting well cements the beginning of the doctor-patient supportive psychotherapeutic relationship.

The patient is then encouraged to discuss the problems in this context, and the doctor does reality-testing psychotherapy with the patient, while the drug is being given. The drug is given with the patient understanding that it will be given for as long as the patient needs it. The length of drug therapy is left as a variable quantity of time, but with a definite implication that when the patient can get along without the drug, the drug will be stopped. By then the patient will have been taught how to use the drug, either with the doctor's help or alone, so that should the patient need further help when things go out of the patient's control, the medicine is available, as well as the doctor's relationship. This is perhaps the trickiest part of the supportive combined psychotherapeutic-pharmacotherapeutic relationship with acutely psychotic patients. Many of these, once they recover, "want no part of anything," including the therapeutic relationship, that reminds them of having been ill (19). The patient must, therefore, be helped to understand the importance of being able to deal with things themselves and handle medicine over a period of time.

In the past, probably the majority of doctors felt that a schizophrenic patient who had had an acute and serious psychotic episode needed ongoing maintenance therapy (i.e. without stop). This author never shared this view for *all* patients, preferring the above-mentioned visualization for many treated in a personalized therapeutic context. The late complications of maintenance neuroleptic therapies, such as tardive or persistent dyskinesia, have done much to bring the need for time-related and time-controlled drug therapies into focus. As a result, many who previously favored ongoing maintenance therapy have adopted a more favorable consideration of a target symptom, patient-physician, cooperation-oriented approach to the chemotherapy, thus tending to introduce more and more of the psychotherapeutic element. In this regard, some studies of "sociotherapy" and pharmacotherapy (3, 6) have shown that the more than two-year progress of patients on neuroleptics and supportive relationship is better as to quality of life, work performance, etc., than straight drug therapy, and this in a straight, once-a-month social work contact.

Treatment of Schizophrenia

A potent neuroleptic, given in adequate dosage, will present its characteristic pharmacological profile in the patient receiving it. Regardless of what this profile is (and it will vary from drug to drug), the neuroleptic drugs have a beneficial effect in schizophrenia when the following conditions seem to be satisfied:

1) The physiological effects (pharmacologic profile) of a drug permit control of a symptom or symptom complex.

2) This symptom complex must express for this particular patient his inability to face himself and his most feared impulses. Here I refer to those specific impulses which, for this particular patient, represent the core of the inner conflict that he cannot solve for himself without regressing into his schizophrenic illness as his best personal compromise.

3) The control of this symptom or symptom complex must be interpreted by the patient as beneficial for him rather than detrimental to him.

4) The patient considers this in terms of his total constellation of impulses, his defences against them, and his present reality situation. Therefore, the patient who benefits from the characteristic pharmacological profile of the neuroleptic medication does so because he interprets the action of the drug in controlling certain symptoms or symptom complexes as a "good" thing for him rather than a "bad" thing for him. For the majority of such patients, much of the efficacy of the medication depends on these external variables which help to give its pharmacological profile the value judgment "good" or "bad." Some of these include the attitude of the doctors, nurses, and orderlies towards both the particular drug and the patient's reaction to receiving it. The unconscious, as well as the conscious, visualization by the patient of what is appropriate to the hospital setting (that is, what is sociologically required of him when under the influence of a drug and therefore is controlled in reference to the standards of behavior in a specific hospital society) may play some role here. Many external factors concerned with interpersonal relations in psychotherapy are vital here.

5) When the above-mentioned symptom complex is controlled by the drug, this lays the foundation for the fundamental process of remitting from a regressed state, that is to say, for ego growth, and the enlarging of neurotic and normal defenses. It is to be emphasized that the patient does not immediately return from a regressed state.

It must be remembered that there are many different types of schizophrenic patients, and there are many approaches to the treatment of patients and to interpersonal dealings with such patients. Not all of these patients need drugs, but in those who do and get better, we feel that the modalities of the treatment are those we are describing.

When a patient with a schizophrenic illness arrives in hospital in an acute phase of his illness, he can be approached from the point of view that you in the hospital are going to help him overcome and master what he is most afraid of in himself and fears in others as stimulating these impulses in him.

Those patients who do well on the drug do so because the drug helps control symptoms expressing the patient's attempts to cope with problems such as intolerable aggression, perverse sexuality, and feelings of total inadequacy producing tremendous frustration, rage and anger. When the physiological effects of the drug help the patient feel that what he most fears in himself has been brought under better control, the stage is set for renewed externalized flow of energy into renewed reality interest and reality testing.

The patient may immediately or very quickly feel changed or see himself as different under such circumstances. He then tests whether this feeling of difference in him is real and, therefore, perceivable by others and accepted by others, or is a transitory thing. He does this by observing very closely the reactions toward him of the hospital staff, as well as other significant figures in the milieu or his family. These testing maneuvers are essentially independent of any drug, but in some patients they come into play through the beneficial action of the drug in controlling the significant symptom complexes.

If the patient improves under these circumstances, he does so because he feels changed as a result of being controlled. He has been made better able to use his powers, for he now visualizes himself as a less fearful and fearsome object. Because he is in better control of himself or feels himself to be a more worthwhile being than before, the world becomes a less fearful place whether actually or potentially. The way in which others (doctors, family, relatives, nurses, hospital staff) regard the patient, what they expect of him, the enthusiasm for or rejection of certain therapeutic agents, all may as a result play important roles here. It is at this point that many patients, previously relatively inaccessible to psychotherapy, become potentially accessible, for they become ready to endow the external world with new interest and to use their energies to deal with it.

When these attempts to reinvest energy (cathexis) on to external objects receive sympathetic responses from his entourage (that is to say, from the significant figures in his milieu, be they doctor, hospital, nurses, or family group), ego reintegration continues and the patient remits from his psychotic episode. It is up to the physician to take full advantage of his knowledge of transference, of the patient's testing maneuvers, of the patient's conflicts, and of the patient's reaction to neuroleptic medication, and to interpret heavily on the side of better interpersonal relations so as to help the patient use his new and very cautiously used "outgoingness" to gain self-confidence. If this is done, the patient responds well. If this situation continues for a sufficiently long time, further ego integration takes place.

Poor Therapeutic Results

When the schizophrenic patient interprets the drug effect as threatening, that is to say, as an assault or manipulative attempt by the physician, or when he feels that it does not help control what he most fears in himself despite the appearance of the characteristic pharmacological effects, the patient either does not get better or can even become worse (13). Sometimes, if the patient initially improves, faulty relationships with his family and significant adults may shatter his newly developing concept of himself as different, and thus curb the externalized flow of energy. Such rejections confirm his worthlessness and his fear of his own impulses; the patient regresses, relapses, or does not get well.

Thus, in schizophrenia the role of medication is to control those "target symptoms" which express the patient's inability to tolerate those of his impulses which represent to him the essence of his conflicts. If these are controlled, this makes the patient more accessible to psychotherapy, more able to channelize energy into externalized contacts and renewed interest in external reality and interpersonal relations. It is at this point that psychotherapy may become more meaningful, and that psychotherapy may be of more direct benefit in the patient's reality testing maneuvers.

Psychotic Decompensation During Psychotherapy

When a patient in psychotherapy (i.e. without concomitant drug therapy) begins to show signs of deterioration of his ego defenses, the signs and symptoms of a threatened eruption of an underlying psychosis can begin to appear. Increased anxiety, restlessness, irritability, and frightening dreams appear. Sometimes the first warning the physician has is the emergence of an acute psychotic episode with florid schizo-affective or florid paranoid symptomatology, with much affect and agitation. The physician must ask himself which of the symptoms most symbolizes for the patient his feared psychotic deterioration. For example, if the patient cannot sleep and is having nightmares—nightmares which represent the patient's disintegrating mind—the capacity to medicate adequately, to guarantee sleep in the context of psychotherapeutic support, can prove to the patient that the doctor understands the process, and is able to do something about it. Generally, if this is done systematically producing several good nights' sleep and counteracting the sleepless exhaustion that the nightmares have been producing, the patient will often pull himself together and the threatened psychotic deterioration will disappear. Meanwhile, the life crisis that produced it can be fruitfully explored in the supportive psychotherapeutic relationship.

This also holds true when one is doing uncovering psychotherapy, and applies to the decompensating crises that can be occasionally seen even during psychoanalysis (the most intensive form of psychotherapy) of a patient. The symptomatology and the downward progression in the patient's ego defenses indicate that interpretations and the therapeutic relationship are at the moment not necessarily enough. This happens rarely, but particularly with some borderline patients during exploration of weaning and separation experiences (5, 21). In these cases it is very important to medicate the patient adequately, so that what is uncontrollable becomes more controllable, while one continues the psychotherapeutic uncovering or psychoanalytic relationship. Sometimes in psychoanalysis it is necessary to sit the patient up during such a crisis, but on many occasions it is possible to carry on with the patient on the couch, provided that the patient is able to feel that the physician can help him master that which becomes much more dubious and more difficult without these interventions (1, 9). The important thing *in the context of psychoanalysis* is to withdraw all the drug treatment as soon as the patient can master the situation himself; thus, the use of drugs in this context is a "parameter" to be introduced when needed but to be withdrawn as quickly as possible and in full collaboration with the patient when not needed.

In short, in all the above situations, the concept of a time-limited intervention of a nonpsychotherapeutic kind, only when needed—and only to strengthen the patient's ego and ego capacities—is the principle around which one uses pharmacotherapy.

Anti-Depressant Drugs and Psychotherapy

Psychotropic medication includes the tricyclics, the quadracyclics, and the MAO Inhibitors. These are active psychotropic agents when given in adequate dosage. Again, they produce a characteristic clinical pharmacological profile and, again, this drug action is not specifically curative, but rather helpful. We must remember that the vast majority of patients who consult the physician with a depressive illness consult him for a Reactive

Neurotic Depression. These conditions are generally time limited and most patients improve in more than thirty days and within six months to a year, with the vast majority improving in the first six months. Thus, there is an inherent time-related improvement pattern. The majority of such patients are seeking support and the recovery of significant object relationships shattered through loss, i.e. losses which have shattered their inner concept of self. This may be the loss of a job, the loss of a loved one, the loss of a boyfriend, girlfriend, wife or husband, a shattering emotional rejection such as a lack of promotion or getting fired from a position which symbolically represented the persona of the individual. It is the symbolic representation of this event that affects the patient. The presence of *unconscious hope* in the patient should be assessed. The patient who is unconsciously hopeless and thus feels helpless and abandoned cannot really aim his symptomatology at the physician with a demand for resolution. The fact that a patient is able to form a therapeutic relationship with a doctor and aims his symptomatology at the physician for resolution, even though the patient looks helpless and hopeless on the surface, is an indication of the presence of at least unconscious hopefulness. Its presence and extent have to be used psychotherapeutically.

The physician should maintain the capacity to be a steady, realistically optimistic person, who helps the patient fight through his difficulties in psychotherapy. The target symptom principle is used here. One must remember that the antidepressant medication may temporarily induce drowsiness and have other side effects, but that the main therapeutic effect of the antidepressants is to increase the patient's inner drive towards outgoingness and object relatedness. This takes three or more weeks to become clinically manifest. In this regard, the spontaneous improvement of many patients in more than thirty days, mainly in neurotic but also in some other depressions as well, must be remembered.

The major indication for the antidepressant drugs, in the presence of a supportive psychotherapeutic attitude on the part of the physician, is in the severe psychotic depressions, or depressions with severe psychomotor retardation. This applies equally to the young, the elderly, or the middle aged (i.e. involutional melancolia, psychotic depressions, with marked psychomotor retardation—the so-called endogenous depressions). Many of these patients cannot relate well while depressed. Here the antidepressants, given in adequate doses, improve the patient's capacity to reach outward and become more outgoing in approximately 70% of such patients after at least three weeks of treatment. Often the drugs must be maintained for the length of the depressive episode, but the patient becomes increasingly available for supportive psychotherapy as the improvement increases.

One must remember these patients' propensities to have nothing to do with any part of treatment or anything that is linked with the depressive psychotic episode of this magnitude—i.e., when they are well, they are in a statebound consciousness of being well, and when they are ill, they are in a time-related statebound consciousness of being ill (19). When one state is present, the other state is absent. Thus, such patients avoid therapeutic contacts of any kind with physicians and with *anything* that reminds them of their illness when they are well. One has to wait for the next episode, if there is one, before one sees the patient again (19).

Antianxiety Agents

Antianxiety agents are not specifically discussed here. They are, as a class, the most abused and overused of all medications. In psychotherapy, mastery of problems is a primary goal; as this is done, it is rare to need antianxiety agents for any length of time.

REFERENCES

1. Azima, H. and Sarwer-Foner, G. J. Psychoanalytic formulations of drugs in pharmacotherapy. *Rev. Canad. Biol.*, (June) 1961, 20:603.
2. Freyhan, F. Neuroleptic effect: Fact or fiction. In: G. J. Sarwer-Foner (Ed.), *The Dynamics of Psychiatric Drug Therapy*. Springfield, Ill.: Charles C Thomas, 1960.
3. Goldberg, S. C., Schooler, N. R., Hogarty, G. E., and Roper M. Prediction of relapse in schizophrenic outpatients treated by drug and sociotherapy. *Arch. Gen. Psychiat.*, Feb. 1977, 34:171.
4. Gottschalf, L. A. Some problems in the use of psychoactive drugs, with or without psychotherapy, in the treatment of non-personality disorders. In: D. H. Efron (Ed.), *Psychopharmacology. A Review of Process 1957-1967*. Washington, D.C.: Public Health Service Publication No. 1836, 1968, p. 225.
5. Harticollis, P. (Ed.). *Borderline Personality Disorders: The Concept, the Syndrome, the Patient*. New York: International Universities Press, 1977.
6. Hogarty, G. E., Goldberg, S. C., Schooler, N. R. et al. Drug and sociotherapy in the aftercare of schizophrenic patients II—Two year relapse rates. *Arch. Gen. Psychiat.*, 1974, 31:603.
7. Lesse, S. Psychotherapy and ataractics: Some observations on combined psychotherapy and chlorpromazine therapy. *Amer. J. Psychother.*, 1956, 10:448.
8. McGhie, A. and Chapman, J. Disorders of attention and perception in early schizophrenia. *Br. J. Med. Psychol.*, 1961, 34:103.
9. Ostow, M. *Drugs in Psychoanalysis and Psychotherapy*. New York: Basic Books, 1962.
10. Sabshin, M. and Ramot, J. Pharmotherapeutic evaluation of the psychiatric setting. *Arch. Neurol.*, 1956, 75:362.

11. Shapiro, A. K. Etiological factors in placebo effect. *J. Amer. Med. Assoc.*, 1964, 187:712.
12. Sarwer-Foner, G. J. and Ogle, W. Use of reserpine in open psychiatric settings. *Canad. M.A.J.*, 1955, 73L187.
13. Sarwer-Foner, G. J. and Ogle, W. Psychosis and enhanced anxiety produced by reserpine and chlorpromazine. *Canad. M.A.J.*, 1956, 74:526.
14. Sarwer-Foner, G. J. Psychoanalytic theories of activity-passivity conflicts, and the continuum of ego defenses. Experimental verification with reserpine and chlorpromazine. *A.M.A. Arch. Neurol. & Psychiat.*, 1957, 78:413.
15. Sarwer-Foner, G. J. *The Dynamics of Psychiatric Drug Therapy.* Springfield, Ill.: Charles C Thomas, 1960.
16. Sarwer-Foner, G. J. and Koranyi, E. K. Transference effects, the attitude of the treating physician, and countertransference in the use of neuroleptic drugs. In: G. J. Sarwer-Foner (Ed.), *The Dynamics of Psychiatric Drug Therapy.* Springfield, Ill.: Charles C Thomas, 1960.
17. Sarwer-Foner, G. J. Some therapeutic aspects of the use of neuroleptic drugs in schizophrenic, borderline states and in short-term psychotherapy of the neurosis. In: G. J. Sarwer-Foner (Ed.), *The Dynamics of Psychiatric Drug Therapy.* Springfield, Ill.: Thomas, 1960, pp. 517.
18. Sarwer-Foner, G. J. The role of neuroleptic medication in psychotherapeutic interaction. *Comprehen. Psychiat.*, 1960, 1:291-300.
19. Sarwer-Foner, G. J. A psychoanalytic note on a specific delusion of time in psychotic depressions. *Canad. Psychiat. A.J. Suppl.*, 1966, 11:S221.
20. Sarwer-Foner, G. J. On psychiatric symptomatology: Its meaning and function in relation to the psychodynamic actions of drugs. In: H. C. B. Denber (Ed.), *Psychopharmacological Treatment in Psychiatry.* New York: Marcel Dekker, 1975.
21. Sarwer-Foner, G. J. An approach to the global treatment of the borderline patient: Psychoanalytic, psychotherapeutic and psychopharmacological considerations. In: *Opus Cite* ref. no. 5, 1977, p. 345-364.
22. Uhlenhuth, E. H., Rickels, K., Fisher, S., Park, L. C., Lipman, R. S., and Mock, J. Drug, doctor's verbal attitude and clinical setting in the symptomatic response to pharmacotherapy. *Psychopharmacologia*, (Berlin), 1966, 9:392.
23. Vaillant, G. E. The prediction of recovery in schizophrenia. *J. Nerv. Ment. Dis.*, 1962, 35:534.
24. Winkelman, N. W., Jr. Chlorpromazine and prochlorperazine during psychoanalytic pyschotherapy. In: G. J. Sarwer-Foner (Ed.), *The Dynamics of Psychiatric Drug Therapy.* Springfield, Ill.: Charles C Thomas, 1960, p. 134.
25. Wittenborn, J. R. and May, P. R. A. *Prediction of Response to Pharmacotherapy.* Springfield, Ill.: Charles C Thomas, 1966.

Name Index

491

Subject Index